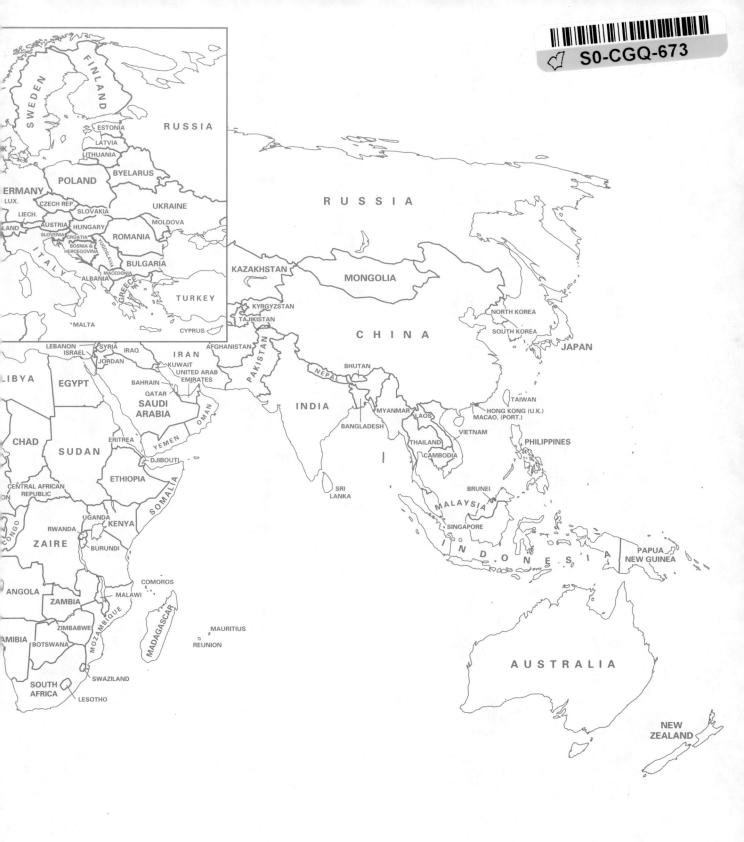

Law for Global Business

Law for Global Business

Eric L. Richards
Indiana University

IRWIN
Burr Ridge, Illinois
Boston, Massachusetts
Sydney, Australia

To my family—Rae Lynn, Jeff, Joey, Nate, and Josh—for the wonder and joy you have brought to my life.

© RICHARD D. IRWIN, INC., 1994

Senior sponsoring editor:	Craig Beytien
Editorial assistant:	Jennifer R. McBride
Senior marketing manager:	Cindy Ledwith
Project editor:	Paula M. Buschman
Production manager:	Diane Palmer
Art manager:	Kim Meriwether
Designer:	Michael Warrell
Compositor:	Graphic Composition, Inc.
Typeface:	10/12 Cheltenham Light
Printer:	R. R. Donnelley & Sons Company

Library of Congress Cataloging-in-Publication Data

Richards, Eric L.
    Law for global business / Eric L. Richards.
        p.   cm. — (Irwin legal studies in business series)
    Includes index.
    ISBN 0-256-11372-6
    1. Commercial law.   2. International business enterprises—Law and legislation.   3. Contracts (International law)   I. Title.
    II. Series.
    K1005.4.R53   1994
    341.7′53—dc20   93–48202

Printed in the United States of America
1 2 3 4 5 6 7 9 0 DO 0 9 8 7 6 5 4 3

Preface

The increasing globalization of business is not surprising when one considers the technological advances transforming our daily lives. As communication barriers crumble, societies are becoming more knowledgeable of each other and, as a result, adopting similar patterns of consumption. Simultaneously, breakthroughs in the transportation industry are permitting global traders to conquer the mountains and seas, joining the lives of people throughout the world.

For astute business managers, the global marketplace offers tremendous opportunities. However, it also is filled with numerous traps for the unwary. Firms that blindly enter the international arena are courting financial disaster. Prudent companies, on the other hand, recognize the increased risks involved in transnational ventures. They carefully design global strategies that balance their goals with the level of risk they are willing to assume.

Accordingly, students of business must broaden their horizons and develop an appreciation for the global environment. However, in a world of accelerating technological, economic, and social change, this is not a simple task. With each passing day, people are swept further along in a stream of new discoveries and fundamental transformations. Only by anticipating and comprehending these changes can managers hope to succeed.

This book provides its readers with the tools for understanding the principles underlying the legal environment of global business. It goes beyond identifying the current legal rules and regulations affecting businesses by presenting insights into new developments and trends that will greatly affect future transactions. The result is a clear, easy-to-ready text that facilitates an understanding of the complexities facing global business managers.

PEDAGOGY

Throughout the materials, Concept Summaries provide immediate reinforcement of important or confusing topics. In addition, chapters contain numerous flowcharts and other visual aids designed to enable students to easily conceptualize the interaction between global firms and the legal environment. Key business forms also are included to more fully illustrate the practical aspects of various transactions.

EMPHASIS ON ETHICS

Brief Ethical Implications sections are presented throughout the text. These comments, questions, and cases permit readers to consider the complex and pervasive nature of the ethical dilemmas confronting businesspeople in the global environment.

CASES

The textual material is further reinforced through the use of high-interest and easy-to-understand cases that have been decided by U.S. courts, various foreign courts, the World Court, GATT panels, and binational panels. They were selected to teach something about business practices as well as the law. Although the case are brief, they include enough facts and discussion to make understandable both the practical business situations and the underlying legal issues. Each case is placed immediately after the textual point it illustrates.

ACKNOWLEDGMENTS

I wish to acknowledge the ideas and insights of the following reviewers. Their contributions to the success of this effort are greatly appreciated.

John Carlson
University of Iowa

William McCarty
Western Michigan University

Carol Miller
Southwest Missouri State University

Fred Naffzinger
Indiana University—South Bend

Daniel Ostas
University of Maryland

Lynda Oswald
Univerity of Michigan
John Wrieden
Florida International University

Special thanks are due to Craig Beytien and Paula Buschman of Richard D. Irwin, Inc. Without their hard work, good cheer, and patience, this dream could not have become a reality. I am also indebted to David Walker, vice president for product development at UNZ and UNZ & Co. of Jersey City, NJ, for permitting the use of selected business forms throughout the text. I am especially grateful to my undergraduate and graduate students at Indiana University. Their frank comments and criticisms of the early manuscripts greatly shaped the final product. Finally, I must thank my good friend and teacher, Sulaiman Zai. His infectious enthusiasm and commitment to excellence in all things inspired me to climb this mountain.

Eric L. Richards

Contents in Brief

Contents

THE INTERNATIONAL LEGAL ENVIRONMENT

Introduction to Global Business

INTRODUCTION

The world that surrounds us is shrinking at an ever-increasing pace. In our lifetime, we have witnessed tremendous advances in both the communications and transportation industries that have made it possible for businesses to efficiently conduct operations throughout the world. The time is rapidly approaching when international transactions may not only be desirable, but they may also be imperative. However, while the global marketplace offers lucrative opportunities for enterprising businesses, it also possesses a wide variety of hazards for the unwary. Accordingly, it is essential that today's managers fully appreciate the benefits as well as the problems that accompany global business.

Chapter Overview

This chapter opens with a brief discussion of the various forces that are encouraging more and more businesses to globalize their operations. It then examines the three basic methods of penetrating global markets, offering a glimpse of the advantages and disadvantages of each. The rest of the material explores the major pitfalls business managers must consider before embarking on the path to globalization. This exploration encompasses dispute resolution problems, limitations on trade, financial uncertainties, expropriation, and political violence against people. Throughout your reading, please keep in mind the introductory nature of this first chapter. Many of the issues raised here are reexamined in greater detail throughout the rest of the book.

BACKGROUND

Global Trade Theory

The predominant explanation for international business is derived from the theory of **comparative advantage.** Under this principle, a country should export goods it can produce more efficiently than its trading partners and import those that can be produced more efficiently overseas.

Suppose a loaf of bread in the United States costs $1 and a dozen oranges sells for $3. In Mexico, the oranges sell for $2 while the bread is priced at $1.

	United States	Mexico
Bread	$1	$1
Oranges	$3	$2

Thus, the United States produces bread more efficiently than Mexico relative to oranges. This is illustrated by the fact that bread sells for one third of the price of oranges in the United States and for one half of the price of oranges in Mexico. Further, Mexico produces oranges more efficiently than the United States relative to bread since Mexican oranges sell for two loaves of bread while U.S. oranges cost three loaves of bread.

Under the theory of comparative advantage, U.S. companies should specialize in the production of bread, while Mexican enterprises should deal in oranges. This is because a U.S. bread producer could sell two loaves of bread in Mexico and receive one dozen oranges. Those oranges could be sold in the United States for three loaves of bread, giving the bread producer a profit of one loaf of bread. Likewise, a Mexican producer could sell one dozen oranges in the United States and, with the proceeds of the sale, purchase three loaves of bread. Two of the loaves could be used to cover the cost of the oranges in Mexico with the remaining loaf constituting a profit on the exchange.

Transfer Costs

Of course, other factors influence an enterprise's decision on whether or not to globalize its operations. For instance, certain **transfer costs** regularly associated with cross-border trade may restrict the profitability of international transactions. They might include packaging and transportation expenses that are unique to ocean travel. Or, as is frequently the case, they may come in the form of government-imposed restrictions such as import duties, quotas, and export restrictions. Thus, in our example of Mexican oranges, U.S. orange growers might lobby for restrictive tariffs or import quotas that greatly increase the cost of shipping oranges to the United States.

When transfer costs are high, international trade is not likely to occur unless there is no domestic source for essential goods or services. However, in some instances, high transportation costs and restrictive import or export regulations may encourage a business to transplant its manufacturing operations overseas, closer to foreign markets.

Globalization Forces

Several developments have converged to spur a surge in international trade. To begin with, as U.S. economic growth slowed during the 1980s, many domestic businesses sought foreign buyers to offset declining demand for their products at home. This strategy was bolstered when the dollar weakened against foreign currencies, making U.S. goods cheaper in comparison with similar foreign products.

Developments in communications technology have stimulated similarities in worldwide patterns of consumption, thereby encouraging global marketing and sourcing efforts. These innovations have been matched by vast improvements in the transportation industry, which have lowered transfer costs and permitted buyers to search the world for high-quality goods at lower prices. Simultaneously, the speed with which modern technology has been changing has shortened the domestic lives of products throughout the developed world. However, many out-of-date goods are still extremely attractive to purchasers in less developed countries, providing an unexpected market for their producers.

The rapid pace of technological change, combined with the growing complexity in modern technology, has boosted research and development costs to tremendous levels. As a result, many companies are obliged to seek out international market opportunities to achieve the economies of scale essential to maintaining or establishing a competitive position. A growing number of nations have facilitated this global search by dismantling many of the restrictive policies that formerly closed their borders to foreign goods, services, and investment.

All of these factors make it clear that future economic success will depend more and more on a business firm's ability to integrate its operations on a worldwide basis. This globalization will place increasing demands on managers to recognize the variety of political and economic risks, as well as the web of legal constraints, that will affect every level of their business operations.

STRATEGIES FOR PENETRATING GLOBAL MARKETS

For a U.S. firm that traditionally has confined itself to domestic activities, the simplest and perhaps safest way to exploit the world market is through a system of global trade. Under this approach, a company maintains its manufacturing operations at home while exporting domestic goods to foreign buyers and importing foreign-made products from overseas suppliers.

Sometimes a producer will want to manufacture its products abroad, closer to its foreign buyers. Overseas production may permit the use of lower-priced labor, better access to raw materials, avoidance of tariffs and other trade barriers, and refuge from costly domestic regulations. A company can arrange production abroad by licensing the technology associated with a product to a new or existing foreign company. Or a U.S. business may decide to invest in its own production and sales facilities abroad.

Each of these strategies for penetrating international markets—trade, licensing, and direct investment—possesses distinct advantages and disadvantages. This section more closely examines each approach.

Trade

Global **trade** (exporting or importing) is the most common form of international transaction for business enterprises. Within this category of globalization strategies, a company might operate within a broad range of international involvement. At the one extreme, a U.S. manufacturer may incidentally sell goods to foreign buyers who seek out the products in the United States. At the other end of the spectrum, the manufacturer may actively solicit business in foreign markets, providing a full array of presale and postsale services.

Active involvement in all aspects of overseas sales provides distinct advantages. For instance, a business can earn greater profits because it will not have to share its revenues with costly middlemen. Simultaneously, it may acquire more direct and intimate knowledge of overseas market conditions, permitting quicker and more accurate responses to changes in demand. Further, it alone will derive the benefits of any goodwill that springs from its product and service reputation. Finally, it will retain control over marketing methods, pricing structure, and service obligations.

Not all businesses are willing or able to extensively involve themselves in overseas trade. An active international presence increases a firm's administrative costs and exposes it to greater risks (i.e., lawsuits in foreign courts, taxation by foreign countries). Further, many companies lack the knowledge and experience to single-handedly cash in on the potential rewards of global trade. Accordingly, enterprises often will start with a marginal international presence and then gradually increase their involvement as they gain practical experience. We now will examine several options available to a business wishing to engage in global trade.

Export Trading Companies

The United States enacted the *Export Trading Company Act* to stimulate the export of U.S. goods. The statute permits domestic producers to combine forces and establish **export trading companies.** It specifically enables banks to invest in those organizations and to simultaneously provide financial backing for their overseas transactions. An export trading company may either buy the products of domestic manufacturers and resell them overseas or sell the producers' goods on a commission basis.

Export Management Companies

Many active global traders still are unable or unwilling to maintain their own export department. Instead, they employ the services of one or more **export management companies** for export advice and related services. While a few of the larger export management companies may actually provide financing for an exporter's foreign sales, most confine their activities to providing market research, background information on potential buyers, and assistance in the negotiation and execution of sales contracts. One advantage of using export management companies is that they often can provide immediate access to foreign markets. However, as with export trading companies, they deprive the manufacturer of close control over the export transaction.

Foreign Buying Agents

It is common for buyers to retain the services of a **buying agent** who is authorized to locate and purchase foreign goods. These agents, who may be employed by private firms or governmental agencies, will then be paid a commission on the resulting sale. While this approach protects producers from many of the risks of exporting, it also deprives them of the valuable insights that can be gained from face-to-face encounters with buyers.

Piggyback Marketing

Sometimes a firm agrees to provide an array of goods and services to a foreign buyer. In instances where the seller does not manufacture all of the products called for in the agreement, it may supplement its own goods with those produced by other U.S. suppliers. While these **piggyback marketing** arrangements relieve the supplemental producers of marketing and distributions expenses, they also deprive them of direct control over their overseas sales.

Foreign Distributors

When a firm believes there are substantial global markets for its products, it often will sell them to overseas merchants who, in turn, will resell them at wholesale or retail under terms and conditions spelled out by contract. Overseas merchants who import goods for such resale purposes are known as **foreign distributors.** They generally purchase the goods at a discount and resell them at a profit, bearing the financial risk if the goods cannot be resold. The parties' distribution agreement frequently will obligate the distributor to confine its activities to specified territories, to refrain from selling competing manufacturers' products, and to maintain certain levels of presale and postsale service.

Sales Representatives

A manufacturer may engage the services of a foreign **sales representative** to solicit purchases from overseas buyers. Sales representatives (frequently called *commission agents*) share many of the attributes of a foreign distributor. For instance, their agreement with the manufacturer generally defines their sales territories as well as the general terms under which they may sell the goods. However, unlike distributors, sales representatives do not take title to the goods and are paid a commission based on their sales volume. Accordingly, they bear no financial responsibility for unsold or damaged goods.

Foreign sales representatives differ from distributors in another important respect. The relationship between the manufacturer and the sales representative is that of principal and agent. That generally is not the case in a distributorship. Under an *agency relationship,* an exporter can exercise extensive control over the overseas selling activities. Of course, with this greater control comes greater responsibility; a producer is more likely to be legally liable for the activities of an agent than for the behavior of a distributor.

Licensing

When transportation costs are high or when a target market is surrounded by steep barriers against imports (e.g., high tariffs, strict quotas), global trade might not be a viable strategy. Under these circumstances, a manufacturer may attempt to penetrate foreign markets through technology **licensing** arrangements. These are contractual agreements in which an enterprise, the *licensor,* makes its *intellectual property* (patents, trade secrets and know-how, trademarks, or copyrights) available to an overseas company, the *licensee.* In return, the licensor will receive compensation (royalties), either in a single payment or in periodic installments pegged to the volume of the licensee's production.

The level of protection given intellectual property varies from country to country. Accordingly, licensing arrangements must be carefully planned, negotiated, drafted, and performed if they are to be successful. (Licensing and the protection of intellectual property are discussed in greater depth in Chapter 13.)

Licensing Restrictions

Some countries restrict the importation of technology or information by requiring that licensing agreements be registered with a governmental agency that can approve or disapprove them. The rules governing approval tend to be complex and permit the governmental agency considerable discretion. Japan, for example, has been accused of using such a program to improve the ability of its manufacturers to obtain more favorable bargaining terms. Instead of having different Japanese manufacturers compete with one another to get a desirable piece of technology from a U.S. licensor, with the licensor awarding the license to the highest bidder, the governmental agency in effect tells the licensor that the large, prosperous Japanese market will not be available to it unless it agrees to accept considerably less favorable terms than would have resulted without the regulation.

In developing countries, licensing regulations may be employed to ensure that the country's scarce resources are not being used to pay royalties unless the licensed technology fits into the country's basic development plans. Technical training of local personnel may be required to get approval, and there may be a requirement that the technology be fully disclosed and become freely available to all nationals after a specified period. The goal of some regulatory schemes is to make licensing so unattractive that the potential licensor will decide it is more profitable to establish a manufacturing facility in the country.

International Franchising

Some licensing agreements specifically permit a licensee to market goods or services overseas under the licensor's trademark. This arrangement, known as international **franchising,** offers several advantages to licensors. First, when the franchisee is a native of the target country, the operation will not be troubled by as many problems stemming from language or cultural differences. Second, the franchisee will be more likely to understand local regulations affecting the business. Third, through the use of a foreign-owned franchise, the licensor possibly can avoid local restrictions on foreign investment. Finally, the local franchisee may be less threatened by political instability than would a foreign company.

The effectiveness of the franchise relationship often will turn on the ability of the parties to reach a comprehensive franchise agreement. In the absence of an agreement to the contrary, the laws of the franchisee's country generally will govern the relationship. And in some matters—patents, trademarks, and antitrust—those laws will apply regardless of the agreement. Many countries will not permit franchise agreements to stand unless the parties agree to the jurisdiction of the local courts. Accordingly, the political stability of the target country is vitally important to the long-term success of a franchising relationship.

Direct Investment The deepest level of international penetration occurs when a business enterprise makes a **direct investment** in a foreign country. This section briefly examines the reasons for direct investment, some important investment considerations, and the fundamental ways in which direct investment is carried out.

CONCEPT SUMMARY
Advantages of International Franchising

1. Franchisee has advantage of franchisor's expertise on numerous matters intimately related to the goods or services
2. Franchisor does not need vast sums of capital to establish distribution network
3. Local management better acquainted with language and culture
4. Local franchisees more in tune with laws of foreign government
5. Franchisee less threatened by political bias against foreigners
6. Avoids the need for detailed supervision of distributors who are many miles away

---

Reasons for Investment

While direct investment generally requires a substantial financial outlay and much greater risks, a firm may choose this option for several reasons. First, as was noted previously, the costs of global trade may be prohibitive when the target market is isolated by restrictive import barriers or high transportation costs. In many instances, a producer may hesitate to overcome these obstacles through licensing out of fear that its intellectual property may be misappropriated. Second, direct investment offers more control and a greater share of potential profits than either trade or licensing. Third, many developing nations will grant generous concessions to entice businesses into establishing new manufacturing facilities within their borders. Fourth, a business may wish to transplant its domestic operations overseas to escape environmental laws, labor laws, or other restrictions imposed by its home country. Finally, some multinational corporations have intentionally dispersed their manufacturing facilities around the globe as part of a strategy to spread risk. In this way, they are less likely to have their entire operation crippled by political or economic upheavals in any single region of the world.

Investment Issues

Before a U.S. firm decides to establish a direct investment abroad, a wide variety of legal issues must be examined. Many of them are peculiar to the country being considered as the location of the facility. Labor laws may be very different from our own and may impose long-term obligations on the employer. Import license requirements and high tariffs may force the firm to use local sources of supplies and raw materials and to manufacture locally a certain percentage by value of the parts used in assembling its final products. Some countries generally prohibit foreigners from having a majority equity interest in any operation within their borders, and many manufacturing activities require licenses from governmental authorities.

Investment Methods

Sometimes an enterprise will penetrate global markets by establishing an overseas **branch.** This form of direct investment offers the home office a great deal of control over its foreign operation. However, because a branch is merely an extension of the home office, it may expose the entire business organization to a whole range of legal liabilities in the foreign nation.

Perhaps the most common form of direct investment is the **wholly owned subsidiary.** While this may provide less control over the overseas operations than a branch office, a subsidiary incorporated in a foreign nation has a separate and distinct legal personality from its parent corporation. As such, the parent corporation might be able to insulate its domestic assets from legal liabilities arising from the subsidiary's overseas activities. Wholly owned subsidiaries may be established in either of two ways: acquisitions or greenfield investments.

Acquisitions occur when the firm purchases an existing business in the foreign market. The major advantage of this method is that the newly acquired unit brings with it established distribution channels and goodwill. *Greenfield investments* refer to situations where the investor erects its own subsidiary. These generally are more costly and risky than acquisitions, although they frequently offer the greatest profit potential. In many underdeveloped nations, there will be no existing operations to acquire, making greenfield investments the only feasible strategy. However, even the greenfield route may be impractical in nations where there is a glaring shortage of trained workers.

Sometimes it is not reasonable to establish a wholly owned subsidiary because the costs or risks are too high. Other times it is not possible because a host country (the target market) may require that at least 51 percent of the enterprise be owned by its nationals. In those instances, a manufacturer may be compelled to carry out its direct investment through a **joint venture.** In a joint venture, two or more firms will join forces to carry out a common business enterprise. The joint venturers may structure their endeavor as a partnership, a corporation, or merely as a contractual obligation establishing their rights and obligations.

DISPUTE RESOLUTION PROBLEMS

Enterprises engaging in trade, licensing, or direct investment across national borders may encounter business and legal problems far different from those that exist in the domestic environment. For instance, when global operations span vast distances and different cultures, the parties are less likely to know each other well or share common business customs. This unfamiliarity increases the risk that misunderstandings and, ultimately, legal disputes will arise.

Multiple Legal Systems

There is no single, international legal system for resolving disputes between businesses. As a result, private lawsuits must be brought before national courts. However, because global conflicts involve more than one nation, there is likely to be confusion over which domestic court system will hear any particular case and which laws will govern the dispute. And, even if the disputants are able to agree on a single forum and set of rules, the prevailing party may have great difficulty enforcing one nation's judgments against a firm doing business in another country.

Contracting to Simplify Dispute Resolution

To avoid the time, expense, and frustrations that often accompany litigation, global contracts often are drafted with an eye toward flexibility so they may be freely renegotiated. This cooperative approach is imperative in foreign cultures where the notion of rigidly enforced obligations is not widely recognized. However, a flexible and cooperative attitude will not always ensure that a satisfactory compromise will be reached. Accordingly, global contracts frequently contain key provisions designed to reduce many of the uncertainties associated with international litigation. They might include **forum selection clauses,** which designate where lawsuits are to be heard, and **choice of law clauses,** which specify the law that governs any dispute. Most of the world's courts enforce these provisions when they are freely negotiated and bear a reasonable relationship to the underlying contract.

Resolving Disputes by Arbitration

The increasing volume of international business transactions, coupled with the complexities they often entail, has led to greater reliance on **arbitration** to resolve contractual disputes. Arbitration, which involves the settlement of disputes by a nonjudicial third party, generally provides a quicker and more private means of resolving disputes than is available under litigation. The increase in commerce with China, Japan, and Korea, where mediation rather than litigation of disputes is traditional, has given added impetus to the arbitration movement.

The growing attractiveness of arbitration has resulted in the establishment of arbitral centers in world capitals, such as London, Paris, Cairo, Hong Kong, and Stockholm, as well as in major cities, such as Geneva and New York. The general accessibility of these forums offers the availability of a neutral location for carrying out arbitration proceedings. Recognition and enforcement of international arbitration agreements and awards are generally ensured through multilateral treaties.

■

REPUBLIC OF NICARAGUA v. STANDARD FRUIT COMPANY
937 F.2d 469 (9th Cir. 1991)

■ **FACTS** Since 1970, Standard Fruit, a wholly owned subsidiary of Standard Fruit and Steamship Company (Steamship), had been involved in the production and purchase of bananas in Nicaragua. In 1979, the Sandinistas overthrew the government in Nicaragua and began efforts to assume closer control over the banana industry. After attempts to negotiate a new contract with Standard Fruit stalled, the government issued a decree that declared the banana industry was to become a state monopoly, all plantation leases would be transferred to a new governmental agency, and all preexisting lease, partnership, and fruit purchase contracts were nullified. Standard Fruit, interpreting this decree as an expropriation of its business, immediately ceased all operations in Nicaragua. In response, Nicaragua requested a "summit meeting" at which Steamship could sort out its differences with the Sandinistas. After three days of intense negotiations, Steamship signed a "memorandum of intent" that envisioned the renegotiation and replacement of the existing contracts between Standard Fruit and the government of Nicaragua. It also contained an arbitration provision that stated: *"Any and all disputes arising under* *the arrangements contemplated hereunder will be referred to mutually agreed mechanisms or procedures of international arbitration."* Although Steamship, Standard Fruit, and Nicaragua all acted as though the memorandum was binding for almost two years, the implementing contracts were never finalized and Standard Fruit left Nicaragua for good in 1982. Nicaragua claimed this action was in breach of contract and petitioned a U.S. district court to compel Steamship to arbitrate the dispute. Steamship argued that the arbitration clause was too vague to be enforceable.

■ **ISSUE** Should the U.S. court compel Steamship to submit to international arbitration?

■ **DECISION** Yes. The standard for demonstrating arbitrability is not a high one; in fact, a district court has little discretion to deny an arbitration motion. As with any other contract, the parties' intentions control, but those intentions are generously construed as to issues of arbitrability. Therefore, the only issue properly before the court is whether the parties entered into a contract that committed both sides to arbitrate the issue of the contract's validity. Where the parties have signed a document that contains an arbitration provision, as here, all questions regarding breach of the agreement must be referred to arbitration. When international companies commit themselves to arbitrate a dispute, they are in effect attempting to guarantee a forum for any disputes. Such agreements merit great deference since they operate as both forum selection and choice of law clauses, and offer stability and predictability regardless of the vagaries of local law. The elimination of all such uncertainties is an indispensable element in international trade, commerce, and contracting. Thus, the most minimal indication of the parties' intent to arbitrate must be given full effect, especially in international disputes.

Parent Liability for Foreign Subsidiaries

A corporation may form a subsidiary corporation to carry out its overseas operations. Such a strategy limits the parent corporation's financial risk to the amount of capital it has invested in its subsidiary. This reduces the likelihood that foreign courts will be able to enforce judgments against the assets of the parent. Recent years, however, have witnessed a growing trend toward holding parent corporations liable for the activities of their foreign subsidiaries. Such liability has arisen in two contexts: the corporation law theory of "piercing the corporate veil" and the tort and agency theory of "direct liability."

Under generally accepted theories of corporation law, a parent corporation is not liable for the debts of its subsidiary; the parent's losses are limited to the amount it has invested in the subsidiary. However, courts may **pierce the corporate veil** and strip away this limited liability when a subsidiary is not adequately capitalized to meet the expected claims that may arise against it. This is even more likely to occur in tort cases where the parent effectively controls the operating decisions of the subsidiary and where the subsidiary was established to carry out inherently dangerous activities in a foreign country.

A parent corporation also may be held responsible for the torts of its foreign subsidiaries under a theory of **direct liability** when the parent fails to intervene and supervise the operations of the subsidiary. More and more, courts impose this special duty on a parent when its subsidiary is dealing with hazardous activities, particularly when the subsidiary is doing business in undeveloped countries that lack the technology needed to protect against the potential harm.

In the following case, *In re Union Carbide,* the victims of an Indian chemical disaster attempted to reach the assets of a subsidiary corporation's U.S. parent. Although the court's decision focuses on whether the lawsuit should be conducted in India or the United States, it raises issues of when corporate parents should be liable for the activities of their foreign subsidiaries.

■

IN RE UNION CARBIDE CORPORATION GAS PLANT DISASTER AT BHOPAL
809 F.2d 195 (2d Cir. 1987)

■ **FACTS** In 1984, the most tragic industrial disaster in history occurred when winds blew a deadly gas from a chemical plant operated by Union Carbide India Limited (UCIL) into densely occupied parts of the city of Bhopal, India. The results were horrendous; estimates of deaths ranged as high as 2,100. Over 200,000 people suffered injuries. UCIL was an Indian corporation although 50.9 percent of its stock was owned by Union Carbide Corporation (UCC), a U.S. corporation. The government of India owned or controlled another 22 percent. UCIL manufactured the chemicals at the Bhopal plant at the request of, and with the approval of, the Indian government. India enacted legislation providing that the government, the Union of India (UOI), had the exclusive right to represent Indian plaintiffs in connection with the tragedy. The UOI sued both UCIL and UCC on behalf of all victims of the Bhopal disaster in a U.S. district court. The complaint against UCC was based on several theories. First, the UOI argued that multinational corporations are absolutely liable to the persons and country in which they have in any manner caused to be undertaken any ultrahazardous or inherently dangerous activity. Second, it alleged that, because UCC knew of the extreme danger posed by the chemicals stored at UCIL's plant, its actions were in deliberate, conscious, and wanton disregard of the rights and safety of the citizens of India. Third, the UOI claimed the disaster was caused by negligence on the part of UCC in originally contributing to the design of the plant and its provision for storage of excessive amounts of dangerous chemicals at the plant. Rather than address the specifics of the UOI's complaint, UCC argued instead that the U.S. district court should dismiss the claim because India, rather than the United States, was the appropriate forum for the lawsuit.

■ **ISSUE** Should the U.S. district court dismiss the complaint because India is the more appropriate forum?

■ **DECISION** Yes. The private interests of the parties weigh heavily in favor of litigating this matter in India. The many witnesses and sources of proof are almost entirely located in India, where the accident occurred, and could not be compelled to appear for a trial in the United States. The Bhopal plant at the time of the accident was operated by some 193 Indian nationals. The great majority of documents bearing on the design, safety, start-up, and operation of the plant, as well as the safety training of the plant's employees, is located in India. UCC's participation in the Indian activities was limited, and its involvement in plant operations was terminated long before the accident. UCC did provide a summary "process design package" for construction of the plant and the services of some of its technicians to monitor the progress of UCIL in detailing the design and erecting the plant. However, the UOI controlled the terms of the agreements and precluded UCC from exercising any authority to detail, design, erect, and commission the plant. The vital parts of the Bhopal plant, including its storage tank, monitoring instrumentation, and vent gas scrubber, were manufactured in India by Indians. Although some 40 UCIL employees were given safety training at UCC's plant in the United States, they represented a small fraction of the Bhopal plant's employees. Further, India has a stronger countervailing interest in adjudicating the claims in its courts according to its standards, rather than having American values and standards of care imposed on it. India's interest is increased by the fact that it has for years treated UCIL as an Indian national, subjecting it to intensive regulations and governmental supervision for the construction, development, and operation of the Bhopal plant, its emissions, water and air pollution, and safety precautions. Moreover, in view of India's strong interest and its greater contacts with the plant, its operations, its employees, and the victims of the accident, the law of India, as the place where the wrong occurred, will undoubtedly govern. In contrast, the U.S. interests are relatively minor.

FIGURE 1–1   Parent Liability for Claims against Subsidiary (Piercing the Corporate Veil)

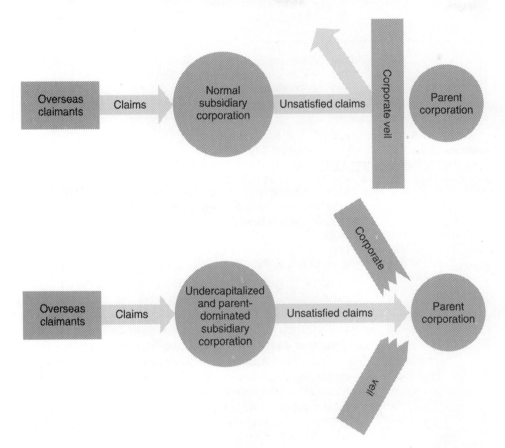

   The Bhopal victims may have pursued their claims against the U.S. corporate parent, Union Carbide Corporation, for several reasons. First, by suing a U.S. corporation directly, the chances were greater that the lawsuit would be heard by U.S. courts, which are attractive forums for personal injury litigation. Second, there might have been concern that Union Carbide India Limited, the subsidiary, did not have sufficient financial resources to meet all the claims against it. (It has been estimated that the Indian subsidiary had a net worth of no more than $27 million and was facing claims in excess of $1 billion.) In any event, after the lawsuit was removed to the Indian courts, Union Carbide Corporation agreed to pay $470 million to the victims of the Bhopal disaster.

ETHICAL IMPLICATIONS   In an intracompany debate to determine the ideal location for a hazardous chemical plant, one company official cites evidence that the potential life earnings of a worker in Country X are 50 percent less than those of a similar worker in Country Y. However, the general level of technological skill in Country Y is much higher, making it less likely that a catastrophic accident would occur there. After balancing these factors, he suggests that it makes economic sense to organize a subsidiary corporation to operate the new facility in Country X because the potential liability for wrongful death suits would more than offset the greater likelihood of a disaster. Should the company's decision be made on this basis?

LIMITATIONS ON TRADE

Governmentally imposed barriers to trade greatly affect a company's decision of whether it should globalize and, after determining that it should, what method of penetration is best. These barriers include tariffs, import controls, and export controls.

Tariffs

A tariff is a tax or duty assessed on goods, generally when they are imported into a country. Through the use of tariffs, governments can restrict imports and protect domestic sales. A sufficiently high tariff will make the product so expensive that most consumers will refuse to buy it; they will do without or turn to domestically produced equivalents. Tariffs have been the most common barrier to free trade and are something that many governments are cooperating to control or eliminate.

One of the most comprehensive efforts at cooperation has been the negotiations under the General Agreement on Tariffs and Trade (GATT), a treaty subscribed to by more than 100 governments. These rounds of negotiations, which last many years, have resulted in significant tariff reductions. The focus of GATT is much broader than tariff reduction, however; its purpose is to reduce all trade barriers and promote a stable world trade environment.

Import Controls

Import restrictions are imposed by countries for a variety of reasons. For instance, sometimes imports are subjected to strict quotas to insulate sensitive domestic industries from foreign competition. Agricultural products, steel, and textiles have historically received such protection. On other occasions, a nation may restrict imports to coerce a trading partner into opening its markets to foreign goods. In the past few years, the United States has forced Japan to limit the number of cars sold in the United States as a way of opening markets for U.S. products in Japan and reducing the unfavorable balance of trade with that country.

A nation may also prevent imports from entering its borders when they threaten the public health, safety, and welfare. Thus, goods that do not meet certain technical standards may be denied entry. In many instances, foreign producers complain that these technical standards are no more than disguised tariff barriers designed to insulate domestic producers from foreign competition.

Export Controls   Most nations impose export controls for political purposes. For example, the sale of militarily sensitive technological goods is restricted by many nations so such goods do not go to countries whose governments are considered unfriendly. The restrictions are agreed on unanimously by the countries that are members of the Paris-based Coordinating Committee for Multilateral Export Controls (Cocom). The restrictions are then enforced through laws passed in each country. Failure to abide by the restrictions can lead to administrative penalties and jail terms for the sellers of the restricted goods.

The Export Administration Act of 1979 is the main law under which exports are controlled in the United States. It authorizes controls for a variety of reasons in addition to national security considerations. These can include preventing the drain of scarce materials, furthering foreign policy, and reducing the inflationary impact of foreign demand.

FINANCIAL UNCERTAINTIES

No matter which form of global penetration an enterprise selects, it will face financial uncertainties far greater than those that exist in its domestic market. These include credit risks, currency fluctuations, and currency controls.

Credit Risks   International trade involves a significant risk that a buyer or seller will not have the financial ability or willingness to fulfill the terms of the contract. If the seller ships the goods without first receiving payment, it faces the risk that the buyer will later be unable or unwilling to pay any or all of the purchase price. However, if a buyer pays in advance of shipment, a possibility exists that the seller will not ship the goods in a timely manner. While this risk also is present in domestic transactions, the long distances and varied legal systems involved in the international realm decrease the likelihood of enforcing contractual obligations against global trading partners.

To solve these problems, the parties frequently will structure an international sale as a **documentary credit.** The first step in this type of transaction is a simple sales contract between the seller and the buyer that conditions shipment of the goods on the seller's receiving a *letter of credit* from a reputable bank. If everything works as planned, the seller delivers the goods to a carrier and is issued a *bill of lading,* which it presents to the bank for payment. The bank then presents the bill of lading, which provides constructive control over the goods, to the buyer who pays the bank. This arrangement minimizes the risk of nonpayment because the seller receives a promise of payment from a bank at the time it ships the goods. The buyer is also protected because the bank will not guarantee the payment unless the seller provides proof the goods have been shipped.

Documentary credit transactions may be structured in a variety of ways, depending on the needs of the parties. Further, the global environment is filled with numerous alternative methods of financing transactions and reducing the credit risks. Accordingly, this topic is explored in greater detail in Chapter 7.

Currency Fluctuations

A special problem associated with global trade stems from the fact that international transactions generally require the exchange of foreign currencies. For instance, German firms that wish to purchase U.S. goods must exchange German marks for U.S. dollars. (Similarly, a U.S. company importing goods from France would have to exchange U.S. dollars for French francs.) Because the exchange rates between currencies vary over time, international traders may face a great deal of uncertainty over these **currency fluctuations.**

Suppose a U.S. seller agreed to sell equipment to a German buyer for 50,000 marks. If one mark would purchase two dollars, the seller ultimately would expect to receive $100,000 for the goods. However, if between the time of contracting and the time of payment, the mark declined in value against the dollar so that one mark would now purchase only 1.5 dollars, the seller would receive only $75,000 for the equipment.

Of course, if the dollar declined against the mark so one mark would purchase 2.5 dollars, the seller would ultimately receive $125,000. However, many sellers do not want to speculate on the possibility of advantageous exchange rate fluctuations. As a result, they frequently insist that foreign buyers make their payment in U.S. dollars. This places the risk of currency fluctuations on the buyer.

In instances where a buyer is unwilling to accept this risk, an exporter may contract with a bank to **hedge** against foreign exchange risks. When this occurs, the bank, in return for a discount or fee, assumes the risk of currency fluctuations by guaranteeing the seller a fixed number of dollars in exchange for the foreign currency the seller receives from the buyer.

■

BANK BRUSSELS LAMBERT, S.A. v. INTERMETALS CORPORATION
779 F.Supp. 741 (S.D. N.Y. 1991)

■ **FACTS** Intermetals Corporation, a New Jersey corporation, traded in steel and other metals on an international basis. For several years, Bank Brussels Lambert, a Belgian bank with a branch office in New York City, provided financing for Intermetals' global transactions. In October 1988, Bank Brussels undertook a foreign exchange transaction to hedge Intermetals' contract for the sale of steel payable at a future date in deutsche marks. The hedge transaction was successfully carried out, protecting Intermetals' profit in the steel sale by shielding it from the risks of fluctuation of the deutsche mark during the period of exposure. The success of the hedge transaction led to discussions of speculative foreign exchange trading, and, ultimately, the bank agreed to conduct a course of foreign exchange trading for Intermetals. Under the parties' arrangement, Bank Brussels would cause Intermetals to enter into a contract for the purchase or sale of a foreign currency at an agreed U.S. dollar price. A

foreign currency would be purchased to speculate that, before settlement, the U.S. dollar would weaken against that foreign currency. A sale of the foreign currency would effect a speculation that the U.S. dollar would gain against that foreign currency. Bank Brussels immediately notified Intermetals of every trade and at no time speculated on a price change over a future period of more than two days. Ultimately, when the bank demanded over $1.5 million from Intermetals to cover losses on its account, the company argued that Bank Brussels had committed fraud by failing to fully inform it of the risks of speculation.

■ **ISSUE** Did Bank Brussels have a duty to disclose the risks of foreign exchange trading to Intermetals?

■ **DECISION** No. The evidence shows that Intermetals was aware of the risks of fluctuations in foreign currency before it began speculative trading. Indeed, Intermetals' first foreign exchange transaction with the bank, the hedge transaction, was motivated by the company's desire to avoid that risk. It had earned a $300,000 profit, payable in the future in deutsche marks. This profit was therefore exposed to the risk that the U.S. dollar might rise against the deutsche mark before payment was re-

ceived. Intermetals made its hedging transaction in awareness of such a risk in order to avoid the risk. The trading it undertook thereafter was equally motivated by awareness of the risk of currency fluctuations. In fact, it hoped to profit from that risk.

Currency Controls   Many countries, particularly those in the developing world, have regulations restricting the conversion of their domestic currency into a foreign currency and the remittance of those funds to another country. In those countries, when a U.S. firm wishes to **repatriate** (bring home) earnings by causing a foreign subsidiary to pay a dividend, permission must be obtained from the currency exchange authorities. These authorities operate under rules that are intended to encourage foreign firms to reinvest their earnings in the country rather than send them home.

Some countries place an absolute limit, stated in terms of a set percentage of the amount a firm has invested (the original amount and any reinvestment of retained earnings), on the amount of earnings that may be repatriated each year. Other countries place a substantial "income withholding tax" on repatriated earnings, which increases in percentage with the amount repatriated. If a U.S. firm wants to sell or liquidate its operations, all proceeds in excess of the original investment are usually considered dividends, and their repatriation may be either prohibited or taxed at a very high rate. A U.S. firm should normally not consider a major investment in a country with such regulations unless it is prepared to make a long-term commitment.

EXPROPRIATION

One of the greatest fears of any business that directly invests in a politically unstable country is the **expropriation** of its property. International law has traditionally offered little protection to businesses whose overseas investments are taken by a host government. There are two fundamental reasons for this state of affairs. First, no international mechanism exists that is capable of legally requiring nations to settle their investment disputes. (These difficulties inherent in the international legal system will be discussed in Chapter 2.) Second, the world community has failed to develop a generally accepted theory on the legality of governmental takings. As one might expect, capital-exporting countries favor strict protection for foreign investments while capital-importing nations claim their national sovereignty outweighs any legal duty owed to foreign investors.

Global Approaches   The predominant view among the capital-importing nations, as well as the socialist
to Expropriation   world, has stressed their sovereign power over both domestic and foreign investors. They insist governmental takings may be both legitimate and necessary to ensure that economic activities are directed toward the best interests of the host nation. This approach asserts that foreign investors are entitled to rights no greater than those

granted to a country's own nationals. Accordingly, a foreign investor's home country should not intervene in an investment dispute if a host country's expropriation does not discriminate against foreigners.

The capital-exporting nations stress that a host nation's sovereignty must be balanced against foreign investors' property rights. This view, strongly supported by the United States, insists that a nation may not expropriate foreign investments unless three basic requirements are met. First, the taking must be for a *public purpose*. Second, it must be carried out in a *nondiscriminatory* manner; that is, foreign investors must not be treated more harshly than domestic investors. Third, investors must be given *prompt, adequate, and effective compensation*.

The level of compensation often varies depending on the nature of the taking. For instance, expropriations that discriminate against foreign investors are labeled as *confiscations* and entitle the property owner to the fullest compensation. However, when a country *nationalizes* an entire industry in a nondiscriminatory manner while pursuing a compelling governmental interest, foreign tribunals are less likely to insist on full compensation. In the case that follows, *West v. Multibanco Comermex,* the court finds that, because the government's interest is so great, no taking has occurred and, accordingly, no compensation is owed.

■

WEST v. MULTIBANCO COMERMEX, S.A.
807 F.2d 820 (9th Cir. 1987)

■ **FACTS** Jack West responded to a solicitation that invited U.S. residents to purchase peso- and dollar-denominated certificates of deposit issued by Mexican banks. At the time of West's initial investment, the banks were privately owned. In the late 1970s, to support its domestic spending programs, Mexico began to borrow extensively from both public and private foreign organizations. This borrowing was predicated on the assumption that Mexico's oil reserves would generate sufficient revenues to meet its debt service. However, when the price of world oil fell significantly, the Mexican government experienced a serious deficiency in the foreign currency reserves it needed to repay its debts. Accordingly, it instituted a program of exchange control regulations designed to provide it with greater ability to monitor and maintain the exchange value of the peso. Exchange control regulations were promulgated, preventing holders of certificates of deposit from receiving payment in currencies other than the peso. The decrees prohibited the use of foreign currency as legal tender and banned the transfer of dollars abroad. Further, the government nationalized the entire private banking system and eliminated all bank deposits in foreign currency, specifying that repay-

ments of those deposits were to be made in pesos at a rate of exchange to be determined by Banco de Mexico. West's account was converted into pesos at the specified rate of 70 pesos to the dollar. When it was reconverted back into dollars in the United States at the prevailing rate of 112 pesos to the dollar, he suffered a loss of approximately one third of his investment. West filed a lawsuit in a U.S. district court, claiming the conversion of his dollar-denominated certificate of deposit to pesos at a rate less than the market rate of exchange was a taking of his property in violation of international law.

■ **ISSUE** Has the Mexican government illegally expropriated West's investment?

■ **DECISION** No. Determining whether an action by a government is a legitimate exercise of the police power in the regulation of its internal affairs as opposed to a taking of property in violation of international law can pose particularly difficult problems. Valid expropriations must always serve a public purpose; that public purpose in some cases may be so strong as to render lawful what otherwise might constitute an "illegal taking." The conclusion that a particular interference is an unlawful expropriation might be avoided if a state had a purpose in mind that is recognized in international law as justifying even severe restrictions on the use of property. A state has such a strong interest in its monetary policy. Under international law, a legislature generally is free to impose exchange controls. Mexico's institution of exchange controls was an exercise of its basic authority to regulate its economic affairs. While West did suffer losses as a result of the exchange controls, the losses were not occasioned by an illegal taking of his property. Thus, he is not entitled to compensation since Mexico had the right to make every effort to stabilize its currency during a time of financial stress.

Judicial Resolution of Investment Disputes

After an expropriation occurs, the investor's first action generally is to challenge the taking in the courts of the host country. If this fails, the investor may seek relief from the courts of a country where the host country owns property. However, this alternative frequently is stifled by the principle of sovereign immunity or the act of state doctrine.

Sovereign Immunity

Historically, there have been two basic theories of **sovereign immunity:** absolute and restrictive. The *absolute approach* holds that whenever a foreign sovereign has formally involved itself in a challenged activity, that involvement renders the activity immune from scrutiny by the domestic courts of other nations. This theory is prem-

FIGURE 1–2   U.S. Judicial Attitude toward Expropriation

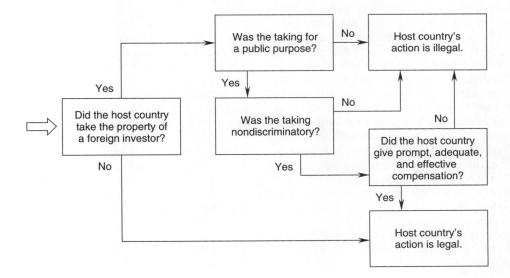

ised on the idea that no nation has the right to judge the internal actions of another nation. The *restrictive approach* shields the public (sovereign) acts of foreign governments from judicial review by domestic courts, but does not protect them from liability for any private acts they might undertake. Today, most of the world community follows the restrictive approach.

Foreign Sovereign Immunities Act

In 1976, the U.S. Congress enacted the *Foreign Sovereign Immunities Act* (FSIA), which codified the restrictive approach in federal law and empowered U.S. courts to determine which actions by foreign sovereigns should be immune from judicial scrutiny. Under the FSIA, foreign nations are granted sovereign immunity unless their actions fall within one of the act's enumerated exceptions. One of these, the **commercial activity** exception, frequently is invoked in investment disputes. No immunity attaches to a country's commercial activities because they are not considered to be sovereign acts. The FSIA states that the commercial character of an activity shall be determined by reference to the nature of the course of conduct or particular transaction, rather than by reference to its purpose. U.S. courts have interpreted this to mean sovereign immunity is warranted only when an activity is peculiar to governments, rather than one that private parties might ordinarily perform.

REPUBLIC OF ARGENTINA v. WELTOVER
112 S.Ct. 2160 (U.S. Sup.Ct. 1992)

■ **FACTS** Since Argentina's currency is not one of the mediums of exchange accepted on the international market, Argentine businesses engaging in global transactions must pay in U.S. dollars or some other internationally accepted currency. In the recent past, it was difficult for Argentine borrowers to obtain such funds, principally because of the instability of the Argentine currency. To address these problems, the Republic of Argentina instituted a foreign exchange insurance contract program (FEIC), under which Argentina effectively agreed to assume the risk of currency depreciation in cross-border transactions involving Argentine borrowers. This was accomplished by Argentina's agreeing to sell to domestic borrowers, in exchange for a contractually predetermined amount of local currency, the necessary U.S. dollars to repay their foreign debts when they matured, irrespective of intervening devaluations. Unfortunately, Argentina did not possess sufficient reserves of U.S. dollars to cover the FEIC contracts as they became due. It then adopted certain emergency measures, including refinancing of the FEIC-backed debts by issuing to the creditors govern-

ment bonds. These bonds provided for payment of interest and principal in U.S. dollars. Under the refinancing program, the foreign creditor could either accept the bonds in satisfaction of the initial debt, thereby substituting the Argentine government for the private debtor, or maintain the debtor/creditor relationship with the private borrower and accept the Argentine government as guarantor. When the bonds began to mature, Argentina concluded it lacked sufficient foreign exchange to retire them. Pursuant to a presidential decree, Argentina unilaterally extended the time for payment and offered bondholders substitute instruments as a means of rescheduling the debts. Several bondholders (two Panamanian corporations and a Swiss bank) refused to accept the rescheduling and demanded full payment. Argentina did not pay, and the bondholders filed a breach of contract suit in a U.S. district court. The Argentine government moved to dismiss the lawsuit on the grounds of sovereign immunity.

■ **ISSUE** Should the U.S. court dismiss the suit on the basis of sovereign immunity?

■ **DECISION** No. Under the Foreign Sovereign Immunity Act (FSIA), a foreign state is immune from the jurisdiction of the U.S. courts unless one of the statutorily defined exceptions applies. The most significant of these is the commercial exception. When a foreign government acts not as a regulator of a market, but in the manner of a private player within it, the foreign sovereign's actions are commercial within the meaning of the FSIA. Because the FSIA provides that the commercial character of an act is to be determined by reference to its "nature" rather than its "purpose," the question is not whether the government is acting with a profit motive or instead with the aim of fulfilling uniquely sovereign objectives. Rather, the issue is whether the particular actions that the state performs (whatever the motive behind them) are the *type* of actions by which a private party engages in "trade and traffic or commerce." Thus, a foreign government's issuance of regulations limiting its foreign currency exchange is a sovereign activity, because such authoritative control of commerce cannot be exercised by a private party; whereas a contract to buy army boots or even bullets is a commercial activity, because private companies can similarly use sales contracts to acquire such goods. The commercial character of these bonds is confirmed by the fact that they are in almost all respects garden-variety debt instruments: they may be held by private parties; they are negotiable and may be traded on the international market; and they promise a future stream of cash income. It is irrelevant *why* Argentina participated in the bond market in the manner of a private actor; it matters only that it did so.

The FSIA also strips a nation of sovereign immunity when it carries out an **unlawful taking** of property under international law. This exception is premised on the notion that each nation has a responsibility to abide by international law; therefore, violations of international law are not sovereign acts. A court is most likely to apply this exception when an expropriation violates a treaty signed by the host country and the foreign investor's home country. In the absence of such a treaty, the exception is not widely used because of the lack of global consensus on what constitutes an unlawful taking.

Act of State Doctrine

When a dispute cannot be resolved without an inquiry into the legality of actions taken by a foreign government, U.S. courts generally will abstain from hearing the case. Known as the **act of state doctrine,** this rule of judicial abstention recognizes the responsibility of every sovereign state to refrain from sitting in judgment on the acts done by the government of another sovereign state within its own territory. In practice, the act of state doctrine is employed by U.S. courts to avoid embarrassing the executive branch in the conduct of foreign affairs.

The act of state doctrine will not prevent a court from examining an investment dispute when the foreign nation is engaging in commercial, rather than governmental, acts. Further, the U.S. Congress enacted the *Hickenlooper Amendment,* which requires federal courts to examine the merits of expropriations claims. This statutory provision overrides the judicially created act of state doctrine in cases where the host country has confiscated property in violation of international law. As with the FSIA, courts are most likely to rule on takings that are discriminatory or otherwise violate an investment treaty ratified by the host country.

Causes of Expropriation

Decisions to expropriate generally stem from two sources: the political and economic climate of the host country and the behavior of the foreign investors. Accordingly, investors must carefully gauge the political and economic environment of a target country. Countries with a recent history of state ownership of property present a risk of expropriating investments. This may be particularly true in nations that are suffering severe economic problems. Governmental leaders may take over foreign-owned industries in an attempt to quickly bolster their political position. Strained relations between the host country and the foreign investor's home country also may induce a host nation to expropriate.

Certain investment behavior is more likely than others to trigger an expropriation. Investments in the extraction of scarce resources, financial institutions, public utilities, and agriculture often are targeted for confiscation by host governments. Further, when multinational corporations penetrate a developing nation through subsidiary corporations, they may burden a host country's balance of payments position by repatriating large amounts of capital. To plug this drain on hard currency and gain control over the multinational's local activities, a nation may resort to expropriation.

Safeguards against Expropriation

Perhaps the most effective safeguard against expropriation is for a business firm to minimize its physical presence in potentially unstable countries. It could do this by limiting itself to exporting, importing, and licensing. If a deeper level of penetration is called for, a firm might carry out its investment activities through joint ventures, thereby reducing its financial exposure. When a foreign presence is necessary, the firm may wish to reduce the inventories, supplies, and capital it maintains in unstable countries. Whenever possible, it should have its intellectual property owned by the parent corporation or by a subsidiary located outside of a risky nation. It should also maintain accurate records of its investment activities outside of the host country. Those documents might be essential in establishing the appropriate level of compensation should a legal tribunal find in favor of the foreign investor.

Insurance

Perhaps the best protection against the risk of expropriation is insurance. To encourage U.S. private investment in developing countries, the U.S. government established the Overseas Private Investment Corporation (OPIC), which offers low-cost expropriation insurance for certain kinds of investment projects in designated countries. If an insured project is expropriated, the U.S. firm receives compensation from OPIC in return for assigning to OPIC the firm's claim against the host government. The program is available only for investments in countries that have signed executive agreements with the United States that recognize in advance the legitimacy of such assignments and provide for arbitration if any dispute arises.

In the case of an uninsured expropriation, the U.S. government has a general policy of using measured diplomatic pressure to aid the U.S. firm involved, but the

FIGURE 1–3   Safeguards against Expropriation

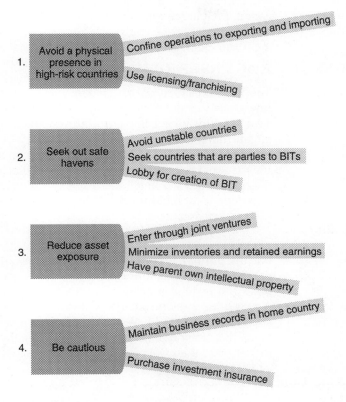

1. Avoid a physical presence in high-risk countries
   - Confine operations to exporting and importing
   - Use licensing/franchising

2. Seek out safe havens
   - Avoid unstable countries
   - Seek countries that are parties to BITs
   - Lobby for creation of BIT

3. Reduce asset exposure
   - Enter through joint ventures
   - Minimize inventories and retained earnings
   - Have parent own intellectual property

4. Be cautious
   - Maintain business records in home country
   - Purchase investment insurance

amount of pressure varies from administration to administration and from case to case. In many instances, this remedy, unlike the purely legal remedies described above, results in at least partial satisfaction of the firm's claim.

Bilateral Investment Treaties

A developed nation may improve the overseas investment climate for its businesses by persuading a potential host country to sign a bilateral investment treaty. Known as a **BIT,** such a treaty often obligates the host country to extend fair and equitable treatment to foreign investors. At its most basic level, this protection includes a pledge of nondiscrimination and a promise of prompt, adequate, and effective compensation whenever a taking occurs.

BITs generally establish formal mechanisms for resolving investment disputes. When the disputing parties are the two contracting nations, their BIT frequently requires that they begin negotiations and, if those fail, that their differences be resolved through arbitration. For disputes between the host nation and a foreign investor, more and more of these treaties call for compulsory arbitration by an international organization, the International Center for Settlement of Investment Disputes (ICSID).

POLITICAL VIOLENCE AGAINST PEOPLE

The focus of much of this chapter has been on the various pitfalls that await the unwary in the global environment. However, this introduction to international business would not be complete if it overlooked the political tensions that undermine global tranquility with depressing regularity. Governmental overthrows, ethnic warfare, kidnappings, and terrorist activities continue to subject corporate personnel and international travelers to very real physical dangers. Global managers must recognize the frequency with which these acts of violence are occurring throughout the world and implement measures to offset their potentially devastating effects.

Legal Implications for Global Businesses

The world community has begun efforts to develop international cooperation among nations in preventing premeditated, politically motivated violence against noncombatants. Further, individual governments have demonstrated a willingness to pursue criminal and civil actions against terrorists. However, particularly in the United States, there has been a growing movement to hold businesses directly liable when their negligence permitted such acts of violence to occur. Thus, in instances where a business knew or should have known that its employees or customers might be exposed to the risk of terrorism, it may have an affirmative duty to take reasonable precautions to safeguard their welfare.

KLINGHOFFER v. S.N.C. ACHILLE LAURO
1993 U.S. Dist. LEXIS 3924 (S.D. N.Y. 1993)

■ **FACTS** On October 7, 1985, four persons seized the Italian cruise liner Achille Lauro in the eastern Mediterranean Sea. During the incident, the hijackers murdered an elderly Jewish-American passenger, Leon Klinghoffer, by throwing him, and the wheelchair in which he was confined, overboard. Soon after the incident, the hijackers surrendered in Egypt. They were then extradited to Italy, where they were charged and convicted of crimes related to the seizure. According to some reports, the seizure was undertaken at the behest of Abdul Abbas, who was reportedly a member of the Palestine Liberation Organization (PLO). The PLO, however, denied any responsibility for the hijacking. Marilyn Klinghoffer and the estate of Leon Klinghoffer filed suit against Crown Travel Service (the agency that sold the Klinghoffers the tour package)

in a U.S. district court. Crown argued that since it did not own or operate the cruise vessel and since the travel tickets sold by Crown specifically disclaimed liability for negligence, it cannot be held liable for the Klinghoffers' injuries. The Klinghoffers urged that the disclaimer did not give them adequate notice they were relinquishing important rights. Further, they claimed Crown explicitly and implicitly agreed to provide reasonably safe travel and knew or should have known that the Achille Lauro would provide inadequate safety measures and yet failed to give a warning.

■ **ISSUE** Should Crown be liable for the injuries suffered by the Klinghoffers?

■ **DECISION** No. Crown did not own, operate, or control the Achille Lauro on the voyage when it was hijacked. Whether the disclaimer is contractually binding or not, it evidences the lack of any express agreement or warranty on the part of Crown for safe passage during the cruise.

Before the 1985 hijacking, the Achille Lauro was well respected within the travel industry, and there had been no complaints about security procedures aboard any Lauro ships. (Note: the owners of the Achille Lauro settled all of the claims filed against them.)

Crisis Contingency Planning

International businesses, particularly when conducting operations in political hot spots, are advised to develop **contingency plans** for responding to acts of political violence. Often these blueprints will closely parallel the procedures a company may have established for natural disasters. At their most basic level, they might include low-key intelligence gathering designed to keep the company informed of potential risks. There also should be a well-defined communication network and a clear preassignment of responsibilities in crisis situations. Further, the organization should maintain up-to-date medical records on all employees. In areas where risks are high, personnel levels should be reduced as much as possible. Finally, security for employees and customers should be substantially upgraded when risks increase.

ETHICAL IMPLICATIONS Northwest Airlines received a telephone call threatening terrorist action against the airline's Paris-to-Detroit flight in retaliation for the prison sentences recently given two Palestinians. Northwest promptly informed the media of the threat and gave all passengers the opportunity to change to other flights or airlines with no penalty. More than three quarters of the passengers canceled their reservations. One week later, Delta gave a similar option to its passengers after receiving a general threat against all of its trans-Atlantic flights. Did the airlines respond in a proper manner?

CONCEPT SUMMARY **Crisis Contingency Plan**	
Gather Information	Maintain discreet intelligence-gathering system to keep abreast of political environment
Establish Communication Network	Establish a method of relaying information in the event of a public communication blackout
Preassign Responsibilities	Develop a clear chain of command for dealing with crises
Maintain Medical Records	Be aware of special medical needs of all at-risk personnel
Reduce Personnel Levels	When crisis looms, evacuate nonessential personnel (develop low-key evacuation plan)
Upgrade Security	Provide adequate security to protect staff and customers when risks increase

QUESTIONS AND PROBLEM CASES

1. What is meant by repatriation of earnings? What problems might hinder repatriation?

2. Under what circumstances might a U.S. parent corporation be held liable for the obligations of its foreign subsidiary?

3. How can parties to an international contract minimize the dispute resolution problems inherent in global transactions?

4. What is hedging? When and why is it used?

5. Brandeis, an international trading company located in England, contracted with Calabrian, a New York corporation, for the purchase of industrial chemical products. Calabrian packaged the chemicals in 1,323 plastic drums, which were placed on 48 pallets and stowed aboard a ship. When the shipment reached Europe, it was discovered that 35 of the plastic drums were damaged due to improper packing by Calabrian. Brandeis advised Calabrian that it rejected the shipment in its entirety and requested a replacement in 30 days. When Calabrian refused the rejection and replacement, Brandeis sought arbitration in accordance with the arbitration agreement in the parties' contract. The arbitrators ruled that Brandeis could reject the entire shipment and was entitled to damages from Calabrian. When Brandeis petitioned a U.S. district court to enforce the arbitral award, Calabrian argued that enforcement would violate U.S. public policy because the arbitrators manifestly disregarded English law in finding for Brandeis. It based this conclusion on the fact that Brandeis was permitted to reject the entire shipment when only a small quantity of the chemicals was damaged. Should the U.S. court refuse to enforce the arbitral award?

6. Northstar Imports, a U.S. company, entered into a distribution agreement with George Philip and Son, Ltd., an English corporation. Under the terms of the contract, Northstar was to be the sole and exclusive agent for the sale of Philip's products in the United States. When Northstar learned Philip was marketing its products in the United States through Time-Life Books and other companies, it filed suit against Philip in a U.S. district court, alleging fraud and breach of contract. Philip moved to dismiss the lawsuit, pointing out a clause in the distribution agreement that provided: *"This agreement is subject to English Law and the English courts shall be the courts of competent jurisdiction."* Northstar argued the clause was invalid because it was ambiguous since it did not give any court exclusive jurisdiction. Does the contract language preclude Northstar from suing in the United States?

7. Bernia Sewing Machine Company (Importer) imported and sold Bernia sewing machines to Bernia Distributors, Inc. (Distributor). Importer paid Swiss francs to purchase the machines from a Swiss manufacturer. Under the terms of the distribution contract, Importer could raise or lower the price of the machines to Distributor to reflect increases or decreases in the manufacturer's invoice price to Importer. For a short time, changes in the exchange rate between dollars and Swiss francs were treated as increases in invoice costs to Importer, which were passed on in the exact amounts of the increases to Distributor. However, when the dollar declined precipitously in relation to the Swiss franc, the reduced value of the dollar in the purchase of Swiss francs had nearly doubled Importer's costs and thus halved its rate of return per dollar invested. As a result, Importer began to surcharge Distributor 10 percent above the increased cost of purchasing Swiss francs so it could retain sufficient profit margin to justify continued sales. Importer argued this increase was permissible since it had not been aware of the risk of currency fluctuations before signing the distributorship contract. Is Importer correct?

8. In 1985, the Italian passenger liner Achille Lauro was forcibly seized in the Mediterranean Sea. During the hijacking, Leon Klinghoffer was shot and thrown into the Mediterranean. Several passengers on the ship sued the Palestine Liberation Organization (PLO), claiming the seizure and murder were done by PLO members. The PLO argued it is a sovereign state and therefore immune from suit under the Foreign Sovereign Immunities Act. Is the PLO correct?

9. U.S. law requires that all grapes must pass governmental inspections before they may be sold in the United States. Both domestic and imported grapes are inspected under the same set of "shipping

point" standards. However, a difference in regulation arises with the time and location of inspection. Domestic grapes are inspected soon after harvest and just before shipment to markets within the United States. Imported grapes, on the other hand, are inspected just before their shipment to the U.S. markets and again at their U.S. port of entry. Chilean grape producers complained this difference meant their grapes were inspected under standards that were in application more stringent than those applied to domestic grapes. Specifically, they argued that, since their grapes must undergo two weeks' transport by refrigerated ship before arriving in a U.S. port, they are less likely to pass inspection than are the more recently harvested domestic grapes. Does the inspection system unlawfully discriminate against imported grapes?

10. International Promotions and Ventures, a U.S. corporation, contracted to supply 52 Starfighter jets to the Republic of Bolivia in return for negotiable promissory notes guaranteed by the Central Bank of Bolivia. Although Bolivia was required to issue the notes upon the signing of the contract, the agreement expressly required International Promotions to return the notes if U.S. governmental authorities failed to approve the transfer of the aircraft. When the U.S. State Department refused to issue the necessary export licenses for the aircraft, Bolivia requested the return of the notes it had issued. However, International Promotions had already sold one of the notes to David Shapiro. When Shapiro sued in a U.S. court to collect on the note, Bolivia argued the court lacked jurisdiction to hear the case under the doctrine of sovereign immunity. Should the suit against Bolivia be dismissed on sovereign immunity grounds?

2

The International Legal System

INTRODUCTION

Nature and Function of International Law

International law may be defined as a body of principles that are commonly observed by the world community. These rules are essential to the orderly management of the relations among nations. This traditional notion of international law, also known as **public international law,** deals with the rights and obligations of sovereign states. Regulation of the activities of individuals and corporations, on the other hand, generally falls within the realm of **private international law.** Often called *conflict of laws,* those rules are part of the domestic legal systems of the individual nations.

Under the doctrine of *incorporation,* most countries recognize the international law as part of their domestic law to some degree. (The *Paquette Habana* case, discussed below, is an example of this phenomenon.) Further, as you will see throughout the remainder of the text, a growing number of international institutions greatly shape the content of private international law. Thus, over time, the two systems are becoming more and more inseparable.

Chapter Overview

This chapter begins with an examination of the basic sources of public international law, indicating how these rules govern the affairs of nations. Attention then shifts to the major families of private international law in the world today. That discussion illustrates how cultural variations around the world affect the different legal environments in which global businesses operate. This is followed by two sections that examine the role of the United Nations in the global legal system. The first looks at its basic structure and method of creating international rules. The second focuses exclusively on how the judicial arm of the United Nations—the International Court of Justice—regulates the legal relationships among nations. The chapter closes with a brief review of several other international organizations that are influential in the creation of both public and private international law.

SOURCES OF INTERNATIONAL LAW

The United Nations, in Article 38 of the International Court of Justice Statute, provides a widely accepted interpretation of how international law is created. Specifically, this provision requires that international disputes be resolved by reference to treaties, customs, general principles of law recognized by civilized nations, and judicial decisions and teachings. Treaties and customs are considered to be the primary sources of international law. General principles and judicial decisions and teachings, on the other hand, are subsidiary sources in the sense that they are used only as evidence of an existing obligation arising from a treaty or a customary practice.

Treaty Law

The most important sources of international law are found in the bilateral and multilateral *treaties* that regulate the affairs between and among nations. Generally, these international conventions make a onetime declaration of the rules that govern their adopting nations. However, they also may establish a procedure for drafting future regulations. For example, U.N. members have delegated ongoing lawmaking power to the General Assembly. And the Organization for Economic Cooperation and Development (OECD) may, in limited circumstances, enact *resolutions* that are binding on its members. Accordingly, **treaty law** may include many of the declarations of international congresses, conferences, and organizations.

As a general rule, international conventions provide a source of law only for their contracting states. Nations that have not ratified a treaty are not obliged to its terms, unless those principles were already a part of customary law. (Customary law is discussed below.) This is because treaty law is based on the consent of sovereign nations. In the absence of such consent, each nation's sovereign right to regulate its own affairs will prevail. However, in response to demands for faster and more effective international lawmaking, the *1969 Convention on the Law of Treaties* articulated a more flexible concept of what actually constitutes a treaty. This convention gives nations complete freedom to determine the required means of expressing consent to the terms of a treaty.

AEGEAN SEA CONTINENTAL SHELF CASE
1978 I.C.J. Reports 39 (International Court of Justice)

■ **FACTS** The Turkish government granted licenses to explore for petroleum in undersea locations of the Aegean Sea, including areas that encroached on the continental shelf of several Greek islands. The Greek government protested Turkey's right to grant licenses over the contested waters. Turkey rejected the protests but expressed a readiness for negotiations to resolve the territorial dispute. Greece then proposed that the nations' differences over the applicable law as well as over the substance of the matter be referred to the International Court of Justice. Turkey answered by expressing hope that Greece would agree to enter negotiations, adding that in principle it considered favorably the proposal to refer the dispute jointly to the Court of Justice. To this effect, Turkey proposed talks between the two governments at the ministerial level. Later, the foreign ministers of Greece and Turkey considered the text of a special agreement concerning submission of the matter to the International Court of Justice. After two weeks of discussions, the prime ministers of both countries met in Brussels and issued a joint communiqué that stated:

> The two prime ministers had an opportunity to give consideration to the problems which led to the existing situation as regards relations between their countries. They decided that those problems should be resolved peacefully by means of

negotiations and as regards the continental shelf of the Aegean Sea by the International Court at The Hague. They defined the general lines on the basis of which the forthcoming meetings of the representatives of the two governments would take place.

The communiqué was issued directly to the media during a press conference at the conclusion of the meeting between the prime ministers and did not bear any signature or initials. The Greek government cited it as evidence that the Court of Justice had jurisdiction to hear the dispute. Turkey responded that the communiqué did not amount to an agreement under international law. The Turkish government reiterated its view that it would not be in the interest of the two countries to submit the dispute to the Court of Justice without first attempting meaningful negotiations.

■ **ISSUE** Was the communiqué an international agreement that bound the two countries to submit their dispute to the Court of Justice?

■ **DECISION** No. On the question of form, there is no rule of international law that might preclude a joint communiqué from constituting an international agreement to submit a dispute to arbitration or judicial settlement. Accordingly, whether the communiqué does or does not constitute such an agreement essentially depends on the nature of the act or transaction to which it gives expression. The question is not settled simply by referring to the form—a communiqué—in which that act or transaction is embodied. On the contrary, in determining what was the nature of the act or transaction embodied in the commu-

niqué, the Court of Justice must have regard above all to its actual terms and to the particular circumstances in which it was drawn up. When considered in this light, the communiqué does not evidence any change in Turkey's original position that the nations should negotiate their differences before submitting the dispute to the Court of Justice.

There are limitations on this relaxation of the importance of form in treaty making. For instance, whenever a treaty includes precise procedures for ratification, other indications of consent are unlikely to bind a nation to the treaty. Thus, a sovereign still must give its consent before it is subject to treaty law. Accordingly, contemporary international law does not recognize a treaty capable of binding all nations unless they specifically have given their consent.

Customary Law

International rules derived from customs and usages preceded the emergence of treaty law. In fact, much of the content of today's international conventions is merely a restatement of the practices that have long been shared by nations. **Customary law** is found by examining the actual practices (usages) of the various countries. Certain conduct that has been carried on for a long period eventually receives the approval of most of the world community. When this occurs, the practice ripens into customary law.

■

THE PAQUETTE HABANA
175 U.S. 677 (U.S. Sup.Ct. 1900)

■ **FACTS** At the outbreak of the Spanish-American War, the U.S. Navy captured two boats that were fishing along the coast of Cuba. Each vessel sailed under a Spanish flag and was owned by a Spanish subject living in Cuba. Until stopped by the blockading squadron of U.S. ships, neither fishing vessel knew of the existence of the war or of any blockade. Their cargo consisted entirely of fish. They had no arms or ammunition and made no attempt to run the blockade after learning of its existence. Both ships were confiscated and sold by auction in the United States as prizes of war. The owners of the fishing vessels sued for the return of the ships, arguing that under international law, fishing vessels are exempt from seizure.

■ **ISSUE** Did the capture and sale of the fishing vessels violate international law?

■ **DECISION** Yes. International law is part of the domestic law of the United States and must be ascertained

and administered by the U.S. courts. For this purpose, where there is no treaty, and no controlling executive or legislative act or judicial decision, resort must be had to the customs and usages of civilized nations. As evidence of these, attention must be given to the works of jurists and commentators, who by years of labor, research, and experience, have made themselves well acquainted with certain subjects. These sources make clear that, by an ancient usage among civilized nations, beginning centuries ago and gradually ripening into a rule of international law, coastal fishing vessels pursuing their vocation have been recognized as exempt from capture as prizes of war. As early as 1403, England and France drafted a treaty that ordained each country's fishing vessels would be granted safe conduct despite hostilities between the nations. Similar edicts were issued by France and the Netherlands in 1536. The doctrine that exempts coastal fishermen with their vessels and cargoes from capture has been familiar to the United States from the time of the War of Independence. Likewise, these terms were included in the Treaty of 1785 between the United States and Prussia. And, in the war with Mexico in 1846, the United States recognized the exemption for coastal fishing boats. Finally, the Empire of Japan (the last state admitted into the rank of civilized nations) promulgated an ordinance at the beginning of the war with China that ex-empted Chinese fishing boats from capture. This review of the precedents and authorities abundantly demonstrates that, by the general consent of the civilized nations of the world, and independently of any express treaty or other public act, it is an established rule of international law that coastal fishing vessels are exempt from capture as a prize of war.

International conferences and organizations are facilitating the discovery of customary law by outlining certain types of acceptable behavior that nations tend to follow. While this suggests some overlap between treaty law and customary law, differences do exist. Lawmaking by treaty requires negotiations and semiformal manifestations of consent. Customary law, on the other hand, arises from actual practice and acceptance of that conduct as law (*opinio juris*).

Actual Practice

It is through *actual practice* that certain behavior becomes part of customary law. It may include active conduct as well as continued abstentions from certain activities. An active manifestation of customary law can be found in the historic practice of states to freely exploit the resources of their coastal waters. Likewise, the general refusal of most nations to threaten or use force against the territorial integrity of other countries is an abstention that has become part of customary international law.

Before practices are elevated to the level of international law, certain requirements must be met. First, they must be widely shared by a broad spectrum of the world community. Of course, there are exceptions to the requirements that the practice be shared by a majority of the nations in the world community. For instance, customary law might arise from common behavior practiced only by nations that share a keen interest in a particular matter (i.e., countries that engage in whaling) and a general acquiescence by the rest of the world. Second, for customary law to arise, national practices must possess sufficient uniformity to clearly indicate the existence of a single standard of behavior. Finally, this uniform and widely followed behavior must continue for sufficient time to identify the conduct as legally required. The emergence of vast numbers of international conferences and organizations, combined with technological breakthroughs in communications, have greatly reduced the amount of time it takes for a practice to become incorporated into international law.

Opinio Juris

Actual practices must be accompanied by a general acceptance that the conduct is required by law before it will become part of customary law. This additional requirement, known as *opinio juris*, prohibits the enforcement of customary rules against the nations that have consistently objected to the legitimacy of particular practices despite their widespread acceptance by the rest of the world community. In instances

FIGURE 2–1   Formulating Customary Law

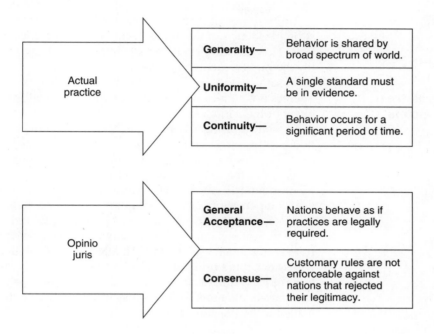

where a country has made no express statements concerning the legality of a particular practice, great weight is given to whether it has consistently followed or deviated from the generally accepted conduct in its own affairs.

General Principles of Law

When the primary sources of international law (treaties and customs) do not offer clear guidance, **general principles of law** recognized by civilized nations may be applied. Although this source was expressly recognized in the Statute of the International Court of Justice, no consensus exists on how these principles are formed. Under the prevailing view today, they may be found by examining the domestic legal systems in the international community. However, as a secondary source of international law, these propositions generally are used to reinforce or identify murky aspects of treaty law or customary law. Because no international or national dispute resolution panel has ever carefully explained the nature of this source of law, its very existence is controversial.

Judicial Decisions and Teachings

Another subsidiary method for determining the content of the rules of international law is found in **judicial decisions and teachings** of the world's most highly qualified publicists. Included in this category are the judgments of the International Court of Justice (discussed below) and the awards of international arbitral panels. Decisions rendered by the national courts are also given deference in determining the existence of international law. (The *Trail Smelter Case* that appears in Chapter 16 provides an example of the legal effect of domestic decisions.)

The writings of highly qualified scholars are given similar effect. They provide strong evidence of the actual legal content of various treaties and customary practices. However, they do not create international law. They are used only to help identify the precise meaning of the primary sources of law.

Alternative Viewpoints

There is not perfect agreement throughout the world over the formation and resulting effect of the various sources of international law. In fact, many underdeveloped nations, while refusing to reject the existence of international law, have strongly criticized its current expression. They view many of today's international rules as a continuation of the European expansion that resulted in the colonization of most of the world.

For instance (as was discussed in Chapter 1), many former colonies reject the modern interpretation of customary law that requires "prompt, adequate, and effective compensation" for expropriations and nationalizations. Similarly, underdeveloped nations often invoke the concept of *unequal treaties* to repudiate overly burdensome obligations imposed on them when they possessed extremely weak bargaining power at a treaty's inception. Finally, many revolutionary governments reject the widely accepted principle that a new government is responsible for the legal obligations of its predecessor. This has important consequences today, as the international community attempts to determine which, if any, of the former Soviet republics are liable for the previous dealings of the Soviet Union.

TRANS-ORIENT MARINE CORP. v. STAR TRADING & MARINE, INC.
731 F.Supp. 619 (S.D. N.Y. 1990)

■ **FACTS** In 1983, Trans-Orient was granted a five-year exclusive agency agreement to represent the Sudan in the United States. Two years later, a military coup deposed the then-head of state in the Sudan, declaring a state of emergency and suspending the constitution. A 12-month transitional military regime followed, which was then replaced by a civilian coalition government. At that time, the name of the country was changed from the Sudan to the Republic of Sudan. In another military coup in 1989, the present military regime overthrew the former civilian administration and suspended the constitution. During 1985, the Sudanese government sent letters advising Trans-Orient that a new agent had been appointed to represent the country in the United States. This termination of Trans-Orient did not provide the one-year termination notice required under the original contract. When Trans-Orient filed a breach of contract suit, the present Sudanese government asserted that it was not liable for

the contractual obligations of the prior sovereign. Trans-Orient responded that neither the 1985 regime nor the present regime was a successor state, but that they represented mere changes in government that did not relieve them from the prior government's contractual obligations.

■ **ISSUE** Did the military coups relieve the present Sudanese government of the country's previous contractual obligations?

■ **DECISION** No. Whether a new administration may terminate the executory portions of its predecessor's contracts is based on the succession of state theory. International law sharply distinguishes the succession of state, which may create a discontinuity of statehood, from a succession of government, which leaves statehood unaffected. It is generally accepted that a change in government, regime, or ideology has no effect on that state's international rights and obligations because the state continues to exist despite the change. However, where one sovereign succeeds another, and a new state is created, the rights and obligations of the successor are affected. While the successor state is permitted to terminate existing contracts originally executed by the former sovereign and a private party, the successor state is liable to that party for any amount due him as of the date of the change of sovereignty. But if the contract is totally executory, the successor state is released from the contract entirely. The Restatement of Foreign Relations Law describes a successor state to include a state that: (1) wholly absorbs another state, (2) takes over part of the

territory of another state, (3) becomes independent of another state of which it had formed a part, or (4) arises because of the dismemberment of the state of which it had been a part. This old and fully accepted principle of general international law has been recognized by writers since at least 1831. A careful study of the events that occurred in the Republic of Sudan show that there has not been a succession of state. Arguments by the Sudanese government that the governmental transitions occurred by way of military coup as opposed to routine, constitutional processes are not persuasive. Treatises, as well as applicable case law, demonstrate that such features do not effect a succession of state.

Jus Cogens

The *1986 Vienna Convention on the Law of Treaties* reaffirmed earlier pronouncements claiming that certain principles of "higher law" govern the affairs of nations. This concept, known as ***jus cogens,*** has been offered as a legal justification for the invalidation of treaties that impose unduly harsh duties on one or more of the signatories. In recent years, it has gained growing acceptance outside of the realm of treaties, particularly in regard to national responsibility for international crimes like terrorism.

The vast cultural differences that distinguish the world community have blunted any widespread acceptance of these natural law notions. The majority of the world community continues to regard national consent as a precondition to the creation of international law. Accordingly, treaties and customs continue to be the only generally accepted, primary sources of international law.

ETHICAL IMPLICATIONS   Is it ethical for multinational corporations and developed nations to extract major concessions from the underdeveloped world as a precondition to investing there?

THE WORLD'S MAJOR LEGAL SYSTEMS

Not all people share the same conception of law. For instance, many cultures distinguish between *ius* (law that is both declared and enforced) and a broader concept known as *lex* (law that is declared but is not necessarily enforced). In the United States, people tend to equate law only with *ius*. This more restrictive view law possesses several fundamental characteristics: (*a*) it is based on general principles; (*b*) it is to be applied universally; (*c*) it is derived from a relationship based on rights and corresponding duties; and (*d*) failure to comply with it should result in the imposition of some type of sanction.

An examination of the domestic legal systems throughout the world reveals wide differences in cultural perceptions of the role of law. Despite these conceptual variations, however, it still is possible to classify the vast number of domestic legal systems into several major categories. This section briefly identifies the primary characteristics of the following legal families: civil law, common law, Islamic law, socialist law, sub-Saharan Africa, and the Far East.

Civil Law

The **civil law** system, derived from ancient Roman law, stresses the importance of formulating comprehensive codes and systematic rules that regulate behavior in advance. In fact, the distinctive feature of civil law countries is their reliance on codified rules. This lends stability and predictability to legal disputes. This civil law family relies on legal scholars for the discovery and formulation of law. Judges then deduce the outcomes for legal disputes from these preestablished sets of abstract rules.

Although the roots of the civil law system lie in continental Europe, through colonization, this family of laws has spread throughout the world. Thus, it is predominant in Latin America and provides an important foundation for the Islamic, socialist, and Far Eastern legal systems as well.

Common Law

While the civil law system approaches legal matters with fixed ideas and deductive reasoning, the **common law** school favors case-by-case analysis. Essentially, common law judges look to prior cases rather than abstract rules in resolving legal disputes. Thus, they tend to be more concerned with the merits of the case at hand than they are with the formulation of general principles of law. As a result of this focus, common law courts tend to place as much importance on procedural rules (e.g., the admissibility of evidence) as they do on substantive issues. This emphasis on the individual case results in lawyers and juries performing extremely important roles in the formation of law.

The common law system evolved from the laws of England and, over time, has spread throughout the former British Empire. The legal system of the United States is part of the common law family. During recent years, in both the United States and throughout the rest of the common law system, demands for business planning and the ordering of social affairs have led to a growing movement to codify legal rules. Simultaneously, the civil law countries have witnessed a trend among judges to take a more active role in the formulation of law. Thus, the two systems seem to be steadily evolving toward one another.

Islamic Law

The Islamic nations share the civil and common law systems' recognition of the fundamental importance of law. However, **Islamic law**, unlike civil law, is not an outgrowth of theoretical legal principles, and it differs from the common law in that it does not spring from practical needs. Instead, it emanates from fundamental religious ideals. Unlike the common and civil law systems, Islamic law does not adapt to reflect changing social conditions. The Islamic system holds that the law of Allah was imparted to the prophet Mohammed for all times. Therefore, society must adapt itself to Allah's will rather than having law respond to social change.

In Islamic society, law holds a paramount place because religious beliefs focus on how people should behave in their day-to-day lives. It stresses the divine nature of law and does not distinguish between legal and ethical duties. Of course, not all

Islamic nations have responded to outside influences in the same way. For instance, the countries of the Arabian Peninsula have rejected other legal philosophies and maintained a traditional system. Similarly, Iran and Libya have revolted against the ways of the outside world and reinstituted fundamentalist notions of Islamic religion. At the other extreme, most of the Islamic world has gradually embraced Western ideas and borrowed legal principles from the common law and civil law families.

Socialist Law   The recent breakup of the Soviet Union, coupled with the democratization of Eastern Europe, makes it difficult to chart the course of **socialist law**. For the most part, the members originally were civil law countries, and they still maintain many of those characteristics. The socialist systems in China, Vietnam, and North Korea have borrowed from the Far Eastern family as well.

The basis of socialist law is derived from abstract principles designed to shape human conduct. It holds that the fundamental basis of social order is grounded in the economic and social conditions of life. Socialist nations confine the role of law to three functions: (1) preservation of national security, (2) development of the production necessary to provide essential goods and services, and (3) education of the populace to the fundamental socialist principles. Thus, the private law aspects of traditional socialist systems are extremely limited with property owned by the state. In general, they share a heavily bureaucratized legal structure. However, this seems to be changing rapidly. China, Vietnam, and Cuba have been opening their doors to outside development and, accordingly, have demonstrated a willingness to modify their legal systems to accommodate the needs of investors.

Sub-Saharan Africa   Despite attempts to transplant civil law and common law notions throughout the African continent, the majority of the population south of the Sahara Desert still retains its adherence to traditional norms. Historically, this region of the world has been characterized by loyalties that center on the family and tribal groupings. Those values are still pervasive. This focus on the group tends to ignore notions of individuality and, as a result, the system lacks refined conceptions of civil rights and liberties. Thus, without an understanding of these core values, **sub-Saharan African law** may appear to an outsider as particularly harsh.

The primary function of law, then, centers on the conservation of community and the maintenance of public order. Most legal disputes are resolved by reference to unwritten customary rules that are evolving to meet changing social conditions. The system places a premium on conciliation, and African judges frequently take on the appearance of arbitrators.

The Far East   The civil law, common law, and Islamic law families share a vision of law as a fundamental basis for society. This view is rejected in **Far Eastern law**. It shares with the sub-Saharan African legal system the idea that the goal of individuals should primarily center on a quest for harmony. Legal action often is seen as arbitrary and a cause of social disorder. Despite the communist revolution in China and the heavy westernization of Japan, this attitude toward legal processes still exists.

Many of the basic characteristics of the Far Eastern legal family can be traced back to its roots in ancient China. Social order was maintained through the Confucian

FIGURE 2–2   The Major Legal Systems of the World

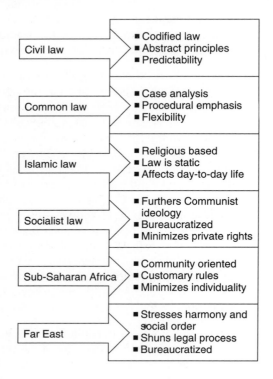

system, which provided an intricate web of social rules and taboos that ensured each individual did nothing to threaten the status quo. However, China also experienced a legalist movement that established an elaborate bureaucratic network that administered the criminal law system through a system of severe sanctions. Although those two influences are still apparent throughout the Far Eastern nations, the national legal systems also show many traces of the civil law, common law, and socialist law families.

THE UNITED NATIONS

The United Nations, more than any other institution, has provided the greatest influence over the formation of international law. Established in the wake of World War II, it was charged with several ambitious goals: to provide for international peace and security, to promote worldwide social progress through a spirit of global cooperation, and to foster a universal respect for international law. It imposes on the nations of the world an obligation to recognize the equality of nations, the right of self-determination, and the responsibility to protect basic human rights.

This section introduces the organizational features of the United Nations, examining its membership requirements and its principal organs. The International Court of Justice, the judicial branch of the United Nations, is covered in the section immediately following this.

Membership of the United Nations

Sovereign states are the primary members of the United Nations, although colonies and constituent republics of sovereign nations also may join. The 51 founding nations automatically became part of the organization as *original members*. Other nations can apply to join as *elective members*. (There are no real differences between the rights and obligations of the original members and those of the elective members.) To be admitted into the organization, a nation must pledge to abide by the United Nations Charter and be capable of fulfilling those obligations. Its application must then be recommended by the Security Council and approved by a two-thirds majority of the General Assembly. (Both of these organs are discussed below.) Today the membership of the United Nations numbers over 160.

Members may be expelled for repeated violations of the charter upon the recommendation of the Security Council. A two-thirds majority of the General Assembly must then concur with an *expulsion* proposal. Permanent members of the Security Council may block decisions to admit applicants or expel members (including themselves) through their veto power. (Permanent members and their veto power are discussed below.) Members also may be subject to *suspension* of their membership, including loss of voting rights, if the Security Council takes enforcement actions against them or if they fail to honor their financial obligations to the United Nations.

The General Assembly

The **General Assembly** is the principal organ of the United Nations. Each member country is represented in the General Assembly and each is entitled to one vote. The General Assembly elects its own president and adopts its own procedural rules. Its tasks are carried out in regular sessions through a number of general and special committees.

Principal Functions of the General Assembly

As a rule, the General Assembly may consider any issue relating to the underlying goals of the United Nations. However, it is precluded from interfering with the internal affairs of individual members. It also may not consider matters that are currently being dealt with by the Security Council. But if Security Council action is blocked by the veto of a permanent member, the General Assembly may then address the issue.

All of the subsidiary agencies of the United Nations must report to the General Assembly. It also prepares the overall budget for the organization and calculates the financial contribution that each member must make to support its activities. A country's financial obligation depends on the General Assembly's determination of its ability to pay.

The Group of 77

Today over two thirds of the members of the General Assembly are newer nations, most of them former colonies. Known as the *Group of 77,* although they now number over 120, these countries have attempted to codify and reform the international legal system through the General Assembly. In particular, they have demanded that the General Assembly assume a more active role in addressing their unique problems. Their efforts frequently have transformed the General Assembly into a battleground between the developed and the developing world.

The Security Council

The **Security Council** has a membership of 15 nations. Five of the countries (China, France, Russia, the United Kingdom, and the United States) are **permanent members.** The other 10 members are elected to two-year terms (five each year) by the General Assembly. A nonpermanent member is not eligible for immediate reelection at the expiration of its term. In electing the nonpermanent members, the General Assembly attempts to make an equitable distribution among the regions of the world.

Voting Rules

The Security Council considers both procedural and substantive issues. *Procedural matters* center exclusively on the internal operation of the Security Council. A decision relating to a procedural issue requires the approval of 9 of the 15 members. *Substantive matters,* on the other hand, extend outside of the internal workings of the Security Council into the international affairs of the member states. Decisions concerning the external application of United Nations principles require the approval of nine members, including all five of the permanent members. Thus, each of the five permanent members has the power to **veto** substantive matters.

Functions of the Security Council

The founders of the United Nations intended that the Security Council would command a military force capable of policing world affairs. However, throughout most of the history of the United Nations, Cold War frictions between the Soviet Union and the United States (both possessing veto power) stymied any significant initiatives by the Security Council. The recent warming of relations between the United States and Russia has rekindled hopes of a permanent United Nations peacekeeping force. United Nations efforts in Somalia and during the Persian Gulf War suggest that such cooperation is possible. However, the powers of the Security Council are not confined to military actions. It possesses broad authority to implement peaceful methods of settling disputes among nations.

Controversies Surrounding the Security Council

The initial selection of the five permanent members was based on their role in defeating the Axis powers in World War II as well as on a prediction of their future influence over world affairs. Their privileged treatment has been a continual source of controversy, in part, because it violates the United Nations principle of equality among nations. Many nations argue that no member should be given permanent status or be granted veto power. If the practice is to continue, some countries argue that the number of permanent members should be expanded. For instance, the underdeveloped world has demanded an increase in the membership of the Security Council so its numbers will be more equitably represented. Further, Germany and Japan can claim that the current distribution of power in the world entitles them to permanent membership status. Finally, the automatic succession of Russia to the former Soviet Union's seat has been criticized by the Ukraine, which has an arguable right to share that position.

The Secretariat

The **Secretariat** provides an international civil service that supports the overall activities of the United Nations. The organizational headquarters in New York has several thousand staff members. More people are employed at the specialized agencies located in major cities throughout the world. Staff members and their activities are regulated by rules promulgated by the General Assembly. They take a pledge of international loyalty that prohibits their seeking or receiving instructions from any individual nation. The Secretariat publishes a daily journal and operates a radio station. It supports numerous studies and circulates their results in books, pamphlets, and magazines published by its Office of Public Information.

The Secretary-General

Presiding over the Secretariat is the **Secretary-General,** who serves as the chief administrative officer of the United Nations. This individual is appointed to a five-year term (with the possibility of reappointment to one additional term) by a majority of the General Assembly, acting upon the recommendation of the Security Council. The Secretary-General must meet the approval of all of the five permanent members to the Security Council since any of them can veto the nomination.

The Economic and Social Council

The Economic and Social Council (**ECOSOC**) was formed to facilitate global cooperation in increasing worldwide standards of living, addressing health problems, and ensuring universal respect for basic human rights. Its 27 member states are elected to three-year terms by the General Assembly. ECOSOC has created numerous committees to study ways of furthering its goals. It has coordinated the efforts of other United Nations' agencies, governmental groups, and nongovernmental organizations that are dealing with similar issues. (The problems with ECOSOC's role in addressing global environmental problems are discussed in Chapter 16.) ECOSOC reports its findings to the General Assembly.

THE INTERNATIONAL COURT OF JUSTICE

The General Assembly and the Security Council are vested with the authority to deal with political issues, while ECOSOC provides assistance in defining and addressing economic and social matters. The Secretariat, under the guidance of the Secretary-General, lends overall administrative support to these efforts. One other United Na-

FIGURE 2–3   The Structure of the United Nations

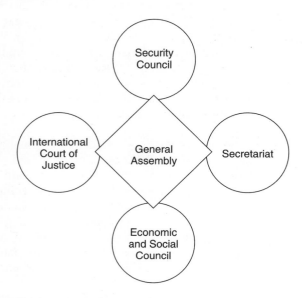

tions institution—the **International Court of Justice**—deserves special mention because of the important role it performs in the adjudication of legal disputes between nations.

Composition of the Court

The International Court of Justice, frequently called the *World Court,* has its headquarters in The Hague. It is composed of 15 judges, no two of whom may be nationals of the same country, who serve nine-year terms. To be elected, candidates must be supported by a majority of the General Assembly and a majority of the Security Council. (In this voting, the permanent members of the Security Council do not have veto power.) While it was envisioned that the court would be staffed by former national court justices, ex-legal practitioners, and ex-law professors, historically its membership has been dominated by ex-ambassadors as well as former politicians and civil servants.

The Chamber System

The Court has developed a **chamber procedure** that enables it to hear cases with as few as three to five judges. By conducting its affairs in this manner, the Court has been better able to meet the growing demands placed on it. Basically, there are three types of chambers. The first, known as the *Chamber of Summary Procedure,* is composed of the president and vice president of the Court as well as three other judges who are designated each year. This preestablished chamber permits conflicts to be addressed immediately. The Court also has authority to designate *special chambers* that can specialize in hearing particular types of cases, such as labor disputes. Finally, when a legal conflict arises, the disputants can call for the creation of an *ad hoc chamber.* The number and identity of the judges in this chamber is determined by the Court with the approval of the disputing countries.

Ad Hoc Membership on the Court

A judge is not disqualified from hearing a case because he or she is a national of one of the disputing countries. In fact, in any case before the Court, each nation involved in the conflict may insist that a judge of its nationality take part in resolving the matter. Thus, if the Court's membership includes a national of one of the disputants but not the other, the unrepresented country may appoint one of its nationals to the Court to hear that particular dispute. If both are unrepresented, each may appoint a judge. These temporary judges are known as **judges ad hoc.**

Standing   The International Court of Justice was designed to resolve legal disputes between sovereign states. As a result, only nations may be parties to contentious litigation. Private parties (corporations and individuals) generally must turn to national courts or international arbitral panels to protect their legal rights. However, in certain circumstances, the World Court may indirectly entertain a lawsuit between a corporation or individual and a foreign country. For this to occur, the private party's national government must bring the claim in the exercise of its right of diplomatic protection for its nationals. The resulting litigation then involves only the two sovereign nations.

BARCELONA TRACTION, LIGHT AND POWER COMPANY, LIMITED
1970 I.C.J. Reports 3 (International Court of Justice)

■ **FACTS** The Barcelona Traction, Light and Power Company was a holding company that formed a number of subsidiaries in Spain to produce and distribute electric power. Although the company was incorporated in Canada and maintained its registered office there, as many as 88 percent of its shareholders were Belgian nationals. Barcelona Traction issued several series of bonds payable in sterling; however, it was later prevented from paying interest on these debts when Spanish exchange control authorities blocked the transfer of the necessary foreign currency. After several Spanish bondholders demanded that the corporation be declared bankrupt because of its failure to pay interest on the bonds, a Spanish court ordered the seizure of corporate assets, including the shares that were held outside of Spain. Later, a Spanish court authorized the issuance of new shares for the subsidiaries. They were purchased by a Spanish corpo-

ration, which then assumed complete control of Barcelona Traction's electric power operations in Spain. Belgium, on behalf of the Belgian shareholders, filed a claim against Spain in the International Court of Justice. Spain argued that Belgium lacked standing to bring an action against it.

■ **ISSUE** Did Belgium have standing to bring this action to protect the Belgian shareholders?

■ **DECISION** No. Generally, modern corporation laws are grounded on a firm distinction between the separate entity of the corporation and that of the shareholder, each with a distinct set of rights. The separation of property rights as between corporation and shareholder is an important manifestation of this distinction. The mere fact that damage is sustained by both corporation and shareholder does not imply that both are entitled to a claim of compensation. Thus, whenever a shareholder's interests are harmed by an act done to the corporation, it is to the latter that she must look to institute appropriate action. Although two separate entities may have suffered from the same wrong, it is only the corporate entity whose legal rights have been infringed. This traditional rule attributes the right of diplomatic protection of a corporate entity to the nation under the laws of which it is incorporated and in whose territory it has a registered office. These two criteria have been confirmed by long practice and by numerous international instruments. In the present case, Barcelona Traction was incorporated in Canada and has its registered office in that country. While it is true that

Canada has not vigorously acted on behalf of the corporation, a nation may exercise diplomatic protection by whatever means and to whatever extent it thinks fit. Should the natural or corporate persons on whose behalf it is acting (or failing to act) consider that their rights are not adequately protected, they have no remedy at international law. The nation must be the sole judge to decide whether its protection will be granted, to what extent, and when it will cease. If the Court of Justice were to adopt the theory of diplomatic protection of shareholders being forwarded by Belgium, it would open the door to competing diplomatic claims. This could create an atmosphere of confusion and insecurity in international economic relations.

Advisory Opinions

The Court of Justice may also issue **advisory opinions** when asked to do so by the General Assembly, the Security Council, or an international organization authorized by the General Assembly to make such a request. This process permits the Court to clarify legal issues involved in disputes between international organizations or between a nation and an international organization. Although countries may have strong interests in the substance of advisory opinions, they do not take an active part in the proceedings. In fact, opinions may be given despite a nation's objections to the process. While the decisions are not formally binding, they create international pressure on countries to abide by the Court's ruling.

Jurisdiction

Because of the fundamental regard given to the sovereignty of nations, the International Court of Justice has only **voluntary jurisdiction.** This means the Court cannot hear legal disputes between sovereign states unless both governments have first consented to its participation. Such consent is given in four fundamental ways. First, after a dispute has arisen, the parties may enter into a special accord, known as a *compromis,* in which they agree to refer the matter to the Court. The *Aegean Sea* case (discussed earlier) involved the Court's interpretation of the terms of a compromis between Greece and Turkey. Second, the nations may be parties to a bilateral or multilateral treaty that requires that disputes concerning the treaty be resolved by the Court. These provisions are called *compromissory clauses.* Third, a nation may have signed a *general treaty* on dispute resolution that designates the World Court as the forum for the settlement of disputes.

The fourth way in which the Court may acquire jurisdiction is known as the *optional clause.* Under this process, a country may deposit its unilateral declaration of acceptance of the Court's jurisdiction with the Secretary-General of the United Nations. These declarations may be made unconditionally or subject to any number of reservations. Under the notion of *reciprocity,* any reservations that a country includes in its declaration may be claimed by a country against which it has filed a claim. For instance, suppose Honduras filed a declaration in which it limited its acceptance of the Court's jurisdiction to disputes that arose after 1988. Mexico, on the other hand, filed an unconditional declaration. If Honduras brought an action against Mexico over a dispute that arose in 1986, Mexico could prevent the Court from hearing the case because of the Honduran restriction.

When a dispute arises over jurisdiction, the matter is to be resolved by the Court. The next case is a landmark decision in which the Court, over the objections of the United States, ruled that it had jurisdiction to hear Nicaragua's claim.

■ MILITARY AND PARAMILITARY ACTIVITIES IN AND AGAINST NICARAGUA (NICARAGUA v. UNITED STATES OF AMERICA)
1984 I.C.J. Reports 392 (International Court of Justice)

■ **FACTS** Nicaragua accused the United States of mining its harbors and covertly aiding mercenaries carrying out military operations against the Nicaraguan government. It also claimed the United States had violated international law through an economic boycott of Nicaragua, as well as through overflights of its territory by military aircraft. On April 9, 1984, Nicaragua filed an action against the United States in the International Court of Justice. It asserted the Court had jurisdiction based on each country's declaration of jurisdiction under the optional clause. Nicaragua's declaration stated it *"recognized as compulsory unconditionally the jurisdiction"* of the Court. The U.S. declaration asserted it was to *"remain in force . . . until the expiration of six months after notice may be given to terminate"* it. On April 6, 1984, three days before Nicaragua filed its claim with the Court, the U.S. government deposited a notification with the Secretary-General of the United Nations asserting that its declaration *"shall not apply to disputes with any Central American State"* and *"notwithstanding the terms of aforesaid declaration, this proviso shall take place immediately."* Nicaragua argued that the U.S. attempt to modify its acceptance of jurisdiction was ineffective because it did not comply with the six months' notice period prescribed by the original declaration.

■ **ISSUE** Does the Court have jurisdiction over this dispute between Nicaragua and the United States?

■ **DECISION** Yes. The United States argued that since Nicaragua's declaration was of indefinite duration, the Nicaraguan government could have immediately terminated it at any time. Thus, the United States claimed that under the principle of reciprocity, it was free to ignore the six months' notice period and immediately withdraw its declaration of jurisdiction. This assumption is not correct. Declarations of acceptance of compulsory jurisdiction are unilateral engagements that nations are absolutely free to make or not to make. In making the declaration, a nation is equally free either to do so unconditionally and without limit of time for its duration, or to qualify it with conditions and reservations. However, the unilateral nature of declarations does not signify that a nation is free to amend the scope and contents of its solemn commitments as it pleases. In establishing these declarations, which constitute the optional clause system, the principle of good faith plays an important role. The maintenance in force of the U.S. declaration for six months after notice of termination is a positive undertaking. But the Nicaraguan declaration contains no express restriction at all. It is therefore clear that the United States is not in a position to invoke reciprocity as a basis for its attempt to immediately withdraw its acceptance of jurisdiction. Further, even if reciprocity did apply here, it is not clear that Nicaragua had the right to immediately terminate its declaration. The requirements of good faith would seem to require a reasonable period of time before a withdrawal would be effective. An attempt to withdraw a declaration three days before a claim is filed with a court would not amount to a reasonable time. In sum, the six months' notice clause forms an integral part of the U.S. declaration and it must be complied with in the case of termination or modification. Consequently, the United States cannot terminate its obligation to submit to the compulsory jurisdiction of the Court.

Failure of a Party to Appear

Under the Court's operating procedures, a nation's refusal to participate does not prevent the continuation of the proceedings once the Court determines it has jurisdiction. Those rules permit the Court to find for a complaining party after satisfying itself that the claim is well founded in fact and law.

Despite the Court's finding that it had jurisdiction to hear the Nicaraguan claim, the United States refused to participate in the hearing. The following statement is abstracted from the official U.S. explanation of its withdrawal from the judicial proceedings.

STATEMENT ON THE U.S. WITHDRAWAL FROM THE PROCEEDINGS INITIATED BY NICARAGUA IN THE INTERNATIONAL COURT OF JUSTICE

24 I.L.M. 246 (U.S. Dept. of State, Jan. 18, 1985)

■ The United States has consistently taken the position that the proceedings initiated by Nicaragua in the International Court of Justice are a misuse of the Court for political purposes and that the Court lacks jurisdiction and competence over such a case. United States policy in Central America has been to promote democracy, reform, and freedom; to support economic development; to help provide a security shield against those—like Nicaragua, Cuba, and the U.S.S.R.—who seek to spread tyranny by force. Nicaragua's efforts to portray the conflict in Central America as a bilateral issue between itself and the United States cannot hide the obvious fact that the scope of the problem is far broader. It involves a wide range of issues: Nicaragua's huge buildup of Soviet arms and Cuban advisers, its cross-border attacks and promotion of insurgency within various nations of the region, and the activities of indigenous opposition groups within Nicaragua. The conflict in Central America, therefore, is not a narrow legal dispute; it is an inherently political problem that is not appropriate for judicial resolution. The conflict will be solved only by political and diplomatic means. The International Court of Justice was never intended to resolve issues of collective security and self-defense and is patently unsuited for such a role. Unlike domestic courts, the World Court has jurisdiction only to the extent that nation-states have consented to it. When the United States accepted the Court's compulsory jurisdiction through the optional clause, it certainly never conceived of such a role for the Court in such controversies. Nicaragua's suit against the United States is a blatant misuse of the Court for political and propaganda purposes. In addition, much of the evidence that would establish Nicaragua's aggression against its neighbors is of a highly sensitive intelligence character. We will not risk U.S. national security by presenting such sensitive material in public or before a Court that includes two judges from Warsaw Pact nations. This problem only confirms the reality that such issues are not suited for the International Court of Justice. We have seen in the United Nations, in the last decade or more, how international organizations have become more and more politicized against the interests of the Western democracies. It would be a tragedy if these trends were to infect the International Court of Justice. With great reluctance, the United States has decided not to participate in further proceedings in this case.

Enforcement

Decisions of the International Court of Justice are final and without appeal. However, they are binding only on the parties to the proceeding. As a condition to membership in the United Nations, each country pledges to voluntarily comply with the decisions of the Court in any matter in which it was a party. In the event that a nation fails to comply with a judgment rendered by the Court, the other party may petition the Security Council to enforce the judgment.

CONCEPT SUMMARY
The International Court of Justice

Standing (only nations)	International organizations may request advisory opinions
	Nations may represent their nationals in contentious proceedings
Jurisdiction (voluntary)	Compromis
	Compromissory clause
	General treaty
	Optional clause
Enforcement	U.N. members promise to comply
	Security Council may bring action to force compliance
	Permanent members may block Security Council sanctions

In the *Nicaragua v. United States* case, the Court ultimately ordered the United States to refrain from further acts of aggression against Nicaragua and to make reparations for the injuries it had caused. When the United States refused to comply with the decision, Nicaragua requested that the Security Council give effect to the judgment. The United States, as a permanent member of the Security Council, promptly vetoed this attempt. When Nicaragua repeated its request one week later, the United States again vetoed the resolution. One week after that, the General Assembly called for full and immediate compliance with the judgment. This nonbinding resolution was ignored by the United States. Several years later, after the Nicaraguan government was replaced by one more sympathetic to the United States, Nicaragua withdrew its claims against the United States.

ETHICAL IMPLICATIONS Was it ethical for the United States to refuse to comply with the Court's judgment? Is it ethical for permanent members of the Security Council to veto attempts to enforce judgments against them?

OTHER INTERNATIONAL ORGANIZATIONS

Many of the international organizations that influence the global business environment are briefly introduced throughout the remaining chapters of the text. However, several are so important that they receive more extensive coverage. They are the European Community (Chapter 3), the North American Free Trade Agreement (Chapter 4), and the General Agreement on Tariffs and Trade (Chapter 9). The remaining pages of this chapter look at four other nongovernmental organizations that have a significant impact on global business: the International Monetary Fund; the World Bank; the International Center for the Settlement of Investment Disputes; and the Organization for Economic Cooperation and Development.

International Monetary Fund

The International Monetary Fund (**IMF**) was created after World War II to promote economic and financial cooperation among the nations of the world. It provides short-term financing to more than 150 member countries and oversees their economic and monetary policies with the goal of maintaining a stable international monetary system. To support its operations, the IMF receives contributions from its members, with each nation's *quota* being based on factors such as national income, gold and dollar balances, and average annual trade balances. A member country's voting rights and borrowing rights are based on the level of its contributions.

Governance

Although the IMF officially is a United Nations specialized agency, it is independently governed by its Board of Governors. This body is composed of the finance ministers and central bank presidents of the member countries. Day-to-day operations are conducted by 22 executive directors. The five largest contributors to the fund each appoint one director and the remaining members select the others. The voting power of each executive director is weighted according to the quota of his or her constituency. Under this system, the directors from France, Germany, Japan, the United Kingdom, and the United States are able to block any policy decisions they jointly oppose.

The Lending Process

The IMF extends temporary financial assistance to member countries to ensure that they correct their balance of payments problems without resorting to currency exchange restrictions. This approach stems from the belief that many of the currency disorders that plague the world economy are instigated by shortsighted domestic responses to foreign exchange shortages. By offering financial resources to offset balance of payments maladjustments, the IMF hopes to persuade member countries to avoid domestic policies that could destroy international prosperity.

Although reference generally is made to IMF loans, in reality, the IMF exchanges hard currency for the member's soft currency. These transactions are called *repurchases*. It is expected that any member may need to avail itself of this process from time to time to offset temporary payments imbalances. However, a country normally may not borrow more than 25 percent of its quota in any year without special permission from the executive directors. When larger and longer-term loans are requested, the IMF often requires that the borrowing country pledge to reform its economic policies. Failure to comply with these requirements results in termination of the line of credit. This practice of tying credit availability to adherence to IMF policies is known as *conditionality.*

Cooperation among Members

The Articles of Agreement of the International Monetary Fund (the Bretton Woods Agreement) require that all member countries cooperate to promote exchange stability and orderly exchange arrangements. In support of this objective, all members agree to refrain from enforcing *exchange contracts* involving the currency of another member when those contracts violate the IMF-approved exchange control regulations of the other country. Exchange contracts generally are defined as contracts for the exchange of one currency against another or one means of payment against another.

■

LIBRA BANK LIMITED v. BANCO NACIONAL DE COSTA RICA
570 F.Supp. 870 (1983)

■ **FACTS** Libra Bank, a British banking corporation with an office in New York, made a $40 million loan to Banco Nacional, a banking concern wholly owned by the Costa Rican government. The loan was made to provide pre-export and export financing of sugar and sugar products from Costa Rica. Before the loan could be repaid, the Central Bank of Costa Rica adopted a resolution designed to remedy Costa Rica's problems in servicing its external debts (i.e., debts to foreign creditors in foreign currency). Costa Rican banking laws require all foreign exchange transactions to be authorized by the Central Bank. The resolution provided that only repayments of external debts to multilateral international agencies would be authorized. Thus, Banco Nacional's requests for foreign currency to repay Libra Bank were denied and it could not make principal or interest payments. As a result, Libra Bank petitioned a New York court to attach Banco Nacional's assets in New York to satisfy its claims against the Costa Rican bank. Banco Nacional argued that the Bretton Woods Agreement made the loan agreement unenforceable in the United States.

■ **ISSUE** Will a U.S. court's enforcement of the loan agreement violate the Bretton Woods Agreement?

■ **DECISION** No. The Bretton Woods Agreement provides: "*Exchange contracts which involve the currency of any member and which are contrary to the exchange control regulations of that member maintained or imposed consistently with this Agreement shall be unenforceable in the territories of any member.*" Both the United States and Costa Rica are signatories to the Agreement. However, a contract to borrow U.S. currency that requires repayment in U.S. currency and designates New York as the situs of repayment is not an exchange contract. Accordingly, the Bretton Woods Agreement is inapplicable to this case. Further, even if the loan agreement were an exchange contract, it is not clear that an intervening change in foreign currency regulations may render a preexisting contract unenforceable. Finally, there is no evidence to demonstrate that Costa Rica's currency regulations were maintained or imposed consistently with the goals of the International Monetary Fund.

World Bank   The international conference that created the International Monetary Fund also gave birth to the **World Bank.** While the IMF was designed to foster stable monetary relations among all nations, the World Bank's core function was to provide economic assistance to the weakest and poorest countries of the developing world. Owned by more than 130 countries, the World Bank consists of the International Bank for Reconstruction and Development (IBRD) and the International Development Association (IDA). The World Bank's primary goals are to promote foreign investment and global trade and to make or guarantee loans for useful projects.

The IBRD obtains most of its funds from selling bonds in the capital markets of the developed world. Its loans generally are for 10 to 15 years and are subject to interest rates that reflect what it must pay on the bonds. The IDA obtains its funds primarily from contributions made by the developed nations. Its loans are made only to the poorest nations of the world at extremely low interest rates. They generally permit repayment over 50 years with no payments due during the first 10 years. Both the IBRD and the IDA offer loans only to governments or to organizations with the guarantees of their governments. Further, the loans are made only for specific projects or well-defined programs.

ICSID

The International Center for the Settlement of Investment Disputes (**ICSID**) was created by the World Bank to promote mutual confidence between private foreign investors and the governments of the developing nations of the world. It provides administrative support for the conciliation and arbitration of investment disputes. Two prerequisites must be met before private investors and host nations are obligated to use ICSID's dispute resolution mechanisms. First, the host nation must become a contracting state by signing and ratifying the ICSID Convention. Second, the parties must give *mutually binding consent* to submit the dispute to ICSID. This consent must be in writing, although it can take many forms, including an arbitration clause in their investment contract.

Nations may freely condition their consent upon the investor first exhausting all its legal remedies in the contracting state. However, unless otherwise stated, the parties' consent to ICSID arbitration prohibits them from pursuing any other legal remedy. Although the conciliation process does not result in a binding decision, arbitral awards do bind the parties and are not subject to appeal.

OECD

After World War II, the Organization for European Economic Cooperation (OEEC) was established to rebuild Europe and liberalize trade among its members. After these objectives were largely achieved, the OEEC was remodeled into the Organization for Economic Cooperation and Development (**OECD**). As such, its membership was expanded to include virtually all of the major capitalist nations of the world. Its primary objectives are the furtherance of international growth, employment, and stability through the expansion of global trade on a multilateral, nondiscriminatory basis. The OECD pursues these goals through the exchange of information, consultation, and joint projects.

The Council of Ministers of the OECD, which is composed of one representative from each of the 24 member states, has the authority to make decisions that are binding on the members. However, since these decisions must first be agreed to by each representative, they tend to take the form of broad recommendations rather than concise legal obligations. Perhaps the most important contribution of the OECD is its regular exchange of information among the member states. Generally, these exchanges first occur between technical experts. Only later, after the information has been carefully considered, is it discussed at a political level. Through this process, the member states can extensively review the economic policies of each nation on a country-by-country basis and arrive at cooperative approaches to economic, energy, and environmental issues.

QUESTIONS AND PROBLEM CASES

1. Identify the primary sources of international law. What are the secondary sources? Explain the difference between a primary source and a secondary source.

2. What is the fundamental difference between the civil law family and the common law family?

3. Describe the basic prerequisites to the creation of customary law.

4. How are judgments of the International Court of Justice enforced? What is the weakness inherent in this enforcement system?

5. In 1911, the Imperial Chinese government sold certain bearer bonds in the United States to help finance the construction of a north-south railway system. In 1912, soon after the bonds were issued, a revolutionary movement culminated in the replacement of the Imperial Chinese government by the Republic of China. The new government made timely interest payments on the bonds until 1930. In the spring of 1937, the Republic of China, which was then led by Chiang Kai-shek, offered a compromise program to extend the due date of the bonds to 1976. Interest payments were never made, however, because of the outbreak of the Sino-Japanese War. From that point until 1949, China was wracked with the turmoil of civil war as the Communist Party fought to take control of the government. During 1947, the prime minister of the national government pledged to repay the bonds. In 1949, the Communist Party seized control of the mainland and established the People's Republic of China. The former national government withdrew to Taiwan. Is the People's Republic of China responsible for the repayment of the bonds?

6. A boundary dispute arose between the United States and Canada over certain areas of continental shelf and fishing zones in the Gulf of Maine. As a result, the two governments signed a special accord in which they agreed to submit their dispute to an ad hoc chamber of the International Court of Justice. However, in an accompanying letter signed by their ambassadors, the two countries emphasized that the chamber had to be formed before the new members of the Court (elected in the previous election) began their terms of office. They further insisted that the number of judges in the chamber be fixed at five and that the identity of the judges be subject to their approval. If these conditions were not met, both countries reserved the right to withdraw the case from the Court and send it to an arbitration panel. A majority of the Court agreed to establish an ad hoc chamber under the conditions imposed by the United States and Canada; however, two judges objected. Explain why a World Court judge might object to the manner in which the United States and Canada submitted their dispute to the Court.

7. Friedreich Nottebohm was born in Germany in 1881. In 1905, he moved to Guatemala and made that country the headquarters of his extensive business activities, although he retained his German citizenship. In 1939, one month before the outbreak of World War II, Nottebohm visited Liechtenstein and applied to become a naturalized citizen there. That country waived its ordinary three-year residency requirement and granted Nottebohm naturalization upon his payment of the required fee and pledge of allegiance. He then obtained a Liechtenstein passport and immediately returned to Guatemala where he resumed his former business activities. During 1943, as a result of war measures, Guatemalan authorities arrested Nottebohm as a German national, and he was interned in the United States until the end of the war. After the war, he was refused readmission into Guatemala and his property was confiscated. Liechtenstein filed a claim against Guatemala on behalf of Nottebohm in the World Court. Guatemala argued that Liechtenstein did not have standing to represent Nottebohm. May Liechtenstein extend diplomatic protection to Nottebohm in the World Court?

8. In response to complaints from Norway, British fishermen refrained from fishing in Norwegian coastal waters for almost 300 years. However, beginning in the early 20th century, British fishing vessels equipped with improved and powerful equipment entered Norway's coastal region, drawing severe criticism from the Norwegian fishing industry. In response to these developments, Norway enacted legislation that formally delineated a zone along the Norwegian coast as reserved exclusively

for fishing by its nationals. Throughout the next several decades, Norway strictly enforced this law by seizing any British vessels caught fishing in the restricted region. Britain instituted proceedings before the World Court, arguing that Norway's claim to the coastal waters violated international law. Norway defended on the basis that it was best able to define its own territorial waters and that British acceptance of its territorial claims for over three centuries gave them the force of law. Are Norway's arguments correct?

9. Germany and the Netherlands agreed to a partial demarcation of their coastal waters. Soon after, Germany and Denmark reached a similar agreement. While the partial boundaries were drawn according to the equidistance principle, the three nations were unable to arrive at an agreement on their respective territorial claims throughout the continental shelf. Denmark and the Netherlands argued that the equidistance principle should also govern that demarcation. Germany resisted, asserting the concave nature of its coastline would limit its claims to the continental shelf area under the equidistance method. Denmark and the Netherlands argued that the three nations were bound to apply the equidistance principle because the 1958 Geneva Convention on the Continental Shelf prescribed that method when parties were unable to reach an agreement. Germany argued it was not bound to the 1958 Geneva Convention because it never ratified the treaty. Denmark and the Netherlands responded that Germany's use of the equidistance principle in their earlier agreements demonstrated its acceptance of this method of defining coastal territory. Will international law require Germany to adhere to the equidistance principle?

10. Maritime International Nominees Establishment (MINE), a Swiss company, contracted with the Republic of Guinea to transport bauxite. Under the terms of the written investment contract, all disputes between the parties were to be arbitrated through the International Center for the Settlement of Investment Disputes (ICSID). The Republic of Guinea was a contracting party to ICSID. Later, when a dispute arose, MINE petitioned a Swiss magistrate to freeze certain assets belonging to the Republic of Guinea in Switzerland to ensure that MINE's monetary claims would be honored. The Republic of Guinea argued that the attachment of its assets by a Swiss tribunal was unlawful because ICSID's jurisdiction over the dispute was exclusive. Is the Republic of Guinea correct?

3

The European Community

INTRODUCTION

One of the greatest challenges facing modern global business is the need to recognize and respond to the profound changes arising from the emergence of a single Europe. As the national barriers that once characterized the European continent crumble and fall, business leaders must develop effective strategies to compete in this new environment. Informed managers realize that an integrated Europe presents both opportunities and challenges for the 1990s. On the one hand, the prospect of a single Europe offers tremendous commercial opportunities for exporters hoping to tap into a unified market of over 345 million citizens. Simultaneously, however, an integrated Europe will give rise to heightened competition as a new breed of European businesses challenge their foreign counterparts in Europe, the United States, and throughout the world.

Chapter Overview

This chapter will familiarize the reader with the developments that now are occurring within the European Community (EC). It first offers a brief glimpse of the current design of the EC and a forecast of the changes yet to come. The focus then shifts to the EC political institutions and the processes by which community laws are made. This discussion includes an exploration of how U.S. business interests might influence the formation of EC law. Attention then turns to the judicial institutions and the adjudicative process within Europe. The chapter closes with a brief discussion of how U.S. businesses can hope to benefit from the rise of the European Community.

THE NEW EUROPE

The European Community embraces 12 countries with a combined population of approximately 345 million people. Belgium, France, Italy, Luxembourg, the Netherlands, and West Germany (now Germany) were the founding members. In 1973, Denmark, Ireland, and the United Kingdom were admitted. Greece joined in 1981, and both Portugal and Spain became members in 1986. The European Community envisions the creation of an economic community fostering free trade within its boundaries. This is to be accomplished by eliminating tariffs among the member states; establishing a common tariff for outside countries; promoting the free movement of workers, goods, and capital among the members; creating a uniform community monetary policy; and generally promoting the welfare of individuals within the union through common economic development.

The Treaties

While we now speak of the European Community, in strict legal terms, today's integrated Europe springs from three separate treaties: the European Coal and Steel Community; the European Atomic Energy Community; and the European Economic Community. Originally, one needed to look to each of these treaties to fully understand the power and authority of the four major institutions of the Community: the Council, the Commission, the Parliament, and the Court of Justice. Their powers were separately assigned in each of those agreements. Still, it is not surprising that we so often speak of the European Community in the singular. The Merger Treaty of 1965 in part unified the original three treaties by providing that they be served by a single Council and a single Commission. Likewise, the 1987 passage of the Single European Act cemented in the minds of most observers the vision of a unified European Community.

Single European Act

During the 1980s, increased economic competition with the United States and Japan refueled the desire of the European Community members to remove the barriers to creation of an internal market. It was believed that increased unification would permit the economies of scale necessary to ward off this perceived competitive threat. A White Paper published by the Commission drew up several hundred legislative proposals designed to bring about a free trade area. Then, in 1987, the original treaties were amended by the Single European Act (SEA).

Designed to facilitate passage of the legislation envisioned by the White Paper, the SEA set a target date of December 31, 1992, for realization of a single Europe. It officially renamed the Assembly as the European Parliament and increased the degree of participation that the Parliament would have in the Community's legislative process. The SEA also revamped the rules requiring unanimity in voting by the Council, thereby facilitating the passage of legislative proposals. (These reforms will be discussed in more detail later in this chapter.)

The Future of Europe

As envisioned by the original treaties and the SEA, the European Community was to become an integrated trade bloc, uniting the economies of its member states. At its simplest, this involved the not-so-easy task of removing barriers to the free movement of goods, services, capital, and persons. The steady dismantling of these obstacles to economic union fueled greater expectations among many powerful interests within the EC. They advocated the need for the EC to likewise achieve a monetary and political union that would culminate in a European superstate stretching from the Mediterranean Sea to the Arctic Ocean.

Removal of Barriers

The Single European Act aimed at removing the physical, technical, and fiscal barriers to an internal market. Removal of the physical barriers entails abolishing the immigration and customs formalities that once sealed the borders of the member states. The technical barriers will be effectively dismantled when the EC successfully harmonizes the patchwork of national health and safety regulations and product standards that once pervaded the continent. Finally, in removing fiscal barriers, the EC aims at eliminating the different rates of taxation among the member states and the collection of tariffs at the national borders. In the *Rewe–Zentral* case that follows, consider how the European Court of Justice determines the legality of national regulations that restrict free trade throughout the EC.

■

REWE–ZENTRAL AG v. BUNDESMONOPOLVERWALTUNG FÜR BRANNTWEIN
European Court of Justice, Feb. 20, 1979, (1979) 3 C.M.L.R. 494

■ **FACTS** Rewe–Zentral AG (Rewe) attempted to import alcoholic beverages from France to resell them in Germany. The German authorities informed Rewe that one particular liqueur, *Cassis de Dijon,* could not be sold in Germany because it contained only 15 to 20 percent alcohol by volume. German law required that liqueurs have an alcohol content of at least 32 percent. Rewe challenged the law in a German court, arguing that it constituted an illegal restriction on the free flow of goods within the European Community. Germany claimed its minimum alcohol content regulation was necessary to protect the public health and to defend consumers from unfair practices. The German court asked the European Court of Justice to provide a preliminary ruling as to the legality of the German regulation.

■ **ISSUE** Does the German law unlawfully restrict the free movement of goods within the European Community?

■ **DECISION** Yes. In the absence of common EC rules relating to the production and marketing of alcohol, the individual member states may regulate all matters relating to the production and marketing of alcohol and alcoholic beverages on their own territory. These national laws will be permitted to restrict the free flow of goods within the EC if the regulations are necessary to protect the public health or defend consumers from unfair practices. Germany suggested that its law met this standard.

First, it claimed the restriction was necessary to protect the public health since alcoholic beverages with a low alcoholic content were more likely to induce a tolerance toward alcohol than more highly alcoholic beverages. However, this argument is not persuasive since consumers can obtain a wide range of weakly or moderately alcoholic products on the market. Furthermore, much of the high alcohol content beverages freely sold on the German market are generally consumed in a diluted form. Second, Germany argued that setting a minimum limit on alcohol contents would protect consumers from unfair practices by distributors. Because of the high taxation rate on alcohol, a lower alcohol content gives a beverage a competitive advantage over one with a higher alcohol content. However, this interest could be protected in a less restrictive manner simply by requiring the display of an indication of origin and of the alcohol content on the packaging of products. It is clear that the German regulation does not serve a purpose that is in the general interest so as to take precedence over the fundamental requirements of the free movement of goods. In practice, the principal effect of this legislation is to promote alcoholic beverages having a high alcohol content by excluding from the German market products from other member states that do not meet that standard.

Monetary Union

The draft treaty on economic and monetary union set as a fundamental goal establishment of a single European currency policed by a European central bank. This monetary integration is to be brought about by the establishment of the European Monetary Institute (EMI) in 1994. Designed to smooth the way toward final monetary union, the EMI would foster greater exchange rate and monetary coordination among the member states. Further, it would encourage greater reliance on the European Currency Unit (ECU), a monetary reserve based on the weighted average of the 12 European Community currencies. In short, the EMI is to lay the groundwork for a full-fledged central bank, which could come into existence sometime during or after 1997.

Political Union

There also were calls for transformation of the EC from an economic bloc into a powerful political union. Advocates of this position argued the need for a single European voice on matters of foreign policy and defense. They urged the adoption of a political union treaty that would give broader powers to the European Parliament, streamline the EC's decision-making structure, and create a more unified foreign policy structure.

An Integrated European Continent?

In 1993, the EC and six members of the European Free Trade Association (EFTA) countries (Sweden, Finland, Norway, Austria, Iceland, and Liechtenstein) agreed to join forces (Swiss voters rejected such a union). Creation of this European Economic Area (EEA) requires the six EFTA nations to incorporate the EC's single market legislation into their legal systems. Similarly, during the previous year, the EC and the Eastern European countries of Poland, Hungary, and Czechoslovakia (now the Czech Republic and the Slovak Republic) negotiated creation of a free trade area that is to be phased in over time.

The Maastricht Treaty

During 1992, the EC member states signed the Treaty for European Union (Maastricht Treaty). This treaty established an ambitious plan for a more comprehensive integration of the EC member states. First, it called for the adoption of a common European Currency Unit by 1999, although it left open the possibility of a common currency being introduced as early as 1997. Second, it reinforced the goal of achieving the free movement of people by providing for broad EC citizenship rights. Third, it encouraged greater cooperation among the member states, urging the development of common policies in the areas of foreign policy and defense. Fourth, the Maastricht Treaty attempted to increase the powers of the Parliament.

The unbridled enthusiasm for a more fully integrated Europe was severely shaken when Danish voters initially rejected the Maastricht Treaty in a national referendum. This was followed by a wave of economic crises and nationalist sentiments that threatened to abort the integration movement. Denmark finally adopted the treaty in a new referendum. In the wake of Maastricht, there have been widely supported calls for greater adherence to the principle of **subsidiarity.** Under subsidiarity, the EC institutions are not to deal with issues that can be better handled at the member state level. This call for greater preservation of national cultures and identities is likely to slow integration efforts.

THE POLITICAL INSTITUTIONS

The treaties went beyond merely enunciating the general guidelines for a unified European Community. They also established four major institutions essential to the realization of these political and economic goals: the Commission; the Council; the Parliament; and the Court of Justice. The major executive and legislative functions of the Community are shared by the first three institutions, while the Court of Justice serves as the judicial branch of government.

This section examines the political institutions: the Commission, the Council, and the Parliament. (The Court of Justice is investigated later in this chapter.) It also looks at two other bodies—the Economic and Social Committee and the European Coun-

FIGURE 3–1   The European Community

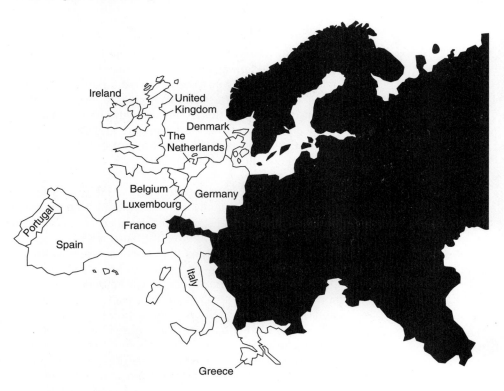

cil. Scrutiny of these political institutions lays the foundation for a later examination of how law actually is made and enforced in the European Community.

The European Commission

Composition

The Commission is composed of 17 members. The five larger member states (France, Germany, Italy, Spain, and the United Kingdom) each appoint two commissioners, while the remaining seven countries appoint one each. Although the commissioners are selected by the national governments, they are charged with representing the entire European Community rather than their own national interests. This is guaranteed in part by the condition that each appointment must be approved by all the member states. Further, commissioners are not permitted to be members of their national parliaments and are expected to devote their full attention to Community matters.

The Commission makes decisions on the basis of majority rule; although, as the *Akzo Chemie* case illustrates, for some administrative matters, authority may be delegated to a single individual. Commissioners are appointed to renewable four-year terms and cannot be replaced during this term by their national governments. However, the European Parliament has the power to remove the entire Commission by a vote of no confidence, and the Court of Justice may remove individual commissioners for cause. The 12 member states select the Commission president who serves a two-year term with the possibility of reelection to one additional term. By convention, this office is rotated among the member states.

Functions

Basically, the Commission serves as an executive arm of the European Community. It alone among the four major institutions has the power to propose legislation to the Council. The Commission also is responsible for ensuring that the EEC Treaty is enforced and to this end may initiate actions against member states before the Court of Justice. The Commission represents the Community in its external relations in the international environment. Thus, upon being authorized by the Council, it negotiates international trade agreements. Finally, in some instances, the Commission has been delegated its own power of decision and may, in these limited circumstances, adopt its own legislation. These expanded powers exist in the area of agricultural policy, antitrust enforcement, and antidumping and antisubsidy matters.

AKZO CHEMIE B.V. v. COMMISSION
European Court of Justice, Sept. 23, 1986, [1986] ECR 2585

■ **FACTS** Acting on complaints that Akzo Chemie had been unfairly pricing its flour additives, the Commission began investigating the company. Later, the commissioner in charge of the inquiry decided to expand the investigation into Akzo Chemie's pricing practices in the plastics industry. He announced to the company that the Commission would begin a search and seizure of all company records relating to such behavior. Akzo Chemie objected to this investigation, claiming that only the Commission acting as a body, rather than a single commissioner, could institute such an inquiry.

■ **ISSUE** Was the Commission's delegation of authority to a single commissioner proper?

■ **DECISION** Yes. Generally, the decisions of the Commission should be subject to collective deliberation so all members of the body bear collective political responsibility for all decisions. However, efficient operation of the Commission's many diverse functions requires exceptions to this policy. Further, ultimately the Commission must accept responsibility for such delegations as it retains the right to reconsider decisions granting delegations of authority. The commissioner's decision to order Akzo Chemie to submit to an investigation of its pricing behavior is a form of preparatory inquiry that can be considered a straightforward measure of management. As such, it falls within the scope of administrative or managerial measures that may be delegated to a single commissioner.

The Council of the European Communities

Composition

The Council is made up of 12 members—one from each of the member states. On general matters the governments usually send their foreign ministers, while on specialized topics they will be represented by their ministers or deputies responsible for that policy area. For instance, if the topic to be discussed is harmonization of taxation, each nation generally will send its finance minister and the session will be called a meeting of the Finance Council. While in legal terms there is but one Coun-

FIGURE 3–2   Makeup of the Commission

Nation	Number of Members
France	2
Germany	2
Italy	2
Spain	2
United Kingdom	2
Belgium	1
Denmark	1
Greece	1
Ireland	1
Luxembourg	1
The Netherlands	1
Portugal	1
Total	17

cil, it can simultaneously conduct several meetings. The Council presidency is rotated among the 12 member states at six-month intervals.

Voting among Council members has been weighted according to the size of the individual member states. France, Germany, Italy, and the United Kingdom each possess 10 votes. Spain has eight votes; Belgium, the Netherlands, Greece, and Portugal have five votes each; Denmark and Ireland each have three votes; and Luxembourg has two. On most matters, the Council acts by a qualified majority, which is defined as 54 out of the 76 total votes. Thus, it would take 23 votes to block most matters before the Council. In some limited circumstances (to be discussed later), the Council cannot act in the absence of unanimity.

Functions

The Council is the institution through which the member states can express their direct interests. It also serves as the primary legislative arm of the Community, although it can act only on legislation proposed by the Commission. The Council, after consultation with the Parliament, ratifies treaties negotiated by the Commission and coordinates the economic policies of the member states. Finally, together with the Parliament, it drafts the Community budget. Meetings of the Council are conducted in private with no publication of the proceedings.

COREPER

An integral part of the Council is its Committee of Permanent Representatives (COREPER), which is made up of resident representatives of each of the member states. COREPER provides necessary continuity to the Council since the nation's ministers generally are able to meet as a group for only short periods. Lower level deputy representatives (COREPER I) work on routine and technical matters, while the permanent representatives (COREPER II) handle more sensitive issues.

FIGURE 3–3   Makeup of the Council

Nation	Votes
France	10
Germany	10
Italy	10
United Kingdom	10
Spain	8
Belgium	5
Greece	5
The Netherlands	5
Portugal	5
Denmark	3
Ireland	3
Luxembourg	2
Total	76

In most cases, Council matters will first be presented to COREPER. If a proposal is unanimously approved by COREPER, it will make the A List on the Council agenda. More contentious matters are relegated to the B List. Issues on the A List generally will be adopted without discussion, while the B List is likely to require more careful consideration and debate by the ministers. Most negotiations with the Commission over legislative proposals occur in COREPER.

**The European
Parliament**

Composition

The European Parliament (formerly called the Assembly) is composed of 518 representatives directly elected for five-year terms by the citizens of the member states. Originally, the members of Parliament (MEPs) were nominated from the national parliaments; however, since 1979, each country has implemented its own electoral system. The treaties have provided that the Community is to fashion a uniform voting procedure for all member states, but the Council has been unable to agree on a single scheme.

Seats in the Parliament are distributed among the member states in rough proportion to their overall population. France, Germany, Italy, and the United Kingdom each have 81 seats. Spain has 60, while the Netherlands is represented by 25 MEPs. Belgium, Greece, and Portugal have 24 representatives each; Denmark has 16; Ireland has 15; and Luxembourg has 6. MEPs, however, directly represent the people that elected them rather than their national governments. In fact, each MEP is affiliated with a transnational political party and sits in the Parliament according to that party rather than according to his or her country.

Functions

The Parliament primarily is a consultative body on most Community issues. Generally, its actions are confined to gathering information, communicating ideas, and forming public opinion rather than to actual decision making. It has no formal legislative

FIGURE 3–4   Makeup of the Parliament

Nation	Members
France	81
Germany	81
Italy	81
United Kingdom	81
Spain	60
The Netherlands	25
Belgium	24
Greece	24
Portugal	24
Denmark	16
Ireland	15
Luxembourg	6
Total	518

power. Before the Commission presents a proposal to the Council, the Parliament examines it and offers its opinion. However, the Parliament cannot force the Commission to modify or otherwise act on the proposal. Yet the Council cannot enact any Commission proposal without first submitting it to the Parliament for an opinion. Under changes implemented by the Single European Act, in some instances, the Parliament can reject certain proposals that could then be enacted only by a unanimous Council. (The actual legislative process and the role of the Parliament is discussed more fully later in this chapter.)

To gather information, the Parliament may submit oral or written questions to the Commission and the Council, although only the Commission is required to answer. The Parliament also considers the budget and has limited powers to amend it. Also, pursuant to the Single European Act, the Parliament, acting by majority vote, may veto either the admission of new member states or the implementation of Community agreements with nonmember nations. Finally, the Parliament, acting by a two-thirds majority vote, may remove the entire body of commissioners. However, this latter power is of limited impact since the Parliament has no power over the appointment of new commissioners and the old Commission will continue to sit until it actually has been replaced. (This power of censure has been attempted only once, and unsuccessfully, when in 1972 the Commission delayed proposing increases in the Parliament's budgetary powers.)

Other Political Institutions

An in-depth examination of all of the institutions of the European Community is beyond the scope of this chapter. However, two others should be mentioned because of their importance to the political and economic processes of the European Community. These bodies are the Economic and Social Committee and the European Council.

Economic and Social Committee (ESC)

This committee is composed of 189 members representing a broad range of professional, labor, and consumer organizations and other public interest groups. It consists of three groups, one representing employers, another representing workers, and the third representing all other interests. Its membership is selected by the Council of the European Communities from a list of candidates supplied by the member states. All of the members are appointed to renewable four-year terms, and the membership is allocated to the member states roughly in proportion to their populations. The ESC is an advisory body and generally must be consulted on all Commission proposals made pursuant to the EEC and the Euratom treaties. (Another committee—the Consultative Committee—carries out a similar function for ECSC Treaty matters.) The ESC is designed to ensure that the legislative process adequately addresses the numerous interests that make up the European Community.

The European Council

The European Council (often confused with the Council of the European Communities) technically was not envisioned as an institution of the European Community. It formally arose out of 1974 agreement pledging that the leaders of the member states, together with their foreign ministers, would conduct regular summit conferences. At these meetings, the nations discuss matters arising out of the treaties as well as general issues of political and economic cooperation. A provision in the Single European Act has given official treaty recognition to the European Council by affirming the right of the Commission president to attend the conferences. (Throughout the remainder of this chapter all references to the "Council" will relate to the Council of the European Communities rather than to this European Council.)

LEGAL MEASURES IN THE EUROPEAN COMMUNITY

The treaties provide the primary source of law in the European Community. They are the foundation of all Community rules and cannot be challenged other than through a cumbersome amendment procedure. In a sense, they serve the role that the federal Constitution fulfills in the U.S. legal system. The EEC Treaty specifies the types of legal measures the Commission and the Council may promulgate. These legal instruments—regulations, directives, decisions, recommendations, and opinions—are secondary sources of law and, as such, are not enforceable if they conflict with the treaties. Each of these secondary sources is discussed below.

Regulations

A regulation is a law that is binding and directly applicable in all of the member states without the need for any implementing legislation at the national level. It automatically becomes part of the domestic law of each nation and is enforceable by anyone to whom it is addressed as soon as it becomes effective. Regulations frequently serve as a foundation for achieving broad aims, establishing general guidelines that may be refined in later legislative enactments.

Directives

A directive is not effective until it has been incorporated into the laws of the individual member states. It instructs the member states as to the results that are to be achieved, but it leaves each nation great discretion over the form that the implementing legislation will take. This can be a great source of confusion for businesses dealing throughout the European Community as they need to consider not only the actual directive, but also each set of implementing legislation. Much of the lawmaking in the European Community is conducted through directives. Member states that fail to implement directives within the allotted transition period may be sued in their national courts or be challenged by the Commission before the European Court of Justice. (The ways in which the European Court will enforce Community law are discussed later in this chapter.)

Decisions

Either the Council or the Commission may issue decisions that are binding only on the parties to whom they are addressed. They may be aimed at member states, businesses, or private persons. No implementing legislation is necessary for decisions to become effective and enforceable through the courts of the member states. It is common to find these legal measures in the competition and antidumping areas.

Recommendations and Opinions

Although recommendations and opinions are not legally binding, they may be adopted by the Council and the Commission and, therefore, may have economic and political weight. Frequently, they provide a means by which the Commission suggests certain policy choices to the Council. For example, the White Paper (discussed earlier in this chapter) was a recommendation on the importance of completing the internal market. Businesses are wise to pay close attention to recommendations and opinions because they may signal the likelihood of impending regulations or directives.

THE LEGISLATIVE PROCESS

Thus far, we have examined the treaties, the major political institutions, and the types of legislation predominant in the European Community. This section moves one step further, illustrating the interplay among the Commission, the Council, and the Parliament in enacting legislation. This discussion explores the two primary methods for adopting laws: the consultation procedure and the cooperation procedure. It concludes with a brief look at how the Commission, acting through powers delegated from the normal legislative process, can implement its own legal measures.

The Consultation Procedure

The consultation process begins when the Commission proposes legislation to the Council. The Council sends the proposal to the Parliament and the Economic and Social Committee, soliciting their opinions. The Commission may then offer amendments incorporating the views expressed in these opinions. At this point, the Council determines whether to enact the proposal into law.

Three general observations can be made about this procedure. First, only the Commission has the authority to propose legislation. In the absence of a Commission-sponsored proposal, legislation cannot occur. (Note, however, that in practice the Council may ask the Commission to offer a particular proposal.) Second, the Parliament clearly has the least significant role in the process. It has no veto power; it merely expresses its opinion on the legislation. Finally, once a proposal has been made, the Council wields the most power of all the institutions. It has the right to unilaterally enact or reject the measure.

Keep these observations in mind as we now more closely examine each of the steps in the consultation procedure. Recognize the checks and balances integrated into the system.

The Commission Proposal

When considering submitting a proposal, the Commission does not act in isolation. As was suggested above, frequently the Commission may be acting in response to a Council request when it introduces legislation. The actual formulation of the proposal generally is accomplished by staff members in working groups made up of civil servants, scholars, and other experts nominated by the national governments. The views of this working group are extremely influential, but in the end only advisory. The formal draft of the proposal must be approved by a majority of the Commission.

The Role of the Parliament

Immediately after receiving the proposal from the Commission, the Council sends it to the Parliament and the Economic and Social Committee for their opinions. (The procedures followed by these bodies are roughly parallel.) A special committee of the Parliament solicits the views of interested parties and prepares a preliminary opinion to be presented to the full body. This may include suggested amendments from the Parliament.

Generally, the full Parliament does not actively consider the proposal until after the Commission has an opportunity to respond to any inquiries or amendments raised by the committee. If the Commission refuses to respond to the Parliament's questions or suggested amendments, the Parliament may delay the proposal by keeping it in committee and refusing to issue an opinion to the Council. Thus, the Parliament frequently can persuade the Commission to amend the proposal in a manner that better reflects the interests of the Parliament. At this point, the proposal, along with any amendments the Commission was persuaded to make, is voted on by the full Parliament. If this receives majority support from the full Parliament, the opinion (called a *resolution*) is reported to the Council. The *Freres* case, which follows, examines the Parliament's power to block legislation by refusing to report an opinion.

■

SA ROQUETTE FRERES v. COUNCIL OF THE EUROPEAN COMMUNITIES
European Court of Justice, October 29, 1980, [1980] ECR 3333

■ **FACTS** In response to a judgment by the Court of Justice invalidating production levies imposed on isoglucose, the Commission presented the Council with a proposal for an amended regulation of the sweetener. On March 13, 1979, the Council sought the Parliament's opinion on the proposal. At that time, the Council emphasized that since the regulation was to apply as from July 1, 1979, it wanted the Parliament to give its opinion at its

April session. Throughout April and May, the Parliament was unable to reach a consensus on the proposal. It then adjourned its session to allow the members to take part in their electoral campaigns. As the Parliament was not scheduled to meet again until July 17, 1979 (after the elections), the Council adopted the proposal on June 25, 1979, without receiving an opinion from the Parliament. The regulation was challenged as invalid because the Council did not adhere to the consultation process by waiting for the opinion of the Parliament.

■ **ISSUE** Is the regulation void due to the absence of an opinion by the Parliament?

■ **DECISION** Yes. While the treaty provisions regarding consultation of the Economic and Social Committee allow Council action in the absence of an opinion, there is no such provision regarding the Parliament. This is because the consultation requirements involving the Parliament are the means by which the Parliament is to play an actual part in the legislative process of the European Community. Such power represents an essential factor in the institutional balance envisioned by the treaties. Although limited, it reflects the fundamental democratic principle that the people should take part in the exercise of power through the intermediary of a representative assembly. Due consultation of the Parliament, therefore, constitutes an essential formality, disregard of which means the measure concerned is void. Observance of that requirement implies the Parliament has expressed its opinion. It is impossible to take the view that the requirement is satisfied by the Council's simply asking for the opinion.

The Actions of the Council

On receiving the opinions of the Parliament and the ESC, the Council submits the proposal to a working group made up of various experts from the national governments and a representative of the Commission. Working through COREPER, a report is prepared for the entire Council. As was discussed earlier, if COREPER fully agrees with the proposal, it is placed on the A List and generally will be approved without debate by the Council. However, if a consensus cannot be reached at the COREPER level, the proposal appears on the B List, which subjects it to more intense scrutiny and debate when the Council meets. The Commission may amend the proposal anytime before its adoption by the full Council.

At this point, there are three potential outcomes. First, the Council may approve the proposal precisely as it was submitted by the Commission. If this occurs, the proposal automatically will become law unless it was a directive or decision. Remember, unlike regulations, a directive or decision may require action by the member states before it becomes effective. Second, if the Council is unable to reach an agreement, the proposal ultimately will lapse. Third, the Council may amend the proposal under its own initiative. These amendments must remain within the general framework of the Commission's proposal and will not be effective unless unanimously approved by the Council.

Problems with the Consultation Procedure

During the 1980s, a general concern arose within the European Community that there had been a disappointing lack of progress in the movement toward a closer union. Increasing economic competition from the United States and Japan, coupled with an economic recession throughout Europe, accentuated the existence of continued barriers to a free market within the Community.

These obstacles to completion of a single market in part were attributed to several problems with the consultation procedure. First, while the treaties envisioned that

Council approval of Commission proposals would be achieved through majority voting, in practice this was not occurring. Pursuant to the Luxembourg Accord of 1966, anytime a nation argued that a proposal affected its vital interest, it could insist on passage only when there was unanimity on the Council. In effect, this gave each member state a veto over most legislative activity, substantially reducing the passage of necessary legislation. Second, there was a general concern that the Parliament—perhaps the most democratic of the political institutions—was effectively frozen out of any meaningful role in the legislative process.

This concern culminated in the adoption of the Single European Act, which amended the treaties with a goal of eliminating these weaknesses. The reform had two major components. First, it provided for greater reliance on majority voting (rather than unanimity) when the Council was considering proposals relating to implementation of the internal market. Second, it created a new legislative process—the cooperation procedure—that would provide the Parliament with more meaningful input into the passage of new legislation.

The Cooperation Procedure

Overview

Generally, the cooperation procedure must be used for legislation designed to implement the internal market program envisioned by the White Paper. Its use also is required for proposals involving employee health and safety, nondiscrimination based on national origin, and the free movement of workers.

Briefly stated, the cooperation procedure involves a two-stage process whereby the Parliament and the Council each review Commission proposals twice before enacting them. The first stage resembles the consultation procedure (discussed above) until the point at which the Council normally would vote to enact the proposal into law. Instead, at that point, the Council merely develops a common position on the proposal. The proposal then returns to the Parliament for a second reading. After this occurs, the Commission has an opportunity to reexamine the proposal and any amendments offered by the Parliament. Finally, the measure returns to the Council for its final decision. In most instances, the Council can enact the proposal into law by a qualified majority (54 out of 76 votes) rather than through unanimity. (Unanimity is still required in certain politically sensitive areas, such as fiscal policy, the free movement of persons, and environmental protection.)

We will now more closely examine the actual implementation of the cooperation procedure. However, because of the parallel between its first stage and the consultation procedure, our discussion assumes the Council has finished the first stage and formulated a common position.

Second Reading by the Parliament

After formulating a common position by qualified majority, the Council presents this to the Parliament. This report includes a discussion of the basis of the position, a statement of the Commission's position, and an explanation of any divergences from the Parliament's original opinion. During this stage, the Parliament has three months to approve, reject, or amend the common position. Failure to act within these time limits is treated as an approval, although an agreement can be made with the Council to give the Parliament one extra month to consider the common position. (Remember, in the first stage, the Parliament could have delayed a proposal in committee indefinitely.)

A simple majority of those present is all that is needed for the Parliament to approve a proposal. Although, as was noted above, the Parliament's failure to act is also treated as an approval. When the Parliament approves the proposal or fails to act within the three months, the Council must enact the common position into law. The Parliament also can reject or propose amendments to the common position, but an absolute majority (260 or the 518 members) is necessary to do so. If the Parliament has rejected the proposal, the Council can pass it into law only by a unanimous vote.

Reexamination by the Commission

When the Parliament proposes amendments to the Council's common position, the Commission has one month to reconsider the measure in light of the Parliament's proposals. If the Parliament can convince a majority of the Commission to endorse its amendments, the Council can adopt them by a qualified majority. However, if the Commission and the Parliament do not agree, the Commission presents the Council with its reexamined proposal along with an explanation of why it rejected the Parliament's position.

Final Consideration by the Council

At this stage, the Council can adopt the Commission's reexamined proposal by a qualified majority. Any of the Parliament's amendments that were not accepted by the Commission can be adopted only through the unanimous support of the Council. The Council may also offer its own amendments, but these require unanimity to be adopted. During this last phase, the Council has three months within which to act. (The Parliament and the Council can agree to extend this by one month.) If the Council does not act within these time limits, the proposal is not adopted. As a final note, the Commission may alter its proposal anytime before the Council takes final action on a measure.

Advantages of the Cooperation Procedure

The cooperation procedure generally increases the level of active cooperation among the Commission, the Parliament, and the Council throughout the life of a legislative proposal. The time restraints the procedure places on each institution, coupled with the provisions governing majority versus unanimous voting in the Council, have resulted in incentives for each institution to more readily compromise with the other two.

The Commission's Delegated Authority

Much of the legislation produced by the processes discussed above requires additional implementation before it can become effective. (We have seen how directives require action by the member states.) In these circumstances, the Council may delegate authority to the Commission to ensure that the legislation is carried out. In certain areas (antidumping duties, antisubsidy duties, and competition law), the Com-

FIGURE 3–5

EEC Legislation from Start to Finish

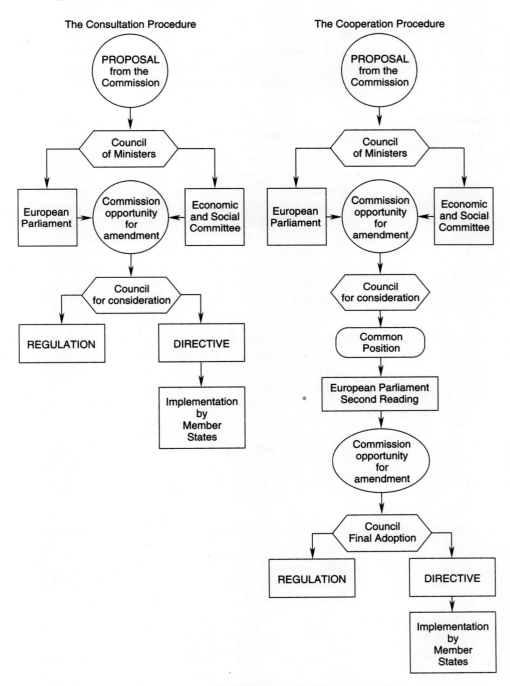

Source: Ernst & Whinney, *Completing the Internal Market* (Commission of the European Communities Current Status Series).

mission may be vested with unqualified power to act. The *Akzo Chemie* case, discussed earlier, was an example of the Commission's power to issue decisions in furtherance of the EC's competition law. Other times (when the Commission may be drafting technical rules with Communitywide effect) the Council may require that the Commission act only in concert with an advisory committee composed of experts representing the member states.

LOBBYING TO INFLUENCE LEGISLATION

Active lobbying of European institutions by U.S. corporations and interest groups is a relatively recent phenomenon. In large part, this increased political activity is a natural outgrowth of the heightened hopes and fears raised by the specter of a single Europe. American businesses—both large and small—have witnessed the events in Europe with mixed emotions. On the one hand, greater integration offers promises of a tremendous market filled with opportunities for the astute businessperson. Simultaneously, however, there are visions of Europe becoming an impenetrable fortress, subsidizing its companies at home so they may unfairly compete with U.S. corporations throughout the globe. One way or the other, U.S. companies recognize more than ever the need to actively influence policy making within the European Community.

Points of Access   Our previous investigation of the legislative process reveals four major points of access for parties wishing to influence legislation. These four points of entry—the Commission, the Economic and Social Committee, the Parliament, and the Council—are discussed in turn.

Entry through the Commission

First, and perhaps most importantly, interested individuals and businesses can make their views known to the Commission, particularly when a proposal is still in the formative stages. The working groups that perform the Commission's background analysis are extremely influential and often approachable.

Entry through the Economic and Social Committee

A receptive ear also might be found among the formal interest groups represented on the Economic and Social Committee. This body plays a consultative role in most legislative efforts. Although its members represent European interests, many of them maintain working relationships with outside interests.

Entry through the Parliament

The increased power of the Parliament under the cooperation procedure makes this an increasingly viable point of entry for businesses hoping to influence the outcome of legislation. As with the Commission, the real power in the Parliament may lie with the special committees that perform the investigative work on potential legislation. Accordingly, those committees might be an ideal place to direct a lobbying effort.

Entry through the Council

A final path to the legislative process lies through the Council. Generally, this is the least desirable avenue because of the confidential nature of the Council's activities. However, it may be possible to wield some influence through COREPER, particularly during the early stages of its deliberations.

Developing a Lobbying Strategy

With the increased worldwide attention focused on the completion of an integrated Europe, the Community's governing institutions are becoming more familiar with and receptive to attempts to influence their activities. However, lobbying tactics that are successful in the United States may not work so well in Europe. As we have already witnessed, the institutional framework of the European legislative process varies in significant ways from the American system. Accordingly, this section offers four things to consider in developing a lobbying strategy for the European Community.

Understand the Process

To effectively influence the lawmaking process, a lobbyist must fully understand the internal workings of that system. One must know the role of the participating institutions and the key actors at each stage in the life of a proposal. The nature of the procedure is such that a proposal frequently is considered by several of the institutions at the same time. This demands a coordinated lobbying effort aimed at each of these institutions simultaneously. Without a sophisticated knowledge of the legislative process, this high level of coordination is not likely to be achieved.

Gain Access to Current Information

At the most basic level, a business should know what laws currently affect its operations as well as those being considered for passage. Some familiarity with the White Paper will help in this regard as it provides a rough map of the path toward integration. It makes good sense to monitor the statements and activities of the political institutions to anticipate their future actions. This can be accomplished by examining the recommendations and opinions they promulgate as well as any annual or semi-annual agenda they circulate. Under some circumstances, it may be necessary to develop some sort of presence in Brussels to gain more insight into the political climate. However, the U.S. government as well as private U.S. trade groups are actively monitoring the events in Europe and often are able to provide timely information.

Act Quickly

Most lobbying efforts fail unless they begin very early in the legislative process. Success is more likely to be achieved at the working group level while the Commission is still contemplating the drafting of a proposal. Likewise, other key points of entry

---

CONCEPT SUMMARY
Lobbying the EC Institutions

Select the Appropriate Points of Access	
	Commission
	Economic and Social Committee
	Parliament
	Council

Develop an Effective Strategy	
	Understand the Legislative Process
	Stay Informed
	Act Quickly
	Be Diplomatic

---

are through the special committees of the Parliament and through COREPER at the Council level. In the cooperation procedure, generally it is too late to have any meaningful impact after the Council has formulated its common position.

Be Diplomatic

American businesses must be sensitive to the fundamental cultural differences between the United States and Europe. Lobbying in Europe is much more low key than in the United States, and, accordingly, it may be necessary to tread lightly. Also, the lawmaking institutions are political bodies, subject to the demands of important political constituencies throughout the European Community. Therefore, the interests of U.S. businesses are likely to carry less weight than those of their European counterparts. This fundamental disadvantage might be offset in either of two ways. First, an American business or industry may be able to align itself with a company or industry group within the Community that shares its views. Second, an American business may decide to make its views known through the U.S. government. Both the executive and legislative branches of government have made clear their strong interest in the removal of trade barriers between the United States and the European Community. Accordingly, they may help U.S. companies hoping to make their views known.

THE JUDICIAL INSTITUTIONS

Thus far, our discussion has been confined to lawmaking and the predominant political institutions of the European Community. An understanding of the various types of legislation and the procedures by which they are enacted is essential for businesspersons hoping to effectively compete in and with Europe. However, one cannot fully appreciate the nature and function of the European legal system without also examining the judicial institutions and activities that complement those political processes. This section briefly introduces the major adjudicatory bodies of the European Community: the European Court of Justice; the Court of First Instance; and the national courts of the member states.

**The European
Court of Justice**

Of all the EC institutions, the European Court of Justice (ECJ) has assumed the most active role as the guarantor of European integration. It has been highly visible in its effort to ensure that Community law is enforced, in resolving disputes between the Community and member states as well as between the EC's political institutions, and in protecting individuals from those political institutions.

Composition

The ECJ is composed of 13 judges appointed by the members of the European Community. By tradition, one judge is appointed by each of the member states, while the 13th selection is rotated among the five larger nations (France, Germany, Italy, the United Kingdom, and Spain). Generally, the court sits in chambers of three or five judges; although major cases are heard by the entire court. Actions brought by a member state or the political institutions are always heard by the full court (plenary session).

Procedures

The procedures of the ECJ are mostly written; oral hearings play a very minor role. In large part, this stems from the multilingual nature of the European Community. There are 10 official languages for ECJ decisions; French is the working language of the court. The court deliberates in secret and, despite private differences of opinion among the judges, issues a single collegiate judgment. (There are no concurring or dissenting views.) This goal of outwardly demonstrating solidarity, coupled with the difficulties of communicating in so many diverse languages, frequently results in terse, unemotional judicial opinions that lack the strength and conviction that so often characterizes decisions handed down in the United States.

Several other features of the ECJ distinguish it from U.S. courts. First, because of the language problems (interpreters are not permitted during the court's deliberations), the European court places little weight on the literal meaning of words, focusing instead on policy considerations. Second, unlike English-based common law with its great emphasis on stare decisis (following past decisions), the ECJ does not feel compelled to make direct reference to relevant precedents. However, the court does seem to follow previous decisions in the majority of cases. Third, decisions of the ECJ are final—they permit no appeal.

Advocate Generals

A final feature of the ECJ places it in sharp contrast with the U.S. judicial process. Pursuant to the EEC Treaty, the Court of Justice is to be assisted by six advocate generals. France, Germany, Italy, and the United Kingdom each appoint one advocate general, while the remaining two selections are rotated among the eight smaller member states. These independent advisers (one is appointed for each hearing) aid the ECJ in interpretation. Thus, before the judges' formal deliberations, the advocate general assigned to the case issues a reasoned, nonbinding opinion that sets out the relevant facts and policy concerns and recommends a final outcome. The judges then meet in private (without the advocate general) and arrive at a formal opinion. They are in no way required to follow the advocate general and frequently depart from his or her views. Still, the advocate general greatly assists the ECJ by providing it with a common starting point in each case.

The Court of First Instance

The Single Europe Act modified the structure of the ECJ by establishing the Court of First Instance (CFI). A major impetus behind this change was the growing number of cases being heard by the ECJ and the increasing amount of time spent on each case. It was believed that the ECJ's performance would be greatly enhanced by transferring cases involving complex factual determinations to the CFI.

At present, the CFI hears three types of cases: staff cases (disputes between the EC institutions and their employees), competition cases, and coal and steel cases arising from application of the ECSC. Several general observations can be made about the CFI cases. First, they may only be brought by natural or legal persons (not by EC institutions or the member states). Second, they are the types of cases that generally require time-consuming investigation of complex facts. Third, CFI decisions may be appealed to the ECJ, although the appeal is limited to points of law only.

The CFI is composed of 12 judges—one representing each member state. While it officially has no advocate generals, one of its members serves that function for each hearing. Finally, like the ECJ, judges in the CFI generally sit in panels of three or five judges when hearing cases.

The National Courts

Although EC law has supremacy over the laws of the member states, the actual application of Community law frequently is left to the national courts. Thus, the courts of the member states often are responsible for giving full meaning and effect to Community law. This supportive role is carried out by the use of preliminary rulings (to be discussed in the next section) and through the doctrine of direct effects.

Direct Effect

One of the strongest forces behind the integration of the European legal system is the principle of direct effect. This doctrine requires the national courts to enforce Community legal rules and mandates that such provisions be given priority over conflicting national laws. The various treaty provisions, regulations, directives, and decisions are all capable of having direct effect and thus prevailing over national rules and regulations. The practical impact of a directly effective legal provision is that it grants private individuals rights that they can enforce against the governments of the member states (vertical effect) and, in limited circumstances, against other private individuals (horizontal effect).

Not all Community law has direct effects. Rules that are too general in nature or that require further action before they become enforceable are not directly effective.

Only those rules that are specific and immediately enforceable grant such rights to private individuals. Basically, Community law must meet three prerequisites before it becomes directly effective: (1) it must have sufficient clarity and precision that it can be readily applied by the courts; (2) it must establish an unconditional obligation on the government or private individuals; and (3) it must not depend on any subsequent action or discretion before it becomes effective.

Originally, it was believed that the doctrine of direct effect did not apply to directives. That is no longer the case, although directives still do not have horizontal effects. The decision by the European court to extend the direct effect principle to directives has probably had a more significant impact on European integration than any other action by the court. This is because the member states have been notoriously resistant and slow in implementing directives. Now private individuals can bring direct effect suits in the national courts against member states that either incorrectly enact a directive or fail to pass one before the implementation period expires. This next case, *van Gend en Loos*, is the ECJ's landmark direct effects opinion.

VAN GEND EN LOOS v. NEDERLANDSE ADMINISTRATIE DER BELASTINGEN
European Court of Justice, Aug. 16, 1962, [1963] ECR 1

■ **FACTS** On September 9, 1960, the company van Gend en Loos imported ureaformaldehyde into the Netherlands from Germany. On the basis of the Dutch revenue laws in effect at that time, the product was assessed an import duty of 8 percent. This amount was challenged by van Gend en Loos on the grounds that on January 1, 1958 (the date on which the EEC Treaty entered into force), the Dutch tariff on ureaformaldehyde was 3 percent. The EEC Treaty provided that member states were to refrain from introducing between themselves any new customs duties on imports or exports and from increasing those that already applied in their trade with each other. After the inspector of customs and excise dismissed the objections, van Gend en Loos appealed to the Dutch Tariefcommissie. This tribunal referred the matter to the ECJ for a preliminary ruling on the correct application of the EC law to the case at hand.

■ **ISSUE** Did the EEC Treaty give van Gend en Loos rights that the Dutch court must protect?

■ **DECISION** Yes. The objective of the EEC Treaty is to establish a Common Market, the functioning of which is of direct concern to interested parties in the EC. This implies this Treaty is more than an agreement that merely creates mutual obligations between the member states. This view is confirmed by the preamble to the Treaty, which refers not only to governments but also to peoples. The EC constitutes a new legal order of international law for the benefit of which the states have limited their sovereign rights and the subjects of which comprise not only member states but also their nationals. Independently of national legislation, EC law not only imposes obligations on individuals but is also intended to confer upon them rights that become part of their legal heritage. These rights arise not only where they are expressly granted by the Treaty, but also by reason of obligations, which the Treaty imposes in a clearly defined way on individuals as well as on member states and on the institutions of the EC. The Treaty language concerning import duties contains a clear and unconditional prohibition. This obligation is not qualified by the need for any implementing legislation by the member states. The very nature of this prohibition makes it ideally adapted to produce direct effects in the legal relationship between member states and their subjects.

THE EUROPEAN JUDICIAL PROCESS

Earlier, we saw how the European Community treaties established the powers of and relationships among the Council, the Commission, and the Parliament. The treaties have simultaneously vested the European Court of Justice with the jurisdiction to ensure that the political institutions carry out their powers in a lawful manner. Besides restraining the political institutions and the member states from exceeding their powers under the treaties, the ECJ has performed a quasi-legislative function by actively interpreting EC legislation in a manner designed to encourage integration. Specifically, the ECJ has the jurisdiction to conduct two major types of proceedings: (1) preliminary rulings and (2) direct actions. Each will now be discussed in greater detail.

Preliminary Rulings   Preliminary rulings (as we saw in the *van Gend en Loos* case) arise when the national courts refer questions to the ECJ to ensure the issues are given uniform treatment throughout the Community. Thus, they involve a special cooperation between ECJ and the national court in the application of Community law. First, a case is brought before the national court, which must determine the relevant facts and decide if the case involves an application of EC law. Next, if the national court decides there are questions of Community law, it refers the matter to the ECJ for a preliminary ruling on the correct interpretation of the law. Finally, the national court will render its judgment, applying the preliminary ruling to the facts of the case.

Generally, three types of legal issues are referred to the ECJ for a preliminary ruling: (*a*) interpretations of EC legislation, (*b*) questions as to the effect of Community law on the legal systems of the member states, and (*c*) the legality of the acts of the EC political institutions. National courts of last resort (those from which there is no appeal) must refer matters of EC law to the ECJ for preliminary rulings. Other national courts have the discretion to refer such questions when they feel such an interpretation is necessary. The national courts are bound by the preliminary rulings handed down by the ECJ. This fact, coupled with the narrow standing of individuals to bring direct actions before the ECJ, has made the national courts an attractive avenue for individuals wishing to challenge or enforce community law. In the case that follows, *CILFIT,* the ECJ addresses the discretion that the national courts possess in requesting preliminary rulings.

SRL CILFIT v. ITALIAN MINISTRY OF HEALTH
European Court of Justice, Oct. 6, 1982, [1982] ECR 3415

■ **FACTS** CILFIT brought suit before the Italian courts challenging certain Italian regulations on wool on the grounds that they conflicted with Community regulations. The lower court rejected CILFIT's argument, and the company appealed to the Italian Court of Cassation (Italy's highest court). That court was in doubt whether it was obliged to refer the issue to the ECJ.

■ **ISSUE** Does the Italian court have the discretion to determine whether the dispute must be referred to the ECJ?

■ **DECISION** Yes. Generally, the courts or tribunals of the member states against whose decisions there is no judicial remedy under national law are to refer questions of interpretation of EC law to the ECJ. However, this is not the case where the question raised is materially identical with a question that has already been the subject of a preliminary ruling in a similar case. Of course, national courts and tribunals remain at liberty to bring such matters before the ECJ. Before a national court of last resort concludes that there is no reasonable question to be resolved, it must be convinced the matter is equally obvious to the courts of the other member states and to the ECJ. The existence of this possibility must be assessed in light of the fact that community legislation is drafted in several languages and often uses terminology that does not necessarily have the same meaning throughout the EC.

Direct Actions

Unlike preliminary rulings that begin and end in the national courts, direct actions are conducted exclusively within the European Court of Justice. These direct actions are of four types: (1) infringement proceedings against the member states for failure to comply with their treaty obligations, (2) annulment actions against the EC political institutions that have improperly issued measures, (3) proceedings to compel the Commission or the Council to act, and (4) actions to establish noncontractual liability.

Infringement Proceedings

These actions are brought by the Commission to compel the member states to comply with their treaty obligations. (They also may be brought by one member state against another, although, for diplomatic reasons, this seldom occurs.) Infringement actions must begin with a precontentious phase in which the Commission writes a letter to the member state warning of the treaty violation and soliciting that nation's views on the matter. Most disputes are resolved at this stage. The Commission then issues a reasoned opinion in which it orders the member state to act within a prescribed time period. If the member state refuses the Commission's request for a dialogue or fails to comply with the Commission's opinion, the matter will be brought before the ECJ, which may declare there to be a treaty violation. The court's judgment is declaratory only (it can issue no sanctions); however, the Commission has the power to withhold various entitlements from the member state.

An infringement action might be brought against a member state that either incorrectly enacts a directive or fails to implement one within the prescribed time period. As may be imagined, such proceedings are often cumbersome and politically difficult. As we saw in the *van Gend en Loos* case, however, there is another way to address a member state's failure to comply with its treaty obligations. This occurs if an injured private person brings a lawsuit before the courts of the noncomplying nation under the doctrine of direct effect. It is not uncommon to find parallel infringement and direct effect proceedings occurring simultaneously.

■ **ETHICAL IMPLICATIONS** In several instances, a member state has refused to comply with its obligations under the treaties. In reality, there is little the court or the Commission can do to force such compliance. Is it ever ethical for a member state to behave in such a manner?

Annulment Actions

These proceedings are brought by the Commission, the Council, or any member state to annul binding community actions (regulations, directives, or decisions) that have been illegally enacted. They may also be brought by private persons under narrow circumstances where the wrongful act concerns them directly and individually. The *Akzo Chemie* and *Freres* cases, discussed earlier, were both attempts to annul community actions. Four major types of illegality support an annulment action: (*a*) acting outside of the authority granted by the treaties, (*b*) failing to comply with the procedural requirements mandated by the treaties, (*c*) acting in violation of any rule of law, and (*d*) exercising power for improper purposes. If a measure has been enacted in violation of any of these principles, the ECJ declares it to be retroactively null and void. Annulment actions for regulations and decisions are brought directly before the ECJ, while actions to annul directives must be brought before the national courts (which may then seek a preliminary ruling from the ECJ).

Proceedings for Failure to Act

Sometimes the EC institutions or the member states may seek to compel the Commission or the Council to take an action that it had a duty to perform. As with the annulment actions described above, private persons may also bring these actions when they are affected directly and individually by the failure to act. Such proceedings are not permitted until the institution has been formally requested to take the action and has refused to comply. When the ECJ finds there to have been a wrongful failure to act, it has no power to actually enact the measure itself. All it can do is rule that the Commission's or the Council's failure violated the EEC Treaty, which, in theory, obligates those institutions to comply with the judgment of the court.

Actions to Establish Noncontractual Liability

The ECJ has exclusive jurisdiction over noncontractual (tort) civil liability claims against the EC for actions of its institutions and servants. In order to establish EC liability, the court has insisted that there be: (*a*) an illegal act on the part of an EC institution or servant, (*b*) damages inflicted on the victim, and (*c*) a causal link between the act and the damages.

As a general rule, contract disputes must be heard by the appropriate national courts rather than the ECJ. The European Court has no jurisdiction over contract disputes because none was granted in the treaties. However, the ECJ may hear a contract dispute if the contract with the EC contained an arbitration clause that designated the ECJ as the appropriate forum. Such arbitration cases are the only instances where a private person may be a defendant in a direct action heard by the European Court of Justice.

CONCEPT SUMMARY
Judicial Action in the EC

Preliminary Rulings	Suit arises in national court
	ECJ gives binding opinion on application of EC law
	National court renders final decision

Direct Action	Infringement proceeding against member state
	Action to annul an unlawful EC action
	Proceeding against Commission or Council for failure to perform obligations
	Noncontractual (tort) claims against EC institutions or servants
	Contract disputes involving EC when ECJ designated in aritration clause

---

KROHN & CO. IMPORT-EXPORT GMBH v. COMMISSION OF THE EC
European Court of Justice, Feb. 26, 1986, [1986] ECR 753

■ **FACTS** Krohn applied to the German Federal Office for the Organization of Agricultural Markets (the Bundesanstalt) for licenses to import manioc from Thailand. Acting in compliance with instructions from the Commission, the Bundesanstalt refused to grant the import licenses. Claiming the Commission's actions were illegal, Krohn brought an action for noncontractual liability against the Commission before the ECJ. The Commission argued that because the decision to deny the licenses was that of the Bundesanstalt, only the German national courts could hear the case.

■ **ISSUE** Does the ECJ have jurisdiction to hear this claim?

■ **DECISION** Yes. The ECJ only has jurisdiction to award compensation for noncontractual damages caused by EC institutions or by their servants in the performance of their duties. Damage caused by national institutions, on the other hand, can give rise only to liability on the part of those institutions in actions brought before the national courts. Thus, it must be determined if the unlawful conduct alleged in this claim was the responsibility of the Bundesanstalt or the Commission. The Commission has not only the right to give opinions on the granting of import licenses, but it may also actually insist that the national institutions comply with its instructions. It follows that since the Bundesanstalt was obligated to comply with the Commission's wishes, the unlawful denial should be attributed to the Commission.

IMPLICATIONS FOR U.S. BUSINESSES

Fortress Europe An integrated Europe is a fact of life. For the most part, all of the regulations essential to the creation of a single market for goods and services have been implemented. Still, there will continue to be variations among the 12 member states that will complicate the economic environment for U.S. businesses. Further, elimination of internal barriers will not automatically translate into a breakdown of external barriers. Burdensome testing and certification requirements and other forms of discriminatory regulations pose serious technical barriers to non-European traders, perhaps ultimately threatening the erection of a "Fortress Europe."

ETHICAL IMPLICATIONS   The European Community is establishing extensive testing and certification requirements for products that are to be sold within the EC. Many U.S. exporters complain that they have been left out of the formation of these standards and, as a result, the regulations will discriminate against non-European goods. Is it ethical for EC officials to favor European goods over foreign goods?

Developing a European Strategy

U.S. businesses must carefully monitor the economic and legal situation in the various member states if they hope to overcome these potential barriers. Despite the single Europe movement, there are still wide variations among the national governments in their implementation and enforcement of internal market directives. Likewise, the many languages and diverse cultures represented in the European continent often result in marked differences in consumer preferences from one region to another. For these reasons, it is more important than ever that U.S. business managers understand the workings of the EC and establish an effective European presence if they hope to take full advantage of the single European movement.

QUESTIONS AND PROBLEM CASES

1. Explain the system of checks and balances that characterizes the role of the political institutions in the legislative process in the European Community.

2. How does the consultation procedure differ from the cooperation procedure for enacting legislation?

3. Explain the cooperative nature of the national courts and the European Court of Justice in the judicial process of the European Community.

4. In the context of the role of the European Court of Justice, what is the difference between a preliminary opinion and a direct action?

5. French law requires cinemas to apply for a performance certificate before public showings of movies. After receipt of this certificate, it would be unlawful for others to sell or rent videocassette versions of the same movie for a period of one year in the absence of special permission from the Ministry of Culture. The film *Merry Christmas, Mr. Lawrence* was first shown in French cinemas on June 1, 1983, although it did not receive its performance certificate until June 28, 1983. Glinwood Films, Ltd., the British copyright owner of the film, granted to AAA Company the exclusive right to show the movie in French theaters. Simultaneously, it gave Cinetheque the exclusive right to produce and sell videocassettes of the film during the same period. AAA Company agreed to the Cinetheque arrangement after being promised a share of Cinetheque's video royalties, although the parties never applied for a waiver from the Ministry of Culture. The Federation Nationale des Cinemas Francais obtained an

order that Cinetheque's videocassettes be seized until the expiration of the one-year waiting period. Glinwood and Cinetheque claimed the provisions of the French law violated EC law. Does the French regulation unlawfully interfere with the free movement of goods within the EC?

6. An Italian wine trader, Foglia, sold wine to be delivered in France to another Italian, Novello. All delivery costs were to be paid by Novello. However, when Foglia sent him the bill, Novello refused to pay certain import fees levied by France. Foglia sued Novello before the Italian courts despite the fact that both Foglia and Novello believed the French import fees to be unlawful. (They hoped to obtain a decision from the European Court of Justice condemning the French action.) The Italian court requested a preliminary ruling as to the legality of the French action. Will the ECJ give a preliminary ruling?

7. Nitrate fertilizers are manufactured from ammonia, and great amounts of energy are required to produce ammonia. Thus, the cost of nitrate fertilizers is largely dependent on the cost of energy. In the Netherlands, the primary source of energy is natural gas, and the Dutch government granted special rebates for Dutch ammonia producers. This subsidy enabled the Dutch nitrate industry to undersell its competitors. The Commission began an investigation of this practice; however, it terminated its inquiry after the Dutch authorities amended their subsidy program. A French nitrate producer claimed the Dutch system was still discriminatory and sought to have the Commission's decision to drop the investigation annulled. Could the French company bring an annulment action before the European Court of Justice?

8. Marshall, a 60-year old woman, was dismissed from her job as a senior dietician with the Southampton and South West Hampshire Area Health Authority (a governmental institution). The only reason for her dismissal was that she was past the retirement age applicable to women. The Authority had a written policy that its female employees must retire at age 60 and its male employees at age 65. She claimed her dismissal violated an EC Council directive that required equal treatment for men and women as regards access to employment. Should the national courts enforce Marshall's claims under the doctrine of direct effect?

9. Grimaldi worked in Belgium as a miner and at various other trades for over 20 years. After retirement, he claimed to be suffering from work-related injuries and applied to the Belgian government for compensation. This request was denied on the ground that Grimaldi's injuries were not listed in the Belgian schedule of occupational diseases. They were contained, however, in the European Schedule of Occupational Diseases, which the EC Commission had recommended be adopted by the member states. (It was not adopted by Belgium.) Should a Belgian court order that Grimaldi be compensated under the doctrine of direct effect?

10. The EC Commission issued a decision addressed to the member states pursuant to Article 118 of the EEC Treaty setting up a prior communication and consultation procedure on migration policies. The member states were to inform the Commission and the other member states of their draft measures and draft treaties with regard to workers from non-EC countries relating to entry, residence, and employment. Such notification could be followed by consultation between the member states and the Commission, arranged by the latter at the instigation of itself or of a member state. The first paragraph of Article 118 confers on the Commission the task of promoting close cooperation between the member states in the social field. The second paragraph provides that, to that end, the Commission is to act in close contact with the member states by making studies, delivering opinions, and arranging consultations. Several member states challenged the authority of the Commission to adopt binding decisions designed to arrange consultations. Does the Commission possess this authority?

The North American Free Trade Agreement

INTRODUCTION

Enterprise for the Americas Initiative

Pondering its place in a newly emerging world order, the United States searched for a way to maintain a prominent role in the global economy. Partially in response to these concerns, the United States proposed the **Enterprise for the Americas Initiative** designed to promote regional economic integration in the Western Hemisphere. The program rests on three pillars: (1) stimulation of market-oriented investment reforms throughout the area, (2) reduction of the debt obligations of the Latin American and Caribbean nations, and (3) elimination of trade barriers. This third pillar—reducing obstacles to free trade in the Western Hemisphere—is the centerpiece of the initiative.

Free Trade Reforms

The ultimate goal of the Enterprise for the Americas Initiative is the creation of a hemispheric free trade area stretching from the Arctic to the southern tip of South America. As a first step in this ambitious plan, the United States is negotiating bilateral framework agreements with each of the nations. These arrangements are designed to increase trading volume and to begin a general harmonization of trade policies.

Despite this progress, the tremendous disparities in political and economic development among the various nations guarantee that the realization of a hemispheric free trade area is years away. Accordingly, the primary focus of the program was on a more immediately attainable goal—the creation of the North American Free Trade Agreement (NAFTA) among Canada, Mexico, and the United States. Only after the economies of the other nations mature will they be granted membership into this core group.

NAFTA

The North American Free Trade Agreement encompasses a market of more than 360 million people and a combined output of over $6 trillion. NAFTA seemed to be a natural starting point for hemispheric integration for several reasons. First, since 1989, the United States and Canada had been partners in a free trade agreement that served as a blueprint for the trilateral accord. Second, the Mexican and Canadian economies offered the prospect of immediate opportunities for U.S. businesses since the United States already provided over two thirds of the goods imported into those two nations. Finally, recent political and economic reforms in Mexico made it an inviting environment for U.S. businesses interested in expanded trade and investment.

In general, NAFTA eliminates barriers to the flow of goods, services, and investment within the free trade area over a 15-year period. Because of political pressures within each nation, the treaty envisions a phased removal of these obstacles with the length of the transition period varying from industry to industry.

Free Trade Agreement versus Common Market

NAFTA is a free trade agreement while the European Community is a common market. A free trade agreement confines itself to the regulation and harmonization of trade and investment among its members. Accordingly, each of the NAFTA partners maintains its own tariff rates for countries that don't belong to the free trade agreement. As a common market, the European Community establishes a common economic policy for trade and investment within the community as well as a common external tariff. Further, the EC has expressed a long-range interest in creating a common monetary policy and a common foreign policy. The NAFTA members have not indicated any similar desires.

Chapter Overview

Rather than detailing the long-range ambitions of the Enterprise for the Americas Initiative, this chapter focuses on the concrete aspects of NAFTA and its likely impact on U.S. businesses. This investigation occurs at several levels. For instance, there is an introduction to the institutions designed to implement the treaty as well as a look at the key provisions governing cross-border trade in goods and services. The chapter also examines the fundamental aspects of NAFTA's dispute settlement procedures.

Because of its recent origin, no NAFTA cases are available for this edition of the text. However, in many instances, the NAFTA provisions duplicate those that were part of the Canada–U.S. Free Trade Agreement. Accordingly, cases from the Canada–U.S. agreement are used to illustrate similar NAFTA issues.

GOALS AND RESERVATIONS

The three NAFTA partners—Canada, Mexico, and the United States—each have their own goals for the free trade agreement and varying levels of commitment to its success. This section offers a general overview of the objectives of the individual participants as well as a glimpse at some of their reservations.

Canada

Goals

Canada may have been the most reluctant participant in the treaty negotiations. While Canada is the number one trading partner of the United States, its access to the vast U.S. market already was secured under the bilateral Canada–U.S. Free Trade Agreement. Because its economic ties with Mexico had been negligible, it saw little advantage to a Canada–Mexico treaty. In fact, numerous Canadian interests feared the NAFTA discussions might result in the country forfeiting certain grudging concessions it previously had received from the United States in the bilateral treaty. Ultimately, Canada's participation seems to be a defensive maneuver premised on the concern that, without a formal role in the negotiations between Mexico and the United States, it might lose many of the rights it gained in the earlier agreement.

Reservations

Certain Canadian interests may suffer hardships under NAFTA. In particular, labor-intensive industries are threatened by the combination of Mexico's immense labor pool (a population of over 90 million) and low wages. Employees in the automobile assembly industry are greatly alarmed over the prospect of mass relocations of factories to Mexican soil.

Mexico

Goals

By many accounts, Mexico has the most to gain from NAFTA. Of the three partners, it has by far the smallest and the most restrictive economy. Mexican leaders envisioned the free trade agreement as a means of attracting large amounts of foreign investment necessary to reverse its international trade deficit.

Mexico already was the third largest trading partner of the United States; thus, their economic links were strong. Much of this trade was generated by the Mexican **maquiladora** industry. Established in 1965 under Mexico's Border Industrialization Program, maquiladoras are factories for the assembly, processing, and finishing of foreign materials and components. Mexico assessed no tariffs on components imported by these factories if the finished products were exported. Their development was aided by U.S. Customs regulations that permitted U.S. businesses to export components to the Mexican factories and, when importing the finished products, to pay tariffs only to the extent of the value added in Mexico. (This special program for U.S. goods assembled abroad is discussed more fully in Chapter 10.)

The economic success of the maquiladora program convinced Mexican leaders of the potential benefits that could follow greater cooperation between U.S. and Mexican businesses. Further, the prospect of tariff-free entry into the vast U.S. market, coupled with the low wage demands of Mexican workers, was certain to attract manufacturers from around the world.

Reservations

Not all Mexican interests view NAFTA as a boon to the country. Some argue that, although many assembly operations will be attracted to the country, those will be the lowest paying, unskilled jobs that add little value to the overall economy. Further, many contend that Mexico's small and medium-sized firms will be unable to compete with the more efficient U.S. companies that soon will dominate the domestic market. Finally, Mexico and Canada share a common concern over the great likelihood that the economic might of the United States eventually will overwhelm their unique cultures and political sovereignty.

United States

Goals

Many U.S. interests view NAFTA as a means of improving access to the growing Mexican market. Mexico's tariffs are much higher than those in Canada and the United States and conceivably could be raised even higher. While some U.S. industries would move to Mexico in order to take advantage of the lower wage scales, the resulting increases to the Mexican economy are seen as indirectly benefiting the United States. First, economic gains in Mexico would strengthen that country's commitment to political and market reform. This would provide a safer environment for U.S. investment. Second, the gains in the standard of living would increase demand for U.S. exports. Third, a strong Mexican economy would help stem the tide of illegal immigration into the United States.

One further advantage of the free trade agreement is that it provides U.S. businesses with easier and cheaper access to the rich resources of Canada and Mexico. This has been described as essential if the United States is to compete more effectively in the world markets, particularly in the face of European integration.

Reservations

Employees in the labor-intensive industries of the United States share the Canadian concern that many factories will shift operations to the low-cost, Mexican labor market. This is extremely likely to occur in the automobile assembly, textile, apparel, steel, and electronics industries. Also, cheaper Mexican imports will drive prices on fruits and vegetables downward, cutting into the profits of domestic growers. Finally, environmentalists have strongly criticized the treaty on the grounds that there will be a mass migration of businesses southward to take advantage of Mexico's weak commitment to environmental protection.

Other Nations' Concerns

Countries outside of the NAFTA region have expressed great concern that the free trade agreement will foster protectionist policies. Special rules of origin for automobiles, televisions, and clothing appear to be designed to shelter domestic producers from foreign competition. Some critics have condemned the pact as further evidence that the global system of trade is splintering into three major regional blocs (North America, Europe, and Asia).

Central American and Caribbean Basin businesses have complained they are losing out as foreign investors have rushed to Mexico. In particular, the electronics and garment industries have been relocating assembly operations to Mexico to take advantage of free access to the U.S. consumer market. Similar migrations from East Asia also are occurring.

GATT Legality

The three NAFTA partners have pledged their continued commitment to the General Agreement on Tariffs and Trade (GATT) and promised that NAFTA will be applied in a GATT-consistent manner. (GATT and the obligations it imposes on its members are discussed more fully in Chapter 9.) At first glance, GATT's requirement that members extend trade concessions to all GATT members in a nondiscriminatory fashion would seem to be violated by the special preferences the NAFTA members are giving one another. However, this is not the case. GATT provides an exception for free trade areas, such as NAFTA, if they do not increase tariffs or other trade restrictions to countries that do not belong to the free trade agreement. Thus, NAFTA may grant special preferences and expand trade among Canada, Mexico, and the United States as long as it does not raise new barriers against the other GATT members.

RATIFICATION

After the leaders of the three nations signed the accord, the widespread enthusiasm for NAFTA throughout Mexico left little doubt that the Mexican Senate would ratify it. Likewise, despite much opposition to a free trade agreement among the Canadian population, legislative approval also seemed certain. Under Canada's parliamentary system, the prime minister had firm control of the ratification process.

Ratification was most questionable in the United States where environmental and labor groups hoped to block its passage. This section briefly explores the nature of those concerns. It also examines the "fast-track" authority that permitted the U.S. executive branch to negotiate the treaty without fearing that special interests would fundamentally alter it during the congressional ratification process.

Environmental Concerns

Environmentalists expressed deep concern that NAFTA would encourage U.S. and Canadian manufacturers to migrate to Mexico where they could benefit from lax environmental protection. NAFTA addressed these complaints in two fundamental ways. First, the treaty requires that no member may lower its health, safety, or environmental standards for the purpose of attracting investment. Second, the three nations negotiated a side agreement that created a process for enforcing each nation's national and subnational environmental standards.

The environmental side agreement established a trinational commission that investigates allegations of a NAFTA nation's persistent failure to enforce its environmental laws. If at least two of the members desire, the complaint must be heard by a panel of environmental experts that can levy fines of up to $20 million. If either Mexico or the United States refuses to pay the fine, the complaining nation may impose trade sanctions in the form of tariffs or quotas. When Canada refuses to pay a fine the panel can seek enforcement through the Canadian courts.

Job Displacement

U.S. and Canadian labor groups warned that NAFTA would result in a tremendous loss of jobs among unskilled workers, arguing that Mexico's weak enforcement of labor laws would act as a magnet for employers. In response to these complaints, the three nations also implemented a side agreement that created a trinational commission on labor issues. Like its environmental counterpart, this body coordinates closer relations among the members on labor issues and provides a fine/trade sanction mechanism for punishing governments that fail to enforce health and safety standards, child labor rules, and minimum wages.

ETHICAL IMPLICATIONS   Is it ethical for U.S. manufacturers to move their operations to Mexico to take advantage of less stringent environmental standards? Is it ethical to move to Mexico to lower wage costs?

Fast-Track Approval   International treaties, such as NAFTA, generally involve delicate negotiations among the executive branches of the participating countries. In the United States, these treaties become federal law once they have been ratified by Congress. However, if this congressional ratification were handled the same as any lawmaking process, the treaties likely would be subjected to numerous special interest amendments and changes. Ultimately, they would become unacceptable to the other treaty partners.

The United States created **fast-track** authority to avoid this situation. Designed to strike a balance between legislative oversight and executive discretion, Congress extends fast-track negotiating authority to the President for a limited time. During this period, presidential agreements with foreign nations are subject only to a straight up or down vote (with no amendments) by Congress within 90 days after implementing legislation has been drafted.

ADMINISTRATION OF NAFTA

Trade Commission   NAFTA's primary administrative body is a three-member **Trade Commission** staffed by trade ministers or cabinet-level officers appointed by each of the member states. The Commission meets at least once a year with each session to be chaired by the representative from each nation on a rotating basis. All Commission decisions are to be taken by consensus, unless the commissioners unanimously decide in advance to agree otherwise.

The Commission supervises implementation of the treaty and resolves disputes that arise over its interpretation or application. However, much of the day-to-day operations of NAFTA are conducted by various ad hoc or standing committees and working groups staffed by officials designated by each of the governments.

Secretariat   The Commission also oversees a permanent **Secretariat** comprised of national sections representing each member country. The fundamental purpose of this body is to provide administrative and technical support to the Trade Commission, dispute settlement panels, and any other committees and working groups that may be established. Through the administrative functions performed by the Secretariat, the treaty is more efficiently managed by the three member states.

Administration of Laws   NAFTA requires that each nation's laws affecting trade and investment are readily accessible and fairly enforced. To ensure some level of due process, each of the nations has promised to provide independent judicial or administrative review of any governmental action that affects matters covered by the treaty. To ensure **procedural transparency,** the member states must notify and inform each other before taking any actions that might interfere with the treaty.

Rules of Origin   Because the free trade agreement ultimately will remove all tariffs on goods originating in Canada, Mexico, and the United States, manufacturers in the United States were deeply concerned that goods produced outside of NAFTA might be transhipped

FIGURE 4–1   Comparison of the NAFTA Partners

	Canada	Mexico	United States
Population	27 million	88 million	253 million
Gross domestic product per person	$21,960	$3,220	$22,420
Hourly pay and benefits (automobile industry)	$19.20	$2.75	$21.90
Hourly pay and benefits (textiles)	$11.90	$1.95	$10.30
Total exports	$128 billion	$27 billion	$417 billion
Total imports	$120 billion	$38 billion	$490 billion
Exports to Canada	—	$2.1 billion	$85.1 billion
Exports to Mexico	$.390 billion	—	$33.3 billion
Exports to United States	$93.7 billion	$31.9 billion	—

Source: International Monetary Fund (1991).

Canada

United States

Mexico

through Mexico or Canada to enter the U.S. market under the preferential tariff treatment. Accordingly, the treaty establishes strict **rules of origin** designed to ensure that NAFTA's benefits are extended only to goods produced wholly, or in large part, within the free trade area.

Goods containing non-NAFTA components will be classified as North American only if they are transformed within a member state to the extent that they undergo a change in tariff classification. In several instances (discussed below), goods will not be eligible for preferential treatment unless they include a specific percentage of North American components.

The treaty permits two ways to determine if goods meet the North American content requirements. Under the "transaction-value" method, the value of the components is calculated from the price paid or payable for the goods. The "net-cost" method, on the other hand, is determined by subtracting the costs of royalties, sales promotion, packing, and shipping from the total cost of the goods. Generally, a producer can elect either approach except in those cases where the transaction value is not acceptable under the GATT Customs Valuation Code. (Net cost also must be used for automotive products.)

Uniform Customs Administration

NAFTA contains several provisions designed to harmonize and streamline the customs procedures of each of the member states. In part, these measures call for common recordkeeping requirements, a standard certificate of origin, and uniform regulations to guarantee consistent interpretation of the rules of origin. Another provision requires the customs authorities from each country to offer advance rulings on the origin of imports. Further, each NAFTA member must give exporters and producers from the other two member states substantially the same rights of review and appeal of its rule of origin decisions that it gives its own importers.

TRADE IN GOODS

General Principles

A fundamental goal of the NAFTA negotiations was elimination of barriers to trade in goods among the three members. The treaty carries out these objectives in two important ways. First, each participant agrees to accord **national treatment** to goods imported from either of the other two nations. This means the NAFTA countries will ensure that none of their national or local laws discriminate against the goods of the other members.

Second, the treaty is designed to secure greater market access for each member state within the borders of the other two. Some of these measures provide for the elimination of tariffs and a reduction in import and export restrictions. However, certain country of origin marking requirements remain in effect.

Elimination of Tariffs

For most goods, tariffs will be eliminated immediately or phased out in 5 or 10 annual stages. Thus, within the first five years, roughly two thirds of all U.S. exports to Mexico will have received duty-free status. In certain sensitive sectors of each nation's economy, the phaseout period might extend up to 15 years. For instance, Mexico may take this longer period to phase out tariffs on some agricultural products, like corn and beans, to give its domestic farmers an opportunity to adjust to new competition.

Elimination of Import Restrictions

Each NAFTA member has pledged to eliminate prohibitions and quantitative restrictions, such as quotas and import licenses, for goods originating in the other member countries. However, the governments retain the right to impose some restrictions designed to protect human, animal, or plant life, or the environment. (Some special rules apply to automobiles, energy, agriculture, and textiles.)

Elimination of Export Restrictions

NAFTA prohibits the imposition of any export taxes unless they also apply to goods that are to be consumed domestically. Other export restrictions are permitted only if they do not reduce the proportion of the supply of the product below the level of the preceding three years. Further, the members cannot impose higher prices on exports to the other NAFTA countries than they do on domestic sales and they cannot disrupt normal supply channels. (Mexico has been granted exceptions from these export restrictions.)

Country of Origin Marking Requirements

NAFTA does not preclude a member from imposing country of origin marking requirements on imports that originated in the other member countries. These labeling requirements are designed to fully inform ultimate purchasers of the national origin of foreign goods, although they are widely condemned as unfair barriers to free trade. (Country of origin marking is discussed more fully in Chapter 10.) The treaty attempts to harmonize these restraints and minimize unnecessary costs on the flow of goods.

The three countries agreed to recognize and protect certain "distinctive products." Canadian Whiskey, Tequila, Mezcal, Bourbon Whiskey, and Tennessee Whiskey fall within this category. Accordingly, products cannot be sold within the NAFTA countries under those names unless they meet the requirements imposed by their country of origin.

Agricultural Products

Agriculture may have been the most politically sensitive area in the NAFTA negotiations, with each of the participants reluctant to open key agriculture sectors to unbridled competition. Not surprisingly, the parties were unable to reach a trilateral accord for reducing barriers to trade in agricultural products. Instead, they crafted two separate bilateral treaties, one between Canada and Mexico and the other between the United States and Mexico. Agricultural trade between the United States and Canada is governed by the Canada–U.S. Free Trade Agreement.

Mexico–U.S. Accord

Before NAFTA, over 25 percent of U.S. agricultural exports were required to obtain import licenses before they could enter the Mexican market. Under the treaty, the United States and Mexico agreed to immediately eliminate those and all other nontariff barriers to agricultural trade. Primarily, this is accomplished through the implementation of ordinary tariffs or **tariff-rate quotas** (TRQs). Under a TRQ, a certain quota for each type of agricultural product is established and no tariffs will be assessed for imports that fall within the quota amount. Any imports in excess of the quota will be dutied at a level that progressively declines to zero during a 10-to-15-year transition period.

The tariffs on roughly half the agricultural trade between the two countries was eliminated immediately. The tariffs on most of the remaining agricultural products is to be eliminated within 10 years. For certain sensitive products—corn and dried beans in Mexico and orange juice and sugar in the United States—the tariff phaseout will take 15 years.

Canada–Mexico Accord

Mexico agreed to eliminate its import licenses and other nontariff barriers for Canadian agricultural products. However, Canada is allowed to maintain production quotas, subsidies, and import quotas (nontariff protection) for its dairy, poultry, and egg producers. Mexico will retain its import licenses for Canadian dairy, poultry, and egg products, but will replace them with tariffs and TRQs for most other goods. Most tariffs will be phased out over 5 to 10 years.

Safeguard Provision

NAFTA provides a special **safeguard provision** that will apply to certain products governed by the bilateral treaties during the first 10 years they are in effect. The mechanism will be invoked when imports of these products reach certain trigger levels established in the agreements. When this level is met, the importing country may impose the lower of either the tariff rate in effect when the treaty became operative or the most-favored-nation rate that was then in effect under GATT. The trigger levels will increase over a 10-year period. (For the Canada–U.S. Free Trade Agreement this "snap-back" provision is triggered by complaints from domestic producers rather than from imports reaching preset levels.)

Domestic Supports and Export Subsidies

The NAFTA nations recognized the importance of domestic price supports to their agriculture sectors and, accordingly, made no effort to eliminate them. However, they agreed to reform their individual programs to minimize their trade-distorting effects.

Likewise, the three members agreed to avoid the use of export subsidies except when they are designed to counter subsidized imports from non-NAFTA countries. For instance, suppose Mexico imports grapes from Chile that have been subsidized by the Chilean government. Nonsubsidized U.S. grape producers would be unable to effectively compete with the Chilean grapes in the Mexican market. Before the United States could subsidize U.S. grape exports to Mexico, it would need to give Mexico three days' notice of that intent. The United States would then enter into consultations with Mexico on measures that Mexico might take to offset the advantages its importers gained from the Chilean export subsidies. If Mexico were to adopt mutually agreed-upon measures to counter the Chilean subsidy, the United States would not introduce its countervailing subsidy.

Automotive Goods

Automotive trade provided another tough area in the trilateral NAFTA negotiations. At stake was a multibillion-dollar North American automobile market and a battle among manufacturers and workers trying to survive in an increasingly competitive international industry. Both the United States and Mexico proposed that only automobiles containing a high percentage of North American content be covered by the pact. Canada strongly resisted the high North American content requirements out of a concern that they might discourage Japanese automobile manufacturing in Canada.

The discussions were complicated further by Mexico's 20 percent tariff on automobiles and other restrictions on automotive trade. For instance, Mexico required that automobiles manufactured in that country have at least 36 percent Mexican-made parts. The law also contained a trade-balancing provision that forced companies importing auto parts into Mexico to export automobiles in an amount greatly exceeding the value of the imported parts.

Despite these difficulties, NAFTA arrived at an automobile pact that opened the growing Mexican market to U.S. and Canadian manufacturers over a 10-year transition period. The agreement committed U.S. and Canadian producers to increasing production within Mexico. By making Mexican automobile production available to U.S. and Canadian investors, automobile manufacturers are expected to build large, efficient assembly plants that can supply the entire NAFTA region. Simultaneously, through stricter content requirements, the treaty increases the obstacles for non-NAFTA manufacturers operating in North America.

Tariff Elimination

The United States immediately eliminated its tariffs on Mexican-made passenger cars. It has reduced its tariffs on Mexican light trucks to 10 percent, which will then be phased out over five years. All other tariffs on Mexican vehicles are to be eliminated over a 10-year period.

Mexico has cut in half its 20 percent tariff on U.S. and Canadian passenger automobiles. The final 10 percent is to be phased out over 10 years. The tariff on light trucks has been halved and will finally be eliminated over five years. All other vehicle tariffs will end after 10 years.

The pact obligated Canada to eliminate its tariffs on Mexican vehicles under the same schedule that regulated U.S. and Canadian vehicles entering Mexico. Canada and the United States already had eliminated tariffs on automobiles under the Canada–U.S. Free Trade Agreement.

North American Content Rules

Passenger cars and light trucks, as well as their engines and transmissions, will not qualify for duty-free trade within the free trade area unless they meet a 62.5 percent North American content rule that will be phased in over eight years. (For other vehicles and automotive parts, the figure is 60 percent.) In assessing the content level, the treaty calls for a **net-cost formula** that traces the value of imports of automotive parts from outside the NAFTA region through the production chain. This calculation will subtract from the price of each car certain costs, such as profit, selling and marketing expenses, packing and shipping expenses, and royalties paid to designers. This discounted amount will be compared to the value of parts and labor from outside the NAFTA countries to determine its North American content percentage.

ARTICLE 304 AND THE DEFINITION OF DIRECT COST OF PROCESSING OR DIRECT COST OF ASSEMBLING
USA-92-1807-01 (Binational Review Panel 1992)

■ **FACTS** In response to an advice request from Toyota Motor Sales, the U.S. Customs Service ruled that interest payments on loans used to finance tools and equipment, payroll, and factory inventory did not fall within the "direct cost of processing" under Article 304 of the Free Trade Agreement. Customs held that this provision was limited to mortgage interest associated with land and buildings. This narrow interpretation substantially reduced the amounts that Canadian automobile assemblers could designate as North American content for rule of origin purposes. Canada requested a binational panel review of the ruling.

■ **ISSUE** Should the binational panel uphold Customs' interpretation?

■ **DECISION** No. It is clear from the objective and scope of the free trade agreement that the members sought to create a trading arrangement whose benefit would accrue primarily, but not exclusively, to the goods and producers of the members. This would enhance employment and income opportunities primarily, but not exclusively, for persons living within the territories of the member states. The question submitted to this panel focuses on the legal form of the transaction giving rise to the interest obligation. However, it follows from our analysis that the form of the debt should not be a controlling circumstance. All interest payments should be attributable to North American content if the producer can demonstrate that they are: bona fide (not incurred as a part of a sham intracorporate loan transaction), payable on arm's-length terms (not artificially inflated to increase the cost of production), and connected to a loan that is objectively assignable to the production of goods. It is recommended that the members adopt such regulations and internal administrative procedures as are necessary to implement this determination.

Textiles and Apparel

The NAFTA talks over textiles and apparel, as with agriculture and automotive goods, were filled with controversy. These industries have historically been carefully protected by the trading nations of the world and, as a result, real trade reform has been difficult to achieve. Not surprisingly, NAFTA's textile and apparel package, while striving to eliminate tariffs and quotas, possesses rules of origin and safeguard provisions that permit the continuation of barriers against free trade.

Rules of Origin

While most tariffs on textiles and apparel have been immediately eliminated or phased out within five to six years, this increased market access has been balanced with strict rules of origin designed to ensure that only North American products receive preferential trade treatment. For most products, a "yarn forward" rule requires that textiles and apparel be produced from North American yarn. For certain cotton and man-made fiber yarns, the treaty imposes a "fiber forward" rule that holds that clothing made from fibers not grown in North America will not receive duty-free status.

In effect, NAFTA has erected a triple rule of origin that requires that clothing be sewn in North America from fabric made in North America that has been derived from North American yarn. To partially offset this protectionist feature, the treaty includes tariff-rate quotas (TRQs were discussed earlier in this chapter) under which textiles and apparel that do not meet the rules of origin might still qualify for preferential treatment up to specified levels. The pact also permits duty-free status for clothing cut and sewn from certain non-NAFTA fabrics (such as silk and linen) that the three countries agree are in short supply.

Safeguard Provisions

All customs duties on North American textiles and apparel will be eliminated within 10 years. However, during this transition period, the NAFTA nations may increase tariffs on imports that meet the NAFTA rules of origin in order to provide temporary relief to producers suffering serious injury as a result of increased imports. For imports that do not qualify as North American products, the safeguard action also can take the form of a temporary quota (with the exception of Canada–U.S. trade).

TRADE IN SERVICES

General Principles   NAFTA has taken great strides toward eliminating the formidable barriers that once prevented cross-border trade in services. For instance, NAFTA service providers may now operate in any member nation without establishing or maintaining a residence in that country. However, as it did with its strict rules of origin for goods, the treaty carefully reserves these benefits to true NAFTA companies. Thus, service providers that are owned or controlled by persons from non-NAFTA nations may not take advantage of these reforms. The services agreement grants NAFTA service providers three fundamental protections: national treatment, most-favored-nation treatment, and procedural transparency in licensing requirements.

National Treatment

The treaty carries forward the obligation of **national treatment** that has long stood as a hallmark to trade in goods under the GATT and other international trade agreements. Under this provision, each NAFTA member must treat the service providers of the other member countries no less favorably than it treats its own. Within each nation, the state and provincial governments must likewise accord no less favorable treatment to service providers of other countries than they do to those of their own nation.

Most-Favored-Nation Treatment

Cross-border trade in services within the free trade area is also accorded **most-favored-nation treatment.** Under this rule, each NAFTA country is required to treat the service providers of the other NAFTA countries no less favorably than it treats providers from any other country.

Licensing Requirements

The negotiators realized that licensing and certification requirements often raise unnecessary barriers to trade. Accordingly, the treaty calls on each of the members to ensure that its licensing and certification procedures are based on objective and **transparent** criteria. Further, they must be based on professional competence and may be no more burdensome than is necessary to ensure quality service.

Reservations

The treaty permits each NAFTA member to retain certain of its laws even if they do not comply with the general principles discussed above. However, the nations are given two years to compile a list of such measures. These reservations may be amended in the future but only if they do not increase the extent to which they already violate the general principles governing cross-border trade in services.

Financial Services   Financial service providers of any NAFTA country may establish banking, securities, and insurance operations throughout the free trade area. Each of the countries now accords national treatment and most-favored-nation treatment to these financial institutions. Thus, they permit their residents to freely purchase financial services and generally may not enact new restrictions on cross-border trade. Notwithstanding these measures, the treaty still permits each nation to impose restrictions for balance-of-payment purposes.

Procedural Transparency

The NAFTA members agreed to process applications for entry into the financial service markets in a transparent manner. This obligates them to:

1. Fully inform interested persons of the application requirements.
2. Update applicants on the current status of their application.
3. Generally complete an administrative determination on an application within 120 days.
4. Publish regulations concerning financial services on or before their effective date and, wherever practicable, allow interested persons to comment on proposed measures.
5. Provide offices to answer questions about the regulation of financial services.

Country-Specific Obligations

Throughout the negotiations, each nation was mindful of the political ramifications of eliminating barriers to trade in the financial services sector. Accordingly, they agreed on varying transition periods for compliance with the NAFTA principles. Further, each country retained certain reservations to protect politically sensitive industries. Finally, the liberalization commitments varied from member to member, depending on the level of each nation's pre-NAFTA restrictions and its ultimate commitment to free trade. As a result, Mexico made most of the concessions in the financial sector, in part, because its financial services industry had been the most protected.

Transportation   Canada strongly demanded that shipping and other forms of transportation be included in the NAFTA negotiations. However, negotiators were constrained by the Jones Act, a U.S. law that restricts maritime trade between U.S. ports to ships built in the United States and operating under U.S. flags. Still, the three nations were eager to move beyond the Canada–U.S. Free Trade Agreement, which had excluded the transportation sector. As a result, the three members agreed to a timetable for the removal of barriers to land transportation services and agreed to harmonize technical and safety standards in the land transportation industry.

Removal of Barriers

The transportation agreement calls for a phased elimination of restrictions on bus, trucking, and rail services, as well as the liberalization of the land-side aspects of marine transport. The treaty grants full access for charter and tour bus operators within the free trade area and, within three years, will allow truckers to freely carry their cargos across the national borders. Further, after 10 years, Canadian and U.S. trucking companies will be permitted to fully own Mexican carriers involved in international commerce. (None of the nations is required to remove any restrictions on truck carriage of domestic cargo.) Likewise, railroads are free to market their services, operate trains, construct and own terminals, and finance their infrastructure throughout the free trade area. Finally, NAFTA companies now are able to invest in and operate the land-side port services (cranes, piers, and terminals) in the ports of all three countries.

Harmonized Standards

An important component of the transportation pact is the agreement to harmonize operating and safety standards, regulations for shipping dangerous goods, and licensing procedures. The partners agreed to make these standard-related measures compatible over a six-year period.

Telecommunications   ### Nondiscriminatory Access

Private companies from the three member countries now receive reasonable and nondiscriminatory access to the telecommunications transport networks throughout the North American region. Restrictions on such access may be imposed only when necessary to safeguard the public service responsibilities of the network operators or to protect the technical integrity of the public networks.

The treaty calls for eliminating restrictions on foreign investment by 1995. However, the NAFTA partners are not required to authorize a person from another member country to provide or operate telecommunications transport networks or services. Likewise, they may prohibit operators of private networks from providing public networks. NAFTA recognizes the right of the countries to grant monopolies to telecommunications service providers. However, it requires that the partners ensure the provider does not engage in anticompetitive conduct that injures persons in the other NAFTA countries.

Removal of Hidden Barriers

The pact also attempts to eliminate hidden barriers in the telecommunications industry by limiting each country's authority to impose standards-related restrictions on the attachment of equipment to public networks. These measures are permitted only when they are necessary to prevent technical damage to, and interference with, the network's services or when they actually ensure user safety and access. Finally, the agreement contains several provisions guaranteeing that the rules governing access to, and use of, public networks and services are publicly available.

Investment

It has been suggested that the primary attraction of the North American Free Trade Agreement had more to do with investment than with trade. Most of the discussions involved efforts by U.S. and Canadian interests to persuade Mexico to relax its severe restrictions on foreign investment and to provide adequate methods for resolving investment disputes. In the end, the negotiators hammered out an investment agreement that contained several broad governing principles as well as various country-specific reservations and obligations.

Governing Principles

Each of the partners will accord national treatment and most-favored-nation treatment to NAFTA investors. (The treaty broadly defines a NAFTA investor as an enterprise with substantial business activities in a NAFTA country.) The members also pledge to treat such investments in accordance with generally accepted international law principles calling for fair and equitable treatment and full protection and security.

Country-Specific Reservations and Obligations

Because of a Mexican constitutional provision reserving petroleum exploitation and profits to Mexican citizens, Canadian and U.S. oil companies will not be allowed to explore for oil, operate refineries, or open gasoline retail outlets in Mexico. Canada has reserved the right to screen foreign investments, and the United States, pursuant to federal legislation, still retains the right to block takeovers of U.S. companies when they might threaten the national security. Mexico may review acquisitions valued at over $25 million, with that threshold gradually rising to $150 million after 10 years. Government procurement and subsidies (discussed below) are exempted from the investment provisions.

The pact also contains several general provisions that seem to be specifically aimed at reforming Mexico's investment climate. For instance, no NAFTA country may impose **performance requirements** as a condition to permitting investment. Before the treaty, Mexico had mandated such obligations on foreign investors, ranging from foreign exchange restrictions to domestic sourcing requirements. Mexico also agreed to remove restrictions on the conversion and free transfer of foreign currency.

The negotiators, mindful of Mexico's history of expropriating foreign investments, also enacted certain rules to govern **expropriation.** In particular, they require that such takings may occur only in a nondiscriminatory manner and for a public purpose. Further, the expropriating country must promptly pay the investor the fair market value of the property, plus any applicable interest. Finally, the accord has a dispute settlement mechanism for remedying violations of the investment rules by a host country. These provisions give a NAFTA investor the option of seeking monetary damages through binding investor-state arbitration or through the remedies available in the host country's domestic courts.

CONCEPT SUMMARY
General Principles of Trade in Services

National Treatment	Treat domestic and foreign providers the same
Most-Favored-Nation Treatment	Treat NAFTA providers as well as any other foreign provider
Transparent Rules	Give full information on licensing requirements

---

SPECIAL GUIDELINES

NAFTA also contains special rules for dealing with several other issues that greatly affect cross-border trade among the NAFTA partners. These guidelines encompass: the implementation and enforcement of safety measures and technical standards, guarantees for the protection of intellectual property rights, uniform competition policy, liberalization of government procurement, and commitments to ease entry for businesspeople.

Safety Measures and Technical Standards

The treaty prevents the countries from using safety codes or technical standards as a ruse to restrict trade. Safety measures are permitted when they: (*a*) are based on scientific principles and a risk assessment, (*b*) are applied to the extent necessary to provide the country's chosen level of protection, and (*c*) do not result in unfair discrimination against trade.

Likewise, NAFTA recognizes each country's right to adopt and enforce technical standards, to choose the level of protection it wishes to achieve, and to conduct risk assessments to ensure those levels are met. However, it requires the partners to ensure that the standards provide both national treatment and most-favored-nation treatment.

With both safety measures and technical standards, the countries will work toward harmonization and compatibility. This will entail cooperation among the standardizing bodies of the partners and public notice before adopting or modifying measures that may affect North American trade.

Intellectual Property Rights

NAFTA sets out specific commitments regarding the protection of patents, copyrights, trademarks, trade secrets, industrial designs, and integrated circuits (semiconductor chips). It ensures that each country will provide effective protection of such intellectual property rights on the basis of national treatment. The countries will enforce intellectual property rights against infringement by both domestic and cross-border violators. To secure this end, the treaty establishes enforcement procedures that include provisions for damages and injunctive relief.

Competition Policy

The NAFTA partners agreed to provide effective enforcement of antitrust laws. Through cooperative enforcement efforts against anticompetitive government and private business practices, they hope to eliminate unnecessary interference with cross-border trade. While recognizing that each nation may grant monopolies in limited circumstances, the treaty mandates that such entities not discriminate against the goods or businesses of the other NAFTA countries. Further, they will be prevented from using their monopoly power to engage in anticompetitive practices outside of their monopoly market.

Government Procurement

The government procurement market for goods and services has been substantially opened to all suppliers within the free trade area. Government purchases over certain threshold amounts ($50,000 for certain goods and services and $6.5 million for construction services) are to be made on a nondiscriminatory basis to suppliers from any NAFTA country. The treaty does not apply to the procurement of weapons and other purchases that directly involve the national security of the partners.

The government procurement obligations require each country to publicize any technical specifications, qualifications of suppliers, and time limits for submitting bids. Further, they prohibit offset practices and other discriminatory, buy-national requirements. Finally, each country has established a bid protest system that allows suppliers to challenge bid procedures and awards.

Temporary Entry

NAFTA makes clear that it has not created a common market for the free movement of labor. Accordingly, each of the countries may still implement its own immigration policies, safeguard its domestic work force, and protect its borders. Despite these national reservations, treaty members have agreed to facilitate the temporary entry of businesspeople from the other NAFTA countries.

Four categories of businesspeople will be granted temporary entry:

Business visitors engaged in global business activities related to research and design, growth, manufacture and production, marketing, sales, distribution, and service.

Traders and *investors* who carry on a substantial trade or commit a substantial amount of capital, provided that they act in a supervisory or executive capacity.

Intracompany transferees employed by a company in a managerial or executive capacity or who have a specialized skill.

Certain categories of professionals who meet threshold educational qualifications and seek to engage in business activities at a professional level.

For the first 10 years of the agreement, no more than 5,500 Mexican professionals will be permitted to enter the United States unless the countries decide to remove the numerical limit.

DISPUTE RESOLUTION

NAFTA's mechanisms for resolving trade disputes have refined the highly successful dispute settlement procedures of the Canada–U.S. Free Trade Agreement. Like the earlier bilateral accord, NAFTA provides elaborate provisions for settling two distinct types of disputes: (1) antidumping and countervailing duty matters, and (2) conflicts over a country's interpretation or application of the treaty. The dispute settlement procedures are subject to strict time limits designed to prevent the lengthy delays that characterize many international dispute mechanisms.

Antidumping and Countervailing Duty Disputes

Dumping occurs when an exporter sells goods in one country for less than the price charged in its home country. If dumping causes material injury to the importing country's domestic industry, the importing nation may assess an antidumping duty to offset the advantaged position of the exporter. Likewise, if imported goods are priced lower than domestic goods because they are subsidized by the exporting country, the importing country may assess a countervailing duty equal to the amount of the subsidy.

NAFTA permits each country to retain its antidumping and countervailing duty laws. (Mexico agreed to amend its procedures to ensure that U.S. and Canadian companies receive a fair hearing.) However, the treaty establishes a panel review process that can overturn domestic antidumping or countervailing duty determinations. It also creates an extraordinary challenge procedure and a safeguard mechanism to protect against interference with the panel process.

ETHICAL IMPLICATIONS   Is it ethical to sell goods in a foreign market for less than you sell them in your home country market?

Panel Review

If a NAFTA member wishes, it may have a five-member **binational panel** (rather than the importing nation's domestic courts) review the importing country's dumping and subsidy determinations. When this occurs, each country will select two panelists from a 75-person roster (25 from each country) maintained by the three countries. A fifth panelist will be selected by agreement of the two disputing parties. If this is not possible, the four designated panelists will select the fifth member. If they cannot agree, the final panelist will be chosen by lot. In reviewing a dumping or subsidy decision, the panel applies the law of the importing country. It will then either uphold the domestic decision maker's findings or remand the dispute back to that body for action not inconsistent with the panel's decision.

■

RED RASPBERRIES FROM CANADA
USA-89-1904-01 (Binational Panel 1989)

■ **FACTS** U.S. growers and packers of red raspberries claimed Canadian exporters were dumping bulk-packed red raspberries in the Pacific Northwest. After comparing the exporters' domestic prices to the prices at which the raspberries were sold in the United States, the International Trade Administration (ITA) determined the Canadian imports were being dumped. For two of the exporters, however, the dumping margins were so low that no antidumping duty was assessed. In a later administrative review, the ITA changed its methodology from the "home market sale" method to a "constructed valuation" method. This resulted in a finding of substantially increased dumping margins and the assessment of antidumping duties on the two companies' exports. Canada called for a binational panel review, pointing out that the U.S. Tariff Act stipulated the use of home market sales in cases such as this. The ITA defended using the constructed valuation since the exporters' home market sales were not large enough to provide a meaningful basis for price-to-price comparisons.

■ **ISSUE**   Should the binational review panel instruct the ITA to recalculate the dumping margins under the home market sales method?

■ **DECISION**   Yes. This case considers when the ITA may disregard sales of such or similar merchandise in the home market of the exporting country and, instead, calcu-

late foreign market value on the basis of constructed value. In reviewing the actions of the ITA, the panel shall hold unlawful any determination found to be unsupported by substantial evidence or otherwise not in accordance with U.S. law. While deference must be given to an administrative agency's interpretation of a statute, agency discretion is not unfettered. Accordingly, the ITA's approach must be supported by clearly articulated reasons. This was not done. Deviation from the home market sales method merely because of the low level of home market sales is not acceptable when that choice is not mandated by statute. Thus, the ITA must recalculate the dumping margins by using home market sales in determining the fair market value of the raspberries. (This resulted in the ITA finding insignificant margins and thereby removing the antidumping duties.)

Extraordinary Challenge Procedure

Either of the countries involved in a dispute may invoke the **extraordinary challenge procedure** to review a panel decision. This 3-person committee will be drawn from a 15-person roster of judges or former judges from the three nations. Each of the disputing countries will select one panelist, and they will then decide by lot which country will select the third panelist.

The extraordinary challenge committee will vacate a panel decision and remand it to the original panel whenever there has been a serious impropriety or gross panel error that materially affects the panel's decision and threatens the integrity of the binational panel review process. This process will not be triggered unless the committee finds that: (a) a panel member was guilty of gross misconduct, bias, or a serious conflict of interest; (b) the panel seriously departed from a fundamental rule of procedure; or (c) the panel manifestly exceeded its powers.

■

FRESH, CHILLED, OR FROZEN PORK FROM CANADA
ECC-91-1904-01USA (Extraordinary Challenge Committee 1991)

■ **FACTS**   The U.S. International Trade Commission (ITC) ruled that the U.S. domestic pork industry was threatened with material injury by the importation of subsidized fresh, chilled, or frozen pork from Canada. Several Canadian parties appealed that determination to a binational panel comprised of three Canadian and two U.S. members. The panel held that the ITC should rehear

the matter because the original findings were based on faulty statistical analysis. During its reconsideration of the case, the ITC gathered additional evidence and again ruled in favor of the U.S. pork industry. Once more, the binational panel remanded the case, ruling that the ITC erred in considering evidence beyond that admitted during the original hearing. The panel severely limited the issues, as well as the legal and economic arguments, the ITC could consider on remand. After following these narrow guidelines, the ITC unanimously concluded that the pork industry was not threatened with material injury by reason of Canadian imports. The United States complained that, in its second remand, the binational panel departed from proper procedures and exceeded its authority. Accordingly, the United States requested the formation of an extraordinary challenge committee to review the actions of the binational panel.

■ **ISSUE** Did the United States raise issues sufficient to support an extraordinary challenge committee inquiry?

■ **DECISION** No. The extraordinary challenge procedure is intended to review binational panel decisions only under exceptional circumstances. While binational panels substitute for judicial review in countervailing duty and antidumping investigations, it is not the function of the extraordinary challenge committee to conduct a traditional appellate review regarding the merits of a panel decision. None of the allegations presented here provides a basis for finding that the panel *seriously* departed from a fundamental rule of procedure or *manifestly* exceeded its powers, authority, or jurisdiction. And none of the alleged errors materially affected the panel decision or threatened the integrity of the panel review process.

Safeguard Mechanism

Any NAFTA country may demand the creation of a **special committee** to decide if the panel process is yielding unfair decisions and should be discontinued. A country may invoke this process when it believes that another NAFTA country has: (*a*) prevented the formation of a panel, (*b*) prevented a panel from issuing a final decision, (*c*) prevented the implementation of a panel decision or denied it binding force and effect, or (*d*) failed to provide judicial review of a final administrative finding in a dumping or subsidy dispute.

A special committee will be selected in the same manner as the extraordinary challenge committee. If the committee should find that a country has interfered with the binational review process in any of the above-mentioned ways, the complaining country may suspend the binational panel system with respect to the offending country or may suspend other benefits under the treaty. The offending country may invoke reciprocal action until the disputing countries resolve the matter.

General Dispute Settlement Procedures

When conflicts arise over the interpretation or application of the treaty, the disputing countries are required to promptly consult on the matter. If these discussions fail to settle the dispute, either nation may call for a meeting of the Trade Commission so all three partners can resolve the conflict. The Trade Commission may use good offices, mediation, conciliation, or any other form of alternate dispute resolution.

Should the efforts of the Trade Commission fail, any consulting country may initiate panel proceedings. When such a dispute could be brought under both GATT and NAFTA, the complaining country may select the appropriate forum. If the third NAFTA member also brings the same complaint, the two complaining countries will try to agree on the forum. If they are unable to do so, the dispute generally will be heard by a NAFTA panel. (For certain disputes involving environmental, safety, or conservation matters, the defending country can insist on a NAFTA panel.) Once a forum is selected, the countries are precluded from using any other forum.

Arbitral Panels

The NAFTA **arbitral panel** generally will make findings of fact and determine whether the defending country has violated its NAFTA obligations. The five panelists will be chosen in a "reverse selection process" from a roster of 30 legal experts from both NAFTA and non-NAFTA countries. (A special roster of experts exists for disputes involving financial services.) Under this mechanism, if the disputing countries cannot agree on a panel chairperson, the disputing country chosen by lot will select someone who is not a citizen of that country. Each disputing party will then select two panelists who are citizens of the other country.

The third NAFTA country may join the panel procedure as a complaining country or it may limit its involvement to written or oral presentations. When it joins the process as a complaining party, it will join the other two countries in selecting the chairperson. If they cannot agree, the party or parties on the side of the dispute chosen by lot will select a person who is not a citizen of such country or countries. The defending nation will then select two panelists—one from each complaining country—and the complaining nations each will select one panelist from the defending country.

Implementation of Panel Reports

Within 90 days of its selection, the arbitral panel will give the disputants a confidential initial report. They then have 14 days to issue comments to the panel. Within 30 days of the issuance of the initial report, the panel must present its final report to the disputants and to the Trade Commission, which will publish it. The countries then have 30 days to resolve their dispute. If they are unable to do so, and the panel findings were that the defending country had violated the treaty, the complaining countries may suspend equivalent benefits against the defending country until the matter is resolved. If a defending country believes the retaliatory action is excessive it may seek a panel ruling on that issue.

WEST COAST SALMON AND HERRING FROM CANADA
CDA-89-1807-01 (Binational Panel 1989)

■ **FACTS** In 1986, Canada enacted regulations prohibiting the export of unprocessed salmon and herring. Responding to complaints by the United States, a GATT panel in 1987 found the Canadian laws to violate GATT. After informing the United States that it would accept the GATT decision, Canada revoked the offending legislation. However, several months later, the Canadian government passed new laws that required that salmon and herring be landed in Canada before they could be exported to the United States for processing. The United States called for the formation of a binational panel, arguing that the new regulations were a trade barrier that discriminated against U.S. processors. Canada defended on the grounds that its landing requirement fell within an exception for measures relating to the conservation of an exhaustible natural resource.

■ **ISSUE** Should the binational panel find the landing requirement to be a trade barrier that violates the free trade agreement?

■ **DECISION** Yes. Canada's landing requirement is a restriction on "sale for export" within the meaning of GATT and, hence, prima facie is incompatible with the free trade agreement. There is no doubt that catch information is vital to Canada's management of its salmon and herring fisheries and that landing requirements can play an important role in obtaining that information. However, the fact that export restrictions had been imposed in the past provides some evidence that this regulation would impede a meaningful volume of exports. It is unlikely that Canada would have found the conservation benefits of a 100 percent landing requirement to have overcome the commercial inconveniences if it had been imposed on Canadian buyers rather than on export buyers.

Private Disputes

The mechanisms described above involve conflicts between and among the NAFTA countries. The treaty also encourages private parties to use arbitration and other means of alternative dispute resolution to settle their commercial disputes. To carry this out, the members agreed to fully recognize and enforce arbitration agreements and arbitral awards.

EXCEPTIONS AND SAFEGUARDS

To secure domestic approval in each of the treaty nations, the NAFTA negotiators included several provisions designed to protect various economic and political interests. Specifically, the agreement contains procedures for the protection of domestic industries adversely affected by increased competition and grants general exceptions for the preservation of vital national interests.

Emergency Safeguard Actions

The treaty permits the NAFTA countries to take **emergency safeguard actions** to provide temporary relief to industries adversely affected by increased competition from foreign sources. Such relief may be granted only for a limited time, and the NAFTA country against which the action is taken is entitled to compensation. If the countries cannot agree on the level and form of the compensation, the exporting country may take countervailing action against the importing nation.

Bilateral Safeguards

A NAFTA member may temporarily suspend an agreed-upon duty elimination or reestablish a pre-NAFTA rate of duty if, during the transition period, increased imports from another member cause serious injury to a domestic industry. This safeguard action may be taken only once and generally may not exceed three years in duration. (For certain sensitive goods, the safeguard action may be extended for a fourth year.) After the transition period (which varies by industry and country), a bilateral safeguard action may not be taken without the consent of the exporting country.

CONCEPT SUMMARY **Exceptions and Safeguards**		
Emergency Safeguards	Bilateral	• NAFTA imports seriously injure domestic industry • May temporarily suspend NAFTA tariff rate • May occur only once
	Global	• International competition seriously injures domestic industry • NAFTA imports account for substantial share of imports • May temporarily suspend GATT preferences
Exceptions from NAFTA Obligations		• Actions to protect national security • Actions to protect public health, safety, and welfare • Actions to protect balance of payments

Global Safeguards

GATT permits both tariff and quota-based safeguard measures to protect domestic industries severely threatened by international competition. When a NAFTA member undertakes such a safeguard action, it must exclude the other NAFTA partners from the action unless their exports account for a substantial share (they fall within the top five suppliers) of the total imports at issue and contribute importantly to the serious injury or threat of injury.

General Exceptions   The treaty recognizes the need for each member country to take measures it considers necessary to protect its essential security interests. Further, it may deviate from its treaty obligations when such a course is essential for the protection of the public health, safety, and welfare. (This assumes such measures are not disguised restrictions on trade.) Finally, each country also may impose limited, trade-restrictive measures when they are necessary to protect its balance of payments.

QUESTIONS AND PROBLEM CASES

1. How does NAFTA differ from a common market?
2. Explain the fundamental barriers to trade that NAFTA is designed to eliminate.
3. Explain why NAFTA has strict rules of origin.
4. What protections are there against companies moving to Mexico to avoid stricter U.S. and Canadian antipollution laws?
5. Pacific Western Brewing Companies, a Canadian brewer, filed a complaint under Canada's Special Import Measures Act (SIMA), alleging that G. Heileman Brewing Company (a U.S. company) was dumping beer in the Canadian market. To determine if dumping exists, SIMA requires the Cana-

dian governmental agency (Revenue Canada) to compare the price of the beer exported to Canada with the price of *like goods* sold in the U.S. market. If the price of the exports is lower, dumping has occurred. SIMA defines *like goods* as: "(*a*) goods that are identical in all respects to the other goods, or (*b*) in the absence of any goods described in paragraph (*a*), goods the uses and other characteristics of which closely resemble those of the other goods." Revenue Canada determined that Heileman had dumped beer based on a comparison of Heileman's domestic and export sales of Lone Star, finding that Lone Star beer sold in Texas was "identical in all respects" to Lone Star beer exported to

Canada. Heileman argued that domestic Lone Star beer is not identical to exported Lone Star beer because of marketing, labeling, and cost differences. If Heileman convinces a binational panel that its objections are meritorious, what remedy will the panel give?

6. Suppose the Canadian government enacted legislation designed to ensure that manufacturers of consumer products eliminate nonrecyclable packaging. The rules required all manufacturers to collect and recycle their product packaging. U.S. manufacturers have complained that the regulation violates NAFTA by discriminating against manufacturers from the United States. The essence of their complaint is that the costs of collecting and transporting the packaging will be greater for U.S. manufacturers since their manufacturing operations are likely to be geographically farther away from Canadian consumers than are the Canadian manufacturers. Is a binational panel likely to agree with the complaint of the U.S. manufacturers?

7. A Japanese corporation established manufacturing operations in Mexico and Canada with the intention of selling automobiles and automobile parts tariff free in the United States. It assembled an instrument cluster housing in Mexico that was composed of $24.50 worth of Japanese parts and $25.50 worth of Mexican labor. This was exported to Canada tariff free as a Mexican product because it had a 51 percent Mexican content. In Canada, the cluster housing was combined with $49 worth of Japanese gauges and wiring and $1 worth of Canadian labor to create a $100 partially completed instrument panel that it classified as North American ($50 Mexican cluster housing plus $1 Canadian labor plus $49 Japanese gauges and wiring). This $100 North American product was then exported back to Mexico tariff free where it was combined with $98 worth of Japanese components and $2 worth of Mexican labor. This completed instrument panel was then exported to the United States as a

North American product since it contained a $100 North American partially completed instrument panel plus $2 of Mexican labor plus $98 worth of Japanese components. Will NAFTA permit the completed instrument panels to enter the United States tariff free? Explain.

8. Suppose the United States enacts food safety legislation that requires all fruit to be sold in the United States to be certified as safe for human consumption by government-licensed inspectors within 48 hours of harvesting. The legislation further requires that fruit imported from foreign countries receive an additional inspection within 72 hours after it arrives in U.S. Customs territory. Mexican fruit growers claim that imposing a double inspection system on them violates NAFTA. Are they correct?

9. The United States prohibited lobsters from entering interstate or foreign commerce for sale within or from the United States if they came from states or nations that allowed the sale of lobsters smaller than the minimum limits permitted by U.S. federal law. Canada argued that the U.S. prohibitions violated the free trade agreement since the members had agreed not to adopt any import restrictions inconsistent with GATT. The United States maintained that, since the catching of undersized lobsters threatened the future of the lobster population, the legislation was an internal measure that fell within the national treatment exception from GATT and the free trade agreement. Should a binational review panel uphold the U.S. restrictions?

10. In Canada, the determination of whether dumping has occurred or subsidies have been given is made by the Assessment Programs Division of the Department of Revenue, Customs and Excise. If dumping or subsidies are found, the Canadian International Trade Tribunal decides if a Canadian industry has suffered a material injury. If the United States challenges the assessment of antidumping duties by the Canadian authorities, what is the standard by which a binational panel will review the matter?

P A R T

II

CONTRACTING IN THE GLOBAL MARKET

5

International Contracts

6

Contracts for the Carriage of Goods

7

International Payment Mechanisms

8

Dispute Resolution

CHAPTER

5

International Contracts

INTRODUCTION

International transactions, while expanding a firm's range of opportunities, simultaneously increase its risk of doing business. Shrewd managers realize not all of these risks can be eliminated. Instead, they work to accurately identify and carefully manage those that attend each international transaction. And they discover, as this chapter demonstrates, that risk management can be accomplished through the careful use of the contracting process.

Nature of Contracts

Contract law elevates a private agreement between two or more people or business entities into a legally binding obligation. In essence, a contract is a private law that is enforced by public institutions (courts). Because of contract law, a party may order its business relationships with others with a high level of confidence that those contracting partners will honor the promises they have made. This certainty facilitates the planning essential to the successful completion of a complex business deal.

Transaction costs would rise to unmanageable levels if managers could not count on suppliers' promises to deliver essential raw materials. Likewise, a manufacturer might be unwilling to commit to purchasing those raw materials if it was uncertain whether distributors would honor their promises to market the finished products. Thus, contract law is of tremendous importance to both domestic and international trade.

Global Issues

Contract disputes involve either one or both of the following questions:

1. Do the parties have a contract?
2. If they have a contract, what rights and obligations does it give to the parties?

Accordingly, the parties generally structure their agreement so it maximizes the likelihood that these questions will be answered in a manner that best carries out their original intent. To facilitate this goal, most business contracts contain three sometimes overlapping dimensions: formation, performance, and dispute settlement.

When both parties are from the same country and governed by the same rules, the judicial resolution of contract disputes often is complex and time consuming. The uncertainty and complexity rise tremendously in the international realm, where it may no longer be clear which legal system will govern the transaction. Compounding these problems are the geographic separation, unfamiliarity, language differences, cultural differences, and large amounts of money that frequently characterize international transactions. For all of these reasons, international contracts generally demand greater precision and caution if the parties hope to avoid economic disaster.

Chapter Overview

Because the success or failure of a contract frequently hinges on which set of legal rules governs its provisions, global business managers should have a basic understanding of the various approaches to contract law throughout the world. Accordingly, this chapter begins by introducing the reader to the contract law orientation of each of the major legal systems of the world. It then examines the fundamental elements of a contract and provides insight into the basic attributes of successful agreements. Throughout this detailed discussion of contracts and the contracting process, the reader will learn methods of effectively managing risk through careful planning.

SOURCES OF CONTRACT LAW

This section briefly introduces the predominant approaches to contract law that exist throughout the world. It begins with an examination of the four major classifications of law: civil law, British common law, socialist law, and Islamic law. This is followed by a quick look at the legal schemes that govern contracts in Africa and the Far East. The special brand of contract law practiced in the United States is covered in a separate section. Likewise, the harmonized body of international contract rules—the United Nations Convention on Contracts for the International Sale of Goods—is treated separately.

Civil Law

Civil law predominates on the European continent and throughout most of the Latin American nations. A unifying feature of the civil law countries has been their reduction of law to a codified set of rules. While judicial discretion still is necessary to fill in the gaps that inevitably arise within any set of rules, the nature of the civil codes lends stability and predictability to legal issues. Often, one finds special commercial courts that include business experts who provide advice as to the applicable business customs. As a consequence, the civil law systems tend to offer businesses clear rules that allow private parties much flexibility in the negotiation and performance of contracts.

Civil law courts are likely to be highly protective of consumers who are contracting with commercial entities. Businesses, on the other hand, are expected to be sophisticated and largely able to take care of themselves. As a general rule, consumer contracts require a writing while none is necessary for a commercial transaction. However, there are variations within this broad classification of law. For instance, under Romano-Germanic civil law, consideration is not needed to create a contract. However, French civil law permits a contract to be rescinded on the basis of inadequate consideration when there is a gross disparity between the parties' obligations.

Common Law

Most of the nations that formerly made up the British Colonial Empire subscribe to the British common law system. While the common law and civil law both grew out of ancient Roman law, their paths have diverged. Unlike civil law, which is gleaned from codified rules, common law is characterized by heavy reliance on specific cases decided over time by judges. Accordingly, the common law system vests much power in its courts and, unlike the civil law, places a great deal of reliance on lawyers.

In theory, the common law is a flexible system that stands in stark contrast to the stable and predictable processes embodied in the civil law. In reality, however, this does not seem to be so true. Under the doctrine of **stare decisis,** common law courts generally decide new cases in a manner consistent with the principles that governed earlier decisions. Over time, this case law has become well established. Further, many of the contract law principles that developed in the common law over time were codified in the Sales of Goods Act. With the exception of the United States, most common law nations have enacted that legislation.

Socialist Law

A thorough understanding of the status of contract law within the socialist nations is difficult for three major reasons. First, the very concept of a private contract is inconsistent with the underlying values of the socialist system. These nations try to limit law to three functions: (*a*) preservation of the national security; (*b*) development of the production necessary to furnish the goods and services that each individual requires; and (*c*) education of the populace to eliminate selfish tendencies. Second, recent years have witnessed a great political and economic upheaval within the socialist sphere. Democratic reforms in the former Soviet Union and Eastern Europe have placed those legal systems in a state of constant flux. Simultaneously, countries, such as China, Vietnam, and Cuba, have shown a tremendous willingness to modify their legal systems to attract foreign investment. Third, while the socialist nations have many similarities, there also exist wide differences in their application of contract law principles.

Despite this turmoil, certain generalizations still can be made. The contracting process in socialist nations, because it is designed to help the state further its national programs, is heavily regulated by the government. Accordingly, contract terms tend to be standardized and the parties should fully document all of their rights and obligations. Further, the agreement generally must be in writing or it will not be enforced. A premium is placed on certainty; therefore, custom and usage seldom play an important role in contractual interpretation. Finally, the principle of socialist cooperation dictates that parties avoid the arm's-length dealings that often characterize contracts in the civil law and common law systems.

Islamic Law

Islamic legal systems combine the body of Islamic religion with a set of civil codes that govern all aspects of peoples' lives. The *Koran* (holy scriptures) revealed to Mohammed by God form the foundation of Islamic law. Those fundamental rules are reinforced by the *Sunna*—the pronouncements of Mohammed. Another source of the law, called the *Ijma*, springs from the interpretations of the *Koran* and the *Sunna* by Islamic scholars. Finally, when novel situations arise, they may be solved by the *Qiyas*, which derives the solution by analogy from the earlier pronouncements.

The Islamic nations have responded to increasing globalization in differing ways. The nations of the Arabian Peninsula are traditionalists in the sense that they have resisted outside influences and have basically preserved a pure Islamic system. They should be contrasted with countries like Malaysia that have followed a reformist path by modifying their laws to accommodate Western culture. Iran and Libya are fundamentalist countries that have eradicated outside influences and restored the Islamic religion to a position of preeminence. Finally, most of the Islamic nations practice a secularism that places religion above political and legal affairs.

Contract law varies widely within the Islamic world. In the more traditional countries, contracts must be carefully drafted to avoid offending certain religious principles. For instance, the *Koran* prohibits charging excessive interest on loans; therefore, financing arrangements must be tailored to avoid breaking the law. Likewise, the *Koran* does not permit gambling or speculative ventures. This places severe limitations on insurance contracts and a premium on agreements that have definite terms. Most of the Islamic world, however, has moved away from these traditionalist notions and, depending on the country, has adopted the approaches of the common law, civil law, or socialist law systems.

Other Systems

Many legal systems throughout the world do not fit neatly into the four major classifications. For instance, economic relationships in Africa historically were determined by tribal custom rather than contractual rules. While modernization brought many Islamic, civil law, and common law ideas to the more developed areas, much of the African interior remained closed to outside influence. Several African countries now are attempting to develop national legal systems that will harmonize the various tribal customs with the foreign rules that were transplanted in the developed regions.

The common law, civil law, and socialist systems have greatly influenced the laws of many East Asian nations. For instance, Vietnam, Cambodia, and Laos (as a result of French colonization) inherited many civil law traditions. However, they are now within the socialist school. Hong Kong follows the common law approach, while Thailand and South Korea were greatly influenced by civil law. Japan has established an extensive set of legal codes derived from the civil law model, although it has also been greatly influenced by ancient Chinese culture.

AMERICAN CONTRACT LAW

The legal system of the United States is a direct descendant of the British common law system. While the U.S. and English political systems diverged sharply after the American Revolution, many U.S. courts voluntarily continued to follow English legal precedents. Despite the many similarities that have grown from this common heritage, the two legal systems also differ in several important respects. For instance, the U.S. law governing contracts has split into two distinct, yet overlapping, branches: the common law rules and the Uniform Commercial Code.

Common Law Rules

Much of the contract law in the United States has slowly developed over time. When a new case arose, the judge would declare the applicable rule of law. However, whenever the facts were similar to those in a previous case, the judge would follow that earlier decision. Over time, thousands of disputes were resolved in this manner, and a large body of common law came into being. Today these common law rules govern service contracts and agreements for the sale of land, stocks and bonds, and intangible property.

Early common law rules in the United States were tailored to face-to-face agreements between parties with relatively equal bargaining strength. Accordingly, courts maintained a hands-off approach that gave private parties a great deal of control over the terms of their contracts. This *classical approach* to contractual relations provided predictable results that facilitated private business planning.

With industrialization and modernization, however, the complexity of contractual relations increased tremendously. Many contracting parties (particularly consumers) frequently had much less knowledge and bargaining power than the business organizations with which they were forced to deal. Contract rules evolved over time to reflect these changing conditions. As a result, American courts today are much more likely to assume a hands-on posture to protect weaker parties and to ensure a fair result. This *modern approach* lacks the clarity and predictability that characterized traditional contract theory.

The common law rules in effect in the United States today combine the principles of both the modern and the classical approaches. When both parties possess relatively equal knowledge and bargaining power (business versus business), one might expect the courts to apply the traditional, hands-off rules. However, when there is a great deal of disparity in the knowledge and the power of the parties (business versus consumer), a court is more likely to assume the modern, interventionist posture.

Uniform Commercial Code

Perhaps the greatest reform in American contract law has been the adoption of the **Uniform Commercial Code (UCC)** by all of the states except Louisiana (which has adopted some of its provisions). The UCC contains a partial codification of the American law governing contracts for the *sale of goods*. In part, it was designed to establish a uniform contract law for goods transactions; although, it should be remembered that some of its language and interpretations vary from state to state. While the UCC is domestic U.S. law, its effect has extended well beyond the United States since global businesses often select it as the governing law for their international contracts.

The UCC does not replace the common law of contracts within the United States. Instead, it provides codified rules only for selected situations. In circumstances where there is no specific UCC provision, courts apply the common law. In general, the UCC has adopted rules that reflect the actual practices of contracting parties. It also attempts to promote fair dealing by imposing a duty of **good faith** on all contracting parties and, in certain situations, requires that *merchants* (businesspersons) follow a higher standard of conduct.

While the UCC theoretically applies only to contracts for the sale of goods (*goods* are defined as movable, personal property), in reality it enjoys a wider application for two fundamental reasons. First, many contracts involve elements of both goods and services. When this occurs, the UCC is the governing law if the goods provide the predominant aspect of the transaction. For example, the UCC would govern a contract where a business bought lawn mowers from a manufacturer. While the contract involved both goods (the lawn mowers) and services (the manufacture and assembly processes), the predominant purpose of the contract was the acquisition of the goods. A contract to have lawn mowers repaired, on the other hand, generally would fall within the common law rather than the UCC.

Second, since its adoption, the UCC has had a tremendous influence on the evolution of the general body of common law contract rules. Many courts liberally apply

---

CONCEPT SUMMARY
The World's Major Legal Systems

System	Fundamental Attributes
Civil Law	• Codified rules. • Stability and predictability are emphasized.
Common Law	• Judge-made rules. • Flexibility emphasized.
Socialist Law	• Heavily regulated by state. • Standardized rules. • Premium placed on certainty
Islamic Law	• Close connection to religious laws. • Codified rules. • Certainty required.
UCC	• Codified rules for selected situations. • Promotes fair dealing.

UCC concepts and standards by analogy to contracts that technically fall outside of its scope. Thus, a court may refuse to enforce a grossly unfair services contract on the grounds that it is unconscionable despite the fact that policy prohibiting enforcement of unconscionable contracts technically is part of the UCC.

CONTRACTS FOR THE INTERNATIONAL SALE OF GOODS

The many national approaches to contract law greatly impeded global trade. Business lawyers were required to spend time researching the different legal schemes in order to draft agreements that would protect the parties' expectations throughout the world. Transactions often were delayed or otherwise burdened by disagreements between the parties over the selection of a particular choice of law provision within the contract. In an attempt to overcome these problems, the United Nations Convention on Contracts for the International Sale of Goods (CISG) was created. The fundamental goal of the CISG is to unify and codify an international law of sales.

History

UNIDROIT

Attempts to develop a uniform international contract law began in the early 1930s when a group of European scholars formed the International Institute for the Unification of Private Law (UNIDROIT). Their efforts were suspended during World War II but resumed after that conflict ended. Although UNIDROIT completed the Hague Conventions in 1964, the documents were rejected by the United States, the socialist nations, and the Third World Nations. After being largely excluded from the drafting process, these non-European nations refused to ratify an international treaty based primarily on West European civil law traditions.

UNCITRAL

UNIDROIT's efforts in drafting the Hague Conventions led to establishment of the United Nations Commission on International Trade Law (UNCITRAL). This global body was formed to promote the harmonization and unification of international trade law. With its membership designed to fairly represent the various regions of the world, UNCITRAL was better able to create a truly international body of contract law.

The UNCITRAL representatives considered each of the major legal systems of the world in fashioning the CISG. As a result, in 1980 (after 12 years of work), the CISG was approved at a United Nations diplomatic conference in Vienna. By its terms, the CISG would not become effective until it was ratified by 10 nations. At the end of 1986, the United States, along with China and Italy, brought the number of ratifying nations over 10 and, on January 1, 1988, the CISG went into effect. By the end of 1992, the CISG had been adopted by 35 nations and that number is expected to be between 40 and 50 by 1996.

General Principles

The CISG contains four parts and 101 articles designed to assist buyers and sellers in creating, performing, and enforcing contracts. To encourage global acceptance, the CISG steered clear of favoring any single set of domestic laws, opting instead to compromise among the world's predominant legal systems. Further, the CISG appears to have balanced the positions of buyers and sellers by ensuring that their respective rights and obligations mirror each other.

Scope

To facilitate worldwide adoption, the CISG contains five important limitations. First, it applies only to *commercial contracts*. Consumer transactions are left to each nation's domestic laws. Second, the CISG governs only *sales of goods*. It does not cover real estate or service contracts. Third, the CISG is concerned with *international contracts* rather than agreements between buyers and sellers who are both doing business primarily in the same nation. Fourth, the drafters found certain topics to be extremely controversial. Accordingly, there are *excluded topics* in the CISG in order to permit universal acceptance among the nations of the world. Finally, the CISG, in the name of promoting *freedom of contract*, liberally permits buyers and sellers through their contract to expressly exclude any or all of its provisions. Each of these five limitations now is briefly examined.

Commercial Contracts

Consumer sales (goods bought for personal, family, or household use) are not encompassed by the CISG. Because of the tremendous disparities in consumer protection among the differing legal systems of the world, the drafters would have been unable to reach any consensus on a harmonized law for consumer sales. This exclusion for consumer sales does not mean consumer goods are never covered by the

CISG. For instance, if a retailer purchases kitchen appliances (consumer goods) from a foreign manufacturer, the transaction may be covered by the CISG. This is a commercial sale because both the seller and the buyer are merchants (they are in the business of making such contracts). However, if a foreign buyer purchases one of the appliances from the retailer to use in her home, the CISG would not apply. Since she bought for personal, family, or household use, she has engaged in a consumer sale. The CISG covers **merchant-to-merchant** sales; it does not govern merchant-to-consumer sales.

Sale of Goods

The CISG is similar to the UCC in that its coverage is limited to **sales of goods** rather than service or real estate transactions. Goods may be thought of as tangible, movable, personal property, although the CISG specifically excludes ships, aircraft, stocks, securities, and electricity from its coverage. Because many contracts incorporate both goods and services elements, it is not always clear if the CISG governs. For instance, retailers may be able to purchase either partially assembled or wholly assembled bicycles from manufacturers. When a retailer orders wholly assembled bicycles, she is contracting for both goods (bicycles) and services (assembly). When there is such a mixture of goods and services, the CISG will apply unless the service element is the *preponderant part* of the seller's obligation. Our bicycle example is likely to be covered by the CISG because the bicycles (rather than the assembly) seem to be the preponderant part of the agreement. However, if the retailers supplied most of the bicycle components (suppose the assembler supplied only the wheels and rims), the contract would be predominantly for the assembly services and the CISG would not apply.

International Transactions

Generally, the CISG automatically applies to commercial sales of goods between buyers and sellers whose places of business are in different ratifying nations. When a party has more than one place of business, the location with the closest relationship to the contract and its performance determines nationality. Thus, if a New York-based wholesaler purchases wine for the U.S. market from a Paris-based producer, the CISG is likely to govern since both France and the United States are ratifying nations.

Even if one of the nations has not ratified, the CISG still might apply. For instance, if the French producer sent wine to a Japanese buyer, the CISG would not automatically apply because Japan has not ratified. However, if the normal choice of law rules would find that French law had the closest connection to the contract, the CISG would govern since France is a ratifying nation. On the other hand, if Japanese law had the closest connection, the CISG would not be used. The CISG permits each nation, at the time of ratification, to declare that it will not be bound by this latter provision. The United States has exercised this reservation. Accordingly, in a sale between a U.S. company and a Japanese company, the CISG would not govern even if U.S. law were found to have the closest connection to the contract.

Excluded Topics

Certain topics were so contentious that the drafters had to exclude them if they hoped to achieve widespread acceptance for the CISG. Product liability, like consumer sales law (discussed above), varies tremendously from legal system to legal system. Accordingly, the CISG steers clear of questions regarding the seller's liability for death or injuries caused by the goods. Likewise, it does not apply to issues concerning the validity of the underlying contract, such as fraud, duress, or illegality. Wherever these gaps occur, the courts look to the appropriate domestic law to resolve any contractual dispute.

Freedom of Contract

Out of deference to the concept of freedom of contract, the CISG permits the parties to the transaction to **opt out** of its coverage. They may either reject its application and select another set of rules to govern their agreement or, in the alternative, accept its coverage but vary any of its provisions. In this respect, the CISG differs from the UCC. In the United States, the UCC is the controlling law for domestic sale of goods transactions and the parties have no freedom to escape its coverage.

The CISG does not specify any particular language or form for opting out. However, as a general rule, the contracting parties make their selection by including in their contract a *choice of law clause* that rejects the CISG and designates the particular domestic law they wish to have govern the transaction.

Buyers and sellers also may expressly **opt in** to the CISG in instances where it might not otherwise apply. This would be accomplished with a choice of law clause designating the CISG as the governing law. In our discussion above, we noted how the issue of whether the CISG automatically applied turned on whether the transaction was commercial (instead of consumer), a sale of goods (rather than services), and international (parties' places of business were in different ratifying countries). At the time of contracting, often it is not clear if all of these steps have been met (i.e., it may be unclear if a transaction predominantly involves goods or services). In these ambiguous situations, the parties may include a choice of law clause in the contract specifying the CISG in order to ensure its application to their agreement.

Interpretation   The CISG and the UCC are similar in that both have numerous gaps in their coverage. In U.S. sale of goods cases when an issue is not specifically encompassed within the UCC's codified rules, the courts will fall back on the common law of contracts. With international sale of goods cases, for those issues not explicitly covered by the CISG, there is no such common underpinning. Accordingly, the contracting parties may wish to designate in their contract a particular domestic legal system that they wish to have serve as the backdrop for their CISG agreement.

International Uniformity and Good Faith

There is no single international tribunal to interpret CISG cases. Instead, international contract disputes are resolved either by national courts or by arbitration tribunals. The CISG specifically instructs these tribunals to interpret its provisions in a manner

FIGURE 5–1   Scope of the CISG

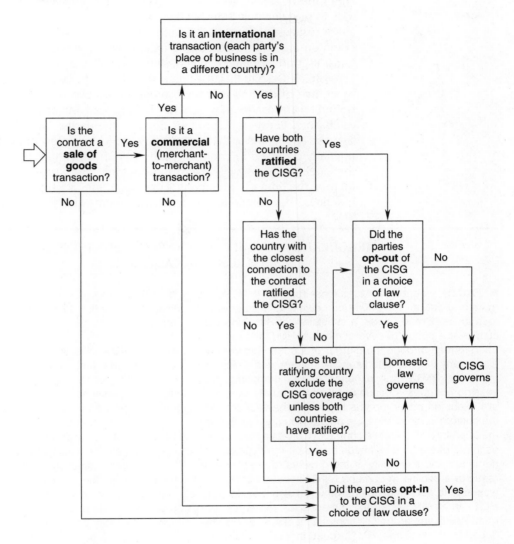

that promotes international uniformity and the observance of good faith. However, this is not an easy task. Arbitration decisions seldom are published; thus, it is difficult to maintain worldwide consistency in their interpretations. Likewise, uniform judicial interpretation is nearly impossible given the wide variety of legal philosophies that distinguish the nations of the world. For these reasons, prudent parties to CISG contracts generally include a *forum selection clause*, indicating which court or arbitration panel will resolve their dispute.

Course of Dealing and Trade Usages

For domestic sale of goods contracts in the United States, the UCC instructs courts to look to past dealings between the parties (course of dealing) and industry standards (trade usages) to supplement and qualify the terms of the contract. While this is common among the developed nations within the civil law and common law systems, it is not widely accepted within socialist legal systems and underdeveloped economies. Despite this resistance, the CISG requires the contracting parties to abide by course of dealing and trade usage under two distinct situations. First, they are bound by any usages to which they have agreed and any course of dealing they have established between themselves. Second, the parties are considered to have agreed to make applicable to the contract any usage they knew or ought to have known was regularly observed in contracts of the type in which they are engaged. To be certain that such practices will govern the contract, the parties should explicitly agree to them at the time of contracting. However, if they wish to avoid the addition of such practices, they should explicitly exclude them when they form the contract.

HEGGBLADE–MARGULEAS–TENNECO v. SUNSHINE BISCUIT
131 Cal.Rptr. 183 (Ct.App. Cal. 1976)

■ **FACTS** Heggblade–Marguleas–Tenneco (HMT) contracted to deliver 100,000 hundredweight sacks of potatoes to Bell Brand Foods, a subsidiary of Sunshine Biscuit, over a period of several months. HMT had recently been formed through the merger of a potato grower and a company that marketed agricultural products. This contract was HMT's first experience with marketing processing potatoes. Because processing potato contracts are executed many months before the harvest season, the custom in the processing potato industry was to treat the quantity called for in a contract solely as a reasonable estimate of the buyers' needs based on their customers' demands and the ability of the growers to supply. As a result of a decline in demand for Bell Brand potatoes, it was able to take only 60,000 hundredweight sacks from HMT. When HMT sued for damages for breach of contract, Bell Brand argued its contractual obligation was reduced by trade usage. HMT argued that since the quantity terms in the contract were definite and unambiguous, there was no reason to fall back on trade usage.

■ **ISSUE** Should the trade usage release Bell Brand from its obligation to purchase the original contractual amount?

■ **DECISION** Yes. A trade usage may be put into evidence in order that the true understanding of the parties as to the agreement may be reached. It should be assumed that usages of trade were taken for granted when the contract was drafted. Unless carefully negated, they become an element of the meaning of the words used. Similarly, the actual performance by the parties is considered the best indication of what they intended their contract to mean. Established trade usage is part of the contract unless the parties agree otherwise. Persons carrying on a particular trade are deemed to be aware of prominent trade usages applicable to their industry. The knowledge may be actual or constructive, and it is constructive if the custom is of such general and universal application that the party must be presumed to know of it.

While the *Sunshine Biscuit* case was decided under the UCC, the result likely would have been the same if it had been governed by the CISG. The UCC formally establishes a hierarchy of interpretation when the express terms of the contract conflict with an applicable course of dealing or trade usage: Express terms control both course of dealing and trade usage, and course of dealing controls trade usage. The language of the CISG is much vaguer, leaving its actual meaning to be discovered over time.

| **ETHICAL IMPLICATIONS** | Suppose Bell Brand knew that HMT was not familiar with the trade usages in the processing potato industry at the time they were negotiating their agreement. Would it be ethical for Bell Brand to enter the contract without first informing HMT of the applicable trade usages? |

FORMATION OF THE CONTRACT

This section examines the key elements that traditionally have been involved in the formation of commercial contracts: offer, acceptance, consideration, and writing. It discusses their treatment under the CISG while simultaneously providing general comparisons to the UCC and other legal systems.

Offer

Elements of the Offer

Under the CISG, a proposal does not constitute an offer unless it meets three formal requirements: (1) it must be addressed to one or more specific persons; (2) it must be sufficiently definite; and (3) it must indicate the intention of the one making the offer (offeror) to be bound in the case of acceptance. Proposals that do not meet these standards are treated as mere invitations to make an offer. Under the UCC, an offer arises if it can be determined that the offeror intended to create a contract and if the terms are definite enough to permit the court to fashion an appropriate remedy.

At first glance, the CISG and UCC tests appear similar. However, there is a fundamental difference. The CISG makes clear that a proposal will not be *sufficiently definite* unless it identifies the goods and specifies the price and quantity or indicates a method for determining the quantity and price. This was a concession to Islamic and socialist legal systems that demanded a great deal of specificity in their contracts. The UCC, on the other hand, frequently finds an offer to exist even in instances where the offeror has left the price term open. (In those cases, the court will find the price to be a reasonable price at the time of delivery.)

Still, the CISG standard is not as onerous as it might at first appear. For instance, an Italian shoe manufacturer might propose to sell shoes at a future date with the price to be the prevailing market price in Italy at some specifically stated future date. This would satisfy the CISG. Further, if a buyer orders goods from the seller's catalog without specifically identifying a price, the CISG probably would imply the buyer is offering to pay the catalog price.

Effectiveness of an Offer

The CISG indicates that an offer becomes effective when it actually reaches the offeree. However, it may be revoked, even if the offeror promises that it is irrevocable, if the revocation reaches the offeree before or at the same time as the offer. Suppose that Nannini, an Italian seller, mails an offer to Isaac, a California buyer. Nannini then telegrams a revocation to Isaac. If the telegram reaches Isaac before or at the same time as the offer, Nannini will have effectively withdrawn the offer. This will be true even if Nannini's offer promised it would not be revoked.

What would have happened if Nannini's telegraphed revocation would have reached Isaac after the mailed offer? The offer still would have been revoked unless one of two things occurred. First, if Isaac already had mailed his acceptance, it would have been too late for Nannini to revoke. This would be true even if Nannini had not yet actually received the acceptance. Under the CISG, an offeror cannot revoke an offer after the offeree dispatches his acceptance. Second, if Nannini's offer had indicated it was irrevocable, he could not revoke it after it was actually received by Isaac.

Irrevocable Offers

The CISG specifies two situations where an offer is irrevocable: (1) when the offeror states it is irrevocable, and (2) when the offeree reasonably relies on its irrevocability. For the first situation to occur, the offeror merely needs to tell the offeree she has a fixed amount of time to consider the offer before giving a reply. This approach is similar to what one would expect to find in a civil law country. Under the common law, the offer still would not be irrevocable unless the offeree had paid a price for the promise. (Such a promise is called an option.) The UCC, on the other hand, would not find the offer to be irrevocable unless the offeror was a merchant who had promised that it was irrevocable in a signed writing.

The second situation described above is similar to the common law notion of estoppel. For instance, a supplier may offer to sell lumber at a fixed price to a builder. The builder then uses the price in that offer in calculating the amount he can bid on a construction job. After the general contractor submits his bid for the construction job, the supplier might not be permitted to revoke her offer to sell the lumber at the original price. To do so would impose an unfair burden on the builder since he might then be unable to find lumber at the price he incorporated in his bid for the construction job.

Acceptance

Time of Acceptance

Mutual consent (or agreement) is the essence of contract law under the CISG. Accordingly, a contract is formed at the moment the acceptance reaches the offeror. This **receipt rule** is widespread in civil law countries. Most common law systems, on the other hand, follow the **mailbox rule.** There a contract is formed at the instant the offeree dispatches her written acceptance unless the offeror had stipulated it would be effective only on receipt. Thus, under the CISG, the offeree bears the risk that her acceptance letter might be lost in the mail. Under the common law, the risk of lost or delayed letters falls on the offeror. (Of course, the offeree would have to convince the court that the acceptance letter actually was dispatched.)

The CISG's receipt rule gives the offeree a strategic advantage when prices or market conditions are fluctuating. Remember from our earlier discussion of offers that an offeror cannot revoke his offer after the offeree has dispatched her acceptance. However, a contract will not be formed until that acceptance actually reaches the offeror. Yet the CISG expressly states the offeree may withdraw an acceptance if the

FIGURE 5–2   Timeliness and CISG Contract Formation

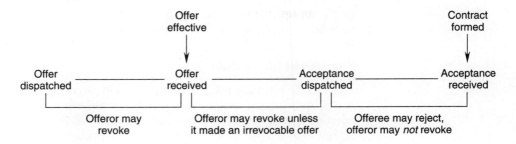

withdrawal reaches the offeror before or at the same time as the acceptance. Thus, after mailing an acceptance, the offeree can change her mind and avoid being bound to the contract if she informs the offeror of her rejection before or at the same time that he receives the acceptance.

Offerors may avoid this quirk in the CISG by placing a short time limit on the offeree's power to accept. (When no time is stated, the offeree must respond within a reasonable time and oral offers generally must be accepted immediately.) A late acceptance still might create a contract if the offeror immediately informs the offeree he will abide by the contract. Or, in instances where an acceptance should have reached the offeror in a timely manner but was unforeseeably delayed, it will create a contract on receipt unless the offeror immediately informs the offeree that he considers the offer to have lapsed.

 **ETHICAL IMPLICATIONS** Cortez, in a letter, offered to sell sugar to Wyatt at a fixed price. After Wyatt mailed an acceptance, the market price for sugar began to fall. Wyatt immediately contracted to buy sugar at a lower price from another supplier and telegraphed a rejection to Cortez. The telegram reached Cortez before the letter of acceptance. Did Wyatt behave in an ethical manner?

Manner of Acceptance

Acceptance generally occurs when the offeror receives a statement from the offeree indicating the offeree's intent to be bound to the terms of the offer. However, sometimes the CISG permits acceptance to occur through the performance of an act without the offeree having to give notice to the offeror. For instance, if a buyer telegraphed a seller requesting prompt shipment of widgets because of an emergency shortfall, the contract would arise at the instant the seller shipped the widgets. Also, an offeree's silence may be an acceptance if past dealings between the parties have made clear that silence should be construed as acceptance. Suppose that over a period of time a seller has regularly shipped goods to a buyer within 10 days after receiving the buyer's order form. The seller never acknowledged the orders other than to ship the goods. If the buyer orders more goods, the seller must either ship them or notify the buyer he will no longer do so because the seller's silence now would be construed as acceptance. These situations would be treated similarly under most common law and civil law systems.

The Mirror Image Rule

The CISG follows the **mirror image rule** in requiring that an acceptance basically match the terms of the offer. Accordingly, if an offeree responds to an offer by proposing additional or different terms that *materially alter* the terms of the original offer, the reply is treated as a rejection that automatically terminates the offer. Basically, the offeree's response becomes a *counteroffer*, which the original offeror is then free to accept or reject. The CISG considers additions or changes relating to the following items to be material alterations: price, payment, quality and quantity of goods, place and time of delivery, extent of one party's liability to the other, and settlement of disputes.

In cases where the offeree proposes additional or different terms that do not materially alter the original offer, that reply constitutes an acceptance unless the original offeror immediately objects. If the offeror does not object, the parties have a contract that contains the offeree's additions or changes. However, if the offeror objects in a timely manner, there is no contract.

The Battle of the Forms

Most legal systems (including the U.S. common law) follow the mirror image rule. However, the UCC deviates from the CISG and the other legal systems when the parties transact business through competing standardized forms. The likelihood that these preprinted forms will agree in every detail is slight. Accordingly, the UCC has devised a *battle of the forms* provision that makes it easier for the court to find the existence of a contract. When the offeree's form indicates the intent to accept but also includes terms additional to those stated in the offer, the additional terms are treated as proposals for addition to the contract. When both parties are merchants, the additional terms become part of the contract unless: (1) the offer made clear no such proposals could be included, (2) the additional terms would materially alter the contract, or (3) the offeror objects to their inclusion within a reasonable time. If any of these three things occur, or if both of the parties are not merchants, the parties still have a contract, but the additional terms are not included in it.

■

FILANTO S.p.A. v. CHILEWICH INTERNATIONAL CORP.
789 F.Supp. 1229 (S.D. N.Y. 1992)

■ **FACTS** Filanto is an Italian corporation that manufactures and sells footwear. Chilewich is an export-import firm with its principal place of business in New York. Chilewich, through an agent in the United Kingdom, signed a contract with Raznoexport, the Soviet Foreign Economic Association, to supply footwear to the Soviets. The written contract between Chilewich and Raznoexport contained a provision requiring that all disputes be arbitrated in Moscow. Chilewich then sent a standard merchant's memo to Filanto in which it offered to purchase the footwear it needed for the contract with Raznoexport. Included in this offer was a provision incorporating the Soviet arbitration clause. Four months later, Filanto sent a return letter to Chilewich in which it agreed to supply the footwear but excluded the arbitration clause. During this time, however, Filanto had been delivering footwear to Chilewich. Later, when a dispute arose, Chilewich argued that it had to be arbitrated in Moscow. Specifically, Chilewich claimed that under the UCC's battle of the forms provision, Filanto's reply was an acceptance and the exclusion of the arbitration clause was a proposal for a material modification, which would not become part of the contract.

■ **ISSUE** Does the arbitration clause remain part of the contract because of the UCC's battle of the forms provision?

■ **DECISION** No. The general principles of contract law relevant to this action do not include the UCC; rather, the law to be applied to this case is found in the CISG. This was a commercial sale of goods, and both the United States (Chilewich's principal place of business) and Italy (Filanto's principal place of business) have adopted the CISG. The CISG varies from the UCC in many significant ways. Specifically, the CISG reverses the battle of the forms rule and reverts back to the common law rule, "A reply to an offer which purports to be an acceptance but contains additions, limitations, or other modifications is a rejection of the offer and constitutes a counteroffer." Although the CISG, like the UCC, does state that between merchants nonmaterial terms do become part of the contract unless objected to, the CISG treats the inclusion (or deletion) of an arbitration clause as "material." Accordingly, Filanto's reply was a counteroffer.

Consideration

Enforceability of Agreements

Common law courts seldom enforce gratuitous promises. This means a promisor need not carry out the terms of his promise unless the promisee has paid a price for the promise. For instance, Ingrid will not be able to persuade a common law court to force George to deliver on his promise to paint her house unless she can show that she gave him legal value or promised him legal value in exchange for his promise. This legal value is known as *consideration*.

Civil law countries have not widely adopted the notion of consideration. The CISG follows the civil law tradition and never mentions the need for consideration. However, this distinction between the CISG and the common law is of limited importance. Since the CISG (like the UCC) encompasses contracts for the sale of goods, consideration generally exists automatically because the parties are each paying a price (the seller delivers goods in exchange for the buyer paying money).

Contract Modifications

Consideration issues often arise when one party to a contract asks the other to modify the agreement. For instance, Todd contracted to build the Carrocias a cabin for $20,000. Before completing his work, Todd informed the Carrocias that he would not complete the job unless they paid him an additional $5,000. Even after completing the construction, Todd would not be entitled to this additional compensation under common law rules because he paid no consideration for the promise of additional compensation. He had a preexisting obligation to build the home for $20,000.

FIGURE 5–3   Formation of a CISG Contract (A Mirror Image)

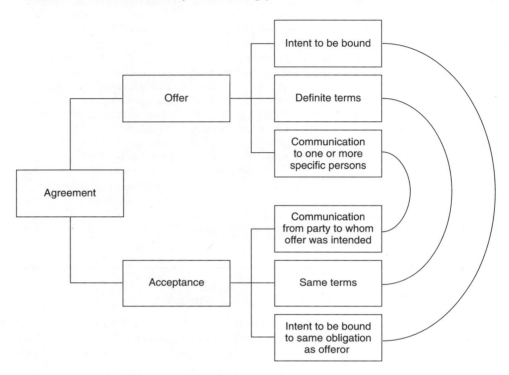

The UCC does not require that new consideration be paid in exchange for the modification of a preexisting contractual obligation as long as the request is reasonable and in good faith. The CISG follows this lead by holding that contracts may be modified or terminated by the mere agreement of the parties. However, if the original contract was in writing and contained a provision requiring that modifications also be in writing, the CISG generally enforces only written modifications.

Writing

Most countries have dispensed with the requirement that contracts be evidenced by a writing. The United States and the socialist nations, however, have not followed this trend. Thus, in the United States, contracts for the sale of goods in excess of $500, contracts for the sale of land, promises to pay the debts of others, and contracts that cannot be performed within one year generally require a writing to be enforceable. Most socialist nations, because of the premium they place on certainty and foreseeability, require written proof of contractual arrangements.

The drafters of the CISG accepted the notion that writing requirements frequently make international contracting slow and unwieldy. Accordingly, the CISG states that contracts need not be evidenced by a writing. However, to induce the socialist nations to ratify the convention, the drafters gave any country the option of declaring that sales contracts be in writing when any contracting party has a place of business in that nation. Argentina, Hungary, and China have made this declaration.

PERFORMANCE OF THE CONTRACT

Warranty Provisions

Buyers involved in international sales frequently have little opportunity to carefully inspect goods before purchasing them. For this reason, most legal systems require merchant sellers to honor the express and implied promises they make concerning the quality, character, and suitability of the goods. The CISG has established general rules governing these express and implied warranties.

Express Warranties

Under the CISG, sellers are required to deliver goods of the quantity, quality, and description called for in the contract. The goods also must be packaged in the manner required by the contract. Similarly, when a seller uses samples or models to induce the buyer to make a purchase, she is expressly warranting that the goods she delivers will be the same.

Implied Warranties

Unless properly disclaimed, sellers in CISG transactions impliedly promise they will deliver goods that are fit for the purposes for which goods of the same description ordinarily would be used. Thus, if a wholesaler sells canned food to a retailer, the wholesaler has impliedly promised the food is edible. This protection, known as the *implied warranty of merchantability,* also is incorporated in the UCC.

Both the CISG and the UCC also have an *implied warranty of fitness for a particular purpose.* This arises when a seller makes known to the buyer that the goods are useful for a specific purpose and the buyer has reasonably relied on the seller's skill and judgment. Thus, if a buyer asks a computer company to select software for use in his computer system, the seller will be impliedly promising the software is compatible with the buyer's system.

Liability and Disclaimers

Despite language differences, the codified rules governing the creation of warranties under the CISG and the UCC are roughly similar. Further, both generally exempt a seller from liability if at the time the contract was made the buyer knew or could not have been unaware of the goods' lack of conformity. The only real point of departure between the two systems seems to be their handling of sellers' attempts to disclaim warranties. Under the UCC, the seller's disclaimer must use very precise language and be conspicuously presented to the buyer. The CISG, on the other hand, states only that the seller must deliver conforming goods unless the parties have agreed otherwise.

SOBIECH v. INTERNATIONAL STAPLE AND MACHINE CO.
867 F.2d 778 (2d Cir. 1989)

■ **FACTS** Sobiech was engaged in the business of growing, packaging, and shipping vegetables. International Staple and Machine Co. (ISM) was a distributor of vegetable packaging equipment and had supplied Sobiech with several "weigh packers" that weighed onions on a mechanical scale and automatically packaged them. After discovering the availability of more efficient machines, Sobiech agreed to have ISM re-outfit one of the machines on a trial basis so he could evaluate its performance before deciding whether to purchase one. At that time, ISM informed Sobiech that the machine was new and experimental. Although he experienced numerous problems with the conversion machine, Sobiech decided to buy one of the new weigh packers from ISM. He also decided to buy the conversion machine. After several years of difficulties with both machines, Sobiech stopped making payments, alleging ISM had breached the implied

warranties of merchantability and fitness for a particular purpose.

■ **ISSUE** Did ISM breach the implied warranties of merchantability and fitness?

■ **DECISION** No. ISM is entitled to the unpaid purchase price for the new weigh packer and the re-outfitted conversion machine. Sobiech was aware of the experimental nature of, and potential problems with, the machines at the time he decided to purchase them. He had been using such machines on a trial basis for several months. His extensive use and actual knowledge of the problems before purchase precluded any implied warranties as to the performance of the conversion machine or any machines of identical design.

Nonconforming Goods

Notice of Lack of Conformity

Most domestic legal systems require that the buyer give timely notice of any nonconformity so the seller can attempt to make repairs. Failure to give prompt notice generally bars the buyer from any remedy. The CISG expands on this notice requirement by insisting that such notice be given no later than two years after the goods actually were handed over to the buyer.

Many Third World countries complained that strict notice requirements would work to the disadvantage of their businesspeople. They argued that they tended to sell raw materials (where defects were rare or easily discoverable) and buy complicated equipment (where defects might not appear until long after delivery). The CISG responded to these complaints in two ways. First, the buyer may be excused from giving timely notice if it can be shown that the seller knew of the nonconformities, yet failed to disclose them to the buyer. Second, buyers may reduce the purchase price if they have a reasonable excuse for failing to give the required notice.

Right to Cure

The **right to cure** permits the seller to repair any nonconformities or defects in the goods. Despite differences in the language used, the CISG and the UCC treat this right identically. It exists in three situations: (1) When the seller makes an early delivery that contains nonconforming goods, she has an absolute right to cure until the actual time of performance (i.e., the time called for in the contract) is due. (2) A seller may

FIGURE 5–4   Seller's Right to Cure

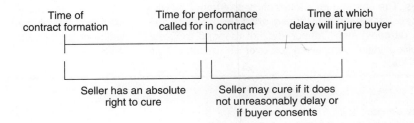

have a right to cure even after the time of performance if the repairs can be made without unreasonable delay and without causing the buyer unreasonable inconvenience (i.e., the buyer already has a surplus of the goods in his warehouse). (3) A seller may cure after the time of performance if the buyer consents to the repairs.

Anticipatory Repudiation

Sometimes the other party's words (i.e., "I will not deliver the goods") or special circumstances (i.e., the seller's factory has been closed for several months because of a strike) make it appear that a contract to be performed at a future date will be breached. When a contracting party has *clear and convincing evidence* that such breach will occur, he should give the other party notice that he considers the contract to be breached. Under both the CISG and the UCC, the contract then will be canceled unless the other party gives **adequate assurances** that she will be able to fully perform when the time of performance is due.

CREUSOT–LOIRE INTERNATIONAL v. COPPUS ENGINEERING CORP.
535 F.Supp. 45 (S.D. N.Y. 1983)

■ **FACTS** Creusot–Loire, a French company, was the project engineer for the construction of ammonia plants in Yugoslavia and Syria. Creusot–Loire contracted with Coppus Engineering for the purchase of burners that were capable of continuous operation using heavy fuel oil with combustion air preheated to 260 degrees Celsius. Coppus warranted the burners for one year from the start-up of the plants but not exceeding three years from the date of shipment. The burners for the Yugoslavia plant were shipped in November 1979, but the plant was not to become operational until the end of 1983 because of construction delays. In 1981, Creusot–Loire discovered that similar burners at the Syria plant (and also at a plant in Sri Lanka) were experiencing serious operational difficulties. Creusot–Loire wrote to Coppus asking for

proof that the burners for the Yugoslavia plant would meet contract specifications. Specifically, Creusot–Loire insisted that Coppus extend its contractual warranty to cover the delay in the start-up of the Yugoslavia plant and post an irrevocable letter of credit for the purchase price of the burners.

■ **ISSUE** Is Creusot–Loire's request for assurances reasonable?

■ **DECISION** Yes. The contract plainly states Coppus was obligated to provide burners that would operate under certain conditions. Because the burners delivered to Syria and Sri Lanka did not conform to those specifications, Creusot–Loire had reasonable grounds for insecurity and, accordingly, was justified in seeking assurances from Coppus. The assurances requested by Creusot–Loire were not unreasonable in light of the circumstances. The demand for a letter of credit comported with accepted international business practices. Further, the record demonstrates Coppus did not respond to Creusot–Loire's initial complaints for over six months. This stalling forced Creusot–Loire to request security in the form of a letter of credit and an extension of the warranty. Accordingly, Coppus' failure to provide any assurance, save its statement that the burners would work if installed, constituted a repudiation of the contract, which entitled Creusot–Loire to a return of its purchase price.

EXCUSES FOR NONPERFORMANCE

Sometimes a party that fails to conform with the terms of the contract may avoid liability if she can prove the existence of compelling circumstances that provide a *legal excuse* for nonperformance. However, most courts hesitate to excuse parties from their contractual obligations, particularly when the parties knew or should have known of the potential hardships at the time of contracting. This section briefly examines the most widely accepted excuses.

Prevention

All legal systems generally excuse someone from the duty to perform on the contract if the failure to act was substantially caused by the other party. Basically, promisees owe promisors a duty to cooperate and not actively hinder the performance of the contract. The CISG also recognizes this doctrine of **prevention.** Thus, a seller may be unable to process an export license without first giving his country's export agency a letter, signed by the buyer, promising that the goods will not be reshipped to certain hostile countries. If the buyer never signs and sends this form, the seller will be excused from delivering the goods.

Impossibility

Most legal systems, including the common law and particularly the civil law, narrowly construe the circumstances under which a party is excused from performance. In these countries, absent prevention by the promisee, the duty to perform is discharged only if the promisor can demonstrate **impossibility.** The fact that performance will be more burdensome than anticipated or unprofitable is not enough to trigger this defense. Instead, the promisor must show that an unforeseeable event arose *after the formation* of the contract that now makes performance objectively (i.e., *nobody* could perform this particular contractual duty) impossible. An event is unforeseeable if neither of the parties would have considered it to be a real possibility at the time of contracting. The most common situations where impossibility occurs are: death or illness of the promisor in a personal service contract; supervening illegality (a new law makes performance unlawful); and destruction of the subject matter of the contract when no viable substitutes are available.

Frustration of Purpose

Some domestic courts excuse performance under a **frustration of purpose** standard. This defense arises when events that occur after formation of the contract make the promisee's return performance worthless to the promisor. For example, suppose

Timmins charters a plane to transport key personnel to a trade convention. If the trade convention is canceled, the plane is no longer of value to Timmins. He may then be excused from the obligation imposed by the charter agreement under the doctrine of frustration. Impossibility would not apply here because Timmins would still be able to perform (pay the charter fee). Most courts in the United States do not recognize the frustration defense.

Commercial Impracticability

Some common law courts have begun to relax the impossibility defense, making it easier for promisor's to escape burdensome contractual obligations. In the United States, the UCC has formally adopted this **commercial impracticability** standard. Basically, this doctrine excuses a promisor's duty to perform when unforeseeable events make performance highly impracticable or unreasonably expensive. In instances where a seller's ability to deliver goods is only partially affected, she may allocate production among her customers. When this occurs, however, her buyers have the option of agreeing to the allocation or terminating the contract.

ALIMENTA (U.S.A.) v. GIBBS NATHANIEL (CANADA) LTD.
802 F.2d 1362 (11th Cir. 1986)

■ **FACTS** Alimenta and Gibbs, each an international dealer in agricultural commodities, entered into several contracts in advance of the 1980 peanut harvest. All of the contracts called for Gibbs to deliver peanuts to Alimenta. Gibbs was not a peanut grower; therefore, it purchased peanuts from numerous growers to meet the demands of Alimenta and 75 other buyers. Before formation of the contracts at issue, the 1980 peanut crop had already been planted and was growing in good condition. After contracting with Alimenta, Gibbs contracted to purchase peanuts from 15 growers in quantities 7 percent in excess of its expected sales. Soon thereafter, a record drought occurred that reduced peanut production to 48 percent of the previous year's crop. As a result, Gibbs received only 52 percent of the peanuts it had contracted to purchase. Gibbs then notified Alimenta that it would allocate its supply among all of its customers, resulting in Alimenta receiving only 87 percent of the amount called for in their contracts. When Alimenta sued for breach of

contract, Gibbs claimed its full performance was excused by the doctrine of commercial impracticability.

■ **ISSUE** Does Gibbs' failure to fully perform fall within the commercial impracticability defense?

■ **DECISION** Yes. Gibbs was entitled to allocate among its customers if it could demonstrate that the drought was not reasonably foreseeable when the contracts were entered into and that, as a result, full performance was made impracticable. A climatology expert testified that the onset and duration of the drought was unprecedented and that the probability of its occurring was "very low, near zero." For Gibbs to have fully performed on its contracts, it would have been forced to pay over $3.8 million. Yet its net worth was only $2.5 million and its anticipated profits on the Alimenta contracts were only $18,000. Measured objectively, the drought's occurrence made performance commercially impracticable.

Force Majeure in the CISG

The CISG contains a **force majeure** provision that appears to lie somewhere between the impossibility and commercial impracticability doctrines discussed above. (Force majeure is an unforeseeable and irresistible event that renders an obligation impossible to perform.) Under the CISG, a promisor is not liable for failure to perform if the nonperformance was caused by an "impediment" beyond the promisor's control that the promisor could not reasonably have been expected to have considered when the contract was formed. As with all of these legal excuses, the CISG provision holds the promisor liable for damages if he fails to give notice of the nonperformance to the promisee within a reasonable time.

The CISG specifically addresses the applicability of force majeure to situations where the promisor's inability to perform was caused by a third party's failure to act. In those instances, the promisor's nonperformance is excused only if the third party's failure also would be exempt under force majeure. For instance, in the *Alimenta* case (discussed above) the seller was unable to deliver all of the peanuts because its suppliers (the growers) failed to fully perform. If this case had been governed by the CISG, the seller's nonperformance would be excused because the growers would not have reasonably expected a drought of that severity to occur when they agreed to supply the seller.

Force Majeure Clauses

Most parties to international contracts will include a **force majeure clause** in their private agreement. These provisions usually list the types of events that will excuse the parties from their contractual obligations. Courts generally enforce these provisions. Still, it is wise to carefully draft the force majeure clause so it fairly reflects the unacceptable risks involved in that specific transaction.

REMEDIES FOR BREACH OF CONTRACT

While some socialist countries punish contractual breaches with fines or imprisonment, most legal systems embrace the idea that a party who breaches a contract should be required to place the nonbreaching party in the same position she would have been in if the breach had not occurred. Although most countries share this objective, there are some fundamental differences in the methods they favor for achieving it. The CISG, drawing from this variety, has established a wide range of remedies. In this final section of the chapter, we examine the major options available to a nonbreaching party upon the occurrence of such a breach.

Avoidance

In some circumstances, the CISG permits a nonbreaching party to walk away from a contract by declaring an **avoidance.** Generally, this remedy is allowed only when there has been a *fundamental breach.* This occurs when the nonconformity is so severe that it substantially deprives the nonbreaching party of what she is entitled to expect. Further, the breaching party must have reasonably foreseen such a consequence. Under the UCC, the buyer has a broader right of *rejection* whenever the seller supplies nonconforming goods.

The UCC gives a buyer similar protection even after goods have been delivered and accepted if the nonconformity substantially impairs their value. To exercise this *revocation of acceptance,* the buyer must show that she accepted the goods: (*a*) without knowledge of the nonconformity because of difficulty in discovering it, or (*b*) based on the seller's promise that the nonconformity would be cured and it was not cured within a reasonable time. The CISG will permit an avoidance under similar circumstances, although its rule is somewhat vaguer. It prohibits the buyer from avoiding the contract unless she does so within a reasonable time after she knew or ought to have known of the breach. In instances where a nonbreaching party is not permitted to avoid (i.e., when the breach was not fundamental), she still may pursue the other remedies described below.

Monetary Damages

The prevailing remedy for contractual breaches in common law countries is monetary damages. Generally, the nonbreaching party will receive **compensatory damages.** They are measured as the difference between the value of the performance the nonbreaching party actually received and the value of the performance she had the right to receive. Thus, if no performance has occurred, the damages are the value of the promised performance. In limited circumstances, the nonbreaching party may suffer additional damages. For instance, a wholesaler may lose a long-term contract with a retailer if its manufacturer does not make timely deliveries. These **consequential damages** generally are not available to the nonbreaching party unless the breaching party should have foreseen that they would occur.

Both the CISG and the UCC share the common law standard for determining compensatory damages. They also permit consequential damages when they should have been foreseeable at the time the parties formed their contract. However, it appears that consequential damages are more easily available under the CISG.

Specific Performance

Sometimes monetary damages do not adequately compensate the nonbreaching party because the goods called for in the contract cannot be purchased elsewhere. This frequently occurs in many socialist systems and underdeveloped economies where substitute goods do not exist. Those nations, as well as most civil law countries, prefer to grant **specific performance.** Under this remedy, a buyer can force a seller to deliver conforming goods and a seller can require the buyer to pay the contract price.

This preference for specific performance is not shared by the common law and the UCC. In those systems, the prevailing remedy is monetary damages. They permit specific performance only when monetary damages are inadequate because the called-for performance is unique and unavailable elsewhere. As a compromise between these conflicting attitudes, the CISG allows specific performance in cases only where there was a *fundamental breach.* It further holds that a court is not bound to award specific performance unless that would be an appropriate remedy under its domestic law. Accordingly, common law courts are likely to order specific performance only sparingly. (Parties may wish to consider this fact when they are deciding if they wish to designate a particular nation's courts in a forum selection clause.)

Reduction in Price

While common law countries favor the monetary damages remedy, civil law systems have traditionally denied such awards unless the breaching party was guilty of fault or fraud. A seller's delivery of nonconforming goods generally would not meet the fault or fraud standard. In instances of nonconforming deliveries, however, buyers are not without a remedy. The civil law systems developed an action for **reduction in price,** which permits buyers unilaterally to reduce the price they pay to offset the

FIGURE 5–5   Countries Ratifying the CISG (as of August 1992)

—Argentina   —Lesotho
—Australia   —Mexico
—Austria   —Netherlands
—Bulgaria   —Norway
—Byelorussia   —People's Republic of China
—Canada   —Romania
—Chile   —Russian Federation
—Czech Republic   —Slovakia
—Denmark   —Spain
—Ecuador   —Sweden
—Egypt   —Switzerland
—Federal Republic of Germany   —Syria
—Finland   —Uganda
—France   —Ukraine
—Guinea   —USA
—Hungary   —Yugoslavia
—Iraq   —Zambia
—Italy

reduced value of the goods that were delivered. Despite objections from the common law nations, the CISG has adopted the reduction in price remedy. However, it is not available to a buyer if a seller can cure the nonconformity without causing the buyer unreasonable delay or inconvenience.

Nachfrist Notice   Another civil law remedy that was adopted by the CISG is a German concept, called **Nachfrist notice.** This procedure permits a buyer to give a seller an additional time period of reasonable length to fulfill contractual obligations. Likewise, a seller can extend to the buyer additional time to pay the purchase price or accept delivery of the goods. During this extension, the nonbreaching party must refrain from pursuing any remedy for breach of contract; however, he is not deprived of later claiming damages for the delayed performance. If a buyer or seller fails to fully perform by the expiration of the extended time period, the nonbreaching party can declare an *avoidance* (even in instances where the breach is not fundamental). While the common law countries do not have a Nachfrist notice provision, the concept is somewhat similar to the UCC notion of *anticipatory repudiation* and *adequate assurances* (discussed earlier).

QUESTIONS AND PROBLEM CASES

1. Why do many underdeveloped economies and socialist countries favor the remedy of *specific performance* over monetary damages?

2. In which legal systems are oral contracts most likely to be unenforceable?

3. When is a contract governed by the CISG?

4. When does the CISG permit a seller to cure non-conforming goods?

5. Eagle Comtronics manufactured and sold addressable descramblers to Cable Holdings for use in the St. Charles Cable TV cable system. The sale resulted from a series of meetings and telephone conversations between Donald Behrman, the chief engineer for Cable Holdings, and Eagle. On October 12, Behrman telephoned an order for 4,000 Eagle descramblers. Following this telephone order, Eagle sent sales acknowledgment forms to Cable Holdings. Each acknowledgment, on its face, stated the price, the number of descramblers, and the warranty period. On the reverse side of the order form, Eagle listed several additional terms, among them a provision stating the buyer would be responsible for freight charges and interest arising out of any contract dispute over defective goods. Cable Holdings never objected to the terms on the acknowledgment form, but no representative of Cable Holdings ever signed the form. Later, a dispute arose over financial responsibility for modifications that needed to be made to the descramblers. Cable Holdings refused to pay the balance due on its bill until Eagle shared in the costs of the modifications. Eagle sued for the balance due on the contract plus interest as well as for freight charges. Would Cable Holdings be liable for the interest and freight charges under the UCC? Explain.

6. What would the outcome to Problem Case 5 be if it were governed by the CISG? Explain.

7. Bende contracted to supply the government of Ghana with 10,000 pairs of boots. Kiffe, who knew Bende was going to resell the boots, agreed to manufacture them for Bende in Korea and deliver them to Ghana. After the boots were manufactured, they were shipped by boat from Korea to the United States. They were then loaded on railroad cars for shipment to the East Coast; however, the train derailed and the boots were destroyed. When Bende was unable to purchase boots from other sources, the government of Ghana canceled its contract. Bende sued Kiffe for breach of contract and Bende claimed its nonperformance was excused under the doctrine of commercial impracticability. Assuming this case is governed by the UCC, will Kiffe's nonperformance be excused?

8. Using the facts of Problem Case 7, assume the contract between Bende and the government of Ghana is governed by the CISG and the government of Ghana sues Bende for breach of contract. Will Bende be able to avoid liability by claiming its nonperformance was excused under the CISG's force majeure provision?

9. For this question use the facts of Problem Case 7 and also assume Kiffe's commercial impracticability defense failed. Bende offers uncontradicted evidence to the court that the government of Ghana had offered to pay $158,000 to Bende once the boots were delivered. However, Bende also admitted the sale to the government of Ghana would have required that it incur $14,815 in freight charges. Kiffe offered uncontradicted evidence that Bende had agreed to pay Kiffe $95,000 when the boots arrived in Ghana. If Bende brings an action against Kiffe for monetary damages, what amount will Kiffe be required to pay? Explain.

10. Tai Wah, a Hong Kong company, contracted to sell two orders of stereo cassette recorders to Ambassador, a New York distributor. After the first order arrived, Ambassador immediately began receiving complaints about the cassettes from its customers. It relayed this information to Tai Wah, requesting that the problems be corrected in future orders. Tai Wah informed Ambassador it was working on the problems but the second order already had been shipped without any changes. Ambassador, knowing of the defective condition of the second order, accepted delivery. It then notified Tai Wah it was revoking its acceptance and would not pay for the second shipment unless and until Tai Wah compensated it for the damages it suffered in the first order. Under the UCC, would Ambassador have the right to revoke its acceptance of the second order? Would the answer be the same if the contract were governed by the CISG?

6

Contracts for the Carriage of Goods

Introduction

Global sales transactions ultimately require that one of the parties arranges for the carriage of the goods from one country to another. Physical delivery generally involves one or a combination of the following methods of transportation: road, rail, air, or sea. The importance of determining which party is responsible for the costs of delivery as well as the risk of loss while goods are in transit should not be underestimated. Thus, the carriage of goods should be an integral part of the contracting process.

Chapter Overview

This chapter begins with a review of the logistical complexities involved in transporting goods from one country to another. It then examines the role that documents of title—particularly bills of lading—play in the carriage of goods. Next, there is an explanation of how trade terms may be used to define the rights and responsibilities of buyers and sellers while goods are in transit. This includes an introduction to each of the 13 Incoterms that have been designed to simplify the allocation of risks and duties between the parties. Finally, the chapter closes with an in-depth examination of the special rules governing the carriage of goods by road, rail, air, and sea.

LOGISTICAL CONCERNS

Global traders often fail to appreciate the difficulties involved in shipping goods across national borders. Great distances, varying regulatory systems, and increased risks frequently combine to make the process both cumbersome and time-consuming. As a result, managers may unwittingly assume obligations that can cripple an otherwise profitable business opportunity. In other instances, sellers may view transportation as an unavoidable cost and automatically insist that their customers bear all responsibility for shipment of the product. That approach may undermine the competitiveness of the seller's product in an international market. Prudent managers become aware of the important transportation options and incorporate those issues into their management process.

Packaging Needs

Global transport often involves perils above and beyond those associated with domestic deliveries. Carriage by oceangoing vessels may subject goods to damage from excessive moisture. Further, containers may be dropped, rattled, and smashed as they are loaded by slings, stacked in the hold, or jostled during violent storms. Further, many foreign ports lack adequate storage facilities, thereby exposing goods to rain or snow as well as to the threat of theft or pilferage. Accordingly, products must be packaged in a manner that will protect against these risks. At the same time, it must be recognized that transportation charges are based on the weight and volume of the goods. The high cost of transportation requires shippers to balance the need for protection against their corresponding costs.

Documentary Requirements

The amount and types of documentation that must accompany an international shipment depend on the regulatory requirements of the exporting and importing nations. Failure to comply with these regulations may prevent the goods from leaving the exporting country or entering the importing country. In extreme cases, the merchandise may be seized. Some of the more common documents that accompany overseas shipments are listed below.

Bill of lading. This document serves, among other functions, as the transportation contract between a carrier and the owner of the goods.

Certificate of origin. Some nations require that imports be accompanied by a document certifying their country of origin.

Commercial invoice. This document describes the merchandise, identifies the buyer and the seller, and discloses the basic delivery and payment terms.

Dock receipt. This is issued when the goods arrive at the dock before the carrier's issuance of a bill of lading.

Export license. Certain types of goods require a validated license before they may be exported.

Inspection certificate. The buyer, a bank that is financing the sales transaction, or a governmental agency may require certification from a third party that the goods meet certain specifications.

Insurance certificate. The terms of the sales contract often require proof that the goods are insured while they are in transit.

Packing list. This document itemizes the contents, type, and number of packages in the shipment.

Shipper's export declaration. The U.S. Department of Commerce requires this form, known as an **SED**, for shipments valued at over $500.

Warehouse receipt. This is issued if the goods are temporarily stored before or after their carriage.

Depending on the merchandise and the countries involved in the transaction, numerous other documents may be required. Further, many countries require special markings that must be legible, clearly visible, and often written in a foreign language.

Transportation Decisions

Buyers and sellers must determine who is responsible for arranging the carriage of the goods; although, in competitive markets, sellers often provide this as a service to their customers. The **shipper** (the party who arranges for the shipment) must decide which form (or combination of forms) of transportation is most appropriate. Then it must contract with a particular **carrier** (the party who actually transports the goods) to ensure that they safely reach the correct destination in a timely manner.

Freight Forwarders

The complexities of transporting goods are beyond the expertise of many global traders. Accordingly, shippers often turn to **freight forwarders** to coordinate their contracts of carriage. Freight forwarders who have developed extensive connections throughout the world can efficiently provide a full range of transportation services. Further, by handling large volumes of goods, they generally can obtain lower freight

COMMERCIAL INVOICE

Copyright © 1989 UNZ & CO.

SHIPPER/EXPORTER	COMMERCIAL INVOICE NO.	DATE
	CUSTOMER PURCHASE ORDER NO.	
	COUNTRY OF ORIGIN	DATE OF EXPORT
CONSIGNEE	TERMS OF PAYMENT	
NOTIFY: INTERMEDIATE CONSIGNEE	EXPORT REFERENCES	

QUANTITY	DESCRIPTION OF MERCHANDISE	UNIT PRICE	TOTAL VALUE

SAMPLE

| PACKAGE MARKS: | MISC. CHARGES (Packing, Insurance, etc.) | |
| | INVOICE TOTAL | |

CERTIFICATIONS

AUTHORIZED SIGNATURE

and insurance rates than most buyers or sellers can on their own. An experienced freight forwarder is aware of special documentary requirements and in many cases can provide smooth passage of the goods through the importing nation's customs procedures.

The relationship between a shipper and a freight forwarder is grounded in the law of agency. As an agent of the shipper, the freight forwarder's duties are created by the parties' contract, their past dealings, industry practices, and the common law of agency. In arranging and supervising the transport of the cargo, the freight forwarder promises to use care and skill and assumes the fiduciary obligations of loyalty and obedience imposed by agency law. (Fiduciary duties and other traditional agency duties are discussed in Chapter 15.)

JOHN BROWN ENGINEERING LIMITED v. HERMANN LUDWIG, INC.
1992 U.S. App. LEXIS 7296 (4th Cir. 1992)

■ **FACTS** John Brown Engineering Ltd. purchased heavy machinery in South Carolina and contracted with Hermann Ludwig, Inc., a freight forwarder, to arrange transport of the machinery to Clydebank, Scotland. When some of the equipment arrived in Scotland damaged, Brown sued Ludwig for breach of the freight forwarding contract. Specifically, Brown charged that the freight forwarder failed to ensure proper packing of the machinery for transportation, failed to select a proper vessel and crew for the carriage, and failed to ensure proper stowing and lashing of the cargo aboard the vessel.

■ **ISSUE** Did Ludwig violate the duties imposed on it by the freight forwarding contract?

■ **DECISION** No. Ludwig's duties as a freight forwarder were governed by the contract between the parties. Nothing in this contract indicated Ludwig was responsible for export packing. Brown's subjective expectations that Ludwig would perform this service were not adequately communicated. The only evidence that Brown instructed Ludwig to perform export packing duties was a facsimile that was never actually sent to Ludwig. A freight forwarder cannot be said to have contracted for a duty of which it was unaware. Daniels Construction Company was primarily responsible for export packing. Brown specifically involved Ludwig in the task of providing containers for electronics, but the very fact that this responsibility had to be specifically delegated bespeaks an understanding that the primary packing responsibility lay elsewhere. Further, Ludwig had no special expertise in export packing. As a freight forwarder, Ludwig was responsible for retaining a carrier for the cargo. It retained the Kestrel Shipping Company, which in turn provided the vessel *Osprey* to ship the goods under Captain Broehan. The *Osprey* was a heavy lift cargo vessel that was perfectly suited for the journey, and Captain Broehan had many years experience transporting heavy lift cargo. The only claim ever registered against Captain Broehan was the damage to this particular cargo. Ultimate responsibility for the stowing and lashing of cargo lies with the captain of the ship. Under ordinary circumstances, a freight forwarder has no contractual duty to attend and supervise the loading. No evidence exists that Ludwig was even aware of any cargo characteristics requiring special care. A freight forwarder has no affirmative duty to investigate special cargo sensitivities.

In-house Transportation Department

When a seller repeatedly supplies the same type of goods to a single set of buyers, it may comfortably handle its transportation arrangements in-house. Further, if a seller anticipates it will be engaging in a high volume of overseas sales over an appreciable time period, it may decide to erect a profit center in its transportation activities. Thus, many companies, after engaging in cost-benefit analysis, establish an **in-house transportation department**. Frequently, the first step in this process is to retain the services of a freight forwarder and contract for complete documentation of its shipping transactions. This provides a road map for future in-house operations. Over time, it may retain the services of transportation consultants who ensure the transportation department keeps pace with new developments in the transportation industry.

ETHICAL IMPLICATIONS	What duties do you owe your freight forwarder? Is it ethical to establish an in-house transportation department after learning the intracacies of international shipping from a freight forwarder?

DOCUMENTS OF TITLE

For the past 400 years, **documents of title** have been widely used to establish the rightful owners of goods involved in global transport. These documents may be either *negotiable* or *nonnegotiable*. When they are negotiable, they provide that the goods are to be ultimately delivered to the bearer or to the order of a named person. This negotiability feature permits the goods' owner to transfer title and constructive possession of the goods to other persons even though the merchandise may be at sea or otherwise located thousands of miles away. It also provides a great deal of security for buyers and creditors when the purchased goods have not yet been delivered. (These uses of documents of title are further discussed in Chapter 7).

Bills of Lading

A **bill of lading** generally is issued by carriers when they receive goods for shipment. Its statutory definition is quite broad, including any document evidencing the receipt of goods for shipment that is issued by a person engaged in the business of transporting or forwarding goods. Accordingly, bills of lading come in many different forms. Some of the more common types include:

Through bills. When a carrier requires the services of other carriers to deliver the goods, it may issue a through bill. Both the receiving and the delivering carrier are liable for damages to the goods although either may seek indemnity from the carrier on whose line the losses occurred.

Destination bills. Sometimes, particularly with air transport, the goods may reach their destination before a bill of lading arrives. In those cases, the bill of lading may be issued by the carrier at the place of destination rather than at the place of shipment.

Forwarder's bill. A freight forwarder may issue a bill of lading on receipt of the goods from the seller. It is then liable for misdescription or nondelivery of the goods.

Negotiable bills. Sometimes called *order bills*, these documents can be held by sellers or creditors who wish to retain a security interest in the goods or sold to subsequent buyers, thereby granting constructive possession of the goods before they actually arrive at their destination.

Straight bills. These are nonnegotiable documents; thus, they permit the title to the goods to be constructively transferred to another party. The face of these documents contains the words *nonnegotiable* or *not negotiable*.

Clean bills. On receiving the goods, the carrier immediately inspects them or their packages. Any visible signs of damage are noted on the bill of lading. When no damages are observed, the carrier issues a clean bill.

On-board bills. These indicate the goods have actually been loaded on a particular vessel.

Received-for-shipment bills. These merely signify that the carrier has received the goods for transport. They do not indicate which vessel will actually carry the goods or when they will be loaded.

In most instances, the bill of lading issued by a carrier combines several of these characteristics. For instance, the carrier may forward to the buyer a clean, on-board, negotiable bill of lading. This signifies the goods were received by the carrier without any visible damage and have already been loaded on a vessel for transport. Further, the buyer may transfer the right to receive the goods to another party merely by selling it the bill of lading.

Uses of the Bill of Lading

Bills of lading may perform three important functions. First, the freight forwarder or carrier issues it as a **receipt** for the goods. On receiving the goods, the carrier carefully inspects them and details their quantity, weight, volume, description, and condition on the bill of lading. Second, the bill of lading generally defines the terms of the **contract of carriage** between the shipper and the carrier. Third, it serves as a **document of title**.

Electronic Bills

Developments in transportation and communications technologies are compelling a movement away from the traditional paper documents. *Containerized shipping* has greatly accelerated the loading, traveling, and unloading times for the carriage of cargo. It has permitted establishment of *multimodal transport systems* whereby various types of carriers (road, rail, air, and sea) integrate their operations. As containers are merely transferred from one carrier to another, the overall transport time has been reduced to such a degree that the goods frequently arrive before the bill of lading. Without the bill of lading, buyers are unable to immediately pick up the goods, resulting in increased storage costs and congested ports. Developments in the electronic data interchange (EDI) technology offer the transportation industry a way to better coordinate and track shipments without the need for traditional paper documents.

Warehouse Receipts

A **warehouse receipt** is issued by a person engaged in the business of storing goods for hire. To be valid, it does not need to be in any particular form; however, a warehouseman may be liable for damages resulting from the failure to include certain information, such as: (*a*) the location of the warehouse where the goods are stored; (*b*) whether the goods are to be delivered to the bearer or to the order of a named

FIGURE 6–2   Straight Bill of Lading

STRAIGHT BILL OF LADING — SHORT FORM — ORIGINAL — NOT NEGOTIABLE

RECEIVED subject to the classifications and tariffs in effect on the date of the issue of this Bill of Lading, the property described above in apparent good order, except as noted (contents and condition of contents of packages unknown), marked, consigned, and destined as indicated above which said carrier (the word carrier being understood throughout this contract as meaning any person or corporation in possession of the property under the contract) agrees to carry to its usual place of delivery at said destination. If on its route, otherwise to deliver to another carrier on the route to said destination. It is mutually agreed as to each carrier of all or any of said property over all or any portion of said route to

destination and as to each party at any time interested in all or any said property, that every service to be performed hereunder shall be subject to all the bill of lading terms and conditions in the governing classification on the date of shipment.

Shipper hereby certifies that he is familiar with all the bill of lading terms and conditions in the governing classification and the said terms and conditions are hereby agreed to by the shipper and accepted for himself and his assigns

From _____

At _____ 19 ___ **DESIGNATE WITH AN (X)** BY TRUCK ☐ FREIGHT ☐   Shipper's No. _____

Carrier _____   Agent's No. _____

(Mail or street address of consignee— For purposes of notification only.)

Consigned to _____

Destination _____ State of _____ County of _____

Route _____

Delivering Carrier _____ Vehicle or Car Initial _____ No. _____

No. Packages	Kind of Package, Description of Articles, Special Marks, and Exceptions	*Weight (Sub. to Cor.)	Class or Rate	Check Column	Subject to Section 7 of conditions of applicable bill of lading, if this shipment is to be delivered to the consignee without recourse on the consignor, the consignor shall sign the following statement:
					The carrier shall not make delivery of this shipment without payment of freight and all other lawful charges.
					Per _____ (Signature of Consignor.)
					If charges are to be prepaid, write or stamp here, "To be Prepaid."
					Received $ _____ to apply in prepayment of the charges on the property described hereon.
					Agent or Cashier.
					Per _____ (The signature here acknowledges only the amount prepaid.)
					Charges Advanced:
					C.O.D. SHIPMENT Prepaid ☐ Collect ☐ $ _____ Collection Fee _____ Total Charges _____
					*If the shipment moves between two ports by a carrier by water, the law requires that the bill of lading shall state whether it is "Carrier's or Shipper's weight."
					†Shipper's imprint in lieu of stamp; not a part of bill of lading approved by the Department of Transportation.
					NOTE—Where the rate is dependent on value, shippers are required to state specifically in writing the agreed or declared value of the property.
					THIS SHIPMENT IS CORRECTLY DESCRIBED. CORRECT WEIGHT IS _____ LBS.
TOTAL PIECES					Subject to verification by the Respective Weighing and Inspection Bureau According to Agreement. Per _____

†The fibre containers used for this shipment conform to the specifications set forth in the box maker's certificate thereon, and all other requirements of Rule 41 of the Uniform Freight Classification and Rule 5 of the National Motor Freight Classification. †Shipper's imprint in lieu of stamp, not a part of bill of lading approved by the Interstate Commerce Commission.

_____ Shipper, Per _____

_____ Agent, Per _____

Permanent post-office address of shipper

Form No. 35-643 © , 1986 UNZCO 190 Baldwin Ave., Jersey City, NJ 07306 - (800) 631-3098 - (201) 795-5400

If lower charges result, the agreed or declared value of the within described containers is hereby specifically stated to be not exceeding 50 cents per pound per article.

This is to certify that the above-named materials are properly classified, described, packaged, marked and labeled and are in proper condition for transportation according to the applicable regulations of the Department of Transportation

_____ SIGNATURE

1

person; (*c*) the rate of storage and handling charges; and (*d*) a description of the goods or of the packages containing them. A warehouseman is liable to a good faith purchaser of the warehouse receipt for any misdescription of the goods unless the receipt conspicuously qualifies the description with a statement such as "contents, condition, and quantity unknown."

INCOTERMS

In drafting their sales contract, the buyer and seller should not underestimate the importance of including *trade terms* that define their respective obligations over the delivery of the goods. Specifically, they should decide in advance: who bears the risk of loss if the goods are lost or damaged while in transit; who is responsible for purchasing insurance coverage; who must pay for the loading, carriage, and unloading of the goods; and who is responsible for securing export and import clearance.

To minimize uncertainties over the parties' duties, the International Chamber of Commerce established an elaborate set of common shipping terms that the parties may incorporate in their contract. However, these trade terms, known as **Incoterms**, do not enter the sales contract automatically. Thus, the agreement should specifically note their applicability.

The 13 Incoterms are divided into four distinct categories: departure terms, main carriage unpaid terms, main carriage paid terms, and arrival terms. This section examines the fundamental features of each of these classifications. However, this discussion of Incoterms is sandwiched between an exploration of two related issues that are not covered by Incoterms: the allocation of delivery obligations when the contract does not include trade terms and the allocation of risk of loss when goods are sold during transport.

Failure to Designate Trade Terms

When a sales contract contains no explicit provisions apportioning the risks and obligations of the parties, it is left to the domestic legal systems of each country to make these determinations. Basically, the court must decide whether the agreement is a shipment contract or a destination contract.

Shipment Contract

In a **shipment contract**, the title to the goods and the risk of loss passes to the buyer when the seller has properly delivered the goods to the carrier for shipment. A shipment contract generally requires the seller to send the goods by carrier to the buyer, but does not obligate the seller to guarantee their delivery. When the parties fail to specify the delivery obligations of the parties, U.S. courts presume they intended to create a shipment contract.

Destination Contract

If the parties do not specifically agree to a **destination contract,** the courts consider the agreement to be a shipment contract. Under a destination contract, the seller agrees to deliver the goods to a particular destination and to bear the risk of loss until the tender of delivery actually occurs. Thus, title to the goods remains with the seller until the goods have reached the specified destination. The category of Incoterms entitled *arrival terms* (discussed below) are examples of destination contracts.

Departure

Ex Works, ex Factory, ex Warehouse—EXW

Of all the Incoterms, the departure terms place the minimum obligation on the seller. **EXW** requires only that the seller make the goods available to the buyer at the seller's premises (i.e., works, factory, warehouse). The buyer bears all costs and risks after the goods have been made available to it.

Main Carriage Not Paid by Seller

Free Carrier—FCA

Under the **FCA** term, the seller's obligations are met when the goods are cleared for export and handed over to the carrier designated by the buyer at the location indicated in the contract. Normally, the seller is not required to arrange the transportation with the carrier. However, if the buyer requests assistance in this regard, or if it is customary practice for the seller to assist, the seller must arrange the transportation unless it promptly notifies the buyer of its refusal. This term was specifically designed to meet the needs of container transport.

Free Alongside Ship—FAS

Under **FAS,** the seller must deliver the goods at the named port of shipment. Its obligations are completed when the goods arrive at the wharf or in lighters alongside the ship. From that point on, the buyer bears all costs and risks. Thus, the buyer is responsible for export clearance as well as freight and insurance.

Free on Board—FOB

Basically, under this trade term, the seller's obligations end once the goods have passed over the ship's rail at the port of shipment designated in the sales contract. However, **FOB** also requires the seller to obtain export clearance and to promptly notify the buyer when the goods have been delivered on board. After that point, it places all freight costs and risks of loss on the buyer.

Main Carriage Paid by Seller

Cost and Freight—CFR

Under this shipment contract, the seller must arrange for the contract of carriage and pay the freight to the designated port of destination. Thus, **CFR** requires the seller to deliver the goods on board the ship and to provide export clearance. The risk of loss passes to the buyer once the goods cross the ship's rail and it is the buyer's responsibility to insure the goods after that point. The buyer must also pay any unloading costs that were not included in the freight charges. CFR can be used only for sea and inland waterway transport.

PHILLIPS PUERTO RICO CORE v. TRADAX PETROLEUM LTD.
782 F.2d 314 (2d Cir. 1985)

■ **FACTS** Phillips Puerto Rico Core agreed to buy approximately 30,000 metric tons of naphtha from Tradax. The contract stated that the sale was to be *CFR Guayama, Puerto Rico,* and that shipment was to be made between September 20 and 28. No dates for delivery were specified. Tradax arranged to have the naphtha transported on the *Oxy Trader,* an integrated tug barge. The *Oxy Trader* loaded the naphtha and embarked for Puerto Rico on September 24. Four hours after the vessel had begun its transoceanic journey, Tradax learned that several newspaper articles had been questioning the safety of using integrated tug barges for deep-sea transport. The following day, the Coast Guard at Gibraltar notified Tradax that the *Oxy Trader* would not be permitted to proceed to Puerto Rico because it was believed to be unsuitable for transoceanic journeys. When it learned the delivery would be delayed several months, Phillips refused to pay for the naphtha and notified Tradax it was terminating the contract.

■ **ISSUE** May Phillips legally avoid paying Tradax because of the detention of the vessel?

■ **DECISION** No. As a CFR seller, Tradax had the duty to deliver the naphtha to an appropriate carrier with which it had contracted for shipment. In return, Phillips was contractually obliged to pay for the naphtha when presented with the shipping documents. Phillips was not relieved of its contractual obligation because of Tradax's selection of the *Oxy Trader.* Incoterms requires that a CFR seller contract for the carriage of goods in a seagoing vessel of the type normally used for the transportation of goods. Although the integrated tug barge was of novel design, this feature did not disqualify the *Oxy Trader* as a ship that might normally be used for transport. The vessel had safely sailed on other transoceanic trips. Thus, there is no basis for concluding Tradax should have known before the vessel left port that it was likely to be found unsafe. Tradax's risks and responsibilities ended and Phillips' began once the naphtha was loaded on the vessel.

Cost, Insurance, and Freight—CIF

CIF is the most widely used trade term found in international sales transactions. It requires the seller to arrange the contract of carriage, pay the freight charges, load the goods on board, provide export clearance, and purchase insurance that covers the goods until they cross the ship's rail at the port of destination. Thus, this term gives the seller the same obligations as under CFR with the addition of the responsibility to purchase insurance. The insurance must cover at least the contractual price of the goods plus 10 percent and be payable in the currency of the contract. Although the seller purchases the insurance, the policy is payable to the buyer since the risk of loss passes to the buyer once the goods cross the ship's rail at the port of shipment. CIF can be used only for sea and inland waterway transport.

Carriage Paid to—CPT

Unlike CFR and CIF, this trade term can be used for road, rail, air, and sea transport or any combination of them involved in multimodal transport. **CPT** gives the seller the duty of arranging the contract of carriage, paying the freight to the named destination, and providing export clearance. The seller's obligations end once it has delivered conforming goods to the custody of the first (or only) carrier. At that point, the risk of loss passes to the buyer.

Carriage and Insurance Paid to—CIP

This trade term also is appropriate for multimodal transport. **CIP** gives a seller the same obligations it had under CPT with the addition of a duty to purchase insurance for the benefit of the buyer. The insurance coverage requirements are the same as those discussed in connection with the CIF term. The risk of loss passes to the buyer once the seller has delivered the goods to the custody of the first (or only) carrier.

Arrival

Delivered at Frontier—DAF

Unlike the previous Incoterms, the arrival terms are destination contracts that extend the seller's delivery responsibility to the country of destination. Under **DAF,** the seller has fulfilled its obligations once the goods are available at the customs border of the designated country of destination. The risk of loss does not pass to the buyer until the goods have reached that frontier and have been placed at its disposal. The buyer must secure any import clearance necessary to bring the goods into the country of destination.

Delivered ex Ship—DES

This Incoterm can be used only for sea or inland waterway transport. **DES** obligates the seller to tender delivery of the goods to the buyer on board a ship that has arrived in the port of the country of destination. The risk of loss passes to the buyer in the port of destination once the goods are placed at its disposal on board the ship. The buyer is responsible for unloading the ship and clearing the goods through customs.

Delivered ex Quay—DEQ

DEQ is used only for sea and inland waterway transport. It requires the seller to make the goods available to the buyer, cleared through customs, at the wharf (quay) at the port of destination. Thus, the seller must pay all loading, carriage, and unloading costs. The risk of loss does not pass to the buyer until the goods are at its disposal on the wharf.

Delivered Duty Unpaid—DDU

This arrival term requires the seller to deliver the goods at a named place in the country of destination. Under **DDU,** the seller must provide export clearance and bears the costs and risks involved in transporting the goods to the delivery point in the importing country. However, the buyer must arrange import clearance and is responsible for all costs associated with clearing the goods through customs. Risk of loss passes to the buyer when the goods are made available to it at the named place in the importing country.

CONCEPT SUMMARY
Incoterms

Group	Term	Contract Type	Carrier Type	Seller's Responsibilities	Buyer's Responsibilities
E Group Departure	EXW	N/A	N/A	Makes goods available at seller's premises	All costs and risks after goods are available
F Group Main carriage *not* paid by seller	FCA	Shipment	All	Deliver goods to carrier; export clearance; assist in arranging carriage if asked	All costs and risks after carrier receives goods
	FAS	Shipment	Sea	Deliver goods at wharf alongside ship in exporting country	All costs and risks after goods reach wharf
	FOB	Shipment	Sea	Load goods on ship; export clearance	All costs and risks after goods are loaded
C Group Main carriage paid by seller	CFR	Shipment	Sea	Load goods; export clearance; arrange and pay freight	Risk passes after goods are loaded
	CIF	Shipment	Sea	Load goods; export clearance; arrange and pay freight; buy insurance for voyage	Risk passes after goods are loaded
	CPT	Shipment	All	Deliver goods to carrier; export clearance; arrange and pay freight	Risk passes after goods reach carrier
	CIP	Shipment	All	Deliver goods to carrier; export clearance; arrange and pay freight; buy insurance for carriage	Risk passes after goods reach carrier
D Group Arrival	DAF	Destination	All	Deliver goods to customs border of importing country	Risk passes when goods are available at customs border
	DES	Destination	Sea	Deliver goods to buyer on board ship at port of importing country	Risk passes when goods available on board ship in port of importing country
	DEQ	Destination	Sea	Deliver goods at wharf alongside ship at port of importing country; export and import clearance	Risk passes when goods available at wharf
	DDU	Destination	All	Deliver goods at named location in importing country	Risk passes when goods available at named location; import clearance
	DDP	Destination	All	Deliver goods at named location in importing country; import clearance	Risk passes when goods available at named location

Delivered Duty Paid—DDP

This final Incoterm, **DDP,** places the maximum obligation on the seller. It requires the seller to place the goods at the buyer's disposal at the named location in the importing country. Thus, the seller must arrange loading, carriage, and unloading, as well as both export and import clearance. Risk of loss does not pass to the buyer until the goods are made available to it at the named destination.

Goods Sold in Transit

While Incoterms define the obligations of the parties in transactions involving one seller and one buyer, the realities of modern global trade are not always that simple. Commodities, such as oil and grain, frequently are bought and sold several times while they are still at sea. When such a *string of sales* occurs, a question arises as to when the risk of loss passes to the new buyers. Neither Incoterms nor the Uniform Commercial Code resolve this issue. However, the Convention on Contracts for the International Sale of Goods (discussed in Chapter 5) suggests that repurchasers of goods sold in transit should assume the risks borne by their immediate sellers unless that reseller knew or should have known the goods already had been lost or damaged.

CARRIAGE OF GOODS BY ROAD AND RAIL

When transporting goods by air or sea, the first leg of the journey often is by road or rail. And then, after the merchandise arrives at a foreign airport or seaport, it is quite likely the final delivery will be by ground carrier. Thus, most overseas deliveries incorporate some form of ground transportation.

Liability of U.S. Ground Carriers

U.S. regulations governing the carriage of goods by road or rail have their roots in the common law. Traditionally, those common law rules imposed almost absolute liability on common carriers whenever goods were lost or damaged while in transit. The carrier was excused from liability only if it could establish that the loss or damage was caused by an act of God, an act of a public enemy, an act or order of the government, an act of the shipper, or the nature of the goods themselves. However, over time, carriers began to limit their liability by issuing bills of lading that included provisions limiting their common law liability. Because of their superior bargaining strength, most carriers were able to impose these conditions on shippers.

Congress enacted the Interstate Commerce Act, in part, to prevent the abuses perpetrated by ground carriers. The regulatory framework made ground carriers liable for any loss or damage except for those specifically exempted. Most carriers relieve themselves from liability for the traditional common law defenses (acts of God and public enemies, acts of the government, negligence of the shipper in packing or loading, and inherent defects in the goods). While ground carriers may not relieve themselves from all liability, they may negotiate with shippers to limit the amount of their liability. However, ground carriers may not reduce their liability unless they pay some consideration to the shipper in return. They generally do this by offering the shipper a lower shipping rate in return for the shipper's agreement to lower the claimed value of the goods. This means a shipper can insist on the carrier assuming liability for the full value of the goods if it is willing to pay a higher shipping charge. The Interstate Commerce Commission must approve these arrangements and the lowered valuation must appear on the face of the bill of lading.

CALVIN KLEIN LTD. v. TRYLON TRUCKING CORP.
892 F.2d 191 (2d Cir. 1989)

■ **FACTS** Calvin Klein, a New York clothing company, used the services of Trylon Trucking hundreds of times to transport goods from New York airports to its facilities. After completing each delivery carriage, Trylon would forward an invoice to Calvin Klein that contained a provision limiting Trylon's liability to not *"more than $50 on any shipment . . . unless a greater value is declared, in writing, upon receipt at time of shipment and charge for such greater value paid, or agreed to be paid, by shipper."* A shipment of 2,833 blouses from Hong Kong arrived at John F. Kennedy International Airport, and Calvin Klein arranged to have Trylon pick it up. After picking up the shipment, Trylon's driver stole both the truck and the blouses. When Calvin Klein sought $150,000 in damages (the alleged value of the blouses), Trylon, while admitting it was grossly negligent in its hiring and supervision of the driver, claimed its liability was limited to $50. Calvin Klein argued the limitation clause was not enforceable because: (1) no agreement existed between it and Trylon to limit liability; and (2) even if an agreement existed, public policy would prevent its enforcement because of Trylon's gross negligence.

■ **ISSUE** Is Trylon liable for more than $50?

■ **DECISION** No. A ground carrier is strictly liable for the loss of goods in its custody. Where the loss is not due to excepted causes (acts of God or public enemies, inherent nature of the goods, or shipper's fault), it is immaterial whether the carrier is negligent or not. The shipper and the carrier may contract to limit the carrier's liability to an amount agreed to by the parties, as long as the language of the limitation is clear, the shipper is aware of the terms of the limitation, and the shipper can change the terms by indicating the true value of the goods being shipped. Such a limitation is valid and enforceable despite the carrier's negligence. These parties' past behavior clearly establishes the existence of such a limitation. Carriers can contract with their shipping customers on the amount of liability each party will bear for the loss of a shipment, regardless of the amount of carrier negligence. Calvin Klein was aware of the terms and was free to adjust the limitation upon a written declaration of the value of a given shipment, but failed to do so with the shipment at issue here. The fact that the limitation was so low is immaterial because Calvin Klein had the opportunity to declare a higher value. Commercial entities can easily negotiate the degree of risk each party will bear and which party will bear the cost of insurance.

Liability of European Ground Carriers

International truck carriage throughout most of Europe is governed by the Convention on the Contract for International Carriage of Goods by Road (CMR). The liability rules for rail transport are encompassed in the International Convention Concerning the Carriage of Goods by Rail (CIM). It has been adopted by most European nations, the former Soviet republics, and several Middle Eastern nations. Under the CMR and the CIM, the shipper and the carrier draw up three copies of a **consignment note.** The shipper and the carrier each retain one copy, and the third is delivered with the goods. Unlike a negotiable bill of lading, a consignment note is not a document of title and it is not negotiable.

Both conventions permit a ground carrier to defend against liability by showing that any loss or damages resulted from the negligence of the shipper, inherent defects in the goods, or other circumstances beyond the carrier's control. If a carrier can establish that one of the above defenses might apply, it avoids liability unless the owner of the goods can affirmatively rebut its defense. The liability of truck carriers is limited to about $4.25 per pound (for rail carriers it is about $8.50 per pound) unless the shipper declares and pays for a higher value. Notwithstanding these limits, willful misconduct by a ground carrier or its employees makes the carrier liable for the full value of lost or damaged goods.

CARRIAGE OF GOODS BY AIR

U.S. Domestic Carriers

Domestic air transporters in the United States are subject to the traditional common carrier liability for lost or damaged goods. That is, they are liable unless they can prove the loss was caused by acts of God or public enemies, something inherent in the nature of the goods, or improper packing or loading by the shipper. Unlike ground carriers, U.S. air carriers are not required to issue a bill of lading. Instead, they normally present the shipper with an **air waybill**. This document is similar to a bill of lading in that it serves as a receipt for the goods and also is the contract of carriage between the carrier and the shipper. However, unlike a bill of lading, the air waybill is not a document of title and is not negotiable. Domestic air carriers may limit the amount of their liability for cargo; however, this limitation need not be shown on the air waybill if it is on file with the tariff they have filed with the Civil Aeronautics Board. In these tariffs, carriers frequently limit their liability to no more than $50 or 50 cents per pound for shipments weighing more than 100 pounds.

Warsaw Convention

The United States and most of its trading partners are parties to the **Warsaw Convention**. This international treaty automatically regulates air carriage between two nations, each of which has adopted the convention. However, most U.S. carriers subject all shipments to the terms of the Warsaw Convention by incorporating it in the contract of carriage. The document of carriage under the Warsaw Convention is known as the *air consignment note*. It is similar to the air waybill and the consignment note issued by European ground carriers.

International air carriers governed by the Warsaw Convention have three defenses to liability for lost or damaged cargo. First, they can prove the loss occurred despite taking all reasonable precautions. (They were not negligent.) Second, they may show the damages resulted from negligence by the pilot in the handling of the aircraft. (This seldom is claimed because of the repercussions it might have on personal injury lawsuits.) Third, they may establish that the loss or damage was caused by the negligence of the shipper.

Damage claims are limited to approximately $8.50 per pound unless the shipper has paid for greater coverage. The carrier may not rely on this limitation, however, if the loss was occasioned by the willful misconduct of the air carrier or its employees. Further, the air consignment note must state that the carriage is governed by the terms of the original Warsaw Convention or the liability limits do not apply.

Amended Warsaw Convention

Numerous nations (but not the United States) have adopted the **amended Warsaw Convention**. It governs international carriage between two countries that both have ratified its provisions. If both countries have adopted the original convention (the United States and the United Kingdom) but only one is a party to the amended convention (the United Kingdom), the original convention governs the shipment.

Under the amended convention, the air consignment note (the document of carriage) has been renamed the *air waybill*. Failure to issue an air waybill or to indicate that the carriage is governed by the amended Warsaw Convention prevents the carrier from limiting its liability to the $8.50 per pound level established by the treaty. The terms of the amended treaty vary from the original version in several respects. First, it does not relieve the carrier from liability for losses caused by negligent handling of the aircraft by the pilot. Second, it allows courts to award claimants their legal costs in actions they pursue to recover from carriers. Third, it strips an air carrier of the liability limitations only if it commits willful acts done with the knowledge that damage probably would result.

CARRIAGE OF GOODS BY SEA

Ocean carriers frequently encounter problems of a different nature and severity than both ground and air carriers. For instance, sea cargo is particularly likely to be exposed to water and salt, as well as violent jostling from high winds and waves. Further, the distances involved in ocean travel are long and the speed of the ships is slow in comparison to ground and air carriage. For these reasons, the regulation of international sea carriage has developed somewhat independently of the other forms of transportation.

The Harter Act

The liability of U.S. sea carriers originally was determined by the rules governing common carriers. Over time, however, carriers began to include provisions in their bills of lading that relieved them from liability for their negligence. Courts were split on whether or not to enforce these provisions.

In 1893, the U.S. Congress enacted legislation, the *Harter Act,* that made liability rules governing sea carriage more certain and simultaneously offered a better balance between the interests of carriers and shippers. Specifically, the statute prohibits carriers from using the bill of lading to relieve themselves from liability for their negligence, fault, or failure in the proper loading, stowage, custody, care, or delivery of cargo. Further, it imposes on carriers the responsibility to exercise due diligence in ensuring that their vessels were seaworthy. Finally, it exempts ocean carriers from liability for faults or errors in the navigation or management of the vessel when the carrier exercised due diligence and provided a seaworthy and properly manned ship. Today the Harter Act still governs domestic ocean carriage between U.S. ports.

 **ETHICAL IMPLICATIONS**   Is it ethical for carriers to use their superior bargaining strength to limit their liability to shippers?

COGSA

The Harter Act was so well received by the major trading nations of the world that it provided the basis for multilateral discussions on sea carrier liability. Those unification efforts culminated in the creation of an international convention known as the *Hague Rules*. The United States ratified this convention and enacted it into law as the *Carriage of Goods by Sea Act* (**COGSA**). As it now stands, the Harter Act governs domestic water carriage (from one U.S. port to another) while COGSA regulates overseas shipments from the time goods are loaded aboard an oceangoing ship until they are discharged in a foreign port.

COGSA prevents carriers from disclaiming liability for negligence in their bills of lading. Further, it requires them to exercise *due diligence* to make their vessels *seaworthy* and to safely load, stow, carry, and discharge cargo. If the carrier meets these requirements, it is exonerated from liability for loss or damage resulting from the following causes:

a. Acts, neglect, or default of the master or the servants of the carrier in the navigation or management of the ship.

b. Fire, unless caused by the actual fault of the carrier.

c. Perils of the sea.

d. Acts of God, war, or public enemies.

e. Legal seizure or quarantine of the ship or its cargo.

f. Act or omission of shippers or owners of goods.

g. Strikes, riots, or civil commotions.

h. Saving or attempting to save life or property at sea.

i. Loss or damage arising from an inherent defect or quality of the goods.

j. Insufficiency of packing or inadequacy of labeling.

k. Latent defects not discoverable by due diligence.

l. Any other cause arising without the fault of the carrier or its agents. (The burden of proof is on the carrier to show that its negligence did not contribute to the loss or damage.)

Burdens of Proof

COGSA places the initial burden on cargo claimants to show that their cargo was lost or damaged while in the custody of the carrier. This burden is met if the carrier issued a clean bill of lading and the cargo was not delivered or arrived at its destination in a damaged condition. The burden then shifts to the carrier to establish its defenses by convincing the court that the cause of the loss or damage fell within one of the COGSA exceptions listed above. If the carrier succeeds, the burden shifts back to the claimants to prove the vessel was unseaworthy and the unseaworthiness was at least a contributing cause of the loss. Even if this is established, the carrier can still avoid liability if it demonstrates it exercised due diligence in loading, stowing, keeping, and discharging the goods and in attempting to make its vessel seaworthy.

Per Package Limitation

A key feature of COGSA is its provision limiting a carrier's liability to *$500 per package* or customary freight unit unless the shipper declares a higher value for the goods on the bill of lading. Of course, the shipper is required to pay extra for this additional coverage. (Many carriers have voluntarily raised their liability limits to $1,000.) However, unlike the rules governing road and rail transportation, shippers and sea carriers may not agree to value the cargo at less than $500 per package.

Although COGSA limits a sea carrier's liability to $500 per package, the statute does not clearly define what constitutes a package. With the advent of containerized transportation, the absence of a precise definition has caused some uncertainty. Frequently, these containers are semi-truck trailers that have been lifted off their wheels and stacked on the vessel. They are then transferred to another set of wheels at the port of destination. Containers create a great deal of confusion because each one may be filled with numerous packages of various sizes and shapes. When a loss occurs, the carrier attempts to show the container was a single package and thereby confine its liability to $500 per container. The owner of the goods, on the other hand, claims up to $500 for each package within the container. While courts differ in their resolution of these disputes, the following case illustrates the approach followed by the majority of U.S. courts.

MONICA TEXTILE CORPORATION v. S.S. TANA
952 F.2d 636 (2d Cir. 1991)

■ **FACTS** Monica Textile Corporation engaged the *S.S. Tana* to transport a single 20-foot shipping container from Africa to the United States. On the face of the bill of lading, the "DESCRIPTION OF GOODS" column stated the contents of the container (which Monica had stuffed and sealed) consisted of 76 bales of cloth. The "NO. of PKGS." column had the number "1" typed in, and a line labeled "TOTAL NUMBER OF PACKAGES OR UNITS IN WORDS (Total Column 19 [No. of Pkgs. column])" had the word "ONE" typed in. On the reverse side of the carrier's bill of lading, Clause 2 provided that: "The word *package* shall include each container where the container is stuffed and sealed by the merchant, although the shipper may have furnished in the Particulars herein the contents of such sealed container." Clause 11 stated in relevant part:

> Where container is stuffed by shipper and the container is sealed, the carrier's liability will be limited to $500 with respect to the contents of each container, except when the shipper declares value on the face hereof and pays additional charges on such declared value. The freight charged on sealed containers when no higher valuation is

declared by the shipper is based on the value of $500 per container.

When the goods were damaged in transit, Monica sought to recover $500 for each of the 76 bales. The carrier replied it owed no more than $500 because the bill of lading articulated an agreement between the parties to treat the container as a single package.

■ **ISSUE** Is the shipping container a single package for purposes of COGSA's $500 per package limitation on carrier liability?

■ **DECISION** No. Unhappily, neither COGSA nor its legislative history provides any clue as to the meaning of *package*. Despite the difficulties this lack of guidance engendered, courts managed to muddle through this oft-litigated issue by generally deferring to the intent of the contracting parties when that intent was both clear and reasonable. Past decisions in noncontainer cases have established a bright-line rule that holds that the number of packages is the number appearing in the "No. of Pkgs."

column of the bill of lading, unless other evidence of the parties' intent plainly contradicts the applicability of that number or unless the item referred to by that number is incapable of qualifying as a COGSA package. COGSA, however, requires that container cases be viewed through a different prism. Courts should have a genuine reluctance to treat a container as a package because to do so violates the fundamental nature of COGSA by permitting carriers to limit their liability unduly. The better rule holds that where the contents of a container are disclosed in the bill of lading, the container is not a COGSA package for purposes of applying the $500 per package limitation. Courts should deviate from this finding only where the bill of lading discloses that the parties agreed to make the container the package in terms that are explicit and unequivocal. Because this bill of lading is ambiguous on its face and Clauses 2 and 11 (both of which appear on the reverse side) appear to be unbargained for, it cannot be stated that Monica unequivocally agreed to treat the container as a COGSA package.

Deviation

Sea carriers lose the protection of COGSA's liability limits if they engage in an unreasonable **deviation** from the contract of carriage. Long before the enactment of COGSA, courts recognized that sea carriers had a responsibility to proceed on their voyage in the direct, shortest, and usual route to the port of destination without unnecessary deviation. This doctrine originally arose in response to complaints by marine insurers that a geographic deviation in a carrier's normal route would saddle insurers with different and unexpected risks. However, by the time COGSA was drafted the concept had expanded to include any significant variation from customary conduct that substantially increased the risk of loss or damage. Nongeographic deviations are known as *quasi-deviations*. Courts commonly consider it to be a quasi-deviation for an oceangoing vessel to transport cargo on its deck unless the shipper expressly consents to this practice in the bill of lading.

Himalaya Clauses

COGSA's liability limitations apply to carriers but not to stevedores and other third parties involved in the handling of cargo. As a result, owners of lost or damaged cargo frequently file claims against these noncarriers to circumvent the damage limitations. However, COGSA permits carriers to contractually extend their liability limitations to their employees, agents, and independent contractors. This is accomplished by including liability extension clauses, known as **Himalaya Clauses,** in the bill of lading. U.S. courts narrowly construe these provisions, and some countries that are parties to the Hague Rules do not enforce them at all.

■

MORI SEIKI USA v. M/V ALLIGATOR TRIUMPH
990 F.2d 444 (9th Cir. 1993)

■ **FACTS** Mori Seiki was the owner of a precision lathe that was being transported from Japan to Texas by Mitsui O.S.K. Lines. The lathe was damaged after it was unloaded from an ocean vessel at the Port of Los Angeles but before it was released from the seaport. The Los Angeles seaport operator was Trans Pacific Container, and the stevedore services firm that actually unloaded and handled the lathe was Marine Terminals Corporation (MTC). Section 5 of Mitsui's bill of lading stated in relevant part:

> The carrier shall be entitled to subcontract on any terms the whole or any part of the handling, storage, or carriage of the goods and any and all duties whatsoever undertaken by the carrier in relation to the goods. . . . Every such servant, agent, and subcontractor shall have the benefit of all provisions herein for the benefit of the carrier as if such provisions were expressly for their benefit.

Mori Seiki filed suit against MTC, claiming the Himalaya Clause found in Section 5 did not extend to the stevedore because it was a subcontractor of Trans Pacific, not of Mitsui.

■ **ISSUE** Does this Himalaya Clause limit the stevedore's liability to $500?

■ **DECISION** Yes. Whether a bill of lading extends limitations of liability to stevedores depends on whether the clarity of the language used expresses such to be the understanding of the contracting parties. Further, whether an entity is an intended beneficiary of a Himalaya Clause depends on the contractual relation between the party seeking protection and the ocean carrier, as well as the nature of the services performed compared to the carrier's responsibilities under the carriage contract. There is no question that MTC's unloading of the lathe was directly related to the carrier's responsibilities under the carriage contract. Further, there is a contractual relationship between Mitsui and MTC. Trans Pacific was acting on behalf of Mitsui when it hired MTC. This is reinforced by the fact that the stevedore service agreement applied only to Mitsui vessels and that MTC invoiced Mitsui, in care of Trans Pacific, for the services of unloading the lathe.

Hague–Visby Rules

Many of the major trading nations became dissatisfied with the Hague Rules' (COGSA's) per package liability limits and the difficulties in determining precisely what constituted a package. Accordingly, an amended version of the Hague Rules, known as the **Hague–Visby Rules**, has now been adopted by a majority of the world's shipping nations. The amended rules apply to ocean carriage between two adopting nations. A shipment between a party to the Hague Rules and a country that has ratified the Hague–Visby Rules would be governed by the Hague Rules. The United States has not adopted the Hague–Visby Rules, although several U.S. carriers have voluntarily incorporated those terms into their bills of lading.

Specifically, the Hague–Visby Rules provide that the number of packages or units enumerated in the bill of lading as packed in a larger article of transport (e.g., container, pallet) is the number of packages for liability limitation purposes. Further, they increased a carrier's liability to over $800 per package or approximately $1 per pound, whichever is higher. Finally, the Hague–Visby Rules deny a carrier the right to limit its liability whenever the cargo is damaged by intentional or reckless acts committed by the carrier with knowledge that damage would ensue.

COMPLAINT OF TECOMAR, S.A.
765 F.Supp. 1150 (S.D. N.Y. 1991)

■ **FACTS** In 1987, the *M/V Tuxpan,* an oceangoing vessel owned by Tecomar, mysteriously disappeared with her crew of 27 and cargo worth $22 million. She had departed from Germany for a final destination in Mexico with intermediate stops in Belgium and the United States. Over the course of its five-year lifetime, the *Tuxpan* sustained over 100 cracks to its tanktops, wing tanks, bulkheads, shell plating, deck plating, and hatch covers. The rules of the vessel's classification society, Germanischer Lloyd (GL), require shipowners to report cracks and other defects to GL's surveyors. If a shipowner fails to abide by these rules, GL may temporarily suspend the vessel's regularly scheduled service or permanently withdraw the vessel's classification certificate. Without a classification certificate, a shipowner cannot obtain insurance for the vessel and, thus, the vessel loses all commercial value. Despite these rules, Tecomar regularly concealed the cracks and attempted repairs from the GL inspectors. The ship also was plagued by chronic engine problems, which Tecomar failed to report. The owners postponed necessary repairs to avoid disrupting the vessel's busy schedule. On its final voyage, the *Tuxpan* encountered 50 mile per hour winds and 30- to 50-foot waves in a severe storm in the North Atlantic Ocean. The owners of the lost cargo claimed Tecomar had failed to exercise due diligence in attempting to make the vessel seaworthy.

■ **ISSUE** Did the carrier fail to exercise due diligence in making the vessel seaworthy?

■ **DECISION** Yes. The cargo that was bound for the United States is governed by COGSA, while the cargo that was bound for Mexico is governed by the Hague–Visby Rules as interpreted by the country in which the cargo was loaded. Thus, the cargo that was loaded in Germany is governed by the German interpretation, while the goods that were loaded in Belgium are regulated by the Belgian version of the Hague–Visby Rules. Under both COGSA and the Hague–Visby Rules, the legal issues of this case are resolved in the following manner. First, the cargo claimants have met their burden

of establishing that Tecomar received the cargo in undamaged condition because they hold clean bills of lading. Second, Tecomar has failed to show that the weather encountered by the ship constituted a peril of the sea that excused it from liability for the loss. While the storm was extremely severe, it is expectable to encounter inhospitable weather conditions in the North Atlantic during the winter. Only unexpected storms will exonerate a carrier for a loss under the peril of the sea exception. Third, even if the *Tuxpan* had experienced conditions severe enough to constitute a peril of the sea, the cargo claimants have met their burden of proving the vessel was unseaworthy at the commencement of its voyage and this condition contributed to the loss. One symptom of a ship's unseaworthiness is the presence of cracks. Fourth, Tecomar might have avoided its liability for the unseaworthiness if it had shown it exercised due diligence in attempting to make the vessel seaworthy. Due diligence consists of whatever a reasonably competent vessel owner would do under similar circumstances. Failure to make necessary repairs in order to maintain a busy schedule clearly demonstrates a lack of due diligence. Under the Hague–Visby Rules, the carrier cannot avail itself of the package limitations when it has engaged in reckless conduct with the knowledge that damage would probably result. Tecomar's continuous course of reckless behavior clearly meets this test. Accordingly, the package limitation on Tecomar's liability for the cargo loaded in Germany and Belgium and destined for Mexico is denied. This is not the case for the cargo loaded in Germany and Belgium and bound for the United States. COGSA is silent on the issue of recklessness; thus, the $500 per package limitation is not abolished by a carrier's reckless conduct.

Hamburg Rules

Many of the world's developing nations complained that traditional maritime law discriminated against their national interests. They registered their complaints in the United Nations and, through the United Nations Conference on Trade and Development (UNCTAD), drew up a radically different liability scheme for oceangoing carriers. This new treaty, known as the **Hamburg Rules,** went into force in 1992 after it was ratified by the 20th country. None of the major trading nations of the world, including the United States, has adopted this treaty.

The Hamburg Rules place liability on the carrier for lost or damaged goods unless it can prove it or its employees and agents took all measures reasonably necessary to avoid both the occurrence and its consequences. This approach is premised on the idea that it is easier for a carrier to prove it was not negligent than for a shipper to prove it was. Unlike both COGSA (the Hague Rules) and the Hague-Visby Rules,

FIGURE 6–3

Percentages of U.S. Trade with Members of the Major Conventions on Sea Carriage (1993)

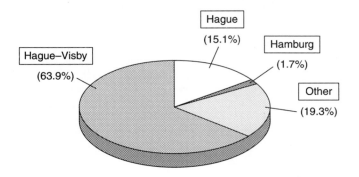

Source: Oversight Hearing of the Subcommittee on Merchant Marine, June 24, 1992, Serial No. 102-101.

the Hamburg Rules cover deck cargo. They have also raised a carrier's liability to approximately $1,000 per package. The Hamburg Rules share the Hague-Visby definition of a package and the policy of abolishing the liability limits when a carrier acts recklessly with the knowledge that damages are likely to result.

Charterparties

The regulatory schemes for oceangoing vessels discussed above pertained to contracts for the carriage of goods at sea that are evidenced by bills of lading. Contracts contained in **charterparties** are another type of international sea transport. These arrangements are commonly used for shipping bulk commodities such as chemicals, coal, grains, oil, ore, and sugar. There are two primary types of charterparties. The first, a *voyage charterparty,* occurs when a shipper leases the entire ship to transport a specified cargo on an agreed on itinerary. The second, known as a *time charterparty,* arises when the shipper hires the ship for a time period during which it may sail the ship to any destination and carry any cargo not forbidden by the contract between the shipper and the shipowner.

The charterparty, rather than a bill of lading, is the governing contract between the shipowner and the shipper (the charterer). The bill of lading generally serves only as a receipt. However, if a charterparty negotiates a negotiable bill of lading to another party, the shipowner is governed by the terms of the bill of lading unless the bill itself gave notice that the terms of the charterparty applied.

The shipowner must provide the charterparty with a seaworthy vessel that is properly manned and equipped. While shipowners also may be liable for negligently loading, handling, and discharging the cargo, the parties often negotiate the terms of the charterparty, including the liability issues. Because shippers who employ charterparties usually have sufficient bargaining strength to protect themselves, the regulatory rules and liability provisions discussed above (COGSA, the Hague-Visby Rules, etc.) generally do not apply to charterparties. However, those rules govern the terms of bills of lading that are negotiated to third parties.

Marine Insurance

Shippers have two options for offsetting the carrier's liability limits in contracts for the carriage of goods by sea. First, they may declare a higher value for the cargo and pay the higher freight charges associated with it. Second, they may purchase insurance to protect against loss or damage during transit. When cargo is lost or damaged, the owner's ability to recover from its insurer turns on the precise terms of the insurance contract. Cargo owners must understand these agreements because most courts place the burden of proving coverage on the insured. Three basic types of losses are covered by marine insurance policies: total, general average, and particular average.

Total Losses

When a cargo owner is insured against a **total loss,** it may recover the full amount stated in the policy. Total losses may arise in several ways. For instance, the goods might be missing due to destruction by fire or they may have disappeared along with their vessel. Or they may be unfit for use, such as grain that has been contaminated by seawater. The insured generally cannot recover for a total loss unless it presents the following documents: evidence of the loss: invoices (showing the value of the lost goods); a copy of the insurance policy or certificate; the original bills of lading (showing the goods were part of the vessel's cargo); and a letter of subrogation that permits the insurance company to sue the party who actually caused the loss.

General Average Losses

Historically, an ocean voyage was considered to be a joint venture involving the carrier and the individual cargo owners. Thus, if part of the cargo was voluntarily sacrificed to save the rest, the owners of the undamaged cargo would prorate the loss among themselves. This concept, known as **general average,** frequently arises when the carrier jettisons some of its cargo to lighten the load during emergency conditions. (In maritime law, the term *average* means *loss.*) A general average loss will not arise unless there exists an imminent danger to the vessel, cargo, or crew that cannot be avoided without sacrificing part of the cargo.

Particular Average Losses

Most cargo losses today stem from breakage due to improper loading or stowage, contamination from rats or seawater, theft, or severe damage to the vessel itself (sinking, burning, stranding, or collision). When the damages from these causes are partial, they are called **particular average** losses. They differ from general average by the fact that they are involuntary losses. The insured must carefully read its marine insurance policy because insurers commonly limit their liability for particular average losses. Many insurance contracts contain a *Free of Particular Average Clause* (FPA Clause) that denies coverage for partial losses other than those expressly provided in the policy. The burden of proving that a partial loss was caused by a peril covered in

---

CONCEPT SUMMARY
Carriers' Liability Limits

Ground Carriage	U.S. Domestic	• Carrier may offer liability limits by offer lower shipping rates. • Shipper may insist on full liability by paying higher shipping rate.
	European	• Liability limits $4.25/lb. road $8.50/lb. rail • Shipper may purchase higher value. • No limits if willful misconduct.
Air Carriage	U.S. Domestic	• $50 or $.50/lb. (for more than 100 lbs.)
	Warsaw Convention (U.S. International)	• $8.50/lb. • Shipper may pay extra for higher value. • No limits if willful misconduct.
	Amended Warsaw Convention	• $8.50 lb. • No limits if willful misconduct done with knowledge that damage was likely.
Sea Carriage	U.S. Domestic (Harter Act)	• May not use bill of lading to relieve carrier from liability for negligence.
	COGSA/Hague (U.S. International)	• $500/package • Shipper may pay extra for higher value.
	Hague–Visby	• $800/package or $1/lb. (whichever is higher). • No limits if willful misconduct done with knowledge that damage was likely.
	Hamburg	• $1,000/package. • No limits if reckless with knowledge that damage was likely.
	Charterparties	• Shipowner and shipper may freely negotiate liability issues.

the policy is on the insured. Ordinarily, insurers cover only particular average losses caused by sinking, burning, stranding, or collision.

QUESTIONS AND PROBLEM CASES

1. Explain the three fundamental functions of a bill of lading.

2. What are Incoterms (trade terms)? What function do they perform?

3. What is meant by a *general average* loss? How does the concept of general average differ from particular average?

4. SPM was the owner and importer of certain plastic injection molding machines that were shipped from Yokohama, Japan, to Norfolk, Virginia, aboard the *Ming Moon,* a container vessel. The shipment consisted of three crates. The *Ming Moon* followed its published itinerary and put in at an intermediate port in New Jersey before sailing on to Norfolk. While in New Jersey, the carrier moved SPM's cargo from the vessel to make room for other cargo on the return trip to Japan and to have SPM's oversized cargo relocated so it would remain accessible for discharge at Norfolk. Such restowage is common in the maritime trade. During this restowage, one of the crates was destroyed. SPM argued that

COGSA's liability limitation should not apply because the restowage constituted a deviation from the carriage agreement. Accordingly, it claimed damages in the amount of $228,000. The carrier responded by asserting the doctrine of deviation is limited to carrier's geographical departures from course and to unauthorized on-deck stowage of cargo. Thus, it claimed its liability should be limited to $500 for the single crate that was destroyed. Did the restowage of the cargo strip the carrier of COGSA's $500 per package liability limitation?

5. Johnson Products contracted to have International Customs Service (ICS), a freight forwarder, arrange the shipment of 25 to 30 40-foot containers from Chicago to Lagos, Nigeria. ICS used Container Overseas Agency (COSA) as an intermediary between itself and the carrier. ICS sent Johnson Products a bill of lading and an invoice charging it $145,000 for ocean freight and other services. The bill of lading stated the freight had been prepaid and the goods were on board the vessel *Nurenburg Express*. ICS knew, however, that this bill of lading was false and the goods were never loaded on that vessel. One month later, COSA arranged to have the goods loaded on the vessel *La Molinara*, owned by Nigerian Star Line (NSL). The bills of lading were stamped "freight to be prepaid," which meant the cargo could not be released until the shipper presented the original bills of lading, which it would receive upon payment in full. During this time, COSA was suffering severe financial problems and was unable to pay the freight charges. Despite its knowledge of COSA's financial distress, ICS paid the freight money to COSA because COSA threatened to hold up shipments of other ICS clients. COSA never passed any of this money on to NSL. Ultimately, Johnson Products was forced to pay $111,000 in freight charges to NSL to secure the release of the goods. Johnson Products sued ICS for the amount of the freight charges. Did ICS breach its duty as a freight forwarder?

6. As a part of its contract to sell steel coils to Associated Metals, Altos Hornos arranged to have the goods transported on a ship owned by Elite Shipping. Altos Hornos contracted with its own stevedore, Maritime Candida, to load and stow the coils on board the vessel. The bill of lading covering the goods contained a provision that shifted liability to the shipper for improper stowage of the cargo. When the vessel arrived in port, it was discovered that some of the cargo was damaged due to improper stowage. When Associated Metals attempted to recover from Elite Shipping, the carrier argued the provision in the bill of lading relieved it of liability for Maritime Candida's negligent stowing of the cargo. Both parties agreed that this shipment was regulated by COGSA. May Associated Metals recover from Elite Shipping for the damaged cargo?

7. Universal contracted with Netumar, a Brazilian sea carrier, to transport a large cargo of tobacco from Brazil to the United States. Universal packed the tobacco into fiberglass cases and then stuffed and loaded the cases into large metal containers supplied by Netumar. The containers then were sealed by Brazilian customs. Each 40-foot-long container held 90 to 99 cases of tobacco. On the bill of lading, the number of large metal containers was typed in under the heading "NO. of PKGS." However, the total number of fiberglass cases of tobacco (1,200) was typed in under the heading, "PARTICULARS FURNISHED BY SHIPPER/DESCRIPTION OF PACKAGES AND GOODS." On the reverse side, under "LIMITATION OF LIABILITY," the bill of lading stated: "Where a container is not stuffed by the carrier, each individual such container, including in each instance its contents, shall be deemed a single package and carrier's liability limited to $500 with respect to each such package." While the ship was at sea, water got into the hold and destroyed six containers (568 cases) of tobacco. Netumar argued its carrier liability was limited to $500 for each of the six metal containers. Is Netumar correct?

8. Continental Food Products shipped frozen meat from Guatemala to Florida. When the ship arrived in port, the meat was hard frozen. However, the Department of Agriculture prevented some of it from entering the United States because the packages contained evidence that they had been thawed and refrozen. There was no evidence of standing, sinking, burning, or collision. Further, there was no evidence of a breakdown of the vessel's refrigeration system other than the appearance of blood stains on some of the cartons. Neither the carrier nor Continental Foods knew how the thawing

occurred. Continental Food's insurance policy contained a provision that stated:

> Warranted Free of Particular Average unless the vessel be stranded, sunk, or burnt. It is, however, agreed that only while stowed in refrigeration compartments this insurance is extended to cover loss, damage, or deterioration caused by breakdown or stoppage of refrigerating machinery, provided such breakdown or stoppage continues for not less than 24 hours.

Will this marine cargo insurance policy cover the partial loss suffered by Continental Foods due to the thawing and refreezing of the meat?

9. Amar agreed to purchase 64 electronic watches from Karinol. The terms of the contract were embodied in a one-page invoice prepared by Karinol. A notation printed at the bottom of the invoice read: "Please send the merchandise in cardboard boxes duly strapped with metal bands via air parcel post to Chetumal. Documents to Banco de Commercio De Quintano Roo S.A." There were no provisions in the contract that specifically allocated risk of loss on the goods while in the possession of the carrier. Further, no trade terms (FOB, CIF, etc.) were mentioned in the agreement. After Karinol arranged to ship the watches from Miami, Florida, to Chetumal, Mexico, Amar paid the full purchase price. When the cartons arrived in Chetumal without any watches in them, Karinol refused to refund Amar's money or to supply new watches at no charge. Did Karinol bear the risk of loss for the watches?

10. Carman Tool purchased two milling machines in Taiwan from Dah Lih Machinery. Pursuant to the established practice between the parties, Dah Lih arranged to have the machines shipped to Los Angeles using the services of Evergreen Lines. Dah Lih then delivered the bill of lading to its bank, which in turn negotiated it to Carman's in exchange for a letter of credit authorizing payment to Dah Lih. After the machines were unloaded from the vessel but before they were delivered to Carman, they were damaged to the tune of $115,000. Evergreen asserted its liability to Carman was limited to $500 per package, pursuant to COGSA and the terms of the contract of carriage as contained in the bill of lading. Carman conceded the bill of lading contained this limitation; however, it claimed the limitation was ineffective since it did not see a copy of the bill of lading until long after the goods had been shipped. It argued that this delay denied it the opportunity to opt for higher liability limits. Will Evergreen be liable to Carman for more than $500 per package?

International Payment Mechanisms

INTRODUCTION

Global transactions frequently involve parties who have little familiarity with one another's commercial and financial status. As a result, these arrangements may involve tremendous financial risks for the unwary. Because of these uncertainties, structuring the method of payment generally is a vital component of negotiations for an international sales contract.

Chapter Overview

The actual number of payment options employed by international traders is too extensive to permit an exhaustive treatment here. Instead, this chapter examines several widely used methods that fairly represent the range of payment terms available to contracting parties. The major alternatives are: (1) open account, (2) cash in advance, (3) documentary collections, and (4) documentary credits. This discussion is preceded by a look at the legal and practical aspects of commercial paper and the role of commercial banks in global sales. The chapter closes with a brief examination of several other commonly used financial devices. This includes an introduction to countertrade and its growing importance in the international arena.

Selecting the Best Option

International traders must carefully tailor their payment terms to the deal at hand if they wish to remain competitive in the global marketplace. As we will see, each option discussed below involves a different apportionment of risk between the buyer and the seller. For instance, requiring that the buyer pay cash in advance of delivery of the goods places a great deal of risk on the buyer with almost no financial exposure for the seller. On the other hand, selling on an open account (permitting the buyer to pay at some time after delivery) may be extremely risky for the seller while involving little buyer risk.

Because of the greater risk and inconvenience it may bear, a buyer generally is not willing to pay as much for goods when the payment terms are cash in advance. Likewise, one might expect a seller to demand a higher purchase price when the goods are sold on an open account. In short, each payment mechanism involves a fundamental trade-off; with greater contract security comes higher monetary cost. Accurately assessing the risk of nondelivery or nonpayment, then, is vitally important if the parties hope to avoid unnecessarily sabotaging what could be a mutually beneficial contract.

MAXIMUM RISK PAYMENT TERMS

Open Account

Under an **open account** arrangement, the seller/exporter delivers the goods (or the documents required to gain possession of the goods) directly to the buyer/importer. This may involve much risk for the seller since it must rely on the willingness or future ability of the buyer to make timely and full payment for the goods. Should a real or feigned dispute arise over the contract, the buyer often has superior bargaining strength in negotiating a settlement since it possesses both the money and the goods.

Several considerations may prompt a seller to contract on an open account basis. First, because this payment method provides minimal risk and inconvenience to the buyer, the buyer may be willing to pay a higher price for the goods. Second, in actuality, the risk of nonpayment by the buyer may be very small. For instance, the buyer and seller may have developed a long-term relationship that shows the buyer is an extremely reliable customer. The buyer's creditworthiness is enhanced even more if it owns assets in the seller's country that the seller could easily attach should nonpayment occur. Finally, if the seller is in an extremely competitive market, it may have little choice over the selection of payment terms. Frequently in international transactions, the seller is forced to provide favorable payment terms if it hopes to make the sale.

The following case, decided by an English court, illustrates the risks a seller faces when dealing with an unscrupulous buyer. Notice how the seller attempted to avoid the risks of an open account transaction by retaining an interest in the goods after the sale.

PFEIFFER G.m.b.H. v. ARBUTHNOT FACTORS
[1988] 1 W.L.R. 150 (Q.B.D.)

■ **FACTS** Pfeiffer, a German exporter, supplied wines to Springfield, an English importer, on an open account. Their sales contract specified Springfield would resell the wine only on immediate payment terms and those resale proceeds would be directly applied to its open account with Pfeiffer. Despite this contract, Springfield then entered into an agreement with Arbuthnot that provided that Arbuthnot would advance money to Springfield and, in return, Springfield's buyers would make their payments directly to Arbuthnot. Springfield entered into this factoring contract without informing Arbuthnot of its prior obligation to Pfeiffer. When Springfield failed to pay Pfeiffer on the open account, Pfeiffer sued Arbuthnot to recover the money Arbuthnot received from Springfield's buyers.

■ **ISSUE** Must Arbuthnot pay the money to Pfeiffer?

■ **DECISION** No. When a buyer is given the right to resell goods before paying its supplier, the normal implication is that it would be doing so for its own account and not as one who was obligated to collect the payments for the supplier. Without any prior knowledge of Pfeiffer's claims to the amounts owed on the open account, neither Springfield's purchasers nor Arbuthnot would be aware of Pfeiffer's claim to the money. As a result, because it was the first to notify the purchasers of its interests, Arbuthnot had first right to the proceeds.

Cash in Advance

From the seller's point of view, **cash in advance** is the ideal arrangement. It involves minimal risk to the seller since it requires the buyer to tender payment before the seller delivers the goods (or documents required to gain possession of the goods) to the buyer. Of course, since prepayment provides the maximum risk and inconvenience to the buyer, the seller may not be able to insist on such terms in a competitive market or may be able to do so only at a substantially reduced price.

Where demand greatly exceeds supply, buyers may have no choice but to accept cash in advance terms. They also might be used where the buyer has a poor credit rating. However, where the seller has an excellent reputation for reliability or where it owns assets in the buyer's country, the risk to the buyer may be minimal.

ETHICAL IMPLICATIONS   When the buyer is in an inferior bargaining position, the seller may be able to demand that the payment terms be cash in advance. Is it ethical for a seller to use its bargaining strength to impose such terms on a buyer?

The Partial Prepayment Compromise

A **partial prepayment** term is a fairly common compromise that divides the risks between the seller and the buyer. Under this option, the buyer prepays an amount sufficient to cover the seller's cost of manufacturing the goods. This minimizes the seller's risk by guaranteeing it may at least break even on the contract. The balance due on the sale would then be an open account that is due later.

COMMERCIAL PAPER

Introduction

Sometimes the buyer and seller have relatively equal bargaining strength. Or each may be unfamiliar or uncomfortable with the other's reliability. On these occasions, payment terms based on cash in advance or open account may be unsuitable for the contract. Instead, the parties may be willing to incur additional expenses to obtain greater security. Documentary collections or documentary credits often provide this extra protection. These payment options are examined in some detail. However, first we look at the role of commercial paper in implementing these devices.

Negotiable Instruments

Commercial paper encompasses any of a number of substitutes for money that are common in international commerce. Basically, it is a contract for the payment of money, although it also can be used to extend credit. Our analysis of commercial paper focuses on **negotiable instruments.** They are called negotiable because of the ease with which they pass through the financial system.

Kinds of Negotiable Instruments

The two basic types of negotiable instruments are: (*a*) promises to pay money and (*b*) orders to pay money. A promissory note is a promise to pay money while a draft (bill of exchange) and a check are orders to pay money.

Promissory Note

A **promissory note** represents the first category of negotiable instruments. With a promissory note one person (the maker) makes an unconditional promise to pay money to another person (the payee) or to someone specified by the payee either on demand or at some particular time in the future.

FIGURE 7–1   A Promissory Note

Payee

$1,000.00   July 1, 1993

    90   Days after Date ____ I ____ Promise to Pay to the Order of

(Amanda Brown)

            One Thousand and no/100 ---------------------------- Dollars

with Interest at Rate of   10   Percent per Annum

No. ____ 1 ____   Due   October 1, 1993

                            (Ronald Ross)

Maker

FIGURE 7–2   A Time Draft

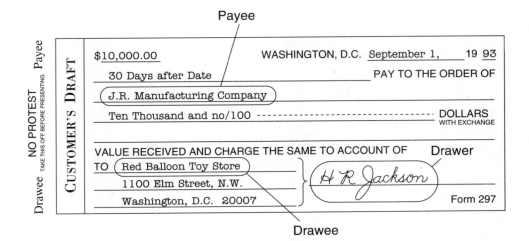

Payee

NO PROTEST — TAKE THIS OFF BEFORE PRESENTING

Payee
Drawee

CUSTOMER'S DRAFT

$10,000.00   WASHINGTON, D.C. September 1,   19 93

    30 Days after Date   PAY TO THE ORDER OF

(J.R. Manufacturing Company)

    Ten Thousand and no/100 -------------------------------- DOLLARS
                                                           WITH EXCHANGE

VALUE RECEIVED AND CHARGE THE SAME TO ACCOUNT OF   Drawer
TO (Red Balloon Toy Store)
    1100 Elm Street, N.W.   (H R Jackson)
    Washington, D.C. 20007   Form 297

Drawee

FIGURE 7–3   A Check

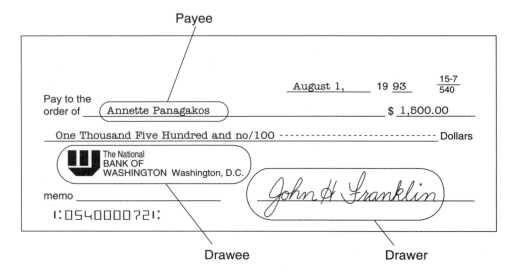

Payee

Drawee   Drawer

Drafts

Drafts (bills of exchange) are orders to pay money rather than promises to pay. With a draft, one person (the drawer) orders another person (the drawee) to pay money to a third person (the payee) or to someone specified by the payee either on demand or at a designated time in the future. A draft that is payable to the payee on demand is known as a **sight draft.** If it is not payable until some particular time in the future, it is called a **time draft.** A drawer is liable to the payee or its transferee for the face amount of the draft. The drawee becomes liable if it "accepts" the draft by signing it. If the drawee that accepts the draft is a bank, it is called a *banker's acceptance.* This chapter focuses on drafts because of their widespread use in international sales transactions.

Checks

A **check** is a special type of draft that is payable on demand. It is also designated by the fact that the drawee of a check is the bank where the drawer has an account from which the proceeds are paid. Thus, with a check, the drawer orders its bank (the drawee) to pay on demand a certain amount of money to the payee or someone designated by the payee. Checks are widely used in domestic transactions.

Negotiability   Negotiable instruments have certain advantages that make them desirable in commercial transactions: They are safer to carry or send than money; yet generally they are accepted readily as a substitute for money. Often a bank is willing to extend cash for a negotiable instrument because it realizes it can become a holder in due course and take the instrument free of many of the risks that would be assumed by an assignee to a contract.

Rights of an Assignee to a Contract

Suppose a seller promised to ship widgets to a buyer on an open account with the $12,000 purchase price due 90 days after delivery. Several days after delivery, the seller (needing money now) assigns its right to collect on the account to its bank in return for an immediate cash payment. If many of the widgets turn out to be defective, the buyer may refuse to pay the entire contract price. Since the bank, as an assignee to a contract, has no greater rights than did its assignor (the seller), it will not be able to recover the full amount from the buyer. As a result of this risk, the bank may not be willing to extend as much money to the seller.

Rights of a Holder in Due Course

If the parties had used a negotiable instrument rather than an open account, the situation would have been different. Upon receiving the goods, the buyer would have drawn a time draft or made a promissory note promising payment in 90 days. The seller could then negotiate this with its bank for cash. Later, even if the widgets proved to be defective, the buyer would be required to pay the full amount of the instrument to the bank. This is because the bank would have taken the negotiable instrument free of the buyer's defenses to the underlying contract with the seller.

Two conditions would have had to be met before the bank could have received this special protection. First, the buyer's promise or order to pay the money must be made in the proper form. Second, the bank would have had to qualify as a holder in due course. We now look at each of these concepts.

Requirements for Negotiability

To be negotiable, commercial paper must:

1. Be in *writing.*
2. Be *signed* by the maker or drawer.
3. Contain an *unconditional promise* or *order* to pay a *sum certain in money.*
4. Be *payable on demand or at a definite time.*
5. Be *payable to order or to bearer.*

If the commercial paper does not meet these strict requirements, it still is collectible by the payee; however, it is nonnegotiable.

Paper that is nonnegotiable is governed by the general rules of contract law. As such, it does not confer any special protection on an assignee. Thus, the importance of making the paper negotiable is to permit a transferee (such as the bank in our example above) to receive the special rights accorded a holder in due course.

Holder in Due Course

To qualify as a **holder in due course**, a transferee must:

1. Have *possession* of a negotiable instrument that is *properly endorsed and delivered* to it.
2. Give *value* for the instrument. (Many civil law nations do not require that value be given.)
3. Take the instrument in *good faith* (obtain it honestly).
4. Be *without notice* that the instrument is *overdue*, has been *dishonored*, or has *any defense* against it.

A transferee who does not meet all of these requirements has only the rights of an assignee under contract law. A holder in due course, on the other hand, takes the instrument free of most of the contract defenses available to the buyer (maker or drawer of the instrument).

Personal Defenses

In commercial transactions, a holder in due course is not subject to any of the buyer's **personal defenses** to the underlying contract. These might include: fraud by the seller in inducing the sale, breach of warranty, or even nondelivery of the goods. Thus (as we saw in our earlier example), once the seller negotiated the note or draft to its bank, the buyer must pay the full $12,000 even though many of the widgets were defective. If the bank had not qualified as a holder in due course, the buyer could have withheld payment to cover the defective widgets.

Real Defenses

Holders in due course still are subject to the buyer's **real defenses.** These are claims by the buyer that go to the "validity" of the instrument, rather than to the terms of the contract. For instance, if the maker of a promissory note could establish that its signature was forged, the instrument would not be a valid negotiable instrument. Or if a person was forced to sign a draft at gunpoint, the draft would not be valid. If the buyer in our earlier example could have proven any of these real defenses, it would not have owed any money to either the seller or the bank.

CARADOR v. SANA TRAVEL SERVICE
700 F.Supp. 787 (S.D. N.Y. 1988)

■ **FACTS** Sana Travel Service drew a check on National Bank of Pakistan (NBP) for $33,000 payable to Al-Bark Turismo. On the line on the face of the check that usually holds memoranda, Sana inserted the words: "JUST TO HOLD FOR THE SECURITY OF FUTURE BUSINESS." After receiving the check at its offices in Brazil, Al-Bark endorsed it and sold it to Carador (a small check broker) for cash. When NBP received the check it telephoned Sana, who directed that it be dishonored. Carador sued for the $33,000 plus interest, alleging that Sana is liable to it as a holder in due course. Sana contends that the notation on the face of the instrument made the check a conditional promise to pay, thereby destroying its negotiability. Sana further argued that Carador's delay in negotiating the check (five months) deprived him of his status as a holder in due course.

■ **ISSUE** Is Carador entitled to payment as a holder in due course of a negotiable instrument?

■ **DECISION** Yes. A check or draft is not a negotiable instrument if the drawer writes on it a promise or order that, when examined on its face, limits the drawer's unconditional promise to pay. By contrast, an instrument that notes on its face that it is a security deposit for future performance of another contract remains negotiable because such a notation does not suggest on its face that the drawer may have reneged on the promise to honor the instrument. Therefore, the notation on this check does not destroy negotiability because it merely indicates

Al-Bark and Sana have agreed that Sana will give Al-Bark a security deposit to ensure future performance on another contract. As a buyer without actual notice of any irregularity, Carador has taken in good faith without notice of any defense against it. He has not lost this status through delay in attempting to negotiate the check. A holder in due course is given a reasonable time to collect on a check. While normally 30 days is deemed to be sufficient time, five months does not seem unreasonable where a check between two small international companies must make its way over two continents. As a holder in due course, Carador takes the instrument free of all of Sana's personal defenses to payment, including the assertion that Al-Bark did not pay valid consideration for the check.

COLLECTIONS AGAINST DOCUMENTS

Clean Collection

Sometimes the goods or the documents representing the goods (discussed below) are forwarded by the seller directly to the buyer. The seller then has its bank forward a draft to the buyer's bank for payment or acceptance. In this procedure, known as a **clean collection,** the buyer acquires title to and possession (actual or constructive) of the goods before payment has been made. Thus, the seller has little protection if the buyer should refuse to accept or pay on the draft.

Documentary Collections

In international transactions, the parties often opt for the greater security provided by **documentary collections.** Under this mechanism, the seller/drawer draws a draft payable to itself on the buyer/drawee. The seller then presents this draft and the shipping documents to its bank (remitting bank), which forwards them to a bank in the buyer's country (collecting bank). The shipping documents (giving control over the goods) are released to the buyer only when it accepts or pays on the draft.

The documents usually called for in a documentary collection are:

1. Sight draft or a time draft.
2. Bill of lading or air waybill (giving constructive possession of the goods and establishing that they have been shipped).
3. Commercial invoice (shows the sales terms).
4. Certificate of origin (necessary for customs evaluation purposes).
5. Export license/health inspection certificate (certifies that goods are cleared for export).
6. Inspection report (certifies that goods meet the standards called for in the contract).
7. Proof of insurance (verifies that goods are insured while in transit).

**Documents
on Payment
of a Sight Draft**

Benefits

When the seller does not want to surrender control of the goods until the buyer has tendered payment, it may employ **documents on payment of a sight draft.** This payment mechanism offers the seller more protection than open account terms because the shipping documents are not released to the buyer until payment has been made to the collecting bank. It also provides the buyer with more security than it would have in a cash in advance transaction. With cash in advance, the buyer cannot be certain the seller will make a timely shipment of the goods after payment has been received. But with documents on payment of the sight draft, by examining the shipping documents, the buyer knows the goods have been shipped.

Costs

As with all commercial transactions, particularly in the global environment, this payment option is not risk-free. The possibility always exists that the buyer will refuse to pay on the sight draft when the documents are presented for collection. Because of the long distances goods often travel in an international transaction, the seller already may have incurred substantial freight charges. If the buyer refuses to accept a shipment, the seller may have either to reship the goods or to try to sell them in an overseas market under distress conditions. The buyer also assumes some risks since it has received documents representing the goods rather than the goods themselves when it tenders payment. There is always the possibility that the documents have been forged or the goods will be lost or damaged in transit.

**Documents
on Acceptance
of a Time Draft**

Benefits

Frequently, the buyer is unable or unwilling to make an immediate payment for the goods. (Perhaps the buyer does not have sufficient cash on hand until after it has had an opportunity to resell the merchandise.) In these instances, the parties may utilize the **documents on acceptance of a time draft** arrangement. Under this option, the remitting bank sends the shipping documents and a time draft drawn on the buyer to the collecting bank. The collecting bank then releases the shipping documents to the buyer when the buyer signs (accepts) the time draft. (This accepted draft is called a *trade acceptance.*) Under the terms of a time draft, the buyer agrees to pay the draft amount at some future date (often 30, 60, or 90 days later). Thus, by permitting the use of a time draft, the seller is extending credit to the buyer.

Costs

Time drafts are risker than sight drafts from the seller's standpoint. With a time draft, the buyer receives the shipping documents (and constructive control of the goods) based on its promise to pay rather than actual payment. During the period between delivery of the goods and the due date on the draft, the seller has, in effect, extended a loan to the buyer. And, as with the sight draft, the seller still faces the possibility that the buyer will refuse to accept the draft after the goods have already been shipped.

■ **ETHICAL IMPLICATIONS**	The seller in a documentary collection always bears the risk that the buyer will refuse to pay or accept when the collecting bank presents the shipping documents. As was noted above, this places the seller in a stressful situation when the shipping charges are great and it has no sales representative in the buyer's country. While the seller has the option of suing the buyer for breach of contract, this can be a long, expensive, and not always fruitful action. Would it be unethical for a buyer to refuse a shipment for no other reason than to force the seller to renegotiate the contract with terms more favorable to the buyer?

The Role of the Banking System

Under documentary and clean collections, the collecting bank does not guarantee that the buyer will either pay on the sight draft or accept a time draft. The bank also does not verify the quantity or quality of the goods described in the shipping documents. Instead, the only obligation the bank assumes is to follow the seller's instructions and accepted banking procedures in releasing the shipping documents upon the buyer's payment or acceptance. For these services, the banks generally charge a fairly low flat rate to cover their administrative efforts.

DOCUMENTARY CREDITS

The Letter of Credit

Under both clean and documentary collections, the possibility exists that the buyer will refuse to pay after the seller already has shipped the goods. When the likelihood of nonacceptance is great, the seller may insist the buyer have a bank issue an irrevocable **letter of credit** guaranteeing that payment will be made upon presentation of the proper documents (the same documents described above under documentary collections). This provides great protection against nonpayment since the seller can look to a commercial bank, rather than the buyer, for payment.

Let's return to our earlier example where the seller contracted to sell widgets to the buyer for $12,000. In that case, there was a chance the buyer would back out of the contract after the goods had been shipped but before payment had been made. Wishing to substantially reduce this risk, the seller may insist on either an unconfirmed or a confirmed letter of credit transaction.

Unconfirmed Letter of Credit

Under an unconfirmed letter of credit, the **account party** (the buyer) instructs the **issuing bank** (buyer's bank) to issue a letter of credit. This documentary credit is the issuing bank's guarantee to the **beneficiary** (the seller) that it will receive payment if it supplies the appropriate documents to an **advising bank.** This advising (or collecting) bank generally is a branch or correspondent of the issuing bank and is located in the seller's country. In return for the issuance of the letter of credit, the buyer is obligated to pay the issuing bank either in advance or, if the buyer's creditworthiness is good, later. After the seller presents the appropriate documents to the advising bank, they are forwarded, through the issuing bank, to the buyer. At the time of presentment, the seller may submit a draft drawn on the issuing bank and receive its payment.

When the issuing bank has a strong international reputation, its guarantee (represented by the letter of credit) provides much financial security to the seller. However, not all banks share the same solid financial reputation. A bank in a nation suffering a severe shortage of hard currency may be unable to obtain sufficient U.S. dollars to honor its commitment to a U.S. seller. Or a nation may prohibit its banks, through a political boycott or some currency restriction, from further dealings with the nationals of certain countries. If the seller questions the future reliability of the issuing bank's guarantee, it may demand a confirmed letter of credit.

Confirmed Letter of Credit

Under a confirmed letter of credit, the seller designates a second bank (usually located in the seller's country) to obligate itself to ensure payment to the seller. The procedure is the same as that described above except the seller presents the documents to the **confirming bank,** rather than to the advising bank. After tendering the documents, the seller may receive payment from the confirming bank. The documents then are forwarded to the issuing bank, which reimburses the confirming bank.

The confirmed letter of credit gives the seller double protection since both the issuing and the confirming bank guarantee payment. Of particular importance is the fact that the confirming bank is likely to be located in the seller's country and familiar to the seller. Thus, the seller will feel more confident that when it presents the documents it will be paid in its own currency. The confirming bank, rather than the seller, bears the risk that the issuing bank will be unable or unwilling to pay. Of course, this additional protection is not free. Adding the assurances of a second bank increases the cost of the transaction to the buyer.

Assessing the Value of a Letter of Credit

Benefits

Only cash in advance offers the seller more protection against nonpayment than the documentary credit. With cash in advance, the seller does not ship the goods until it is paid. While this satisfies the seller, it can be very risky for the buyer since there is no guarantee the seller will ship the goods after receiving payment. Under a documentary credit, the seller does not ship the goods until a bank guarantees it will be paid. (The bank assumes the risk that the buyer might refuse to pay.) But, unlike cash in advance, the letter of credit transaction also protects the buyer. Through the requirement that the seller forward shipping documents, the buyer gains some degree of assurance that the goods have been shipped.

Costs

Of course, these advantages do not come without a cost. In arranging to have a letter of credit issued, buyers usually discover that the process is more time consuming than the other payment options. Also, a letter of credit is similar to a loan to the buyer. Thus, its issuance ties up a portion of the buyer's available line of credit at the issuing

CONCEPT SUMMARY
A Confirmed Documentary Credit Transaction

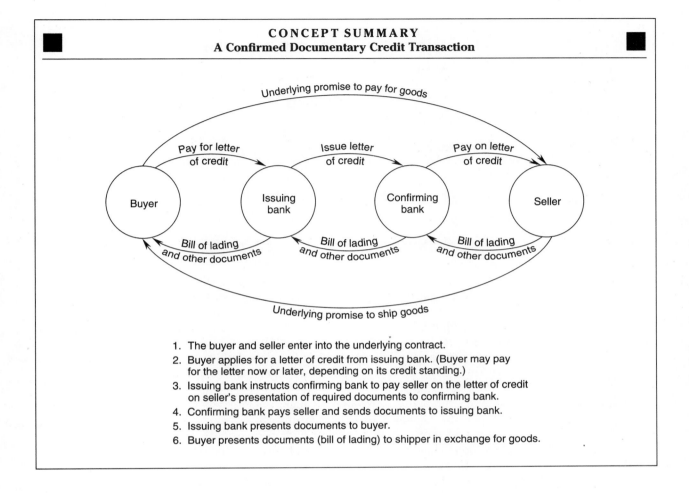

1. The buyer and seller enter into the underlying contract.
2. Buyer applies for a letter of credit from issuing bank. (Buyer may pay
    for the letter now or later, depending on its credit standing.)
3. Issuing bank instructs confirming bank to pay seller on the letter of credit
    on seller's presentation of required documents to confirming bank.
4. Confirming bank pays seller and sends documents to issuing bank.
5. Issuing bank presents documents to buyer.
6. Buyer presents documents (bill of lading) to shipper in exchange for goods.

bank. Further, letters of credit are more expensive than the other alternatives. The bank charge for a letter of credit may be from ⅛ to ½ percent of the face amount plus additional administrative fees. If the credit is confirmed, there would be an additional fee of between 1/20 and ½ percent of the face amount. Accordingly, in an extremely competitive market, sellers may find that their insistence on letter of credit terms may sabotage the sale.

Governing Law   Article 5 of the Uniform Commercial Code generally governs domestic letter of credit transactions between U.S. businesses. Although it defines the rights and responsibilities of the parties to most letter of credit situations, there are gaps in its coverage. The Uniform Customs and Practice for Documentary Credits (UCP), on the other hand, was drafted with the day-to-day operation of credits in mind.

The UCP was drafted by the International Chamber of Commerce and, as such, is not a formal law. However, the parties to international and domestic sales contracts

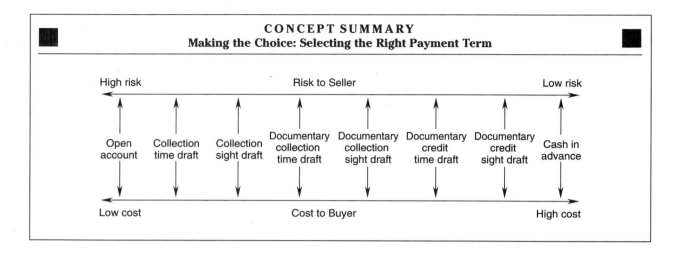

CONCEPT SUMMARY
Making the Choice: Selecting the Right Payment Term

often elect to have it govern their documentary credits. All that it takes to incorporate it into the transaction is to state on the letter of credit: "This letter of credit is issued subject to the UCP." It is so popular, in fact, that the banks of the United States, as well as those in over 160 countries, subscribe to it.

As a general rule, however, Article 5 and the UCP are consistent and complementary. Therefore, no effort is made to distinguish their coverage in this chapter.

Revocability

Generally, the parties agree that the letter of credit will be **irrevocable.** That means it cannot be canceled or amended unless the beneficiary and the account party (seller and buyer) both give their written consent. Under a revocable credit, the seller/beneficiary has much less security because the issuing bank could unilaterally decide to cancel or modify its obligation to pay. If a letter of credit failed to indicate on its face that it was irrevocable, it was treated as revocable. Accordingly, the beneficiary had to take great care to ensure the credit was designated as irrevocable if that was the intent of the parties. However, under the 1993 amendments to the UCP (known as UCP 500), letters of credit now are treated as irrevocable unless they state otherwise.

The Three Principles Underlying Documentary Credits

While the laws governing letter of credit transactions impose numerous obligations on banking institutions, three fundamental principles underlie all such arrangements. They are:

1. The Independence Principle.
2. The Strict Compliance Principle.
3. The Documents Only Principle.

Most legal disputes involving documentary credit transactions invoke the operation of one or more of these three legal rules.

The Independence Principle

The documentary credit transaction contains a series of interrelated contracts. The issuance of the letter of credit involves an agreement between the issuing bank and the account party, as well as an obligation by the issuing bank to the beneficiary. If the credit is confirmed, there also are agreements between the confirming bank and the beneficiary and between the issuing bank and the confirming bank. Finally, underlying all of these arrangements is the basic sales contract between the buyer and the seller.

Much of the success of documentary credits depends on the idea that the letter of credit contracts are independent of the underlying sales contract. Thus, if the seller presents documents that conform to the terms of the letter of credit, the bank must pay even if the goods are somehow defective. Because of the **independence** principle, the buyer's only recourse would be to sue the seller for breach of contract.

The Strict Compliance Principle

The **strict compliance** principle complements the idea that the letter of credit is independent of the underlying contract. Since the bank's obligation extends no further than to inspect the documents presented by the seller, the only real safeguard available to the buyer is its right to specify precisely the form and substance of those documents. Accordingly, the courts have developed the idea that the beneficiary is not entitled to payment unless the documentation strictly conforms to the terms specified by the buyer in the letter of credit. Under this reasoning, the mere misspelling of an individual's name has excused the issuing bank from paying on the letter of credit.

TEXPOR TRADERS v. TRUST COMPANY BANK
720 F.Supp. 1100 (S.D. N.Y. 1989)

■ **FACTS** Texpor and Oxford entered into a sales contract in which Texpor was to sell high-quality cotton sweatshirts to Oxford. In connection with the purchase orders, Oxford arranged for Trust Company Bank to issue an irrevocable letter of credit in favor of Texpor for $242,000. The parties later amended this letter of credit to accommodate Texpor's delay in delivering the first two shipments. On January 20, Texpor made the first shipment and, upon presentation of the shipping documents, received payment under the letter of credit. After receiving the shipment, Oxford discovered that most of the sweatshirts were defective. On February 3, Texpor made the second shipment and again presented identical documents to Trust Company Bank. On this occasion, the bank refused to honor the credit, claiming the documents did not conform to the requirements of the letter of credit. Among the discrepancies were a missing room number,

a misdescription of the address on the invoice, and an omission of the word *Oxford* as it appeared on the letter of credit. In a suit against the bank for wrongful dishonor, Texpor claimed the documents were satisfactory since there was no possibility they would mislead the bank.

■ **ISSUE** Did the issuing bank wrongfully dishonor the letter of credit?

■ **DECISION** No. The prevailing judicial view is that the issuing bank normally is obligated to honor the beneficiary's request for payment only when the documents presented are in strict compliance with the letter of credit. There is no room for documents that are almost the same or that will do just as well. Texpor claimed the real reason behind the dishonor was Oxford's request that the bank not pay. It argued that this was evident by the fact that the bank honored the request for payment on the first shipment when it was presented with identical documents. However, Texpor's argument has no legal effect. Merely because Oxford in one instance chose to waive discrepancies in the letter of credit does not require that it do so again, nor does it authorize the issuing bank to similarly waive such discrepancies. Trust Company Bank properly refused to honor the request for payment since the documents presented did not strictly conform to the requirements of the letter of credit.

ETHICAL IMPLICATIONS

Suppose the sweatshirts in the first shipment had not been defective. However, after receiving them, Oxford discovered that another manufacturer would sell sweatshirts of similar quality for a substantially lower price. Thus, Oxford now either wants out of the contract or to renegotiate the price. Under these circumstances, would it be ethical for Oxford to instruct the bank to refuse payment on the second shipment because of the discrepancies in the documents?

The Documents Only Principle

A corollary to the independence and strict compliance principles is the rule that banks should deal in **documents only.** Their obligation to make payment should not be based on matters outside of the documents. This means a bank generally will not issue a letter of credit when the beneficiary's compliance with the terms of the credit cannot be determined exclusively from a review of documents. Thus, if a buyer does not want its bank to pay the seller unless the goods meet certain quality standards, it will not ask the bank to inspect the goods. Instead it requires, as part of the documentary exchange, that the seller present an inspection certificate to the bank.

Some buyers are tempted to require detailed documentation to ensure that the seller lives up to the terms of the underlying contract. However, by inserting complex documentary requirements, the buyer may greatly increase the likelihood that the seller's documentary presentation will somehow fail the strict compliance requirement. When this occurs, the seller may be given an opportunity to resubmit the documents if the credit has not yet expired. Or the buyer may decide to waive the need for complete conformity. In any event, the result is likely to be delay and perhaps a breakdown of the sales transaction. For this reason, both Article 5 and the UCP specifically discourage the use of extensive detail in documentary credits.

Exceptions to the Three Principles

Fraud

Despite the independence principle, payment on the letter of credit may be withheld when the beneficiary to the credit has committed a serious act of fraud. This deception may be manifest in either of two ways. First, a required document may be shown to be forged or materially altered. Thus, the seller might forge the name of an inspector on an inspection certificate. Or if the bill of lading correctly listed 20 cases of widgets, the seller might fraudulently change the number to 200 to conform to the amount called for in the letter of credit. These are examples of **fraudulent documents.**

Second, the beneficiary may have committed an act of **fraud in the transaction.** This may occur when the seller ships goods that are fundamentally different from those called for in the underlying contract. For example, suppose the seller agreed to ship cotton fabric in return for payment under a letter of credit. Although all of the documents described the goods as cotton fabric, the seller shipped worthless scraps of paper. If the buyer discovers this before payment to the seller has been made, it may obtain a court injunction to prevent the bank from honoring the documentary credit.

The courts have made clear that these exceptions to the independence principle should be limited to instances of active and intentional fraud by the beneficiary. Thus, they do not apply to mere breaches of warranty or actions by individuals other than the beneficiary. Further, the fraud exception does not excuse the issuing bank from paying on drafts presented by a holder in due course. Finally, if the bank has already paid on the credit before receiving notice of the beneficiary's fraud, it is not liable to the account party as long as it exercised reasonable diligence before making payment.

BANK OF NOVA SCOTIA v. ANGELICA-WHITEWEAR LTD.
36 D.L.R. (4th) 161 (Sup.Ct. Canada 1987)

■ **FACTS** Protective Clothing Company, a Hong Kong manufacturer, contracted to sell men's industrial uniforms to Angelica-Whitewear, a Canadian importer. At the request of Whitewear, the Bank of Nova Scotia opened a letter of credit in favor of Protective in the amount of $350,000 to cover the full invoice costs of the uniforms. Later, after several drafts had been presented to the bank for payment, Whitewear discovered the prices in one invoice had been fraudulently inflated in the amount of $19,000. It informed the bank that "the amount claimed was not correct," but never specifically stated there was a fraudulent increase in the price. Despite Whitewear's request that no payment be made, the bank paid on the letter of credit. Whitewear sued the bank for wrongfully honoring the letter of credit under a theory of fraud in the transaction.

■ **ISSUE** Did the bank wrongfully honor the letter of credit because of Protective's fraudulent inflation of the price?

■ **DECISION** No. A fundamental principle governing documentary credits is that the bank's obligation to pay is independent of the performance of the underlying contract. An exception to this general rule has been recognized when the beneficiary commits a fraudulent act to gain the benefit of the credit. However, the potential scope of the fraud exception must not be a means of creating serious uncertainty and lack of confidence in the operation of letter of credit transactions. At the same time, the rule of independence must not facilitate or encourage fraud in documentary transactions. Keeping this balance in mind, courts have held that the fraud exception applies as long as the fraud has been brought to the knowledge of the issuing bank before it has paid under the letter of credit. Thus, an issuing bank generally does not have to make an independent inquiry to determine whether fraud has occurred when it has been presented with documents that appear on their face to be regular. It is only when fraud appears on the face of the documents or when fraud has been brought to its attention that it must refuse payment. In this case, it is impossible to conclude from the words "the amount claimed was not correct" that it was made clear to the bank before payment that fraud had been committed. This message did not make obvious to the bank that the higher price was a product of fraud rather than an increase in price that may have been permitted under the agreement between the parties.

Substantial Compliance

Some U.S. courts have replaced the strict compliance principle with a "substantial compliance" rule. In these cases, the courts have held banks liable on letters of credit when the deviations from the required terms were inconsequential. For instance, a bank was ordered to pay a company called Blow Out Products, even though the letter of credit called for payment to Blow Out Prevention because the court did not believe the difference to be material since no confusion was likely to result.

The development of the substantial compliance standard faces severe criticism for several reasons. First, it forces bankers to look beyond the documents to glean the true intent of the parties. Second, it has added uncertainty to documentary credit transactions as bankers are required to speculate as to which deviations are acceptable and which are not.

A trend seems to be emerging that reverses the hardships the substantial compliance rule was placing on banks. Under this approach, substantial compliance would be used only in lawsuits brought against a bank for wrongfully honoring the letter of credit. In these cases, the bank would not be liable if it could demonstrate that it paid on documents that substantially complied with the terms of the credit. In suits by the beneficiary for wrongful dishonor or by the account party to enjoin payment, the court would use the traditional strict compliance standard.

Special Types of Credits

There are numerous varieties of documentary credits and, accordingly, the parties should carefully tailor the required terms to meet their precise needs. We have already seen that credits can be confirmed or unconfirmed or they can be irrevocable or revocable. This section examines several other widely used variations.

Transferable Credits

Sometimes the seller of the goods is a middleman who serves as a conduit between a supplier and the buyer. In these instances, the seller/beneficiary may wish to transfer all or part of its rights under the letter of credit to the supplier/transferee. However, a letter of credit is not transferable unless the issuing bank expressly agrees to those terms at the time the credit is issued. Even then, the seller/beneficiary has to request the transfer in writing before it is permitted. The transferee then must comply with the original terms of the credit before funds are disbursed by the issuing or confirming banks.

Back-to-Back Credits

When the seller is a middleman, it might use a back-to-back credit to serve the same function as the transferable letter of credit. Under this mechanism, the seller asks a bank to issue a letter of credit guaranteeing that the supplier will be paid for the goods it supplies to the seller. That bank uses the original letter of credit issued by the buyer's bank as collateral for its documentary credit.

Red Clauses

A red clause helps the seller/beneficiary obtain financing so it can manufacture the goods the buyer wishes to purchase. (This provision generally is indicated by a notation written on the credit with red ink.) Under a red clause, the advising or confirming banks advance money to the seller in return for its promise to present the shipping documents. The buyer instructs the issuing bank to authorize the advising or confirming banks to make this loan. When the goods are actually manufactured and the shipping documents presented, the issuing bank makes payment. The advising or confirming bank deducts the amount of the advance plus interest from this payment to the seller.

Revolving Credits

Sometimes the underlying sales contract is a long-term arrangement. A revolving credit permits the seller to make a series of draws against the face amount of the letter of credit as it ships installments to the buyer.

Electronic Credits

Some electronic reporting systems permit companies to process documentary credits faster by making a direct interface with their banks' credit systems. In many instances, this permits same-day payment rather than the two to three days that may be required under traditional credits. The future of this innovation, however, is still uncertain. As of yet, there is no clear consensus on a satisfactory means of transmitting bills of lading and other documentary requirements by wholly electronic means. EDIFACT, a standardized electronic format for transmitting data, has been considered as a means of overcoming this hurdle. However, there is still great controversy over the reliability of these electronic systems in eliminating fraud.

Standby Letters of Credit

Up to now, the discussion has focused on letters of credit that are designed to supplement sale of goods transactions. Such devices are commonly called **straight credits.** Letters of credit also are quite useful in providing assurances that the account party will perform some service that it has promised to undertake. These specialized credits are called **standby letters of credit.**

In our earlier example, a seller promised to supply widgets to the buyer for $12,000. Suppose the buyer insisted the seller warrant the widgets against any defects for six months after delivery. A standby letter of credit gives the buyer assurance that the seller actually will honor this promise. Under this arrangement, the seller has its bank issue a credit to the buyer assuring the buyer that it will receive a certain payment if the goods prove to be defective and the seller does not repair the defect within a prescribed time period.

As with the straight letter of credit, this standby credit also is a documents-only transaction. Thus, if the seller refuses to live up to the warranty terms, the buyer presents a document (perhaps a letter from some independent arbiter) asserting that the seller has breached. (The parties will have stipulated the proper form of documentation in the application for the standby credit.) The issuing bank then pays the buyer and seeks reimbursement from the seller.

Standby letters of credit can be used to reinforce almost any type of performance obligation undertaken by the account party. The rules governing their operation are substantially the same as those governing straight credits.

RECON/OPTICAL, INC. v. GOVERNMENT OF ISRAEL
816 F.2d 854 (2nd Cir. 1987)

■ **FACTS** Recon/Optical contracted with the Israeli government to develop and produce a unique aerial reconnaissance system for the Israeli Air Force. The agreement between the parties required Recon to obtain an irrevocable standby letter of credit in favor of Israel in the amount of $33 million. The contract allowed Israel to draw against the letter of credit in any amount not exceeding its advance payments to Recon if Israel certified to the issuing bank that it was entitled to such amount because of material breach by Recon. A dispute arose between the parties over Israel's responsibility to pay for millions of dollars of modifications that Recon made to correct problems in its original design. While this conflict was being arbitrated, Recon refused to continue work until it was paid for the modifications. Israel declared the work stoppage constituted a material breach of the contract and attempted to draw $21.5 million (the total payments it had made to Recon up to that point) under the letter of credit. Recon, claiming Israel's draw against the credit was fraudulent, sued to enjoin the issuing bank from honoring the letter of credit.

■ **ISSUE** Should the issuing bank pay on the standby letter of credit?

■ **DECISION** Yes. The purpose of the standby letter of credit provision was to allow Israel to have immediate access to the funds necessary to secure procurement from a second source if performance under the original contract ceased. This allowed Israel to decide unilaterally that a material breach had occurred and to certify that determination to the bank. This was not fraudulent. There was no evidence that Israel acted in bad faith or impeded Recon's continued performance. Far from constituting fraud, the drawdown by Israel was consistent with the parties' contractual intent.

ALTERNATE METHODS OF FINANCE

Introduction

As the global markets become more competitive, it becomes increasingly difficult for sellers to insist on letter of credit transactions. However, many sellers cannot afford to tie up precious resources by selling on open credit terms or on the basis of documents against a time draft. Instead, they opt for alternate methods of **nonrecourse financing** for their cross-border transactions.

The advantage of nonrecourse financing is that the seller receives payment from some third party whether or not the buyer ultimately pays. (Letters of credit are nonrecourse payments.) Thus, while the seller is still liable to the buyer for any product disputes (e.g., defective goods, failure to deliver the goods), all credit risk is borne by the third party.

Factoring

International **factoring** allows the seller to extend open account payment terms to the buyer while simultaneously permitting the seller to be paid immediately. The process is carried out through a network of factoring companies located throughout the world. First, the seller contracts with a U.S. member of the factoring group. Second, the U.S. factor already will have a contractual relationship with a factor located in the buyer's country. That overseas factor, after investigating the buyer's creditworthiness, guarantees the buyer's payment. Third, based on the assurances from the overseas factor, the U.S. factor also guarantees payment. These guarantees permit the seller to receive immediate financing from either the U.S. factor or a local bank. Finally, when the buyer's payment is due, it is collected by the overseas factor and forwarded to the seller. The seller can then repay the advance. (A variation on this factor arrangement was briefly explored in the *Pfeiffer* case that appeared earlier in this chapter. There the middleman/reseller used a factor to gain an advance on its resale of the goods.)

Forfait Financing

Another form of nonrecourse financing—**forfaiting**—was developed after World War II to provide financing for trade between the countries of Eastern and Western Europe. Under a forfaiting arrangement, the underlying sales contract generally requires the buyer to provide a promissory note or time draft in return for the shipping documents. The seller then takes this negotiable instrument and sells it to a commercial bank (the forfait house) at a discount. Forfait is attractive to the seller because, as a nonrecourse device, the seller walks away from the transaction with immediate access to payment and no credit risk. The forfait house assumes this risk; although frequently it requires that the buyer's bank guarantee the buyer's promise.

Forfait is widely used in Europe and Asia, and several European banks have been trying to establish a presence in the United States. However, U.S. exporters and banks have been slow to accept this method of finance. One factor that has limited its use is that most forfait houses do not finance export sales of less than $500,000.

Acceptance Financing

Under **acceptance financing** a bank accepts drafts drawn by either the seller or the buyer and advances them discounted funds. For instance, the terms of a sales contract may require the buyer to arrange for a letter of credit payable at sight. However, the buyer may not have sufficient funds to pay for the goods until after it has had an opportunity to resell them. In this case, the buyer could draw and endorse a time draft drawn on its bank. The bank will accept the draft (called a banker's acceptance) and provide discounted funds to the buyer, who will repay the face amount at maturity (after it has had an opportunity to resell the goods). Between the time of the bank's acceptance and the buyer's repayment, the bank has the option of holding the draft or rediscounting it in the open market.

Leasing

Overseas sales also can be financed through a **leasing arrangement.** Under this alternative, the lessor (the party receiving the rental fees) might be the exporter/seller. However, it is more likely that an international leasing company buys the goods from the seller and then leases them to the lessee/buyer. In many instances, the lessee reserves the option to buy the goods at the expiration of the leasing term. Leasing, which often provides for long-term financing, is commonly found in transactions involving expensive capital goods and equipment.

Eximbank

Commercial banks often are reluctant to provide loans to small and midsize companies engaged in international transactions. The Export-Import Bank of the United States (**Eximbank**) attempts to alleviate this problem by making guarantees to banks that extend working capital loans to U.S. exporters or provide financing to overseas customers of U.S. exports (at least 50 percent U.S. origin). Eximbank guarantees an approved lender up to 90 percent of principal and interest on a single transaction or on a revolving basis. The loans generally are short term (no more than 12 months), and the borrower must provide collateral of at least 90 percent of the face amount of the loan. Frequently, Eximbank requires that the goods be financed on terms of an irrevocable letter of credit.

Under the Federal Credit Reform Act of 1990, Eximbank was required to reevaluate its programs to give the government a better idea of the true cost of federal credit programs. After determining that loan guarantees might actually cost the government more than direct loans, Eximbank has indicated it might shift its emphasis away from guarantees toward more direct loans. This has raised a clamor among commercial banks, which fear that Eximbank may become a major competitor in international trade financing.

Foreign Credit Insurance Association

The **Foreign Credit Insurance Association** (FCIA), the insurance arm of Eximbank, was established to protect against the commercial and political risks that attend extending credit terms to foreign buyers. Because FCIA insures the exporter against nonpayment, it greatly aids U.S. exporters attempting to discount their foreign receivables to obtain immediate financing. Basically, the exporter pledges its FCIA-insured receivables as collateral for a bank loan. This can be done in either of two ways. First, the exporter could borrow from a commercial bank that already has its own FCIA policy to cover open account transactions or unconfirmed documentary credits. Second, the exporter could secure its own FCIA policy and assign its right to collect on the policy to the lender as collateral for the loan.

COUNTERTRADE

Introduction

With global demand for credit on the increase and many banks hesitant to finance international sales, more and more exporters are forced to resort to less desirable options. **Countertrade** is one such option. In general, it involves linking two or more trade obligations using some form of product-for-product exchange. Thus, the seller, in order to secure a contract with the buyer, may agree to purchase goods designated by the buyer.

There is no single form of countertrade transaction; instead, the parties usually individualize their contract by combining different types of countertrading techniques. And while numerous nations practice countertrade, no uniform national or international legislation governs its use. In 1979, the United Nations Commission on International Trade Law (UNCITRAL) adopted the position that countertrade took too many different forms to be fit for uniform international regulation.

These uncertainties make countertrade a cumbersome and risky financing alternative that should not be undertaken without a great deal of caution and preparation. Yet, despite these problems, countertrade transactions are on the upswing, and today countertrade accounts for perhaps one third of all international trade. This section briefly explores the fundamental reasons behind the prevalence of countertrade in the global market. This is followed by a quick look at the major countertrading techniques. Finally, it examines some difficulties that must be overcome if the parties hope to successfully carry out a countertrade transaction. This section aims to highlight some basic issues that must be considered in structuring a countertrade deal so the reader will better understand how to minimize the attendant risks.

Rationale

Most of the impetus behind the increase in countertrade today stems from a shortage of convertible currencies in many of the developing nations of the world. (It has been estimated that at least 70 percent of the world's economies have soft currencies.) U.S. exporters are finding that consumers in these cash-strapped nations want to buy U.S. products, but they lack ready access to U.S. currency. By purchasing an equivalent amount of goods from the buyer or someone else in the buyer's country, the seller can generate the foreign exchange needed to consummate the original sale. While this is an awkward and often inefficient way of structuring a sale, U.S. exporters frequently are willing to assume the additional burden because, by penetrating a soft-currency market today, they may cement a market share in what will someday be a hard-currency country.

Types of Countertrade Transactions

As was mentioned above, the terms and conditions of countertrade have not been standardized. Accordingly, there are no universally accepted categories or descriptions. However, a countertrade transaction might take several generally recognizable forms. Three of these principal types are explored in this section.

Barter

The simplest form of countertrade—**barter**—probably is the earliest form of trade. At its most basic level, barter occurs when two parties exchange goods with each other. Pure barter exchanges between private parties are rare today. Perhaps the most common form of barter involves a transaction where two traders swap deliveries of equivalent products destined for delivery to other customers in order to lower transportation costs. For example, suppose a Saudi Arabian company has contracted to sell petroleum products to a U.S. company. At the same time, a Mexican company is under contract to sell similar products to a German business. To save on shipping

FIGURE 7–4   Barter

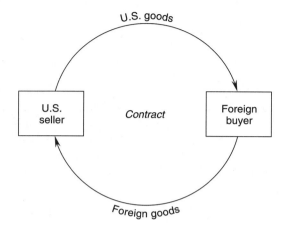

charges, the Saudi and Mexican oil producers swap their obligations; the Mexican oil goes to the U.S. buyer and the Saudi oil goes to the German purchaser.

Buy-backs

Under a **buy-back,** the buyer agrees to purchase a factory or equipment from the seller on the condition that the seller will buy the output produced by the factory or equipment. These arrangements generally are long-term, high-value transactions that should not be entered without careful consideration. They have a great likelihood of turning sour since the original seller often has little control over the quality of the goods produced from the original factory or equipment.

Counterpurchase

In a **counterpurchase** agreement, the buyer purchases goods from the seller on the condition that the seller either obligate itself to buy unrelated goods from the buyer or from someone else designated by the buyer. In another variation of this device, the original seller may be required to arrange for a third party to buy goods from the original buyer or from someone designated by the buyer. This is the most widely used of all the countertrade categories.

Potential Pitfalls   The risks accompanying a countertrade arrangement extend well beyond those associated with normal commercial transactions. Countertrade may include three or more interrelated agreements involving as many or more different parties. Not only

FIGURE 7–5   Buy-backs

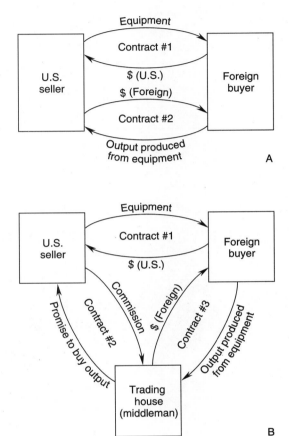

must the parties concern themselves with the content of each contract for the purchase of goods, but they also must carefully define the linkages between each set of agreements.

For these reasons, countertrade is not recommended for smaller companies or businesses new to the international market. Most large multinationals rely on countertrade consultants or special in-house departments, while other firms rely on international trading houses to assist them in selling their countertraded merchandise. Recognizing the pitfalls that often attend countertrading deals (and hoping to offset the greater countertrading experience of European and Japanese firms), the U.S. Department of Commerce has established an Office of Barter to monitor global trends in countertrade and assist U.S. countertraders.

FIGURE 7–6   Counterpurchases

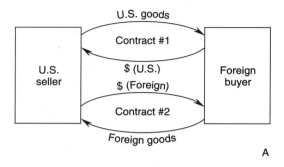

A

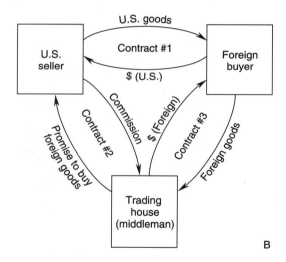

B

■

PAGNAN S.p.A. v. GRANARIA B.V.
[1986] 2 Lloyd's Rep. 547 (C.A.)

■ **FACTS** Pagnan had contracted with a German company to purchase 65,000 tons of Thailand tapioca in a number of separate shipments. In another transaction, Granaria had purchased 21,000 tons of Chinese manioc for shipment in January/February 1984. Pagnan and Granaria then began negotiating a countertrade arrangement in which Granaria would sell Pagnan the 21,000 tons of Chinese manioc for delivery to an Italian port in January/

February 1984 and Pagnan would sell to Granaria an equivalent amount of Thai tapioca for shipment to a north European port in September/October 1984. When Pagnan refused to go forward with the transaction, Granaria sued under a theory of breach of contract. Pagnan argued there was no contract since the parties had not formally agreed on a price differential or on the type of export certificate each would provide.

■ **ISSUE** Were the parties legally bound to this countertrade transaction?

■ **DECISION** No. The idea is that each would buy from the other and there would be a "swap" transaction. This was a complicated deal that had ample scope for misunderstanding. It was not a case of selling just one product; it involved selling two products and integrating the two contracts. In a deal such as this, one of the principal terms that needed to be negotiated was the price differential between the Chinese manioc and the Thai tapioca to reflect the difference in quality. (Manioc is the same product as tapioca except the Chinese product is of slightly better quality than the Thai product.) Agreeing on the price differential was even more important because Pagnan would have to pay in January/February 1984 while Granaria would not be required to pay until the following September or October. There was a further complication. Thai tapioca faces an import duty of only 6 percent if it is covered by a Thai export certificate. Chinese manioc can attract an import duty of between 6 and 30 percent, depending on whether it falls within the quota determined by the European Community licensing authority. The parties had agreed neither to the differential in prices nor to what type of export certificates would be available. As a result, neither party was contractually bound to the other.

QUESTIONS AND PROBLEM CASES

1. What are the risks under an open account sales arrangement? Why might a seller contract on an open account rather than under a documentary credit?

2. How do the rights of an assignee to a contract differ from the rights of a holder in due course?

3. Briefly identify and explain the three principles underlying letters of credit.

4. Briefly describe three types of countertrade. Why do parties resort to countertrade?

5. The *Times-Herald* of Bermuda (T-H) arranged with National Park Bank to issue an irrevocable letter of credit to induce R&M to ship 1,000 tons of newsprint paper. The letter of credit conditioned payment on the bank's receipt of a commercial invoice, weight returns, and a bill of lading. Shortly before delivery, T-H learned that R&M had been delivering an inferior grade of paper to its other customers. Accordingly, T-H instructed National Park Bank not to pay on the letter of credit unless the three required documents were accompanied by a certified report from an independent testing agency that the newsprint was of reasonable quality. When R&M refused to supply such a report, the bank refused to pay. Should the bank be required to honor the letter of credit? Explain.

6. Culver entered into a business relationship with Kalliel whereby Kalliel would handle the financial aspects of Culver's business while Culver would manage the day-to-day operations. Subsequently, when Culver notified Kalliel that he urgently needed money, Kalliel arranged to have the bank transfer $30,000 to Culver's account. Culver believed Kalliel would be responsible for repayment of the loan. A week later, Culver was approached by one of Kalliel's employees who told Culver that the bank "wanted to know where the money went for their records." He had Culver sign a document that he represented to be a receipt for the $30,000. In reality, Culver had signed as maker of a preprinted promissory note that contained a blank space for the principal amount. The amount was later filled in as $50,000. Although Culver received only $30,000, the bank deposited the full $50,000 in an account controlled by Kalliel. When the FDIC later took control of the bank's operations, it brought suit against Culver to collect on the $50,000 note. Culver defended on the grounds that since he had been tricked into signing the note, his defense was good against the FDIC even though it was a holder in due course. Is Culver correct? Explain.

7. Norwest Bank issued a letter of credit payable to Conoco. The following provision was printed on the letter:

   This Commercial Letter of Credit shall remain in force for a period of six (6) months from August 5, 1981, and will be available to Conoco, Inc., on its sight draft for 100 percent invoice cost to be accompanied by a letter of demand from Conoco, Inc., and supported by commercial invoices.

Norwest revoked the letter of credit on November 12, 1981. On the following day, Conoco presented its sight draft and the supporting documents. When the bank refused to pay, Conoco sued Norwest for wrongful dishonor of an irrevocable letter of credit. Norwest defended by claiming its promise was revocable. Was the letter of credit irrevocable?

8. Beyene agreed to sell Mohammed Sofan two prefabricated houses. As part of the contract, Sofan arranged to have the Yemen bank issue a letter of credit in favor of Beyene. Among the documents required under the letter of credit was a bill of lading indicating Sofan should be notified by the shipping company upon arrival of the goods. When the documents were presented for payment, the bill of lading listed Mohammed So*r*an instead of Mohammed So*f*an as the party to be notified. Will this misspelling be sufficient grounds for the issuing bank to refuse payment on the letter of credit? Explain.

9. Worldwide Tire contracted to sell tires to Auto Servicio. A letter of credit in favor of Worldwide was issued by Banco de Maracaibo. Hibernia National Bank was to serve as the confirming bank for this documentary credit. When the requested documents were presented, Hibernia paid on the letter of credit. It was later discovered that the documents had been forged and no tires had been shipped. Auto Servicio argued that Hibernia could have easily discovered the fraudulent scheme by looking beyond the face of the documents presented. If this is true, should Hibernia be liable for negligently honoring the letter of credit? Explain.

10. Sztejn contracted to purchase bristles from Transea Traders. To pay for the bristles, Sztejn arranged to have the Schroder Banking Corporation issue an irrevocable letter of credit in favor of Transea. Payment would be made upon shipment of the bristles and presentation of an invoice and a bill of lading covering the shipment. Instead of shipping bristles, Transea filled 50 crates with cowhair and rubbish that it hoped to pass off as bristles. When Sztejn learned of this deceit, he instructed Schroder Bank to refuse payment on the letter of credit even though the documents, on their face, appeared legitimate. Should the bank refuse payment? Explain.

8

Dispute Resolution

INTRODUCTION

Each day, more and more businesses realize the countless benefits that await those who internationalize their operations. Prudent managers have expanded their horizons and now scour the globe for investment, sourcing, and distribution opportunities. Despite this tremendous potential, however, not all world traders recall their international experiences with fondness. Global transactions frequently span great distances and bring together people of diverse cultures who may have vastly different methods of doing business. These characteristics greatly increase the likelihood that the parties will, at some point, be confronted with a contractual dispute of sufficient magnitude to scuttle the deal.

Chapter Overview

Even meticulously planned transactions between familiar and well-intentioned partners sometimes result in unresolvable conflicts. Experienced managers are well aware of this and, accordingly, anticipate the inevitability of disputes and carefully prepare for their eventuality. This chapter examines the fundamental issues that arise in dispute resolution. It begins with a look at litigation—the alternative with which business students generally are most familiar. As this discussion reveals the numerous problems that confront litigation efforts in the international environment, it paves the way for a following section emphasizing the importance of dispute awareness at the contract formation stage. That material illustrates how careful planning enhances the likelihood that problems will be handled quickly and efficiently. The chapter closes with an investigation of the growing role of arbitration as the preferred method for resolving international contractual disputes.

LITIGATION

Background

Disputes frequently arise during the life of a contractual relationship; however, in most instances, the parties can adjust their expectations and arrive at a peaceful solution. In those instances where a voluntary settlement cannot be reached, more drastic measures may be contemplated. One such action, **litigation**, occurs when the disputants petition the courts to settle their differences.

Problems with Litigation

Litigation generally is the option of last resort rather than a favored dispute resolution strategy. For one reason, the costs (both in time and money) associated with litigation tend to be extremely high. Further, lawsuits frequently place irreparable strains on business relationships, destroying the likelihood of future cooperation. Perhaps most importantly, litigating international contracts can be extremely cumbersome and of-

---

CONCEPT SUMMARY
Costs of Litigation

Delay	Crowded court dockets make process time consuming
Expensive	Court costs and attorneys' fees may be exorbitant
Enforceability Problems	There is no global treaty ensuring enforcement of foreign judgments
Adversarial	May severely strain or destroy potentially profitable business relationships
Public	Competitors may gain access to business secrets

---

ten ineffective because there is no international court system available for resolving commercial disputes between private parties.

Public International Law

No single set of rules or legal machinery governs contractual relationships between private parties. The body of international rules and procedures that we generally refer to as international law (also called *public international law*) primarily is addressed to the relations between nations. Likewise, while the International Court of Justice (World Court) sometimes deals with commercial issues, only nations may bring an action before it.

Private International Law

Private parties, then, must bring their lawsuits before the domestic court systems. Their litigation is part of the *private international law*, which is composed of the rules of national legal systems for resolving disputes involving litigants from different countries. These procedures determine in what country or countries a lawsuit may be brought, how evidence may be gathered, what nation's laws will govern the dispute, and when the courts of one nation will recognize and enforce a judgment issued by the courts of another. Because the domestic court systems of the world vary tremendously, litigation of private international disputes can be a confusing and frustrating experience.

Jurisdiction
Despite wide differences among the world's national courts, certain generalizations can be made. For instance, a court normally must have authority over the issues involved in the conflict (subject matter jurisdiction) and over the parties being sued (personal jurisdiction) before it may properly hear the dispute. This personal jurisdiction generally does not exist unless the defendant has some close connection (minimum contacts) with the territory where the suit is brought. Further, most legal systems have formal rules (service of process) ensuring that defendants are properly notified of any lawsuits filed against them. Finally, most judicial systems have established elab-

orate procedures for the discovery of the evidence necessary to a proper resolution of the dispute. This section briefly examines each of these issues.

Subject Matter Jurisdiction

All courts operate under some set of procedural rules that determine the type of cases or issues with which they may deal. For instance, many countries have established specialized courts that deal exclusively with commercial disputes. Or, in the federal district courts of the United States, a dispute involving a U.S. citizen and a citizen from a foreign country must involve a claim of more than $50,000. Failure to file a lawsuit with the court that has **subject matter jurisdiction** may, in some legal systems, result in the plaintiff forfeiting her cause of action entirely. And, even if the plaintiff is permitted to refile in the proper court, her initial mistake can result in the loss of valuable time and money.

Personal Jurisdiction

A court also is precluded from adjudicating a legal dispute unless it has **personal jurisdiction** over the defendant. This generally is not a problem if the defendant is a resident of the country where the court is located. However, the situation is more uncertain when the plaintiff files a lawsuit against a nonresident. In those instances, the court does not have personal jurisdiction unless it can be shown that the nonresident defendant has certain **minimum contacts** with the country where the suit is brought.

In the United States, the minimum contacts requirement often is met if the defendant intentionally conducts business in the United States or was served process (notified of the suit) while physically present in the United States. French courts adhere to a more expansive notion of personal jurisdiction for contractual disputes between French citizens and foreign nonresidents. They claim personal jurisdiction over the nonresident regardless of whether the contract was transacted in France or in another country.

■

GULF CONSOLIDATED SERVICES v. CORINTH PIPEWORKS
898 F.2d 1071 (5th Cir. 1990)

■ **FACTS** Gulf Consolidated Services, a Texas corporation operating under the name of International Materials & Services (IMS), purchased 1,260 joints of steel oil field casing from Corinth Pipeworks, a Greek corporation with its principal office in Athens, Greece. After the joints arrived in Texas, IMS had them threaded and then sold 66 of them to United Pipe & Supply (United). During drilling operations, several of the casings failed, costing United over $400,000 in losses. Analysis of the failed casings indicated they contained weld seam defects that were traceable to Corinth. When suit was filed against Corinth in the U.S. District Court for the Southern District of Texas, the Greek company argued it lacked sufficient contacts with Texas for it to be subject to the personal jurisdiction of the district court. In particular, Corinth argued that it purposefully structured its conduct so as to avoid being subject to the jurisdiction of the courts of Texas. For instance, it maintained its offices and factory in Greece and was not registered to do business in the United States. It had no agent, office or assets in the

United States. Further, IMS and Corinth negotiated their contract by telegram and the actual sale occurred in Greece.

■ **ISSUE** Did the U.S. district court have personal jurisdiction over the Greek company?

■ **DECISION** Yes. A party can, through its actions, avoid being haled into a foreign jurisdiction. However, the simple fact that a transaction is consummated outside a jurisdiction does not prevent the sale from forming the basis of personal jurisdiction. The *minimum contacts* requirement is satisfied, and personal jurisdiction is proper, where a foreign defendant delivered a product into the *stream of commerce* with the expectation that it would be purchased by or used by consumers in the state where the court is located. Here, Corinth's expectation that the casings would be used in Texas is indisputable.

ETHICAL IMPLICATIONS Corinth admitted it tried to structure the transaction so as to avoid being subject to the jurisdiction of the courts of Texas. And, in the first line of its decision, the court states that a foreign company can permissibly attempt to avoid the jurisdiction of a state where it does business. Is it ethical to sell goods in a country while trying to shield yourself from the damages they might cause?

Jurisdiction over Corporate Parents

Many multinational corporations structure their overseas operations to insulate themselves from the personal jurisdiction of the courts in the foreign countries where they wish to do business. For instance, Corinth, the Greek corporation in the previous case, might have formed a wholly owned subsidiary corporation in Texas. The subsidiary would purchase casings from Corinth in contracts that occurred entirely in Greece. It could then resell the casings to IMS. When the casings failed, the Texas court would have jurisdiction over the subsidiary but not over Corinth, the corporate parent.

These corporate strategies will not succeed when the corporate parent becomes too closely involved with the ultimate purchaser. Further, if the subsidiary corporation is undercapitalized (it does not have enough assets to pay expected claims against it) or is the alter ego of its parent (they share the same officers and directors) the foreign court may have personal jurisdiction over the parent.

Service of Process

A defendant generally is not subject to the personal jurisdiction of a court unless he has received **service of process**. This formal notification provides the defendant with documents that give him legally sufficient notice of the lawsuit that has been filed against him. Personal jurisdiction occurs automatically if the defendant is physically present in the state where the court is located when the papers are served. Should the defendant fail to appear at the hearing after receiving adequate notice, he generally will lose the lawsuit through a default judgment.

When both parties are in the same state, service frequently is carried out through registered mail or by a process server. The jurisdictional issues become cloudier when service of process occurs across national borders. First, because the defendant is physically located in a foreign nation, there must be some minimum contacts (instead of mere physical presence) for personal jurisdiction to arise. Second, it may be difficult and expensive to ensure that the defendant is properly served. Many courts do not permit service of process on a foreign person by registered mail. They require plaintiffs to comply with the cumbersome requirements of the 1965 Hague Service Convention.

The Hague Service Convention is a multilateral treaty designed to facilitate the service of process across national borders and to provide proof that timely notice actually has been given. In serving process on a defendant in a ratifying country, a plaintiff may: (1) formally petition a central authority established by the country to serve the papers on the defendant, (2) request its diplomatic or consular agents in the foreign country to effect the service, (3) petition the judicial officers of the foreign nation to make the notification, (4) follow any other procedures established by treaty between the foreign nation and the nation where the court is located, or (5) comply with any method approved by the foreign nation. The United States and over 30 other nations have ratified the treaty.

BANKSTON v. TOYOTA MOTOR CORPORATION
889 F.2d 172 (8th Cir. 1989)

■ **FACTS** Charles Bankston, Sr., filed suit in the U.S. District Court for the Western District of Arkansas against Toyota Motor Corporation, a Japanese corporation, seeking damages resulting from an accident involving a Toyota truck. Bankston attempted to serve process on Toyota by sending a summons and complaint by registered mail, return receipt requested, to Tokyo, Japan. The documents were in English and did not include a translation into Japanese. The receipt of service was signed and returned to Bankston. Toyota filed a motion to dismiss the suit against it, claiming there had been an improper service of process.

■ **ISSUE** Was the service of process by registered mail proper?

■ **DECISION** No. At issue in this case is the correct interpretation of Article 10 of the Hague Service Convention, which provides in relevant part: *"Provided the State*

of destination does not object, the present Convention shall not interfere with (a) the freedom to send judicial documents, by postal channels, directly to persons abroad." Two distinct lines of Article 10(a) interpretation have arisen in recent years. Some courts hold that since the purported purpose of the Hague Convention is to facilitate service abroad, the reference to *"the freedom to send judicial documents, by postal channels"* includes sending such documents for the service of process. A second line of reasoning is that the words *"send judicial documents"* in Article 10(a) do not include service of process. Subscribers to this interpretation maintain that Article 10(a) merely provides a method for sending subsequent documents after service of process has been obtained by other means. This second line of reasoning is more persuasive. Sending a copy of a summons and complaint by registered mail to a defendant in a foreign country is not a method of service of process permitted by the Hague Convention.

Gathering Evidence Abroad

Collecting the evidence necessary to successfully prove a case often is the most expensive and time-consuming part of international litigation. The courts of the United States place a great deal of emphasis on *discovery* (the pre-trial gathering of evidence) to avoid unfair surprises and to encourage private settlement of lawsuits. In other nations, particularly the civil law systems, the courts rely less on the discovery efforts of the litigants.

To facilitate the discovery process in litigation involving foreign parties, the United States and many Western European countries have adopted the Hague Evidence Convention. (Few countries outside of Western Europe have ratified the treaty.) Under the convention, a lawyer may gather evidence abroad by requesting the courts of the foreign country to assist in the collection of the information. The foreign courts perform the discovery process as long as the request does not violate their national laws. To date, the Hague Evidence Convention has not been widely used, in part, because the treaty vests a great deal of discretion in foreign officials as to when and how they respond to discovery requests. However, the U.S. State Department generally assists U.S. residents in their efforts to gather evidence from foreign parties.

Where to Litigate?

Frequently, more than one court has jurisdiction over the parties and the subject matter of their dispute. It is then necessary to determine which court is the proper place for the lawsuit to be brought. This concept is known as **venue**. When contracts cross national borders, venue often is proper in both the country of the seller and the country of the buyer. If the contract is formed in a third country and will be performed in a fourth, courts in at least four nations could have proper venue.

Where the lawsuit actually is brought can be crucial to the outcome of the dispute since the laws of the forum determine which body of substantive rules governs the conflict. Further, the procedural rules controlling admissibility of evidence and the conduct of the trial may vary greatly from legal system to legal system. Finally, being summoned into a foreign court can cause an unwilling defendant a tremendous psychological and financial burden.

When contractual disputes arise, each of the parties opts for the court offering it the greatest tactical advantage. This frequently results in one party questioning the suitability of that particular forum. Or, after a race between each of the parties to file a claim in its favored location, two separate courts might be called to simultaneously try the same dispute. These two situations, an inconvenient forum and parallel litigation, now are briefly examined.

Forum Non Conveniens

Sometimes a court meets jurisdictional and venue requirements, but the trial would be more convenient and just if it were conducted in another forum. Under these circumstances, a judge is permitted to dismiss the case under the doctrine of **forum non conveniens**. This defense has assumed great importance in the United States due to the tremendous growth of international business transactions. More and more it is utilized by multinational corporations attempting to block access to foreign injury victims hoping to take advantage of the liberal tort and product liability laws in the United States. Forum non conveniens is not widely found outside of the common law legal systems.

In deciding if a case should be dismissed on the basis of forum non conveniens, U.S. courts utilize a three-step process that considers certain private and public interests.

1. The court looks to see if there are any **alternative forums** with subject matter jurisdiction over the dispute and personal jurisdiction over the defendant. If there are none, the court will not dismiss the suit. In some instances, a court will not dismiss on forum non conveniens grounds unless the defendant first agrees to submit to the jurisdiction of another forum acceptable to the plaintiff.

2. In this part of the inquiry, the court weighs various **private factors** to evaluate the relative advantages and obstacles to a fair trial. Included among the private interests are: (*a*) the ease of access to evidence, (*b*) the costs of summoning witnesses, (*c*) the need to actually view any premises, and (*d*) the enforceability of the court's judgment.

3. Finally, in deciding if the lawsuit should be removed to another forum, the court considers certain **public factors**. These include: (*a*) the amount of congestion the court is experiencing, (*b*) the desire to avoid burdening jurors with issues that have little relevance to the community, (*c*) the importance of having the trial in a community with a strong interest in the outcome, and (*d*) the desire to have the case decided in a forum that is familiar with the law governing the dispute.

U.S. courts seldom disturb the plaintiff's choice of forum unless the balance tilts strongly in favor of the defendant. Further, the scales are weighted even more heavily in the plaintiff's favor if she is a resident of the United States. When the plaintiff does not reside in the United States, the court is far less deferential to her choice. (This stands in stark contrast to most foreign legal systems where the venue provisions tend to favor the defendant.) Consider the following case where, despite the strong presumption in favor of the American plaintiff's choice of a U.S. forum, the court dismissed the case under forum non conveniens.

INTERPANE COATINGS v. AUSTRALIA & NEW ZEALAND BANKING GROUP
732 F.Supp. 909 (N.D. Ill. 1990)

■ **FACTS** Interpane Coatings, a Wisconsin corporation, delivered goods to McDowell Pacific, an Australian buyer. The parties utilized a documentary exchange whereby McDowell would receive the bills of lading covering the goods upon its acceptance of drafts promising payment to Interpane. To facilitate this documentary transfer, Interpane and McDowell enlisted the services of Australia & New Zealand Banking Group (ANZ), an Australian bank. Out of concern that McDowell might fail to honor its promise to pay on the drafts, Interpane instructed ANZ not to release the bills of lading unless the bank would guarantee the debt. ANZ misunderstood these instructions and delivered the bills of lading to McDowell. After taking possession of the goods, McDowell refused to honor its obligation to pay on the drafts. Interpane filed suit against ANZ for negligence and breach of contract. It brought suit in an Illinois federal district court because ANZ maintained an office in Chicago and thus could easily be served with process there. ANZ asserted that the U.S. district court was a highly inconvenient forum in which to litigate Interpane's claims and the suit should have been brought in Australia.

■ **ISSUE**   Should the U.S. district court dismiss the case on the grounds of forum non conveniens?

■ **DECISION**   Yes. The application of forum non conveniens presupposes the existence of an adequate alternative forum. Interpane argued that Australia would not meet this requirement because that nation requires foreign plaintiffs to pay a security deposit to cover the defendant's costs. It stated that it did not wish to expose additional monies to risk. However, an alternative forum is not adequate only if the remedy provided there is so clearly inadequate that it is no remedy at all. The financial burden posed by Australia's security deposit requirement does not disqualify the Australian courts as an alternative forum. The private factors involved in this dispute completely favor an Australian forum. Most of the witnesses, particularly on the negligence claim, live in Australia. Further, the bulk of the evidence is located in that country also. Finally, McDowell (the Australian buyer) is located in Australia and is not subject to the process of the U.S. court. The public factors also favor Australia. The Northern District of Illinois has no interest in this litigation. Australian law probably will govern both the negligence and the contract claims. Permitting the suit to go forward in the United States would require expert testimony to establish contract principles and Australian business custom and practice. Because both the private and public interest factors come out so heavily on the Australian side, this suit should be dismissed under the forum non conveniens doctrine.

Parallel Proceedings in Different Jurisdictions

International disputes over commercial matters sometimes end up being litigated simultaneously in two different courts. For example, suppose a buyer, Panama Processes, brought a breach of contract suit against a seller, Cities Service, in a U.S. district court. After the U.S. court denied Cities Service's motion to dismiss on forum non conveniens grounds, Cities Service filed its own suit against Panama Processes, on the same issues, in a Brazilian court. Panama Processes might then petition the U.S. court to enjoin Cities Service from participation in the Brazilian trial, but such a request is likely to be denied. When two sovereigns have concurrent personal jurisdiction over the parties, one court ordinarily does not try to restrain the proceedings before the other. This is because most courts are reluctant to interfere with foreign proceedings that parallel their own trials out of deference to the integrity and authority of the foreign tribunal. Failure to exercise such restraint could start a retaliatory cycle among the courts of the world.

In the contract dispute between Panama Processes and Cities Service, the first final judgment generally binds the other court. Thus, if the Brazilian court issues a final judgment first, the U.S. court will abide by the decision despite the fact that the Brazilian suit was the second to be filed and even though trial procedures in Brazil differ significantly from those in the United States.

What Law Governs?   When the parties' contract does not specify which body of law governs their dispute, it is determined by the rules of the forum where the lawsuit occurs. The process by which a court chooses the appropriate law is known as **conflict of laws**. Most legal systems have well-established conflict of laws rules. For instance, when the dispute is over a sale of goods contract, the courts of many nations apply the laws of the seller's country. In the civil law systems, conflict of laws determinations tend to be derived from a mechanical application of each nation's codified procedures for selecting the governing law.

In the United States, courts handle conflict of laws issues in several ways. For sales of goods under the Uniform Commercial Code, courts have much discretion since they are to apply the law that bears an appropriate relation to the contract. The common law has two predominant approaches. Under the simpler approach, if the dispute is over the actual formation of the agreement, the applicable law is that of the place where the contract is made. When the conflict concerns the actual performance of the contract, the governing law generally is that of the place where performance was to have occurred. The second (and most widely used) approach applies the law of the jurisdiction with the **most significant contacts**. For contracts, this involves an examination of: (*a*) the place of contracting, (*b*) the place of negotiation, (*c*) the place of performance, (*d*) the location of the subject matter of the contract, and (*e*) the domicile, place of incorporation, and place of business of the parties.

For tort claims, the majority of U.S. courts discover the jurisdiction with the most significant contacts by examining four factors: (*a*) the domicile, place of incorporation, and place of business of the parties; (*b*) the place where the tortious conduct occurred; (*c*) the place where the relationship of the parties is centered; and (*d*) the place where the injury occurred.

WALPEX TRADING v. YACIMIENTOS PETROLIFEROS
756 F.Supp. 136 (S.D. N.Y. 1991)

■ **FACTS** Walpex Trading Company, an American export company, brought a breach of contract suit against Yacimientos Petroliferos Fiscales Bolivianos, a Bolivian government-owned corporation that purchased supplies for the Bolivian government's national oil program. The parties first made contact after Yacimientos publicly invited bids for a supply of piping. The invitation appeared in Spanish in several Bolivian newspapers and was read by Walpex's Bolivian sales agent. After Walpex filed suit in a U.S. district court in New York, Yacimientos argued that the dispute was governed by Bolivian law.

■ **ISSUE** Should the U.S. court try the lawsuit under Bolivian contract law?

■ **DECISION** Yes. Although it is unclear whether the parties agreed in advance to be bound by the laws of Bolivia, that issue need not be resolved because this action should be governed by Bolivian law even in the absence of such an agreement. Pursuant to the conflict of laws rules of this forum, the law governing the contract should be the law of the jurisdiction having the greatest interest in the litigation. The defendant is a Bolivian resident and an instrumentality of the Bolivian government. The solicitation of bids was published only in Spanish and only in Bolivia. All the events underlying formation of the contract occurred in Bolivia. New York has only two significant contacts with the transaction: (1) plaintiff was a New York resident, and (2) Walpex's letter of credit was obtained from a New York bank. Bolivia's interest in having the litigation governed by its laws far outweighs that of New York. The piping involved in the contract was to be used in Bolivia's national oil industry. While New York has a strong interest in regulating transactions conducted within its borders, there is no indication the state has a paramount interest in applying its law whenever a New York business entity contracts with anyone anywhere. The resolution of this case is more likely to affect international confidence in the stability of Bolivia's commercial and legal systems than those of New York.

Enforcement of Judgments

At the conclusion of the lawsuit, the court instructs the losing party to pay damages or otherwise abide by its decision. While many parties voluntarily obey the court, many others do not readily comply. The winning party may then have to return to court and request a judicial order demanding enforcement of the judgment. If the losing party is physically present within the original court's jurisdiction or owns assets in that territory, it may be fairly simple to compel compliance. However, if the losing party and its assets are located outside of that jurisdiction, the winner is forced to seek enforcement from a foreign tribunal.

In the ideal situation, the foreign court *enforces* the original judgment by ordering the losing party to fully comply with its terms. Should that not occur, the foreign court may at least give *recognition* to the judgment. In that case, it enforces some aspects of the decision while permitting the parties to relitigate others. In many instances, the foreign court neither enforces nor recognizes the judgment, thereby forcing the plaintiff to relitigate the entire dispute.

Enforcing U.S. Judgments Abroad

At present, there is no worldwide system for the international enforcement of judgments from U.S. courts. Further, while many nations have established bilateral agreements and there exist a few regional accords (i.e., the European Community, the South American nations) calling for mutual enforcement of judgments, the United States has not participated in these efforts. Thus, while many nations give partial recognition to U.S. judgments, most do not fully enforce them.

Certain nations, like Indonesia, refuse to enforce all foreign judgments. Others (Norway and Saudi Arabia) only enforce foreign judgments from countries with which they have an enforcement treaty. Many nations require *reciprocity;* that is, they will not enforce U.S. judgments if their judgments are not enforced in the United States. Both Austria and Korea, among other nations, take the position that the United States does not have reciprocity with them.

The most frequent justification for refusing to enforce a foreign judgment is that the original court lacked subject matter or personal jurisdiction. Some countries, such as France and Brazil, claim to have exclusive jurisdiction over their own nationals unless they consented to the jurisdiction of the foreign court. Other countries raise numerous public policy reasons for their refusal to enforce judgments. For instance, Greece and Thailand refuse to enforce any judgments from abroad unless the plaintiff's claim was one that would have been actionable in their country. Other countries (India and the Philippines) reject a judgment if their courts believe the foreign court applied the wrong governing law.

Sometimes a nation enforces only part of a U.S. judgment or may otherwise diminish its value. For example, many Islamic nations refuse to enforce the interest portion of a foreign money judgment. Other countries may have currency controls that either prohibit repatriation of funds or require that judgments be paid in their local currency.

U.S. Enforcement of Foreign Judgments

The U.S. Constitution requires that each state fully recognize and enforce the judgments of the courts of the other 49 states. While this *full faith and credit clause* does not extend to foreign nations' judgments, state courts have the discretion to enforce them if they choose. Most of the state and federal courts in the United States do recognize and enforce the judgments of foreign tribunals.

Generally, U.S. courts fully enforce a foreign judgment when that judgment does not violate any strong public policy. Courts frequently base this decision on the doctrine of *comity,* which refers to the voluntary deference and respect the institutions of one nation give to those of another. Recognition and enforcement are extended to foreign judgments where there has been a full and fair trial before a court with proper subject matter and personal jurisdiction. Mere procedural differences from the rules followed by the enforcing court do not justify nonenforcement. However, a court will refuse to recognize or enforce a judgment if it believes the foreign tribunal was biased against the losing party.

A few U.S. courts base their enforcement decision on the doctrine of reciprocity. Thus, a foreign judgment would not be given conclusive effect unless the courts of the nation that rendered the judgment would give the same effect to a comparable judgment from a U.S. court. However, most U.S. courts today have rejected or ignored reciprocity, in part, because it seems unjust to penalize private litigants for the enforcement policies of the various nations.

■

BANQUE LIBANAISE POUR LE COMMERCE v. KHREICH
915 F.2d 1000 (5th Cir. 1990)

■ **FACTS** Banque Libanaise, a French banking corporation, operated a branch office in Abu Dhabi, one of the seven emirates comprising the United Arab Emirates. Hanna Elias Khreich, a former resident of Abu Dhabi who is now a naturalized U.S. citizen and a resident of Texas, was sued by the Banque Libanaise in an Abu Dhabi court. After the Abu Dhabi court rendered a judgment for 200,000 dirhams against Khreich, the bank petitioned a U.S. federal court to enforce the judgment.

■ **ISSUE** Should the U.S. court enforce the Abu Dhabi judgment?

■ **DECISION** No. Historically, foreign country judgments have not been entitled to full faith and credit, but only to comity. Although comity is not a rule of law, it is more than mere courtesy and accommodation. Still, notwithstanding comity concerns, judges retain the discretion to refuse to recognize foreign judgments due to lack of reciprocity. Evidence was presented that suggested Abu Dhabi courts demonstrate a certain skepticism toward the unquestioning application of legal principles adopted from the developed Western nations, particularly where these appear to work to the disadvantage of local parties. Given this evidence, it is not an abuse of discretion to deny enforcement of the foreign judgment against Khreich.

ANTICIPATING LEGAL DISPUTES

The previous section demonstrated that the litigation of international disputes can be confusing, time consuming, expensive, and frequently unfruitful. As importantly, by resorting to judicial remedies, the parties risk destroying what still could be a profitable relationship. For these reasons, many managers prefer to explore less con-

---

■   **CONCEPT SUMMARY**   ■
                                 Choosing a Forum for Litigation

Will the Court Have Jurisdiction?	• Subject matter jurisdiction
	• Personal jurisdiction
Will the Court Hear the Case?	• Improper venue
	• Forum non conveniens
Will the Court Have Access?	• Access to witnesses
	• Access to evidence
	• Access to defendant
Will the Court's Judgment Be Enforceable?	• Defendant has assets in the court's jurisdiction
	• Defendant has assets in a jurisdiction that will recognize and enforce the judgment

tentious alternatives before considering litigation. This section examines the importance of anticipating disputes and preparing for their smooth resolution.

Flexible Approaches

In many cultures, the concept of rigidly enforced obligations is alien. Under those circumstances, rather than insisting on a detailed contract, it might be better to fashion a flexible agreement that envisions frequent renegotiation. Even when dealing with parties who insist on certainty and predictability in their agreements, it is possible to craft a carefully worded contract that anticipates and defuses future conflicts.

Adjustment Provisions

The global environment holds so many surprises that conflicts and misunderstandings are almost inevitable. Accordingly, it is essential that contracting partners (particularly in long-term agreements) maintain flexible attitudes at both the drafting and performance stages. This flexibility frequently can be incorporated into a contract through the use of some type of **adjustment provision**.

These clauses can take several forms. For instance, sometimes it is clear at the contract formation stage that certain details need to be negotiated later. This might occur in a licensing agreement that involves the transfer of new technology. Until the parties acquire more experience, they are unable to predict all of the issues upon which agreement is required. At other times, the parties may anticipate that a key condition upon which the contract is based could change. For example, the contract may establish a price for a long-term supply of electrical power while recognizing that future events may drastically alter the conception of what is a fair price. Finally, the parties often realize that events beyond their control (i.e., wars, earthquakes, droughts) can render their original agreement exceedingly more difficult to perform.

In anticipation of these events, a contract may include a wide variety of clauses calling for many actions, ranging from price escalation to renegotiation to termination.

Renegotiation

Most businesses realize that nobody really wins a lawsuit. The time, expense, and uncertainty involved in litigation spurs many disputing parties to seriously pursue contract **renegotiation**. As discussed above, sometimes the contract itself mandates renegotiation through an adjustment provision. However, even in the absence of such a requirement, the parties may find it to be in their best interest to voluntarily restructure their obligations.

Settlements

Even after disputants have become embroiled in litigation, they may simultaneously pursue **settlement** efforts. Some courts actively encourage litigants to consider that action. At the culmination of a successful settlement effort, the parties draft a formal agreement designed to terminate all or part of their legal dispute.

Because settlement agreements are meant to be legally binding, certain precautions should be taken in their negotiation and execution. First, in negotiations with a corporate entity, the discussions must be conducted with a representative who is authorized to legally bind the corporation. Second, the settlement agreement must be carefully worded so it resolves the key issues involved in the dispute without obligating the parties to additional, unintended responsibilities. Finally, judicial procedures governing settlement agreements vary greatly around the world. The parties must be aware of the applicable rules if they hope to arrive at an enforceable settlement.

Key Contractual Provisions

The previous discussion introduced several ways of avoiding the costs and uncertainties associated with litigation. While the contract itself frequently calls for the use of those methods, they are most successful when the parties voluntarily pursue their ongoing relationship with cooperative spirits and flexible attitudes. The focus now shifts from an examination of attitudes to a look at several formal contractual provisions that permit the parties to renegotiate with a reasonable degree of certainty as to the costs and convenience of potential litigation.

Choice of Language Clause

International contracts often involve parties who speak different languages. While each receives a copy of the contract written in her own native language, differences in interpretation are inevitable. Accordingly, the parties should agree in advance on an **official language** text of the contract that will govern any misunderstandings that arise. They may also wish to specify that the official language be used for all future communications, including any nonjudicial dispute resolution that might be called for in the contract. (Nonjudicial, or alternate, dispute mechanisms are discussed below.)

Forum Selection Clause

Increasingly, international contracts include a **forum selection clause**, which specifies the place where litigation is to be brought. These provisions may be either exclusive or nonexclusive. An *exclusive clause* requires that lawsuits be filed only in the designated location. When enforced, such a provision prevents either party from suing anywhere else even though another court might also have jurisdiction. A *nonexclusive clause* permits litigation to be brought in the designated court, but it does not preclude a party from suing in another forum. Thus, in a nonexclusive clause, the parties voluntarily consent to the jurisdiction of the designated forum without waiving their right to litigate in any other court.

While a few nations' courts do not honor forum selection clauses, most enforce the parties' choice if it is not unreasonable. Generally, there is no enforcement problem if the parties select the courts of either of their countries or those of a third country that has some relationship to the contract. The courts of the United States will uphold a freely negotiated forum selection clause unless doing so would be grossly unfair. In the following landmark decision, the U.S. Supreme Court examines these criteria.

THE BREMEN v. ZAPATA OFF-SHORE CO.
407 U.S. 1 (U.S. Sup. Ct. 1972)

■ **FACTS** Unterwester, a German corporation, agreed to tow a drilling rig owned by Zapata, a U.S. corporation, from Louisiana to Italy. After submitting the low bid for the towage, Unterweser sent Zapata a contract that contained a forum selection clause mandating: "*Any dispute arising must be treated before the London Court of Justice.*" After reviewing the contract and making several changes, but without altering the forum selection clause, Zapata signed and returned the contract to Unterweser. While the rig was under tow at sea, it was damaged by a storm and Zapata ordered Unterweser to tow it to Florida (the nearest port of refuge). After Zapata filed a damage claim in a U.S. district court, Unterwester, citing the forum selection clause, petitioned the U.S. court to dismiss the suit for want of jurisdiction.

■ **ISSUE** Should the U.S. court enforce the forum selection clause and dismiss Zapata's lawsuit?

■ **DECISION** Yes. The expansion of American business and industry will hardly be encouraged if we insist on a parochial concept that all disputes must be resolved under our laws and in our courts. We cannot have trade and commerce in world markets and international waters exclusively on our terms, governed by our laws, and resolved in our courts. Foreign businesspersons prefer, as do we, to have disputes resolved in their own courts, but if that choice is not available, then in a neutral forum with experience in the subject matter. Plainly the courts of England meet the standards of neutrality and competence. This forum selection clause was made in an arm's-length negotiation by experienced and sophisticated businesses, and, absent some compelling and countervailing reason, it should be honored by the parties and enforced by the courts. There are important reasons why a freely negotiated private international agreement, unaffected by fraud, undue influence, or overweening bargaining power, such as that involved here, should be given full effect. In the course of the voyage, Unterweser's ship was to traverse the waters of many jurisdictions. Much uncertainty and great inconvenience to both parties could arise if a suit could be maintained in any jurisdiction in which an accident occurred or in any place where the ship might happen to be found. Eliminating all such uncertainties by agreeing in advance on a forum acceptable to both parties is an indispensable element in international trade, commerce, and contracting. It would be unrealistic to think the parties did not conduct their negotiations, including fixing the monetary terms, with the consequences of the forum selection clause figuring prominently in their calculations. Thus, the court should enforce the clause unless Zapata can clearly show that enforcement would be unreasonable and unjust.

Choice of Law Clause

Contracting partners can eliminate a great deal of uncertainty by placing a **choice of law clause** in their agreement. The courts in most of the world's major trading nations enforce such a provision when there is some connection between the chosen legal system and the contract. U.S. courts require that the chosen law bear a *reasonable relation* to the transaction. Generally, the parties meet this test if they select the law of either of their home countries or that of a third country where the contract was negotiated or might be performed.

Despite the growing trend toward enforcement of freely negotiated choice of law clauses, they still should be approached with caution. A few nations (i.e., Chile, Peru) require that contracts performed within their territory be governed by their domestic law. Further, sometimes the legal system selected by the parties changes drastically after the contract has been formed. There may then be controversies over which interpretation governs the contract.

Choice of Currency Clause

The nature of international transactions is such that it is crucial that traders in some way account for foreign exchange risks. As a result, sellers often insist they be paid either in their own currency or in some other freely convertible foreign currency. The various legal systems of the world differ in how they treat such provisions. Although there is no legal prohibition against it, U.S. courts have not been willing to render judgments in foreign currencies. British common law tribunals occasionally do so, and, as a general rule, the civil law courts issue judgments in a foreign currency.

Alternate Dispute Mechanisms

The numerous problems associated with litigation have spurred many global traders to pursue alternate avenues for resolving their business disputes. These devices generally work best when the original contract calls for their use and carefully describes their operating procedures. This section discusses four mechanisms: (*a*) negotiation, (*b*) mediation, (*c*) mini-trial, and (*d*) arbitration. Following this brief overview, the chapter more carefully examines the arbitration alternative.

Negotiation

Unlike litigation where a judge presides over the conflict, in a **negotiation**, the parties personally engage in discussions over how to resolve the matter. As you may imagine, this is unlikely to succeed unless both parties make a good faith effort to arrive at a solution. After reaching an agreement, the parties generally draw up a binding contract spelling out their new obligations.

┌───┐

CONCEPT SUMMARY
Key Contractual Provisions

Choice of Language Clause	• Minimizes interpretation problems by designating the official language for the contract
Forum Selection Clause	• *Exclusive*—requires lawsuits to be filed only in designated forum
	• *Nonexclusive*—consents to suits filed in designated forum but does not preclude others
Choice of Law Clause	• Selects the law that will govern the dispute
	• Chosen law must have reasonable relation to the transaction
Choice of Currency Clause	• Minimizes foreign exchange risks by designating currency in which payment should be made

└───┘

Mediation

With **mediation**, the disputants call in a neutral third party to help them reach a compromise. While some mediators may have the power to force a solution, generally their role is to persuade the parties to voluntarily agree on a common position. As with negotiation, after resolving a dispute through mediation, the parties are likely to draft a contract incorporating their new agreement.

Mini-trial

A **mini-trial** is similar to litigation in that lawyers from each side formally present their legal and factual arguments to each other. Frequently, there is a discovery process in which the parties exchange relevant information. Like mediation, mini-trials generally are officiated by a neutral third party who may be called on to issue a nonbinding decision at the culmination of the lawyers' presentations. As with negotiation and mediation, however, it is up to the parties themselves to voluntarily reach a settlement agreement.

Mini-trials seem best suited for disputes involving complex facts (i.e., licensing of new technology). They permit the parties to avoid complicated legal issues and, instead, focus on the practical business aspects of their dispute.

Arbitration

The generally preferred method of resolving international business disputes is through **arbitration**. This involves the settlement of legal controversies by a nonjudicial third party. Frequently, the arbitrator issues a binding decision; although nonbinding arbitration also is common. As with the three previous alternate mechanisms, the parties must voluntarily agree to arbitrate. They have the power, through their

---

CONCEPT SUMMARY
Alternate Dispute Resolution

Negotiation	• The disputing parties voluntarily hold discussions to resolve the dispute
	• Requires good faith and willingness to compromise
Mediation	• Neutral third party facilitates resolution of dispute
	• Generally nonbinding so good faith is essential
Mini-trial	• Formal presentation of evidence by lawyers
	• Officiated by neutral third party
	• Parties voluntarily reach settlement so good faith is essential
Arbitration	• Most common method for resolving international disputes
	• Judgment is rendered by neutral third party
	• Decision often is binding
	• Widely enforced throughout the world

---

agreement, to select the arbitrator as well as the rules that will govern the arbitration process.

THE ARBITRATION ALTERNATIVE

As a result of cooperation among many of the world's developed nations, the parties' decision to arbitrate is widely honored. Likewise, the arbitral award generally has a better chance of being enforced than a judgment issued by a foreign court. For these reasons, international contracts often designate arbitration as the exclusive form of dispute resolution. This section takes a closer look at the predominant arbitration systems as well as the legal issues accompanying enforcement of arbitration clauses and arbitral awards.

**Arbitration
Institutions**

Private parties have a great deal of discretion over the arbitration forum and the substantive rules that will govern their dispute resolution process. Generally, they make these choices during the contract negotiation stage (before any disputes arise) and incorporate them into their final agreement. Numerous international institutions are available to parties who opt for arbitration.

American Arbitration Association

Headquartered in New York City, the *American Arbitration Association* (AAA) hears mostly domestic disputes; however, it also handles international cases. It takes care of the administrative aspects of the proceedings as well as designates the actual arbitrators if that is what the disputants desire. The AAA's arbitration rules, in part, provide that: (*a*) the arbitrator must make a decision within 30 days after the hearing closes; (*b*) arbitrators may consider custom and trade usage in deciding the case; and (*c*) while the parties may present evidence and call on witnesses, they also may agree that the arbitrators' decision will be based exclusively on documentary evidence.

International Chamber of Commerce

While the *International Chamber of Commerce* (ICC) has its headquarters in Paris, it has regional offices throughout the world. It conducts proceedings in any of these locations under whatever law the parties select. At present, the ICC is the most widely used of the various arbitral institutions. Its most fundamental rules provide that: (*a*) decisions must be made within six months after the hearings close unless an extension is given, which is common; (*b*) arbitrators may consider custom and trade usage; and (*c*) the right to present evidence and call on witnesses is left to the arbitrators' discretion, although the parties may stipulate that decisions must be based on documents only.

London Court of International Arbitration

An advantage of the *London Court of International Arbitration* (LCIA) is the close support it receives from the English courts. They readily enforce an arbitrator's discovery orders as well as remove an arbitrator who does not proceed within a timely manner. On the whole, its procedural rules are more detailed than the other arbitral institutions; although they also are both simple and flexible. Under the rules of the LCIA: (*a*) the arbitrators must issue a decision "as soon as practicable" (there is no set time limit); (*b*) there is no provision for the use of custom and trade usage and, following the usual English practice, the arbitrators might not take them into consideration; and (*c*) the parties may present evidence but the arbitrators can prevent the cross-examination of witnesses. As with the AAA and the ICC, under the LCIA procedures, the disputants can require that the final decision be based solely on the documentary evidence.

Stockholm Chamber of Commerce

The *Arbitration Institution of the Stockholm Chamber of Commerce* (SCC) grew in prominence because of the expanding contacts between U.S. businesses and foreign trade associations of the former Soviet Union during the 1970s. The SCC was the institution of choice for the Soviet trade organizations. Chinese and Eastern European interests also came to favor this arbitral forum when dealing with Western businesses. Under its rules: (*a*) each party selects one arbitrator and the SCC selects a third who serves as chairperson; (*b*) the arbitral award must be rendered within one year of the close of the hearing; and (*c*) the arbitrators have wide discretion over the rules of evidence and the calling of witnesses.

Ad Hoc Arbitration

Rather than select an institutional arbitration forum, the contract may call for *ad hoc* arbitration. Under this approach, the parties must furnish all of the administrative services normally applied by the arbitral institutions, agree on the procedural rules that will govern the hearing, and formulate a mechanism for choosing the arbitrators. This path may be chosen to minimize the expense and delay frequently associated with the institutional forums. Ad hoc arbitration also tends to be more private than institutional proceedings. In selecting the governing procedures, the parties are free to designate the rules of any of the formal arbitration institutions.

UNCITRAL Arbitration Rules

There has been widespread global acceptance of the *UNCITRAL Arbitration Rules*. They were formulated by the United Nations Commission on International Trade Law for the express purpose of accommodating the differences and similarities among the world's major legal systems. Although the UNCITRAL Arbitration Rules were initially intended for ad hoc arbitration, each of the formal arbitral institutions will abide by them if the parties call for those procedures in their agreement. The UNCITRAL Arbitral Rules provide: (*a*) no time limit for issuing a decision; (*b*) that the arbitrators must consider custom and trade usage; (*c*) considerable discretion to the arbitrators in determining the admissibility of evidence and the participation of witnesses; and (*d*) that the losing party will bear all of the costs of the proceedings unless the arbitrator believes they should be shared.

Enforcing the Agreement to Arbitrate

Businesses cannot be forced to submit their contractual disputes to arbitration. Instead, they must voluntarily agree to the use of an arbitral forum. While the decision to arbitrate can be made after a disagreement has arisen, generally the parties make their choice during the contract formation stage by including an **arbitration clause** in their agreement.

The New York Convention

In the wake of World War II, most of the developed world strongly supported development of an international arbitration treaty. In part, this was a response to the fear that the absence of global cooperation over economic policy posed a serious threat to world peace. However, it also reflected a growing recognition of the fact that private parties generally favored arbitration over litigation as a means of dispute resolution.

In 1958, the United Nations drafted the Convention on the Recognition and Enforcement of Foreign Arbitral Awards. This treaty, known as the *New York Convention,* establishes a presumption in favor of enforcing arbitration clauses contained in an international commercial contract. The more than 70 nations that have adopted the New York Convention require their courts to rigorously enforce agreements to arbitrate that meet the following four-part test:

1. There must be a *written agreement* to arbitrate.
2. The arbitration agreement must provide for *arbitration in a territory or country that has adopted the New York Convention.* (This *reciprocity requirement* is followed by the United States and at least 30 other nations. The remaining signato-

ries enforce the agreement to arbitrate even if it is to occur in a country that has failed to adopt the convention.)

3. The arbitration agreement must arise out of a *legal relationship*. (Many countries, including the United States, apply the New York Convention only to *commercial,* business-versus-business, disputes.)

4. The *disputing parties must be from different countries* or their legal relationship must have some reasonable relation with a different nation.

Despite passing this four-step inquiry, an agreement to arbitrate is not enforced if it is subject to an internationally recognized defense such as duress, mistake, fraud, or when the agreement contravenes a fundamental policy of the forum state. The following case examines these defenses.

TENNESSEE IMPORTS v. FILIPPI
745 F.Supp. 1314 (M.D. Tenn. 1990)

■ **FACTS** Tennessee Imports, a U.S. corporation with its principal place of business in Tennessee, contracted with Prix Italia, an Italian corporation doing business in Venice, Italy. Under the terms of their agreement, Tennessee Imports was given the exclusive sales rights over Prix Italia's pricing and labeling machines in the United States. The contract, which was drafted by Prix Italia, contained an arbitration clause requiring that all contractual disputes be settled by the Arbitration Court of the Chamber of Commerce in Venice. When a dispute arose, Tennessee Imports filed suit against Prix Italia in a U.S. district court. Prix Italia, citing the arbitration clause, petitioned the U.S. court to dismiss on the grounds of improper venue. Tennessee Imports claimed the arbitration clause was not enforceable because the bargaining power between the two parties was unequal. In essence, it argued that since the machines manufactured by Prix Italia were unavailable from any other source, it was forced to accept the terms of Prix Italia's contract.

■ **ISSUE** Should the U.S. court enforce the parties' agreement to arbitrate in Italy?

■ **DECISION** Yes. The contract between Tennessee Imports and Prix Italia clearly evidences a commercial relationship between the parties: the sale and purchase of

goods by corporate entities. This transaction also is an international one. Each of the two parties is incorporated and has its principal place of business in a different signatory country. The sales contract contains an express agreement to arbitrate and provides for arbitration in Italy, a signatory to the New York Convention. Clearly, the arbitration agreement between Tennessee Imports and Prix Italia is the type of agreement contemplated by the convention. Tennessee Imports has not demonstrated any internationally recognized defense against enforcement of the agreement to arbitrate. Tennessee Imports made no allegation that it was unfairly surprised by the presence of the arbitration clause in its contract with Prix Italia. It was not hidden in the small print boilerplate of a standard form contract. It was not the product of a battle of the forms. It was not buried among the provisions of a lengthy and complex sales agreement. On its face, the contact appears to be one specifically drawn to define the relationship between these two parties. It may be true that Tennessee Imports had no choice other than to take or leave the contract as presented by Prix Italia, including the unwanted arbitration clause. Nevertheless, Tennessee Imports *chose* to take it, a choice made in anticipation of enjoying the profits of an exclusive distributorship. Having made its choice, Tennessee Imports must now abide by it.

ETHICAL IMPLICATIONS Can Tennessee Imports afford to arbitrate this dispute in Italy? Is it fair for a large company to insist on arbitration in a distant country when dealing with small distributors?

Countries Not Subject to the New York Convention

While the New York Convention has met with wide acceptance in much of the developed world, it has been rejected by an equal number of countries. It has been resisted most strenuously in Latin America, in part, out of a fear of exploitation by foreign influences. Despite this reluctance, however, at least 10 Latin American countries, as well as the United States, have ratified the *Inter-American Convention on International Commercial Arbitration.* The provisions of this regional accord are similar to the New York Convention.

Enforcing the Arbitration Award

Perhaps the most important issue when drafting an arbitration clause is ensuring that the arbitration award will be enforceable. Most of the countries that have adopted the New York Convention enforce the arbitration awards rendered in any other country. However, as noted above, the United States and 30 other ratifying nations enforce only those awards made in the territory of another party to the convention.

Under very limited circumstances, the New York Convention authorizes a ratifying nation to deny enforcement of a foreign arbitral award. The instances where enforcement may be avoided occur when:

1. The agreement to arbitrate was invalid, perhaps due to duress, fraud, or incapacity.
2. A party was not given notice of the appointment of the arbitrator, notice of the arbitration proceedings, or was otherwise unable to present her case.
3. The arbitration award deals with matters outside of the scope of the arbitrator's authority.
4. The composition of the arbitral panel or the procedures it followed violated the parties' arbitration agreement or violated the laws of the country where the arbitration occurred.
5. The arbitral award has been set aside by the courts of the country where the arbitration occurred.
6. The arbitration award violates the laws or public policy of the country where enforcement is sought.

These exceptions are narrowly construed and the burden of proving their occurrence falls on the party seeking to prevent enforcement.

CONCEPT SUMMARY
Enforceability of Arbitral Awards

Parties Must Agree to Arbitrate	• May consent before dispute arises • May consent after dispute arises
Arbitration Agreement Must Be Valid	• Cannot be induced by fraud or duress • Parties must have capacity to contract
Arbitration Proceeding Must Be Fair	• Parties must have notice of hearing • Hearing must comply with the terms of the arbitration agreement • Award cannot exceed terms of the arbitration agreement
Award Must Not Violate Public Policy	• Must be legal in country where arbitration occurred • Must be legal in country where enforcement is sought

AMERICAN CONSTRUCTION v. MECHANISED CONSTRUCTION OF PAKISTAN
659 F.Supp. 426 (S.D. N.Y. 1987)

■ **FACTS** American Construction, a Cayman Islands corporation, contracted with Mechanised Construction of Pakistan (MCP). The contract, which called for American Construction to supply MCP with goods and services, contained an arbitration clause that designated the International Chamber of Commerce as the arbiter of any commercial disputes. When a contractual dispute arose, American Construction filed a claim with the ICC. Despite receiving proper notice of the arbitration hearing, MCP elected not to attend. Instead, it convinced a Pakistani court to rule that the arbitration clause and proceeding were void. After receiving a favorable ruling from the arbitrator, American Construction sought to enforce the award in a U.S. district court. MCP argued that the arbitration award was against public policy and therefore unenforceable.

■ **ISSUE** Should the U.S. court refuse to enforce the arbitration award because it violates public policy?

■ **DECISION** No. A general pro-enforcement bias is manifested in the New York Convention, to which the United States is a party. The party opposing enforcement of an arbitration award bears the burden of proof, and MCP has failed to meet this burden. The public policy defense is very narrow and is applicable only when enforcement would violate the forum state's most basic notions of morality and justice. This is hardly such a case. MCP argues that U.S. public policy would be offended by enforcing an arbitral award in the face of a Pakistani judgment that the arbitration clause and proceeding were invalid. In fact, public policy would be violated if the court declined to confirm the award. The Pakistani proceeding was, according to the arbitrator, marked by MCP's "omissions and misstatements." MCP agreed to arbitrate and then sought to circumvent the process. In light of this strategy, enforcing the award in no way violates this forum's notions of justice.

Commercial Disputes with Foreign Nations

The discussion up to this point has focused on the resolution of disputes between private business entities. However, commercial disagreements also may arise between sovereign nations or between a private foreign investor and a host nation. Disputes between nations may be resolved by the World Court (International Court of Justice). Further, sometimes a private investor may persuade its home country to pursue its private claim against the host nation before the World Court.

Currently, more than 90 countries are parties to the Washington Convention, which established the International Center for the Settlement of Investment Disputes (ICSID). As part of the World Bank, ICSID provides a forum for the arbitration of disagreements between nations and investment disputes between private parties and host countries. Many countries also have bilateral treaties that provide for arbitration of disputes involving at least one sovereign state.

QUESTIONS AND PROBLEM CASES

1. Explain how the parties to an international agreement can use their contract to minimize the confusion that might otherwise arise over the appropriate governing law or jurisdiction.

2. What is meant by *personal jurisdiction?*

3. Why are international arbitration awards more likely to be enforced than the judgments issued by foreign courts?

4. How does negotiation differ from mediation? In what ways are they similar?

5. OMS is a Canadian corporation with its principal place of business in Canada. Command-Aire is incorporated in Texas and has its principal place of business there. The OMS president met with Command-Aire representatives at a convention in Chicago and discussed the possible purchase of heat pump equipment manufactured by Command-Aire. At one point, OMS representatives traveled to Texas to deliver and discuss design specifications. Contract negotiations were conducted, and the contract was finally consummated by use of telephonic and mail services. Although the initial sales agreement contemplated that Command-Aire would deliver the equipment in Canada, the parties ultimately agreed that OMS would take possession in Texas. OMS installed the pumps in Canadian condominiums. Later, when the heating pumps proved to be defective, OMS refused to make further payments. Command-Aire filed suit in a federal court in Texas and OMS moved to dismiss for lack of personal jurisdiction. Does the Texas court have personal jurisdiction over OMS?

6. Eulala Shute purchased passage on a ship operated by Carnival Cruise lines. Her ticket contained language informing her that the contract of passage was subject to certain terms and conditions. One such term was a forum selection clause stipulating that all disputes were to be litigated before a court located in the state of Florida. While the ship was in international waters off the Mexican coast, Shute was injured when she slipped and fell during a guided tour of the ship's galley. After returning to her home in Washington, Shute brought suit against Carnival in a federal district court in the state of Washington. When Carnival asked for a summary judgment on the grounds that the suit must be brought in Florida, Shute argued that the forum selection clause was unenforceable because it was not the product of negotiation between the parties. Is the forum selection clause enforceable?

7. McDonnell Douglas Corporation (MDC) contracted to supply Iran with military aircraft parts. Because of the political turmoil that erupted in Iran in the latter part of 1978, MDC became concerned for the safety of its employees in Iran and ordered their evacuation. Further, the U.S. Air Force ordered that no foreign military sales items be released for shipment. Following these events, MDC suspended

all work in progress under its basic agreement with Iran. The new Iranian government sued MDC on the grounds that the American company had breached its contract. Iran claimed the trial should be conducted in Iran because the contract between the parties contained a forum selection clause that stated *"disputes should be settled through the Iranian Courts."* MDC argued that the forum selection clause was unenforceable because: (1) an agreement providing that disputes *"should"*, rather than *"shall"*, be settled by Iranian Courts was optional rather than binding; and (2) the new Iranian legal system would not fairly adjudicate the dispute. Will a U.S. court uphold the forum selection clause?

8. Chhawchharia, a citizen and resident of India, died in an airplane crash in Japan. The airplane was designed and manufactured by the Boeing Company, a Delaware corporation with its principal place of business in the state of Washington. As part of a settlement with Japan Air Lines, owner of the airplane, Mrs. Chhawchharia (also a citizen and resident of India) signed a release of all claims against Boeing. She later claimed the release was induced by fraud and filed a lawsuit against Boeing in a U.S. district court. Mrs. Chhawchharia contended the Indian courts were inadequate to hear her claim because they were overcrowded. Boeing argued that all of the witnesses to the settlement negotiations and signing of the release are living in India. Mrs. Chhawchharia responded that she would be willing to travel to the United States and the only other witness was Boeing's own agent. Boeing then claimed that in order to determine an appropriate amount of damages, the court would need access to Mr. Chhawchharia's financial records, all of which were located in India. It also asserted that India, the country where Chhawchharia's wife and children live, has the strongest interest in the outcome of the litigation. Finally, Boeing stated that Indian law would govern the validity of the release.

Should the U.S. court grant Boeing's motion that the lawsuit be dismissed on the grounds of forum non conveniens?

9. Commerce Consultants International, a U.S. corporation, contracted with Vetrerie Riunite, an Italian corporation. The written agreement was drafted in English for Commerce Consultants by its employee, Michael Galbraith, who was fluent in Italian but not a lawyer. He included a clause in the parties' contract that stated: *"The validity, enforceability, and interpretation of this agreement shall be determined and governed by the appropriate court of Verona, Italy."* Later, when a dispute arose, Commerce Consultants filed suit in a U.S. district court. Riunite moved to dismiss the complaint for improper venue, claiming the contract required that suits be brought in Verona, Italy. Commerce Consultants argued that the contractual provision was a choice of law clause rather than a forum selection clause. Is Commerce Consultants correct? Explain.

10. Mitsubishi, a Japanese corporation, distributed automobiles through Chrysler dealers outside of the continental United States. Soler, a Puerto Rican corporation, entered into a distributorship agreement with Mitsubishi that permitted Soler to sell cars in Puerto Rico. The agreement provided that disputes would be arbitrated in Japan in accordance with the rules and regulations of the Japan Commercial Arbitration Association. When the new car market slackened, Soler attempted to cancel several shipments of cars and also tried to transship cars to Latin America and the continental United States. Mitsubishi denied these requests and sought to compel arbitration of the parties' resulting disputes. Soler filed an antitrust suit against Mitsubishi in a U.S. district court, arguing the arbitration agreement was not enforceable since only U.S. courts could hear antitrust claims. Should the U.S. court enforce the parties' arbitration agreement despite Soler's antitrust claims?

U.S. POLICIES ON GLOBAL TRADE

U.S. Law and the General Agreement on Tariffs and Trade

INTRODUCTION

The General Agreement on Tariffs and Trade (GATT) is the predominant international mechanism regulating business transactions today. However, GATT's rules cannot be separated from the economic and political policies of the various nations of the world. Global traders must understand the relationship between GATT and the domestic legal systems if they hope to make sense of international trade policy.

Background

Lawmakers have been regulating international trade throughout the history of the United States. The first major legislative effort of the first Congress was the *Tariff Act of 1789*. The import duties established by this statute, while defended as an important source of revenue, also were designed to protect U.S. industry from competition. During the ensuing years, the country continued to erect barriers to foreign goods, sowing the seeds for the Civil War between the pro-tariff forces of the industrial North and the free traders of the agricultural South.

By 1930, protectionist forces in the United States were bitterly complaining of the unfairness of having to compete against heavily subsidized imports. In response, Congress enacted the *Smoot-Hawley Tariff Act,* which empowered the president to increase tariffs by as much as 50 percent whenever the Tariff Commission (now called the International Trade Commission) believed the costs of foreign production offered an advantage over domestic goods. The country's major trading partners immediately implemented retaliatory measures that drastically reduced U.S. exports and helped push the nation (and the world) into a severe economic depression.

In an effort to undo the damage caused by high tariffs, free trade forces engineered the passage of the *Reciprocal Trade Agreements Act of 1934*. This legislation delegated to the president broad authority to negotiate with foreign nations for reciprocal reductions in tariffs. Although the duration of these grants of authority was never more than several years, the executive power was regularly renewed through new legislation. Basically, these trade acts gave the president the authority to negotiate tariff reductions and to proclaim them as part of the domestic law of the United States.

The success of these tariff-reduction efforts stimulated a movement to construct a regular mechanism for conducting multilateral trade negotiations on a worldwide basis. This process, known as the *General Agreement on Tariffs and Trade* (GATT), sponsors rounds of negotiations (each lasting several years) designed to remove barriers to global trade. Throughout the post-World War II years, Congress regularly has delegated authority to the president to participate in the GATT negotiations. However, during the past decade, Congress has insisted on greater oversight of the negotiating process. Thus, recent trade acts have been marked by greater wrangling between the executive and legislative branches as special interests clamor for protection from international competition. This phenomenon is not unique to the United States. Throughout the world, protectionist forces seem to be on the rise.

Chapter Overview

This chapter examines the process by which the United States regulates global trade. It begins with a discussion of the complementary (and conflicting) roles of the executive and legislative branches, as well as a look at the constitutionality of state regulations that affect foreign trade. That is followed by a brief introduction to the governmental agencies that are the key participants in the U.S. regulatory process. The rest of the chapter provides an overview of the GATT. This includes a review of its administration, major principles, exceptions, dispute settlement procedures, and future role in the world economy.

U.S. REGULATION OF GLOBAL TRADE

The drafters of the U.S. Constitution, fearful of concentrations of power, fashioned a system of *checks and balances* that distributed power among the three branches of government (executive, legislative, and judicial) and between the national and state governments. This section illustrates how the political processes affect the way international economic affairs are regulated in the United States.

The Treaty-Making Power

While treaties provide the principal source of international law in the world today, the way in which nations enter these pacts varies widely. In the United States, the Constitution confers **treaty-making power** on the president with the advice and consent of two thirds of the Senate. This means the president, after negotiating an international accord, must persuade the Senate to approve its terms.

U.S. courts broadly construe the treaty power. They hold that it extends to any issue that involves negotiations with foreign governments, even those that greatly influence domestic affairs. Despite this judicial deference, however, the cumbersome nature of the traditional treaty-making process renders it too unwieldy for many international economic agreements. As a result, the government has developed alternate procedures for implementing international pacts. These executive agreements fall into two fundamental categories: those that require congressional participation and those the president may enter into on his own under inherent executive power.

Congressional Participation Agreements

As U.S. influence in world affairs increased, several treaty-like procedures emerged that facilitated the negotiation and implementation of executive agreements. Three of these methods are similar to treaty power in that they require cooperation between the president and Congress. They are treaty-authorized agreements, prior congressional approval agreements, and subsequent congressional approval agreements.

Treaty-Authorized Agreements

Sometimes a treaty delegates advance authority to the president to conclude supplemental pacts to carry out the terms of the original accord. These **treaty-authorized agreements** require no new participation from the legislative branch. They are particularly well suited for the environmental field where frequent scientific discoveries necessitate ongoing refinements to international conventions (see Chapter 16).

Prior Congressional Approval Agreements

Congress may pass a statute authorizing the president to bind the country to an international agreement. Historically, the United States has followed this approach in negotiating tariff agreements with its trading partners. These **prior congressional approval agreements** differ from treaties and treaty-authorized agreements by requiring the approval of both the Senate and the House of Representatives.

The Constitution grants the primary authority to regulate international economic policy to Congress. Accordingly, courts review prior congressional approval agreements to ensure the legislature does not extend too much negotiating authority to the president. A proper *delegation of power* requires that Congress establish an objective standard that clearly confines presidential discretion.

Courts are aware of the complex and delicate nature of international economic affairs. Simultaneously, they recognize the special competence of the executive branch in the foreign policy realm. For these reasons, the judiciary frequently permits more open-ended delegations to the executive branch when foreign affairs are involved. This is particularly true when the president is empowered to respond to certain emergencies. For instance, after the courts permitted the president to rely on the *Trading with the Enemy Act* to regulate outside of the wartime context, Congress enacted the *International Economic Emergency Act* to subject those executive powers to congressional review. (Both statutes are discussed in Chapter 12.)

UNITED STATES v. YOSHIDA INTERNATIONAL
526 F.2d 560 (C.C.P.A. 1975)

■ **FACTS** During the summer of 1971, the United States was faced with an economic crisis. The nation suffered under an exceptionally severe and worsening balance of payments deficit. Foreign exchange rates were being controlled by several of the country's major trading partners in such a way as to overvalue the U.S. dollar. That action, by stimulating U.S. imports and restraining U.S. exports, contributed substantially to the balance of payments deficit. As one step in a program designed to meet the economic crisis, the president issued a proclamation declaring a national emergency and assessing a 10 percent surcharge on imports. The president relied on the *Trading with the Enemy Act* (TWEA) as authority for this action. The TWEA expressly delegated to the president the power *"during any period of national emergency declared by him . . . [to] regulate, prevent, or prohibit the importation of any property in which any foreign country . . . has any interest."* An importer claimed the proclamation was unconstitutional because the surcharge exceeded the authority delegated to the executive branch.

■ **ISSUE** Did the surcharge fall within the powers delegated to the president?

■ **DECISION** Yes. The Constitution granted the power to *lay and collect duties* and to *regulate commerce* to Congress. However, beginning as early as 1794, Congress has delegated the exercise of much of the power to regulate foreign commerce to the executive branch. It is incontestable that the TWEA delegates to the president, for use during war or during national emergency only, the power to regulate importation. The delegation is broad and extensive; it could not have been otherwise if the president were to have the flexibility required to meet problems surrounding a national emergency. It is not surprising that Congress did not *specify* that the president could use a surcharge in a national emergency. Having left the battlefield, it would hardly do to dictate all the weapons that could be used in the fight. It cannot be lightly dismissed that the TWEA is operative only during (war or) national emergencies, which inherently preclude prior prescription of specific detailed guidelines. Further, it is clear that the surcharge had as its primary purpose the curtailment (i.e., the regulation) of imports. What was sought was an offset to actions of foreign nations that had led to the loss of a favorable balance of trade. The relationship between the action taken and the power delegated was thus one of substantial identity. Finally, through its impact on imports the surcharge had a direct effect on the balance of trade and, in turn, on the balance of payments deficit. Therefore, the president's action in imposing the surcharge bore an eminently reasonable relationship to the emergency confronted.

Subsequent Congressional Approval Agreements

With a **subsequent congressional approval agreement,** Congress enacts a presidential proposal into law after the negotiations are complete. While this type of executive agreement may be negotiated by the president alone, it is not binding until it has been confirmed by both houses of Congress. Generally, this mechanism does not require advance authorization from the legislative branch before the president may begin negotiations. However, under the *1988 Omnibus Trade and Competitiveness Act,* Congress authorized the president to negotiate international trade agreements before June 1, 1993, for the reduction of tariff and nontariff barriers. It then stipulated that any resulting executive agreement would not have domestic legal effect unless it was subsequently approved by the Senate and the House of Representatives.

During recent years, Congress has favored the subsequent approval process because it permits a final check on the content of executive agreements. The executive branch and foreign governments, on the other hand, object to this approach because special interests are likely to unravel the negotiated proposal once it reaches Congress. The United States has created a *fast-track* mechanism that addresses both of these concerns. There are four steps to the fast-track procedure. First, the president must consult with Congress during the drafting of the proposal. Second, legislative committees are required to report the bill to the floor of each house within a relatively short time. Third, debate on the measure is subject to strict time limits. Fourth, Congress must approve or reject the proposal through a straight up or down vote (with no amendments) within 90 days after it was drafted. (Fast-track authority is discussed in Chapter 4.)

Inherent Executive Authority

In limited circumstances, the president can bind the country to executive agreements without prior or subsequent approval from Congress. This **inherent executive authority** arises from the president's general power as chief executive, his authority as commander in chief of the armed forces, and his power to appoint and to receive ambassadors and foreign ministers. Courts have narrowly construed the inherent power and prevented it from being exercised over issues that have substantial domestic effects. This type of executive agreement is most likely to be upheld when it involves the disposition of the U.S. armed forces overseas or the diplomatic recognition of foreign governments.

Legal Effects of Treaties and Executive Agreements

Some treaties and executive agreements automatically become part of U.S. domestic law without further action by the legislative or executive branches. They are called **self-executing** agreements. Others have no domestic legal effect until they are implemented by further governmental action. The language and history of each agreement

CONCEPT SUMMARY Presidential Authority to Regulate Global Trade		
Treaty-Making Powers	• President negotiates terms of agreement.	
	• Treaty must be approved by two thirds of the Senate.	
	• Treaty overrides conflicting terms in previously enacted statutes or treaties.	
Delegated Powers	Treaty-Authorized Agreements	Treaty delegates authority to President to proclaim supplemental pacts.
	Congressional Approval Statutes	Prior approval—Statute authorizes President to proclaim agreement.
		Subsequent approval—Congress enacts statute codifying president's proposed agreement.
Inherent Powers	• No congressional approval is necessary.	
	• Generally confined to diplomatic and military affairs.	
	• Does not override prior statutes or treaties.	

must be scrutinized to determine if it was intended to be self-executing. While nonself-executing treaties may create obligations under international law, U.S. courts will not enforce their terms until they are properly implemented by some further governmental act.

Under the U.S. Constitution, self-executing treaties (along with federal statutes) are the "supreme law of the land." When they conflict with other agreements or statutes, whichever was enacted most recently will govern. For the most part, treaties and executive agreements have the same legal effect. However, this is not the case for executive agreements that arise pursuant to the president's inherent powers. They may not conflict with prior federal statutes, treaties, or the other types of executive agreements.

This distinction between international law and domestic law is not shared by all nations. Some countries do not recognize the notion of a self-executing treaty. All of their international agreements must be implemented by further legislation before they will assume a domestic law effect. Other countries automatically extend domestic effect to all of their international agreements without requiring further governmental action.

GOLDSTAR (PANAMA) S.A. v. UNITED STATES
967 F.2d 965 (4th Cir. 1992)

■ **FACTS** The armed forces of the United States invaded Panama on December 20, 1989, and "occupied, pacified, and controlled" an area of Panama City. During the occupation, the Panamanian Defense Force, which also served as Panama's police force, was effectively eliminated. A group of Panamanian businesses, collectively known as Goldstar, sued the United States for taking inadequate precautions to prevent mobs from looting their commercial establishments. They asserted that the *Hague Convention* imposed a duty on the United States to provide protection for the residents of an occupied territory. The *Hague Convention,* a multilateral treaty to which the United States is a signatory, states that an occupying country may be liable to pay compensation if it fails to maintain public order. The United States claimed Goldstar had no right to recover damages under the *Hague Convention* because the treaty was not self-executing.

■ **ISSUE** Is the *Hague Convention* a self-executing treaty?

■ **DECISION** No. International treaties are not presumed to create rights that are privately enforceable.

Courts find a treaty to be self-executing only if the document, as a whole, evidences an intent to provide a private right of action. The *Hague Convention* does not explicitly provide for a privately enforceable cause of action. Moreover, a reasonable reading of the treaty as a whole does not lead to the conclusion that the signatories intended to provide such a right. Article 1 of the treaty states, *"[t]he Contracting Powers shall issue instructions to their armed land forces which shall be in conformity with the Regulations."* This language suggests that the *Hague Convention* is not self-executing, and that, instead, the signatories contemplated that individual nations would take subsequent executory actions to discharge the obligations of the treaty. Because it is not self-executing, it does not, by itself, create a private right of action for its breach.

ETHICAL IMPLICATIONS   The U.S. Supreme Court has stated: "a treaty is primarily a compact between independent nations which depends for the enforcement of its provisions on the interest and the honor of the governments which are parties to it." Suppose the U.S. government had negligently failed to provide adequate personnel, equipment, and orders to protect the residents and businesses of Panama City. Is it ethical (or honorable) for the United States to avoid paying compensation to Goldstar because the *Hague Convention* was not self-executing?

State Regulations   While states have broad powers to regulate activities that have no significant effects outside of their borders, their authority over international economic activities is extremely narrow. This is because the Constitution grants the federal government the power to regulate commerce with foreign nations. States still may govern activities that only incidentally affect foreign trade; however, that authority is subject to two important restrictions. First, the Supremacy Clause of the Constitution holds federal laws superior to state laws. Thus, state regulations may not conflict or otherwise interfere with federal statutes, treaties, executive agreements, or policies. Second, the Constitution expressly prohibits certain types of state regulation. For instance, states may not tax either imports or exports. (The federal government also is precluded from taxing exports.)

ITEL CONTAINERS INTERNATIONAL v. HUDDLESTON
113 S.Ct. 1095 (U.S. Sup.Ct. 1993)

■ **FACTS** The use of large steel containers to transport goods by truck, rail, and oceangoing carrier was a major innovation in transportation technology. In 1990, the United States shipped, by value, 60 percent of its marine imports and 52 percent of its marine exports in these containers. Itel's primary business is leasing cargo containers to participants in the international shipping industry, and all its leases restrict use of its containers to international commerce. The Tennessee Department of Revenue assessed $382,000 in sales tax, penalties, and interest on the proceeds Itel earned from leased containers delivered in Tennessee for the period of January 1983 through November 1986. Itel maintained the Tennessee tax violates foreign commerce clause principles as well as the Import-Export Clause of the Constitution.

■ **ISSUE** Does the Tennessee sales tax on containers used in international trade violate the Constitution?

■ **DECISION** No. A state tax that affects foreign commerce must satisfy the following test: (1) it must be applied to an activity with a substantial nexus with the taxing state; (2) it must be fairly apportioned; (3) it must not discriminate against interstate or foreign commerce; (4) it must be fairly related to the services provided by the state; (5) it must not create a substantial risk of interna-

tional multiple taxation; and (6) it must not prevent the federal government from speaking with one voice when regulating commercial relations with foreign governments. The sales tax is a fair measure of the state's contacts with the container leasees in Tennessee. Thus, steps 1 through 4 of the inquiry are easily met. This confirms both the state's legitimate interest in taxing the transactions and the absence of any attempt to interfere with the free flow of foreign commerce. Step 5 is not violated because Tennessee offers a credit against its tax for any tax properly paid in another jurisdiction on the same transaction. Further, step 6 is passed because both Congress and the executive branch have given strong indications that Tennessee's method of taxation is allowable. Finally, Itel's Import-Export Clause argument also fails. This tax is not a tax on importation or imported goods, but a tax on a business transaction occurring within Tennessee. The tax does not draw revenue from the importation process and so does not divert import revenue from the federal government.

STRUCTURAL ASPECTS OF U.S. TRADE POLICY

Although the Constitution delegates the power to regulate foreign commerce to Congress, the executive branch has long been the dominant force in U.S. foreign affairs. Both the legislature and the judiciary recognize that, of the three branches of government, only the executive has the continuing, spontaneous capacity for making quick and decisive responses to international problems. Certainly Congress has a complex committee system that permits strict scrutiny of foreign policy. However, the fragmented nature of its organizational structure makes it ill-suited to negotiate and implement national policy with foreign leaders.

Recognizing the special competence of the presidency, Congress has delegated authority to numerous agencies within the executive branch. While the sheer numbers of these agencies with some jurisdiction over trade regulation results in reduced coordination, the president's powers and effectiveness still are formidable. This section examines the major agencies that assist the president in shaping and administering U.S. trade policy.

U.S. Trade Representative

Carrying the rank of ambassador, the **U.S. trade representative** (USTR) plays a key role in negotiating international agreements. The appointment to this cabinet-level post is a politically charged process. Besides coordinating the president's global trade agenda, the trade representative heads numerous interagency committees that formulate trade policy. When negotiating international trade packages, the U.S. trade representative is required to closely consult with congressional leaders.

PUBLIC CITIZEN v. OFFICE OF THE U.S. TRADE REPRESENTATIVE
970 F.2d 916 (D.C. Cir. 1992)

■ **FACTS** The U.S. trade representative was negotiating the Uruguay Round of the General Agreement on Tariffs and Trade on behalf of the president. No agreement had been reached. The Sierra Club and Friends of the Earth sued the trade representative, claiming that in negotiating the agreement she had failed to prepare an environmental impact statement. The *National Environmental Policy Act* (NEPA) requires an impact statement for every recommendation or report on proposals for legislation. The trade representative maintained she is under no legal obligation to prepare such statements for trade agreements.

■ **ISSUE** Was the trade representative legally obligated to prepare an environmental impact statement on the Uruguay Round negotiations?

■ **DECISION** No. The trade representative is responsible for conducting international trade negotiations, developing and coordinating U.S. international trade policy,

and imposing retaliatory trade sanctions on other countries. Trade agreements involving nontariff barriers and bilateral trade agreements involving tariff and/or nontariff barriers are to take effect only if implementing bills are enacted by both the House of Representatives and the Senate. The approval occurs on a fast-track basis, which precludes Congress from amending the president's proposal. Of course, Congress retains the power to modify the fast-track rules at any time. Because no final agreement has been reached in the Uruguay Round negotiations, there has been no final agency action to trigger the environmental impact statement requirement. Any argument that a statement must be prepared before final action because there would not be time to do so during the fast-track process is not persuasive. Congress retains the power to change its rules and extend the statutory 90-day limit on its consideration of trade agreements during the fast-track process. It can easily do so if it wishes to postpone consideration of the agreement pending preparation of a statement.

Commerce Department	In recent years, the Commerce Department has assumed a growing role in the ongoing operation of U.S. trade policy. It takes an active part in the promotion of exports and in the issuance of export licenses (see Chapter 12). A branch of the Commerce Department, the *International Trade Administration,* helps conduct antidumping and countervailing duty investigations. (This is discussed in Chapter 11.)
Treasury Department	Because it administers the U.S. Customs Service (see Chapter 10), the Treasury Department carries out vital import policies. These include tariff classification and valuation as well as the supervision of foreign trade zones. Further, it combines with the Federal Reserve System in implementing U.S. financial policies. The Treasury Department also negotiates international tax agreements and enforces the U.S. tax laws against foreign businesses.
Other Departments	Numerous other agencies and departments have jurisdiction over the regulation of international economic issues. For instance, the Labor Department protects U.S. workers displaced by imports from foreign countries. The Agricultural Department regulates the conduct of international trade in agricultural products. Both the Defense Department and the State Department have substantial influence over U.S. export controls.

International Trade Commission

Unlike the executive agencies discussed above, the **International Trade Commission** (ITC) is an independent agency. Formerly known as the U.S. Tariff Commission, the ITC is bipartisan. This means the president must appoint the six commissioners from both political parties and the appointments are subject to confirmation by the Senate. Commissioners serve nine-year terms. The ITC staff supplies both Congress and the president with extensive information on international economic issues. Further, it performs a formal fact-finding role in unfair trade complaints against imports. (These functions are discussed more fully in Chapter 11.)

THE GENERAL AGREEMENT ON TARIFFS AND TRADE

Historical Origins

During World War II, the United States and its allies acknowledged the growing economic interdependence among the nations of the world. They concluded that the way to prevent future economic disasters and world wars was through greater international cooperation and coordination. The Bretton Woods Conference of 1944 addressed these concerns through creation of the *International Monetary Fund* (IMF) and the *World Bank* (both are discussed in Chapter 2). The *International Trade Organization* (ITO) was to be the third pillar of this global economic structure. Envisioned as an international trade organization with the power to reduce worldwide tariffs, the ITO never came into existence because the U.S. Congress failed to approve it. This rejection occurred even though the United States, through its executive branch, was the principal architect of the ITO charter. Congressional dissatisfaction with the ITO has been attributed, in part, to a growing reluctance to weaken U.S. economic sovereignty during the recessionary period following World War II.

The efforts to establish the ITO were not totally unsuccessful. Throughout the discussions, negotiators simultaneously were preparing mechanisms, known as the **General Agreement on Tariffs and Trade,** for the creation and maintenance of global standards for the stabilization and reduction of tariffs.

The Nature of GATT

While GATT has become the principal system governing global trade, in reality, it is more of a mechanism than an organization. (The ITO was designed to be the structure that would implement the GATT process.) Further, the nature of GATT has changed over the past half century. It began in 1947 with 23 founding members, which were predominantly developed nations with common economic interests. By 1993, GATT membership had swollen to 111 countries, three fourths of which were developing nations.

In reality, GATT is composed of almost 200 treaties that provide a *legal framework for trade relations* among members. It also has established a *forum for multilateral trade negotiations.* Discussions are conducted through a series of rounds that generally last several years. The members have conducted eight major trade rounds to date. The latest, the *Uruguay Round*, began in 1986 and has yet to be completed,

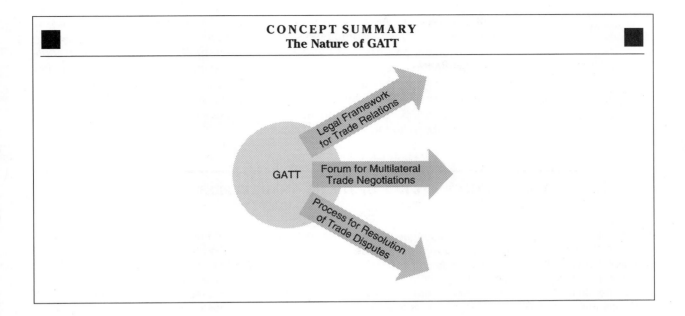

CONCEPT SUMMARY
The Nature of GATT

despite being originally scheduled to end in 1990. Finally, the GATT system includes a *dispute resolution process.*

Institutional Framework

The ITO was envisioned as the institutional body that would administer GATT. When it did not come into being, GATT's operations were conducted by its member countries. However, in 1960, the members created the *GATT Council* (officially known as the Council of Representatives) to serve as an executive organ. The Council, which regularly meets throughout the year, consists of all member countries that request representation. Generally, about 70 percent of the member countries serve on the Council.

Frequently, the Council or the member countries establish committees, working parties, or panels of experts to deal with special problems or issues. GATT also has a *Group of Eighteen* that meets several times a year to address major commercial issues. Its 18 members are chosen to reflect the economic characteristics of GATT's total membership. The *Director-General* of GATT serves as the chairperson for the Group of Eighteen and also leads trade negotiations. However, the post has no real means of compulsion over member countries. Finally, GATT's operations are supported by a *secretariat* composed of several hundred staff members.

GATT's Legal Status

The executive branch of the United States originally negotiated GATT under a 1945 renewal of the *Reciprocal Trade Agreements Act.* Under this statute, the president was delegated the authority to proclaim GATT into law without further congressional approval. Because this authority would soon expire, the president was eager to quickly arrive at an agreement. Other nations needed legislative ratification before they could adopt an agreement. Accordingly, they did not wish to move on GATT until the negotiations over the ITO were completed so they could ratify both as a package deal.

By way of compromise, GATT was adopted under the *Protocol of Provisional Application.* When the president agreed to its terms, it became a part of U.S. domestic law as a prior congressional approval agreement (discussed earlier). However, its domestic legality can be overridden by subsequent federal statutes and treaties. In the following case, a U.S. district court finds that, because GATT is not a Senate-ratified treaty, it is subservient to any federal statute.

■

PUBLIC CITIZEN v. OFFICE OF THE U.S. TRADE REPRESENTATIVE
804 F.Supp. 385 (D.D.C. 1992)

■ **FACTS** The U.S. trade representative regularly submits to GATT panels proposals to resolve specific trade disputes between the United States and other GATT member countries. The trade representative also receives decisions from those panels before the panel decisions are adopted by the membership of the GATT Council. A U.S. citizen made a series of requests under the *Freedom of Information Act* (FOIA) to the trade representative, requesting submissions and panel decisions relating to U.S. involvement in four controversies being resolved by GATT panels. When the trade representative did not comply, the citizen filed suit. The FOIA requires governmental agencies to make documents available for inspection and copying when they are "statements of policy and interpretation which have been adopted by the agency."

■ **ISSUE** Must the U.S. trade representative release to the public copies of her proposals to the GATT panels and the advance reports of the panel decisions?

■ **DECISION** Yes. When contracting countries are unable to resolve a trade dispute among themselves, they may refer the dispute to a panel established by the GATT Council. The panel accepts briefs, hears arguments, and eventually issues a final report. That report is then submitted to the GATT Council for approval after the parties have had a chance to review the panel decision and attempt to resolve their dispute. The submissions to GATT panels contain statements of policy and interpretations adopted by the trade representative. They constitute the agency's interpretation of U.S. international legal obligations, even if not personally approved by the trade representative herself. While the panel decisions are not interpretations or statements of policy by the trade representative, they must be released pursuant to the FOIA's provision requiring prompt release of nonexempt records. The trade representative's argument that GATT rules forbid disclosure is not persuasive. GATT and its subsequent modifications are not Senate-ratified treaties. Thus, the provisions of the FOIA, a federal statute, prevail over GATT.

GATT'S MAJOR PRINCIPLES

As noted above, GATT is unlike most international institutions in that it focuses on policy rather than structure. Thus, to fully comprehend its role in global trade, one must understand its primary objectives. It has four major principles: (1) tariff-based import restrictions, (2) most-favored-nation treatment, (3) national treatment, and (4) reciprocity.

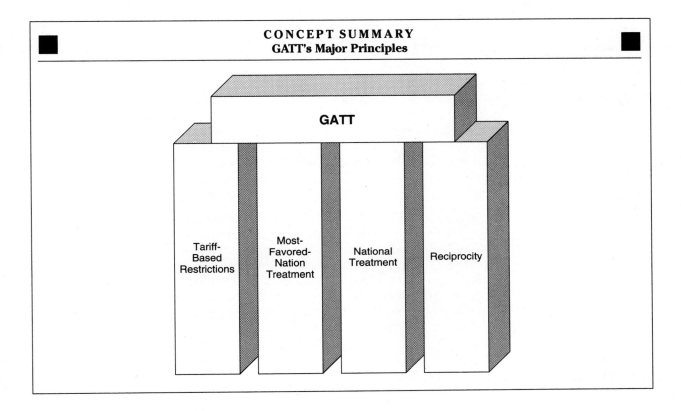

CONCEPT SUMMARY
GATT's Major Principles

GATT

| Tariff-Based Restrictions | Most-Favored-Nation Treatment | National Treatment | Reciprocity |

Tariff-Based Restrictions

Hoping to avoid the protectionist economic policies that preceded the Great Depression, GATT's founders sought a multilateral approach to the elimination of restrictive trade barriers. They selected a **tariff-based approach** that had two fundamental goals. First, GATT members were to engage in regular negotiations designed to systematically reduce import duties. Second, tariffs were to be the only form of import protection permitted by GATT. Specifically, GATT prohibited the use of nontariff barriers, such as quotas and quantitative restrictions to trade. As will be seen later, however, there are numerous exceptions to this policy.

Most-Favored-Nation Treatment

An essential attribute of the GATT process is the notion of **most-favored-nation treatment** (MFN) in the relations between member countries. In general, this requires that any privilege, advantage, or benefit granted to imports from one GATT member be extended to imports of similar products from all other GATT members. Thus, the lowest tariff the United States agrees to offer to a class of goods from any GATT member must be extended to the products of all other GATT members. Through MFN treatment, GATT permits member countries to engage in bilateral negotiations while bringing about uniform, multilateral reductions in tariffs. GATT permits several exceptions to the MFN policy, including customs unions and free trade areas (discussed in Chapter 4) and the generalized system of preferences for imports from certain developing countries (discussed below).

National Treatment

GATT also prohibits members from treating imports from other members—once they have been dutied and cleared customs—less favorably than domestic products. This **national treatment** requirement applies to a wide variety of regulations affecting taxation, transportation, and distribution. As a part of its ban on discrimination, national treatment requires that regulations be *transparent* so foreign producers can comply with their terms.

Reciprocity

A final principle underlying the GATT process is the notion of **reciprocity**. Specifically, GATT envisions that negotiations for the reduction of tariffs occur on a reciprocal and mutually advantageous basis. Within each round, GATT members negotiate reductions in tariffs on a reciprocal basis. Reciprocity, combined with MFN treatment, is designed to ensure a balanced and worldwide reduction in tariffs. However, as the gap between developed and developing members has widened, reciprocity often has been diluted by special exemptions for developing nations.

GATT EXCEPTIONS AND SAFEGUARDS

Political realities dictated that GATT provide exceptions from its free trade policies. For instance, it contains a *grandfather clause* excusing members from complying with GATT obligations that conflict with trade legislation that was in effect before a country joined GATT. This simplified the adoption process by permitting executive officials to approve GATT without the need for subsequent legislative authority. Other exceptions and safeguards (discussed below) recognize the special needs of developing countries, national security interests, and politically sensitive industries. (Antidumping and countervailing duties are covered in Chapter 11.)

Generalized System of Preferences

After GATT's first decade of operation, it became obvious that its developing members were unable to extract meaningful concessions from the developed members. As a result, few items of export interest to the developed world had been the subject of meaningful tariff reductions. When GATT did not heed their calls for preferential treatment, the developing countries (under the leadership of the former Soviet Union) initiated the first *United Nations Conference on Trade and Development* (UNCTAD) in 1962. Six years later UNCTAD implemented the **Generalized System of Preferences** (GSP). Under this program, developing nations do not have to pay duties on their exports to developed countries, while exports from developed countries are subject to the MFN tariffs. The GSP, despite its discriminatory character, is not illegal because the GATT membership granted the preferences a waiver from the

MFN clause. This waiver allows each developed country to erect its own GSP program. (The operation of the GSP is discussed further in Chapter 10.)

Multifiber Arrangement

For over 30 years, international trade in textiles and clothing has been restricted by a series of agreements known as the **Multifiber Arrangement.** These pacts were initiated by the United States and other developed countries after their domestic textile industries faced stiffening competition from Japan and several developing countries. The Multifiber Arrangement is a system of bilateral treaties that establish quotas on the amount of textiles a country can export to another each year.

By replacing most-favored-nation treatment with quantitative restrictions, the Multifiber Arrangement clearly violates GATT's underlying principles. However, these textile agreements contain provisions requiring their signatories to refrain from asserting their GATT rights. During the latest round of GATT discussions, the negotiators tentatively have agreed to phase out the Multifiber Arrangement over a 10-year period.

International Commodities Agreements

GATT permits an exception from its nondiscrimination (MFN treatment) requirement for **international commodity agreements** between governments. These quantitative restrictions on imports and exports are allowed when they are essential for the protection of governmental and economic stability. They are common in the sugar, coffee, rubber, tin, timber, and wheat industries. Sometimes international commodity agreements are implemented for balance of payment reasons. In many instances, the GATT membership approves them under special *waiver provisions* that suspend GATT obligations when authorized by a two-thirds majority vote.

Agricultural Trade

The politically sensitive nature of **agricultural trade** historically has entitled it to special consideration. Throughout the world, national governments have considered their agricultural industries to be particularly vulnerable to foreign competition. Accordingly, many nations heavily subsidize farmers through extensive price supports and restrictive import barriers.

GATT has done little to combat the many decades of managed agricultural trade. In fact, farm products have been expressly exempted from GATT's prohibitions against import quotas and export subsidies. However, in recent years, the United States has been pushing for an end to these trade-distorting policies. Hoping to open new markets for its agricultural exports, the United States has been pressing the European Community and Japan to reduce their agricultural subsidies and dismantle their import barriers. This has been perhaps the most volatile issue during the latest round of GATT negotiations.

Government Procurement

Another controversial topic during the most recent GATT negotiations involves **government procurement.** GATT provides an exception to its national treatment obligation for purchases by governmental agencies for governmental purposes. Few nations were willing to risk their national security by opening government procurement to unrestricted trade. This exception has become increasingly controversial as the government sectors of more and more nations are growing. There has also been substantial debate over the precise definition of what constitutes a governmental purpose. In the United States, both the federal government and as many as 36 states have *Buy American* statutes that require government purchasers to give a preference to domestically produced goods.

■

K.S.B. TECHNICAL SALES CORP. v. NORTH JERSEY
381 A.2d 774 (Sup.Ct. N.J. 1977)

■ **FACTS** The North Jersey District Water Supply Commission, a governmental agency, was created to develop a water supply for municipalities in the northern part of the state. The commission is recognized as an instrumentality exercising public and essential governmental functions. Pursuant to a directive from the State Department of Health, the commission began constructing a water treatment plant to improve the quality of the water. It invited bids on the construction project, specifying "only manufactured products of the United States, wherever available, shall be used." The commission was required to include this provision by the New Jersey Buy American statute. A taxpayer challenged the Buy American provision, claiming it impermissibly interfered with GATT's prohibition on discrimination against imported products.

■ **ISSUE** Does the Buy American provision violate the obligations imposed on the United States by GATT?

■ **DECISION** No. A state law must yield when it is inconsistent with or impairs the provisions of a treaty or international agreement. For the purposes of this case, GATT may be considered the equivalent of a treaty. New Jersey's Buy American statute appears to be in direct conflict with GATT's requirement that imports "shall be accorded treatment no less favorable than that accorded to like products of national origin." However, GATT makes an exception for "procurement by governmental agencies of products purchased for governmental purposes and not with a view to commercial resale." The commission is a public body, exercising essential government functions in the interest of the public health and welfare. In transmitting water to municipalities, the commission, unlike a commercial enterprise, operates at cost. Its purchases for the water treatment plant are for governmental purposes and not with a view to commercial resale.

Escape Clause

GATT contains safeguards that authorize governments to increase tariffs or impose quantitative restrictions if imports are harming their domestic economy. For instance, if a nation is suffering a balance of payments deficit, it may impose quotas to protect its monetary and financial situation.

The **escape clause** is perhaps the best known safeguard. It recognizes that a rapid increase in imported goods may devastate certain industries in a nation's economy. To minimize the dislocations that attend free trade, GATT permits countries to extend temporary protection to these besieged industries while they adjust to the new competition.

To trigger the escape clause, it must be shown that an increase in imports is causing injury or a threat of injury to a domestic industry. When this occurs, the importing nation may take temporary measures to prevent or remedy the harm. The importing nation is then expected to grant alternative concessions to the exporting countries as a form of compensation for the temporary suspension of its GATT obligations. If an agreement cannot be reached, the exporting countries may suspend equivalent concessions. Many GATT members have incorporated various versions of an

FIGURE 9–1   GATT's Escape Clause

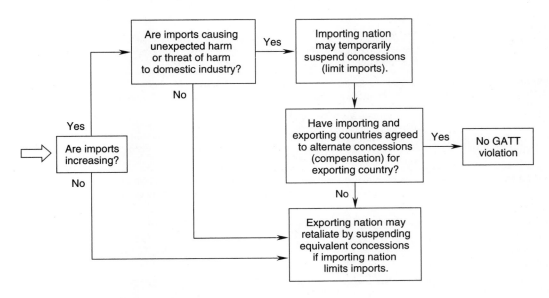

escape clause into their trade regulations. (The U.S. escape clause is examined in Chapter 11.)

GATT'S DISPUTE SETTLEMENT PROCEDURES

In application, the GATT process is complex. And, while the entire system is grounded on only four basic principles (tariff-based restrictions, most-favored-nation treatment, national treatment, and reciprocity), over the years, numerous exceptions have been carved out. These factors, coupled with frequent outbursts of protectionist sentiments throughout the world, have triggered numerous trade disputes among the GATT members. To resolve these inevitable conflicts, the GATT system has constructed flexible dispute settlement procedures.

This section briefly examines GATT's dispute resolution mechanisms. It begins with a look at the prerequisites to filing a GATT claim. It then explores the formal steps that conflicting parties are to follow: consultation, panel proceedings, action by the Council, and compliance.

Nullification and Impairment

When a country fails to honor its GATT obligations and that violation deprives another member of GATT benefits, the breach is referred to as a **nullification and impairment.** Only GATT members have *standing* to use GATT's dispute settlement procedures to redress these wrongs. This means injured people and businesses can-

---

CONCEPT SUMMARY
GATT Exceptions and Safeguards

Generalized System of Preferences	Developed nations may deviate from most-favored-nation treatment by importing goods from developing nations duty-free.
Multifiber Arrangement	Nations limit imports of textiles and clothing. These agreements substitute quantitative restrictions for tariff-based, most-favored-nation treatment.
International Commodities Agreements	Governmental agreements restrict the importation of commodities that threaten economic and governmental stability. They often are exempted by GATT's waiver provisions.
Agricultural Trade	Farm products are exempted from GATT prohibitions against import quotas and export subsidies.
Government Procurement	Governmental purchases for governmental purposes are exempted from GATT's national treatment principle.
Escape Clause	Importing nations may temporarily suspend concessions when imports threaten domestic industry. Must offer alternate and equivalent concessions as compensation.

---

not formally lodge complaints. Private complaints are heard only if a member country files a claim on behalf of its nationals. It is up to the discretion of each government whether it will do so. As a part of their GATT obligations, all members pledge to avoid unilateral retaliation and instead to rely exclusively on the GATT dispute resolution procedures.

Consultation

The GATT procedures are typical of the dispute resolution mechanisms of most international economic institutions. Rather than focusing on fault or the imposition of sanctions, the process is designed to bring about a prompt and voluntary compromise between the member nations. Therefore, when a dispute arises, it is suggested that the disputing countries voluntarily negotiate a settlement to the conflict.

If informal negotiations break down, the complaining member may initiate GATT's formal **consultation** process. In the past, GATT violators could undermine this conciliation stage by unfairly prolonging the discussion. Now, under reforms that are in force on a trial basis during the Uruguay Round, strict time limits have been imposed. An offending party is required to enter into consultation within 30 days of the complaining country's request. The parties have 60 days from the date of the request to reach a settlement. If either of these timetables are not met, the complaining party may insist on the formation of a panel.

Panel Procedures

When consultations are unsuccessful, the GATT Council appoints a **panel** that assists the GATT membership in examining the dispute. Panels normally consist of three members unless both disputants agree to have five panelists. Historically, GATT violators were able to delay the panel process indefinitely by refusing to agree on the selection of panel members. Current trial reforms have addressed this problem. If the disputants cannot agree on the choice of panelists within 20 days, either party may request GATT's Director-General to fill the positions within 10 days.

During deliberations, the panel will hear from the disputing parties as well as from any other interested contracting members. To prevent the stalling tactics that formerly plagued the panel inquiry, GATT's trial reforms require that the panel issue a report within six months. In the spirit of compromise, the panel initially submits its report to the disputants. This gives them an opportunity to voluntarily abide by its terms or negotiate their own settlement.

Council Action

After the disputing parties have had 30 days to examine the panel report, it is forwarded to the GATT Council for consideration. The panel's findings are not binding. Thus, the parties to the dispute can register their objections to the report during the Council's deliberations. The Council's decision on the **adoption** of the panel report must be given within 15 months from the complaining party's initial request for consultation unless both disputants agree to an extension. However, since the Council's decision must be unanimous, either one of the disputing members can block adoption of the panel report.

Despite this veto power, the Council approves many panel reports. This may be attributable, in part, to the political weight a panel decision carries. However, it also springs from the conciliatory approach GATT panels generally take.

■ **ETHICAL IMPLICATIONS**   Is it ethical for a GATT member to block an adverse panel report when the rest of the GATT membership agrees with the report?

Compliance

Once the Council has adopted the panel report, the breaching party must come into **compliance** with those recommendations. Generally, a country is given a reasonable adjustment period (no longer than six months) to make the necessary changes. When a nation fails to implement the recommended action, the GATT members may authorize the complaining country to retaliate by suspending equivalent concessions it owes the noncomplying country. This **suspension** of obligations is extremely rare, and when it occurs, the offending nation may withdraw from GATT.

■

EEC—PAYMENTS AND SUBSIDIES PAID TO PROCESSORS AND PRODUCERS OF OILSEED AND RELATED ANIMAL-FEED PROTEINS
Report of the Panel L/6627 (Jan. 25, 1990)

■ **FACTS** In a 1962 trade agreement with the United States, the European Community pledged to give duty-free treatment to imports of oilseeds, such as soybeans, rapeseed, and sunflowers. As a result of this zero rate of duty, oilseed imports to the EC swelled as farmers used cheaper soybean and sunflower imports to feed their live-

stock. In response, the EC implemented a subsidy program that paid EC oilseed processors the difference between EC prices and the lower world market prices. The United States claimed the payments to processors were made on conditions that gave them an incentive to purchase domestic rather than imported oilseeds. It considered this to be contrary to GATT's national treatment principle and to impair the benefits it could reasonably expect to accrue to it under the 1962 tariff concessions for oilseeds. The EC claimed the subsidy scheme did not impair U.S. benefits under the concessions because it did not displace or impede imports. In support of this claim, the EC pointed out that oilseed imports from the United States had risen from 4.5 million tons in 1966 to 20.4 million tons in 1988.

■ **ISSUE** Did the subsidies program illegally impair benefits accruing to the United States under GATT?

■ **DECISION** Yes. GATT's national treatment principle provides that "the products of the territory of any contracting party shall be accorded treatment no less favorable than that accorded to like products of national origin." Subsidy payments made to EC oilseed processors are capable of creating an incentive to purchase domestic rather than imported products. The exposure of a particular imported product to a risk of discrimination constitutes, by itself, a form of discrimination. Thus, the subsidy program must be considered to be according imports less favorable treatment in violation of the national treatment principle. The main purpose of the tariff concession granted to imports of U.S. oilseeds by the 1962 agreement was to provide an assurance of better market access through improved price competition. To the extent that the subsidy program counteracts the price effect of those concessions, it impairs benefits accruing to the United States under GATT. It does not matter that U.S. oilseed sales in Europe had been rising even in the face of the subsidies. GATT concessions are commitments on the conditions of competition for trade, not on volumes of trade. Accordingly, the EC should consider ways to eliminate the impairment of its tariff concessions for oilseeds.

In response to the panel report, the EC slightly altered its subsidy program. However, the United States was not satisfied and filed another complaint. When a new GATT panel ruled against the reforms, the EC blocked adoption of the panel report through its veto power. The EC promised to resolve the issue by offering compensation to the United States and other oilseed exporters.

Under GATT rules, a country may abandon previous trade agreements by extending fair compensation to injured parties. The breaching member is given 60 days to arrive at a settlement. If that deadline passes without a resolution, the GATT Council may recommend a course of action to the member states. Should the violator still refuse to comply with its GATT obligations, an aggrieved party can retaliate one month after giving written notice to the other GATT members.

In the oilseeds case, the EC's 60-day deadline passed without a settlement and the United States threatened to impose 200 percent tariffs on French white wines and other EC goods. The EC promised to counterattack any unilateral U.S. measures. Then, in November 1992 (four years after the initial complaint by the United States), the United States and the EC reached an agreement that required the EC to cut subsidies to its grain exporters by 21 percent and to reduce the amount of land it uses for oilseed production.

THE FUTURE OF GATT

The failure to meet the original 1990 Uruguay Round deadline shook world confidence in the GATT process. Part of this failure may be attributable to the increasingly ambitious goals negotiators are tackling in each succeeding round of discussions.

FIGURE 9–2   GATT Dispute Resolution

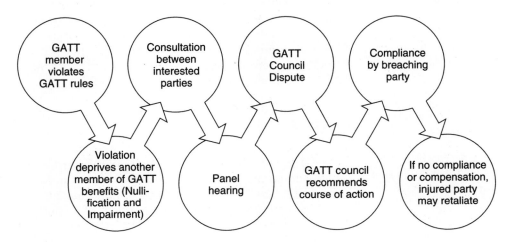

Progress also has been stymied by a rising protectionist tide in Europe and the United States. This section briefly explores the various factors influencing the future of the GATT system.

Protectionist Forces   In recent years, the downward trend in restrictive trade practices has been interrupted by a distressing growth in managed trade. Despite GATT's goal of confining import barriers to tariff-based restraints, quantitative restrictions still abound. These barriers to the free flow of commerce may be visible and openly negotiated or they may be hidden.

Visible Restraints

Visible trade barriers have taken three basic forms: agreements between governments; agreements between exporters and importers; and agreements between governments and exporters or importers. The arrangements between governments, sometimes called **orderly marketing agreements** (OMAs), generally fall within the reach of the GATT rules. Likewise, agreements between private exporters and private importers can be policed under the antitrust laws (discussed in Chapter 14).

Perhaps most distressing to free traders has been the growing reliance on **voluntary export restraints** (VERs) by developed nations. VERs are private understandings between foreign producers and importing governments in which the producers agree to limit their exports. For instance, both the United States and the European Community have regularly persuaded Japanese automobile manufacturers to rein in their exports of cars and trucks. Because they are not formal agreements between

GATT countries (they involve a government and a private party), VERs presently do not violate the GATT rules.

Similarly, the United States, particularly in its dealings with Japan, has been insisting on **voluntary import expansions** (VIEs). These require an importing country to guarantee the purchase of a specific quota of goods from the exporting country. Thus, the United States has insisted that U.S. semiconductor producers be granted a 20 percent share of Japan's domestic market. Such arrangements run counter to GATT's emphasis on rules rather than results.

Hidden Restraints

VERs, VIEs, and OMAs tend to be openly negotiated, thereby permitting buyers and sellers to plan for their effects. Some nontariff barriers, on the other hand, are less visible and so may be more crippling to global trade. For instance, some nations impose elaborate licensing schemes without making the rules available to foreign suppliers. Or a country may erect a system of technical standards (product safety, pollution) without fully informing foreign producers. GATT has attempted to address these problems by insisting that regulatory policies be *transparent* so all producers (domestic and foreign) can discover them and fully understand their terms. Likewise, the *GATT Standards Code* is designed to harmonize standard-setting procedures throughout the world.

GATT's Expanding Reach

Much of the paralysis currently plaguing the GATT process may be attributable to the ever-widening scope of the negotiations. First, the economic status of the growing number of GATT members has been becoming more diverse. As a result, consensus is much harder to achieve today than it was when the membership shared common economic interests. These problems are bound to multiply as the GATT members try to find a place for the Soviet Union's successor states and the Eastern European economies within the GATT framework.

Second, the Uruguay Round took on an extremely ambitious agenda. Historically, the GATT process was confined to global trade in goods. Services and investment issues largely were excluded. Attempts to bring these topics within GATT's orbit have tremendously increased the complexity of the negotiations. There have also been attempts to develop GATT rules for the protection of intellectual property (patents, trademarks, etc.). Finally, the United States has been pushing hard to open overseas markets for its agricultural production. These politically volatile issues have occupied the minds and emotions of the negotiators throughout the Uruguay Round.

Growing Regionalism

The increasing complexity of international trade issues has raised worldwide concern over the continued vitality of the multilateral negotiations. The early successes of the European Community, the Canada–United States Free Trade Agreement, and the North American Free Trade Agreement negotiations suggested that regional and bilateral trade arrangements might be better suited to the current political and economic environment. The next few years should be critical in determining if GATT's multilateral approach can survive these challenges.

QUESTIONS AND PROBLEM CASES

1. Describe the U.S. president's authority to enter into international trade agreements.

2. What is meant by most-favored-nation treatment in the context of the GATT process?

3. What are voluntary export restraints? How do they differ from orderly marketing agreements?

4. Describe the basic steps in GATT's dispute settlement procedures.

5. Under the Agricultural Act of 1948, the United States implemented a potato support program that committed the government to purchase from eligible potato growers all table stock and seed potatoes that could not be sold commercially at parity prices. The statute further provided that whenever the president believed potatoes were being imported into the country under such conditions as to render the program ineffective, he was to cause an immediate investigation to be made by the United States Tariff Commission. If that investigation revealed a threat to the program, the president was instructed to impose quantitative limits on potatoes that may be imported for consumption. In an attempt to protect the potato market and the support program from an influx of Canadian-grown potatoes, the acting Secretary of State entered into an executive agreement with the Canadian government. This arrangement limited the availability of export permits to Canadian exporters who could give evidence that their potatoes would not be used for table stock purposes in the United States. Will a U.S. court uphold the executive agreement with Canada?

6. Intelcom hired 146 citizens of the Philippines to work at the U.S. Air Force base on Wake Island. Throughout this employment relationship, a treaty was in effect between the United States and the Philippines. Pursuant to the terms of the treaty, the Philippine government, through the Philippine Overseas Employment Agency (POEA), approved both the recruitment process and the standard employment agreement for the employment of the Filipino workers. While the treaty specified that employees were entitled to certain benefits, it made no mention of whether individuals would have recourse to the courts of the United States to enforce its terms. However, it did state, "[t]he Government

of the Philippines shall have the responsibility of ensuring that contracts are consistent with the provisions of the treaty." After a dispute between Intelcom and the POEA, Intelcom terminated all of the Filipino employees. The terminated employees brought suit in a U.S. court, claiming Intelcom had violated the terms of the treaty. Intelcom argued the treaty did not permit private lawsuits. Is Intelcom correct?

7. Kraft General Foods operated a business throughout the United States and in several foreign countries. Because part of its business was conducted in Iowa, Kraft was subject to the Iowa Business Tax on Corporations. If a domestic subsidiary transacts business in Iowa, its income is taxed, but if it does not do business in Iowa, neither its income nor the dividends paid to its parent are taxed. In the case of a foreign subsidiary doing business abroad, Iowa does not tax the corporate income, but does tax the dividends paid to the parent. Kraft argued that this taxing scheme violates the Constitution because it discriminates against foreign commerce. Is Kraft correct?

8. After concluding that imported sugar was undermining the price support operations conducted by the Department of Agriculture, the president issued a proclamation imposing duties on sugar imports. The proclamation was issued in 1978 pursuant to discretion delegated by Congress to the president by the 1948 and 1951 amendments to the Agricultural Adjustment Act. Because the proclamation exempted sugars of Malawian origin, sugar exporters from Argentina claimed the exception for Malawian sugar violated the most-favored-nation principle contained in a 1941 trade agreement between the United States and Argentina. Accordingly, they argued that the importation of their sugar was entitled to similar treatment. Are they correct?

9. The purchasing department of the City and County of San Francisco invited bids for the furnishing of equipment for its Canyon Generating Station. The bid invitation contained a provision stating, "All materials, supplies, and equipment covered by this contract proposal shall be manufactured in the United States." This place of manufacture specifi-

cation was included in the contract proposal to-comply with the California Buy American statute. A California court concluded the equipment was to be used to produce electricity for sale to consumers. It further held that electricity is a commodity, which, like other goods, can be manufactured, transported, and sold. Will the California court find the place of manufacture specification to be legal?

10. In all but two of Canada's provinces, imported beer had access to fewer points of sale than domestic beer. This was because domestic brewers could establish private retail stores and also had access to government outlets. Imported beer could be sold only in government outlets. The United States complained that the system violated GATT's national treatment principle. Canada argued that its beer retail system was excluded from GATT rules because it was in effect before Canada became a GATT member (it was grandfathered). That legislation restricted the sale of beer to sales by the liquor board and sales by federally licensed Canadian brewers "duly authorized by the Dominion of Canada." Has Canada violated GATT by not according imported beer national treatment?

10

Customs Laws

INTRODUCTION

Generally, foreign goods may be imported into the United States only after they have been processed by the U.S. Customs Service. The customs procedures often are confusing and highly technical and, if not properly followed, can result in long and expensive delays. Accordingly, it is extremely important for businesspeople to familiarize themselves with the legal framework of the customs and tariff laws.

Chapter Overview

This chapter begins with an examination of the actual operating procedures followed by the U.S. Customs Service. It introduces the reader to the various ways in which importers and customs officials cooperate in the implementation of U.S. customs law. This is followed by a detailed investigation of how Customs actually determines the appropriate tariff for imported articles. The reader sees how this dutiable status formula is made up of three major components: classification, valuation, and rate of duty. Finally, the chapter closes with a brief look at several duty savings devices available to prudent importers.

The Customs Service

Functions

The United States Customs Service, an agency of the Treasury Department, is responsible for the administration and enforcement of the customs laws. Its primary functions include the assessment and collection of duties, taxes, and fees on imported goods. This encompasses the classification and valuation of imports as well as the determination of the proper rate of duty. To carry out its responsibilities, Customs supervises the entry and unloading of vessels, vehicles, and aircraft into the United States. It also combats smuggling and, through cooperation with other governmental agencies, helps enforce a variety of federal regulations.

Organization

The Customs Service is headed by the Commissioner of Customs, who is appointed by the Secretary of the Treasury. It oversees the customs territory of the United States, which encompasses all 50 states, the District of Columbia, and Puerto Rico. This territory is divided into seven customs regions, and each of those is headed by a regional commissioner. Each region is further divided into customs districts (headed by district directors), which oversee some 300 ports of entry and customs stations.

The Customs Service operates in a highly decentralized fashion; most determinations are made by customs officials in the field at the point of entry. With this fact in mind, importers should acquaint themselves with the operating procedures of their particular district. Close attention to local preferences might help avoid costly delays in the importation of goods. However, since the Commissioner of Customs establishes policy for the entire network of offices, extremely arbitrary decisions at the local level may be appealed to the regional or national office.

THE ENTRY PROCESS

Requirements   Most importations begin with an **entry.** The actual entry process generally involves two steps: (1) The importer files entry documents that enable the customs officials to determine whether the goods may be released from custody. (2) The importer files an entry summary that provides Customs with information necessary for duty assessment and statistical purposes.

The Entry Documents

The **entry documents** are to be filed with the district or port director at the port of entry within five working days after the goods reach the United States. There are numerous types of entry, including entry for consumption, entry for storage in a customs warehouse at the port of entry, and entry for transportation to another port of entry where they may be entered under the same conditions as at the point of arrival. The documents required for customs entry generally include:

1. An entry manifest or other form of merchandise release required by the district director.
2. A bill of lading, carrier certificate, or other evidence of a right to make entry.
3. A commercial invoice or pro forma invoice.
4. Packing lists (if appropriate) detailing the specific contents of each package, case, or container.
5. Any other documents necessary to determine if the goods are admissible.

The Entry Summary

Within 10 days of the release of the goods, the importer must file an **entry summary.** Copies of the invoice, a packing list, and a document of title are attached to the entry summary. This information helps Customs assess the value of the imported goods. When the importer submits the entry summary, it pays the estimated duties. Customs generally also requires that the importer post a bond to cover the possibility that the final calculation of duties will exceed this initial estimate.

Invoices

The **commercial invoice** is an integral part of the entry process because it provides the basic information on which the applicable duty is calculated. Federal law and customs regulations prescribe the form and content of the invoice. In its barest form, it must be signed by the seller or shipper and include information as to the kind, quantity, price, and value of the goods. (A sample commercial invoice appears in Chapter 6.)

Sometimes (perhaps because the exporter delayed sending it) a commercial invoice is not available at the time the goods are presented for entry. If this occurs, a

FIGURE 10–1   The Entry Summary

ENTRY SUMMARY

DEPARTMENT OF THE TREASURY UNITED STATES CUSTOMS SERVICE	1. Entry No.	2. Entry Type Code	3. Entry Summary Date	
	4. Entry Date	5. Port Code		
	6. Bond No.	7. Bond Type Code	8. Broker/Importer File No.	

9. Ultimate Consignee Name and Address	10. Consignee No.	11. Importer of Record Name and Address	12. Importer No.
		13. Exporting Country	14. Export Date
		15. Country of Origin	16. Missing Documents
	State	17. I.T. No.	18. I.T. Date

19. B L or AWB No.	20. Mode of Transportation	21. Manufacturer I.D.	22. Reference No.
23. Importing Carrier	24. Foreign Port of Lading	25. Location of Goods/G.O. No.	
26. U.S. Port of Unlading	27. Import Date		

28. Line No.	30. A. T.S.U.S.A. No. B. ADA CVD Case No.	29. Description of Merchandise 31. A. Gross Weight B. Manifest Qty.	32. Net Quantity in T.S.U.S.A. Units	33. A. Entered Value B. CHGS C. Relationship	34. A. T.S.U.S.A. Rate B. ADA/CVD Rate C. I.R.C. Rate D. Visa No.	35. Duty and I.R. Tax
						Dollars / Cents

SAMPLE

36. Declaration of Importer of Record (Owner or Purchaser) or Authorized Agent

I declare that I am the ☐ importer of record and that the actual owner, purchaser, or consignee for customs purposes is as shown above. **OR** ☐ owner or purchaser or agent thereof.

I further declare that the merchandise ☐ was obtained pursuant to a purchase or agreement to purchase and that the prices set forth in the invoice are true. **OR** ☐ was not obtained pursuant to a purchase or agreement to purchase and the statements in the invoice as to value or price are true to the best of my knowledge and belief.

I also declare that the statements in the documents herein filed fully disclose to the best of my knowledge and belief the true prices, values, quantities, rebates, drawbacks, fees, commissions, and royalties and are true and correct, and that all goods or services provided to the seller of the merchandise either free or at reduced cost are fully disclosed. I will immediately furnish to the appropriate customs officer any information showing a different state of facts.

Notice required by Paperwork Reduction Act of 1980. This information is needed to ensure that importers/exporters are complying with U.S. Customs laws, to allow us to compute and collect the right amount of money, to enforce other agency requirements, and to collect accurate statistical information on imports. Your response is mandatory.

↓ U.S. CUSTOMS USE ↓		TOTALS
A. Liq. Code	B. Ascertained Duty	37. Duty
	C. Ascertained Tax	38. Tax
	D. Ascertained Other	39. Other
	E. Ascertained Total	40. Total
41. Signature of Declarant, Title, and Date		

pro forma invoice may be filed. This includes all the information Customs requires for its entry and valuation purposes. The importer must also post a bond guaranteeing the commercial invoice will be produced within 120 days from the date of entry.

Mail Entries

It often is advantageous for an importer to transport goods into the United States through the mail. This may simplify the entry process because the duties on parcels valued at $1,250 or less are collected by the letter carrier. All such parcel post packages must have a customs declaration (available at the post office) firmly attached that gives the value and an accurate description of the goods. A commercial invoice also must accompany each commercial shipment.

Customs officials prepare the entry forms for mail importations, and the mail carrier delivers the parcel to the addressee upon payment of the duty owed. If Customs determines the value of the imported goods exceeds $1,250, the addressee is instructed to prepare and file a formal customs entry at the nearest entry port.

Right to Make an Entry

When goods arrive by commercial carrier, they may be entered only by the owner, the purchaser, a regular authorized employee of the owner, or an authorized customs broker. While U.S. Customs employees often give advice and assistance, they may not act as agents for the importation of goods. Generally, a "carrier's certificate" provides sufficient evidence of the right to make an entry. This certificate describes the goods and states that the named person or company is the owner or consignee for customs purposes. If the goods do not arrive by common carrier, the person who possesses them at the time of arrival generally is permitted to make an entry.

Customs Brokers

Other than employees of the importer, the only persons authorized to act as agents in the entry process are customs brokers. These private individuals and firms must be licensed by the Customs Service before they are permitted to represent the importer. When properly licensed and authorized, the customs broker can prepare and file the necessary documents, arrange for payment of duties, and effect the release of the goods. It has been estimated that 99 percent of all customs entries are filed by brokers.

The relationship between the importer and its broker is governed by the law of agency. Consequently, the importer ultimately is liable for most of the broker's actions in entering the goods. Accordingly, it is important for the importer to understand the customs regulations and ensure that the broker comply with those legal obligations.

Power of Attorney

Before a customs broker may make an entry for an importer, it must be granted power of attorney from the owner, purchaser, or consignee. Likewise, an employee wishing to enter goods for her employer is advised to secure a power of attorney to establish her authority to do so. In general, power of attorney occurs when one individual gives another person express authority to act on his behalf. Customs provides a specific

FIGURE 10–2 A Power of Attorney

Department of the Treasury
U.S. Customs Service
141.32, C.R.

POWER OF ATTORNEY

Check appropriate box:
☐ Individual
☐ Partnership
☐ Corporation
☐ Sole Proprietorship

KNOW ALL MEN BY THESE PRESENTS: That, ______________________________
(Full Name of person, partnership, or corporation, or sole proprietorship [Identify])

____

a corporation doing business under the laws of the State of ______________ or a ______________

doing business as ______________ residing at ______________

having an office and place of business at ______________, hereby constitutes and appoints each of the following persons

____
(Give full name of each agent designated)

____

as a true and lawful agent and attorney of the grantor named above for and in the name, place, and stead of said grantor from this date and in Customs District ______________, and in no other name, to make, endorse, sign, declare, or swear to any entry, withdrawal, declaration, certificate, bill of lading, or other document required by law regulation in connection with the importation, transportation, or exportation of any merchandise shipped or consigned by or to said grantor; to perform any act or condition which may be required by law or regulation in connection with such merchandise; to receive any merchandise deliverable to said grantor;

To make endorsements on bills of lading conferring authority to make entry and collect drawback, and to make, sign, declare, or swear to any statement, supplemental statement, schedule, supplemental schedule, certificate of delivery, certificate of manufacture, certificate of manufacture and delivery, abstract of manufacturing records, declaration of proprietor on drawback entry, declaration of exporter on drawback entry, or any other affidavit or document which may be required by law or regulation for drawback purposes, regardless of whether such bill of lading, sworn statement, schedule, certificate, abstract, declaration, or other affidavit or document is intended for filing in said district or in any other customs district;

To sign, seal, and deliver for and as the act of said grantor any bond required by law or regulation in connection with the entry or withdrawal of imported merchandise or merchandise exported with or without benefit of drawback, or in connection with the entry, clearance, lading, unlading or navigation of any vessel or other means of conveyance owned or operated by said grantor, and any and all bonds which may be voluntarily given and accepted under applicable laws and regulations, consignee's and owner's declarations provided for in section 485, Tariff Act of 1930, as amended, or affidavits in connection with the entry of merchandise;

To sign and swear to any document and to perform any act that may be necessary or required by law or regulation in connection with the entering, clearing, lading, unlading, or operation of any vessel or other means of conveyance owned or operated by said grantor;

And generally to transact at the customhouses in said district any and all customs business, including making, signing, and filing of protests under section 514 of the Tariff Act of 1930, in which said grantor is or may be concerned or interested and which may properly be transacted or performed by an agent and attorney, giving to said agent and attorney full power and authority to do anything whatever requisite and necessary to be done in the premises as fully as said grantor could do if present and acting, hereby ratifying and confirming all that the said agent and attorney shall lawfully do by virtue of these presents; the foregoing power of attorney to remain in full force and effect until the ______ day of ______________, 19 ______, or until notice of revocation in writing is duly given to and received by the District Director of Customs of the district aforesaid. If the donor of this power of attorney is a partnership, and said the power shall in no case have any force or effect after the expiration of 2 years from the date of its receipt in the office of the district director of customs of the said district.

SAMPLE

IN WITNESS WHEREOF, the said ______________________________

has caused these presents to be sealed and signed: (Signature) ______________________________

(Capacity) ______________________________ (Date) ______________

WITNESS: ______________________________ ______________________________

______________________________ ______________________________

(Corporate seal) *(Optional)

form for extending this authority, although the parties may draw up their own agreement.

Liability of Importer

Importers generally must accept personal liability for all duties owed on goods entering the U.S. customs territory. However, sometimes the importer of record is merely a middleman, rather than the actual owner of the imported goods. In that case, it can be relieved of liability for any additional duties that may be assessed after payment of the estimated duties. To qualify for this relief, the importer must declare its status and provide the name and address of the actual owner.

Any individual in whose name an entry is made must vouch for the accuracy of all information provided in the entry documents. Knowing falsification of the entry documents can result in a penalty equal to the domestic value of the imported goods.

Recordkeeping Requirements

Any importer who knowingly causes goods to be imported into the customs territory of the United States must maintain records of the transaction for five years from the date of entry. Customs brokers also are obligated to retain these records. Since records need be retained only by a single entity, a company may rely on its customs broker, accountant, or attorney to provide this service. A company that orders goods from an importer is excused from the recordkeeping requirement unless it controls the terms and conditions of the order or provides technical data or production assistance used in the manufacture of the imported goods.

Customs Authority to Inspect Records

As a general rule, all of the documents filed with an entry should be retained. Purchase orders, proof of payment documents, bookkeeping materials, resale contracts, and other documents kept in the ordinary course of business should also be preserved. Customs is authorized to inspect all of these records. It may use three procedures to obtain them:

1. It can inspect them with the consent of the importer after giving reasonable notice.
2. It can issue an administrative summons enforceable by a court order.
3. It can seize the information after obtaining a search warrant from a court.

Sanctions for Noncompliance

Failure to comply with a summons ordering access to records demanded by Customs subjects the noncomplying company to contempt sanctions. These include the normal penalties of monetary fines and jail sentences. A court also may impose two additional sanctions on an importer that fails to make its records available: (1) The importer may be barred from importing any more goods into the United States. (2) Customs may withhold the delivery of the imported goods.

UNITED STATES v. $1.5 MILLION LETTER OF CREDIT
1992 WL 204357 (S.D. N.Y. 1992)

■ **FACTS** Synergy is a Hong Kong corporation that imports into the United States denim and leather goods produced in the People's Republic of China. Synergy hired Andrew Olding as vice president of finance and administration and controller at its New York office. Olding's responsibilities provided him with access to Synergy's financial books and records, its invoices, and its import records. After reading Synergy's financial records and import documents, Olding concluded Synergy was valuing goods it imported into the United States lower than their correct dutiable value by using false invoices, which fraudulently undervalued the goods being imported. Without informing Synergy, Olding provided the Customs Service with numerous documents that detailed his dis-

covery. In addition, Olding had a special agent of the Customs Service hired as a junior accountant at Synergy, and for six months the two engaged in an undercover investigation of the company. As a result of the information acquired in this investigation, the government obtained several search warrants and seized documents, bank accounts, and merchandise from Synergy's New York office. Synergy then posted a $1.5 million letter of credit as a substitute for the $4.3 million seized from its bank accounts. Synergy petitioned the court to dismiss the government's case on the grounds that the undercover activities conducted by Olding and the Customs Service agent constituted an illegal search.

■ **ISSUE** Was the Customs Service's undercover investigation illegal?

■ **DECISION** No. Undercover operations in and of themselves do not violate the privacy rights of corporations. There is no violation of the Fourth Amendment when someone cooperating with the government permits a search of premises to which that person had access and either common authority or permission to exercise that access. The broad range of responsibility given to Olding by Synergy's management demonstrates that he possessed the required authority over the documents and offices to permit their being searched. Synergy has produced no evidence indicating the undercover agent conducted a search that was unlawfully broad in scope, unbounded in time, or that included areas over which neither Olding nor the agent had authority.

The Automated Commercial System

The U.S. Customs Service is moving to establish a totally electronic environment for importing cargo into the United States. This innovation permits importers and customs brokers to file customs documents electronically without sending in the paper backup. According to Customs, 75 percent of all import transactions will be processed electronically by 1997, and there will be an almost total electronic exchange of information with the trade community by the year 2000.

Methods of Paperless Trade

Customs currently has three ways of filing entry summaries electronically. The first is a bar code-based system that clears millions of entries along the U.S.–Canada border. The second is an all-electronic filing that is available to only a few highly sophisticated companies. The third method involves standard agreements between Customs and importers who make many repeat entries. Customs officials visit these companies' facilities and, after a thorough inspection, grant preclearance for a series of entries. This preclassification program (also called *line review*) is discussed later in the chapter.

National Entry Processing

Paperless trading technology paves the way for the implementation of national entry processing. Under this program, sometimes called *triangle processing,* a customs broker at one location could clear goods entering the country at another site for a customer that could be at a third location. Thus, cargo could be cleared anywhere in the country regardless of the point of entry.

Global Harmonization of Paperless Trade

The Customs Service has been an active promoter of worldwide customs automation. Those efforts have been buoyed by the broad global acceptance for **Edifact** (Electronic Data Interchange for Administration, Commerce, and Transport). Edifact is a United Nations-backed organization that establishes guidelines for carrying out business dealings with electronic messages rather than with paper documents and telephone calls.

To date, the United Nations has approved 19 globally standardized messages for transport, customs, and financial purposes. Included in this list are an invoice and a purchase order. Four other messages apply exclusively to customs matters. They are a customs declaration, a customs response, a customs cargo form, and a customs report.

Opposition to Automation

Despite Customs' eager embrace of total automation, many importers and customs brokers are outspoken critics of paperless trade. For instance, while Edifact is widely used in Europe and Asia, the changeover in the United States has been much slower. One reason behind this delayed acceptance is that numerous U.S. companies and brokers have already invested in computer programs based on non-Edifact standards and now cannot afford to switch.

Brokers often complain that automation will be paperless for Customs but not for them. They argue that many of their carriers and customers are not automated. Thus, while they can make a paperless entry to Customs, they still must print out copies for the carrier and the customers. Brokers have also expressed concern over the impact of automation on their recordkeeping responsibilities. They argue that the move to paperless trade will increase the demands by Customs for audits and investigations of the information brokers have stored.

Despite these complaints, Customs seems determined to break its link with the processing of paper documents. Formerly, information on the release of shipments processed electronically was distributed on paper to companies that were not linked with its computer systems. Now such information is posted in the form of computer printouts at local customs houses. Nonautomated companies are required to send messengers to check the lists.

ASSESSMENT OF DUTIES

To survive in increasingly competitive markets around the world, businesses require accurate and timely information as to their costs and revenues. This necessitates a thorough understanding of the impact of customs laws and rulings on the imported goods. In this section, we examine the rights of importers both before and after Customs has assessed an import duty.

Self-Assessment and Cooperation

The entry documents filed by the importer or its customs broker are designed to assist Customs in determining:

1. If the goods are admissible into the country.
2. The dutiable status of the goods.
3. Whether the goods should be specially labeled.

Customs' ability to carry out these functions relies largely on the importer's self-assessment and voluntary cooperation in accurately and honestly preparing the entry documents.

Examination of Imported Goods

Before goods are released to the importer, the district or port director may designate that representative quantities be examined. Some trade sensitive goods (textiles) or goods from nations with a history of customs violations are inspected more frequently and more extensively than others. If Customs discovers goods that are not specified in an invoice or are improperly invoiced, they are confiscated if it appears that the misstatement was fraudulent.

Liquidation

After Customs has classified and valued the imported goods (these processes are fully discussed below), it formally assesses an import duty. This determination—called a **liquidation**—generally is the point at which the tariff on the goods becomes final. In the case of mail entries, the duty assessed by the local official where the entry was prepared is treated as the final duty.

Liquidated as Entered

In most instances, the liquidation is made by the customs officers at the port of entry and is based on the information contained in the required documents. Where the entry summary is accepted as submitted, the entry is "liquidated as entered." Customs then posts a formal notice in a conspicuous place in the customhouse in the port of entry. Frequently, Customs sends the importer a "courtesy notice" that provides informal notice of a liquidation. However, this letter, unlike the posted notice, has no legal effect.

Liquidated as Corrected

Sometimes the information provided in the entry summary is not correct. Or the local officials may decide their original tariff classification or valuation was not correct. Under these circumstances, the importer is notified that the initial estimate was too low. If the importer does not respond to this "notice of adjustment" or Customs decides its protests are without merit, the tariff is "liquidated as corrected." Notice is posted at the customhouse and the higher duty is assessed.

If the liquidated duty exceeds the estimated duties that were paid upon release of the goods, Customs bills the importer for the difference. However, if the estimated duty exceeded the liquidated amount, the importer receives a refund.

Time Limits

Generally, Customs must make its liquidation within one year of the date of entry. Up to three one-year extensions can be granted by the district director after giving notice to the importer. Extensions may be granted if the information needed to make the assessment is not currently available to the customs officials. The importer also can receive an extension if more time is needed to provide information pertinent to the assessment decision. Failure by Customs to make a final liquidation within the prescribed time limit results in the goods being liquidated at the rate asserted by the importer in its entry summary.

When the liquidated duties exceed the earlier estimates, the importer is required to pay within 15 days of the date on which the liquidation notice was posted. (The date of any courtesy notice is irrelevant.) If payment has not been made after 30 days from the date of liquidation, the debt will be delinquent and bear interest from the 15th day after liquidation.

Protests

A liquidation is final unless the importer files a written **protest** at the port of entry within 90 days after the date of notice of liquidation. Because the protest is filed with the district director who was responsible for the original duty assessment, most appeals are denied. However, the importer can file a request for further review if it desires to have the matter examined by the regional office or the national headquarters.

A protest must be allowed or denied within two years from the date it was filed. However, an importer may request an accelerated disposition when goods are being denied entry into the United States. This appeal must be resolved within 30 days. If the protest is not reviewed within the time limits, it is deemed to have been denied. A denied protest can be appealed to the Court of International Trade, and adverse rulings there can be appealed to the Court of Appeals for the Federal Circuit.

Petitions

Sometimes a party other than the importer is interested in the rates at which goods are allowed into this country. For instance, a competitor of the importer may be alarmed if it learns the importer received an extremely favorable rate of duty. Any "domestic interested party" may submit a petition to the Commissioner of Customs challenging such a liquidation. Notice of the petition is published in the *Federal Register*, and Customs invites written comments on the matter. The commissioner then rules on the challenge.

Binding Rulings

One valuable service provided by Customs is its issuance of **binding rulings** on import matters. These rulings are made only for prospective transactions; therefore, a request will not be processed after the arrival or entry of goods. Only the Customs headquarters in Washington and the regional commissioner for the New York region may make such rulings. It generally takes from six to nine months for a ruling to be made.

After the importer receives a ruling letter, it must attach a copy of it to the entry documents. The ruling then is binding on all customs officials for any customs transactions involving goods identical to those that were the subject of the ruling letter. However, if Customs should later withdraw the ruling, it will individually notify only the person who requested the ruling. Thus, others should be cautioned against relying too much on another person's ruling letter.

Preentry Classification Program

The earlier discussion of Customs automation efforts referred to the availability of preclearance reviews for companies that make numerous repeat entries. These "line reviews" permit a high-volume importer to receive a binding ruling on an entire line of goods that will be imported in the future. As with all binding rulings, the preentry classification program is not available for goods that have already arrived in the United States.

DUTIABLE STATUS OF GOODS

All goods imported into the U.S. Customs territory are either **dutiable** or **duty-free.** Their duty status can be discovered only after they have been properly classified under the Harmonized Tariff Schedule of the United States, which recently replaced the Tariff Schedule of the United States (TSUS). The changeover was mandated in 1988 to synchronize the U.S. classification system with the procedures employed by most of this country's trading partners.

Dutiable Status Formula

If the goods fall in a classification that is dutiable, Customs ascertains their value. This valuation, combined with the appropriate rate of duty, determines the amount of duty owed upon final liquidation. Thus, three basic steps are necessary to determine the dutiable status of imported goods:

1. Classification.
2. Valuation.
3. Rate of Duty.

The next three sections of this chapter explore each of these steps in fuller detail.

CLASSIFICATION

The Harmonized Tariff Schedule

The classification of imports plays a central role in whether they are subject to customs duties and, if they are, the rate at which the duties are assessed. Since 1989, the United States has classified goods according to a system that conforms to the procedures followed by the major trading nations of the world. Known as the Harmonized Tariff Schedule, this scheme was designed to simplify the classification process. While this goal has been achieved to a great extent, classification still remains a highly technical procedure involving numerous complicated issues.

Structure

Under the Harmonized Tariff Schedule, goods are divided according to type and makeup. The system is divided into 22 sections, which are further subdivided into 99 chapters. Each section covers a particular industry beginning with agricultural products and ending with industrial and high-technology products. For instance, section I covers "Live Animals and Animal Products" while section XI relates to "Textiles and Textile Articles."

As a rule, the system classifies all goods that are derived from a single raw material into one chapter or series of chapters, moving from basic component to final product. However, this progression is not possible in all instances since many goods have numerous components. Some of the sections list commodities by function or use. For instance, section XII encompasses "Footwear, Headgear, etc."

The harmonized system classifies items by utilizing a 10-digit number. The first eight digits represent the chapter headings and subheadings where the goods are described. The final two digits are a statistical reference for information gathered by the U.S. government. Many developed nations have adopted a six-digit version of the harmonized system, while less developed countries may utilize only four digits.

Despite the logical structure of the Harmonized Tariff Schedule, correctly classifying an import is not simple. Almost all goods could easily fall into several different categories, each of which might well have a greatly different rate of duty. For this reason, importers requiring certainty as to the applicable duties often request binding rulings from Customs in advance of importation.

Statutory Interpretation

When classification disputes are appealed to the Court of International Trade or the Court of Appeals for the Federal Circuit, the courts follow certain well-recognized rules of statutory construction. Their major objective is to render a decision consistent with the legislature's intent when it established the classification. When the legislative intent is not clear from the face of the statute, the courts seek to find it in the legislative history of the tariff act. Generally, the court looks to the **common meaning** of the disputed article in the belief that Congress intended it to govern the classification unless Congress clearly has indicated that a commercial designation is to apply.

C. J. VAN HOUTEN & ZOON v. UNITED STATES
644 F.Supp. 514 (C.I.T. 1987)

■ **FACTS** Van Houten & Zoon imported over 80,000 pounds of sweetened molten chocolate from Canada into the United States in two tank trucks. The U.S. Customs Service classified the chocolate under item 156.30 as "Chocolate: . . . Sweetened: . . . In any other form. . . ." Van Houten & Zoon contested this designation, arguing that the merchandise should be classified under item 156.25 as "Chocolate: . . . Sweetened: In bars or blocks weighing 10 pounds or more each. . . ." The company argued that the "bars or blocks" language in item 156.25 was flexible enough to include chocolate in molten form. They further alleged that Congress intended the provision to cover commercial imports of chocolate; and the language employed merely reflected how chocolate was transported in 1929 when the provision was enacted.

■ **ISSUE** Does molten chocolate fall within the definition of *bars* and *blocks?*

■ **DECISION** No. Initially, it must be determined whether the definitional aspects of *bars* and *blocks* encompasses liquid or molten material. The common meaning of the words applies unless Congress clearly designated that a commercial designation is to prevail. Since it is a well-settled axiom that classification is determined based on the condition of the article as imported, the chocolate at issue does not comport to the definitions of bars or blocks. Altering the state of an article temporarily to facilitate transportation without changing the essential nature of the goods should not control classification. However, the process must not result in the conversion of the product into another commodity with a separate and distinct tariff classification. The legislative history of the classification scheme does not demonstrate a clear congressional intent to classify chocolate based on whether it is used for commercial purposes. Accordingly, the common meaning of the words must prevail.

FIGURE 10–3   The Harmonized Tariff Schedule

HARMONIZED TARIFF SCHEDULE of the United States (1992) -- Supplement 1
Annotated for Statistical Reporting Purposes

II
8-4

Heading/ Subheading	Stat. Suf. & cd	Article Description	Units of Quantity	Rates of Duty General	Rates of Duty 1 Special	2
0805		Citrus fruit, fresh or dried:				
0805.10.00		Oranges......................................	....	2.2¢/kg	Free (E,IL,J) 0.4¢/kg (CA)	2.2¢/kg
	20 1	Temple oranges...........................	kg			
	40 7	Other....................................	kg			
0805.20.00		Mandarins (including tangerines and satsumas); clementines, wilkings and similar citrus hybrids....................................	....	2.2¢/kg	Free (E,IL,J) 0.4¢/kg (CA)	2.2¢/kg
	20 9	Tangerines...............................	kg			
	40 5	Other....................................	kg			
0805.30		Lemons (<u>Citrus limon</u>, <u>Citrus limonum</u>) and limes (<u>Citrus aurantifolia</u>)				
0805.30.20	00 7	Lemons...................................	kg......	2.75¢/kg	Free (E,IL,J) 0.5¢/kg (CA)	5.5¢/kg
0805.30.40	00 3	Limes....................................	kg......	2.2¢/kg	Free (CA,E,IL,J)	4.4¢/kg
0805.40		Grapefruit:				
0805.40.40	00 1	If entered during the period from August 1 to September 30, inclusive, in any year.............................	kg......	2.2¢/kg	Free (E,J) 0.2¢/kg (IL) 0.4¢/kg (CA)	3.3¢/kg
0805.40.60	00 6	If entered during the month of October...	kg......	1.8¢/kg	Free (E,J) 0.2¢/kg (IL) 0.3¢/kg (CA)	3.3¢/kg
0805.40.80	00 2	If entered at any other time.............	kg......	2.9¢/kg	Free (E,J) 0.3¢/kg (IL) 0.5¢/kg (CA)	3.3¢/kg
0805.90.00	00 8	Other, including kumquats, citrons and bergamots..................................	kg......	0.9%	Free (A,E,IL,J) 0.1% (CA)	35%
0806		Grapes, fresh or dried:				
0806.10		Fresh:				
0806.10.20	00 0	If entered during the period from February 15 to March 31, inclusive, in any year.............................	m³ ....v kg	$1.41/m³	Free (E,IL,J) 84.6¢/m³ (CA)	$8.83/m³
0806.10.40	00 6	If entered during the period from April 1 to June 30, inclusive, in any year......	m³ ....v kg	Free		$8.83/m³
0806.10.60	00 1	If entered at any other time.............	m³ ....v kg	$2.12/m³	Free (E,IL,J) $1.272/m³ (CA)	$8.83/m³
0806.20		Dried:				
		Raisins:				
0806.20.10		Made from seedless grapes............	....	2.2¢/kg	Free (E,IL,J) 0.4¢/kg (CA)	4.4¢/kg
	10 8	Currants.........................	kg			
	20 6	Sultanas.........................	kg			
	90 1	Other............................	kg			
0806.20.20	00 8	Other raisins........................	kg......	4.4¢/kg	Free (E,IL,J) 0.8¢/kg (CA)	4.4¢/kg
0806.20.90	00 3	Other dried grapes......................	kg......	5.5¢/kg	Free (E,IL,J) 1.1¢/kg (CA)	5.5¢/kg

The General Rules of Interpretation

Anticipating that goods might frequently fall within more than one classification, the Harmonized Tariff Schedule contains a body of general rules designed to facilitate its interpretation. Known as the general rules of interpretation, these internationally accepted rules provide the key to properly understanding the classification scheme.

Most Specific Description

The search for the appropriate classification should begin by examining first the headings, and then the subheadings, for the **most specific description** of the imported item. If the goods are unassembled or incomplete articles, they often fall under the same heading as a corresponding completed object. Thus, an unassembled automobile would fall within the category of motor vehicles. However, an unassembled automobile without an engine would not fall under that same heading.

Composite Goods

When the import contains a combination of elements that could fall within more than one heading, a three-step progression determines the proper classification. First, the heading that provides the most specific description is favored over headings with more general descriptions. If this does not resolve the matter, the second step has the classification turn on the heading describing the component that gives the item its **essential character.** When goods still cannot be accurately classified, they fall under the heading that occurs last in numerical order among the headings that otherwise merited equal consideration. Cases, boxes, and containers should be classified with the articles that are imported inside of them if they usually are sold together. Thus, a camera case generally falls within the same heading as a camera if they were imported together.

Most Closely Akin

When an imported item cannot be categorized pursuant to the previous interpretive rules, it is classified under the heading of goods to which it is **most closely akin.** This rule applies only when all other efforts have failed to resolve the matter. In deciding to which item it is most akin, Customs looks at factors such as: its components, its intended use, its normal designation, and its production process.

The Special Rules of Interpretation

In this country, the general rules of interpretation have been supplemented by several additional U.S. rules of interpretation. These special rules focus on instances where the proper classification depends on the use of the imported article or where parts or textiles are being imported.

Use

Sometimes the tariff classification of an article turns on its use. To qualify under the **actual use** subheadings, the goods must meet two conditions. First, they must be directly used for the purpose listed in the description and that intent must be declared to Customs at the time of entry. Second, the importer must provide Customs with verification that the goods have continued with this use within three years of the date of entry. If these conditions are not met, the imports are assessed duties at the rate of most specific heading or subheading describing the article.

Problems sometimes arise when a classification is determined by use (other than actual use) since many goods have more than one use. In those instances, the **principal use** governs. That concept is defined as the use that exceeds any other individual use.

Parts

The **parts** of an imported article do not fall within the same classification as the actual article unless the tariff description specifically includes a provision for parts. This generally would be language to the effect: "widgets and parts thereof." Customs has developed guidelines for determining if an item is a part. First, the part generally could not be used on its own. It would have to be combined with other items to be of use. Second, a part must be essential for the proper functioning of the article to which it is to be attached.

SEARS, ROEBUCK & CO. v. UNITED STATES
723 F.Supp. 805 (C.I.T. 1989)

■ **FACTS**   Sears imported tuners, amplifiers, turntables, and dual cassette decks from Japan and sold them at retail as a stereo rack system. The Customs Service classified the articles as individual components and assessed duties at the following ad valorem rates: tuner (7.7 percent); amplifier (5.9 percent); turntable (4.5 percent); and dual cassette deck (4.2 percent). Sears protested the classification, contending the imported merchandise constituted an "entirety" that should be assessed at the rate of 4.2 percent ad valorem.

■ **ISSUE**   Should the stereo equipment be classified as an entirety rather than as separate components?

■ **DECISION**   No. Under the doctrine of entireties, when an importer imports a set of components designed to form a single salable unit, the merchandise is classifiable as that unit. The components are classified as an entirety if, when combined as a unit, they become an inseparable part of an entity and the changed article becomes more than that which it formerly was. However, if the individual components retain their individual identities and are not subordinated to the identity of the combination, duties are imposed on the individual components in the combination as though they had been imported separately. Since the articles in question retain their essential characteristics as components, the customs doctrine of entireties does not apply.

Textiles

The United States also has developed a special interpretive rule for goods made up of a mixture of textile materials. When an article is composed of more than one textile material, it is classified according to the material that constitutes the **predominant weight** of the combination. The relative monetary value of the components is irrelevant. Thus, if cotton comprises 70 percent of the weight of a fabric and the remaining 30 percent is wool, it would be classified as cotton.

VALUATION

After imported goods have been properly classified, the Customs Service is required by law to determine their value. This valuation serves two important functions: (1) Most duty rates are assessed as a percentage of the value of the imported articles. (These ad valorem rates are discussed in the next section.) (2) The valuation provides statistical information useful in accurately measuring the country's international trade balance.

The United States has adopted valuation procedures that conform with the provisions of the Multilateral Trade Negotiations (MTN) of the General Agreement on Tariffs and Trade (GATT). This international system is designed to promote uniform, fair, and neutral procedures for determining the value of imported goods. Under these global standards, the preferred method of valuation is based on the transaction value (the price actually paid or payable by the buyer) of the goods. However, in some instances, there will have been no arm's-length transaction between the importer and the exporter. When that occurs, the valuation system provides a list of secondary methods for determining the value of the imported articles.

This section examines each of the customs valuation methods in their order of precedence. They are:

1. Transaction value of the imported goods.
2. Transaction value of identical or similar goods.
3. Deductive value.
4. Computed value.
5. Adjusted valuation.

These methods are to be employed sequentially. That is, Customs would use the second method only if it were unable to determine the value under the first method. Likewise, it would not resort to step three unless steps one and two were inapplicable.

Transaction Value   By far, the customs value of most articles imported into the United States is based on the **transaction value** of the imported goods. Transaction value is calculated by adding the price actually paid or payable for the goods when sold for exportation to this country to the following amounts:

a. Packing costs incurred by the buyer.
b. Selling commissions paid by the buyer.
c. The value of any assists.
d. Royalty or license fees the buyer is required to pay as a condition of the sale.
e. Any proceeds of the subsequent resale, disposal, or use of the goods that accrues to the seller.

The dollar amount of each of these items is added to the price paid or payable only if it has not already been included in that price.

If Customs does not have sufficient information to accurately assess the amount attributable to any of these items, it does not base its valuation on the transaction value of the imported goods. Instead, it moves to the second method of valuation and attempts to measure the transaction value of identical goods.

Packing Costs

The packing costs, if they are not already included in the price of the goods, must be added to the price to calculate their transaction value. They consist of all the costs incurred by the buyer for containers and coverings, including the labor and materials, needed to package the goods for export to the United States.

Selling Commissions

The transaction value also must include any selling commissions incurred by the buyer in purchasing the goods. Selling commissions are any amounts paid to the seller, manufacturer, or an agent of either. Thus, selling commissions are paid to a party that is the exclusive intermediary between the buyer and the seller or manufacturer. That individual must be acting on behalf of and under the control of the seller or manufacturer or acting on her own behalf as an independent reseller.

This category often is the subject of legal disputes since buying commissions are excluded from the dutiable value of the goods. A buying commission arises only when the intermediary is acting on behalf of and under the control of the buyer. The buyer's agent must not have independent power to change the terms of the contract and should not be financially related to the seller.

 **ETHICAL IMPLICATIONS** In many cases, an importer is hesitant to exert too much control over the purchasing agent because it does not want to assume legal responsibility for the contracts or torts of this intermediary. Despite this fact, the importer often claims a deduction for payments to the intermediary as buying commissions. Is this ethical?

Assists

Assists are items or services the buyer provides to the seller or manufacturer at no charge or at a reduced charge as part of the sales transaction. They are included in the calculation of the dutiable value of the import. Assists are defined as materials, components, parts, and similar items incorporated into the imported goods. Thus, tools, dies, and molds used in producing the goods generally are assists if they are provided, in whole or in part, by the importer. Engineering, development, artwork, and plans and sketches undertaken outside of the United States also are included in the transaction value to the extent that they are supplied by the importer.

To qualify as an assist (and be included in the transaction value), the goods or services supplied by the buyer must be used directly in the production of the imported articles. Thus, if an importer supplies sewing machines free to an exporter of textiles, the cost of the sewing machines would be added to the dutiable value of the imported textiles. However, if the importer also supplied air-conditioning for the exporter's factory, that would not be an assist since it would not be used directly in the production of the textiles. The value of an assist generally is considered to be the importer's cost of buying and supplying it to the exporter.

Royalty or License Fees

Royalty or license fees are included in the dutiable value of imports if the buyer is required to pay them, either directly or indirectly, as a condition to buying the goods. If the payment of these fees is required by the contract between the importer and the exporter, they are added to transaction value even if they were paid to a third party.

Charges for the right to reproduce certain imported articles in the United States are not included in the transaction value. This exclusion applies to the following types of reproductions: originals or copies of artistic or scientific works; originals or copies of models and industrial drawings; model machines and prototypes; and plant and animal species.

Proceeds from Resale

The transaction value also includes the proceeds from any resulting use or sale of the imported articles that ultimately must be paid to the seller. This is because such payments form an indirect part of the actual purchase price of the goods.

Exclusions from the Dutiable Value

Freight and insurance charges are excluded from the dutiable value of the imported articles, even when they were originally included in the purchase price. Reasonable charges for the construction, erection, assembly, or maintenance of the goods after importation also are not included in the customs valuation. And the customs duties and federal taxes for which the importer generally is liable are not part of the transaction value of the imports. Finally, finance charges are not dutiable if: (*a*) the payment is separately identifiable from the purchase price, (*b*) the financing agreement is agreed on in writing, and (*c*) the buyer can prove that the charge does not exceed the prevailing interest rates.

NISSHO IWAI AMERICAN CORP. v. UNITED STATES
1992 WL 382393 (Fed.Cir. 1992)

■ **FACTS** The Metropolitan Transportation Authority of New York City (MTA) agreed to purchase 325 rapid transit passenger cars from Nissho Iwai Corporation (NIC) for use in the New York City Transit System. Kawasaki

---

CONCEPT SUMMARY
Transaction Value

The Sum of:		The Sum of:		
• Purchase price • Buyer's packing costs • Selling commissions paid by buyer • Value of assist • Royalty and license fees paid by buyer • Proceeds of resale paid to seller	**Minus**	• Freight fees • Insurance charges • Construction and assembly expenses incurred after importation • Customs duties and federal taxes • Bona fide finance charges	**Equals**	Transaction Value

---

Heavy Industries (KHI) then contracted to build the cars in accordance with MTA's specifications. The vehicles subsequently manufactured and delivered by KHI were intended for sale to MTA and could not be used for any other purpose. Duties were assessed by Customs on the basis of the transaction value of the imported cars. For the first 120 cars, this transaction value was determined on the basis of the price NIC paid KHI. The remaining 205 cars, however, were appraised by Customs at the higher price that MTA paid NIC pursuant to their contract. NIC appealed, claiming the transactional value of the cars should have been the manufacturer's (KHI) price to the middleman (NIC).

■ **ISSUE** Should Customs have based the transaction value on the manufacturer's price to the middleman?

■ **DECISION** Yes. The transaction value of imported merchandise is the price actually paid or payable for the merchandise when sold for exportation to the United States, subject to certain additions and deductions. Two legal points are significant here. First, a sale need not be to purchasers located in the United States to provide the basis for valuation. Second, if the transaction value between the manufacturer and the middleman falls within the statutory provision for valuation, the manufacturer's price, rather than the price from the middleman to the customer, is used for appraisal. Once it is determined that both the manufacturer's price and the middleman's price are statutorily viable transaction values, the rule is straightforward: the manufacturer's price, rather than the price from the middleman to the purchaser, is used as the basis for determining transaction value. The manufacturer's price constitutes a viable transaction value when the goods are clearly destined for export to the United States and when the manufacturer and the middleman deal with each other at arm's length, in the absence of any nonmarket influences that affect the legitimacy of the sales price. In this case, the vehicles that were the subject of the contract between KHI and NIC were manufactured for a specific U.S. purchaser (MTA). They were unquestionably intended for exportation to the United States and had no possible alternative destination.

Identical or Similar Goods

Sometimes the transaction value of the actual imports cannot be accurately appraised. This might occur because the relationship between the importer and the exporter was too close to permit an arm's-length contract (a parent corporation transferring goods to a wholly owned subsidiary). Or it could be that the seller has placed severe restrictions on the importer's use of the goods, thereby substantially affecting the value of the articles.

When these things occur, Customs looks to the value of **identical goods.** Goods are identical if they are the same in all respects and produced by the same manufacturer and in the same country as the imported articles. If identical goods cannot be found or properly appraised, the dutiable value is the transaction value of **similar**

goods. Goods are similar if they are commercially interchangeable with the imported items and produced by the same manufacturer in the same country.

All of the additions and exclusions to the transaction value of the imported goods (discussed above) also apply to the identical goods/similar goods determination. However, this second method of valuation contains several additional factors.

> **Exportation date.** The identical/similar goods must have been sold for export and actually exported at about the same time as the imported articles.
>
> **Sales level/quantity.** The identical/similar articles must be sold at the same commercial level (wholesale or retail) as the imported items. They also must be sold in a similar quantity.
>
> **Order of precedence.** Sometimes the identical/similar valuation method results in more than one transaction value. When this occurs, the lowest value is used for customs valuation purposes.

Deductive Value

When a transaction value cannot be obtained for the imported articles, identical goods, or similar items, Customs attempts to appraise the dutiable value under the **deductive value** method. The importer might avoid the deductive value if it has designated a preference for the computed value method (discussed below) in the entry summary. However, if computed value does not work, Customs may revert back to deductive value.

Basically, the deductive value is the resale value of the imported goods in the United States with certain additions and deductions. Under this method, Customs calculates a "unit price" of the imported articles, identical goods, or similar items. Costs related to the packaging of the goods are then added to this unit price. The following amounts are deducted from the unit price: commissions, transportation costs, insurance expenses, customs duties, federal taxes, and the value of any further processing after importation.

Computed Value

When the dutiable value of imports cannot be discovered through any of the previous methods, Customs uses **computed value.** Under this procedure, the value of imported articles is calculated as the sum of four factors: (1) the cost of materials, fabrication, and other processing used in manufacturing the goods; (2) the manufacturer's profits and general expenses if they are usual in the exporting country; (3) the value of any assists unless they were already included in the previous two steps; and (4) the costs of packaging the materials for export to the United States.

Adjusted Valuation

Sometimes none of the valuation methods discussed above proves satisfactory in calculating the dutiable value of the goods. In those circumstances, Customs determines a value by making necessary adjustments to any of the mechanisms. For instance, under the transaction value for identical goods method, Customs might flexibly interpret the notion that the identical merchandise should be exported at about the same time as the imported articles. Or it could waive the requirement that identical goods be from the same country as the imported items.

RATE OF DUTY

After classification and valuation of the import, Customs assesses the liquidated duty. This amount varies depending on what type of duty is appropriate. Accordingly, this section begins with an examination of the various types of customs duties. Attention then is focused on the importance of identifying the country where the imported goods originated. Finally, in a world of ever-increasing competition, importers often try to structure their international sourcing decisions so as to qualify for one or more of the special Customs programs that reduce or eliminate import duties. The section closes with a brief look at several of these programs.

Types of Duties

The three principal types of duties are: ad valorem rates, specific rates, and compound rates. Most duties are levied on the basis of **ad valorem** rates. This is a percentage of the value of the goods. Thus, if the rate is 6 percent ad valorem, goods valued at $100 would face $6 in duties. The appropriate ad valorem percentage is discovered for each classification in the Harmonized Tariff Schedule. A **specific rate** is calculated as a predetermined amount per unit of weight or other quantity, such as 7.2 cents per dozen. A **compound rate** is some combination of the ad valorem and specific rate procedures. For instance, goods may be levied on the basis of 4.3 cents per dozen and 5 percent ad valorem.

Country of Origin

Both duty-free status and the actual rate of duty on imports often depends on the country of origin of the goods. Because of this fact, an importer frequently can save a great deal of money by sourcing goods from countries that receive the most preferential customs treatment. In the absence of special tests for determining the actual country of origin, enterprising importers merely route their imported goods through countries that receive preferential rates. For instance, a company may purchase Japanese widgets that are subject to a 6.4 percent tariff. However, rather than directly importing them into the United States, it might first ship them through a Caribbean basin country to qualify for duty-free status.

Substantial Transformation

Generally, the country of origin is the place where the imported article was grown, manufactured, or produced. However, in many instances, the goods are a composite of numerous materials, many of which originated in different countries. When this is the situation, Customs applies a rule of origin test to determine the appropriate country of origin.

The fundamental test employed by Customs is known as the doctrine of **substantial transformation.** It is used when materials from one country are processed in a second country and then exported to the United States. Under this test, the goods are treated as a product of the second country only if a substantial transformation occurred. Basically, this happens if the original materials acquired a new "name, character, and use" after undergoing processing in the second country. Thus, if thread is shipped from Canada to Mexico where it is used to sew cloth into shirts, the shirts will be a Mexican product since the thread and cloth underwent a substantial transformation.

Labeling Requirements

The country of origin of goods is important for another fundamental reason. Most foreign goods imported into the United States must be labeled so the ultimate purchaser knows the country of origin. This labeling requirement raises two fundamental issues. First, imported materials might be further processed in the United States before being sold to the public. If this processing constitutes a substantial transformation, the final product does not have to be labeled since it is a U.S. article rather than foreign goods.

The second important issue is the determination of who actually is the **ultimate purchaser** of imported goods. The ultimate purchaser of goods is a buyer who receives the product in substantially the same form as when it was imported. Labeling is not required beyond the ultimate purchaser level. Suppose sticks were imported into the United States where they were combined with domestic ice cream to form ice cream bars. If the ice cream producer is the ultimate purchaser of the sticks, the country of origin label would need to appear only on the cases containing the sticks. However, if the consumer were the ultimate purchaser, each individual stick would need to be properly labeled. As you might imagine, this could be expensive. In the case of the ice cream bars, the producer would be the ultimate purchaser because the sticks lost their original identity when they were processed with the ice cream.

UNIROYAL v. UNITED STATES
542 F.Supp. 1026 (C.I.T. 1982)

■ **FACTS** Uniroyal manufactured footwear uppers, consisting of complete shoes except for an outsole, in Indonesia and imported them into the United States. After the importation, Uniroyal sold the uppers to Stride-Rite, which completed the manufacturing process by attaching preshaped outsoles to the uppers and then marketed the finished shoes to retail sellers. Before exportation to the United States, the uppers were packed in cartons marked "Made in Indonesia." The U.S. Customs Service prohibited the entry of the uppers on the ground that each upper was not marked with its country of origin. Uniroyal claimed such labeling was not necessary because Stride-Rite was the ultimate purchaser since the uppers were substantially transformed during the final manufacturing process.

■ **ISSUE** Is Uniroyal exempt from the labeling requirement because Stride-Rite substantially transformed the imported uppers?

■ **DECISION** No. Every article of foreign origin imported into the United States must be labeled in such a manner that its ultimate purchaser in the United States is aware of its country of origin. Accordingly, each individual upper must be properly labeled unless Stride-Rite's attachment of the outsole constitutes a substantial transformation, which results in the final product having a name, character, or use differing from that of the imported article. This clearly is not the case here. A substantial transformation of the upper has not occurred since the attachment of the outsole to the upper is a minor manufacturing or combining process that leaves the identity of the upper intact. The upper was substantially a complete shoe when it was imported. The manufacturing process performed by Stride-Rite required only a small fraction of the time and cost involved in producing the uppers.

Most-Favored-Nation Treatment

As a member of GATT, the United States has promised that the rate of duty available to one GATT member will be available to all other trading members that belong to GATT. Under this **most-favored-nation** principle (see Chapter 9), most goods entering the United States qualify for mid-level rates. However, not all nations of the world are GATT members and, in some instances, GATT may permit discriminatory treatment. Accordingly, goods imported from some nations may be subjected to substantially lower or higher rates of duty. For instance, imports from Canada and Israel may qualify for low rates or duty-free status under GATT's limited exceptions for commerce among members of free trade associations. At the other extreme, imports from Communist nations may be prohibited from entering the country or subjected to extremely high ad valorem rates. Finally, under special development programs, imports from many of the poorest nations of the world often receive duty-free treatment.

Generalized System of Preferences

The United States and 18 other nations are participants in a worldwide effort to encourage the economic growth of certain developing countries. Under this **Generalized System of Preferences,** the U.S. provides duty-free treatment for more than 3,000 types of imports from over 130 beneficiary nations. (Both the number of eligible products and countries may vary from year to year.)

Eligibility

To ensure that the program actually enhances economic development in the target countries, certain requirements must be met before a product receives special treatment. First, the goods must be imported directly to the United States from the beneficiary nation. Second, at least 35 percent of the cost or value of the product must be derived from processing that occurred in the developing country. This "value-added" requirement is designed to prevent businesses from securing favorable tariff treatment merely by using the beneficiary countries as transshipment points.

A company may include the cost or value of materials imported into the developing nation when calculating the 35 percent value-added total. This is possible when the materials are substantially transformed into new and different articles that are then processed into the eligible product. For instance, the importer might export raw skins from Canada to the Dominican Republic (an eligible country). The skins could then be processed into leather in the Dominican Republic and used for the manufacture of leather purses. When the importer then brought the purses into the United States, the value of the raw skins could be used to meet the 35 percent requirement.

Periodic Reviews

The President of the United States is authorized by law to designate which countries and which articles are eligible for preferential treatment. He also is required to conduct periodic reviews of all eligible products and to remove the duty-free status from those that have attained a sufficient level of competitiveness. Under the statutory provisions, the president must suspend the eligibility of any product from a country when that country supplied more than 50 percent of the value of U.S. imports or more than a certain monetary level (to be adjusted each year).

Caribbean Basin Initiative

The United States also provides duty-free status for most imports from approximately 24 countries and territories in the Caribbean Sea under the Caribbean Basin Initiative. The actual list of beneficiary nations is subject to change over the life of the program. The eligibility requirements for preferential rates are similar to those that govern the Generalized System of Preferences.

U.S. Goods Returned

Customs regulations provide special treatment for U.S. goods that have been exported and then returned to the United States. However, importers are advised to seek professional assistance before attempting to utilize these programs since eligibility is contingent on strict compliance with complicated documentation requirements. The remainder of this section provides a general overview of the more common transactions that fall within the scope of these limited exemptions.

Goods Not Improved Abroad

No duty is assessed on American-made goods that are reimported into the United States if they have not been advanced in value or otherwise improved by manufacture while abroad. Under this section, samples sent abroad for inspection, prototype models exported for testing, or shipments rejected by an overseas buyer may reenter the United States duty-free. Likewise, containers used in previous export transactions may be returned without the payment of an import duty. In some instances, duty-free entry may be permitted for goods that have been sorted or repacked overseas if their essential condition has not been changed or improved.

Goods Exported for Repairs

When goods are exported for repairs or alterations and reimported into the United States, duty is assessed only to the extent of the repairs or alterations. In calculating the appropriate duty, Customs first looks to the cost to the importer of any such change. If no charge is made for the alterations or if the charge shown on the invoice or entry papers is not sufficient, Customs constructs a value. To qualify for this program, the owner or exporter of the goods must file a certificate of registration. This permits Customs to inspect the goods before exportation.

CONCEPT SUMMARY
Dutiable Status Formula

(Rate of duty*) × (Valuation) = (Customs duty)

*Classification of goods determines the rate of duty

Goods Assembled Abroad with U.S. Components

Due to the high labor costs in the United States, many manufacturers seek to export their labor-intensive operations overseas. These manufacturers may take advantage of special customs rules that apply to U.S. components that are exported abroad for assembly and then imported into the United States. The fully assembled goods are dutiable according to their normal classification. However, the cost or value of the U.S. components and the costs of shipping them to the port of export in the United States is deducted from this dutiable value.

To be eligible for this exemption, the components must be a product of the United States. If the components contain any foreign materials, they must be substantially transformed into a new and different article in the United States before being exported abroad for assembly. At the time they are shipped abroad, the components must be ready for assembly without any further fabrication. Under this restriction, garments sewn abroad did not qualify for an exemption when fabric was cut abroad. However, certain incidental operations—such as cleaning, sorting, or folding—have been permitted when the assembled component retains its physical identity.

DUTY-SAVING DEVICES

We have seen how businesses can use certain preferential programs and various customs exemptions to reduce the duty owed on goods assembled or produced abroad. This last section of the chapter examines three special duty-saving devices that frequently are available to prudent businesspersons. It begins with a brief look at how importers can reduce (or eliminate) duties by utilizing customs warehouses. Next, there is a quick look at the advantages of importing goods into foreign trade zones. The section (and the chapter) closes with a general survey of the mechanics and advantages of the duty drawback system.

Customs Bonded Warehouses

A **customs bonded warehouse** permits a U.S. business to import and store goods without having to pay an import duty. In some circumstances, depending on the type of warehouse, the goods can be cleaned, sorted, repacked, manufactured, or otherwise manipulated without incurring any duty. The Customs Service closely regulates the operation of the warehouses through audits, random inspections, and general supervision by the district directors.

When the goods are entered into a bonded warehouse, the importer and warehouse operator must post a bond as security for the payment of duties. The actual classification and liquidation does not occur until the goods are withdrawn from the warehouse for consumption within the United States. If the goods are exported, no duty is assessed. No merchandise is permitted to remain in a bonded warehouse for more than five years.

Advantages

Importing goods into a bonded warehouse avoids the assessment of a duty if the goods are exported rather than consumed within the United States. These warehouses also permit an importer to delay the payment of duties on goods. For instance, an importer may import goods with the intent of reselling them within the United States. However, it may wish to store many of the articles in a bonded warehouse until it finds actual buyers for them. In this way, the importer does not have to pay any duties on the goods until it finds a buyer, receives payment, and removes the goods from the warehouse. Finally, an importer might save on import duties when it expects the tariff rate to be reduced within the near future. Thus, an importer may buy goods from a country that will soon receive most-favored-nation treatment. Rather than immediately enter the goods and pay a higher tariff rate, it may store them in a warehouse until the lower duty rate becomes effective.

Foreign Trade Zones

A **foreign trade zone** (free trade zone) is similar to a customs bonded warehouse in that both permit goods to be imported and stored without the actual payment duties. The foreign trade zone, however, permits the importer many more opportunities to manufacture or otherwise manipulate the goods while they are in storage. Unlike the bonded warehouse, there is no time limit on how long goods may be stored in a foreign trade zone.

Generally, the foreign trade zone is adjacent to a customs port of entry and, like the bonded warehouse, is closely supervised by the Customs Service. Private companies that are unable to take advantage of the free trade zones may be permitted to establish subzones near their private facilities.

Advantages

Since the foreign trade zones technically are outside of the U.S. customs territory, they offer numerous advantages for importers hoping to delay, reduce, or avoid their liability for import duties. Since a duty is not assessed until the goods leave the free trade zone and enter the country, an importer may store the goods during slow seasons and remove them when actual sales are made. Merchandise also may be exhibited in the foreign trade zone for an unlimited time, although retail trade may not occur there. Tariff savings might occur in instances where goods are assessed a duty based on their weight. In such instances, the merchandise might be dried in the free trade zone and entered at a reduced weight. Finally, manufacturing processes that involve a lot of unrecoverable waste may be performed within a foreign trade zone. The importer can then avoid paying duties on the wasted components.

NISSAN MOTOR MFG. CORP. v. UNITED STATES
884 F.2d 1375 (Fed.Cir. 1989)

■ **FACTS** Nissan established a foreign trade zone sub-zone at its motor vehicle manufacturing plant in Tennessee. The company then imported production machinery for use in the subzone. The machinery consisted of a highly automated, integrated system of industrial robots, automated conveyor and stamping systems, and a complex computerized interface. Customs valued the production equipment at $116 million and assessed over $3 million in duties. Nissan protested the liquidation by claiming that, because a foreign trade zone is considered to be outside the customs territory of the United States, the equipment would not be dutiable until after it left the subzone and entered U.S. customs territory.

■ **ISSUE** Is the production machinery subject to customs duties despite the fact that it will not leave the subzone?

■ **DECISION** Yes. Nissan's argument that duties cannot be imposed on any article brought into a foreign trade zone unless or until it is sent into the customs territory of the United States is overbroad. Congress signaled its intention to make the imposition of immediate duties dependent on the operations that occur in a foreign trade zone. The applicable legislation provides that merchandise brought into a foreign trade zone may be "stored, sold, exhibited, broken up, repacked, assembled, distributed, sorted, graded, cleaned, mixed with foreign or domestic merchandise, or otherwise manipulated, or be manufactured. . . ." It does not say imported equipment may be "installed," "used," "operated," or "consumed" in the zone, which are the kinds of operations Nissan performed in the subzone with the production equipment. Since the equipment was to be used (consumed) in the subzone for the production of motor vehicles, it is subject to immediate customs duties.

Duty Drawbacks

Businesses that import goods used in the manufacture of other articles that are exported may receive a **duty drawback** for up to 99 percent of the original import duty. Thus, a substantial drawback may be available to a company that can establish that: (1) goods were imported, (2) a duty was paid on the imported articles, and (3) the imported items were used in the production of articles that were exported.

Drawback offers great opportunities for companies to save money when sourcing materials from overseas suppliers. For instance, a U.S. manufacturer might purchase low-cost components from a supplier located in China despite the fact that Customs would assess a very high duty on Chinese goods. After using the Chinese components in its manufacturing process, the U.S. manufacturer could export the finished product and recover 99 percent of the duty it paid through the drawback program. While there are many types of drawbacks, most of the common types fall within two broad categories: same condition drawback and manufacturing drawback.

Same Condition Drawback

If the imported goods are not used in the United States and are exported in the condition they were in when they were imported, they may fall within the **same condition drawback.** Thus, if crates of golf balls are imported into the United States where they are placed in packages of 12 and then exported, they can qualify for the same condition drawback. Likewise, the company could substitute identical U.S.-made balls for the imported ones and still receive a drawback when they were exported.

Manufacturing Drawback

Imported goods used in the manufacture of products that later are exported may qualify for the **manufacturing drawback.** This category permits the U.S. company to use either the actual imported goods or domestic merchandise of the same kind and quality and still qualify for the drawback. Thus, if transportation problems delay delivery of the foreign goods to the manufacturing site, the U.S. company may substitute domestic goods without losing its right to a drawback.

QUESTIONS AND PROBLEM CASES

1. What are the major components of the dutiable status formula employed by the U.S. Customs Service?

2. What is a foreign trade zone? Why might an importer wish to import goods into such a zone?

3. Why are many importers opposed to automation of the Customs procedures?

4. What is the importance of knowing the country of origin of an imported article? How does the concept of substantial transformation relate to this inquiry?

5. The U.S. Customs Service issued an opinion advising that containers of imported frozen concentrated orange juice must be individually labeled with their country of origin. The imported orange juice went through two levels of production. First, before importation into the United States, fresh oranges were run through an extractor and transferred to an evaporator, where the juice was reduced to approximately 14 percent of its original volume. During this stage, the essential oils and flavoring ingredients also evaporated. The second level of production occurred within the United States after importation. It involved blending the concentrate with other ingredients (primarily water) to create the end product of frozen concentrated orange juice. Is the Customs Service correct in requiring that the frozen concentrated orange juice containers be labeled with the country of origin? Upon what does this answer depend?

6. Pflueger Corporation exported fishhooks from the United States to Hong Kong. While overseas, the hooks were sorted by size and shape and placed into containers holding 40 hooks each. These packages were then imported back into the United States where they were sold to fishermen who wanted an assortment of hooks. Should Pflueger be required to pay customs duties on hooks that are imported into the United States? Explain.

7. Camel Manufacturing imported nylon tents into the United States. The tents were designed to hold approximately five to nine persons and weighed between 29 and 33 pounds each. They were used as shelter by people who wished to camp outdoors, either purely for that purpose or to engage in a variety of other outdoor activities. The U.S. Customs Service classified the tents as "textile articles not specially provided for," which subjected them to a duty of 25 cents per pound plus 15 percent ad valorem. Camel protested, claiming the tents should be classified as "sports equipment," which would result in a duty of 10 percent ad valorem. Is the Customs Service correct? Explain.

8. Federal legislation requires that "all articles of foreign manufacture . . . shall be marked . . . in a conspicuous place . . . so as to indicate the country of origin." The Customs Service interpreted this language to permit importers of frozen vegetables to place the country of origin labels on the rear panel of their packages. After its share of the frozen vegetable packaging market declined significantly due to increased imports of foreign produce, Norcal/Crosetti Foods complained that foreign vegetables should be marked on the front panel of the packages. Should importers be required to place the country of origin labels on the front panel of the packages?

9. Samsonite assembled luggage in Mexico and imported it into the United States. As part of this pro-

cess, Samsonite manufactured steel strips in the United States and shipped them to its assembly plant in Mexico. After arrival at the assembly plant, the strips were bent by a machine, cleansed of their oil coatings, covered with vinyl, riveted to sheets of plastic, and fastened to luggage as part of the frame. Samsonite argued that the value of the steel strips should be deducted from the customs valuation of the luggage since they are American-fabricated articles assembled abroad. Is Samsonite correct? Discuss.

10. During the fall of 1990, J.C. Penney, a U.S. retailer, provided Synergy, a Hong Kong corporation with offices in the United States, with specifications for pants that J.C. Penney wished to buy. Synergy arranged to have the China National Textiles Import and Export Corporation (Chinatex) manufacture a sample production pant. After seeing the sample, J.C. Penney ordered pants from Synergy at a price of $123.48 per dozen. Synergy contracted with Chinatex to fill the J.C. Penney order and then attempted to enter the merchandise into the United States at $58.00 per dozen, the price Synergy had paid to Chinatex in their arm's-length contract. Customs rejected this attempted entry and valued the pants at $123.48 per dozen. Did Customs correctly assess the transaction value of the imported merchandise?

11

Import Relief

INTRODUCTION

The last decade has witnessed a growing departure from the free trade principles nurtured by the GATT process. Government intervention has risen markedly as more policymakers challenge the assumption that the free play of market forces maximizes global welfare. They view the theory of comparative advantage underlying modern trade theory to be poorly suited for international commerce because it is premised on the existence of perfectly competitive markets. However, competitive success in the global environment often requires conducting operations on such a large scale that only a few dominant firms ultimately can survive within each industry.

Most political systems are unwilling to permit their domestic firms to be replaced by large, multinational competitors. Accordingly, they gravitate toward activist policies that ensure the maintenance of economic viability for domestic firms, even when it means discriminating against foreign businesses.

Modern U.S. Trade Policy

Despite its free trade rhetoric, the United States has been pursuing an activist policy over the past 20 years. Described as **strategic intervention,** this approach incorporates varying combinations of import barriers and export assistance. The United States has gone beyond earlier protectionist policies motivated primarily by the desire to insulate domestic firms from global competition. Recent trade initiatives have conditioned access to the domestic market on reciprocal opportunities for U.S. businesses abroad.

Chapter Overview

This chapter explores the major U.S. trade policies that influence the accessibility of domestic markets to imports from foreign countries. It assumes the reader possesses a general understanding of the U.S. policy-making process and the GATT system (both are discussed in Chapter 9). The chapter begins with a brief look at the governmental institutions that play prominent roles in administering import relief in the United States. The next two sections examine national policies directly affecting the ability of foreign goods to penetrate the U.S. market. The first of these sections explores three measures designed to safeguard domestic industries from market disruptions. This is followed by a discussion of governmental initiatives designed to counteract the threat of unfair import competition. The chapter closes with a review of the various ways the government uses import barriers (and threats of restrictions) to open overseas markets.

KEY PARTICIPANTS IN U.S. IMPORT POLICY

The U.S. Constitution gives primary responsibility for regulating international commerce to the legislature. However, over the years, Congress delegated so much authority to the executive branch that U.S. trade policy today reflects a careful balance between both branches of government. Of course, because of the complexity and magnitude of modern global trade issues, neither the president nor Congress can manage the day-to-day conduct of U.S. trade. Thus, to cope with the immensity of the

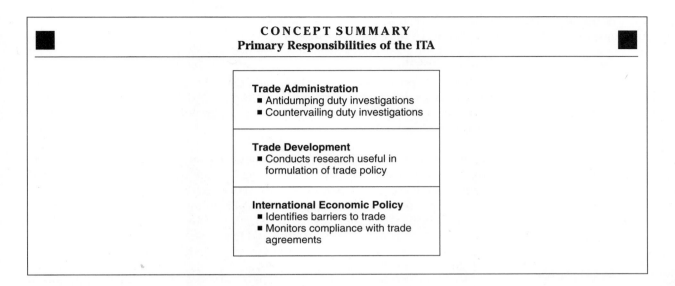

CONCEPT SUMMARY
Primary Responsibilities of the ITA

Trade Administration
- Antidumping duty investigations
- Countervailing duty investigations

Trade Development
- Conducts research useful in formulation of trade policy

International Economic Policy
- Identifies barriers to trade
- Monitors compliance with trade agreements

task (and to place an additional check on the executive branch), Congress has delegated much of the responsibility over U.S. import policies to several administrative agencies. This section briefly examines those institutions. It then looks at the judicial body primarily responsible for adjudicating import trade issues.

U.S. Customs Service

The **U.S. Customs Service** is the agency most frequently associated with import transactions. This division of the Treasury Department has primary responsibility for the administration and enforcement of the U.S. customs and tariff laws (see Chapter 10). As the overseer of the hundreds of entry points to the United States, the Customs Service plays a key role in blocking imports that violate U.S. trade law.

International Trade Administration

As a part of a governmental reorganization growing out of the *Trade Act of 1979,* the Secretary of Commerce created the **International Trade Administration** (ITA). Headed by the under Secretary for International Trade, the ITA is charged with strengthening the competitive position of the United States in world trade.

When the ITA was created in 1980, it assumed the Treasury Department's role in administering the U.S. antidumping and countervailing duty (export subsidy) statutes. As part of its trade development function, the ITA conducts much of the economic research underlying U.S. trade policy and assists U.S. companies in their export and overseas investment efforts. The ITA also assists U.S. negotiators in their dealings through GATT and other international economic institutions. It identifies overseas barriers to U.S. trade and investment and offers suggestions on how they might be dismantled. As a part of this function, the ITA plays a vital role in monitoring foreign compliance with international trade agreements.

International Trade Commission	The ITA is assisted in handling antidumping and foreign subsidy complaints by the **International Trade Commission** (ITC). The ITC also investigates charges of unfair competition brought under Section 337 of the Tariff Act of 1930 and requests for import relief under Section 201 of the Trade Act of 1974 (both are examined below). To maintain its political independence, the ITC has been designated as a bipartisan agency whose six commissioners must equally represent both major political parties. Presidential appointments to the ITC must be confirmed by the Senate. (The ITC is discussed in Chapter 9.)
U.S. Trade Representative	Through the *Trade Act of 1974,* Congress created an Office of Special Trade Representative that was to serve as a permanent agency within the executive branch. Part of the motivation for this congressional action was to ensure that future trade representatives would cooperate with the legislative branch. In a governmental reorganization precipitated by the *Trade Agreements Act of 1979,* the special trade representative was renamed the **U.S. trade representative** and her responsibilities were codified. Her primary functions include the development and coordination of U.S. trade policy, negotiating international trade agreements, advising the president on trade matters, and protecting U.S. rights under trade agreements. She also assists the Commerce Department in imposing antidumping and countervailing duties. The trade representative holds the rank of ambassador. As such, her appointment by the president must be approved by the Senate. (See Chapter 9 for further discussion of the role of the U.S. trade representative.)
Court of International Trade	The **Court of International Trade** (CIT) has exclusive jurisdiction over most lawsuits involving U.S. trade laws. Its nine judges are appointed by the president and must be confirmed by the Senate. No more than five of the judges may be from the same political party. The CIT has the same powers as any federal district court, including the authority to conduct jury trials.

Most lawsuits filed with the CIT require a trial *de novo,* which means the court decides for itself all issues of fact and law. However, in antidumping, countervailing duty, and adjustment assistance cases (all are discussed below), the CIT reviews the administrative record only to ensure that the governmental agencies did not abuse their discretion. Decisions of the CIT may be appealed to the Court of Appeals for the Federal Circuit and from there to the U.S. Supreme Court.

PROTECTION FROM MARKET DISRUPTIONS

Some U.S. policies are designed to protect domestic industries from unfair imports. Others call for the government to close its borders to goods from countries that unfairly restrict opportunities for U.S. exports. These regulatory responses (they are examined in the following sections) share one fundamental trait; each is triggered by an *unfair trade* practice.

However, unfairness is not a prerequisite for all governmental remedies against foreign competition. This section examines three U.S. programs sheltering domestic industries from imports entering the United States under *fair trade* conditions. They are: the escape clause, adjustment assistance, and relief from increased imports from Communist countries. Despite their protectionist appearance, these measures are designed to provide only temporary relief while domestic producers adjust to the disruption caused by foreign competition.

The Escape Clause

When the United States adopted GATT's process for reducing tariffs and other import barriers, it insisted on including a safeguard against unforeseen and injurious consequences to domestic industries. Accordingly, the GATT agreements permit members to temporarily suspend their treaty obligations when increased imports threaten serious injury to domestic producers. This safety valve, known as the **escape clause,** is codified in U.S. law as *Section 201 of the Trade Act of 1974* (Section 201). (GATT's escape clause is briefly discussed in Chapter 9.)

The Escape Clause Procedure

The Section 201 process begins when the International Trade Commission receives a *petition* to undertake an investigation. This request may be made by firms, trade associations, unions, the president, the U.S. trade representative, the House Ways and Means Committee, the Senate Finance Committee, or the ITC itself. On receiving a petition, the ITC must promptly investigate to see if import relief is merited.

The ITC *investigation* involves collecting economic and legal information from the affected industry, importers, foreign exporters, trade associations, and governmental agencies. It includes a *public hearing* in which interested parties may present their views. Within 120 days of receiving a petition, the ITC is required to make a *final decision.* Three or more of the six ITC members must recommend to the president that Section 201's remedies be invoked before relief may be granted. Escape clause relief is not legally permitted in the absence of an ITC recommendation.

Standards for Escape Clause Relief

Section 201 remedies may not be implemented unless the ITC investigation concludes: (1) imported articles are entering the United States in increasing quantities; (2) the imports are affecting a domestic industry producing an article like or directly competitive with the imported goods; (3) the domestic industry is suffering serious injury or faces a threat of injury; and (4) the increased imports are a substantial cause of the injury or threat of injury. We now briefly examine each of these elements.

Increasing Imports

Section 201 states imports must be entering the country in *increased quantities* before relief may be granted. However, this requirement may be met by either finding an absolute increase in the number of imports or showing that imports merely have increased relative to domestic production. Thus, in periods of declining domestic production, there is a relative increase in imports when their actual numbers have remained constant or are declining at a slower rate than domestic production. The time period over which imports are analyzed can greatly affect the ITC's findings on this point. As a general rule, the ITC considers data relating to the five years immediately preceding the filing of the petition.

Domestic Industry

Only a *domestic industry* producing an article *like or directly competitive* with the imported article is entitled to Section 201 relief. In making this determination, the ITC interprets "like articles" as goods that share intrinsic characteristics (appearance, quality, texture) with the imports. "Directly competitive" refers to products that are substantially equivalent for commercial purposes (they essentially are interchangeable). U.S. producers requesting import relief generally urge the ITC to define the domestic industry very narrowly so the injury appears more severe. Foreign producers and importers, on the other hand, usually argue for a broader interpretation.

Injury

Section 201 relief is not appropriate unless the domestic industry suffers *serious injury* or faces the *threat of serious injury.* In investigating these issues, the ITC examines a broad range of economic evidence. For instance, a finding of serious injury might result if there is significant unemployment or underemployment in the domestic industry. Further, a significant idling of production facilities or the inability to generate a reasonable profit across the entire domestic industry might show the existence of a serious injury.

Congress has instructed the ITC to consider certain factors in determining if there has been a threat of serious injury. Included among them are a decline in sales or market share, a growing inventory, and a downward trend in production, profits, wages, or employment. Other evidence of such a threat may be the inability to generate capital needed for the modernization of domestic plants or the maintenance of existing levels of research and development.

Causation

The final precondition to escape clause relief is a finding that increased imports are a *substantial cause* of the injury or threat of injury to the domestic industry. This requirement generally is met when the ITC investigation uncovers an increase in imports matched by a decline in the U.S. producers' share of the domestic market. However, the decline must be a result of the increased imports. It should not stem from normal cyclical changes or recessionary factors.

Escape Clause Remedies

When all of Section 201's elements are met, the ITC recommends to the president that remedial action be taken. (No relief may be granted in the absence of an ITC recommendation.) This relief may come in many forms, including increased tariffs (no more than 50 percent ad valorem), quotas, adjustment assistance (discussed below), or international negotiations. Failure to comply with an import order may subject violators to fines of $100,000 per day or twice the value of the wrongfully imported goods, whichever is greater.

The president may accept, modify, or reject the remedies recommended by the ITC. He may deny relief if he does not believe it to be in the best economic interests of the country. However, after receiving the ITC report, he must inform Congress of the actions he will take. In cases where the president intends to pursue a course different from the ITC recommendation, Congress may enact legislation requiring the ITC recommendation be followed. (The president may veto this legislation.)

Section 201 remedies generally terminate after five years, although they may be extended for up to three more years. Any measures that are to last more than three years must be phased down during their effective period. Thus, tariffs should be gradually reduced or quotas should be gradually increased. Under GATT rules, when the United States implements escape clause relief, it is required to offer equivalent concessions to the affected countries.

MAPLE LEAF FISH CO. v. UNITED STATES
762 F.2d 86 (Fed.Cir. 1985)

■ **FACTS** The American Mushroom Institute, a trade association representing domestic canners and growers of mushrooms, filed an escape clause petition. The ITC investigated to determine whether mushrooms classifiable under the U.S. tariff code as "mushrooms otherwise prepared or preserved" were being imported in such increased quantities as substantially to cause or to threaten serious injury to a like or competing domestic industry. After making an affirmative finding, the ITC report to the president recommended import relief taking the form of import quotas for a three-year period. The president accepted the ITC's determinations but decided to give import relief in the form of increased duties. Maple Leaf Fish Company, a mushroom importer, protested Customs' assessment of increased duties on imports of "frozen battered and breaded mushrooms." It filed suit in the Court of International Trade, claiming frozen and battered mushrooms were not in the ITC's determinations and accordingly were beyond the scope of the president's power to award import relief. Maple Leaf also argued that if frozen battered and breaded mushrooms were intended by the ITC to be covered in its report, the evidence uncovered during the investigation did not support their inclusion.

■ **ISSUE** Was the president authorized to impose supplemental duties on frozen battered and breaded mushrooms?

■ **DECISION** Yes. Maple Leaf's frozen battered and breaded mushrooms are encompassed in the category of *mushrooms otherwise prepared or preserved*. While the ITC report heavily emphasized canned mushrooms, this is not surprising because 97 percent of all imported mushrooms are canned. Nothing in the report indicates frozen mushrooms were meant to be excluded, especially since part of the report details statistics on "dried, frozen, and fresh mushrooms." A critical element in this review is the fact that the escape clause legislation involves the president and his close relationship with foreign affairs. More than that, Congress has vested the president with broad discretion and choice as to what he decides to do affirmatively, or even whether he should do anything. Similarly, the ITC has great leeway to consider the economic factors it deems relevant to making a final determination. This gives reviewing courts a very limited role. For a court to interpose, there has to be a clear misconstruction of the governing statute, a significant procedural violation, or action outside the delegated authority. The president's finding of fact and the motivations for his actions are not subject to judicial review. The same is true of the ITC's actions that are preparatory to, and designed to aid, presidential action. A court may not review the ITC's ultimate factual determination that there was injury to frozen mushroom producers. It is enough that the ITC made the ultimate finding that there was an injury.

Adjustment Assistance   When the ITC receives an escape clause petition, it immediately notifies the Secretaries of Commerce and Labor so they may investigate whether affected employees or firms are eligible for **adjustment assistance.** Similarly, the president may forgo the imposition of import barriers when fashioning a Section 201 remedy and offer instead direct assistance to domestic workers and firms. Under this program, workers may

CONCEPT SUMMARY
The Escape Clause Procedure

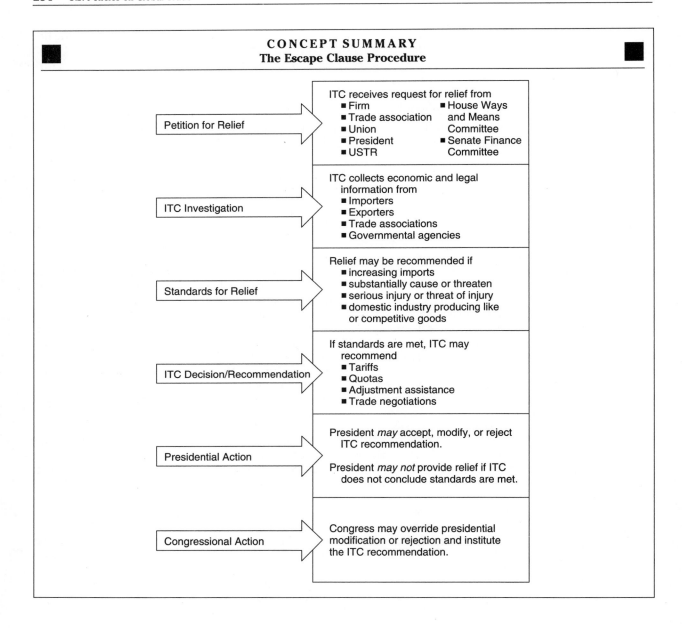

Petition for Relief

ITC receives request for relief from
- Firm
- Trade association
- Union
- President
- USTR
- House Ways and Means Committee
- Senate Finance Committee

ITC Investigation

ITC collects economic and legal information from
- Importers
- Exporters
- Trade associations
- Governmental agencies

Standards for Relief

Relief may be recommended if
- increasing imports
- substantially cause or threaten
- serious injury or threat of injury
- domestic industry producing like or competitive goods

ITC Decision/Recommendation

If standards are met, ITC may recommend
- Tariffs
- Quotas
- Adjustment assistance
- Trade negotiations

Presidential Action

President *may* accept, modify, or reject ITC recommendation.

President *may not* provide relief if ITC does not conclude standards are met.

Congressional Action

Congress may override presidential modification or rejection and institute the ITC recommendation.

receive additional unemployment benefits as well as funds for retraining, relocation, and job searches. Private companies are limited to receiving technical assistance in the development of action plans for coping with foreign competition.

Workers and firms also may request adjustment assistance independently of Section 201's escape clause. Although workers apply through the Secretary of Labor and firms petition the Secretary of Commerce, the criteria for relief are parallel. Before workers or firms can be certified for adjustment assistance, the secretary must find that:

1. A significant number or proportion of workers have become totally or partially separated or threatened with total or partial separation from employment with the firm.
2. The firm's sales or production have decreased absolutely.
3. Increased imports of like or directly competitive articles have contributed importantly to the separations or threat of separations and the decline in sales and production.

Within 60 days after receiving a petition, the secretary must rule on a petitioner's request for adjustment assistance.

WESTERN CONFERENCE OF TEAMSTERS v. BROCK
14 C.I.T. 657 (CIT 1990)

■ **FACTS** Great Western Sugar Company was one of the nation's leading processors of sugar beets, with 12 plants in five states. Great Western produced refined sugar from sugar beets under contract with growers. The sugar produced at the various Great Western facilities was marketed primarily to soft drink producers and food manufacturers. In March 1985, Great Western closed its plants and filed for bankruptcy. Western Conference of Teamsters, on behalf of the former Great Western employees, petitioned the Secretary of Labor for certification of eligibility for trade adjustment assistance. Despite the fact that raw sugar imports had increased absolutely during three of the four years immediately before Great Western's bankruptcy, the Secretary of Labor denied the petition. Western Conference of Teamsters argued that the Labor Department erred by not considering the impact of raw sugar imports when making its determination.

■ **ISSUE** Should the Secretary of Labor reconsider the petition for adjustment assistance?

■ **DECISION** No. Virtually all commercial sugar is produced from either sugar cane or sugar beets. Unlike sugar beets, which are converted directly into refined sugar, sugar cane is first milled to produce an intermediate product, raw sugar. The refined sugar derived from sugar cane is indistinguishable from that derived from sugar beets. The Labor Department's determination acknowledged that raw sugar may be considered like or directly competitive with refined sugar. However, it believed the significance of that fact was tempered by the operation of a sugar price support program that insulated the domestic raw and refined sugar market from the effects of increased imports. As a result of the price support mechanisms, the price of sugar rose to a level sufficient to allow Great Western to operate profitably. Further, data revealed that, during this time, domestic suppliers of high fructose corn syrup had increased their market share from 9.2 to 41.5 percent of the market. This was confirmed by a Labor Department survey showing that large bottling companies had greatly reduced their purchases of refined sugar from Great Western, buying instead from domestic high fructose corn syrup suppliers. Thus, there was ample evidence for the Secretary of Labor to conclude that Great Western's demise was caused, not by the effect of increased imports, but by competition from domestic high fructose corn syrup suppliers and management decisions.

Relief from Communist Imports

When Congress authorized the president to grant most-favored-nation treatment to nonmarket countries, it feared that centrally planned economies might flood the U.S. market by targeting selected industries. Thus, *Section 406 of the Trade Act of 1974* created a special escape clause to protect against disruptions caused by increased imports from Communist countries. Section 406 is similar to Section 201's escape clause in that the ITC must conduct an investigation on receiving a petition from an interested party. If the ITC determines a market disruption exists, it recommends to the president that remedial action be taken.

However, there also are differences between the two escape clauses. For instance, because of congressional concern over the increased threat posed by nonmarket economies, the ITC must complete its investigation within 90 days (it is 120 days under Section 201), and the president may proclaim temporary emergency relief before the ITC has made its determination. Such measures are terminated if the ITC ultimately rejects the petition. Further, adjustment assistance is not an available remedy for disruptions caused by Communist countries. Finally, it is easier to prove a Section 406 case. When imports from a nonmarket country are increasing rapidly, relief may be granted if the goods are a *significant cause of material injury* or threat thereof. This is a less onerous burden than Section 201's *substantial cause of serious injury* or threat thereof.

PROTECTION FROM UNFAIR IMPORTS

Remedies against unfair imports constitute an integral, yet controversial, part of U.S. trade policy. When these measures are used to offset the market distortions caused by unfairly traded imports, they do not necessarily violate GATT's free trade principles. However, foreign exporters and domestic importers often complain that, in practice, these mechanisms have become protectionist devices that artificially raise the price of foreign goods. This section examines the three most frequently used weapons in the U.S. arsenal against unfairly traded imports: antidumping duties, countervailing duties against subsidized goods, and the general prohibition against unfair acts in the importation of goods (Section 337).

Dumping

Dumping refers to the selling of products in an export market for *less than fair value*. For instance, a Japanese widget producer might sell widgets in the United States for less than it sells them in Japan. It can carry out this marketing strategy if Japanese import barriers allow it to charge artificially high prices in Japan. While importers and consumers in the United States benefit from the lower prices associated with dumped goods, domestic producers complain the benefits are only temporary; as soon as the foreign manufacturers gain control of the U.S. market, they will raise their prices.

While GATT does not prohibit dumping, its *Antidumping Code* permits members to impose special tariffs when dumped imports cause or threaten to cause *material injury* to competing industries in the import market. These **antidumping duties** should equal the difference between the home market sales price and the export sales price, known as the *dumping margin*.

U.S. Antidumping Rules

The United States assesses antidumping duties equal to the dumping margin when (1) imports are sold or offered for sale in the United States at less than fair value, and (2) a U.S. domestic industry is materially injured, threatened with material injury, or prevented from being established. Two governmental agencies—the International Trade Administration and the International Trade Commission—jointly administer the U.S. antidumping rules. Initially, the ITA checks to see if foreign goods are being sold, or offered for sale, in the United States for less than fair value. If such dumping is discovered, the ITC investigates to determine if there has been, or is likely to be, material injury to a domestic industry. When both inquiries are affirmative, the ITA issues an order imposing antidumping duties on the imported articles.

The Dumping Investigation

Although domestic producers trigger most antidumping actions by petitioning the ITA for relief, the ITA may initiate an investigation itself. The ITC then conducts a *preliminary investigation* to determine if there is a reasonable indication that dumping is causing or threatening to cause material injury to a domestic industry. During this phase of the inquiry, the ITC sends questionnaires to importers and domestic producers in the relevant industry, gathering market information.

If the ITC concludes there is a likelihood of material injury (or the threat of injury), the ITA investigates to determine the probability that dumping is occurring. This preliminary inquiry is conducted both in the United States and overseas, involving an on-site examination of the foreign producer's business records. If the findings suggest dumping has occurred, the Secretary of Commerce orders for each entry of the goods under investigation the posting of a bond or other security equal to the estimated dumping margin. He also suspends the final assessment (liquidation) of duties on those imports until the dumping investigation is completed.

In these preliminary investigations, both the ITC and ITA generally make affirmative findings if there are any facts supporting the petition. However, during the next phase, the *final determinations*, they are more demanding. First, the ITA makes a final decision (even when its preliminary finding was negative) as to whether the foreign goods are being, or are likely to be, dumped in the United States. If this conclusion is negative, the proceedings are terminated. If it is affirmative, the ITC makes its final determination on the injury issue. This includes a hearing if the parties request one. When at least three of the six commissioners conclude the requisite injury (or threat of injury) has occurred, the Secretary of Commerce directs the Customs Service to assess the antidumping duties.

ETHICAL IMPLICATIONS   The low evidentiary threshold required during preliminary investigations can be disastrous for foreign producers. The expense of posting a bond and the uncertainty attending the suspension of liquidation of import duties often induces importers to drop their foreign suppliers. Thus, domestic producers may greatly benefit from dumping investigations even where the ITA or ITC ultimately rules in favor of the foreign producer. Is it ethical for domestic producers to petition the ITA for antidumping relief for the sole purpose of placing obstacles in the path of foreign competitors?

FIGURE 11–1   The Dumping Equation

The ITA Inquiry

It is the ITA's responsibility to establish the existence and degree of dumping. In deciding if imports are being sold at less than fair value, the ITA looks to see if the imports' foreign market value exceeds their U.S. price. Thus, the ITA inquiry has two fundamental components: foreign market value and United States price.

There are four basic methods for calculating **foreign market value:** (1) sales in exporter's home market, (2) sales for exportation to third countries, (3) constructed value, or (4) in cases of dumping from nonmarket countries, the value of the factors of production in a market economy similar to the nonmarket exporter. Home market sales is the method preferred by the ITA. However, if home market sales are negligible or if that information is not available, the ITA uses one of the other methods for determining foreign market value.

There are two methods for calculating **U.S. price.** First, when the foreign producer sells goods to an unrelated customer in the United States, the U.S. price is based on the *purchase price* before the date of importation. Second, when the foreign seller and the U.S. importer are related (e.g., a parent corporation and its subsidiary), U.S. price is the *exporter's sales price*. This is based on the price at which the goods are resold to an unrelated buyer in the United States.

Under both methods for determining U.S. price, the ITA generally makes *adjustments* for special costs associated with exporting the goods. For instance, the costs of containers, import duties, and export taxes are added to the U.S. price. Further, special buying inducements in the home market (rebates, accessories) that are not available in the U.S. market are deducted from foreign market value. These adjustments can be very important because any additions to U.S. price or deductions from foreign market value reduce the dumping margin.

LMI-LA METALLI INDUSTRIALE S.p.A. v. UNITED STATES
712 F.Supp. 959 (CIT 1989)

■ **FACTS** LMI-La Metalli Industriale, S.p.A. (LMI), an Italian manufacturer of brass sheet and strip, challenged a final determination of the ITA that brass sheet and strip from Italy was being sold in the United States at less than fair value. Specifically, LMI claimed the ITA erred in refusing to deduct home market selling commissions and technical service salaries when determining the foreign market value of LMI's brass sheet and strip. LMI argued that the ITA should have made sale adjustments for the commissions and salaries because they were reasonably identifiable, quantifiable, directly related to sales under consideration, and caused a difference between foreign market value and U.S. price.

■ **ISSUE**   Did the ITA err by not deducting the commissions and technical services from the foreign market value?

■ **DECISION**   No. Allowances generally are made for commissions paid for home market sales that are not paid on U.S. sales. In this case, however, the ITA was correct in denying the adjustment because LMI's exclusive home market sales agent is LMI's wholly owned subsidiary. There is a clear distinction between commission payments to individual salespeople and payments to wholly owned subsidiaries. A foreign producer could avoid a determination of sales at less than fair value merely by increasing the amount of its commission payments to its subsidiary company. Such an intracompany transfer of funds would not decrease the foreign producer's total revenue, but it could enable foreign corporations to sell in the United States at less than fair value. The ITA also was correct in denying an adjustment to foreign market value for the technical service salaries. If the home market sales obligations specifically included providing goods and technical services, while the sales obligations in the United States included only providing goods, a deduction from foreign market value would be appropriate. However, in this case, the technical services were provided for independent purposes such as basic research and benefited both the home market and the U.S. market. It would be unfair to adjust for such expenses in one market and not the other.

The ITC Inquiry

In deciding if dumped imports cause or threaten to cause material injury to a U.S. industry or materially retard the establishment of a domestic industry, the ITC considers three major factors: (1) the volume of imports, (2) the effect of imports on prices in the United States for like products, and (3) the impact of the imports on domestic producers of like products. Thus, **material injury** is likely to be found when a significant volume of imports is underselling domestic goods, resulting in declining profits, market share, productivity, or employment in the domestic industry.

Several factors may lead the ITC to find a **threat of material injury.** For instance, an increase in production capacity or existing unused capacity in the exporting company that is likely to result in a significant increase in imports to the United States may pose such a threat. Further, rapid increases in U.S. market penetration that are likely to reach an injurious level also may be perceived as threatening material injury. Because the ITC has never concluded that the establishment of an industry in the United States has been **materially retarded** by dumped imports, there is no clear guidance on how this standard will be met.

Government Subsidies

Foreign governments frequently offer **subsidies** that enable their businesses to export goods at artificially low prices. Recognizing the trade-distorting effects these direct and indirect payments can cause, the GATT *Subsidies Code* authorizes nations to assess **countervailing duties** to offset export subsidies that cause, or threaten to cause, material injury to a domestic industry. However, GATT does not disapprove of all subsidies. First, it recognizes that domestic subsidies may serve important social and economic policy objectives and should be permitted if they do not cause harm to other countries'

FIGURE 11–2   The Dumping Investigation

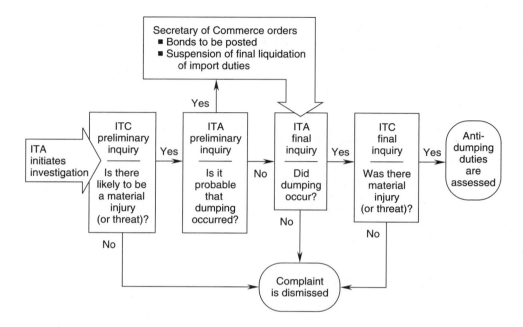

domestic economies. Second, it believes subsidies are essential to the economic development plans of many developing nations. As a result, it approves countermeasures against subsidies from developing nations only when their subsidized exports distort trade in other countries or capture an unfair share of the global market.

U.S. Antisubsidy Law

The antisubsidy law of the United States is broader than the GATT Subsidies Code. It covers any type of export subsidy as well as domestic subsidies, such as the provision of capital, loans, goods or services at preferential rates; the forgiveness of debt; and the assumption of any costs or expenses of manufacture, production, or distribution. The U.S. regulatory scheme permits the assessment of countervailing duties against any of these domestic subsidies unless they are generally available to all industries in the foreign country. Thus, domestic subsidies are countervailable only when made to a specific enterprise or industry.

■

PPG INDUSTRIES, INC. v. UNITED STATES
928 F.2d 1568 (Fed.Cir. 1991)

■ **FACTS** PPG Industries, a U.S. manufacturer of float glass (a type of flat glass), appealed an ITA determination that unprocessed float glass from Mexico was not subject to countervailing duties. PPG asserted that FICORCA, a

Mexican-sponsored trust fund for the coverage of exchange risks, constituted a bounty or grant that permitted Mexican manufacturers to export float glass to the United States at artificially low prices. FICORCA was a trust fund set up by the Mexican government. It permitted all Mexican firms with registered debt in foreign currency and payable abroad to purchase, at a controlled rate, the amount of dollars necessary to pay principal on the debts. The program was available to all Mexican firms with foreign indebtedness; it was not targeted to a specific industry or enterprise. Further, FICORCA was not tied in any way to exports. PPG argued the legal test for determining if a benefit is a subsidy for countervailing duty purposes is whether that benefit allows goods to be sold for less in the United States than would otherwise be possible.

■ **ISSUE** Should the ITA have treated the trust fund as a countervailable subsidy to Mexican float glass manufacturers?

■ **DECISION** No. The countervailing duty statute contemplates two types of subsidies that give rise to counter-

vailing duties: (1) export subsidies, that is, a benefit conferred only on goods that are exported, all of which are countervailable unless *de minimis,* and (2) domestic subsidies that may or may not be countervailable. With respect to domestic subsidies, the ITA has interpreted U.S. law as requiring a two-part specificity test. If the domestic subsidy is provided by its terms to a particular enterprise or industry, it is countervailable without further inquiry. If the benefit appears by its terms to be nominally generally available to all industries, the benefit may nevertheless be countervailable if, *in its application,* the program results in a subsidy only to a specific enterprise or industry. PPG's definition of a countervailable subsidy would nullify the congressional purpose of conforming U.S. law with GATT. The view that U.S. regulations have only one purpose, namely, to protect domestic industries from every competitive advantage afforded by foreign governments, is simplistic and myopic. There is no indication that FICORCA confers a benefit *de facto* on the float glass industry as a discrete, selective, or targeted class. Thus, it does not meet the ITA's specificity standard.

The Injury Requirement

In keeping with the GATT rules, the United States generally assesses countervailing duties only when a governmental subsidy causes or threatens to cause material injury to a domestic industry. However, material injury is not required when the subsidized goods are exported from a country that has not ratified the GATT Subsidies Code or has not negotiated similar trade agreements with the United States. Although a minority of the GATT members have adopted the code, most of the world's major trading nations have done so. The United States uses the material injury test for subsidized imports from GATT members that have not ratified the code in cases where the imports originally were granted duty-free status.

Subsidized Imports from Nonmarket Countries

The U.S. countervailing duty statute does not apply to subsidized imports from nonmarket countries. This is because Congress enacted the legislation under the belief that U.S. companies generally could compete effectively against foreign sellers that were subject to similar market pressures and constraints. Thus, it attempted to protect U.S. firms from the unfair competitive advantage gained by subsidized foreign sellers that could sell in the United States in instances where it would otherwise not be in the seller's best economic interest to export. This type of unfair competition does not exist in cases involving imports from nonmarket countries because those economies are riddled with distortions. Further, even if the incentives offered by nonmarket gov-

FIGURE 11–3 The Subsidy Investigation

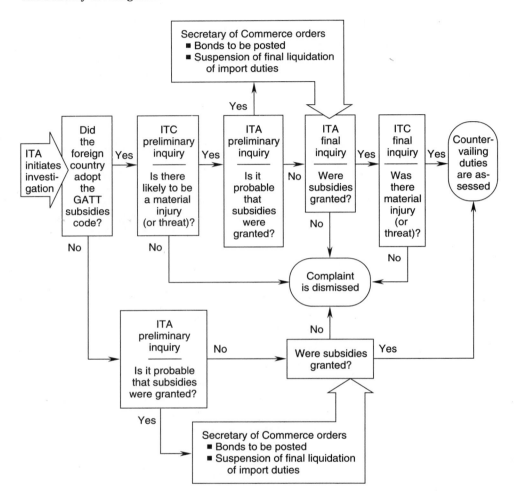

ernments were considered to be subsidies, the governments would in effect be subsidizing themselves. In instances where goods from nonmarket countries are entering the United States at unreasonably low prices, domestic industries may file a petition for relief under the antidumping laws.

The Subsidy Investigation

Countervailing duty proceedings in the United States parallel the dumping investigations described above. Investigations generally are triggered by petitions from a domestic producer, although the ITA may commence an inquiry itself. The ITA investigates the complaint through the use of questionnaires, meetings, and hearings to determine if a subsidy has been provided. If a preliminary inquiry establishes a likelihood that subsidization has occurred, the Secretary of Commerce requires the posting of a bond and the suspension of liquidation for future entries.

The ITC looks to see if a domestic industry has been materially injured or threatened with material injury. In cases where there is no material injury requirement (the subsidized imports are from a country that has not ratified the GATT Subsidies Code), the ITA conducts the investigation alone. As in dumping cases, when the final determinations of the ITA and ITC support the subsidization petition, the Secretary of Commerce directs the Customs Service to assess countervailing duties equal to the amount of the subsidy.

Information Issues

Throughout both antidumping and countervailing duty investigations, important issues arise concerning the information gathered by the government. For instance, whenever a party refuses or is unable to produce the information requested in a timely manner, the ITA or ITC may proceed by using the *best information available*. They often use this rule as leverage against uncooperative foreign producers.

Both agencies maintain public reading files on every antidumping and countervailing duty case, so interested persons may stay informed on their progress. These files contain summaries of all matters discussed during meetings with the parties. Of course, business proprietary information should not be freely disclosed. When confidential information is requested during an investigation, companies often offer nonconfidential summaries or refuse to comply. The ITA or ITC frequently makes confidential information available to attorneys or other representatives under an *administrative protective order*. Under this procedure, the information is released only on a showing of substantial need. Further, the recipient is subject to legal sanctions if she discloses the confidential information in violation of the order.

MATSUSHITA ELECTRIC INDUSTRIAL CO. v. UNITED STATES
929 F.2d 1577 (Fed.Cir. 1991)

■ **FACTS** During a dumping investigation involving imports of high-information content flat panel displays, Matsushita Electric Industrial Co. submitted certain business proprietary information to the ITC. Tandy Corporation, one of Matsushita's competitors, also was a party to the proceedings. Tandy's in-house counsel, Hershel Winn, requested access to Matsushita's confidential information under an administrative protective order. In his application, Winn certified he was general legal counsel for Tandy and he was not involved in competitive decision making. Matsushita objected to Winn receiving confidential information under the administrative protective order in light of his additional roles as senior vice president and secretary of Tandy. It asserted he was not adequately isolated from Tandy's competitive decision making to remove the risk that he might disclose Matsushita's confidential information to those involved in Tandy's day-to-day pricing and policy decisions.

■ **ISSUE** Should the ITC grant Tandy's in-house counsel access to Matsushita's business proprietary information?

■ **DECISION** Yes. The parties authorized to have access to confidential business proprietary information include both retained counsel and, under certain circumstances, in-house counsel. Both the ITC and the ITA permit such access for an in-house corporate attorney of a party to the proceedings, if the attorney is not involved in competitive decision making for her company. Winn's primary duties at Tandy were legal in nature. He was not involved in competitive decision making. While his position brought him into regular contact with executives involved in competitive decision making, the appropriate standard is not *regular contact* with other corporate officials who make competitive policy.

ETHICAL IMPLICATIONS   Suppose Winn inadvertently discloses Matsushita's trade secrets to Tandy officials. Would it be ethical for Tandy to use the information?

Administrative Review

Until passage of the *Trade and Tariff Act of 1984*, all countervailing duty and anti-dumping orders were to be reviewed every year. Because of the heavy burden this placed on the ITA and the ITC, Congress now mandates a review once each year only if it is requested by the parties. For instance, after an antidumping order has been in place for one year, a domestic producer may petition the ITA to increase the supplemental tariffs because it believes the dumping margin has increased. In another case, a foreign producer or domestic importer may request removal of an antidumping or countervailing duty order if domestic industries are no longer facing material injury. If nobody requests a review for four consecutive years, the Secretary of Commerce announces an intent to revoke the supplemental duty order. Interested parties then have one additional year within which to make such a request; otherwise the order is revoked.

Unfair Competition   In addition to the protections against unfair pricing (antidumping duties) and governmental subsidies (countervailing duties), the United States has another formidable weapon for attacking unfair competition. Known as Section 337 (it actually is *Section 1337 of the Tariff Act of 1930*), it authorizes the ITC to investigate complaints of unfair methods of competition and to exclude offending articles from entry into the United States. Section 337 may be used to combat unfair practices, such as improper marking, deceptive advertising, predatory pricing, and bribery. Despite its broad scope, however, approximately 90 percent of Section 337 investigations involve violations of intellectual property rights (particularly patent infringements) by imports.

The Section 337 Procedure

Section 337 inquiries generally begin at the request of domestic producers, although the ITC may independently decide to investigate. The initial investigation is carried out by an administrative law judge who determines if a violation has occurred. The judge's decision becomes final unless the ITC decides to review it. In an ITC review, the parties submit legal briefs and make oral arguments before the ITC. In addition, the ITC appoints a commission investigative attorney who represents the public interest by participating fully in the hearing.

CONCEPT SUMMARY
Standards for Section 337 Relief

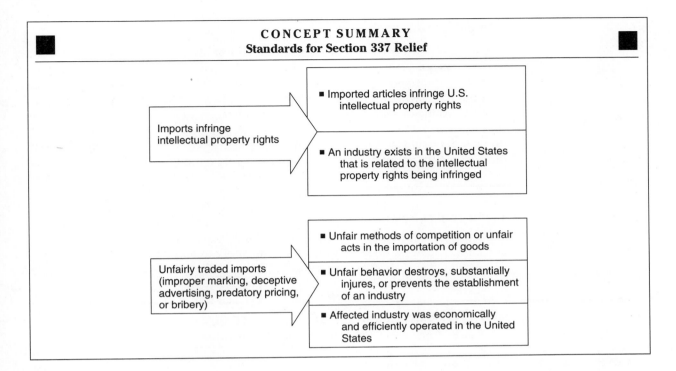

Imports infringe intellectual property rights

- Imported articles infringe U.S. intellectual property rights

- An industry exists in the United States that is related to the intellectual property rights being infringed

Unfairly traded imports (improper marking, deceptive advertising, predatory pricing, or bribery)

- Unfair methods of competition or unfair acts in the importation of goods

- Unfair behavior destroys, substantially injures, or prevents the establishment of an industry

- Affected industry was economically and efficiently operated in the United States

At the conclusion of the investigation, the ITC either dismisses the complaint or makes a recommendation of relief to the president. The recommended remedies may include any combination of exclusion orders, cease and desist orders, or forfeitures. The president has the power to accept, reject, or modify the ITC decision and recommended remedy.

Standards for Section 337 Relief

Traditionally, Section 337 relief would not be granted unless three prerequisites were met. First, there had to be unfair methods of competition or unfair acts in the importation of articles. Second, the unfair behavior had to destroy, substantially injure, or prevent the establishment of an industry. And third, the affected industry must have been economically and efficiently operated in the United States.

Congress amended Section 337 in 1988 to make it easier to grant import relief when imported articles infringed U.S. intellectual property rights (patents, copyrights, trademarks, trade secrets). As a result, in intellectual property cases, the appropriate inquiry has only two steps: (1) imported articles must infringe U.S. intellectual property rights, and (2) an industry existing (or about to exist) in the United States must have some relation to the intellectual property rights infringed by the imports. The ITC still uses the original three-step test for investigations that do not involve intellectual property rights.

The Future of Section 337

Section 337 is a powerful tool for domestic industries, providing them with several advantages not available to foreign producers that have complaints against U.S. competitors. For instance, U.S. companies may pursue unfair competition challenges either through Section 337 or in a federal district court. Section 337 is not available to foreign producers who are injured by the unfair practices of U.S. companies. This can result in a foreign company, but not a U.S. firm, having to defend itself in both forums. Section 337 also has rigid time limits that severely limit the ability of foreign defendants to mount a successful defense. Further, the Customs Service automatically enforces Section 337's exclusion orders, while successful plaintiffs in court cases must bring additional proceedings for injunctive relief.

In short, Section 337 offers distinct advantages over pursuing an unfair competition complaint in federal district court. Since only U.S. producers may file Section 337 complaints, the statute offers advantages to U.S. firms that are not available to foreign companies. Because of this discriminatory treatment, a GATT panel (in the following case) ruled that Section 337 violates GATT's national treatment principle.

■

UNITED STATES—SECTION 337 OF THE TARIFF ACT OF 1930
Report of the Panel, BISD 36S/345 (November 7, 1989)

■ **FACTS** After the ITC issued an exclusion order against a European company whose goods infringed a patent held by a U.S. firm, the European Community requested a GATT panel. It argued that Section 337 violates GATT's national treatment principle by extending to foreign goods less favorable treatment than is available to goods of U.S. origin. For instance, U.S. complainants have the choice of pursuing claims either through a Section 337 investigation or in a federal district court, while only the latter path is available to foreign companies with complaints against U.S. competitors. Because a Section 337 inquiry offers certain advantages over a judicial hearing, the European Community asserted it discriminates against foreign producers. The United States claimed that any instances of unfavorable treatment accorded foreign goods were offset by instances where foreign goods received more favorable treatment than their U.S. counterparts. In particular, it pointed out that relief in Section 337 cases might be modified or rejected on public interest or policy grounds. That possibility does not exist in judicial proceedings.

■ **ISSUE** Does Section 337 violate GATT's national treatment principle?

■ **DECISION** Yes. A showing of more favorable treatment for foreign goods is relevant only if it always accompanies and offsets an element of less favorable treatment. There is no reason to believe a public policy inquiry always favors a foreign defendant. Further, a U.S. complainant always has the choice of whether to proceed before the ITC or before a federal court. No equivalent choice of forum is available to foreign companies injured by products of U.S. origin. Other aspects of the U.S. law that discriminate against goods of foreign origin are: the automatic enforcement of ITC exclusion orders; the rigid time limits in Section 337 proceedings (thereby favoring complainants); the inability of Section 337 defendants to raise counterclaims; and the possibility that importers of products of foreign origin may be exposed to investigations by both the ITC and a federal district court. For these reasons, the United States should bring its procedures into conformity with its obligations under GATT.

Although the United States adopted the GATT panel's report, it stipulated its compliance would be conditioned on the success of efforts to strengthen protection for intellectual property in GATT's Uruguay Round of negotiations.

Thus, while the Section 337 procedure may be the subject of future amendments, it currently provides a potent weapon for U.S. producers seeking relief from unfair imports.

 **ETHICAL IMPLICATIONS**   Is it ethical for the U.S. government and U.S. producers to continue using the Section 337 process after a GATT panel ruled it violates U.S. obligations under GATT?

RETALIATION AGAINST FOREIGN TRADE BARRIERS

The trade remedies discussed up to this point were designed to offset the adverse effects of imports into the United States. In this section, the focus shifts to several measures intended to open foreign markets to U.S. goods, services, and investment and to protect U.S. intellectual property rights abroad. However, these provisions still have a significant impact on import trade since they authorize the imposition of import restrictions against the goods of foreign countries that refuse to dismantle barriers unfairly hindering U.S. businesses overseas.

The three devices examined here—Section 301, Super 301, and Special 301—are part of an aggressive campaign by the United States to expand its presence in foreign markets. They have been severely criticized throughout the world because their *unilateral retaliation* feature disregards GATT's dispute settlement procedures (discussed in Chapter 9) and its system of multilateralism.

Section 301

Section 301 of the Trade Reform Act of 1974 (**Section 301**) is a direct result of congressional frustration with GATT's ineffectiveness in removing governmental barriers to U.S. export trade. Congress has amended the statute several times, generally out of concern that U.S. presidents have not aggressively used Section 301's trade sanctions. Thus, most of the administrative responsibility over Section 301 has been removed from the president and transferred to the U.S. trade representative.

The Scope of Section 301

Section 301 has several important features. First, it requires the U.S. trade representative to inform interested parties of the effects foreign governmental trade policies have on various industries. Second, it orders the trade representative to submit annual reports, known as *national trade estimates,* to the Senate Finance Committee and the House Ways and Means Committee. The reports must identify trade-distorting behavior by foreign countries and estimate its impact on U.S. commerce. Perhaps the most important feature of Section 301 is the power it gives the U.S. trade representative to investigate, and take all appropriate action, to remove foreign trade barriers.

FIGURE 11–4 A Section 301 Case

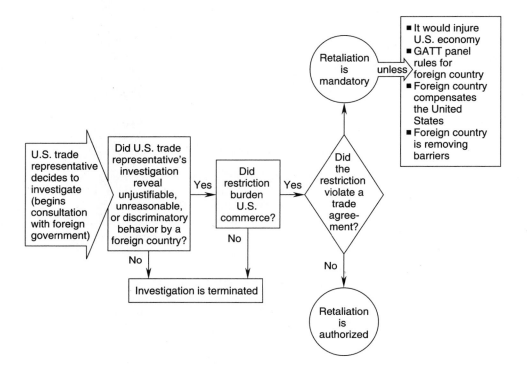

Section 301 Procedures

An interested person may ask the U.S. trade representative to investigate a Section 301 complaint or the trade representative's office may self-initiate an inquiry. (The U.S. trade representative has complete discretion over whether to accept a petition.) Once an investigation begins, the trade representative is required to request consultations with the foreign government. If these discussions do not yield a satisfactory agreement and the investigation reveals unfair trade practices, the U.S. trade representative decides if retaliation is appropriate.

Retaliation is *authorized* if an act, policy, or practice of a foreign country is unjustifiable, unreasonable, or discriminatory and burdens U.S. commerce. This broad language gives the trade representative considerable leverage in trade negotiations with foreign governments. Retaliation is *mandatory* when a nation denies U.S. businesses rights guaranteed under a trade agreement. However, mandatory retaliation is waived if the president proclaims that it would hurt the U.S. economy. Further, it does not apply if a GATT panel rules against the U.S. position, the foreign country is making satisfactory efforts to remove the barriers, or the foreign country offers equivalent trade concessions.

The U.S. trade representative has broad discretion in fashioning responses to restrictive trade practices. She may suspend or withdraw U.S. obligations under various trade agreements, impose import duties or quotas on the goods and services of the offending country, or enter into agreements binding the foreign government to eliminate the restrictive practices or otherwise compensate the United States. The trade representative frequently uses the threat of retaliation to pry concessions from U.S. trading partners. For instance, in the case that follows, a Section 301 investigation induced Thailand to take part in a GATT panel investigating Thai import restrictions. Ultimately, Thailand adopted the panel's report and has begun dismantling the trade barriers.

THAILAND—RESTRICTIONS ON IMPORTATION OF AND INTERNAL TAXES ON CIGARETTES

GATT Doc. D510/R (November 7, 1990)

■ **FACTS** Thailand restricted the importation of cigarettes under its Tobacco Act of 1966, which states, "The importation of tobacco is prohibited except by license of the Director-General." Import licenses for cigarettes had not been granted for over 10 years. The United States requested the GATT panel to find the cigarette import law inconsistent with GATT's prohibition against restrictions made effective through import licenses on the products of other GATT members. Thailand argued its ban on the importation of cigarettes fell within GATT's exception for measures necessary to protect human life or health.

■ **ISSUE** Does Thailand's quantitative restriction on the importation of cigarettes violate its obligations under GATT?

■ **DECISION** Yes. Smoking constitutes a serious risk to human health and consequently measures designed to reduce the consumption of cigarettes fall within the scope of GATT's exception for measures necessary to protect human life or health. Accordingly, nations may impose laws restricting the sale of cigarettes, provided they do not treat imported cigarettes less favorably than domestic cigarettes. The Thai import restrictions do not meet this standard because they permit the sale of domestic cigarettes while preventing the importation of foreign cigarettes.

■ **ETHICAL IMPLICATIONS** The GATT panel proceeding in the trade dispute between the United States and Thailand was instigated by a Section 301 investigation by the U.S. trade representative. That inquiry came at the request of the U.S. Cigarette Exporters Association. At a time when widespread opposition to smoking exists in the United States, is it ethical for the trade representative to use Section 301 to force open overseas markets for U.S. tobacco products?

Super 301

Section 310 of the Omnibus Trade and Competitiveness Act of 1988, known as **Super 301,** strengthened the U.S. response to restrictive trade practices. It required the U.S. trade representative to: (1) identify priority countries (those nations with significant trade barriers), (2) specify their significant trade restrictions (priority practices), and (3) estimate their effect on U.S. commerce. Within 21 days after forwarding this report

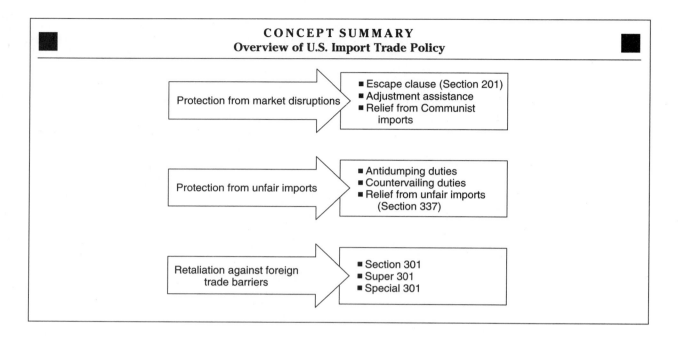

CONCEPT SUMMARY
Overview of U.S. Import Trade Policy

Protection from market disruptions →
- Escape clause (Section 201)
- Adjustment assistance
- Relief from Communist imports

Protection from unfair imports →
- Antidumping duties
- Countervailing duties
- Relief from unfair imports (Section 337)

Retaliation against foreign trade barriers →
- Section 301
- Super 301
- Special 301

to Congress, the trade representative was to initiate a Section 301 investigation and consult with the targeted countries. Each nation was to negotiate an agreement that would eliminate or compensate for the priority practices within three years. U.S. exports to the priority country were to increase incrementally over the three-year period. The U.S. trade representative was required to retaliate against any country that refused to meet these guidelines.

Under its legislative terms, Super 301 was applicable only in 1989 and 1990. During the first year, the U.S. trade representative identified three priority countries—Brazil, India, and Japan—and six priority practices. By 1990, only India had not made significant progress in removing its priority practices. Still, it is difficult to measure Super 301's effectiveness because no country admits to altering its trade practices in response to the threat of retaliation. However, the *Structural Impediments Initiative*, an arrangement by which Japan agreed to remove various obstacles impeding U.S. businesses, came on the heels of Japan's designation as a priority country.

Super 301's future is not clear. Although it has not been in effect since 1990, in recent years, Congress has repeatedly threatened to revive it. This has been met by some resistance from the executive branch and a sharp outcry from U.S. trading partners.

Special 301

Within 30 days after submitting the annual national trade estimate report, the U.S. trade representative is directed to designate foreign countries that: (1) deny effective protection of intellectual property rights, or (2) deny fair access to U.S. persons who rely on intellectual property protection. This process, known as **Special 301,** is similar to Super 301 in that it requires the trade representative to identify priority countries. However, unlike Super 301 (which expired after two years), Special 301 is a permanent feature of the U.S. trade laws. The objective of Special 301 is to compel foreign countries, through the threat of economic retaliation, to provide stronger intellectual property protection for U.S. businesses. Thus, it complements Section 337 (discussed earlier). While Section 337 strives to eliminate the unfair use of intellectual property in the import market, Special 301 strengthens those rights in export markets.

QUESTIONS AND PROBLEM CASES

1. Modern U.S. trade policy has been described as *strategic intervention*. What is meant by this?

2. Describe when the United States might award escape clause relief even though the absolute level of imports has not been increasing.

3. Describe the division of responsibility between the ITA and the ITC in antidumping investigations.

4. Explain when retaliation is mandatory under Section 301. What are the exceptions to this mandatory retaliation policy?

5. Former employees of RCA Corporation's Marion, Indiana, plant petitioned the Secretary of Labor for adjustment assistance. The employees contended that increased imports of televisions contributed importantly to a decline in sales and production of color television picture tubes at the Marion plant. A subsequent investigation disclosed that all of the workers had been engaged in the production of color television picture tubes. It further revealed that the decline in production at the Marion plant was due to a decrease of RCA's export sales and a decrease in the volume of intracompany shipments over the relevant period. More than half of the picture tubes produced by RCA were shipped to the company's consumer electronics division to be used in assembling television receivers. The consumer electronics division did not import color television picture tubes. Are the RCA employees eligible for adjustment assistance?

6. In its original dumping investigation, the ITA concluded Tai Yang, an exporter from Taiwan, was selling malleable cast iron pipe fittings in the United States at less than fair value. It calculated the dumping margin at 37.09 percent. When Tai Yang's sole

U.S. importer challenged the methodology used in the investigation, the ITA sent out new questionnaires. Tai Yang failed to supply any of the requested information, explaining, "The company lacks the resources to repeat the gargantuan effort of the fair value investigation for an investigation period some three times larger than the original case." The ITA warned Tai Yang that failure to furnish the requested data could result in adoption of the original dumping margin. When Tai Yang still refused to furnish new data, the ITA imposed the 37.09 percent antidumping duty without reexamining the record in the original dumping investigation. Did the ITA err by not reviewing its original dumping determination?

7. Brother Industries is a Japanese manufacturer and an importer of portable electric typewriters from Japan. During a dumping investigation, the ITA deducted certain expenses from the foreign market value of Brother's typewriters, thereby reducing the dumping margin. Specifically, the ITA made adjustments for after-sale rebates offered in Japan and not in the United States. Was the ITA correct in reducing the dumping margin by the cost of the rebates?

8. Amax-Chemical Incorporated and Kerr-McGee Chemical Corporation filed petitions with the ITA, alleging the Soviet Union and the German Democratic Republic (East Germany) has provided subsidies for potash imported into the United States. The dumping complaints and the resulting investigation occurred before the Soviet Union and East Germany abandoned their Communist systems of government. The alleged subsidies provided by the

Soviet Union and East Germany were the receipt on export sales of foreign exchange rates higher than the official rates. Are these export subsidies countervailable?

9. Hyundai, a Korean corporation, had a manufacturing agreement with General Instrument Corporation. It obligated Hyundai to serve as a foundry for erasable programmable read only memories (EPROMs) with the technical assistance of General Instrument. In exchange, General Instrument agreed to purchase certain quantities of the EPROMs. On payment of a royalty to General Instrument, Hyundai was free to use EPROMs manufactured in excess of General Instruments' requirements for its own purposes. After conducting a Section 337 investigation, the ITC ruled the EPROMs manufactured for General Instrument infringed several patents belonging to a U.S. corporation. It issued an order excluding from entry into the United States EPROMs manufactured abroad pursuant to designs and process technology provided by General Instrument. It also excluded from entry Hyundai computers containing infringing EPROMs. Part of the exclusion order required importers to certify they had made an appropriate inquiry and believed that infringing EPROMs were not incorporated in the Hyundai computers. Hyundai demanded a review, claiming the ITC exceeded its authority by including Hyundai's secondary products (computers) in the exclusion order. Did the ITC act properly?

10. In 1972, antidumping duties were assessed against dry-cleaning machinery that was sold in the United States at less than fair value by a West German manufacturer. By 1984, despite the antidumping duties, the German manufacturer held a competitive position in the U.S. market. This was attributable, in part, to a new machine the company had designed especially for the U.S. buyers. The machine was superior in quality to competing products and also could be sold at a lower price. During the years that the antidumping duties were in effect, domestic consumption of dry-cleaning machinery increased; however, U.S. producers did not make any sizable gains in market share. The ITC denied the German manufacturer's request for a revocation of the antidumping duty order. Was the ITC correct in leaving the order in place?

12

Export Controls

INTRODUCTION

As global trade and investment opportunities become increasingly accessible to U.S. businesses, many companies are discovering their goods and services have tremendous export potential. Despite these attractions, managers must first familiarize themselves with the U.S. export licensing requirements before selling goods overseas. This is because every export of goods or technology from the United States is subject to some form of export control. Violation of these regulations may subject an exporter to civil fines and criminal punishment.

Chapter Overview   This chapter begins with a brief review of the basic nature of the U.S. export controls. It examines why they exist, the types of articles they regulate, and the manner in which they are implemented. This is followed by an overview of the major legislation governing export transactions. The focus then shifts to the institutions involved in export licensing. Because more than 19 federal agencies regulate export trade, only the major actors are covered here. Attention then turns to more practical aspects of the export licensing process, providing insight into the regulatory maze that makes up the U.S. export control system. The chapter ends with a quick look at the Arab boycott of Israel and the legal effect of U.S. antiboycott regulations on global businesses.

THE NATURE OF U.S. EXPORT CONTROLS

Throughout its history, the United States has closely regulated export trade. Courts have long accorded the government broad authority to implement controls, upholding export restrictions on national security grounds as well as out of deference to the president's authority to conduct military and foreign affairs. This section examines the nature of the U.S. export control system. First, it discusses the fundamental justifications for export controls. This is followed by a look at the primary types of export regulations. The section ends with a glimpse at the expansive reach of the U.S. export licensing system.

Justifications for Export Controls   Throughout history the U.S. government has offered three primary justifications for regulating export trade: (1) protecting the national security, (2) promoting foreign policy, and (3) preserving goods that are in short supply.

National Security Controls

Export controls often have been implemented to protect the **national security** during times of war. Beginning as early as the War of Independence, the United States enacted embargoes to deprive its enemies of products and technology. However, export barriers also are erected for national security reasons in times of peace. For instance, before the thawing of relations with the former Soviet bloc, the United States imposed stringent limitations on trade with the Communist world. Currently, exports to Iraq and Libya are subject to national security restrictions.

In administering national security controls, the president compiles a list of countries that pose a threat to the national security. These nations are known as **controlled countries.** The following factors are considered in deciding if a nation should be placed on the list:

- The extent to which its policies are adverse to the national security interests of the United States.
- The country's Communist or non-Communist status.
- The present and potential relationship of the country with the United States and countries friendly or hostile to the United States.
- The country's nuclear weapons capability and its compliance with multilateral nuclear weapons agreements.

A country may be added to (or deleted from) the list if the president determines that exports to it would (or would not) significantly contribute to that nation's military potential.

The president's authority to prohibit or curtail the transfer of goods or technology to controlled countries is quite broad. It often results in a comprehensive ban on all types of trade with the controlled countries because of the difficulty in preventing them from diverting critical goods and technologies to military use. Trade with friendly nations may be restricted also when there is a genuine threat that critical goods or information may be reexported to a controlled country.

Foreign Policy Controls

During the 20th century, export regulation was expanded to encompass **foreign policy** concerns. As early as 1912, Congress authorized the president to prohibit the exportation of weapons to any nation in the Western Hemisphere that might use them for domestic violence. Since then, the United States regularly has conditioned nations' access to goods and technology on their compliance with U.S. foreign policy objectives.

While export controls assist the government in pressuring countries to conform their behavior to U.S. policies, they also impose substantial economic costs on U.S. exporters. For this reason, Congress reviews foreign policy controls on a yearly basis. Further, the president may impose, extend, or expand export controls for foreign policy reasons only after determining:

- The likelihood the controls will achieve the foreign policy objective (this includes an examination of the availability of similar goods and technology from other countries).
- The proposed controls are compatible with the foreign policy objectives of the United States and its overall policy toward the target country.
- The potential reaction of other countries to imposition of the export controls.
- The likely impact of the controls on the competitive position of individual U.S. exporters and the reputation of the United States in the global market.
- The ability of the United States to enforce the controls.

Under a concept, known as **contract sanctity,** exporters generally are free to complete contracts they formed before the establishment of new foreign policy controls. However, the president may prohibit such exports if he certifies to Congress that the controls are necessary to protect the strategic interests of the United States from a serious breach of the peace.

ETHICAL IMPLICATIONS   When the United States restricts exports to another nation on foreign policy grounds, it seeks cooperation from the rest of the world. Is it ethical for the United States to threaten countries that refuse to enforce its embargoes with trade sanctions or the withdrawal of economic aid?

Short Supply Controls

When essential goods are scarce, the United States has enacted **short supply** controls. These are common during major wars. However, they also existed in the aftermath of World War II. At that time, the United States implemented a short supply program to ensure the availability of materials crucial to the rebuilding of Western Europe.

The secretary of commerce is instructed to monitor exports and contracts for exports when he suspects they may threaten the domestic economy. In particular, he investigates each type of export to determine if:

- There has been a significant increase in relation to domestic supply and demand.
- It has caused a significant increase in domestic prices or a shortage of domestic supply relative to demand.
- The domestic price increase or shortage has significantly adversely affected (or may significantly adversely affect) the national economy or any sector of the economy.

When such a threat exists, the president may order further monitoring, quantitative limits on exports, or a prohibition on exports of the scarce goods. If a quantitative restriction is imposed, a portion of the export licenses will be allocated to importing countries based on their treatment of U.S. importers during times of short supply. Short supply controls are most likely to be imposed on metallic materials, petroleum products, agricultural commodities, and building supplies.

Types of Export Controls

The form and substance of export controls frequently depends on the nature of the type of goods or information involved. Four specific types of exports currently are subject to export regulations: munitions, nuclear materials, equipment and data related to chemical and biological weaponry, and dual-use items.

Munitions

Pursuant to the *Arms Export Control Act*, the president is authorized to regulate the export of munitions. This responsibility has been further delegated to the secretary of state who, together with the secretary of defense, compiles a list of defense articles and defense services known as the **Munitions Control List.** This list contains numerous categories ranging from firearms, ammunition, and explosives to vessels of war, aircraft, and spacecraft. Manufacturers and exporters of articles and services appearing on the list must be registered. No item appearing on the list may be exported without first receiving an export license. An application for a license must be rejected if the transaction threatens U.S. national security or foreign policy.

UNITED STATES v. NISSEN
928 F.2d 690 (5th Cir. 1991)

■ **FACTS** Customs officials set up an undercover business, called Plane Things, Inc., primarily to ferret out smugglers who transported drugs by aircraft. Karl Nissen, a resident and citizen of Sweden, came to the United States with a large list of military parts he wished to purchase for Iran. He gave this list to Plane Things. Under U.S. law, the licensing requirements for military aircraft parts include filing an end-user certificate, a statement by the applicant attesting to the truth of the designated ultimate user, and a pledge of the applicant's intent not to divert the arms from the declared use. When informed that the State Department would not issue licenses to sell military aircraft parts from the Munitions List, Nissen indicated he would falsely designate the aircraft parts were destined for Malaysia. After procuring 13 venturi heaters (parts for Phantom F-4 fighter aircraft) in this fraudulent manner, Nissen transported them through Germany and Sweden to Iran. This delivery of venturi heaters apparently was a preliminary venture by Iran to see if Nissen could get the materials out of the United States and into Iran because Nissen followed it up with a return trip to arrange the purchase of a Boeing 707 and an entire planeload of equipment. He was arrested when he attempted to depart the United States with the plane and over $4 million in parts. After being fined $10,000 and sentenced to 44 months in prison, Nissen claimed the penalty was unduly harsh.

■ **ISSUE** Did the court abuse its discretion in assessing the criminal penalty against Nissen?

■ **DECISION** No. Under federal sentencing guidelines, Nissen's punishment was appropriate if *sophisticated weaponry* was involved. The government's proof demonstrated the venturi heater is designed as a structure control item located in the vertical fin of the F-4 Phantom. Its purpose is to protect the air pressure flowing through the vertical stabilizer. Because the venturi heater ensures proper steerage, it is integral to the fighting effectiveness of the aircraft. Any definition that could reasonably be given to the term *sophisticated weaponry* would include the Phantom F-4 fighter aircraft. Clearly, then, the heaters were involved in a tangible way with sophisticated weaponry. Further, in determining the sentence within the applicable guideline range, the court may consider the degree to which the violation threatened a security interest of the United States, the volume of commerce involved, the extent of planning or sophistication, and whether there were multiple occurrences. Supplying a device that ensures smooth steerage of a fighter jet clearly implicates a U.S. security interest, particularly when the country targeted for export is Iran. Nissen's lengthy negotiations and travel demonstrate he extensively planned this venture, contemplating numerous exports of a high volume of military parts.

Nuclear Materials

The United States strictly regulates the export of nuclear technology and fissionable materials. While the Department of Energy's *Nuclear Regulatory Commission* possesses primary responsibility for the licensing of nuclear materials, it must confer with the Departments of Commerce, Defense, and State before approving an application. The president compiles a **Nuclear Referral List** that identifies items requiring special consideration because their exportation may threaten the goal of nuclear nonproliferation. Frequently, items appearing on the list are not granted export licenses unless the government receives assurances from the importer and its country that they will not be used for prohibited purposes. The United States may insist on the right to verify the actual use of the articles or technology.

Chemical and Biological Weaponry

Modern export controls have been particularly concerned with prohibiting non-ally nations from developing, acquiring, or delivering chemical and biological weapons. Pursuant to this goal, the Commerce Department maintains a list of chemicals that are subject to strict licensing requirements. Many of these chemicals are not themselves chemical or biological weapons. Instead, they are *precursor chemicals* that might be used in the development of more deadly weapons. Similarly, greater emphasis is being placed on the export of commodities potentially useful in the production of missiles capable of delivering chemical and biological payloads.

These regulations impose strict requirements on exporters to be aware of the end use and the end user of goods and technical data. They identify 28 regions and countries that raise special chemical or biological weapons proliferation concerns and prohibit exports there. Further, they specifically include freight forwarders and financial institutions among the entities that can be held liable for supporting the development, export, or delivery of chemical or biological weapons.

Dual-Use Items

The Department of Commerce has primary responsibility for administering export controls over commercial goods. Its 162-page **Commodity Control List** contains over 200 entries. However, many commercial items also have multiple applications and might appear on the Nuclear Referral List or the Munitions Control List, or be useful in the development of chemical or biological weapons. Some commercial goods and technical information may also appear on the **Militarily Critical Technologies List** administered by the Defense Department.

Controls over these dual-use items are the most controversial of the export regulations. By appearing on more than one control list, the exports may trigger the need for consultations among the various departments. This frequently subjects exporters of dual-use goods and technical data to great confusion and long delays in gaining export clearance.

Reach of Export Controls

All exports of goods and technological data originating in the United States are subject to U.S. export controls. Because these regulations encompass a wide variety of transactions that might surprise the average person, businesses must acquaint themselves with the regulatory regime. In particular, they must understand what constitutes exportation, what is included within the concept of technological data, and who may be liable for failure to comply with U.S. export controls.

CONCEPT SUMMARY
Justifications for U.S. Export Controls

	National Security	Foreign Policy	Short Supply
Munitions			
Nuclear materials			
Chemical and biological weaponry			
Dual-use items			

Exportation

Goods are not covered by U.S. export controls unless they leave the United States. However, the government defines the *exportation* of goods in an expansive manner. Thus, an Indian company's sale of an electric generator to a Malaysian company is governed by U.S. export laws if the generator was manufactured in the United States. And the purchase of a Japanese computer by a Czech company is an exportation if any of the computer's components originated in the United States. Further, foreign goods that are shipped to the United States and reexported to another country are encompassed by the regulations. Finally, whenever a U.S. citizen or corporation operating in a foreign country transfers goods or technological data (of either U.S. or foreign origin) to another country, the transaction is treated as an exportation.

Technological Data

The exportation of **technological data** also is subject to export controls. Technological data are defined as any information that can be used, or adapted for use, in the design, production, manufacture, utilization, or reconstruction of articles or materials. This includes both tangible (models, blueprints, manuals, software) and intangible (training by an employee) data.

Businesspersons often are surprised by the wide variety of transactions that qualify as the exportation of technological data. For instance, when foreign nationals receive technical information as part of employment training in the United States, this is an export of technology if it is reasonable to assume they intend to return to their home countries. Further, when a foreign buyer receives operating manuals to accompany the sale of U.S. goods or is permitted to tour a U.S. manufacturing facility, there has been an exportation of technological data. Whenever technical information is transferred from a U.S. citizen or corporation to a foreign person, the transfer is considered an export of technology.

Export Control Responsibility

As the person with the principal economic interest in the export transaction, the exporter has primary responsibility for ensuring compliance with U.S. export controls. However, a broad range of individuals also are legally accountable. All persons related to the transaction who possess information, authority, or functions that enable them to ensure compliance may be liable for illegal exports. Thus, freight forwarders and other intermediaries may be liable for violating U.S. export laws, even when they are following the instructions of the exporter or importer.

An exporter cannot escape liability by relying on the services of a shipping agent. Similarly, a U.S. supplier may be legally responsible when it transfers goods or technological data to another U.S. company with the knowledge that they are to be resold to a foreign purchaser. These rules make it imperative that suppliers, exporters, and intermediaries familiarize themselves with the export regulations and with the circumstances surrounding each export transaction.

THE U.S. EXPORT CONTROL REGIME

Trading with the Enemy Act

The *Trading with the Enemy Act* (TWEA) was enacted in the midst of World War I. This legislation prevents U.S. individuals and corporations from exporting goods to the enemies of the United States unless they are issued an export license by the Treasury Department. For 40 years, the TWEA permitted the president to regulate exports during any national emergency; however, since 1977 it has applied only to wartime conditions. Still, many pre-1977 TWEA sanctions remain in effect, restricting trade with Cuba, North Korea, and Vietnam.

International Emergency Economic Powers Act

The *International Emergency Economic Powers Act* (IEEPA) fills the peacetime void left when the TWEA reverted back to being solely a wartime measure. It permits the president to regulate or prohibit exports whenever he declares a national emergency caused by an unusual and extraordinary threat to the national security, foreign policy, or economy of the United States from an outside source. In the recent past, the IEEPA has authorized economic sanctions against Iran, Nicaragua, Panama, and South Africa. At present, trade with both Iraq and Libya is prohibited.

■

VETERANS PEACE CONVOY, INC. v. SCHULTZ
722 F.Supp. 1425 (S.D. Tex. 1988)

■ **FACTS** The Veterans Peace Convoy, Inc., (VPC) was created to provide humanitarian aid to the people of Nicaragua. It collected humanitarian supplies and transported them to Nicaragua in a convoy of older model pickup trucks, vans, and buses. After delivering the supplies to various schools, hospitals, and churches, 29 of the vehicles were left in Nicaragua. Before these deliveries, the president formally declared the policies and actions of the Nicaraguan government constituted an unusual and extraordinary threat to the United States. Thus, pursuant to his authority under the International Emergency Economic Powers Act (IEEPA), he prohibited exports to Nicaragua unless they were licensed by the Office of Foreign Assets Control. Notwithstanding this emergency declaration, the IEEPA exempted humanitarian aid donations from the executive regulation unless the president made further findings that the humanitarian aid would seriously impair his ability to deal with the emergency or would endanger the armed forces of the United States. The president never made such findings. There was no dispute that the contents of the convoy vehicles constituted humanitarian aid and were exempted from the IEEPA's licensing requirement. However, U.S. Customs officials argued the vehicles required a license. VPC contended the vehicles were humanitarian aid that did not require a license because they were used to relieve human suffering.

■ **ISSUE** Were the exported vehicles exempt from the IEEPA's licensing requirement?

■ **DECISION** Yes. The IEEPA does not create a scheme whereby all persons seeking to donate articles to a blocked country must obtain advance approval from the Office of Foreign Assets Control. On the contrary, it provides that the president may not regulate qualifying humanitarian aid donations directly or indirectly. Thus, the president may not impose a licensing requirement on articles the donor intends to be used to relieve human suffering if the articles can reasonably be expected to serve that purpose. The vehicles delivered to Nicaragua qualified as humanitarian aid and need not be licensed in the absence of a finding that they would seriously frustrate resolution of the national emergency or would endanger U.S. armed forces engaged in hostilities.

Arms Export Control Act

During the 1930s, the United States sought to control its growing munitions industry. With the passage of the *Neutrality Act* in 1935, commercial weapons exporters were required to comply with a comprehensive licensing system. The legislation has been amended numerous times and still exists today, now known as the *Arms Export Control Act* (AECA). Under the AECA, the State Department regulates the commercial export of military-related goods and services. Its licensing scheme is designed to ensure that defense articles and services are not exported if they conflict with U.S. foreign policy or national security interests.

Through passage of the AECA, Congress sought to play a more active role in weapons export policy. For instance, at least 30 days before issuing an export license for commercial arms, the executive branch must notify Congress. The legislature then has 30 days within which it may issue a joint resolution blocking the transaction.

Atomic Energy Act

As the leader in nuclear technology, the United States is concerned about the unauthorized spreading of fissionable materials and nuclear information. Thus, its willingness to share the peaceful benefits of nuclear energy is conditioned on pledges of global cooperation in limiting the reexport of nuclear-related equipment and technology. Under the *Atomic Energy Act* (amended by the *Nuclear Non-Proliferation Act*), the Nuclear Regulatory Commission regulates the export of nuclear materials, technology, and technical data. Licensing decisions are reviewed by the Departments of Energy, Commerce, Defense, and State.

Export Administration Act

In 1940, the president instituted a licensing scheme regulating a broad range of non-military exports. It restricted the export of both weapons and any additional materials essential to their manufacture or operation. These limits on dual-use exports were justified on national security grounds. Over time the controls were extended to

ETHICAL IMPLICATIONS	Although the United States has a nuclear weapons arsenal, it maintains export controls designed to prevent other nations from developing nuclear weapons capability. Is this ethical?

protect against the exportation of scarce materials (steel, medicine, building supplies). After World War II, the onset of the Cold War triggered congressional efforts to strengthen the export control acts. Specifically, the United States sought multilateral cooperation from its allies in blocking Soviet access to strategic trade items.

As Cold War tensions relaxed, so did the severity of the restrictions on trade with the Soviet bloc. The emerging policy of peaceful coexistence reduced national security objections to expanding trade with the Communist nations. Further, the United States was no longer suffering a scarcity of any essential resources or materials. At the same time, the U.S. allies were following a less restrictive trade policy toward the Soviet Union and Eastern Europe and, as a result, were benefiting economically. Finally, Congress was concerned that U.S. export control policies were hurting the country's balance of payments by unnecessarily foreclosing export sales.

Congress enacted the *Export Administration Act* (EAA) in part to encourage trade with the Soviet bloc. The EAA also sought to better coordinate export trade policies with U.S. allies as well as offset the effects of the Arab boycott of Israel. Later amendments were designed to simplify and expedite the export approval process and substantially reduce the number of controls imposed for foreign policy purposes.

Enhanced Proliferation Control Initiative

The collapse of Communism in the former Soviet Union and Eastern Europe has induced the United States to redefine its export control objectives. However, at the same time that export restrictions with the Communist world are being loosened, U.S. policy makers are refocusing their attention on certain non-ally governments that are producing and stockpiling chemical and biological weapons. The urgency of this emerging threat to national security and foreign policy interests was magnified by the war and continuing hostilities between the United States and Iraq.

To address these new concerns, the United States issued the *Enhanced Proliferation Control Initiative* (EPCI) in 1991. These regulations impose controls on exports of chemical and biological equipment to 28 regions and countries. The restrictions focus on certain end users involved in chemical and biological weapons and missile activities.

KEY INSTITUTIONS

Numerous U.S. and international agencies are involved in the administration of export controls. Within the United States, the Departments of Commerce, Defense, Energy, State, and Treasury play active roles in the licensing process. This section examines the key agencies that assist in the formulation, implementation, and enforcement of the U.S. export policy.

Bureau of Export Administration

The Department of Commerce has authority over the export of equipment, materials, software, and technology that have both civilian and military applications. It has delegated most of these functions to the *Bureau of Export Administration* (BXA). As the agency with primary authority over dual-use items, the BXA is perhaps the most influential institution in the regulation of exports. Heading the BXA is an under secretary of commerce who is appointed by the president and confirmed by the Senate.

The Offices of Export Licensing (OEL), Technology and Policy Analysis (OTPA), and Export Enforcement (OEE) provide substantial administrative support for the BXA. The OEL processes export applications and routes them to the appropriate agencies for review. Its decisions are based on policies formulated by the OTPA. The OTPA also represents the United States at multilateral discussions. Finally, the OEE provides special agents who enforce the export regulations by making arrests and issuing subpoenas.

Office of Defense Trade Controls

Licensing decisions regarding defense articles and services rest primarily with the Department of State, which has delegated its day-to-day administrative authority to the *Office of Defense Trade Controls* (ODTC). Manufacturers and exporters of items appearing on the Munitions Control List must register with the ODTC and may not export items without receiving a license from that agency. In processing export licenses, the ODTC works closely with the U.S. Arms Control and Disarmament Agency, which determines if a particular export might contribute to the arms race, support terrorism, or otherwise disrupt world peace.

Defense Technology Security Administration

The Department of Defense established the *Defense Technology Security Administration* (DTSA) to enhance its influence over the licensing of dual-use items and weaponry. It coordinates licensing referrals from the Commerce Department (dual-use items) and the State Department (munitions), directing them to the appropriate agencies within the Defense Department.

Office of Foreign Availability

When export controls are implemented, the president is required to negotiate with foreign governments to secure their cooperation in enforcing the restrictions. If these efforts are unsuccessful, the secretary of commerce must ascertain the **foreign availability** of the good or technology subject to the export restrictions. Responsibility for gathering and analyzing this information has been delegated to the *Office of Foreign Availability* (OFA). It is headed by the under secretary of commerce for export administration.

The OFA considers a wide range of information in determining foreign availability. Private parties as well as the U.S. intelligence agencies assist it in this investigation. A finding of foreign availability is likely if:

- There is a non-U.S. source for the goods.
- The foreign goods are comparable in quality to the prohibited U.S. exports.
- There is an adequate supply of the foreign goods.
- The foreign goods actually are reaching the controlled country.

When it is found that goods or technology are available in sufficient quantity so controls are likely to be ineffective, an export license generally must be approved unless

FIGURE 12–1   CoCom Members

Australia	Japan
Belgium	Luxembourg
Canada	Netherlands
Denmark	Norway
Germany	Portugal
Greece	Spain
Italy	Turkey
United Kingdom	United States
France	

the president determines that granting a license would prove detrimental to the national security.

Office of Foreign Assets Control

Responsibility for administering the Trading with the Enemy Act and the International Emergency Economic Powers Act resides in the Treasury Department's *Office of Foreign Assets Control* (OFAC). Its regulations frequently involve broad proscriptions on trade with targeted countries as well as the freezing of foreign assets. In making licensing decisions, OFAC works closely with the State Department. OFAC currently is administering the Iraqi Sanctions Regulations. Similar controls over trade with Kuwait, South Africa, and Cambodia have recently been terminated.

CoCom

After World War II, the United States and its allies formed the *Coordinating Committee for Multilateral Export Controls* (**CoCom**). This 17-nation organization was established primarily to prevent the former Soviet Union from further developing its military capability. Its members hoped to achieve this objective by curbing the export of potentially dangerous goods and technology to the Soviet Union and other Communist countries.

The CoCom Control Lists

CoCom maintains three lists of goods and technologies that may not be exported to controlled countries. The *International Munitions List* contains restricted weaponry, the *International Atomic Energy List* regulates radioactive materials, and the *International Control List* is composed of prohibited dual-use items. While these lists are not made public, their contents generally are reflected in the national control lists of the individual CoCom members.

CoCom's Role in Coordinating Export Controls

CoCom recognizes the ineffectiveness of unilateral controls as well as the importance of uniform enforcement in a multilateral system. Thus, it provides members with an opportunity to coordinate their policy-making and enforcement efforts. For instance, whenever a member nation wishes to export listed goods or technology to a controlled country, it first seeks permission from CoCom. Further, CoCom restricts attempts to divert controlled items by requiring exporters to obtain certification from importing nations that articles will not be reexported without CoCom approval. It also requires importers to provide governmental verification that the controlled items have been delivered in accordance with their export license.

The Future of CoCom

With the thawing of the Cold War, CoCom began to shift from its original anti-Soviet, East-West orientation. The breakup of the former Soviet Union and the democratization of Eastern Europe has accelerated this transformation. CoCom has greatly reduced the core list of goods and technology subject to export controls. Similarly, it has been assisting former Communist nations in developing effective export control systems so they may qualify to purchase sensitive Western goods and technology. Finally, CoCom is now directing its export control efforts to nations such as China, India, Iraq, North Korea, and Pakistan.

THE EXPORT LICENSING PROCESS

The U.S. government controls exports through a complex licensing system. An exporter's failure to abide by these procedures may result in expensive delays and, in extreme cases, civil and criminal liability. Accordingly, this section provides an overview of the fundamental components of the licensing process. It begins with a brief look at the two major types of licenses. This is followed by an introduction to the export classification scheme that determines which type of license is required. An examination of the most common export documents follows. The section closes with a glance at the basic steps involved in the licensing procedure.

Types of Licenses   Export licenses fall into either of two main categories. One type, the general license, does not require governmental approval before exportation. The other category, the validated license, requires written approval from the government before the goods or technology may be shipped out of the country.

General Licenses

Most goods and technology are exported under a **general license.** It permits any person to export low-level items to most destinations. Exports within this category require neither a licensing application nor any written approval from the government. Instead, the exporter merely identifies the appropriate general license on its shipping documents. There are over 20 types of general licenses for commodities and 2 for technological data. For example, *G-Dest* may be used for any commercial item to any destination not requiring a validated license. *G-Temp* permits U.S. companies to temporarily exhibit or display their products overseas. Severe penalties may be assessed against persons who wrongly export items under a general license.

Validated Licenses

When items do not qualify for a general license, they may not be exported without first receiving a **validated license** from the government. Validated licenses are extremely restrictive in that they must be used within strict time limits and may not be transferred to similar transactions. There are four basic types of validated licenses.

1. *Individual validated licenses* provide a specific grant of authority to a specific person to export a specific item to a specified purchaser on a specific date.

2. *Distribution licenses* allow a specific person to make repeated exports of specific items to a specified destination over a one-year period.

3. *Project licenses* permit a specific person to export all items necessary for the completion of a specified activity for a limited period (usually one year).

4. *Service supply licenses* permit for a limited time the export of replacement parts for items that were sold previously.

UNITED STATES v. SHETTERLY
971 F.2d 67 (7th Cir. 1992)

■ **FACTS** Donald Shetterly, a U.S. citizen residing in Indiana, was charged with attempting to export a controlled microwave amplifier to (then) West Germany without a validated license. Shetterly was approached by Karl Mann, a German businessman, who wished to purchase the equipment. When Shetterly attempted to procure an amplifier from Berkshire Technologies (a California company), the company became suspicious because it had become aware of significant attempts by the Soviets to obtain the amplifier. (The case arose before the breakup of the former Soviet Union.) Berkshire immediately contacted the Department of Commerce and agreed to cooperate in an investigation. This culminated in Shetterly's arrest and conviction for attempting to export a controlled item without a validated license. At the trial, the judge instructed the jury that it should find Shetterly guilty if the government proved: (1) Shetterly exported or attempted to export the amplifier; (2) he did so without receiving a validated license; (3) such a license was required; and (4) he did so knowingly. On appeal, Shetterly contended the

instructions failed to make clear whether *knowingly* modified only the first element and therefore removed from the jury the issue of whether he knew a validated license was needed.

■ **ISSUE** Should the conviction be overturned because the judge's instructions were erroneous?

■ **DECISION** No. One who knowingly violates or attempts to violate the Export Administration Act commits a crime. Shetterly contends an exportation or attempted exportation of a controlled commodity without a validated license becomes a crime only when the exporter knows a validated license is required. That assertion is not correct. A specific intent is not required for a criminal violation to occur. To prove that Shetterly violated the law, the government was required to prove beyond a reasonable doubt only that he knowingly exported or attempted to export a controlled commodity without obtaining a validated license.

Classifying the Export

To determine which type of license is required, the exporter must properly *classify* the goods or technology. The factors essential to this process include the intended and potential uses for the exports, the country of destination, and the identity of the end user.

FIGURE 12–2   The New Commerce Control List (CCL) and How to Read It

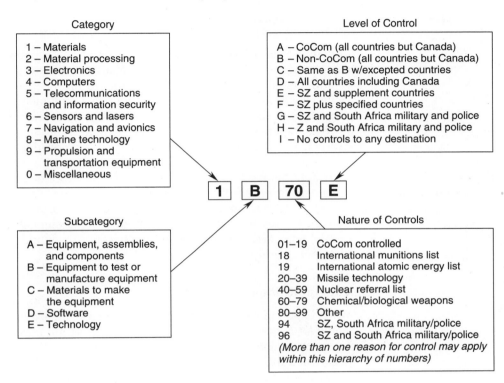

Source: Reprinted from *The OEL Insider*, 3, no. 3, October/November 1991, p. 5.

The Control List

Accurate classification of an export begins with an examination of the Commodity Control List to discover the appropriate **export control classification number** (ECCN). This requires finding the category in the control list that most closely describes the items to be exported. The ECCN identifies the primary characteristics of the good or technology, the countries to which it can or cannot be exported, and the type of license required for each country.

Country Restrictions

Exporters must look beyond the ECCN numbers when determining which export licenses govern their transactions. The information listed in the ECCN frequently is modified or overridden by special country restrictions. Those restrictions, which often appear in the Foreign Assets Control Regulations, list particular countries that may be subject to special embargoes due to foreign policy or national security reasons.

Individual Restrictions

Certain individuals are not permitted to purchase U.S. exports. Persons found guilty of violating the U.S. export laws may be made subject to a **denial order.** This administrative penalty prohibits the offender from receiving goods or technology from the United States for several years. The Commerce Department prints a list of all persons subject to denial orders twice each year. This *Table of Denial Orders* is kept current by regular entries in the *Federal Register.* Exporters may be charged with violating the export laws if they sell goods or technology to an individual subject to a denial order.

Export Documentation

After determining the appropriate license, the exporter must provide proper documentation to ensure the exports clear U.S. Customs. Commercial invoices, bills of lading, and air waybills (necessary for most export transactions) are discussed in Chapter 6. This section focuses on the export documentation required for export control purposes: the export license application, a shipper's export declaration, and certain import documents.

The Application for Export License

When exported items require a validated license, the exporter must submit an *Application for Export License* to the Bureau of Export Administration. Failure to provide correct information on the application may result in criminal liability for the exporter, even when the inaccuracies merely are the result of ignorance. In short, exporters must fully understand what they are exporting, where it is going, who is using it, and how it is being used. A validated license generally is issued within 10 to 20 days after submission of a properly completed application, unless the application must be reviewed by another agency. Turnaround time generally is shorter for exporters who use the Commerce Department's electronic submission process.

The Shipper's Export Declaration

Most items are exported under general licenses. Because exporting under a general license is basically a self-licensing process, there is a great risk that sensitive goods and technology may leave the country in violation of the export laws. To lessen this likelihood, the Commerce Department requires that most exports be accompanied by a properly completed *Shipper's Export Declaration* (SED). The Office of Export Enforcement routinely reviews the SEDs for irregularities. When an entry raises questions or contains discrepancies, Customs officials may detain the exported articles until the problem is cleared up.

All exports requiring a validated license must be accompanied by an SED. An SED is not necessary for articles exported under a general license unless they are valued at more than $1,500 (the amount is $500 for mailed exports).

FIGURE 12–3 An Application for Export License

BB FORM **BXA-622P**
(REV. 6-89)
FORM APPROVED: OMB No. 0694-0005

U.S. DEPARTMENT OF COMMERCE
Bureau of Export Administration
APPLICATION FOR EXPORT LICENSE

Information furnished herewith is subject to the provisions of Section 12(c) of the Export Administration Act of 1979, 50 U.S.C. app. 2411(c), and its unauthorized disclosure is prohibited by law.

APPLICATION CONTROL NUMBER
This is NOT an export license number.
C 546854

DATE RECEIVED
(Leave Blank)

1. CONTACT PERSON

Name — Telephone Number

2a. FORMS ATTACHED	BXA-622P-A	BXA-622P-B	BXA-6031P	TECH. SPEC'S.
2b. DOCUMENT(S) ON FILE WITH APPLICANT	BXA-629P	LETTER OF ASSURANCE	OTHER	

I.C. and/or END-USE CERTIFICATE(S)
COUNTRY # — COUNTRY #

3. RESUBMISSION OF CASE NUMBER

4. SPECIAL PURPOSE

5. APPLICANT
ADDRESS
CITY
STATE — ZIP CODE

7. PURCHASER — Same as Item #6
ADDRESS
CITY — POSTAL CODE
COUNTRY — TELEPHONE NO.

6. ULTIMATE CONSIGNEE
ADDRESS
CITY — POSTAL CODE
COUNTRY — TELEPHONE NO.

8. INTERMEDIATE CONSIGNEE — Same as Item #7
ADDRESS
CITY — POSTAL CODE
COUNTRY — TELEPHONE NO.

9 (a) QUANTITY	(b) COMMODITY PDR	MANUFACTURER'S DESCRIPTION OF COMMODITY (*Place model # before description, followed by a colon. End description with ECCN Paragraph Reference*)	PROCESSING CODE	(c) ECCN	(d) NET VALUE U.S. DOLLARS UNIT PRICE	TOTAL PRICE
				TOTAL OF ENTIRE TRANSACTION $		

SAMPLE

10. PARTY OTHER THAN APPLICANT AUTHORIZED TO RECEIVE LICENSE
ADDRESS
TELEPHONE NO.
CITY — STATE — ZIP CODE

11. MANUFACTURER(S)

12. SPECIFIC END-USE OF COMMODITIES OR TECHNICAL DATA BY CONSIGNEE IN ITEM #6 ABOVE

13. END-USER if different from Item #6
NAME
ADDRESS
CITY — POSTAL CODE
COUNTRY — TELEPHONE NO.

14. FOREIGN AVAILABILITY SUBMISSION ATTACHED — YES — NO

15. ADDITIONAL INFORMATION

16. APPLICANT'S CERTIFICATION. I hereby make application for a license to export, and I certify that (a) to the best of my knowledge, information and belief all statements in this application, including the description of the commodities or technical data and their end-uses, and any documents submitted in support of this application are correct and complete and that they fully and accurately disclose all the terms of the order and other facts of the export transaction; (b) this application conforms to the instructions accompanying this application and the Export Administration Regulations; (c) I obtained the order from the order party who has completed item 17, or I negotiated with and secured the export order directly from the purchaser or ultimate consignee, or through his or their agent(s); (d) I will retain records pertaining to this transaction and make them available as required by §787.13 of the Export Administration Regulations; (e) I will report promptly to the U.S. Department of Commerce any material changes in the terms of the order or other facts or intentions of the export transaction as reflected in this application and supporting documents, whether the application is still under consideration or a license has been granted; and (f) if the license is granted, I will be strictly accountable for its use in accordance with the Export Administration Regulations and all the terms and conditions of the license.

SIGN HERE IN INK ______ (SIGNATURE of person authorized to execute this application)
Type or Print ______ (NAME and TITLE of person whose signature appears on line to the left)
______ DATE OF APPLICATION

17. ORDER PARTY'S CERTIFICATION (See §772.6 (b) of the *Export Administration Regulations*) - The undersigned order party certifies to the truth and correctness of item 16(a) above, and that he has no information concerning the export transaction that is undisclosed or inconsistent with representations made to the Department of Commerce and agrees to comply with items 16(d) and 16(e) above.

Type or Print ______ (Order Party)
SIGN HERE IN INK ______ (Signature of Person authorized to sign for the order party)
Type or Print ______ (NAME and TITLE of person whose signature appears on line to the left)

BB

ORIGINAL

This license application and any license issued pursuant thereto are expressly subject to all rules and regulations of the Department of Commerce. Making any false statement or concealing any material fact in connection with this application or altering in any way the validated license issued is punishable by imprisonment or fine, or both, and by denial of export privileges under the Export Administration Act of 1979, and any other applicable Federal statutes. No export license will be issued unless this form is completed and submitted in accordance with Export Administration Regulation 772.4 (50 U.S.C. app. Sec. 2401, et seq., 15 CFR Part 772).

USCOMM-DC 89-24379

FIGURE 12–4   A Shipper's Export Declaration

U.S. DEPARTMENT OF COMMERCE—BUREAU OF THE CENSUS—INTERNATIONAL TRADE ADMINISTRATION

FORM **7525-V** (1-1-88)   **SHIPPER'S EXPORT DECLARATION**   OMB No. 0607-0018

1a. EXPORTER *(Name and address including ZIP code)*

| | ZIP CODE | **2.** DATE OF EXPORTATION | **3.** BILL OF LADING/AIR WAYBILL NO. |

b. EXPORTER EIN (IRS) NO.

c. PARTIES TO TRANSACTION
☐ Related ☐ Non-related

4a. ULTIMATE CONSIGNEE

b. INTERMEDIATE CONSIGNEE

5. FORWARDING AGENT

6. POINT (STATE) OF ORIGIN OR FTZ NO.   **7.** COUNTRY OF ULTIMATE DESTINATION

8. LOADING PIER *(Vessel only)*   **9.** MODE OF TRANSPORT *(Specify)*

10. EXPORTING CARRIER   **11.** PORT OF EXPORT

12. PORT OF UNLOADING *(Vessel and air only)*   **13.** CONTAINERIZED *(Vessel only)*
☐ Yes ☐ No

14. SCHEDULE B DESCRIPTION OF COMMODITIES, *(Use columns 17-19)*
15. MARKS, NOS., AND KINDS OF PACKAGES

D/F (16)	SCHEDULE B NUMBER (17)	CHECK DIGIT	QUANTITY— SCHEDULE B UNIT(S) (18)	SHIPPING WEIGHT *(Kilos)* (19)	VALUE (U.S. dollars, omit cents) *(Selling price or cost if not sold)* (20)

SAMPLE

21. VALIDATED LICENSE NO./GENERAL LICENSE SYMBOL   **22.** ECCN *(When required)*

23. Duly authorized officer or employee   The exporter authorizes the forwarder named above to act as forwarding agent for export control and customs purposes.

24. I certify that all statements made and all information contained herein are true and correct and that I have read and understand the instructions for preparation of this document, set forth in the "Correct Way to Fill Out the Shipper's Export Declaration" (available Bureau of Census, Wash., DC 20233). I understand that civil and criminal penalties, including forfeiture and sale, may be imposed for making false or fraudulent statements herein, failing to provide the requested information or for violation of U.S. laws on exportation (13 U.S.C. Sec. 305; 22 U.S.C. Sec. 401; 18 U.S.C. Sec. 1001; 50 U.S.C. App. 2410).

Signature

Confidential—For use solely for official purposes authorized by the Secretary of Commerce (13 U.S.C. 301 (g)).

Title

Export shipments are subject to inspection by U.S. Customs Service and/or Office of Export Enforcement.

Date   **25.** AUTHENTICATION *(When required)*

Form 15-780 Printed and Sold by *UNZ&CO* 190 Baldwin Ave., Jersey City, NJ 07306 • (800) 631-3098 • (201) 795-5400

The Import Documents

The Bureau of Export Administration frequently insists on verification of the end use and end user of the exported articles. Thus, it may require the exporter to obtain an *International Import Certificate* from the importing nation. In this statement, the government of the importing country certifies that the goods or technology will not be reexported to a prohibited destination. Because many countries are very slow in processing these requests, prudent exporters urge their foreign buyers to apply for this document as soon as possible.

The exporter may also need to provide a *Statement by Ultimate Consignee and Purchaser*. This form contains the foreign buyer's assurance it will use the goods in the manner described in the original export license application. To ensure it is properly completed, the exporter often fills out the document and has the purchaser or consignee sign it.

Delays in the Review Process

As noted earlier, the Commerce Department and its Bureau of Export Administration do not have exclusive authority over the licensing of exports. In many instances, the application is referred to another agency for review. Applications involving extremely sensitive goods or technology must be reviewed by the CoCom countries. Interagency reviews greatly increase the amount of time it takes to process an application, creating delays that can prove costly to an exporter. While the export regulations establish time limits for the review process, they are routinely disregarded by the reviewing agencies. Consider the following case.

DAEDALUS ENTERPRISES, INC. v. BALDRIGE
563 F.Supp. 1345 (D.D.C. 1983)

■ **FACTS** Daedalus entered into an agreement with the Romanian government, whereby Romania agreed to purchase a Daedalus multispectral airborne scanner. Because Romania was a country to which exports were controlled for national security purposes, the Commerce Department indicated the export application would be referred to the Departments of State, Defense, and Energy and would also require multilateral review by CoCom. Under Export Administration Act regulations, the secretary of commerce must formally issue or deny a license within 180 days of the date of application or within 240 days if a CoCom review is necessary. Despite these time limits, the Commerce Department did not refer the application until 300 days after the application had been filed. Some 29 months after the filing of the license application, the Commerce Department still had not reached a final decision to grant or deny the license. As a result, Daedalus filed suit to force the Commerce Department to comply

with the regulatory timetable for issuing or denying export licenses. The secretary of commerce argued the delay was not unreasonable because of the complexities involved in reviewing applications of sensitive materials to controlled countries. Further, he argued that Daedalus should be compelled to request the secretary to comply with the time periods before petitioning a court to intervene in an administrative matter.

■ **ISSUE** Should the court order the Commerce Department to make a decision on whether to grant or deny the export license?

■ **DECISION** Yes. The secretary's first argument is that the delay was understandable in light of the multitiered process of review stemming from the foreign policy and national security considerations implicated. The difficulty with this argument is that since Congress has carefully prescribed a series of deadlines measured by the number of days—rather than months or years—the court may not simply interpret an additional period into the procedural scheme. The fact that Daedalus failed to make a written petition to the secretary of commerce also does not bar its claim here. When an agency already has made it abundantly obvious it would not conform its actions with the strictures of the export regulations, it would be meaningless to compel a hapless exporter to pursue further administrative remedies simply for form's sake.

The *Daedalus* decision may have provided no more than an illusory remedy for exporters confronted by delays in the license approval process. The court only ordered Commerce to make its decision; it did not stipulate what that decision should be. Thus, exporters may hesitate to pressure the government to meet the statutory deadline out of fear their applications may be denied.

Enforcement

Any of the departments or agencies with export control functions may enforce their regulatory policies within U.S. territory. Overseas investigations also are common. For instance, the Department of Commerce may conduct prelicense investigations and postshipment verifications outside the United States. Further, U.S. Customs officials are authorized to search, detain, and seize items they have reasonable cause to suspect are in violation of U.S. export laws. They also possess the power to arrest individuals suspected of breaking the law. Officers from the Office of Export Enforcement have similar arrest powers.

Criminal Liability

Knowing violations of the U.S. export laws may result in the imposition of criminal sanctions. Criminal fines equal to the greater of $50,000 or five times the value of the illegal export may be imposed, and an individual may be imprisoned for up to five years. The criminal penalties are more severe for willful violations involving exports to controlled countries or to nations that export to controlled countries. An individual may be fined up to $250,000 and sentenced to 10 years in prison. A corporation may have to pay criminal fines equal to the greater of $1 million or five times the value of the exports.

Civil Liability

Violations of the export laws also may subject the importer to civil penalties and administrative sanctions. For each offense, the secretary of commerce may impose a civil fine of up to $10,000. If the export violated national security controls or controls imposed on the export of defense articles and services, the civil penalty may be as much as $10,000 per offense. Serious offenses may result in the issuance of a denial order that revokes a person's export privileges.

Corporate Compliance Programs

Exporters should develop compliance programs that communicate throughout the organization upper management's commitment to strict observance of U.S. export control laws. This should include a clear identification of the company officials with

FIGURE 12–5   Commerce Enforcement Statistics Show Dramatic Increase in Criminal Convictions
                      (October 1989 to September 1991)

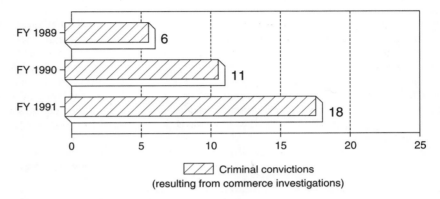

Source: Reprinted from *The OEL Insider* 3, no. 3, October/November 1991, p. 6.

compliance authority, a manageable records-retention system, and a review mechanism to ensure compliance. Employees must be taught to recognize the **red flags**
that create a reasonable suspicion a violation might be occurring. Management officials should encourage a free flow of information, both within the organization and
from potential buyers, to ensure they are aware of the actual end uses, end users,
and countries of destination for the company's products. When red flags do arise,
employees need to understand the importance of immediately reporting them to the
compliance officers so the circumstances can be investigated.

CAESAR ELECTRONICS, INC. v. ANDREWS
905 F.2d 287 (9th Cir. 1990)

■ **FACTS** Fairchild Camera and Instrument Corporation manufactured computer hardware used for testing
semiconductor chips. Because the hardware could have
been diverted to unfriendly governments and used for
military purposes, the Commerce Department classified
it at the highest level and strictly regulated its availability
for export. Caesar Electronics placed an order with Fairchild for the hardware. Caesar was purportedly acting as
a broker for the French firm, Development Engineering
and Electronics, which in turn allegedly received the order from another French company, C.S.F. Thomson. Although the paperwork appeared to be in order, Fairchild's

suspicions were aroused by the following *red flags*: Caesar was not one of Fairchild's established customers; the
order could have been routed through Fairchild's French
affiliate; and the ultimate purchaser was not interested in
receiving any training or service for the hardware. A
check revealed that C.S.F. Thomson had placed no such
order with Development Engineering. Fairchild contacted
the U.S. Customs Service, which instructed the company
to proceed with the transaction and cooperate with the
government in its investigation. Concerned that its actions might lead to civil or criminal liability, Fairchild
sought and obtained letters from the Departments of

Commerce and Justice confirming it would not be subject to liability for possible violations in U.S. export laws as a result of its cooperation in the investigation. The investigators instructed Fairchild to manufacture a dummy facsimile of the hardware for eventual shipment to France. Then, acting as Caesar's agent, Fairchild prepared documents to ensure it would receive its payment of $762,240 through a letter of credit. Upon the dummy hardware's arrival in France, Fairchild collected on the letter of credit. One week later French customs agents seized the dummy hardware at the Swiss border when an attempt was made to divert it to Switzerland. After Caesar and Development Engineering were indicted for violating U.S. export laws, Caesar sued Fairchild for fraud and breach of fiduciary duty for failing to inform it of the government investigation.

■ **ISSUE** Did Fairchild have a duty to disclose the investigation to Caesar?

■ **DECISION** No. Caesar argued that, as its agent, Fairchild had a fiduciary obligation to disclose all pertinent confidential information to it. Thus, by withholding from Caesar that it was the target of a federal criminal investigation, Fairchild violated that fiduciary duty. This argument is meritless. First, the major premise is patently false and finds no support in the law. However high the duty an agent may owe its principal, society's interest in preventing the commission of criminal acts overrides that duty. Second, under California law, which governs this case, citizens generally are immune from civil liability for their good faith cooperation with the government in its criminal investigations.

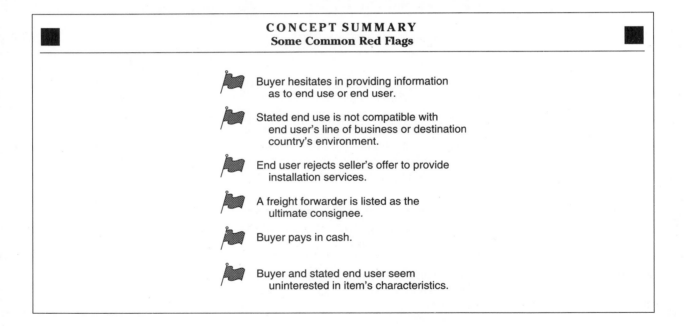

CONCEPT SUMMARY
Some Common Red Flags

- Buyer hesitates in providing information as to end use or end user.

- Stated end use is not compatible with end user's line of business or destination country's environment.

- End user rejects seller's offer to provide installation services.

- A freight forwarder is listed as the ultimate consignee.

- Buyer pays in cash.

- Buyer and stated end user seem uninterested in item's characteristics.

ANTIBOYCOTT REGULATIONS

The Arab Boycott   Many Arab countries engage in a trade boycott of Israel. To further this goal, the boycotting nations **blacklist** any firm doing business with Israel as well as any buyer or seller contracting with such a firm. Blacklisted companies are denied all trading privileges in the boycotting nations. As a means of enforcing the boycott, the Arab nations, through their boycott offices, send inquiries to companies they believe are violating the terms of the boycott. In these questionnaires, the firms are asked about their relationships with Israel and any blacklisted company. Failure to complete and return the form often results in the firm being blacklisted.

The U.S. Response   The United States has enacted **antiboycott regulations** prohibiting U.S. persons from complying with, furthering, or otherwise supporting the boycott. A business violates these rules if it refuses to do business with Israel or with a blacklisted firm. Further, it must report any boycott-related request to the Department of Commerce, whether or not the company intends to comply with the request. (Most enforcement actions involve failure to report boycott requests.) Finally, as the following case illustrates, a firm violates the U.S. antiboycott regulations when it answers an Arab questionnaire seeking information about its business relationships with Israel. Accordingly, companies doing business in the Middle East must establish strong corporate compliance programs to ensure they do not unwittingly run afoul of U.S. antiboycott rules.

BRIGGS & STRATTON CORPORATION v. BALDRIGE
539 F.Supp. 1307 (E.D. Wis. 1982)

■ **FACTS** Briggs & Stratton is a manufacturer of internal combustion engines. Manufacturers in Australia, England, France, Germany, Japan, and the United States sell products powered by Briggs engines to customers all over the world. Briggs received a letter from Kabbabe, a distributor of Briggs products in Syria. Kabbabe wrote that a request for an import license for Briggs products had been refused because Briggs was on a blacklist. He enclosed a letter from the Syrian "Economical Department" that contained a series of questions asking if Briggs had economic ties with Israel. Briggs responded to this letter, answering all the questions in the negative. The response was not accepted because Briggs failed to have it authenticated by an Arab consular officer. However, before Briggs could have this done, the Commerce Department implemented regulations prohibiting companies from responding to such questionnaires. After failing to return the authenticated response, Briggs was blacklisted by Syria, Saudi Arabia, Bahrain, Oman, and Kuwait. This cost the company over $15 million in lost sales. Briggs blamed its losses on the U.S. regulations. In a legal challenge, Briggs argued they were unconstitutional because they were irrational.

■ **ISSUE** Should the court invalidate the U.S. regulations?

■ **DECISION** No. Briggs argues the boycott authorities send out questionnaires haphazardly and seek information that either is not useful or is readily available from public sources. It maintains that once a company fails to answer an inquiry, the boycott authorities consider whether the firm's products are readily available from other sources. If they are, the company is blacklisted. Thus, Briggs argues that by prohibiting answers to such inquiries, the Commerce Department has simplified the task of the boycotters and shifted commerce to foreign competitors. It argues that this is irrational. However, questionnaires such as that received by Briggs were a major focus of the congressional prohibition on the passing of information. Congress believed the information sought would be available from other sources, but it determined the prohibition should include such matters. While the law does explicitly permit the furnishing of normal business information in a commercial context, there is little justification for permitting U.S. persons to supply information when they know it is being sought for boycott enforcement purposes. Thus, the Commerce Department's regulations are not an irrational implementation of the congressional intent; they adequately translate Congress' concerns about cutting off the flow of information to boycotters.

The Future of the Boycott

The recent peace accord between Israel and the Palestine Liberation Organization has raised hopes that the boycott of Israel may soon end. Many of the gulf Arab states already have softened their policies, refusing to automatically prohibit trade with blacklisted companies. While a lifting of the embargo would not result in a massive surge of new U.S. trade, it would help U.S. firms compete against European and Japanese companies that have not had to deal with antiboycott regulations.

ETHICAL IMPLICATIONS   Is it ethical for a company to sever its business relationships with Israel so it may become eligible to conduct trade with an Arab nation?

QUESTIONS AND PROBLEM CASES

1. What are the primary justifications for imposing export controls?

2. What is meant by contract sanctity?

3. Explain the difference between a general license and a validated license.

4. Explain the role of CoCom in the export licensing process.

5. In response to the former Soviet Union's invasion of Afghanistan, former President Jimmy Carter imposed a grain embargo on the Soviet Union. This action was taken pursuant to authority vested in the president under the Export Administration Act. The owners of a family-run farm in Iowa claimed severe losses due to the implementation of the embargo. They asserted the embargo was an unconstitutional taking of their property since it deprived them of a potential market for their wheat crop. Must the government compensate the farm owners for their economic losses resulting from the embargo?

6. Geissler was charged with violating U.S. law when he attempted to export aircraft tires for F-14 military aircraft to Iran without a validated export license. The Commerce Department argued the tires fell within Group Four of the Commodity Control List, which contained the following description: "Other aircraft parts and components . . . and specifically designed parts for the above equipment." This category specifically required a validated license for commodities exported to Iran. In his defense, Geis-

sler pointed to Category VII of the U.S. Munitions List, titled "Aircraft, Spacecraft, and Associated Equipment," which specifically excluded aircraft tires from the list of defense articles requiring a validated license from the State Department. Thus, Geissler claimed tires were not governed by the Commodity Control List and, as such, did not require a validated license. In the alternative, he argued that if they were included within the Commodity Control List, such a strained interpretation rendered the regulations unconstitutional as impermissibly vague. Has Geissler raised a good defense?

7. Van Ameringen became part of a plan involving the sale of counterfeit Winston cigarettes manufactured in Cuba. Van Ameringen contacted Ortiz de Zevallos, a Peruvian citizen residing in Chile, who conducted business in the Panamanian free trade zone. The plan also involved Macko, a U.S. citizen, who was a former engineer with R. J. Reynolds Tobacco Company and had substantial knowledge about manufacturing cigarettes. Macko obtained the necessary items in the United States and shipped them to Ortiz de Zevallos in Panama, who sent them to Van Ameringen in Cuba. Macko gave a freight forwarder, American Overseas Transport Corporation, power of attorney to complete the necessary documentation to ship the machinery to Panama. York, an employee of the freight forwarder, filled out the Shipper's Export Declaration. She was given written instructions from Macko that the goods were to be shipped to Panama in transit.

York believed that "in transit" meant the cargo would be shipped to another country from Panama and she also knew the SED required information regarding the "ultimate destination." However, without obtaining further information from Macko, York listed the ultimate destination as Panama. Macko was charged with making a false statement as to a material fact on the SED because the country of ultimate destination was listed as Panama rather than Cuba. He never saw the form until after he was charged with the crime. Should Macko be found guilty?

8. Dart was charged with attempting to export two wafer polishers to Czechoslovakia without export licenses. In this case, the polishers had been upgraded to approximate more advanced models that could not be exported to Czechoslovakia for national security reasons. During the early stages of planning the export transaction, an official from the firm doing the upgrading vowed to travel to Washington, D.C., to determine if export licenses were needed or available. Dart furnished the name of someone at the Commerce Department who would be appropriate to contact on the issue. During that trip, the representative from the upgrading firm was recruited by the government as an informant. He never told Dart that licenses were required or unobtainable for the upgraded polishers. Indeed, the status of the polishers was never clarified. Based on this information and Dart's lack of expertise with wafer polishers, an administrative law judge (ALJ), after five days of hearings, dismissed the charges against Dart. On review, the secretary of commerce overturned the ALJ's decision and imposed a $150,000 fine and a 15-year ban on Dart's export privileges. Dart appealed the penalties on the grounds that the secretary exceeded his authority. Export regulations permit the secretary to affirm, modify, or vacate the ALJ's rulings. Did the secretary exceed his authority?

9. Helmy pled guilty to illegally exporting 436 pounds of an ablative carbon composite fabric, called MX-4926, which was a critical component in the construction of rocket nozzles. The court increased the penalty against Helmy because his crime involved sophisticated weaponry. Helmy challenged this upward adjustment to his sentence on two grounds. First, he argued that because the distinction between sophisticated and unsophisticated weaponry is ill-defined, the court should not have increased his sentence. Second, he claimed the upward penalty adjustment only applies to weapons, not to weapons components. Are Helmy's arguments persuasive?

10. Bozarov was an international trade official who resided in Bulgaria. While serving as the deputy general manager of a trade organization devoted to developing industry in Bulgaria, Bozarov entered into negotiations with a Dutch company for the purchase of computer disc manufacturing equipment. The Dutch company then contracted with an American company to supply the equipment. The relevant commodities were listed on the Commodity Control List for national security reasons. After the goods were shipped without a validated license, a 10-count indictment was issued against Bozarov. Apparently under the impression that the charges against him had been resolved in his favor, Bozarov hosted a trade show in San Francisco. He was arrested when he arrived there. Bozarov challenged the constitutionality of the export regulations. He argued that the secretary of commerce's authority to list items on the Commodity Control List violated the separation of powers doctrine because only Congress possesses the power to legislate. Is Bozarov correct?

REGULATORY ISSUES IN GLOBAL TRADE

Licensing and Technology Transfers

INTRODUCTION

Many businesses desire a deeper level of global penetration than is afforded by importing and exporting activities; yet they are unwilling to face the economic and political risks associated with direct investment overseas. For these companies, technology licensing provides an attractive alternative because it permits a quick and relatively inexpensive entry into foreign markets. Licensing arrangements allow a firm to license for a fee its **intellectual property** (patents, copyrights, trademarks, and trade secrets) to foreign companies that may then conduct production, sales, and service activities abroad.

While licensing agreements can provide extensive business opportunities, they must be approached cautiously. Businesses that hastily share their core technology with overseas companies risk permanently losing it. Accordingly, global business managers must acquaint themselves with the legal and practical issues involved in the licensing of technology.

Chapter Overview

The chapter begins with an introduction to the basic types of intellectual property, briefly noting the differences in legal protection throughout the world. Attention then turns to the legal aspects of transferring technology. This involves an examination of the basic nature of licensing, including the advantages and risks commonly associated with technology transfers. Included in this section is a general review of the basic provisions found in most technology licensing agreements. The focus then shifts to an overview of the basic types of regulatory schemes governing licensing arrangements. This is followed by a look at the legal problems involved in global counterfeiting and piracy of intellectual property, including a special discussion of the legal and practical issues related to gray market imports.

INTELLECTUAL PROPERTY RIGHTS

While the United States and much of the world support competitive markets, they also value private research and development. Recognizing that ruthless competition is likely to undermine incentives to innovate, most countries offer some degree of legal protection for creative products, processes, and services. Unfortunately, no single regulatory scheme provides universal protection for intellectual property rights. This means global businesses often must register their intellectual property interests in their home country, the countries where they do business, the countries where their competitors do business, and countries where counterfeiting is rampant.

The four basic types of intellectual property are: patents, trademarks, copyrights, and trade secrets. This section introduces these forms, briefly sketching the legal protection each is given throughout the world.

Patents

A **patent** provides its owner with the exclusive right to make, use, or sell an invention during the patent period. In the United States, the patent generally is effective for 17 years; although design patents last for only 14 years. In many developing countries, the patent period is much shorter. The major advantage of a patent is that it deprives competitors of the opportunity to use the invention without the patent holder's consent. This temporary monopoly is expected to encourage the creation and utilization of new products and technologies.

Patentable Creations

Most patents involve inventions of commercially useful goods or novel processes for producing such items. However, many developing countries do not extend patent protection for inventions involving food or drugs. Others protect only the processes for producing these articles.

In the United States, the following things may be patented: *processes; machines; products; compositions* of elements (new chemical compounds); *improvements* of processes, machines, and compositions; *ornamental designs* for products; and *plants* produced by asexual reproduction. Articles or processes falling within these categories may be patented if they are novel and useful.

DIAMOND v. DIEHR
450 U.S. 175 (U.S. Sup.Ct. 1981)

■ **FACTS** Diehr wished to patent his process for molding raw, uncured synthetic rubber into cured precision products. The process used a mold for shaping rubber under heat and pressure and then curing it while still in the mold. Previous efforts at curing and molding synthetic rubber had failed because of the inability to accurately measure and control the temperature inside the molding press. Diehr's process constantly measured the temperature inside the mold, feeding the information to a computer that constantly recalculated the curing time so the molding press would open at the correct time. A U.S. patent examiner rejected Diehr's patent application, asserting that processes involving the laws of nature and physical phenomena are not eligible for patent protection.

■ **ISSUE** Is Diehr's process eligible for patent protection?

■ **DECISION** Yes. A process is a mode of treatment of certain materials to produce a given result. It is an act, or a series of acts, performed on the subject matter to be transformed and reduced to a different state or thing. If new and useful, it is just as patentable as is a piece of machinery. The machinery pointed out as suitable to perform the process may or may not be new or patentable, while the process itself may be new and produce a new result. Transformation and reduction of an article to a different state or thing is the clue to the patentability of a process claim that does not include particular machines. That Diehr's claim involves the transformation of an article (raw, uncured synthetic rubber) into a different state or thing cannot be disputed. Industrial processes such as this historically have been eligible to receive patent protection. Excluded from patent protection are laws of nature, physical phenomena, and abstract ideas. Thus, a new mineral discovered in the earth, a plant found in the wild, or a mathematical formula are not patentable. Such discoveries are manifestations of nature, free to all people and reserved exclusively to none. While Diehr's process involves a well-known mathematical equation, he does not seek to preempt use of that equation. He seeks only to foreclose from others the use of that equation in conjunction with all the other steps in his process. It is now common that an application of a law of nature or mathematical formula to a known structure or process may be deserving of patent protection.

Standards for Patentability

The United States awards patent privileges based on a **first to invent** standard. Under this approach, the exclusive rights over patentable subjects belong to the inventor of the product or process, rather than to the first individual to file an application. This differs from the approach of most nations in the world. They follow a **first to file** standard that rewards the first person to apply for a patent, even when that person is not the inventor.

Corporations often are accused of buying patents and then failing to actively exploit them. Instead, they merely prevent others from utilizing the goods or processes during the patent period. To prevent this, many countries strip patent holders of their patent privileges if they fail to use or license others to use the patented articles or processes. To achieve a similar result, some countries issue an *inventor's certificate.* While this certificate does not entitle its holder to exclusive use of the creation, it does require all users to pay her royalties when they exploit the invention.

 **ETHICAL IMPLICATIONS**   Many drug producers are accused of preventing competitors from producing their patented drugs and then pricing the products out of the reach of patients in Third World countries. Are such practices ethical?

Patent Infringement

Under U.S. law, patent infringement occurs when a person makes, uses, or sells the patented invention in the United States without the patent holder's authorization. Anyone who assists the infringer in these unlawful activities may also be liable. When an infringement occurs, the patent holder is entitled to monetary damages (up to three times the losses caused by the infringement) as well as an injunction to prevent future violations. U.S. businesses may petition the government to block the importation of foreign goods that infringe U.S. patent rights.

When an infringement occurs overseas in violation of a company's patent rights in a foreign country, the patent holder must look to the courts of that nation for redress. However, in many instances, foreign officials do not aggressively enforce their intellectual property laws. If this is a recurring problem, a U.S. business may petition the U.S. trade representative to impose import sanctions on goods from that nation. (This remedy is discussed in Chapter 11.)

Trademarks   A **trademark** is a distinctive word, name, symbol, or device used by a business to distinguish its goods or services from those of its competitors. Descriptive terms that identify the businesses themselves, rather than their products or services, are called *trade names.* In this chapter, both types of identifying marks are referred to as trademarks.

Reasons for Legal Protection

Trademarks are given legal protection to assist purchasers in distinguishing among the many firms, products, and services in existence within a particular market. For this reason, they generally must be distinctive to merit legal protection. A trademark owner can lose its protection if the name or symbol becomes so widely used that it acquires a generic meaning. (This happened to aspirin.)

BERNER INTERNATIONAL CORPORATION v. MARS SALES COMPANY
987 F.2d 975 (3rd Cir. 1993)

■ **FACTS** Mars Sales Company and Berner International Corporation compete in the production and sale of devices that use a barrier of moving air directed across an open doorway or other opening for temperature and insect control. These devices, which were first manufactured in the United Kingdom under the name *air curtains,* originally were marketed in the United States under that name by Berner. When Mars began selling air curtains, it coined and adopted the term *air door* to distinguish its device from others on the market. When other manufacturers used the term *air door* in connection with or on their products, Mars objected and the companies refrained from using the name. Early in 1989, Mars learned Berner had begun using the term *air door* in the promotion of its products.

■ **ISSUE** How will a court decide whether it should order Berner to refrain from using the term *air door?*

■ **DECISION** A term can be protected as a trademark only if the public recognizes it as identifying the claimant's goods or services and distinguishing them from those of others. There are four basic categories of distinctiveness: arbitrary (or fanciful) terms, which bear no logical or suggestive relation to the actual characteristics of the goods; suggestive terms, which suggest rather than describe the characteristics of the goods; descriptive terms, which describe a characteristic or ingredient of the article to which they refer; and generic terms, which function as the common descriptive name of a product class. If a term is arbitrary or suggestive, courts will treat it as distinctive and automatically qualify it for trademark protection. If a term is descriptive, trademark protection will exist only if a claimant proves the term conveys to consumers a secondary meaning of association with the claimant. Finally, if a term is generic, courts are unwilling to afford it trademark protection. Thus, the court must inquire whether the primary significance of the term *air door* in the minds of the consuming public is with the product or with Mars.

The Registration Process

Most countries provide a registration system for trademarks; however, the legal significance of this process varies from nation to nation. For instance, in the United States and most common law countries, a trademark is not eligible for registration in the absence of prior commercial use. And, even after registration, legal protection can be lost if the holder fails to use the trademark. U.S. trademarks are registered for 10-year terms; although the holder generally can renew the registration repeatedly.

Throughout the rest of the world, the first person to register a trademark becomes its legal owner. This legal protection is given to the first person to register even when that individual was not the first person to use the trademark. Many successful U.S.

businesses have been surprised to discover when entering foreign markets that local entities already own their trademarks in those countries.

Trademark Rights

U.S. courts issue injunctions and provide monetary damages for trademark holders who prove that another person has used a similar mark in connection with the sale of goods or services where such use is likely to cause confusion. Customs officials may block the importation of goods likely to infringe the trademark of a U.S. holder.

As with patents, many foreign countries are extremely lax in enforcing their trademark laws. Further, some nations do not allow foreign trademark holders to collect royalties from local businesses that are licensed to use their trademarks. The United States also restricts the licensing of trademarks. For example, a trademark holder is not permitted to license its trademarks to another person unless the owner retains the right to control the nature and quality of the goods or services sold under the trademark.

Copyrights

A **copyright** prohibits the unauthorized reproduction of creative works such as books, magazines, poems, drawings, paintings, musical compositions, sound recordings, films, and videotapes. While most developed countries extend copyright protection to computer software, much of the world offers it little or no protection. In the United States, a copyright generally lasts for the life of the author plus 50 years. However, because copyright laws vary tremendously throughout the world, each nation's laws must be examined individually to understand the extent of legal protection available for copyrighted works.

Creation and Notice

In the United States and many other countries, a copyright comes into existence automatically on the creation of the work. Although owners may register their copyrights with the appropriate governmental office, they are not required to do so. Copyright owners often provide notice of their copyright by indicating its existence on copies of their works. In the United States, a copyright infringer generally is prohibited from reducing its liability by claiming innocent infringement if proper notice has been given.

Enforcement

Global businesses frequently are unaware of the subtle ways in which copyright issues might arise. For instance, the manuals, specification sheets, and sales literature provided to distributors and franchisees generally are protected by copyrights. Even an inadvertent reproduction of these copyrighted materials can subject a firm to liability for copyright infringement. In the United States, a copyright holder may collect its actual damages plus the profits earned by the infringer. In the alternative, the copyright holder may elect to receive statutory damages between $500 and $20,000 for inadvertent violations or $100,000 for willful infringement. Thus, a U.S. software company recently paid a $100,000 settlement for violating another company's copyrights by electronically distributing a dozen of its telecommunications newsletters.

When an infringement occurs abroad, a U.S. exporter may discover it has little recourse against the infringer. Some countries offer no copyright protection, and many others lack the will or the resources to enforce their copyright laws. Even when enforcement occurs, the penalties assessed may be extremely weak.

Trade Secrets

A **trade secret** generally is developed by a firm over the course of its business activities. Sometimes called *know-how,* this type of intellectual property includes secret formulas, devices, processes, techniques, and compilations of information (e.g., customer lists). A trade secret generally does not receive legal protection unless its owner took reasonable precautions to keep it a secret. Further, it must be established that the secret product, process, or idea provides its owners with a distinct advantage over competitors.

A business may attempt to maintain a trade secret when it has a process or product that is not novel enough to receive patent protection. Or it may choose to forgo the patent route because the monopoly period for patents is relatively short. Trade secret protection, on the other hand, can last forever if nobody is ever able to independently discover the secret. For example, the formula for Coca-Cola has remained a trade secret over 100 years. If the formula had been patented, it would have been available to anyone within 17 years.

Maintaining Secrecy

As a precondition to receiving trade secret protection, the owner must take reasonable means to maintain secrecy. This may include limiting the number of persons to whom the secret is disclosed, advising employees of the importance of confidentiality, and having those given access sign contracts containing nondisclosure clauses. Whether the precautions taken are reasonable or not varies with the competitive importance of the secret, the costs of the measures, and the likelihood that someone will discover the secret.

Businesses often fail to appreciate the range of things that could be protected as trade secrets. For instance, safety procedures, sources of various raw materials, training programs, and quality control systems all can make substantial contributions to the competitiveness of an enterprise. By placing reasonable limitations on the external flow of information concerning these processes and lists, a company possibly could claim them as trade secrets.

Misappropriation

In the United States, an individual is liable for disclosing or using a trade secret if she:

1. acquired it by improper means (e.g., theft, trespass, spying, or bribery),
2. obtained it from one who acquired it by improper means, or
3. breached a duty of confidentiality regarding the secret.

FIGURE 13–1 Misappropriation of a Trade Secret

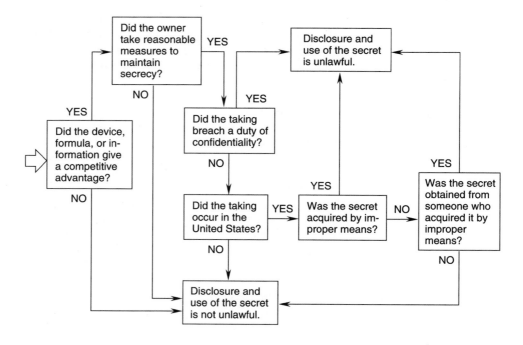

When a misappropriation occurs, the owner generally is entitled to compensatory damages and, in cases of willful misappropriations, punitive damages. An individual may freely use the trade secrets of another if he discovers them through proper means, such as reverse engineering.

Throughout much of the world, trade secret protection is much more limited. Thus, many countries confine liability for misappropriation to individuals who have violated the terms of an agreement to maintain confidentiality. Third parties who did not sign such a contract would not be liable. Further, some underdeveloped nations either refuse to enforce confidentiality provisions or greatly limit the time period during which secrecy must be maintained.

ETHICAL IMPLICATIONS Is it ethical to spy on competitors to discover their trade secrets?

TECHNOLOGY TRANSFER AGREEMENTS

A technology transfer occurs when a business licenses its intellectual property to another firm. These contractual agreements generally permit a company to quickly penetrate a foreign market without incurring the substantial financial and legal risks associated with direct investment. This section examines the fundamental nature of licensing. It then discusses the advantages and the risks associated with technology transfers. This is followed by a brief look at the issues involved in negotiating a licensing agreement. The section closes with a review of the basic contractual provisions included in a technology transfer agreement.

Nature of Licensing

While intellectual property owners generally have the right to prevent others from exploiting their creations, they may selectively authorize individuals to use them. This is the principal purpose of a licensing agreement; it permits an intellectual property owner to grant to another the right to use protected technology in return for some form of compensation. The actual contract may take a variety of forms depending on the needs of the parties, the nature of the intellectual property, and the controlling laws.

Parties to the Licensing Agreement

The person who owns the intellectual property is known as the **licensor.** In return for some type of payment, the licensor permits another, the **licensee,** to produce, use, or sell the intellectual property. Sometimes the licensee is permitted to sublicense all or part of its rights in the technology to a sublicensee. Whether this right or others exists is determined by the licensing agreement itself and the laws of the country where the licensing activities occur.

As a general rule, persons who buy from patent holders or their licensees are not restricted by the original licensing contract. Thus, a patent holder may prevent its competitors from selling its patented products. However, after a customer buys a patented product, she may freely resell it without fear of violating the original patent.

The Need to License

Frequently, an intellectual property owner has few options other than licensing its technology to others. For instance, many inventors do not have production facilities or marketing networks capable of profitably using or selling their creations. In these cases, an inventor may license a manufacturer or sales representative to produce or sell the product. Further, in some nations it is not legally permissible or practical to do business without some level of participation by a local person or company. Thus, a foreign intellectual property owner may be compelled to license its technology to a local firm.

Advantages of Licensing

Licensing provides numerous benefits for both licensors and licensees. Licensors directly benefit by receiving royalty payments as well as by gaining a presence in a market that might otherwise be inaccessible. As was previously noted, licensing allows a firm to penetrate foreign markets much more quickly than direct investment. Further, by licensing rather than directly investing, a business minimizes its physical

---

CONCEPT SUMMARY
Intellectual Property

	Coverage	Formalities for Protection	Duration of Protection
Patent	New and useful products, processes, machines, compositions of elements, ornamental designs, and plants produced by asexual reproduction.	• Must register in countries where protection is sought. • Must be first to invent in the United States. • First to file elsewhere.	Generally protected for 17 years in the United States. The patent period is both longer and shorter in other nations.
Trademark	Distinctive words, names, symbols, or devices that identify the goods and services of a company from its competitors.	• Most countries have registration process. • Must have prior commercial use in the United States. • First to file elsewhere.	Protected for a 10-year period in the United States. May be renewed repeatedly unless the name becomes generic. Period varies from country to country.
Copyright	Creative endeavors, such as books, magazines, poems, drawings, paintings, musical compositions, sound recordings, films, videotapes, and computer software.	• Most countries have a registration system. • May be protected in absence of registration.	Generally lasts for the life of the author plus 50 years. Period maybe shorter in other countries.
Trade Secret	Secret formulas, devices, processes, techniques, and compilations of information that give a company a competitive advantage.	• No registration system. • Owner must take reasonable efforts to maintain secrecy.	Indefinite. Protection continues until someone discovers the secret by proper means.

---

and financial presence overseas, thereby reducing the risk of suffering losses in the event of an expropriation. Some firms select licensing over exporting activities because it provides a method of escaping the tariff and nontariff barriers erected by many importing nations.

Licensees also derive benefits from licensing arrangements. It may provide them with access to products and ideas that otherwise might not be available. They may also gain tremendous competitive advantages through close association with a licensor's established reputation.

Risks of Licensing   Despite its many benefits, technology licensing is not without its drawbacks. Perhaps the greatest risk is that the licensee, after gaining access to the licensor's technology, will sever the licensing relationship and become a competitor. While the licensor may attempt to contain this risk through a carefully constructed contract, many countries refuse to enforce restrictive provisions. In fact, if the restrictions are too severe, they may violate antitrust laws.

If a licensor does not closely monitor the activities of a licensee, it runs the risk that the licensee will produce inferior products or provide inferior service. This could erode goodwill the licensor has taken years to develop. Further, some licensees cannot be trusted to honestly report their use of the licensed technology. If this occurs, and if royalty payments are based on such use, a licensor may be cheated out of large amounts of money. Only by regularly auditing a licensee's business records can a licensor be certain this is not occurring.

Negotiating the Agreement

Global licensing agreements require meticulous planning and a great deal of flexibility. Businesses generally agree that the key to successful collaboration is the development of trust between the licensor and licensee. However, licensors are justifiably wary about entrusting their intellectual property to overseas companies, especially when the agreement encompasses core technologies or vital markets. Similarly, licensees are reluctant to invest their resources establishing a foothold if they fear they will be replaced by the licensor once the venture becomes highly profitable.

Principal Considerations

Licensing agreements require a careful partner selection process that clearly identifies each firm's objectives and details how each plans to meet the other's expectations. Likewise, they necessitate a hands-on, personal interaction during both the negotiation and implementation phases. The actual licensing agreement should be drafted only after identification of areas of potential conflict. Further, it should include provisions detailing the rights and obligations of the licensor and licensee in the event the relationship is terminated. Finally, as with all business agreements, the licensing contract should establish mechanisms for resolving disputes.

Limits on Negotiating Authority

The range of issues that may be governed by the technology transfer agreement often is severely limited. Many developing nations have enacted legislation designed to protect local licensees from the superior bargaining strength possessed by foreign businesses. Much of this legislation is a direct outgrowth of past instances where multinational corporations originally penetrated overseas markets through licensing agreements with local companies. Once the foreign operation became a viable concern, the licensor replaced the licensee with one of its own subsidiaries. In response to these practices, host countries frequently refuse to enforce contractual provisions granting liberal termination rights to the licensor.

Key Contractual Provisions

The precise terms of a licensing agreement depend on the objectives of the parties and their relative bargaining strength, the nature of the intellectual property, and the national laws governing the relationship. Thus, technology transfer agreements assume many forms. Despite these differences, however, certain fundamental provisions can be found in most licensing contracts.

Scope of the License

The **granting clause** indicates the precise scope of the license. It generally describes in great detail exactly what rights are to be transferred. It should explain whether the license is *exclusive* (the licensor cannot license the technology to others in the licensee's territory) or *nonexclusive*. The granting clause also may determine whether the licensee may grant sublicenses in the technology.

Sometimes the granting clause contains a *grant-back* provision that requires the licensee to transfer any inventions it derives from the licensed technology to the licensor. Thus, when a patent licensee improves on the patented technology covered by the licensing agreement, it must assign the new intellectual property rights to the licensor. Many developing countries prohibit grant-back clauses because they deprive local businesses of ownership rights in new technology and increase the market power of foreign licensors. When the agreement involves the transfer of trade secrets, the licensee may insist on the inclusion of a *technical service* clause that requires the licensor to supply various types of assistance throughout the life of the agreement.

Warranties

Licensees frequently ask licensors to guarantee that no other person has a legal claim to the licensed technology. Further, they may insist on **warranties** that the intellectual property meets certain performance standards. Likewise, the licensor may demand that the licensee meet certain **quality standards** in the performance of its contractual responsibilities. Such a condition is common when the licensing agreement authorizes the licensee to produce goods or supply services under the licensor's trademark.

Confidentiality

When the licensed technology is a trade secret, the agreement should contain a **confidentiality clause** that restricts the licensee's right to disclose the information. There are three distinct time frames when secrecy provisions are utilized. First, a licensee may insist on a limited right to inspect the licensor's technology before entering the licensing agreement to ensure the licensing relationship will be worthwhile. When this occurs, the licensee generally is required to sign a contract prohibiting it from using the technology or disclosing it to others. Second, during the life of the licensing agreement, the licensor may wish to restrict the number of people with whom the licensee will share its trade secrets. Finally, the licensor generally insists the licensee promise not to use or disclose the trade secrets after the licensing agreement has ended.

Restrictions on Use

Most licensing agreements include some type of **territorial restriction.** While the licensee may wish to fully exploit the licensed technology throughout the world, the licensor often prefers to reserve certain markets for itself or for other licensees. The licensor's objectives may be achieved either by confining the licensee to a spe-

FIGURE 13–2   Time Frames for Confidentiality Clauses

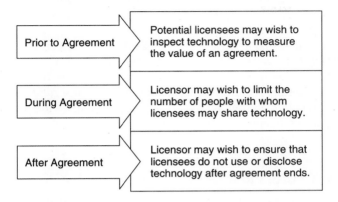

cific geographic region or by imposing quantitative limits on the licensee's exploitation of the licensed technology so it is able to service only its local market.

Licensors may also insist on **requirements clauses** that prevent licensees from purchasing goods, services, or technology from sources other than the licensor. These provisions sometimes preclude a licensee from developing its own technology. Another common provision in licensing agreements is an **exclusive dealing clause,** which prohibits the licensee from providing goods or services that are competitive with those supplied by the licensor. All these provisions have anticompetitive tendencies and, accordingly, are closely regulated by national antitrust laws. (Their antitrust consequences are discussed in Chapter 14.)

Compensation

The licensee's payments for use of the licensed technology may be structured in any number of ways. Sometimes the parties may agree on a single lump sum payment due in advance of the technology transfer. In most cases, however, the licensee makes running royalty payments based on a percentage of sales or actual use of the technology. When compensation is tied to actual use, the licensing agreement generally imposes strict record-keeping obligations on the licensee. The agreement also is likely to grant the licensor broad rights to inspect the records. It is common for compensation clauses to specify the currency in which royalty payments must be made. When they are to be made in a currency other than the one in which a licensee's sales were made, the agreement may stipulate a method for determining the exchange rate.

Duration

The term of the technology transfer agreement often depends on the bargaining strength of the parties. For instance, licensees may insist on long-term licenses to ensure they can recover their investments. In other cases, the duration of the agreement is determined by the nature of the intellectual property rights. Thus, an agreement transferring rights in patented equipment is not likely to exceed the life of the patent. The length of the arrangement frequently is governed by national law. Some nations impose minimum terms to ensure local licensees recover their investments, while others fix maximum limits and award the technology to the licensee at the expiration of the agreement.

Most licensing agreements recite the circumstances under which either party may terminate the relationship. For instance, a licensor might be able to rescind the contract if the licensee breaches the duty of secrecy or fails to make timely royalty payments. The agreement might give the licensee the right to terminate if the licensor fails to provide certain technical services or licenses the technology to another company in the licensee's territory.

REGULATION OF INTELLECTUAL PROPERTY

This section begins with a discussion of the national character of most licensing regulations. This is followed by a look at the differences in how the developed and developing nations regulate licensing agreements. Attention then turns to three basic methods of giving extraterritorial effect to domestic protections for intellectual property. Finally, the section closes with an overview of five international accords designed to harmonize intellectual property rights throughout the world.

National Character Global businesses often are overwhelmed by the costs and complexities involved in protecting their technology abroad. Intellectual property rights depend on national laws for both their existence and their level of protection. For example, when a company registers its trademark in the United States, it can exclude other businesses from using that symbol or term within U.S. territorial limits. However, unless it also has fully complied with Brazil's registration scheme, it cannot prevent a competitor from using the trademark there. If a Brazilian firm registers the trademark there before the U.S. company does, it can prevent the U.S. company from using the trademark in Brazil. Consider the following case.

■

AMGEN v. U.S. INTERNATIONAL TRADE COMMISSION
902 F.2d 1532 (Fed. Cir. 1990)

■ **FACTS** Erythropoietin is a hormone that controls the synthesis of red blood cells in bone marrow and is useful for treating patients suffering from anemia. Scientists from the emerging field of biotechnology have used recombinant DNA technology to produce genetically altered cells (host cells) that produce large amounts of erythropoietin. To simplify the recombinant DNA procedure, the particular DNA sequence responsible for the production of erythropoietin is isolated and removed from human cells. The isolated DNA sequence is then "recombined" with the DNA present in the host cells. As a result, the host cell is genetically altered so as to produce synthetic erythropoietin (rEPO). Amgen owned the U.S. patent for the recombinant DNA sequences, vectors, and host cells used to produce rEPO. This patent gave Amgen no rights over the product rEPO itself and no rights over any process of making rEPO. Chugai Pharmaceutical of Japan made rEPO overseas by a process that used the DNA sequencers, vectors, and host cells protected by Amgen's U.S. patent. It then imported the rEPO into the United States through Chugai Pharm U.S.A. (its U.S. subsidiary). Amgen complained that Chugai violated its U.S. patent rights by importing the rEPO into the United States.

■ **ISSUE** Does U.S. patent law protect against the importation of articles made abroad by a process in which a product protected by a U.S. patent is used?

■ **DECISION** No. The process Chugai performed abroad to produce the rEPO would have infringed Amgen's patent if it had been performed in the United States. Further, the U.S. patent laws prohibit the importation of products made abroad through a process that is protected by a U.S. process patent. However, those laws do not prevent the importation of goods made by a process that merely used abroad a product, apparatus, or material patented in the United States.

Licensing Restrictions

The national character of intellectual property protection has great significance for companies wishing to license their technology abroad. Unless their intellectual property rights are recognized in the country where they hope to do business, they have nothing to license. And even when their basic intellectual property rights are recognized by the host country, licensors must be alert if they hope to comply with the numerous restrictions countries place on licensing agreements. While these restrictions vary from country to country, some generalizations can be made. In particular, fewer licensing restrictions tend to be imposed by developed nations (technology exporters) than by developing nations (technology importers).

Developed Countries

In the developed world, antitrust laws often provide the greatest restrictions on technology licensing agreements. By nature a certain antagonism exists between antitrust enforcement and intellectual property protection; antitrust laws promote competition, while intellectual property laws grant limited monopolies to creative individuals. Many developed nations scrutinize licensing agreements that threaten to stifle competition more than is necessary to stimulate genuine research and development. Thus, licensing contracts that include severe territorial restrictions or exclusive dealing provisions may violate antitrust laws.

WINDSURFING INTERNATIONAL v. COMMISSION OF THE EUROPEAN COMMUNITIES
European Court of Justice, [1986] 2 E.C.R. 611

■ **FACTS** Windsurfing International manufactures sailboards. In the 1970s, the company extended its operations to Europe, where it submitted patent applications in Germany. Windsurfing's German patent application covered only the sailing rig for the sailboard and not the board. To manufacture and distribute its sailboards, Windsurfing concluded licensing relationships with several German undertakings. After a number of companies competing with Windsurfing's German licensees registered complaints, the European Commission investigated the licensing agreements. It ruled the following clauses in the licensing agreements violated the competition (antitrust) rules of the European Community:

1. The obligation on the licensees to exploit the licensed patents only for the manufacture of sailboards using boards that had been given Windsurfing's prior approval.

2. The obligation on the licensees to affix to boards offered for sale a notation stating "licensed by Windsurfing International."

Windsurfing argued that its approval was required for the boards to ensure they were not of inferior quality and did not interfere with the rights of other licensees. It further claimed the obligation on licensees to attach "licensed by Windsurfing International" on the boards did not distort competition because no consumer would infer from such a notice that the board was manufactured with Windsurfing's know-how, only that Windsurfing had issued a license to sell a complete sailboard.

■ **ISSUE**   Do the two clauses in Windsurfing's licensing agreements violate European competition rules?

■ **DECISION**   Yes. Standards of quality and safety in patent licensing agreements are exempted from the competition rules only if they relate to a product actually covered by the patent. Yet Windsurfing's German patent covers only the sailing rig and not the board. However, even if the patent did cover the complete sailboard, and therefore included the board, such controls must be based on objective criteria. If it were otherwise, the discretionary nature of these controls would enable a licensor to impose its own selection of models on the licensee. Despite Windsurfing's contention that the notice requirement was not intended to distort competition, it is nonetheless true that by requiring such a notice, Windsurfing encouraged uncertainty as to whether or not the board too was covered by the patent. It thereby diminished the consumer's confidence in the licensees so as to gain a competitive advantage for itself.

Most developed nations strictly regulate the export of products and technology that might be useful to their enemies. As a result, licensors of goods and information that can be adapted for military purposes must comply with elaborate governmental regulations or face civil and criminal liability. These export controls (discussed in Chapter 12) often impose extensive delays and financial burdens on licensors.

The developed nations also are actively involved in regulating **franchising** relationships. This form of technology licensing occurs when a licensor/franchisor permits a licensee/franchisee to use its trademark for the marketing of goods and services. In much of the developed world, franchisee organizations have persuaded legislators to impose extensive disclosure requirements on franchisors to ensure franchisees are fully apprised of the risks and profit potential of the franchising venture.

Developing Countries

The developing nations often view licensing agreements as a means of gaining access to modern technology. At the same time, they recognize that local licensees may be at a tremendous disadvantage when negotiating with multinational corporations. Further, countries suffering shortages of hard currency dislike licensing agreements that obligate licensees to make large royalty payments to a foreign licensor.

These concerns have motivated many developing nations to require the registration of agreements to license technology. Sometimes the registration must be completed to gain basic governmental approval of the licensing contract. On other occasions, a licensee will not be able to obtain the foreign exchange needed to make royalty payments unless the agreement has been registered. In either case, the registration requirement notifies regulators of the existence of a licensing agreement, providing an opportunity for government supervision of the relationship.

When a country suspects that foreign licensors wield superior bargaining power, it may intervene on behalf of local licensees. For instance, many governments limit royalty payments, the duration of the duty of confidentiality, and restrictions on a licensee's right to export licensed goods or services. Sometimes they insist the licensee be given complete control over the intellectual property within a certain time period.

Multinational corporations frequently are accused of filing for patent protection abroad and then failing to introduce the patented technology overseas. This effectively denies the foreign country of access to the patented articles or processes during the patent period. To ensure that they gain access to technological innovations, many lesser developed nations grant **compulsory licenses** that authorize local persons to work the patent.

Extraterritorial Enforcement

The limited reach of intellectual property laws (a country's laws are not effective beyond its borders) has motivated numerous countries to explore ways of giving extraterritorial protection to intellectual property. These efforts have taken the form of unilateral, bilateral, and multilateral initiatives.

Unilateral Action

The United States, in particular, has pursued the unilateral path by imposing trade sanctions on nations that fail to adequately protect the intellectual property rights of U.S. businesses. By erecting import barriers against goods from those countries, the United States hopes to pressure global compliance with U.S. conceptions of proper protection. This response has been heavily criticized by the rest of the world as being both heavy-handed and a clear violation of GATT's prohibition against unilateral reprisals in trade disputes. (The nature of these trade restrictions and their GATT legality are discussed in Chapters 9 and 11.)

Bilateral Action

A growing number of countries are pursuing bilateral efforts to ensure the fair protection of intellectual property. For instance, the United States has negotiated a number of bilateral investment treaties (**BITs**) that obligate various trading partners to respect the intellectual property rights of U.S. businesses that engage in direct investment or licensing activities in those countries. (BITs are discussed in Chapter 1.) In recent years, the United States has negotiated BITs with the countries of Eastern Europe and the former Soviet Union as a precondition to economic aid and access to the U.S. market. Similar agreements have been reached with China, Taiwan, Singapore, and Indonesia.

Multilateral Action

Although there is no single global scheme for the protection of intellectual property and licensing agreements, multilateral progress has been achieved on a regional basis. For instance, 14 European nations, through the Convention on the Grant of European Patents, have created a European Patent Office that issues patents recognized in member states. All of the European Community nations (except Ireland and Portugal) have signed the convention. To obtain a European patent, the applicant must be a national of one of the parties to the convention. However, U.S. companies may become eligible by applying through a European subsidiary.

Canada, Mexico, and the United States, through the NAFTA negotiations, have made substantial progress in harmonizing intellectual property regulations within North America. The treaty prohibits discriminatory treatment in the regulation of intellectual property. Further, it is the only international treaty that extends protection to trade secrets.

Global Cooperation   Global efforts to harmonize intellectual property protection have culminated in the signing of several important international conventions. Although these agreements do not preempt national laws, they have established general guidelines that facilitate the licensing of technology throughout the world. The most important of these international agreements are the Paris Convention, the Patent Cooperation Treaty, the Madrid Agreement, the Berne Convention, and the Universal Copyright Convention.

The Paris Convention

The most important treaty governing the international protection for patents and trademarks is the *Paris Convention for the Protection of Intellectual Property.* Signed by over 100 countries (including the United States), the Paris Convention has two fundamental principles. First, under **national treatment,** each member country promises to extend to foreigners the same patent and trademark rights that it gives its nationals. Second, the treaty establishes a 12-month **right of priority** for a person who filed a patent application in another member country. (The priority right lasts six months for trademarks.) Thus, once a company files for a patent in the United States, it may wait up to 12 months before filing in any other Paris Convention country. As long as it files within this grace period, its patent application is given priority over other applicants who filed before it in the other countries.

While the convention does not eliminate the need to separately file in each country where protection is desired, it does grant intellectual property owners a reasonable time to determine where protection is needed. Further, before the treaty, some patents were denied overseas after an application had been filed in the United States because the invention no longer was considered novel. The Paris Convention eliminates this result as long as the inventor applies for the additional patents within the priority period.

The Patent Cooperation Treaty

Over 40 countries (including the United States) are parties to the *Patent Cooperation Treaty.* An applicant from any member country may file an international patent application that designates the member states in which it seeks protection. After this filing, an international search is undertaken to determine the patentability of the applicant's creation. Applicants are given 20 months after the date of the initial filing to comply with the patent laws of each nation where they are seeking protection.

The Madrid Agreement

The *Madrid Agreement Concerning the International Registration of Marks* has been ratified by over 30 countries. Under the Madrid Agreement, an applicant from a member state may file a single application for trademark protection with the International Bureau of the World Intellectual Property Organization. The registration then is forwarded to each member country. The trademark automatically becomes effective in every member country except those that reject the application within 12 months.

Before the international bureau will accept a trademark application, it must have been registered in the applicant's country of origin. The United States refused to ratify the Madrid Agreement because of its objections to this provision. U.S. officials argued that this prerequisite favored applicants from countries that had the least stringent trademark requirements. U.S. businesses still may take advantage of the Madrid Agreement by establishing a subsidiary in one of its member states and applying for trademark protection through that country.

The Berne Convention

More than 80 countries (including the United States) have signed the *Berne Convention for the Protection of Literary and Artistic Works*. This treaty requires all member states to extend copyright protection to the published and unpublished literary and artistic works of authors who are nationals of any ratifying country. Authors from nonmember countries may have their works protected if they either first publish in a member country or publish in a member state within 30 days of publishing elsewhere. Copyrights must be protected for at least the life of the author plus 50 years.

The Berne Convention requires its members to follow the principle of national treatment in providing copyright protection. Further, it prohibits conditioning copyright protection on notice or registration once a work is protected in another member state. However, the treaty has no effect on the copyright restrictions a member country places on its own nationals.

The Universal Copyright Convention

China, the former Soviet Union, and the United States originally rejected the Berne Convention (the United States finally signed in 1988). As an alternative they established the *Universal Copyright Convention*. Under its terms, member states generally must protect a copyright for at least the life of the author plus 25 years. However, nations that already had more restrictive terms for certain classes of works could limit the copyright terms to 25 years from the date of first publication. Countries that are members of both the Berne Convention and the Universal Copyright Convention must comply with the terms of the Berne Convention wherever the two treaties conflict.

Currently, more than 80 countries are parties to the Universal Copyright Convention. They agree to extend national treatment to the published works of nationals from other member states. The contracting states further promise to extend adequate

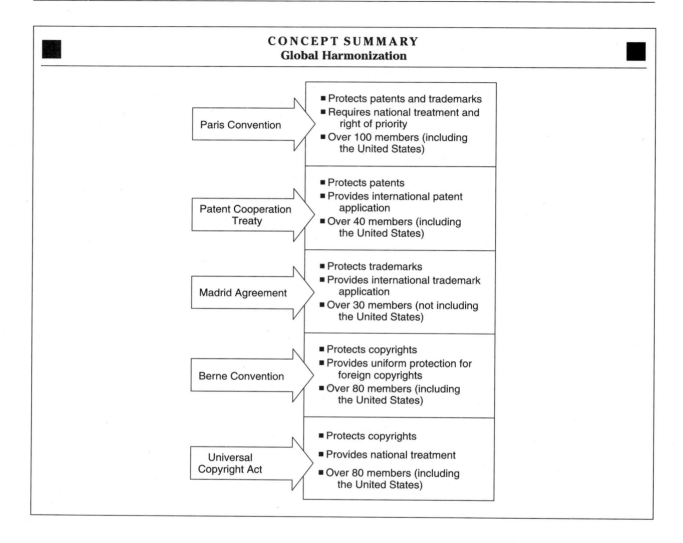

CONCEPT SUMMARY
Global Harmonization

Paris Convention
- Protects patents and trademarks
- Requires national treatment and right of priority
- Over 100 members (including the United States)

Patent Cooperation Treaty
- Protects patents
- Provides international patent application
- Over 40 members (including the United States)

Madrid Agreement
- Protects trademarks
- Provides international trademark application
- Over 30 members (not including the United States)

Berne Convention
- Protects copyrights
- Provides uniform protection for foreign copyrights
- Over 80 members (including the United States)

Universal Copyright Act
- Protects copyrights
- Provides national treatment
- Over 80 members (including the United States)

and effective protection to the literary, scientific, and artistic works of authors and other copyright owners.

ENFORCEMENT ISSUES

Businesses lose billions of dollars each year to commercial counterfeiters. While counterfeiting is rampant in all industries, in recent years there has been a virtual explosion of piracy involving video and audio recordings and computer software. This section explores several methods of enforcing intellectual property rights against unfair competition from foreign pirates. The chapter closes with a brief look at the special problems raised by gray market imports.

Section 43 of the Lanham Act

Section 43(a) of the Lanham Act provides general protection against unfair competition. It permits U.S. commercial enterprises to sue competitors who engage in a wide variety of false or misleading acts. In particular, whenever a firm deceives consumers by imitating another company's trademarks or trade names it might have to pay civil damages.

Section 337 of the Tariff Act

Section 337 of the Tariff Act prohibits the importation of goods that infringe a valid U.S. patent, trademark, or copyright. Foreign goods are refused entry into the United States if the International Trade Commission finds: (a) a U.S. company possesses valid intellectual property rights; (b) the imported goods violate those rights; and (c) there currently is, or soon will be, an industry in the United States relating to the intellectual property. (Section 337 is discussed more fully in Chapter 11.)

The Trademark Counterfeiting Act

Congress strengthened the weapons against international counterfeiting through passage of the *Trademark Counterfeiting Act of 1984*. Under this legislation, international pirates can be sentenced up to 15 years in prison and fined as much as $1 million ($5 million for corporations). Further, it permits the U.S. government to seize and destroy the counterfeit goods.

Gray Market Goods

Up to this point, the discussion in this section has focused on *black market* goods; that is, imports that are counterfeit or otherwise violate a domestic firm's intellectual property rights. However, when a manufacturer sells goods overseas or licenses its trademark abroad, it runs the risk that items bearing its trademark will find their way back into the United States and compete with its domestically produced goods. This phenomenon is known as the **gray market.** Thus, a gray market good is a genuine product bearing a valid U.S. trademark that is bought overseas and then resold in the United States by unauthorized importers and distributors.

Gray Market Sources

For the gray market to arise, the overseas price of the goods generally must be much lower than the domestic price. Sometimes this occurs because of a distress sale abroad. It also may stem from a conscious program of dumping goods overseas (price discrimination). In many instances, the price differential is caused by fluctuations in foreign currency exchange rates. Finally, some gray marketers are *free riders* who sell goods identical to the trademarked articles but cut costs by neglecting to provide the presale and postsale services (e.g., advertising, repairs) required of domestically licensed dealers.

ETHICAL IMPLICATIONS   Some price discounters are able to sell gray market goods at low prices by free riding on the marketing efforts of U.S. trademark owners. Is this practice ethical?

Gray Market Scenarios

There are three general contexts within which the gray market arises:

Case 1. In the **prototypical** gray market scenario, a domestic firm purchases from an independent foreign company the U.S. trademark for foreign-produced goods. This gives the domestic firm the right to register and use the trademark in connection with its domestic sales of the foreign-made goods. The foreign company then imports the trademarked goods and distributes them in the United States or sells them abroad to a third party who resells them in the United States. If the foreign manufacturer (licensor) is permitted to import and distribute the trademarked goods in the United States, the domestic firm (licensee) will be faced with stiff intrabrand competition. This same threat occurs when a third party buys the goods overseas and resells them in the United States. In either situation, the gray market jeopardizes the U.S. firm's investment.

Case 2. This situation, known as the **common control** scenario, arises in three ways. First, a foreign parent corporation may license the use of its trademark in the United States to one of its U.S. subsidiaries. Second, a U.S. trademark holder (the parent corporation) may license one of its foreign subsidiaries to manufacture the goods overseas. Third, a U.S. firm may produce the U.S. trademarked goods abroad through an overseas division. (A U.S. firm and its overseas division are considered to be the same legal entity.) The goods are then imported into the United States where they are sold in competition with the U.S. trademarked goods.

Case 3. In the **authorized use** scenario, a U.S. trademark owner grants to an independent foreign company the license to use the trademark in a particular location overseas. Generally, the trademark holder conditions the trademark license on the foreign manufacturer's promise not to import the trademarked goods into the United States. If the foreign licensee or some third party imports and distributes the foreign-made goods in the United States, they will compete with the goods of the U.S. trademark holder.

Legal Responses to the Gray Market Problem

Domestically licensed dealers complain that gray market goods unfairly undercut their sales efforts. In particular, they assert that gray marketers ultimately destroy the reputation of the U.S. trademark by failing to provide consumers with presale information and postsale service. Discount stores, on the other hand, argue that consumers greatly benefit from the availability of low-priced imports.

When the U.S. Customs Service refused to block the importation of all gray market goods, an association of U.S. trademark holders filed suit. In the case that follows, *K Mart Corp. v. Cartier,* the U.S. Supreme Court examines when gray market imports should be prohibited.

■

K MART CORP. v. CARTIER
486 U.S. 281 (U.S. Sup.Ct. 1988)

■ **FACTS** A gray market good is a foreign-manufactured good, bearing a valid U.S. trademark, that is imported without the consent of the U.S. trademark holder. The prototypical gray market case (Case 1) is a domestic firm that purchases from an independent foreign firm the rights to register and use the latter's trademark as a U.S. trademark and to sell its foreign-manufactured products in the United States. The second context (Case 2) arises when a domestic firm registers the U.S. trademark for goods that are manufactured abroad by an affiliated manufacturer. (The companies are under common legal control.) In the third context (Case 3), the domestic holder of a U.S. trademark "authorizes" an independent foreign manufacturer to use the trademark overseas. Section 526 of the Tariff Act prohibits importing "into the United States any *merchandise of foreign manufacture* if such merchandise . . . bears a trademark *owned by* a citizen of, or by a corporation . . . created within, the United States, and registered in the Patent and Trademark Office . . . unless written consent of the owner . . . is produced at the time of making entry." However, the Customs Service regulations implementing Section 526 furnished "common control" (Case 2) and "authorized use" (Case 3) exceptions to this ban on gray market imports.

■ **ISSUE** Are the Custom Service's common control and authorized use exceptions consistent with Section 526 of the Tariff Act?

■ **DECISION** Yes and no. If an agency regulation is not in conflict with the plain language of the statute it implements, the courts must give deference to the agency's interpretation of the statute. Under this standard of review, the Customs Service clearly may interpret Section 526 to bar importation of gray market goods in the Case 1 context. Similarly, it may carve out a statutory exception for gray market imports that arise under the Case 2 situation. In the common control scenario, there is sufficient ambiguity over who "owns" the U.S. trademark and if the imports are "merchandise of foreign manufacture" that the Customs Service is entitled to choose any reasonable interpretation of the statute. However, the authorized use exception cannot stand. Under no reasonable construction of Section 526 can goods made in a foreign country by an independent foreign manufacturer be excluded from the reach of the statute. Thus, the Customs Service must prohibit the importation of gray market goods arising in the Case 3 context.

Section 42 of the Lanham Act

After the *K Mart* decision, U.S. trademark owners insisted that *Section 42 of the Lanham Act* prohibited the importation of gray market goods. That statute provides that foreign-manufactured goods that *copy or simulate* a U.S. registered trademark shall not be admitted into the United States. However, as with Section 526, the U.S. Customs Service declined to bar imported goods when the foreign producer and U.S. trademark owner were under common control. In the case that follows, *Lever Brothers v. United States*, a U.S. court of appeals examines the legality of a common control exception to Section 42 of the Lanham Act.

LEVER BROTHERS COMPANY v. UNITED STATES
981 F.2d 1330 (D.C. Cir. 1993)

■ **FACTS** Lever Brothers Company (Lever U.S.), a U.S. company, and its British affiliate, Lever Brothers Limited (Lever U.K.), both manufacture deodorant soap under the "Shield" trademark. While the trademarks are registered in each country, the products have been formulated differently to suit local tastes and circumstances. Unlike the British product, the U.S. soap lathers more, smells different, has a bacteriostat that enhances its de-

odorant properties, and contains colorants that have been certified by the FDA. Further, the packaging of the two soaps is somewhat different. Lever U.S. complained that the unauthorized influx of the British soap created substantial consumer confusion and deception in the United States in violation of Section 42 of the Lanham Act. However, the Customs Service permitted importation of the British soap under its common control exception, which provided that foreign goods bearing U.S. trademarks are not forbidden when the foreign and domestic trademark owners are subject to common ownership or control. Lever U.S. brought suit, arguing that the Customs Service's common control exception violated the terms of the Lanham Act when the foreign-made goods are materially different from their U.S. counterparts.

■ **ISSUE** Should the Customs Service be required to exclude the British soap from the United States?

■ **DECISION** Yes. There is nothing in the language or legislative history of Section 42 suggesting that Congress intended to allow third parties to import physically different trademarked goods that are manufactured and sold abroad by a foreign affiliate of a U.S. trademark holder. Customs argued that the British soap did not "copy or simulate" the U.S. trademark because a trademark applied by a foreign firm subject to the common control of the domestic trademark owner is by definition genuine, regardless of whether or not the goods are identical. This argument is fatally flawed. It rests on the false premise that foreign trademarks applied to foreign goods are genuine in the United States. Trademarks applied to physically different foreign goods are not genuine from the viewpoint of the American consumer. Thus, Section 42 of the Lanham Act bars the importation of physically different foreign goods bearing a trademark identical to a valid U.S. trademark, regardless of the validity of the trademark's genuine character abroad or the affiliation between the producing firms.

CONCEPT SUMMARY Gray Market Scenarios		
Case 1 Prototypical Scenario	Domestic firm purchases U.S. trademark for foreign-made goods.	Customs Service *may prohibit* importation of gray market goods.
Case 2 Common Control Scenario	a. Foreign parent corporation licenses trademark to domestic subsidiary. b. Domestic parent corporation licenses foreign subsidiary to produce U.S. trademarked goods overseas. c. Domestic firm produces trademarked goods overseas through a corporate division.	Customs Service *may permit* importation of gray market goods, *unless* foreign-made goods are materially different.
Case 3 Authorized Use Scenario	Domestic firm licenses an independent foreign firm to use U.S. trademark overseas.	Customs Service *must prohibit* importation of gray market goods

---

QUESTIONS AND PROBLEM CASES

1. What is the basic difference between the U.S. patent procedure and the approach followed by most nations?

2. What is the gray market? Explain how it arises and what U.S. firms can do to offset it.

3. Under what circumstances may an individual be held liable for misappropriation of a trade secret?

4. What is meant by a grant-back clause?

5. Atkins, a Massachusetts corporation, was the owner of the distinctive trademark "B & W" used in connection with the sale of stereo speakers in the United States. The English manufacturer of the speakers, B & W Loudspeakers, Ltd., originally registered the trademarks in England. It assigned the

U.S. rights to them to Atkins, which registered the trademarks with the U.S. Patent Office. Atkins complained that Sixth Avenue Electronics City, a New York corporation, was importing and selling speakers bearing the B & W trademark through its retail stores in the United States. Sixth Avenue contended its sale of speakers under the B & W trademark was not illegal because the goods were genuine, having been lawfully produced and trademarked in England. Did Sixth Avenue's importation and sale of the speakers unlawfully infringe Atkins' trademark rights?

6. Rolfe and Gary Christopher were hired by persons unknown to take aerial photographs of new construction at a plant that Du Pont was building to exploit a highly secret unpatented process for producing methanol. The process gave Du Pont a competitive advantage over other producers. All the photographs were taken from public airspace and violated no governmental aviation standard. Further, the Christophers did not have any confidential relationship with Du Pont and did not violate any laws while taking the photographs. Du Pont sued the Christophers for misappropriation of its trade secrets. Are the Christophers liable for misappropriation of Du Pont's trade secrets?

7. Windsurfing International owned a U.S. patent covering a sailboard. AMF Incorporated alleged that Windsurfing had misused its patent through a restriction in its patent licensing agreements that stated: "LICENSEE hereby acknowledges that the terms WINDSURFER, WINDSURFING, and WIND SURF . . . are all valid trademarks. LICENSEE hereby agrees not to use . . . (these) trademarks . . . in any form or fashion in its company name or any of its literature or advertising or promotional material or on any products whatsoever." Has Windsurfing abused its patent rights by including this provision in its patent licensing agreements?

8. Rano, a professional photographer and citizen of Great Britain, entered into an oral copyright license agreement with Sipa Press, a French corporation that is a photograph distribution syndicate. Rano granted Sipa a nonexclusive license of unspecified duration to reproduce, distribute, sell, and authorize others to reproduce, distribute, and sell his photographs. In return, Sipa agreed to store and develop the negatives and to pay 50 percent of the net royalties generated from its sales and distributions.

After eight years, Rano attempted to terminate the licensing agreement, claiming Sipa failed to pay royalties in a timely manner. At the time Rano sought to terminate the agreement, Sipa had paid approximately 99.9 percent of the royalties owed him, excluding royalties due for photographs published in the United States during the previous year. Of those Sipa had paid 86.8 percent of the royalties due. Under the governing law, Rano could not terminate the licensing agreement for 35 years unless Sipa materially breached the agreement. Should Rano be permitted to terminate the licensing agreement?

9. Balmain, a Netherlands corporation, filed for U.S. registration of the trademark *Ivoire De Balmain* for fragrances and related cosmetics. A foreign applicant seeking U.S. trademark registration must comply with Section 44 of the Lanham Act, which says: "No registration of a mark in the United States by a . . . (foreign person) shall be granted until such mark has been registered in the country of origin of the applicant, unless the applicant alleges use in commerce." Balmain submitted a certified copy of its Benelux registration for *Ivoire De Balmain* to the U.S. Patent and Trademark Office (PTO). Afterwards Balmain assigned the U.S. application for registration to De Luxe, N.V., another foreign company. The PTO refused to register this assignment unless De Luxe provided evidence that it also was the current holder of the Benelux registration. De Luxe argued that a foreign applicant need only be the owner of its home country registration at the time when the U.S. application is originally filed. Is De Luxe entitled to U.S. registration of the trademark despite the fact that it does not own the foreign registration?

10. Weil Ceramics & Glass, Inc., was the wholly owned, U.S. subsidiary of Lladro Exportadora, S.A., a Spanish corporation, which manufactures fine porcelain in Spain. Weil registered the Lladro trademark in the United States and became the exclusive distributor of Lladro porcelain in the United States. Later, Jalyn Corporation legally obtained porcelain in Spain from Lladro distributors and sold it in the United States without the consent of Weil. Should the U.S. Customs Service, under the authority of Section 526 of the Tariff Act, prevent Jalyn from importing and selling Lladro porcelain in the United States?

Competition Law

INTRODUCTION

With the growth of national and international markets, the world has witnessed an important development on the economic scene: the emergence of large industrial combines and trusts. Many of these huge business entities engage in practices aimed at destroying their competitors. The general purpose of antitrust law is to encourage and protect competition by controlling the behavior and structure of these organizations.

The prime focus of U.S. antitrust enforcement is to protect American consumers from anticompetitive conduct. In an increasingly global environment, this sometimes entails bringing antitrust actions against foreign defendants or prohibiting conduct that occurs outside of the actual territory of this country. The United States is not alone in its maintenance of domestic and international competition through the enforcement of antitrust laws. Most of the industrial nations have such legislation. International businesses must be more and more alert to the reach of these antitrust laws as they expand their operations around the world.

Chapter Overview   The topic of international antitrust cannot be fully investigated in a single chapter. Accordingly, this chapter provides no more than a general overview of the most significant aspects of antitrust enforcement affecting international business transactions. The prime focus of this coverage is the major U.S. antitrust statutes—the **Sherman Act,** the **Clayton Act,** and the **Robinson-Patman Act**—and their applicability to business activities around the globe. Attention then turns to a brief examination of antitrust enforcement by the European Community. The chapter closes with a glimpse at several international efforts designed to harmonize antitrust enforcement throughout the world.

PROCEDURAL ISSUES

Criminal Penalties   Under U.S. law, the Sherman Act makes contracts in restraint of trade and monopolization illegal. It provides *criminal* penalties for violations of its provisions (up to a $350,000 fine and/or three years in jail for individuals and up to a $10 million fine for corporate violators). It also gives the federal courts broad injunctive powers to remedy antitrust violations. The courts can order convicted defendants to divest themselves of the stock or assets of other companies or to divorce themselves from a functional level of their operations (e.g., they can order a manufacturer to sell a captive retail chain). In extreme cases, the courts can order dissolution—force the defendant to liquidate its assets and go out of business.

Civil Liability   Private individuals who have been injured by antitrust violations have strong incentives to sue under the *civil* provisions of the U.S. antitrust laws. A successful antitrust plaintiff may recover **treble damages** (three times actual losses) plus costs and attorney's fees. This can mean tremendous potential liability for antitrust defendants.

**Non-U.S.
Enforcement
Systems**

Japan

The penalty and private action provisions of U.S. antitrust law substantially differ from the enforcement systems that otherwise predominate throughout most of the world. For instance, in 1992, Japan raised its maximum penalty for violations of its anti-monopoly law to 100 million yen ($769,000). That is only one thirteenth of the U.S. criminal penalty. (Previously, it was only $38,000.) In Japan, the government's power to break up cartels is preferred to monetary fines, and the Japanese legal system makes criminal prosecutions extremely difficult. In fact, between 1947 and 1992, criminal charges against antitrust violators in Japan were brought only twice.

The European Community

The procedural aspects of European competition law also differ markedly from U.S. enforcement measures. Like most of the world, the European Community does not provide for private causes of action for damages. Instead, any anticompetitive agreement that violates European law is simply declared null and void. However, the European Commission is empowered to impose fines of up to 1 million European Currency Units (about $1.15 million) or up to 10 percent of the annual turnover of business firms that violate the European competition laws. The absence of the incentives to sue raised by the availability of private causes of action and the prospects of recovering treble damages may greatly explain the reduced incidence of antitrust litigation outside of the United States.

EXTRATERRITORIAL REACH OF U.S. ANTITRUST

Antitrust violations that occur within the territory of the United States (whether committed by U.S. or foreign entities) fall squarely within the jurisdictional reach of the U.S. antitrust laws. However, U.S. antitrust enforcement is not limited to conduct that occurs within U.S. borders. The Sherman Act has been interpreted to reach actions of foreign entities that have an anticompetitive effect in the United States as well as acts that limit American access to markets abroad. In general, U.S. courts have followed the rule that before they exert jurisdiction over conduct that has an extraterritorial effect, the behavior must be shown to have had a substantial effect on U.S. commerce.

**Foreign Trade
Antitrust
Improvements Act**

Responding to the controversy surrounding the extraterritorial application of U.S. antitrust laws, Congress passed the *Foreign Trade Antitrust Improvements Act* in 1982. Specifically, this statute provides that the Sherman Act shall not apply to nonimport trade unless such conduct has a direct, substantial, and reasonably foreseeable effect on trade or commerce within the United States, on import trade, or on the activities of U.S. exporters. While this act is specifically confined to Sherman Act violations involving nonimport trade with foreign nations, the U.S. Department of Justice, under its enforcement guidelines, applies the standard to import commerce and mergers as well.

McGLINCHY v. SHELL CHEMICAL CO.
845 F.2d 802 (9th Cir. 1988)

■ **FACTS** Dan-De Products, owned and operated by McGlinchy, contracted with Shell Chemical. The agreement established Dan-De as Shell's exclusive representative for the promotion and solicitation of orders for PB pipe resin throughout Southeast Asia. In 1982, Shell notified Dan-De that these various contracts would be terminated. McGlinchy and Dan-De brought suit against Shell under Sections 1 and 2 of the Sherman Act, claiming Shell's refusal to deal injured Dan-De's Southeast Asian operations. Shell moved to dismiss the suit on the grounds that the U.S. courts did not have jurisdiction to hear the antitrust claim.

■ **ISSUE** Do the U.S. courts have jurisdiction to hear this antitrust claim?

■ **DECISION** No. McGlinchy and Dan-De have failed to show the requisite antitrust injury to competition. The antitrust laws were enacted for the protection of competition, not competitors. The elimination of a single competitor, without more, does not prove anticompetitive effect. Here, other than establishing injury to itself, Dan-De has only claimed injury to customers or potential customers in Southeast Asia. The *Foreign Trade Antitrust Improvements Act* makes clear that the Sherman Act reaches only conduct that has a "direct, substantial, and reasonably foreseeable" effect on the U.S. domestic market, import commerce, or U.S. export trade. Thus, it exempts from U.S. antitrust law conduct that lacks such domestic effects, even where the conduct originates in the United States or involves U.S.-owned entities operating abroad. Dan-De's claim relates only to foreign commerce without the requisite domestic anticompetitive effect.

Jurisdiction over Foreign Firms

Starting in 1988, the Justice Department instituted a policy of limiting its extraterritorial enforcement of the antitrust laws against foreign firms only to anticompetitive conduct that had a direct impact on U.S. consumers. This changed in 1992 when the policy was broadened to include actions against foreign cartels that restrict U.S. exports overseas. Thus, as it now stands, the U.S. antitrust laws reach the activities of U.S. or foreign firms, regardless of where the anticompetitive restraint occurred, if the conduct has a **direct, substantial, and reasonably foreseeable effect** on U.S. commerce, import trade, or export trade.

Extraterritoriality and International Law

The Territorial Principle

International law generally recognizes the right of a nation to exercise jurisdiction over persons and property within its national borders under a concept known as the **territorial principle.** Emanating from this universally accepted notion is a more controversial idea known as the **effects test.** This doctrine suggests that a nation may exert jurisdiction over conduct that occurs outside of its borders if that behavior has adverse effects within its territory.

The expressed intent of the United States to extend its antitrust jurisdiction to punish foreign firms that injure U.S. overseas exports has been condemned by much of the world as violative of the territorial principle. Likewise, this extension of antitrust enforcement is out of step with the jurisdictional reach that most other nations grant to their own antitrust laws. For instance, the European Community generally limits its antitrust powers to conduct by undertakings within the European Community that affect intra-Community trade. Although the European Commission has levied fines against non-Community companies, these occurred because those enterprises effectively controlled European subsidiaries that were limiting competition within the European Community.

Retaliation against U.S. Antitrust

Much of the world has responded to the revised U.S. approach with a chorus of criticism and threats of reprisals. Such retaliation is not unprecedented. In the recent past, several nations implemented **blocking legislation** that prohibited the submission of documents necessary for U.S. antitrust investigations or the enforcement of such judgments. Further, some nations enacted **clawback** provisions that permitted foreign companies to claim U.S. assets within that country in order to offset antitrust damages levied by U.S. courts.

Mindful of these possibilities, U.S. governmental officials pledged to be cautious about applying antitrust laws to situations outside of the country. Thus, the primary enforcement activities probably will be confined to foreign subsidiaries or branch offices that are actually operating within the United States.

**Limits on
Extraterritoriality**

Sovereign Immunity

When foreign governments are involved in commercial activities affecting U.S. competitors, our antitrust policy may be at odds with our foreign policy. Accordingly, the *Foreign Sovereign Immunities Act* of 1976 provides that the governmental actions of foreign sovereigns and their agents are exempt from antitrust liability. The commercial activities of foreign sovereigns, however, are not included within this **sovereign immunity** doctrine. Significant international controversy exists over the proper criteria for determining when a governmental activity is commercial.

Act of State Doctrine

The **act of state** doctrine provides that a U.S. court should not adjudicate a politically sensitive dispute that would require the court to determine the legality of a sovereign act by a foreign nation. This doctrine is based on the notion that any such judicial examination of the laws of sovereign nations would raise foreign policy issues better left to the executive branch of government. Under its antitrust enforcement guidelines, the U.S. Department of Justice will not pursue an antitrust action involving foreign jurisdictions without first ascertaining that there would be no conflict between the antitrust interests of the United States and the policies of the foreign nation.

■

W. S. KIRKPATRICK & CO. v. ENVIRONMENTAL TECTONICS CORPORATION
110 S.Ct. 701 (U.S. Sup. Ct. 1990)

■ **FACTS**   W. S. Kirkpatrick, Inc., hired Akindele, a Nigerian national, to act as its local agent in all matters pertaining to Kirkpatrick's bid for selling aircraft equipment to the Nigerian Air Force. On Akindele's advice, Kirkpatrick arranged to bribe various Nigerian political and military officials to gain their approval of Kirkpatrick's bid. Kirkpatrick made over $1.7 million in such payments. When Environmental Tectonics Corporation (ETC) discovered that Kirkpatrick had received the contract, despite the fact that ETC's bid was considerably lower, it investigated. After uncovering the bribes, ETC brought an antitrust action in the U.S. courts. Kirkpatrick argued that ETC's antitrust suit was barred by the act of state doctrine.

■ **ISSUE** Should ETC's suit be barred by the act of state doctrine?

■ **DECISION** No. The act of state doctrine does not establish an exception for cases and controversies that may embarrass foreign governments but merely requires that, in the process of deciding, the acts of foreign sovereigns taken within their own jurisdiction shall be deemed valid. The doctrine has no application to the present case because the validity of no foreign sovereign act is at issue.

Sovereign Compulsion

Closely related to the act of state doctrine is the foreign **sovereign compulsion** defense to U.S. antitrust jurisdiction. Under this doctrine, private parties may be excused from complying with our antitrust laws when their anticompetitive conduct has been directed or compelled by a foreign government. This defense serves two purposes. First, like the act of state doctrine, it insists that courts give due deference to the laws and policies of sovereign nations. And, second, it protects U.S. and foreign businesses from being punished for anticompetitive conduct that was not voluntary. The U.S. Department of Justice imposes two requirements on private firms before they may qualify for the sovereign compulsion defense: (1) The foreign government must have compelled the anticompetitive action under the threat of some significant penalty. The fact that the behavior is merely encouraged or permitted is not sufficient to support the exemption from antitrust. (2) The sovereign compulsion defense does not apply when the anticompetitive conduct has occurred primarily within the territory of the United States.

Frequently, a U.S. or foreign firm may have lobbied for the foreign governmental mandate to engage in anticompetitive behavior. The issue then arises whether this active solicitation prohibits the private business from availing itself of the sovereign compulsion defense. Under the **Noerr Doctrine,** U.S. courts permit businesses to lobby U.S. governmental officials for legislation that may harm their competitors or otherwise limit competition. While the U.S. Supreme Court has never ruled on whether this exemption applies to the lobbying of foreign governments by U.S. or foreign firms, the Justice Department follows a policy of not prosecuting in cases where legitimate lobbying has prompted the anticompetitive compulsion.

Export Trading Companies

As the U.S. trade balance worsened and its imports began to exceed its exports, the importance of facilitating exports was recognized. One response to this was passage of the *Export Trading Company Act* of 1982. This act allows exporters whose goods or services will not be resold in the United States to apply to the Department of Commerce for a "certificate of review." If the exporter's activities will not unduly restrain trade or affect domestic prices nor unfairly compete against other exporters of the same type of goods, the Commerce Department, with the concurrence of the Justice Department, issues the certificate.

	CONCEPT SUMMARY **Extraterritorial Application of U.S. Antitrust**	
Actions Must Have:	Direct, substantial, and reasonably foreseeable effect on U.S. commerce, U.S. imports, or U.S. exports	
Will Not Reach:	Noncommercial, foreign governmental actions	(Sovereign immunity)
	Politically sensitive, foreign governmental policies better left to the executive branch	(Act of state doctrine)
	Overseas private activity compelled by foreign sovereigns	(Sovereign compulsion)
	Anticompetitive lobbying activities	(Noerr Doctrine)
Gives Lenient Treatment to:	Certified U.S. exporting activities	(Export Trading Company Act)

For example, in 1992, the National Pork Producers Council used the *Export Trading Company Act* to launch a trade consortium designed to expand global demand for U.S. pork products. By securing a certificate of review, the various competitors that make up the consortium could be permitted to share market data and prices as part of their strategy to globalize their operations. Or they might combine certain operations to reduce the costs of shipping, processing, and packaging exports. Without a certificate of review, such horizontal collusion clearly would violate the Sherman Act.

The export trade certificate imparts a presumption of legality on the certified conduct of the export trading company and, even if an injured party can prove that a violation has occurred, it may receive only actual (rather than treble) damages. These safeguards apply only to the conduct described within the scope of the certificate and, if the certificate was obtained by fraud, it offers no protection. Finally, the Commerce Department may modify or revoke an export trade certificate if it determines the trading company is no longer complying with the statutory requirements for obtaining the certificate. Thus, if it was found that the American pork consortium was using the shared information or its joint operations to limit competition in the United States, the certificate would be revoked.

SECTION 1 OF THE SHERMAN ACT

Introduction

Section 1 of the Sherman Act provides:

> *Every contract, combination in the form of trust or otherwise, or conspiracy, in restraint of trade or commerce among the several states, or with foreign nations is declared to be illegal.*

A contract is any agreement, express or implied, between two or more persons to restrain competition; a combination is a continuing partnership in restraint of trade; and a conspiracy occurs when two or more persons join to restrain trade.

Joint Action   The purpose of Section 1 is to attack **joint action** in restraint of trade. Accordingly, unilateral actions, even if they have an anticompetitive effect, do not violate Section 1. For instance, a wholesaler may "suggest" a retail outlet sell an item at a certain price. As long as the two businesses did not "agree" that the goods would be sold at that price, Section 1 has not been violated. Further, a manufacturer may terminate a dealer who has failed to follow a "suggested marketing practice" (e.g., selling below the suggested resale price or failing to provide a service department) even though such a practice may tend to raise prices and lower competition. Such a unilateral refusal to deal is not joint action and therefore cannot be prohibited by Section 1.

Determining when a court will infer an agreement from the actions of the defendants is a constant problem for businesses. Some areas are fairly clear-cut. For example, it has long been held that a corporation cannot conspire with itself or with its employees. And the Supreme Court has ruled that a corporation could not conspire with a wholly owned subsidiary. Consignments have also been held to be unilateral action. A consignment agreement is one in which the owner of goods delivers them to another who is to act as the owner's agent in selling the goods. If a manufacturer delivers all goods to its dealers on a consignment basis, it can lawfully fix the price of those goods since the goods remain its property and are not the property of the dealers. U.S. courts appear to be more likely to infer joint action if the defendants are both competitors (as opposed to dealings between a supplier and a distributor) and/ or if the dealings involve discussion of price.

ETHICAL IMPLICATIONS   An agreement between a manufacturer and an independent distributor fixing the retail price at which the manufacturer's products will be sold to the public would be illegal joint action. However, because of the express language in Section 1, a suggestion by the manufacturer (which was complied with by the distributor) would be perfectly legal since it would be unilateral action. Yet if the suggestion is strongly worded, the ultimate effect would be the same as an agreement. Is it ethical to circumvent Section 1 through such verbal gymnastics?

Section 1 Analysis   After a finding of joint action, the court must examine the nature of the alleged violation to determine its legal status. Such joint action is treated as either a **per se** or a **rule of reason** violation. Per se activities are automatically illegal, while the legality of a rule of reason action can be determined only after examining the behavior's ultimate effect on competition.

Per Se Restraints   When faced with the difficult problem of deciding what kinds of joint action amounted to a restraint of trade, the courts concluded some kinds of behavior always have a negative effect on competition that can never be excused or justified. These kinds of acts are classed as per se illegal; they are conclusively presumed to be illegal. While per se rules have been criticized as shortcuts that sometimes oversimplify economic realities, they do speed up lengthy trials and provide sure guidelines for business.

Price-Fixing

The essential characteristic of a free market is that the price of goods and services is determined by the play of forces in the marketplace. Attempts by competitors to interfere with the market and control prices are called **horizontal price-fixing** and are illegal per se under Section 1. Price-fixing may take the form of direct agreements among competitors about what price they will sell a product for or what price they will offer for a product. It may also be accomplished by agreements on the quantities to be produced, offered for sale, or bought. Whether done directly or indirectly, horizontal price-fixing is always illegal and can never be legally justified.

Attempts by manufacturers to control the resale price of their products are also within the scope of Section 1. This kind of behavior is called **vertical price-fixing** or resale price maintenance. As was discussed above, manufacturers can lawfully state a "suggested retail price" for their products, since this does not involve joint action. If the manufacturer gets the retailer to "agree" to follow the suggested price, however, such an agreement is joint action in restraint of trade and is illegal per se under Section 1. Recent decisions have cast doubt on the future application of per se analysis for resale price maintenance. The following decision hints that the Supreme Court may be preparing to abandon per se analysis in some vertical price-fixing cases.

ATLANTIC RICHFIELD CO. v. USA PETROLEUM CO.
110 S.Ct. 1884 (U.S. Sup.Ct. 1990)

■ **FACTS** USA Petroleum claimed that Atlantic Richfield (ARCO) violated Section 1 of the Sherman Act by conspiring with its retail service station dealers to fix retail prices at below-market levels. USA asserted that ARCO's strategy was to eliminate the independent dealers by fixing and subsidizing below-market prices and siphoning off the independents' volumes and profits. ARCO claimed that USA did not have standing to sue because ARCO's maximum resale price maintenance scheme increased rather than decreased competition. It argued that maximum resale price maintenance brings prices lower, not higher. Thus, if competitors failed, it was because they were not able to match the low prices charged by ARCO's dealers.

■ **ISSUE** Is USA Petroleum entitled to antitrust damages due to ARCO's resale price maintenance scheme?

■ **DECISION** No. A private antitrust plaintiff may not recover damages unless it proves that it suffered an injury of the type the antitrust laws were designed to prevent. Resale price maintenance schemes have been held per se illegal because of their potential adverse effects on dealers and consumers. But USA is not a dealer or consumer; it has suffered losses only as a result of competition with the ARCO dealers that are following the vertical, maximum price-fixing agreement. When a group of firms adhering to a maximum resale price agreement maintains prices above predatory levels, the business lost by rivals cannot be viewed as an anticompetitive consequence. A firm complaining about the harm it suffers from nonpredatory price competition is really claiming it is unable to raise prices. This is not an antitrust injury; cutting prices to increase business often is the very essence of competition. The antitrust laws were enacted for the protection of competition, not competitors. USA's argument that an antitrust injury need not be shown where a per se violation has occurred is erroneous. The per se rule is a method of determining whether Section 1 has been violated, but it does not indicate whether a private plaintiff has suffered antitrust injury that calls for the recovery of damages. It is a presumption of unreasonableness based on business certainty and litigation efficiency even though some per se actions may have some procompetitive effects. Vertical, maximum price-fixing may have such procompetitive interbrand effects. In this case, it would be unwise to dilute the antitrust injury inquiry requirement because that might encourage competitors to enforce the rule against vertical, maximum price-fixing. However, if this scheme causes anticompetitive consequences to consumers or to ARCO's own dealers, they may bring suit.

ETHICAL IMPLICATIONS   *Atlantic Richfield* suggests that U.S. manufacturers may have few problems under U.S. antitrust laws when they enter into resale price maintenance agreements with their overseas dealers. (The decision forecloses suits by their U.S. competitors and the overseas consumers and dealers will not be able to show the requisite effect on U.S. domestic commerce.) Is it ethical for courts to interpret the law in a manner that permits overseas anticompetitive injuries to occur?

Group Boycotts and Concerted Refusals to Deal

A single firm can lawfully refuse to deal with certain firms or agree to deal only on certain terms. However, any such agreement by two or more firms to boycott or terminate another is a per se violation of Section 1. Thus, if a distributor persuades a manufacturer to refuse to deal with a rival distributor, the two conspiring parties would have committed a per se violation of Section 1.

Division of Markets

Any agreement among competing firms to divide the available market by assigning each other exclusive territories is a horizontal division of markets and is illegal per se. The idea is that each firm is given a monopoly in its assigned territory.

Rule of Reason Violations

Any behavior that has not been classified as a per se violation is judged under rule of reason analysis. Rule of reason trials involve a complex, often lengthy attempt by the court to balance the anticompetitive effects of the defendants' acts against any competitive justifications for their behavior. If the court concludes the defendants' conduct had a significant anticompetitive effect that was not offset by any positive impact on competition, their behavior is held illegal. Recent antitrust decisions indicate the Supreme Court is moving away from per se rules in favor of rule of reason treatment for many kinds of economic activity. This trend is consistent with the Court's increased willingness to consider new economic theories seeking to justify behavior previously declared illegal per se.

Vertical Nonprice Restraints on Distribution

A manufacturer can lawfully, as a matter of business policy, "unilaterally" assign exclusive dealerships to its dealers or limit the number of dealerships it grants in any geographic area. (Since there is no joint action, there is no violation of Section 1.)

However, manufacturers may run afoul of Section 1 if they require their dealers to "agree" to refrain from selling to customers outside their assigned territories or to unfranchised dealers inside their assigned territories. Such vertical, nonprice restraints are analyzed under the rule of reason.

Joint Ventures and Strategic Alliances

Joint ventures (or strategic alliances) are arrangements in which two or more entities collaborate with respect to research, development, production, marketing, or distribution. Because they generally involve cooperation between actual or potential competitors, joint ventures could possibly violate Section 1 of the Sherman Act. Recognizing the tremendous competitive advantages the United States might gain from joint research and development, Congress enacted the *National Cooperative Research Act,* which mandates that U.S. courts examine research and development joint ventures under rule of reason analysis. Further, if the venture partners have complied with the act's notification requirements, they are liable for only actual (rather than treble) damages in any civil suits that successfully challenge the arrangement.

Although production, marketing, and distribution joint ventures do not fall within the *National Cooperative Research Act,* they generally are scrutinized under rule of reason analysis. The Justice Department recommends a four-part test for examining these arrangements. First, does the collaborative effort harm competition in the market in which the joint venture operates—the *joint venture market?* Second, will there be competitive injury in the *spillover markets* where the venture partners compete (or are likely to compete) outside of the joint venture? Third, what *anticompetitive effects* attend any vertical nonprice restraints that are imposed as a part of the joint venture? (For instance, in a production joint venture, the parties may agree that they will purchase products exclusively from the joint venture.) Finally, even if the first three steps indicate anticompetitive effects, the joint venture is legal if that harm is offset by *procompetitive efficiencies.*

Courts do not employ rule of reason analysis unless the arrangement truly constitutes some form of economic integration. If the cooperation actually is no more than a "sham" joint venture designed to restrict output or maintain prices, it is treated as a per se violation of Section 1.

NORTHWEST WHOLESALE STATIONERS v. PACIFIC STATIONERY & PRINTING
472 U.S. 284 (U.S. Sup.Ct. 1985)

■ **FACTS** Northwest Wholesale Stationers is a purchasing cooperative made up of approximately 100 office supply retailers. It acts as the primary wholesaler for its member retailers. While nonmembers also may buy supplies from Northwest, members effectively buy supplies at substantially lower prices than nonmembers. Pacific Stationery, a member of Northwest, sold office supplies at both the wholesale and retail level. Pacific continued doing this even after Northwest amended its bylaws to prohibit members from engaging in sales at both levels. (A grandfather clause in the amendment permitted Pacific to continue its membership rights.) However, later and without explanation, Northwest's membership voted to expel Pacific from the cooperative venture. Pacific brought an antitrust suit, claiming its expulsion amounted to a per se illegal group boycott.

■ **ISSUE**   Has Northwest committed a per se violation of the Sherman Act?

■ **DECISION**   No. Group boycotts generally are per se unlawful, in part, because their likelihood of having anticompetitive effects is clear and the possibility of countervailing procompetitive effects is remote. However, not every cooperative activity involving a restraint or exclusion possesses these significant anticompetitive consequences. Wholesale purchasing cooperatives, such as Northwest, are not a form of concerted activity characteristically likely to result in predominantly anticompetitive effects. Rather, such cooperative ventures seem designed to increase economic efficiency and render markets more, rather than less, competitive. The arrangement permits the participating retailers to achieve economies of scale in both the purchase and warehousing of wholesale supplies and also ensures ready access to a stock of goods that might otherwise be unavailable on short notice. The cost savings and order-filling guarantees enable smaller retailers to reduce prices and maintain their retail stock so as to compete more effectively with larger retailers. The act of expulsion from such a venture does not necessarily imply anticompetitive animus and thereby raise the probability of anticompetitive effect. These ventures must establish and enforce reasonable rules in order to function effectively. Nor would the expulsion characteristically be likely to result in predominantly anticompetitive effects, unless the cooperative possesses market power or exclusive access to an element essential to effective competition. Absent such a showing with respect to cooperative buying ventures, courts should apply rule of reason analysis.

Licensing Arrangements

A firm frequently attempts to exploit the global market by licensing its intellectual property (e.g., patents, copyrights, trade secrets, and know-how) to foreign manufacturers or distributors. These licenses give the licensee the right to use the licensor's technology (generally for a limited period) for certain purposes. They permit the licensor to combine its intellectual property with the manufacturing or distribution skills of the licensee to more efficiently exploit its special technology. Licensing arrangements often raise antitrust issues as they generally involve restraints on the competitive activities of the licensor and/or licensee. (For example, an exclusive license of a product innovation means no one other than the licensee can manufacture or sell the product in the designated territory. Thus, competition among products using that same technology might be limited.)

Despite their restrictive characteristics, licensing arrangements may maximize consumer welfare by ensuring that new technology reaches the marketplace in the quickest and most efficient manner. Further, by guaranteeing that new ideas realize their maximum return, the licensing arrangements encourage the development of new technology. For these procompetitive reasons, the Justice Department examines such technology transfers under a rule of reason analysis parallel to the four-step scrutiny it accords joint ventures.

SECTION 2 OF THE SHERMAN ACT

Introduction   When a firm acquires monopoly power—the power to fix prices or exclude competitors—in a particular market, the antitrust laws' objective of promoting competitive market structures has been defeated. Monopolists have the power to fix price

FIGURE 14–1   Section 1 of the Sherman Act

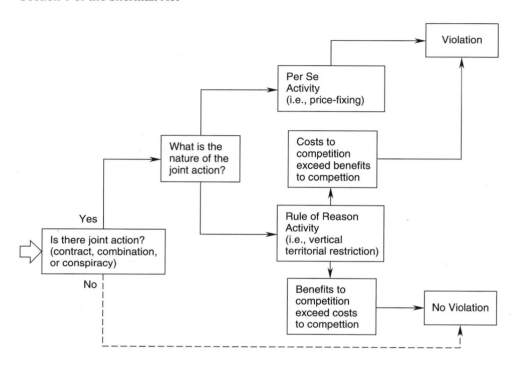

unilaterally, since they have no effective competition. Section 2 of the Sherman Act was designed to attack monopolies. It provides:

Every person who shall monopolize, or attempt to monopolize, or combine or conspire with any other person or persons to monopolize any part of trade or commerce among the several states, or with foreign nations shall be deemed guilty of a felony.

The first thing a student should note about the language of Section 2 is that it does not outlaw monopolies. It outlaws the act of "monopolizing." To show a violation of Section 2, the government or a private plaintiff must show not only that the defendant firm has monopoly power but also that there is an intent to monopolize on the defendant's part. Second, joint action is not necessary to violate Section 2; a single firm can be guilty of "monopolizing" or "attempting to monopolize."

Intent to Monopolize

Courts look at how the defendant acquired monopoly power. If the defendant intentionally acquired monopoly power or attempted to maintain it after having acquired it, intent to monopolize has been shown. However, if the defendant acquires a dominant market position through superior products and service or other demonstrations of business acumen, the intent to monopolize is not found.

FIGURE 14–2   Monopolization

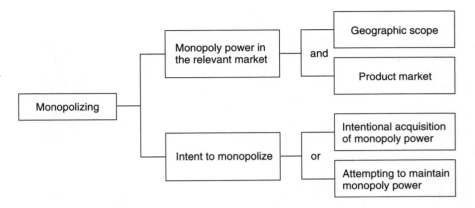

The defendant must convince the court that its monopoly power simply happened and is not the result of a conscious attempt to acquire or maintain it. If the defendant has monopoly power because it "built a better mousetrap," made wise decisions when other competitors did not, or simply was the first entrant or only survivor in a market that can support only one firm of its kind (e.g., the only newspaper in a small town), no violation of Section 2 exists.

Monopoly Power Monopoly power exists when a firm controls a very high percentage share of the relevant market. The decided cases in this area indicate a firm must have captured approximately 70 percent or more of the relevant market to have monopoly power. To determine the defendant's market share, the court in a Section 2 case must define the relevant market. This is a crucial part of the proceedings, since the broader the relevant market is drawn, the smaller the defendant's market share will be. Two components to a relevant market determination are: the geographic market and the product market.

Geographic Market

The relevant **geographic market** is determined by economic realities. Where do the sellers of the goods or services in question customarily compete? Transportation cost often limits geographic market size. Thus, the relevant geographic market may be a small area for cement but the whole world for transistors.

Product Market

The **relevant product market** is composed of those products that are "reasonably interchangeable by consumers for the same purposes" (the *functional interchangeability* test). The idea here is that a firm's power to fix price is limited by the availability of competing products that buyers find acceptable.

THE CLAYTON ACT

The Clayton Act was passed in 1914 to supplement the Sherman Act by attacking specific practices that monopolists had historically followed to gain monopoly power. The idea was to "nip monopolies in the bud" before a full-blown restraint of trade or monopoly power was achieved. The Clayton Act was intended to be preventive, and in most cases only the **probability** of a significant anticompetitive effect must be shown to establish a violation.

Since the Clayton Act deals with probable harms to competition, there is no criminal liability for Clayton Act violations. Treble damages are available to private plaintiffs, however, and the Federal Trade Commission has the power to enforce the act through the use of cease and desist orders.

Section 3

Section 3 of the Clayton Act was basically designed to attack three kinds of anticompetitive behavior: tie-in (or tying) contracts, exclusive dealing contracts, and requirements contracts. Section 3 makes it illegal to lease or sell commodities or to fix a price for commodities on the condition or agreement that the buyer or lessee will not deal in the commodities of the competitors of the seller or lessor if doing so may "substantially lessen competition or tend to create a monopoly in any line of commerce."

Section 3 applies only to **commodities** (goods), so tie-in, exclusive dealing, and requirements contracts that involve services must be attacked under Section 1 of the Sherman Act. Section 3 does not apply to cases where a manufacturer has entered true consignment arrangements with its distributors, since no "sale" or "lease" occurs in such cases. No formal agreement is required for a violation of Section 3; any use of economic power by the seller to stop buyers from dealing with the seller's competitors is enough to satisfy the statute.

Tie-in Contracts

Tie-in contracts (tying contracts) occur when a seller refuses to sell a product (the tying product) to a buyer unless the buyer also purchases another product (the tied product) from the seller. If Acme Seeds, Inc., refuses to sell its seeds (the tying product) to farmers unless they also agree to buy fertilizer (the tied product) from Acme, this is a tie-in contract; the sale of fertilizer is tied to the sale of seeds.

The economic harm from such contracts is that Acme's competitors in the sale of fertilizer are foreclosed from competing for sales to Acme's buyers, since Acme has used its power in the seed market to force its buyers to buy its fertilizer. There is no legitimate reason Acme's buyers would ever want to enter tie-in contracts, and therefore the courts have treated such agreements harshly. Tie-in contracts are illegal under Section 3 if: (1) the seller has monopoly power in the tie-in product; or (2) the seller has foreclosed competitors from a substantial volume of commerce in the tied product. So, if Acme has monopoly power in its seeds or has managed to tie in a substantial dollar volume in fertilizer sales, its tie-in contracts violate Section 3. Tie-in

FIGURE 14–3   A Tie-in Case under Section 3 of the Clayton Act

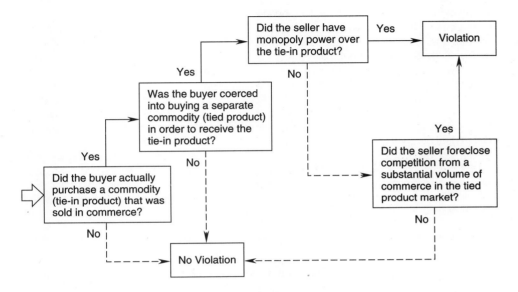

contracts can also amount to an illegal restraint of trade under Section 1 of the Sherman Act if both of the above conditions are met.

Exclusive Dealing and Requirements Contracts

An **exclusive dealing contract** occurs when a distributor agrees not to sell competing products of any other manufacturer. The manufacturer often wants such a provision because it encourages the distributor to devote its full efforts to sales of the manufacturer's product line.

A **requirements contract** is created when a buyer agrees to purchase all of its needs in a certain item from one seller, like a candy manufacturer that agrees to buy all the sugar it requires from one sugar refiner. The economic harm of such contracts is that the competitors of the seller are foreclosed from competing for sales to the buyer for the duration of the contract.

Courts recognize that exclusive dealing and requirements contracts can benefit both the buyer and the seller by reducing selling costs and assuring buyers of a supply of needed items. Therefore, in determining their legality, courts look at the percentage share of the relevant market foreclosed to competition by the contract.

ROLAND MACHINERY v. DRESSER INDUSTRIES
749 F.2d 380 (7th Cir. 1984)

■ **FACTS**   Roland, a substantial dealer in construction equipment, was for many years the area's exclusive dis- tributor of International Harvester construction equipment. After buying Harvester's construction equipment division, Dresser signed a dealership agreement with Roland. The agreement was terminable at will by either party on 90 days' notice. It did not contain an exclusive dealing clause. Eight months later, Roland signed a similar agreement with Komatsu. Several months after discovering this, Dresser gave notice to Roland of its intention to terminate its dealership. Roland argued that Dresser's decision to terminate the dealership demonstrated the existence of an implied exclusive dealing contract in violation of Section 3 of the Clayton Act.

■ **ISSUE**   Did Dresser and Roland have an illegal exclusive dealing contract?

■ **DECISION**   No. Roland would have to show both that there was an agreement not to carry equipment competitive with Dresser's and that the agreement was likely to have a substantial anticompetitive effect. Nothing in the

dealership agreement hints of such an agreement, and the fact that Roland applied for a dealership with Komatsu suggests Roland did not believe it had such a commitment. Dresser's hostility to dealers that carried other manufacturers' products does not establish such an agreement. However, even if there was such an arrangement, it is unlikely it would be anticompetitive. Such agreements should be examined under rule of reason analysis. Under this test, the agreement would be illegal only if two things were shown. First, it must be proved that at least one significant competitor is being excluded from the relevant market. Second, it must be shown that the prices are likely to rise above the competitive level. Komatsu does not appear likely to be excluded from the market. It is a large competitor, and the nationwide practice of terminable at will contracts permits it to enter any area by outbidding its competitors.

Section 7

Section 7 of the Clayton Act was designed to provide a tool for attacking **mergers**— a term broadly used in this section to refer to the acquisition of one company by another. It prohibits any corporation engaged in commerce from acquiring all or part of the stock or assets of any other corporation engaged in commerce, except for investment purposes only, where the effect of the acquisition may be to "substantially lessen competition" or "tend to create a monopoly" in "any line of commerce in any section of the country."

The "line of commerce" and "section of the country" concepts in Section 7 are similar to the relevant product and geographic market concepts in Section 2 of the Sherman Act, but they may be more loosely applied due to the preventive nature of Section 7. Similarly, Section 7 invalidates mergers that involve a probable anticompetitive effect at the time of the merger.

The fact that both of the firms involved in a merger are foreign might not preclude its prohibition under Section 7. The Justice Department would focus on the merger's likely competitive effects within the United States. However, if neither firm has assets in this country, the Justice Department probably would not challenge the merger because of the probable conflict with the interests of the other nations and the practical difficulties in bringing an enforcement action.

Horizontal Mergers

A court seeking to determine the legality of a horizontal merger (between competitors) under Section 7 looks at the market share of the resulting firm. In recent years, the Supreme Court has been less willing to presume that anticompetitive effects result whenever a horizontal merger produces a firm with a large market share. Instead, the

---

CONCEPT SUMMARY
Types of Mergers

Category	Description	Example
Horizontal	Between competitors	One automobile manufacturer merges with another automobile manufacturer
Vertical	Between a supplier and its customer	An oil producer merges with an oil refiner
Conglomerate	Between two largely unrelated businesses	A candy company merges with a greeting cards company

---

Court has been insisting on a higher level of proof that a contested merger is likely to have a negative effect on competition.

Vertical Mergers

A vertical merger is a supplier-customer merger. Vertical mergers occur when a firm acquires a captive market for its products or a captive supplier of a product it regularly buys, thereby becoming a vertically integrated operation (operating on more than one competitive level). The anticompetitive effect of vertical integration is that a share of the relevant market is foreclosed to competition. The competitors of a manufacturer that acquires a chain of retail stores are no longer able to compete for sales to the acquired stores. The competitors of a supplier acquired by a larger buyer are no longer able to compete for sales to that buyer. Analysis of vertical mergers is very similar to that accorded exclusive dealing arrangements.

Conglomerate Mergers

Conglomerate mergers are neither horizontal nor vertical. A conglomerate (a large firm that controls numerous other firms in diverse industries) may acquire a firm in a new product market or a firm in the same product market as one of its captive firms but in a different geographic market.

Conglomerate mergers that create a potential for reciprocal dealing have been successfully challenged under Section 7. If a conglomerate purchases a firm that produces a product that another member of the conglomerate regularly buys, or buys a product that another member firm regularly sells, the potential for reciprocal buying is obvious. A conglomerate may also acquire a firm that manufactures products that the conglomerate's suppliers regularly purchase. Suppliers that are eager to continue selling to the conglomerate may therefore be induced to purchase their requirements from the acquired firm.

Sometimes, a conglomerate merger can injure competition by eliminating a "potential entrant" in the product market. This would occur if a manufacturer of detergents merged with a producer of bleach. Arguably, the detergent manufacturer, since its product line is so closely related to bleach, imposes a competitive check on the bleach industry by the very fact that it might independently enter the market if bleach producers begin reaping monopoly profits.

Hart-Scott-Rodino Antitrust Improvements Act

Proposed mergers or acquisitions affecting U.S. commerce that exceed certain size thresholds must be reported to the Federal Trade Commission and the Department of Justice. Then, under the terms of the *Hart-Scott-Rodino Antitrust Improvements Act,* there is a prescribed waiting period before the transaction can be completed. This waiting period can be extended if the government requests additional information regarding the proposed deal. Mergers involving foreign firms may be required to comply with this act; however, those with an insignificant connection to U.S. commerce are exempted.

THE ROBINSON-PATMAN ACT

Direct Price Discrimination

Section 2(a) of the Robinson-Patman Act prohibits discrimination in price between different purchasers of "commodities of like grade and quality" where the effect of the price discrimination may be to "substantially lessen competition or tend to create a monopoly" in any relevant market, or to "injure, destroy, or prevent competition with any person who either grants or knowingly receives the benefits of such discrimination, or with the customers of either of them." To violate Section 2(a), the discriminatory sales must occur roughly within the same time period and involve goods of like grade and quality. Some substantial physical difference is necessary to justify a different price to competing buyers. A manufacturer that sells "house brand" products to a chain store for less than it sells its own brand name products to the chain's competitors has violated Section 2(a) if the only difference between the products is their label. The Robinson-Patman Act, like the Clayton Act, requires only that price discrimination have a probable anticompetitive effect.

Defenses to Direct Price Discrimination

A severe jurisdictional limitation on the reach of the prohibitions against direct price discrimination is that the commodities sold must be "for use, consumption, or resale within the United States." In the context of foreign commerce, this means this restriction does not apply to exports out of this country; it **reaches only imports** into the United States.

A seller who can **cost-justify** discriminatory prices by showing that the difference in price is solely the product of actual cost savings, such as lower transportation or production costs, has a defense under Section 2(a). Sellers can also lawfully discriminate in price when doing so reflects **changing conditions** in the marketplace that

FIGURE 14–4   Price Discrimination under the Robinson-Patman Act

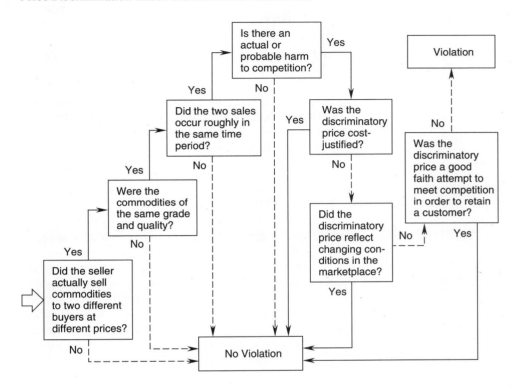

affect the marketability of goods, such as their deterioration or obsolescence. Finally, Section 2(b) allows sellers to **meet competition** in good faith by granting a discriminatory price to retain a customer who has been offered a lawful, lower price by one of the seller's competitors.

| **ETHICAL IMPLICATIONS** | It is unlawful for a buyer to knowingly induce or receive a discriminatory price. However, the buyer is not liable if the seller reasonably believes it is matching a lower price extended to the buyer from a competing seller. Thus, there is no violation if the buyer fraudulently informs the seller she has received a lower price from a competitor. Is it ethical for the buyer to make such a false statement? |

Indirect Price Discrimination   In passing the Robinson-Patman Act, Congress recognized that sellers could indirectly discriminate among competing buyers by making discriminatory payments to them or by furnishing them with certain services that were not available to their competitors. Section 2(d) prohibits sellers from making discriminatory payments to competing customers for services (such as advertising or promotional activities) or facilities (such as shelf space furnished by the customers in connection with the marketing of the goods). Section 2(e) prohibits sellers from discriminating in the services they furnish to competing customers. Thus, a seller violates this provision if he provides a favored customer with a display case or a demonstration kit.

Sellers may lawfully provide such payments or services only if these are made available to competing customers on proportionately equal terms. This means notifying customers of the availability of such services and distributing them according to some rational basis, such as the quantity of goods the customer purchases. The seller must devise a flexible plan that enables various classes of buyers, large chains or small independents, to participate.

THE EUROPEAN COMMUNITY COMPETITION LAW

The antitrust policy of the European Community has provided strong support for the single market concept as its seeks to ensure that competition is the prime force in the economy. Protection of the economic interests of the European consumer is a central theme of this competition policy. In this section, we briefly examine the two primary laws governing competition within the European Community—Articles 85 and 86 of the Treaty of Rome. We see how the substantive provisions of Articles 85 and 86 roughly parallel the U.S. antitrust laws we have just discussed. The section closes with a look at the notification and exemption process that distinguishes European Community competition law from antitrust enforcement in the United States.

Article 85

Article 85 states *"all agreements . . . which may affect trade between member states and which have as their object or effect the prevention, restriction, or distortion of competition within the common market"* are null and void, and fines may be imposed on parties entering into such agreements. This provision encompasses conduct that would violate Section 1 of the Sherman Act, Section 3 of the Clayton Act, and the Robinson-Patman Act under U.S. law. Article 85's concern with concerted action has evolved in a fashion similar to the Sherman Act's joint action concept in that parent corporations and their subsidiaries generally are treated as single economic entities. As such, an anticompetitive agreement between a U.S. parent corporation and its European subsidiary would not violate Article 85 because of the absence of concerted action. However, if the subsidiary was not effectively controlled by the parent (e.g., where the parent was not a majority shareholder of the subsidiary), Article 85 could apply.

Article 86

Article 86 encompasses the same type of conduct that would be governed under Section 2 of the Sherman Act (monopolization) or Section 7 of the Clayton Act (mergers) under U.S. antitrust law. It prohibits "[a]ny abuse by one or more undertakings of a dominant position within the common market or in a substantial part of it." It is similar to Section 2 of the Sherman Act in two important ways. First, Article 86 does not require concerted (joint) action. A single entity may violate its provisions. Second, it does not make dominant position (monopoly power) in and of itself unlawful. Something more—an abuse—is required. This is similar to Section 2's requirement of a monopoly intent before a violation can occur. (Contrast this with Japan's antimonopoly statute that permits the Japanese Fair Trade Commission to proceed against a firm with monopoly power even when there is no evidence of predatory conduct.)

Europe's Preapproval Process

We have already seen how the European and U.S. antitrust schemes differ in the availability of treble damages for successful private actions under the U.S. system. They also differ in several other extremely important ways. These are explored in the following sections discussing Europe's notification, negative clearance, and exemption procedures.

Notification

Conduct that might violate Article 85 must be **notified** to the European Commission. By filing this notification, the firm is not admitting it has violated the competition laws. Instead, it is giving the Commission an opportunity to examine the conduct and rule on its legal effect. There are several advantages to such a notification. First, between the filing and the Commission's response, the behavior is immune from any fines. Second, through its scrutiny, the Commission may give the firm warning of whether the transaction will be challenged as anticompetitive. Thus, while most U.S. antitrust analysis is decided after the fact in the courts, the European Community has developed an administrative preapproval process that permits companies to avoid serious commitment to endeavors that might later be declared null and void.

Negative Clearance

The Commission has developed a series of administrative responses to notification. In some instances, the Commission may respond with a "comfort letter," indicating it does not find the proposed arrangement to violate the competition rules. This declaration that conduct does not fall within the prohibitions of Articles 85 or 86 is known as **negative clearance.** Other times, the Commission may provide "settlement arrangements" by advising the parties how to modify their transaction in a manner that would not be illegal.

Exemptions

The Commission may grant an **exemption** to a restraint when it determines it possesses certain beneficial elements. This exemption cannot be given unless the transaction satisfies *all* of the following four requirements.

1. It must contribute to improvement in production or distribution, or promote technical or economic progress.

2. Consumers must realize a fair share of the resulting benefits.

3. The restriction must be indispensable to the achievement of these beneficial results.

4. The activity must not eliminate competition.

Basically, this exemption system operates like the rule of reason analysis used in U.S. antitrust law. (There are no per se violations of Articles 85 and 86.)

The notification requirement resulted in the Commission being deluged with notified agreements. Accordingly, **block exemptions** were devised to ease the administrative burden on the Commission in dealing with certain areas where the Commission might have received thousands of notifications. Under these exemptions, certain types of transactions (e.g., research and development joint ventures, patent license agreements, know-how licensing, franchising, motor-vehicle distribution and servicing, maritime transport) are automatically exempted from the reach of European competition law. The Commission may inform the parties of individual and block exemptions with comfort letters or through settlement arrangements in a manner similar to the negative clearance procedure described above. However, with many block exemptions, the transaction may be exempted automatically if the Commission does not object within a certain time period after notification.

TETRA PAK RAUSING *SA* v. COMMISSION
[1991] 4 C.M.L.R. 334 (Ct. First Instance 1990)

■ **FACTS**   Tetra Pak, the world's largest producer of paper cartons for packaging milk and other liquids, controlled approximately 90 percent of the European Community market for sterilized cartons and sterilized packaging machines. Despite this, Tetra Pak acquired Liquipak International. At the time of this acquisition, Liquipak had exclusive patent and know-how licenses covering potentially significant advances in packaging. These licenses qualified for the European Community's patent-licensing block exemption. By acquiring Liquipak, Tetra Pak would take over the exclusive licenses and also qualify for the block exemption. The European Commission ruled that Tetra Pak's acquisition of the exclusive license violated European competition law by preventing other potential competitors from entering the sterilized packaging market. According to the Commission, this action unduly strengthened Tetra Pak's position in the market, thereby constituting an abuse of dominant position in violation of Article 86. Tetra Pak argued that its conduct was protected under the block exemption.

■ **ISSUE**   Has Tetra Pak unlawfully abused its dominant position despite the block exemption?

■ **DECISION**   Yes. Tetra Pak possessed a dominant position in the sterilized packaging market throughout the European Community because it had the power to act without paying attention to rivals, suppliers, or purchasers. By acquiring the exclusive patent licenses, Tetra Pak strengthened its existing dominance and further prevented, or considerably delayed, the entry of new competition. This was an abuse of its dominant position since it afforded Tetra Pak competitive advantages disproportionate to the firm's legitimate business interests. While the Commission will not deny a block exemption to a dominant firm, such exemptions will not shield a company against allegations of abuse of dominant position. Exemptions do not relieve a dominant firm from its responsibility not to abuse its position of dominance. Thus, once a dominant firm commits an abusive act, any protection afforded by a block exemption ceases.

CONCEPT SUMMARY
Comparison: U.S. Antitrust with European Competition Law

Section 1 of the Sherman Act
  (contracts, combinations, and conspiracies in restraint of trade)

Section 3 of the Clayton Act   **Article 85**
  (tie-ins, exclusive dealing, and requirements contracts)   (concerted action that distorts competition)

Robinson-Patman Act
  (price discrimination)

Section 2 of the Sherman Act
  (monopolization and attempts to monopolize)   **Article 86**
                                                                 (abuse of dominant position)
Section 7 of the Clayton Act
  (mergers)

GLOBAL COOPERATION IN ANTITRUST

The accelerating pace of globalization of business activities clearly indicates the growing need for uniformity and cooperation in antitrust enforcement throughout the world. Such cooperative efforts already are under way in the guise of both bilateral and multilateral agreements and consultations.

Bilateral Agreements

In 1991, the United States and the European Community signed an agreement that would enable the antitrust authorities in the United States and the EC to exchange information as well as actively assist each other in preventing antitrust abuses. Each side pledged to consider the other's legitimate interests before exercising extraterritorial jurisdiction. The United States has established similar bilateral accords in the past with nations such as Canada, Germany, and Australia.

Currently, the United States also is promoting establishing in Eastern Europe antitrust policies similar to those in effect in the United States. Justice Department and Federal Trade Commission officials have been carrying on a regular antitrust dialogue with the Eastern European nations as a part of their efforts to create market-oriented economies.

Multilateral Cooperation

International efforts at harmonizing antitrust enforcement date back as far as 1927 and the League of Nations World Economic Conference. Efforts of more recent vintage can be traced to the Organization for Economic Cooperation and Development (OECD) and its 1986 Recommendation for Antitrust Cooperation. The OECD provides a regular forum (twice yearly) for the industrialized nations of the world to cooperate on antitrust matters. Specifically, the 1986 recommendations call for a system of notification, exchange of information, and coordination of action on antitrust issues. This program also urges bilateral consultation and conciliation between nations when their interests collide in the antitrust arena.

The OECD and the United Nations Trade and Development Committee (UNCTAD) each have adopted voluntary **codes of conduct** for private businesses to follow. These codes list anticompetitive behavior that multinational companies should avoid and set out principles for nations to follow in regulating economic matters.

QUESTIONS AND PROBLEM CASES

1. Explain the difference between per se and rule of reason analyses under Section 1 of the Sherman Act. Give an example of each.

2. Identify two fundamental differences between European competition law and U.S. antitrust law.

3. What is an export trading company? What are the advantages of becoming one?

4. Identify and describe the limits on the extraterritorial application of the U.S. antitrust laws.

5. Sylvania, in an attempt to increase its share of the U.S. television sales market, adopted a franchise plan that limited the number of Sylvania franchises granted in a given area and allowed its franchisees to sell only from specified store locations. Continental T.V., a Sylvania franchisee, became dissatisfied when Sylvania appointed one of Continental's competitors in the San Francisco area as a Sylvania franchisee. Continental was then refused permission to sell Sylvania televisions in the Sacramento area. Continental claimed Sylvania's location restrictions were per se violations of Section 1 of the Sherman Act. Is Continental correct? Explain.

6. California Computer Products (CalComp) manufactured disk drives and controllers that were "plug compatible" with central processing units (CPUs) manufactured by IBM. CalComp's business strategy consisted of copying and, if possible, improving on IBM designs and then underselling IBM to its own customers. In response to CalComp's tactics, IBM substantially reduced its prices on existing IBM disk drives and controllers. (Although IBM's prices were substantially lower, they still were profitable for IBM.) CalComp sued IBM, arguing it had monopolized or attempted to monopolize the market for disk products by cutting prices on existing IBM disk drives and controllers. Assuming IBM possessed monopoly power in the relevant market, should CalComp prevail? Explain.

7. IAM brought suit against the OPEC nations claiming the cartel's price-fixing activities in the petroleum industry were in violation of U.S. antitrust laws. The U.S. court held that it lacked jurisdiction to try the case since the OPEC members were foreign sovereigns. Was the court correct? Explain.

8. L'Oreal SA is a French-based company that manufactures and markets perfumes and other beauty products throughout Europe. It owns a subsidiary, L'Oreal NV, that is its exclusive distributor of L'Oreal products in Belgium. De Niewue A.M.C.K. wishes to sell L'Oreal products in Belgium. Accordingly, De Niewue challenges L'Oreal's exclusive distribution scheme as a violation of Article 86. What must be shown if the court is to find an Article 86 violation?

9. Tampa Electric entered into a requirements contract to buy all the coal for its Gannon Station from Nashville Coal for 20 years. A minimum price was set for the coal, and a cost escalation clause was included in the contract. After Tampa Electric had spent $7.5 million converting its operations to burn coal instead of oil, Nashville Coal announced it would not honor the contract, claiming it violated Section 3 of the Clayton Act. What must be shown if a court is to find the contract unenforceable as a violation of Section 3 of the Clayton Act?

10. Travel Impressions, a wholesale tour operator, is a New York corporation with its principal place of business in New York. Liamuiga Tours is a St. Kitts (a Caribbean island) corporation that provides tours and tourist information solely on that island.

Travel Impressions engaged Liamuiga Tours as its "destination service operator" (local representative) on St. Kitts. This specifically included running hospitality desks for Travel Impressions customers in the Royal St. Kitts Hotel. After a dispute arose between the Royal St. Kitts Hotel and Liamuiga, the hotel persuaded Travel Impressions to terminate its relationship with Liamuiga. In response, Liamuiga Tours brought an antitrust suit against Travel Impressions in the United States. Does the court have jurisdiction to hear this antitrust complaint? Explain.

Agency and
Employment Law

INTRODUCTION

Regardless of which market strategy a global business pursues—trade, licensing, or direct investment—it cannot conduct its operations profitably without the assistance of qualified personnel. Companies frequently hire individuals as employees to obtain the benefits of their efforts and loyalty on a full-time basis. However, on many occasions businesses find it prudent to retain the services of trade experts for only selected transactions. Either way, the relationship between the firm and its personnel is subject to a broad array of domestic and foreign regulations based on agency and employment law. Global managers must fully appreciate the nature of these rules.

Chapter Overview

The chapter begins with a survey of the agency law rules that most concern global business managers. This includes an introduction to the duties that agents and principals owe each other, the contractual authority and liability of agents, and the rules regarding termination of the agency relationship. Attention then turns to the *Foreign Corrupt Practices Act* and the responsibilities it places on U.S. companies that retain the services of overseas agents. This is followed by an overview of the major employment issues arising in the international environment. This section examines labor relations, job security, employee participation in management, and discrimination. The chapter closes with a review of the special U.S. immigration rules governing the employment of foreign workers in the United States.

INTERNATIONAL AGENCY AGREEMENTS

Agency relationships often are essential to an exporter's global marketing strategy. This is particularly true for small and medium-sized companies that lack the sales volume or economic resources to directly establish an overseas presence. Importers and direct investors also rely heavily on agents as the complexities of international transactions mandate the assistance of global trade experts (freight forwarders, import brokers, lawyers). Although many businesses believe their domestic agency agreements can be used without modification in foreign markets, this is frequently not true. Differences in agency law from one legal system to another caution against this attitude.

Nature of Agency

An agency arises when one person (the **agent**) acts for the benefit of and under the control of another (the **principal**). Agency agreements trigger three overlapping legal relationships: (1) special duties the agent and principal owe to each other; (2) legal liability between the principal and third persons as a result of the agent's activities; and (3) legal responsibilities the agent may have to third persons.

Formalities

Agency relationships generally are created by contract, although they may be found in the absence of such an agreement. In the United States, they may be written or oral; however, many countries require that they be evidenced by a writing.

Throughout the world, an agency results from any indication of consent by the principal that the agent may act on the principal's behalf and under her control. This can be proven not only by express agreements between the parties, but also by their behavior and the circumstances surrounding their relationship. Courts often find agencies to exist even though the parties expressly agreed they did not intend to create one. For instance, a U.S. manufacturer may control the selling activities of an overseas franchisee so closely that the local courts will treat the franchisee as an agent.

Exporters must recognize the legal formalities governing agency relationships in each country where they do business if they hope to avoid legal problems. For example, some nations in the Middle East and North Africa insist that foreign suppliers retain local persons as agents. Like many other countries, they also require that an agency agreement be drafted and filed with an official registry. Further, much of the world prohibits recently retired governmental officials from acting as agents for contracts involving their former departments.

Commercial Agents

Several characteristics commonly distinguish **commercial agents** from distributors and other nonagents. First, agents generally do not maintain their own inventory of goods; instead, they take orders on behalf of their principal. Second, agents usually are compensated through the payment of a commission when a sale is completed. Third, agents seldom bear the financial risk of nonpayment by the purchaser. Fourth, agents often possess the authority to contract on behalf of their principals.

Sales Representatives

Sometimes courts distinguish between a commercial agent and a **sales representative.** Both are agents. However, the term *sales representative* often is used to describe agents who do not possess the authority to contract on behalf of their principal. While a commercial agent can bind his principal to a contract with third persons, a sales representative may only solicit business. The principal must finalize the agreement.

Independent Agents

There are wide differences in the level of control a principal chooses to exercise over its agents. **Independent agents** (they are called independent contractors in the United States) are permitted to work according to their own methods. They are under the control of their principals as to the *result* that is to be achieved, but not as to the means used to accomplish that result.

Principals often wish to structure their agreements so as to maintain an independent agency. Most nations have few restrictions on the right to terminate independent agents. Further, principals are less likely to be liable for their independent agents' torts and crimes when they exercise little control over their agents' daily activities.

Employees

Employees are under the control of their employer/principal as to both the *objective* of their work and the *means* used to achieve it. Thus, employers generally give detailed directions over their employees' day-to-day activities. Most nations closely regulate employment relationships. Thus, when exporters closely control their agents' hours and working conditions, they run the risk of becoming subject to restrictive labor laws. In some nations, particularly in Latin America, these labor laws apply unless the agent is a corporation.

Distributors

International **distributors,** unlike agents, typically purchase products directly from the manufacturer and bear the risk of no sale or nonpayment by the ultimate purchaser. They are compensated by the profits they earn on their operations. Distributors generally are not agents, and, as a result, manufacturers are less likely to be legally responsible for their contracts, torts, or crimes. Further, many nations place few restrictions on the retention or termination of distributors.

Businesses must be careful not to inadvertently transform their foreign distributors into agents. In many countries, failure to explicitly disavow an agency relationship in a distributorship contract may result in the creation of an agency. Further, notwithstanding the language of the parties' agreement, an exporter's strict control over its distributors' day-to-day activities may persuade local courts to treat the distributors as agents.

Agent's Duties

The agency relationship establishes several distinct duties the agent owes her principal. The following duties generally exist even when the agency contract is silent: the duty of loyalty, the duty to obey instructions, the duty to exercise reasonable care and skill, the duty to communicate information, and the duty to account for funds and property.

Of all the duties an agent owes the principal, the most important is the fiduciary duty of loyalty. A **fiduciary** is one who is entrusted to act for the benefit of another rather than pursuing his own interests. This duty demands complete honesty from the agent in all dealings with the principal. It also requires avoidance of conflicts between the interests of the agent and those of the principal unless they are fully disclosed to, and approved by, the principal. Another aspect of the duty of loyalty is the obligation of agents to avoid disclosing or using the principal's confidential information without consent. Trade secrets such as formulas, processes, and mechanisms are included within this duty; so are customer lists, special selling techniques, and sales manuals. However, many developing nations severely restrict a company's right to restrain local agents from using its confidential technology after the agency relationship has ended.

Principal's Duties

A well-drafted agency contract should clearly indicate the duties the principal owes the agent. However, if the agreement is poorly drafted, or if there is no express contract, certain duties still are likely to be found. They generally include: the duty to compensate, the duty to reimburse and indemnify, and the duty to keep accounts.

The agency agreement should specify the amount of compensation due the agent and when it has been earned. Many disputes arise because no clear agreement has been reached. Some developing countries regulate the minimum amounts of compensation and establish strict rules for when commissions are earned. In many instances, these rules override the terms of the agency agreement.

Sometimes agents make advances from their own funds in conducting the principal's business. If the agent is acting within the scope of her authority, the principal has a duty to reimburse her for expenses she incurred for the principal. Or if the agent suffers losses while acting for the principal, the principal has a duty to indemnify her. Of course, the principal need not pay for unauthorized expenses incurred by the agent. Further, the agent is not entitled to indemnification if her losses were caused by her failure to exercise reasonable care or skill.

■

F. W. MYERS & CO. v. HUNTER FARMS
319 N.W. 2d 186 (Iowa Sup.Ct. 1982)

■ **FACTS** Hunter Farms sought to obtain a supply of a farm herbicide called Sencor. It received an offer to sell from a grain and feed company in Canada. An import specialist with the U.S. Customs Service estimated the import duty for the Sencor at 5 percent, although a precise rate could be determined only by examining the shipment at the time of importation. This information was forwarded to Hunter Farms, which eventually ordered the Sencor. In the meantime, Hunter Farms employed F. W. Myers & Co., an import broker, to assist in moving the Sencor through U.S. customs. The import duty imposed on the shipment turned out to be over 20 percent because the Sencor contained chemicals not listed on its label. As a result, the duty increased from $30,000 to over $128,000. Myers paid the additional amount under protest and requested Hunter Farms to reimburse it for the additional expense. Hunter Farms refused to do so, claiming Myers was under a duty to notify it that the 5 percent figure was only advisory.

■ **ISSUE** Did Hunter Farms have a duty to reimburse Myers?

■ **DECISION** Yes. An agent is entitled to reimbursement for reasonable expenses unless he fails to exercise such skill as is required to accomplish the object of the agency. There was no breach of duty by Myers. The standard of care for import brokers does not include a special duty to render advice to the importer unless requested to do so. There was no evidence that Hunter Farms requested advice on import laws. Contrary to Hunter Farms' contention, Myers has not violated its duty to communicate information to its principal. Myers was never informed of Hunter Farms' lack of experience in the business, nor was it aware of the problem in labeling the herbicide that caused the import duty to increase. Absent knowledge of Hunter Farms' special need for advice concerning the open-ended nature of the initial assessment, Myers breached no duties to Hunter Farms. Thus, it was entitled to reimbursement for the additional expenses it incurred.

Agent's Contractual Authority

Commercial agents frequently are able to bind their principals to contracts with third persons. When this occurs, the principal and the third person are liable just as if they had dealt with each other personally. However, this is not always the case. (Remember from our earlier discussion that sales representatives generally are not permitted to contract for their principals.) A clear understanding of the contractual liability of

FIGURE 15–1   Agency Duties

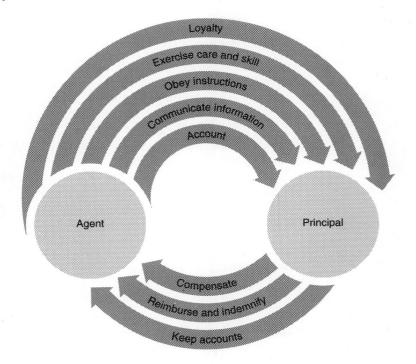

a principal to a third party for a contract created by an agent requires an examination of the authority possessed by the agent.

Actual Authority

Actual authority is the true authority granted to the agent by the principal. It is proper authority in the sense that an agent acting with actual authority is not in violation of her agency duties. Actual authority may be either express or implied.

Authority is **express** when the principal specifically describes the extent of the agent's powers. Generally, this may be done orally, although some nations require a writing. The test of an agent's actual authority is *the specific language the principal used in granting the authority.*

Often, express authority is incomplete and does not cover every contingency because the principal seldom can foresee every circumstance where the agent may need to act. Therefore, an agent also possesses the **implied** authority to do whatever else is reasonably necessary to accomplish the objectives of the agency. This may include what is customary for agents to do in the particular business of the principal or in similar transactions in the nation where the agent conducts business. The test used for determining the extent of an agent's implied authority is *the justifiable belief of the agent.* (In the previous case, *F. W. Myers & Co. v. Hunter Farms,* the import broker had the implied authority to pay the extra import duties assessed by U.S. Customs.)

Apparent Authority

Apparent authority arises when a principal's words, actions, silence, or inaction lead a third person to reasonably believe someone has authority to bind the principal. It may exist if the principal has intentionally or by want of ordinary care induced and permitted third persons to believe a person is her agent even though no actual authority exists. The source of apparent authority is the principal, just as it is for express and implied authority. Words or actions of an agent or purported agent alone cannot create apparent authority.

The test for determining the existence of apparent authority is *the justifiable belief of a third party based on the words, actions, silence, or inaction of the principal.* It may arise from customs in the trade. Thus, when a principal wishes to impose limitations on an agent's authority that are not customary, the restrictions must be communicated to third persons. Former agents often possess apparent authority if the principal does not notify third persons of the termination of the agency relationship. The exercise of apparent authority, in the absence of actual authority, violates the agent's duties to the principal. Thus, a principal who is bound to a contract with a third person based on an agent's apparent authority may sue the agent for damages.

Ratification

One may become liable through **ratification** for an unauthorized act that was done by an agent. Ratification may be of either an act of an agent who has exceeded the authority she was given or an act by someone who never was appointed an agent. For ratification to be effective, the agent or purported agent must have acted on behalf of the principal. Only the entire act may be ratified; the principal may not ratify what is beneficial and deny what is burdensome. Further, the ratification must occur before the third person discovers the agent's lack of authority and cancels the contract. After ratification, the agent is released from any liability for having exceeded her authority and the principal is entitled to the full benefit of the contract.

Agent's Contractual Liability

Generally, the agent is representing the principal when making contracts and all three parties (the agent, the principal, and the third party) intend that the agreement bind only the principal and third party. As a result, agent's normally are not personally liable on the contract. However, an agent may become personally liable on the contract with the third person under several special circumstances.

Unauthorized Actions

A person who represents that she is making a contract on behalf of a principal, without the authority to do so, does not bind the principal. Under those circumstances, the purported agent is liable to the third person. The same is true whenever an agent

	Category	Definition	Test	Contractual Liability*
		CONCEPT SUMMARY **Agency Authority**		
Actual	Express	Specific authority (oral or written)	The explicit agency agreement between the principal and the agent	Principal is liable to the third party.
	Implied	Supplementary authority reasonably necessary to accomplish the agency objectives	The justifiable belief of the agent	Principal is liable to the third party.
Apparent		Appearance of authority in the agent created by the principal	The justifiable belief of the third party dealing with the agent	Principal is liable to the third party, but the agent is liable to the principal.

*Liability is based on a fully disclosed agency.

exceeds her actual or apparent authority. Of course, the agent or purported agent is relieved from personal liability whenever the principal ratifies the unauthorized contract.

Agreements by the Agent to Assume Liability

When an agent makes a contract in his own name, rather than acting on behalf of the principal, the agent is personally liable. Or an agent may become a party to a contract along with the principal, assuming joint liability. An agent normally does not insure the collectibility of payments due on sales; however, a *del credere* agent is required to indemnify his principal when customers do not pay. The agency agreement should indicate if the parties have selected a *del credere* arrangement. Finally, in some instances, an agent is asked by the third party to guarantee the principal's performance on the contract.

Fully Disclosed Agency

Usually a person who is dealing with an agent is aware of that fact and knows for whom the agent is acting. However, to avoid liability because of confusion over whether or not an agent is acting for herself or for a principal, the agent should conduct all contractual negotiations carefully. If she intends to bind only the principal, the agent should (1) fully disclose the identity of the principal and (2) clearly indicate her capacity as an agent. When there is a **fully disclosed agency,** an authorized agent is not a party to the agreement and has no personal liability. Civil law countries refer to this situation as a *direct agency.*

Partially Disclosed Agency

In situations where the third party realizes it is dealing with an agent but does not know the identity of the principal, there is a **partially disclosed agency.** This is likely to occur when an agent signs a contract indicating his status as an agent but fails to properly identify the principal. When the agency is partially disclosed, the principal may intervene and enforce its contract rights against the third party. If this does not occur, the third party can hold the agent liable or, if it discovers the identity of the principal, enforce the contract against him. Whenever an authorized agent is forced to honor the contract with the third party, he is entitled to reimbursement from his principal.

Undisclosed Agency

Sometimes principals do not want their identities known to those who deal with their agents. For example, many individuals and firms demand a higher price when they know they are selling to a multinational corporation. Thus, the corporate principal might retain local agents to purchase the property in their own names. If neither the principal's identity nor the existence of an agency relationship is revealed to the third party, there is an **undisclosed agency.**

When the agency is undisclosed, the third party believes the agent is acting personally and may hold her liable on the contract. Of course, if the agent was authorized to contract for the principal, she may then seek reimbursement from her principal. In common law countries, an undisclosed principal may intervene and enforce the contract on its own behalf. Further, if the third party discovers the principal's identity, it may elect to hold the principal liable on the contract.

In civil law countries, an undisclosed agency is called an *indirect agency.* Those nations consider the contract to be between the third person and the undisclosed agent. Thus, the agent is liable to the third person and neither the principal nor the third person acquires any contractual obligations to the other. Of course, the agent has a duty to account to the principal for any profits earned on the transaction. In civil law countries, the undisclosed agent is known as a *commissionaire.*

 **ETHICAL IMPLICATIONS**   One reason a principal may insist on an undisclosed agency is because the third party might demand a larger payment for land, goods, or services if it knew the identity of the principal. Yet contract law frequently suggests a party has a duty to disclose all material facts to its contracting partners. Is it ethical to contract through an undisclosed agent when it is clear the identity of the principal matters to the third party?

Termination of the Agency

A well-drafted agency agreement usually discusses when or how the agency will end. The relationship then terminates at that time. In the United States, when the duration of the agency has not been agreed on, either party generally may end the relationship at any time. This doctrine is known as **agency at will.**

Most of the world does not share the U.S. notion of agency at will. Accordingly, it may be extremely difficult to terminate an overseas agent in the absence of *good cause*. And even when terminations are permitted, the principal may be required to give reasonable notice and offer some amount of severance pay. Sometimes this can place a considerable burden on the principal. For instance, in some Middle Eastern countries, it is not possible to appoint a new agent until the former agent agrees on a reasonable level of compensation. Since those countries do not permit exporters to resume business without a local agent, the former agent possesses considerable bargaining strength in the severance pay negotiations.

THE FOREIGN CORRUPT PRACTICES ACT

In the mid-1970s, it was discovered that hundreds of U.S. companies had bribed high-level foreign officials to obtain goods and services contracts. Officers of those companies, even while admitting the payments were bribes, argued they were customary and necessary in business transactions in many countries. In a significant number of cases, the bribes were accounted for as commission payments, as normal transactions with foreign subsidiaries, or as payments for services rendered by professionals or other firms. They generally were recorded as normal business expenses and then deducted as business expenses in the income tax returns filed with the U.S. Internal Revenue Service.

In an attempt to prevent **bribery** and other questionable payments, the United States enacted the *Foreign Corrupt Practices Act* (FCPA). This statute has two basic provisions. First, under the antibribery prohibition, it is unlawful for any U.S. individual or firm to offer, promise, or make payments or gifts of anything of value to foreign officials for the purpose of obtaining business. Second, the FCPA also establishes recordkeeping and internal control requirements for U.S. corporations. Curiously, although most countries treat bribery of their own governmental officials as a crime, the United States is the only country that prohibits bribery of the officials of another nation.

The Antibribery Prohibition

It now is unlawful for a U.S. company or individual to bribe a foreign governmental official to obtain business. An offer or promise to make a prohibited payment is a violation, even if the offer is not accepted or the promise is not otherwise carried out. Payments of kickbacks to foreign businesses and their corporate officials are not prohibited by the FCPA (although they may violate the antitrust laws), unless the U.S. firm has knowledge that the payments will be passed on to government officials or other illegal recipients.

Permissible Payments

The FCPA allows a company to pay governmental officials to secure *routine governmental action*. These **grease payments** are not illegal if the recipient has no discretion in carrying out a governmental function. For instance, suppose a U.S. corporation applies for an import license in China and makes a payment to the government official responsible for issuing licenses. If the official grants licenses to every applicant and the payment merely accelerates the processing time, the FCPA is not violated. On the other hand, if only a few applicants are granted licenses and the payment is made to ensure the U.S. company will obtain an import license, the payment is illegal.

Payments to foreign governmental officials also are permitted by the FCPA when they are legal under the *published laws* of the country where the payments were made. However, this is an extremely narrow exception because, even in those countries where bribery is rampant, there generally are written statutes prohibiting it. Finally, a U.S. company also may reimburse foreign officials for the costs they incur in connection with visits to promotions, product demonstrations, and tours of business facilities. Thus, if a company invites a foreign governmental official to the United States to inspect the company's assembly operations, it lawfully could cover the costs of her travel and lodging.

Liability for Actions of Foreign Agents

A U.S. firm is liable for bribes made by its foreign agents when it had *knowledge* of the illicit payments. This requirement is met if the company was aware of the bribery or was aware of the high probability that such behavior was occurring. Thus, a company cannot consciously ignore the activities of its foreign agents. Instead, it should exercise a reasonable amount of diligence to ensure compliance with the FCPA's antibribery provisions.

Recordkeeping and Internal Controls

The FCPA also imposes recordkeeping and internal controls requirements to prevent unauthorized payments and transactions as well as unauthorized access to company assets. The controls require companies to *maintain records* that accurately reflect all their transactions. Further, they mandate the establishment and maintenance of a system of *internal auditing* controls that provide reasonable assurances that unauthorized transactions are not occurring.

Each company must maintain its records in a manner that permits it to prepare financial statements that conform to generally accepted accounting principles. Furthermore, at reasonable intervals, management must compare the records with the actual assets available to ensure they are accurate. If they are not, it must find out why.

Failure to comply with the recordkeeping requirements violates the FCPA even when there have been no illegal payments. Further, the requirements apply to domestic as well as foreign business activities.

Penalties

Substantial penalties may be imposed for violations of the FCPA's antibribery prohibitions. A corporation may be fined up to $2 million and an individual may have to pay as much as $100,000 for *willful* violations. Individuals also may be imprisoned for up to five years. Further, the FCPA prohibits companies from indemnifying officers, directors, and employees for their criminal fines. Finally, the statute permits the imposition of civil penalties as high as $10,000 per violation.

Violations of the recordkeeping and accounting provisions may trigger the criminal penalties established by the U.S. securities laws. They permit fines as high as $2.5

million and imprisonment for up to five years. These criminal penalties only apply to knowing violations and, unlike the fines imposed for bribery, permit companies to indemnify their officers, directors, and employees.

LAMB v. PHILLIP MORRIS
915 F.2d 1024 (6th Cir. 1990)

■ **FACTS** Lamb and other Kentucky growers produced burley tobacco for use in cigarettes and other tobacco products. Phillip Morris, Inc., routinely purchased such tobacco not only from Kentucky growers but also from producers in several foreign countries. Thus, tobacco grown in Kentucky competes directly with tobacco grown abroad and any purchases from foreign suppliers necessarily reduced Phillip Morris' purchases of domestic tobacco. A Phillip Morris subsidiary, known as C.A. Tabacalera National, entered into a contract with La Fundacion Del Nino (the Children's Foundation) of Caracas, Venezuela. The agreement was signed on behalf of the Children's Foundation by the organization's president, the wife of the president of Venezuela. Under the terms of the agreement, the subsidiary would donate approximately $12.5 million to the Children's Foundation. In exchange, the subsidiary would obtain price controls on Venezuelan tobacco, elimination of controls on retail cigarette prices in Venezuela, tax deductions for the donations, and assurances that existing tax rates applicable to tobacco companies would not be increased. Lamb complained that the donations by the subsidiary violated the Foreign Corrupt Practices Act since they were gifts of money designed to influence foreign officials. Phillip Morris argued that businesses injured by unlawful payments to foreign governmental officials have no private right to sue under the FCPA.

■ **ISSUE** Does the FCPA give private parties a right to sue companies that bribe foreign governmental officials?

■ **DECISION** No. In determining whether to infer a private cause of action from a federal statute, the central focus is on congressional intent. As a guide for discerning that intent, courts rely on four factors: (1) whether the plaintiffs are among the class for whose special benefit the statute was enacted; (2) whether the legislative history suggests congressional intent to prescribe or proscribe a private cause of action; (3) whether implying such a remedy for the plaintiff would be consistent with the underlying purposes of the legislative scheme; and (4) whether the cause of action is one traditionally relegated to state law so it would be inappropriate to infer a cause of action. The FCPA was primarily designed to protect the integrity of American foreign policy and domestic markets, rather than to prevent the use of foreign resources to reduce production costs. Thus, domestic growers cannot claim the status of intended beneficiaries of the statute. While the Senate initially included a provision that expressly conferred a private right of action under the FCPA, that provision was deleted before the bill was enacted. This refutes any claim that the legislative history displays a congressional intent that there be a private right of action. Further, the FCPA evidences a careful scheme designed to encourage compliance in lieu of prosecution. The introduction of a private right of action would change the law's focus to postviolation enforcement rather than previolation compliance. Finally, while the regulation of bribery directed at foreign governmental officials cannot be characterized as a matter traditionally relegated to state control, there still is no compelling reason to imply a private right to sue. The potential for recovery under the antitrust laws refutes any contention that a private right of action under the FCPA is imperative.

Ensuring FCPA Compliance

Global traders often have little choice but to use foreign agents in their overseas operations. Sometimes the costs of staffing a foreign office with U.S. employees are too great. In other instances, customer preferences or governmental rules demand the appointment of a local agent. Whatever the reason, whenever a U.S. company retains foreign agents to solicit business abroad, it should establish an **FCPA compliance program.**

Background Checks

At its most basic level, the company should have a procedure for conducting a background check of each potential agent. This should include an investigation of the agent's overall reputation for honest dealings. Further, since payments to government officials generally are prohibited, it is important to determine the relationship between the agent and the foreign government.

Red Flags

Company officials must be on the lookout for **red flags** that warn of the likelihood of illicit payments. For example, bribery seems to be much more widespread in some countries than in others. Thus, companies should exercise extreme caution when retaining agents in nations where bribery is rampant. Further, some industries tend to be more prone to corrupt practices than others. The defense, oil, and construction industries have well-known reputations for illicit payments. When an agent requests that payments be made in cash or that the money be delivered to a third country, company officials should be suspicious. Likewise, when the agent requests an extremely high commission, there is a probability that bribes are being made.

Regular Audits

To discourage the likelihood of corrupt payments, a company should conduct **regular audits** of the expenditures of its agents. It might also request that agents sign agreements verifying they will not make illegal payments. When a U.S. parent corporation holds a majority interest in a subsidiary, the FCPA requires it to maintain accounting records and internal audit controls. If the U.S. company owns less than a majority interest in the foreign corporation, it still is required to make a good faith effort to encourage the company to comply with the recordkeeping and internal auditing rules.

 **ETHICAL IMPLICATIONS**   Suppose you are competing with several companies for a contract to supply goods to a foreign government and your overseas agent informs you that you will not land the deal unless you bribe certain key governmental officials. You are fairly certain your competitors have bribed officials in the past and are likely to do so again. Should you pay the bribe?

CONCEPT SUMMARY
An FCPA Compliance Program

Conduct Background Checks	· Investigate agent's reputation for honesty · Verify agent's relationships with foreign officials
Investigate Red Flags	· Exercise extra caution in high-risk countries · Be wary in high-risk industries · Investigate suspicious payment requests by agent: cash; payment in third country; high commission
Conduct Regular Audits	· Verify agent's expenditures · Maintain records and conduct audits of majority-owned subsidiaries · Encourage recordkeeping and audits in minority-owned subsidiaries

---

INTERNATIONAL EMPLOYMENT ISSUES

Corporations often maintain a direct presence abroad to reap the benefits of greater control and a closer relationship with their overseas markets. However, these advantages are not likely to be captured in the absence of carefully designed operating procedures adapted to the host country. A fundamental component of such a system is the decision over how to staff the foreign office. There are three basic approaches: (1) employing **expatriates** (nationals of the company's home country), (2) hiring personnel from the host country, or (3) staffing key slots with expatriates and filling the remaining positions with local personnel.

Depending on the option it selects, the global business may be subject to the employment laws of its home country, the host country, or both nations. Accordingly, managers must familiarize themselves with the extraterritorial reach of their home country's employment laws as well as the rules of the host country.

Labor Relations

During 1993, U.S. labor unions mounted a furious campaign against the North American Free Trade Agreement (discussed in Chapter 4). They complained its passage would spur companies to relocate in Mexico to take advantage of that nation's less restrictive labor policies. Similar criticisms are rampant in the European Community as numerous multinational corporations have abandoned continental Europe for less costly locations in Great Britain where workers' rights are less protected.

U.S. employment policies in the nonunion sector largely favor employers. However, workers' rights are even less protected in many developing nations where labor policies are specifically designed to attract foreign investment. Canada and most of Europe, on the other hand, provide comprehensive employment benefits for both union and nonunion workers. Labor supporters currently are struggling to stem the flight of jobs from worker protective environments. The following case illustrates an unsuccessful attempt to use U.S. labor laws to enforce an agreement between an overseas company and its foreign work force.

LABOR UNION OF PICO KOREA v. PICO PRODUCTS
968 F.2d 191 (2nd Cir. 1992)

■ **FACTS** Pico Korea, Ltd., a South Korean corporation doing business in Seoul, was a wholly owned subsidiary of Pico Products, a New York corporation with its principal place of business in New York. Pico Korea was incorporated in 1985 to manufacture electronic components in South Korea, all of which were sold to its U.S. parent. In 1988, Pico Korea's employees (Korean nationals) formed a labor union under the laws of South Korea. Several months later, because of Pico Korea's problems (increasing labor costs, low productivity, and lack of operating capital), Pico Products decided to cease providing working capital to the Korean subsidiary. This resulted in Pico Korea shutting down its operations and going out of business. The Korean workers claimed the shutdown violated their collective bargaining agreement and sued Pico Products under Section 301 of the Labor Management Relations Act. Section 301 is a U.S. law that provides that suits for violations of labor contracts may be brought in federal courts without regard to the citizenship of the parties if the employees work in an industry affecting commerce between a foreign country and the United States.

■ **ISSUE** Should the U.S. court enforce the workers' collective bargaining agreement with the South Korean corporation?

■ **DECISION** No. Merely because Section 301 grants federal jurisdiction without regard to the citizenship of the parties does not mean federal jurisdiction exists without consideration of the nature of the collective bargaining agreement at issue. In this case, the employees of Pico Korea are citizens and domiciliaries of South Korea, doing work in South Korea, for a South Korean company. The fact that Pico Korea is a wholly owned subsidiary of a U.S. corporation does not change the character of this labor dispute into one Congress can be presumed to have intended Section 301 to control. In the present "global economy," ever-expanding trade makes it increasingly possible that an overseas industry might affect commerce between a foreign country and the United States. But to construe Section 301 as governing collective bargaining agreements in such an industry would inevitably lead to embarrassment in foreign affairs and be infeasible in actual practice. Such a result would conflict with the general and almost universal rule that the character of an act as lawful or unlawful must be determined wholly by the law of country where the act is done.

ETHICAL IMPLICATIONS Is it ethical for corporations to lay off their U.S. workers and move their manufacturing facilities to lower-cost countries like Mexico where workers receive only minimal wages and job benefits?

Job Security

Nonunion employment relationships in the United States largely are governed by the **employment at will** doctrine. This permits an employer to freely fire employees for any reason in the absence of a contract guaranteeing a specific term of employment. Because most U.S. employees do not belong to a union and are not under the protection of employment contracts, they hold their jobs at the pleasure of their employers. While some U.S. courts offer workers relief from abusive discharges that are against public policy or violate implied promises to fire for only good cause, these exceptions to the employment at will doctrine are of limited scope.

Throughout the remainder of the developed world, all employees (both union and nonunion) receive a great deal of job security. In most countries, workers generally may be terminated only for **cause** and, unless there has been employee misconduct, the employer must give adequate *notice* of the impending discharge. Further, much of the world requires the employer to provide *severance pay*. The notice period and amount of severance pay often are tied to the discharged employee's seniority.

Employee Participation in Management

Labor relations in the United States traditionally have been marked by an adversarial relationship between labor and management. This is in sharp contrast to the European civil law model, which espouses **worker consultation** and **worker participation** in management decisions. Under this approach, employers notify labor representatives before instituting important changes (i.e., mergers, operational restructurings) in the working environment. This provides employees with an opportunity to help shape implementation of the measures. Thus, as U.S. corporations penetrate these markets, they must be fully prepared for the prospect of sharing information as well as managerial authority with their work force.

U.S. employers are not unfamiliar with this concept. For instance, the *Worker Adjustment and Retraining Notification Act* mandates that U.S. businesses with more than 100 full-time employees warn their work force before mass layoffs or plant closings. However, this notification statute is not as broad as its European counterpart, which also obligates management to negotiate with employees over how to conduct the dismissals.

While there are no similar laws in Japan, the Japanese courts scrutinize major work force reductions. They require management to offer proof of a business necessity before making mass terminations. Further, the employer must have exhausted its other alternatives before resorting to the layoffs. Finally, businesses must establish fair and reasonable procedures for deciding who will be dismissed.

Antidiscrimination Laws

Most U.S. businesses already appreciate the need to extend equal treatment to their employees. For three decades, their domestic operations have been subject to *Title VII of the Civil Rights Act*, which prohibits discrimination on the basis of race, color, religion, sex, or national origin. Title VII also has been interpreted to prevent *sexual harassment* in the workplace. In addition, employers are prohibited from discriminating against people 40 years old and older because of their age by the *Age Discrimination in Employment Act*. Further, the *Americans with Disabilities Act* provides extensive protection against employment discrimination on the basis of disability.

Antidiscrimination regulations generally are more comprehensive in the United States than in the rest of the world. While both the European Community and Japan proscribe sex discrimination in pay, they offer few real safeguards against sexual harassment. (This is likely to change as more women enter the international work force.) And, unlike the United States, most countries do not actively prevent age discrimination.

U.S. Employers Abroad

Multinational corporations must comply with the laws of each country where they maintain a foreign office. Thus, a U.S. company located in Brazil and employing both Brazilians and U.S. expatriates is subject to Brazilian employment law. Where the host nation offers little protection for employees, this requirement poses few problems for the employer. However, this does not mean it can freely discriminate. When American-controlled businesses employ U.S. citizens overseas, the employment relationship also is governed by the U.S. antidiscrimination laws.

Some companies feared that extraterritorial application of the U.S. civil rights laws might force them to violate the local laws of some host countries. However, both Congress and the courts have largely eliminated this possibility. For instance, discrimination based on religion, sex, or national origin is permitted when one of those characteristics is reasonably necessary to the normal operation of the job. Under U.S. case law, this *bona fide occupational qualification* (BFOQ) defense is triggered when compliance with the American civil rights laws would violate the host country's laws. Congress later reinforced this exception through legislation. However, as the following case illustrates, this compulsion defense has been narrowly construed.

MAHONEY v. RFE/RL, INC.
818 F.Supp. 1 (D.D.C. 1992)

■ **FACTS** RFE/RL, Inc., is best known under the names of its broadcast services, Radio Free Europe and Radio Liberty. It is a Delaware corporation with its principal place of business in Munich, Germany. It employs more than 300 U.S. citizens at its facility in Munich. Mahoney was employed at the Munich facility until he was terminated when he reached the age of 65. RFE/RL conceded it terminated Mahoney because of his age. However, it claimed this was not unlawful discrimination because the union contract covering its employees in Germany expressly provided for mandatory retirement at age 65. Thus, it argued the termination fell within a statutory exemption to the Age Discrimination in Employment Act (ADEA) in cases where compliance with the ADEA would cause an employer "to violate the laws of the country in which the workplace is located." RFE/RL pointed out that immediately after the ADEA was amended by Congress to apply to overseas employees, the company tried to implement individual contracts that would permit certain employees to continue working past the age of 65. However, the German labor courts ruled the union contract did not permit a retirement age higher than 65.

■ **ISSUE** Was the mandatory retirement at age 65 exempted from the ADEA?

■ **DECISION** No. RFE/RL is essentially arguing that the German unions simply will not allow it to eliminate the mandatory retirement policy. But the U.S. Congress will not allow it to *retain* the policy. Of the two, only Congress makes law. The mandatory retirement provision in the union contract had "legal" force in Germany in the sense that it was legally binding. Yet that does not mean it was a German "law." First, the provision is part of the contract between an employer and unions—both private entities—and has not in any way been mandated by the German government. Second, the provision does not have general application, as laws normally do, but binds only the parties to the contract. While a mandatory retirement age is a deeply embedded concept in German labor practice, that does not elevate it to the status of a law. The foreign laws exception to the ADEA applies only where another country's *laws* would be violated by compliance with the ADEA. The German labor court decisions, while holding that the union contract did not permit a retirement age higher than 65, did not hold that anything in German law compelled the decisions reached. If overseas employers could avoid application of the ADEA simply by embedding an age-discriminatory provision in a contract, having a foreign court enforce the contract, and calling the court's decision law, the ADEA's extraterritorial provisions would be largely nullified because employers could easily contract around the law.

Foreign Employers in the United States

Foreign corporations operating within the United States generally must comply with the civil rights laws. However, they are permitted to discriminate against Americans and in favor of their own citizens when authorized to do so under a *Treaty of Friendship, Commerce, and Navigation* between the United States and their home country. This exception is designed to permit foreign employers to staff key positions with citizens from their home country. Thus, it does not permit discrimination on the basis of race, color, religion, sex, national origin, or age.

The treaty defense traditionally was afforded only to companies incorporated overseas. It generally was not available to their U.S. subsidiaries because they were not foreign companies encompassed by the treaties. In the next case, however, the court extends the treaty exception to a Japanese parent's wholly owned U.S. subsidiary.

FORTINO v. QUASAR COMPANY
950 F.2d 389 (7th Cir. 1991)

■ **FACTS** Quasar Company is an unincorporated division of a U.S. corporation wholly owned by Matsushita Electric Industrial Company, Ltd., of Japan. Quasar markets in the United States products made in Japan by Matsushita, which assigns several of its own financial and marketing executives to Quasar on a temporary basis. They are employees of Quasar and are under its day-to-day control but they also retain their status as employees of Matsushita and are designated as Matsushita personnel on Quasar's books. In 1986, 10 Japanese expatriate executives were working for Quasar. When Quasar lost over $20 million, Matsushita ordered a reorganization and eliminated half of Quasar's management positions. Despite the fact that numerous U.S. executives were discharged, none of the 10 Japanese expatriate executives were dismissed. Far from being discharged, the expatriates received salary increases. The U.S. executives who were retained did not. Several discharged executives charged Quasar with discriminating against its U.S. executives on the basis of their national origin.

■ **ISSUE** Was Quasar's preferential treatment of the Japanese citizens illegal discrimination on the basis of national origin?

■ **DECISION** No. The Friendship, Commerce, and Navigation Treaty between Japan and the United States permits the companies of either party to engage within the territories of the other executive personnel of their choice. By virtue of the treaty, Japanese businesses clearly have the right to choose citizens of their own nation because they are such citizens. Further, the U.S. civil rights laws do not forbid discrimination on grounds of citizenship. Of course, especially in the case of a homogeneous country, like Japan, citizenship and national origin are highly correlated. But to use this correlation to infer national origin discrimination from a treaty-sanctioned preference for Japanese citizens who happen also to be of Japanese national origin would nullify the treaty. This was favoritism all right, but discrimination in favor of a foreign employer's expatriate citizens is not equivalent to discrimination on the basis of national origin. Quasar, even though it technically is not a Japanese company, still can rely on the treaty since its discriminatory conduct was dictated by Matsushita. A judgment that forbids Quasar to give preferential treatment to the expatriate executives that Matsushita sends would prevent Matsushita from sending its own executives to manage Quasar in preference to employing U.S. citizens.

EMPLOYMENT AND U.S. IMMIGRATION RULES

All foreign nationals are required to comply with U.S. immigration laws before entering the United States. Foreign workers cannot enter the country without first obtaining a **visa** from an overseas U.S. consul. These visas are of two types: immigrant and

FIGURE 15–2   Application of U.S. Antidiscrimination Laws

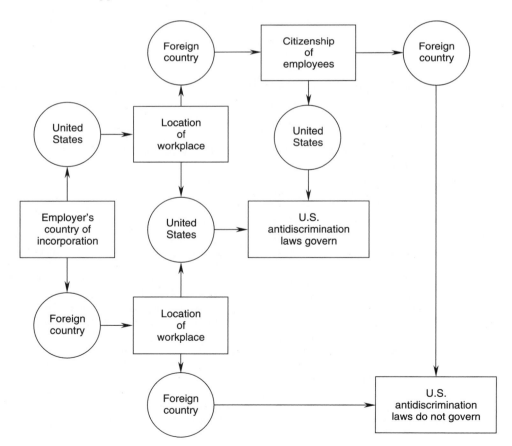

nonimmigrant. An *immigrant visa* grants permanent entry, while a *nonimmigrant visa* allows a foreigner to enter the country for a temporary stay. Because these rules primarily are designed to preserve jobs for U.S. workers, employers must carefully comply with them when staffing their domestic operations with foreign employees.

This final section begins with a brief look at employment-based immigrant visas. Attention then turns to the various nonimmigrant visas available to foreign workers wishing to temporarily enter the United States. The chapter closes with a review of the legal responsibilities placed on domestic employers to ensure compliance with the U.S. immigration laws.

Employment-Based Immigrant Visas

For many years, immigrants seeking entry for employment purposes faced a complicated application procedure before receiving a visa. First, the foreign national needed a firm job offer. Second, the applicant had to receive *labor certification* from the Department of Labor verifying that domestic workers were not available to fill the employment position. Finally, approval from the *Immigration and Naturalization Service* (INS) was necessary. This process frequently took between two and four years to complete.

Congress substantially revised the rules governing employment-based immigration in the *Immigration Act of 1990*. This legislation sought to strengthen the nation's global competitiveness by using immigration to satisfy the need for highly skilled and specially trained personnel. To promote these goals, the statute streamlined the entry procedures for skilled immigrants and increased the number of permanent employment visas from 54,000 to 140,000 per year. The new immigration policy facilitates the admission of four types of immigrants of special interest to U.S. businesses: (1) priority workers, (2) professionals with advanced degrees and aliens of exceptional ability, (3) skilled workers and professionals holding bachelor's degrees, and (4) foreign investors.

Priority Workers

Three types of foreign workers are admitted into the United States as priority workers. First, immigrants of *extraordinary ability* in business, the sciences, the arts, education, or athletics may be admitted, even without a specific job offer, if they submit evidence they will continue their work. Second, *outstanding professors and researchers* are given a preference if they have at least three years' experience in their discipline. Third, *multinational executives and managers* fall within the category of priority workers if they have been employed for at least one of the preceding three years with an overseas affiliate or branch of the U.S. company for which they will be working. Under the 1990 revisions to the immigration rules, priority workers are not required to obtain labor certification.

Advanced Degree Professionals

Professionals holding advanced degrees and aliens with a level of expertise above that ordinarily encountered in the sciences, arts, or business also are given a preference for employment-based visas. To receive a visa, an immigrant with an advanced degree must have a job offer and meet the labor certification requirement. Those formalities are not required for an alien with exceptional skills if the INS determines the visa application is in the national interest.

Skilled Workers and Professionals with a Bachelor's Degree

The INS provides a preferential treatment for visa applications filed by foreign workers capable of performing jobs requiring at least two years of experience or training. Aliens holding a bachelor's degree are treated similarly. These individuals must have a job offer and obtain labor certification. Under this category, a limited number of visas are made available to unskilled foreign workers (people capable of performing jobs requiring less than two years' training or experience).

Foreign Investors

Borrowing from the practices of Australia and Canada, the United States implemented an *alien investment policy*. Under this program, foreigners who invest between $500,000 and $3 million in domestic businesses that employ at least 10 full-time employees may receive preferential treatment for their permanent visa applications. Foreign investors do not need labor certification; however, the visas are conditional for two years to ensure the actual creation of legitimate enterprises.

Nonimmigrant Business Visas

Nonimmigrant visas are available for foreign workers seeking temporary residency in the United States. Four types of nonimmigrant visas are of particular interest to global businesses. They are available to: (1) business visitors, (2) temporary workers, (3) intracompany transferees, and (4) treaty traders.

Business Visitors

Among the easiest business visas to obtain are those for business visitors. They are available to applicants who retain a foreign residence they do not intend to abandon. While this nonimmigrant visa allows foreign workers to remain in the United States for periods up to one year, the visitors must be paid by a foreign employer. Business visitor visas are routinely issued to aliens temporarily visiting the United States to solicit business, conduct contract negotiations, or attend business meetings.

Temporary Workers

Nonimmigrant visas are available for various types of temporary workers including registered nurses, prominent businesspeople, and foreigners participating in formal training programs. This visa requires domestic employers to pay the transportation costs of temporary workers who are discharged before their contracted term expires. Further, the INS will not approve a temporary worker visa until the employer files a *Labor Condition Application* with the Department of Labor. This form certifies that the temporary employment will not hurt domestic employees or working conditions.

Temporary employees generally may be employed in the United States for up to six years.

■

INTERNATIONAL LONGSHOREMEN'S AND WAREHOUSEMEN'S UNION
v. MEESE
891 F.2d 1374 (9th Cir. 1989)

■ **FACTS** Kingcome Navigation Company, Ltd., is a Canadian company engaged in transporting logs in the coastal waters of Canada and the United States. It has two logging vessels equipped with mounted cranes specifically designed for use on board the ships. Kingcome's crane operators do not always travel with the ship on Canadian trips. Rather, they are frequently flown to the vessel solely to load or unload the cargo and then flown out again. To satisfy U.S. immigration laws, the crane operators always enter U.S. waters on the vessels and remain on them until their return to Canada. Temporary worker visas generally are denied to aliens seeking to enter the United States to perform skilled or unskilled work unless the Secretary of Labor has certified that there are not sufficient domestic workers available to do the work at the time of the application. However, this certification is not required for alien crewmen performing in any capacity required for normal operation and service on board a vessel or aircraft. The International Longshoremen's and Warehousemen's Union (ILWU) challenged the Immigration Service's decision characterizing the Canadian crane operators as "alien crewmen" entitled to enter the United States.

■ **ISSUE** Should the crane operators be permitted to temporarily enter the United States as alien crewmen?

■ **DECISION** No. The purpose behind the certification requirement is to protect U.S. workers from an influx of foreign skilled and unskilled workers. However, it does provide an exception for alien crewmen. To qualify for nonimmigrant status, an alien crewman must be serving in good faith in any capacity required for *normal operation and service* on board a vessel. Three factors are relevant to this classification: (1) the nature of the employee's duties, (2) when those duties are performed, and (3) whether the employee has a permanent connection with the ship. Applying these factors, it is obvious that the Kingcome crane operators are not alien crewmen for purposes of the immigration laws. First, cargo handling is not an activity associated with traditional crewmen but is ordinarily associated with longshore laborers. Second, these operators do not aid in the ship's navigation because their primary and substantial duties occur not while the vessel is under way, but rather once the ship has entered U.S. territorial waters to load or unload the cargo. Third, these operators do not have a permanent connection with the ship. Although they travel with the ships on trips to the United States, it is undisputed that they frequently fly to the ship on trips within Canada when it is time to load or unload the cargo. This fact also demonstrates that the crane operators are not in "good faith" necessary for the operation of the vessel.

Intracompany Transferees

Another nonimmigrant visa allows multinational companies to temporarily transfer to their U.S. office foreign executives, managers, and persons with specialized knowledge working for them overseas. Managers and executives may work in the United States for up to seven years and workers with specialized knowledge may remain for five years. To qualify for this visa, the foreign worker must have spent at least one of the preceding three years working overseas in one of the U.S. company's branches, subsidiaries, or affiliates.

CONCEPT SUMMARY Employment-Based Visas		
IMMIGRANT (permanent)	Priority Workers	• Immigrants of extraordinary ability • Outstanding professors and researchers • Multinational executives/managers
	Advanced-Degree Professionals	Labor certification required
	Skilled Workers and Professionals with Bachelor's Degree	Labor certification required
	Foreign Investors	
NONIMMIGRANT (temporary)	Business Visitors	
	Temporary Workers	Labor certification required
	Intracompany Transferees	
	Treaty Traders and Investors	

Treaty Traders and Investors

These visas are provided for foreign nationals who are either trading or investing in the United States. Treaty trader visas permit foreign-owned companies to hire their nationals to work in their U.S. offices. These visas are not available to foreign companies unless the U.S. operations do at least 50 percent of their business with the applicant's nation. Foreign investors may receive similar visas if they can demonstrate a need to enter the United States to manage U.S. investments. Both types are called *treaty* visas because they generally are available only to the nationals of countries that have reciprocal treaties with the United States. The Japanese expatriates in the *Fortino v. Quasar* case (discussed earlier) entered the country with treaty trader visas.

**Employers'
Responsibilities**

Congress enacted the *Immigration Reform and Control Act of 1986* to stem the flow of illegal aliens entering the United States. The statute established civil and criminal sanctions that can be assessed against employers who knowingly hire unauthorized immigrants. At the same time, Congress feared that these penalties might discourage employers from hiring any workers who looked foreign. As a result, the statute penalizes companies that discriminate on the basis of national origin or citizenship in their hiring decisions.

Sanctions for Hiring Illegal Aliens

Any U.S. employer that *knowingly* hires an illegal alien may be liable for civil penalties of up to $5,000 per violation. The *regular, repeated, and intentional* hiring of unauthorized immigrants may lead to the imposition of criminal penalties. These sanctions also apply to companies that retain foreign employees after their visas have expired.

Documentation Requirements

To further strengthen enforcement efforts, the statute requires employers to implement *compliance systems* that verify each worker's identity and status. This requirement generally is met if the job applicant provides the employer with one of the following documents: a U.S. passport, a certificate of U.S. citizenship, a foreign passport that permits U.S. employment, or a resident alien card (green card) that authorizes U.S. employment.

Discrimination Penalties

Employers who refuse to hire workers based on their national origin or citizenship may be forced to pay civil penalties as well as front pay and back pay. Illegal discrimination often results when employers refuse to accept genuine-looking documents that verify worker identity and status or insist on additional documentation beyond those mentioned above.

QUESTIONS AND PROBLEM CASES

1. When is an agent personally liable on a contract she negotiates for her principal?

2. When does the Foreign Corrupt Practices Act permit U.S. businesses to make cash payments to foreign governmental officials?

3. What is meant by employment at will? How does it differ from the employment policies of most countries?

4. What are the two major types of employment-based visas available to foreign nationals desiring to enter the United States?

5. Wade Kern, a U.S. citizen, entered into an employment contract with Dynalectron Corporation, a U.S. corporation, to perform duties as a helicopter pilot. Dynalectron was under a subcontract with Kawasaki Heavy Industries to provide pilots to work in Saudi Arabia. Kern's job consisted of flying a helicopter over crowds of Moslems making their pilgrimage along the path to Mecca. The purpose of the flights was to protect against any violent outbreaks and to help fight the fires that frequently resulted from marchers cooking too close to their tents. Saudi Arabian law, based on the tenets of the Islamic religion, prohibits the entry of non-Moslems into the holy area (Mecca) under penalty of death. Thus, Dynalectron, in accordance with its contract with Kawasaki, required all pilots to be (or become) Moslem. Dynalectron regularly sent pilots to indoctrination courses where they were taught the basic formulation of the Islamic faith, converted thereto, and received a certificate manifesting said conversion. Kern attended such a course and converted from Baptist to Moslem. However, he immediately changed his mind and, as a result, was denied employment as a pilot. Kern charged Dynalectron with discrimination against him because of his religious beliefs. Has Dynalectron violated Title VII of the Civil Rights Act?

6. Elizabeth Nicol began working as a secretary in Ben Line's Aberdeen, Scotland, office in 1981. At that time, the normal retirement age for the company's male/female employees was 65/60 respectively, and the company pension scheme was arranged accordingly. In 1983, upon learning that legislation would soon be introduced equalizing male/female retirement ages, Ben Line implemented a common retirement age of 60 years for both men and women. To ease the transition for existing male employees, the company announced a phased retirement scheme for men. If at the date of the 1983 change a male employee was older than 55, he would retire at 65; if over 50, at 64; if over 45, at 63; and if under 45, at 62. In 1986, the United Kingdom enacted the *Sex Discrimination Act,* which prohibited unlawful discriminatory

retirement ages between men and women. In 1988, Ben Line forced Nicol to retire at 60 despite the fact that she was over 55 years old when the new retirement scheme was implemented. Nicol complained this amounted to sex-based discrimination since similarly situated men were permitted to work until age 65. Ben Line argued its program was fair because men originally had an expectation they would work until 65 and would not qualify for a state retirement pension until that age, while women already qualified for a pension at 60. It claimed that if the new retirement age had been introduced immediately for men, a significant number of them would have had little or no time to make provision for their changed circumstances. Did the company's phased retirement scheme constitute unlawful discrimination on the basis of sex?

7. Tammy Ward, an Alabama resident, claimed an employee of W & H Voortman, a Canadian corporation, met with her in Alabama and encouraged her to apply for a job with the company as its products distributor in middle and southern Alabama. According to Ward, after she was offered the job and accepted it, she was either fired or never even officially hired because of her sex. She filed a sex discrimination suit against Voortman in a U.S. district court. The company moved to dismiss on the grounds that, as a foreign corporation, it was not subject to the U.S. antidiscrimination laws. Is Voortman correct?

8. Mitsubishi Bank, Ltd., is a Japanese corporation with a branch office in New York City. Mitsubishi regularly assigns executive and managerial employees from its home office in Japan to the New York branch on assignments of limited duration. Several U.S. employees complained that this practice constituted intentional racial discrimination against persons of non-Oriental ancestry and origin. They alleged that Mitsubishi reserved the overwhelming majority of its top management positions for the rotating Japanese staff. Will the Friendship, Commerce, and Navigation Treaty between Japan and the United States permit Mitsubishi to discriminate on the basis of race and national origin?

9. McGhee and Rudh, then residing in California, were hired by Aramco, a U.S. corporation, and sent to work in the company's compound in the King-

dom of Saudi Arabia. Their contracts expressly incorporated Aramco company rules, which, as required by Saudi law, included provisions making Aramco liable for terminating its employees without a valid reason. During their period of residence in Saudi Arabia, McGhee and Rudh rented videotapes to fellow Aramco employees out of their homes. American expatriates living in Aramco's compounds were prohibited from operating commercial businesses. This prohibition derived from Saudi commercial law that proscribed the operation of any commercial business without a license. Because licenses are generally unavailable to non-Saudis, expatriates on Aramco compounds were effectively foreclosed from operating commercial businesses. Aramco distributed several notices to its employees concerning the prohibition of commercial businesses, although videotape rental was not listed as a prohibited activity. After Aramco received an anonymous letter claiming McGhee and Rudh were operating a very big business, Aramco officials informed the chief of police of the Eastern Province. He agreed to let Aramco handle the matter internally, provided McGhee and Rudh were terminated and repatriated to the United States. Their videotapes were confiscated and destroyed. McGhee and Rudh complained they were fired without a valid reason in violation of the Saudi law standards incorporated in their contract. They provided evidence that many members of Aramco's personnel division, including the company's lawyer and the head of its security division, had been aware of their activities. In fact, several of these individuals were members of their video club. A jury found Aramco liable for wrongful termination. Should the jury's verdict be upheld?

10. Two U.S. citizens, Judy Corbeille and Fernando Watson, were employees on cruise ships belonging to Kloster Cruise, Ltd., a Bahamian corporation doing business as Norwegian Cruise Lines. Corbeille alleged she was discriminated against and discharged from her position because of her pregnancy, and Watson claimed Kloster discriminated against him on account of his race. Kloster asserted that, as a foreign corporation that does not conduct business in the United States, it was not subject to the U.S. antidiscrimination laws. Is Kloster correct?

16

Environmental Law

INTRODUCTION

Environmental issues transcend national borders and threaten the quality of life for both present and future generations. Acid rain, global warming, depletion of the ozone layer, and the disposal of hazardous wastes are not merely local concerns. They are serious and far-ranging problems that are unlikely to be resolved in the absence of global cooperation.

As a result of the growing list of transnational environmental dangers, there has been a clamoring for the international law regime to take a more active role in preserving the natural resources of the world. However, since most pollution sources and many of the resources needing protection are situated within the territory of sovereign nations, international regulatory efforts must carefully consider national sovereignty issues. Still, despite the reluctance on the part of national governments to sacrifice their sovereign powers, the past two decades have witnessed a growing reliance on global institutions to address the environmental crisis.

Chapter Overview   Environmental law is among the most rapidly growing areas of the international law system. Domestic laws, bilateral treaties, and multilateral conventions abound. In many instances, they have created a complex web of overlapping institutions that can make the global business manager's compliance task overwhelming.

This chapter surveys the fundamental environmental issues confronting global businesses today. It begins with a brief look at the sources of international environmental law and then shifts to an examination of the major environmental events that have shaped the international legal system. This is followed by discussion of the predominant governmental and nongovernmental institutions that promote international cooperation in the formation and enforcement of environmental law. Attention then is directed to the problems inherent in a transnational legal system and the influence they have on the form and substance of global rules. Then, after looking at the role of domestic law enforcement in the environmental realm, the chapter closes with some suggestions on how businesses can establish a responsible environmental management scheme.

SOURCES OF INTERNATIONAL ENVIRONMENTAL LAW

The changing economic and political configuration of the world frustrates any attempt to precisely identify the prevailing norms of international environmental law. For instance, today many undeveloped countries, over the objections of the developed world, are claiming that policies such as compensation and redistribution of wealth are binding upon the developed nations as part of a new legal order. Despite such differences, there do exist some guiding principles that assist in the discovery of the current state of the law. Basically, environmental law, like all international law, is derived from several sources: customary practices, international conventions (treaties), general principles of civilized nations, judicial decisions and teachings, and resolutions of international organizations. (The sources of international law are discussed more fully in Chapter 2.)

Customary Practices

Customary international law arises when it becomes apparent that nations are following a certain course of conduct under the belief that their behavior is mandated by the international legal order. Because of the widely varying philosophies of the nations of the world, these **customary practices** generally provide no more than vague guiding principles. Even then, many developing nations refuse to accept the existence of customary law, considering those practices to be unpleasant vestiges of the colonial and imperialist policies that retarded their political and economic development.

Despite this confusion, it still is possible to identify certain practices that have been elevated to the level of international law. For instance, it has long been recognized that countries have sovereign rights to exploit and conserve the marine resources of their coastal waters. Further, it is generally accepted that a country should not use its territory to harm the environment outside of its borders. Complementing this norm is an accompanying responsibility to issue a prompt warning when events that occur within a nation's territory threaten the environment of other countries.

International Conventions

Perhaps the clearest sources of international environmental law are the numerous **conventions** (treaties) implemented by the nations of the world. As a general rule, the great disparity in national commitments to environmental issues dictates that global accords can contain no more than the most general principles (offering the lowest common denominator) if they are to achieve widespread adoption. Similarly, the reluctance of most nations to sacrifice their sovereignty, even for the sake of pressing environmental issues, greatly limits the obligations and restrictions that these treaties can impose on participating countries.

Because of these political realities, global conventions frequently confine themselves to a research and reporting role. They require adopting nations to keep records of certain types of conduct and to periodically report their environmental activities to an international organization. International environmental treaties also may insist that ratifying countries cooperate in implementing monitoring systems.

General Principles of Civilized Nations

Another source of international law springs from certain **general principles** recognized by civilized nations. Similar to customary law, these principles are derived from fundamental notions that can be found in virtually all the major legal systems. Included in this category of international environmental law are the principles that nations should avoid damaging the environment and that compensation should be paid when such damage occurs.

Judicial Decisions and Teachings

The Statute of the International Court of Justice provides that **judicial decisions** and the **teachings** of the most highly qualified publicists of the various nations also may constitute a source of international law. Global environmental law may be discovered in the decisions of the International Court of Justice as well as from arbitral rulings and the judgments of national courts.

TRAIL SMELTER CASE (U.S. v. CANADA)
3 R.Int'l Arb. Awards 1938 (1941)

■ **FACTS** Consolidated Mining and Smelting Company, a Canadian corporation, operated a smelter plant at Trail, British Columbia. As the corporation increased its smelting activities, it emitted more and more sulphur dioxide fumes into the air. Over a 12-year period, these emissions caused considerable environmental damage to the state of Washington in the United States. Under previous agreements and arbitration, the Canadian government agreed to pay over $400,000 in damages. The United States then asked an arbitration tribunal to enjoin the company from causing any further environmental damage to the state of Washington.

■ **ISSUE** Does international law require that the Trail Smelter refrain from causing further damage to the state of Washington?

■ **DECISION** Yes. According to Professor Eagleton (*Responsibility of States in International Law*, 1928, p. 80): "A state owes at all times a duty to protect other states against injurious acts by individuals from within its jurisdiction." To date, there has been no air pollution case dealt with by an international tribunal. The nearest analogy is that of water pollution, although there also no decision of an international tribunal has been found. There are, however, as regards both air pollution and water pollution, certain decisions by the Supreme Court of the United States that legitimately can be taken as a guide when no contrary rule prevails in international law. These decisions, taken as a whole, provide an adequate basis for the conclusion that, under the principles of international law, no state has the right to use or permit the use of its territory in such a manner as to cause injury by fumes in or to the territory of another when the case is of serious consequence and the injury is established by clear and convincing evidence. Accordingly, Canada is responsible in international law for the conduct of the Trail Smelter and must ensure that the company causes no further environmental damage to the state of Washington.

Resolutions of International Organizations

Global environmental law also may be discovered in the **resolutions** and declarations of various international organizations. Actions by the United Nations General Assembly or by the various environmental conferences sponsored by the United Nations have the potential of rising to the level of international law in two ways. First, in very limited instances, an international organization adopts a *binding resolution*. For instance, the Organization for Economic Cooperation and Development (OECD) has imposed an obligation on the industrialized nations that make up its membership to exchange information concerning certain chemicals. Second, and much more frequently, these international organizations promulgate recommendations, programs of action, and declarations of principles. While these are *nonbinding resolutions*, they may enter the realm of international law when they are followed by an overwhelming majority of nations.

LANDMARK GLOBAL INITIATIVES

International environmental conventions, as well as bilateral treaties, are the predominant sources of global environmental law. While there have been more than 1,000 of these conferences and treaties, a few stand out as watershed events in the development of international environmental law. This section introduces six land-mark initiatives.

The Stockholm Conference

While environmental protection efforts date back at least as far as medieval times (England made it illegal to burn soft coal during certain times of the year), international environmental laws are a relatively recent phenomenon. Perhaps the most important event in the development of international cooperation in confronting environmental problems occurred in 1972 at the *United Nations Conference on the Human Environment.* Convened in Stockholm after two years of extensive preparations, the Stockholm Conference brought together delegations from over 100 nations who laid the groundwork for most of the international environmental proposals that have surfaced during the past 20 years.

In the *Stockholm Declaration on the Human Environment,* the conferees recognized a global responsibility to preserve the environment for present and future generations. To achieve this ambitious goal, the Stockholm Conference unveiled a basic action plan that called for worldwide environmental assessment and management. To carry out the assessment functions, a program, called **Earthwatch,** was established to facilitate international cooperation in research activities, monitoring efforts, and information exchanges.

Several important principles were recognized at the Stockholm Conference. For instance, the delegates squarely confronted the fact that the differing levels of economic development among nations posed a serious obstacle to international cooperation in protecting the environment. Accordingly, they called for financial and technical assistance for underdeveloped countries. Perhaps most importantly, the conference adopted a middle ground between nations' sovereign rights over natural resources and their responsibilities to the rest of the world. While conceding that nations possess sovereign rights to exploit their resources pursuant to their domestic environmental policies, the delegates balanced those rights with corresponding duties to ensure that their activities do not cause environmental damage to areas outside of their national borders. Starting with this fundamental rule of customary international law, the Stockholm Conference urged national governments to cooperatively develop international rules concerning liability and compensation for environmental harms that cross national borders.

The World Charter for Nature

In the years immediately after the Stockholm Conference, international environmental lawmaking efforts increased as global and regional conferences addressed a wide range of environmental issues. These activities culminated in the U.N. General Assembly's declaration of the **World Charter for Nature** in 1982. Attempting to implement the principles that emerged from the Stockholm Conference, the World Charter recognized that mankind had a responsibility to maintain the quality of nature and conserve the world's natural resources. To honor this obligation, individual nations were expected to incorporate conservation efforts into their economic planning and domestic lawmaking.

Public and private entities were instructed to cooperate in conserving nature. Specifically, the World Charter envisioned a worldwide exchange of environmental information. Nations were expected to enact environmental protection regulations and to develop effective methods for assessing the impact of government activities on the environment. Each country was expected to grant equal access to both nationals and foreigners in the formulation and enforcement of environmental protection measures. Further, nations were expected to ensure that businesses did not unnecessarily damage the environment both within their borders or in areas outside of their territory.

The Brundtland Report

As concern for the world environment increased, it was matched by a growing awareness of the need to narrow the wide differences that separated the positions of the developed and developing nations. Many developing nations viewed environmental protection proposals as a direct threat to the pace of their economic growth. They resented the fact that the developed world, which had pursued environmentally destructive paths in attaining its industrialized position, was now trying to force them to retard their own development for the sake of the world environment.

Addressing these concerns in 1987, the *World Commission on Environment and Development* concluded that a clean environment was essential to any nation's economic development. In its *Brundtland Report,* the commission asserted that countries would be unable to develop economically if they had a deteriorating environmental base. Stressing the importance of environmental protection to the developing world, the report introduced the concept of **sustainable development,** which it defined as economic development that meets the demands of the present without compromising the ability of future generations to meet their own needs. The Brundtland Report argued that conservation efficiency, technological improvements, recycling, and reducing population growth were essential prerequisites to sustainable development.

The Montreal Protocol

During the mid-1980s, scientists warned that a significant hole was developing in the ozone layer over the Antarctic each spring. This problem seemed to stem from chlorofluorocarbons (CFCs) and halons, chemicals that were widely used for air-conditioning, solvents, styrofoam, and spray aerosol propellants. Depleting the ozone layer would expose the world's surface to larger amounts of ultraviolet radiation, which would lead to increased skin cancer and decreased plant productivity. Acting on this warning, 57 nations signed the *Montreal Protocol on Substances That Deplete the Ozone Layer* in 1987. The Montreal Protocol, which became effective in 1989, agreed to freeze world consumption of CFCs at 1986 levels and to cut production and consumption in half by 1999. However, developing nations were given a 10-year exemption during which they could actually increase CFC use before being required to meet the 50 percent reduction.

Immediately after the Montreal Protocol became effective, several new developments shocked the world. First, scientific data conclusively proved that CFCs were posing a much more serious threat to the environment than was originally theorized. Second, it was discovered that the ozone layer was being destroyed by a wider variety of chemicals than originally believed. Finally, it became obvious that Third World nations would not participate in the Montreal Protocol unless they received technical and financial support from the developed world.

The Montreal Protocol stands as a landmark example of international environmental cooperation, in part, because of its prompt response to these new concerns. Because the original agreement called for regular reassessments of its measures, the adopting countries were able to quickly reconvene to address the new developments. As a result, 93 nations agreed to amendments that instituted a more comprehensive and aggressive program that would phase out CFCs by the year 2000. Developing countries still retained their 10-year grace period. However, a $240 million interim fund was created to assist developing nations in reaching the revised goals. Previous international agreements only acknowledged the responsibility of the developed world to assist developing nations in meeting their environmental goals. This was the first time developed nations actually agreed to extend financial assistance.

Two years later, 86 countries agreed to an accelerated schedule for phasing out ozone-destroying chemicals, calling for their elimination in the developed world by 1996 instead of 2000. Further, the previously established interim fund (due to expire by 1993) was replaced by a permanent fund designed to help developing countries replace ozone-depleting gases with environmentally safe substitutes.

The Basel Convention

Many lesser developed nations are struggling to improve their economic condition and, consequently, do not share the environmental protection concerns or capabilities of the developed world. These differing levels of commitment and enforcement resulted in the underdeveloped world becoming a dumping ground for the rest of the world's waste. Responding to this reality, the United Nations in 1989 convened the *Basel Convention on the Control of Transboundary Movements of Hazardous Wastes and Their Disposal.*

The 54 countries that adopted the Basel Convention established an international **notice and consent** structure for the export of toxic wastes. The types of wastes that are covered under this requirement of **prior informed consent** are listed in an annex to the agreement. Specifically, whenever a nation intends to export hazardous wastes, it must first notify competent authorities in the export country, the import country, and any country through which the waste will be transported. The exporting nation must not permit the shipment to be made until it receives written confirmation from these authorities that they agree to the shipment and evidence that the waste will be disposed of in an environmentally sound manner. Further, all transboundary shipments of hazardous waste must be covered by insurance. Finally, the Basel Convention requires each adopting nation to treat any violation of its terms by private parties to be a criminal act. Thus, each country must enact domestic legislation designed to prevent and penalize illegal transboundary waste shipments.

The Earth Summit

In 1992, delegates from over 150 countries (including the leaders of 103 nations) met in Rio de Janeiro for the *United Nations Conference on the Environment and Development.* This 12-day meeting, known as the **Earth Summit,** was intended to gain sustained, top-level attention for environmental issues.

CONCEPT SUMMARY
Landmark Initiatives

Event	Date	Contribution
Stockholm Conference	1972	• Established Earthwatch to carry out environmental assessment • Recognized that sovereign rights are balanced by global responsibilities
World Charter for Nature	1982	• Declared that nations should incorporate conservation efforts in economic planning • Called for global cooperation
Brundtland Report	1987	• Recognized differing agendas of developed and developing nations • Called for sustainable development
Montreal Protocol	1989–1992	• Demonstrated quick global response to environmental crisis • First time developed world agreed to finance environmental conservation efforts
Basel Convention	1989	• Recognized problem of transboundary shipments of hazardous wastes • Established system of prior informed consent
Earth Summit	1992	• Revealed continued existence of wide gap in environmental priorities between developing and developed world • Established Sustainable Development Commission to track global compliance

---

Despite its lofty goals, the Earth Summit provided few concrete results. More than anything else, it illustrated the extent to which global environmental issues touch on vital national interests. Developing nations insisted their active participation in preservation of the environment would require massive levels of financial assistance. The developed nations acknowledged they have a greater obligation to preserve the environment because they are the greatest users of the world's resources. However, while they agreed in principle to provide additional financial assistance, their pledges fell far short of the levels requested by the United Nations.

Two binding treaties were signed at the conference. A *climate change treaty* requires the industrialized nations to limit their emissions of earth-warming, greenhouse gases. A *biodiversity agreement* requires its signatories to establish policies aimed at preserving flora and fauna. The treaty also calls on developed and developing nations to cooperate in their research efforts. (The United States refused to sign the biodiversity treaty out of concern that the pact did not provide adequate patent and copyright protection for U.S. biotechnology.)

Perhaps the greatest benefits from the Earth Summit are less easily measured. First, the United Nations created a *Sustainable Development Commission,* designed to track each country's compliance with the pledges it made at the Rio conference. Second, despite its open-ended treaties and weak declarations, the Earth Summit may have performed a valuable *educational function.* Over 9,000 reporters attended the conference, providing the greatest exposure ever to an environmental convention. The worldwide attention the Earth Summit received may mobilize public opinion and pressure the world community to fully commit itself to a serious, global initiative to preserve the environment.

PREDOMINANT INTERNATIONAL INSTITUTIONS

Nations are not the predominant forces behind most international environmental lawmaking and cooperation. Instead, a highly decentralized system of transnational institutions and nongovernmental organizations has been the primary catalyst for ongoing cooperation in preserving the world environment. Although these international bodies have varied roles, they frequently share the following functions: conducting environmental research, collecting and sharing information, recommending new international treaties and rules, and monitoring compliance with current treaties and rules. Three fundamental types of institutions greatly influence the formation of global environmental law: coordinating agencies, intergovernmental organizations, and nongovernmental organizations.

Coordinating Agencies

The institutional framework of the world's environmental regulatory system is best characterized as a confusing array of distinct organizations with overlapping responsibilities. Recognizing the inefficiency and frustration brought about by this state of affairs, the United Nations has made several efforts to coordinate the functions of these institutions.

Economic and Social Council

In an early attempt to coordinate the activities of the growing number of transnational institutions operating in the international community, the United Nations created an *Economic and Social Council* (ECOSOC). This required various specialized organizations, including several environmental bodies, to participate in a free and regular exchange of information. ECOSOC also gave each agency the right to attend the others' meetings.

Administrative Committee on Coordination

ECOSOC's efforts proved unwieldy, in part, because information generally was channeled through ECOSOC and then back down to the other organizations. It stimulated very little ongoing dialogue and coordination among the organizations. To address these problems, ECOSOC formed the *Administrative Committee on Coordination* (ACC), which requires twice yearly meetings between the Secretary-General of the United Nations and the heads of the participating agencies to resolve coordination problems. However, this reform was not well suited for the environmental crises confronting the world. First, many of the organizations covered by the ACC had little interest in environmental concerns. Second, ECOSOC and the ACC included only a limited number of organizations, excluding many transnational agencies and nongovernmental organizations that were big contributors to the coordination problems. Finally, the twice yearly meetings were too infrequent to keep pace with the rapid developments of the environmental field.

United Nations Environment Program

The delegates of the Stockholm Conference recognized the fundamental importance of transnational and nongovernmental organizations. Accordingly, the Stockholm Declaration stated, in part, that nations should "ensure that international organizations play a coordinated, efficient, and dynamic role for the protection and improvement of the environment." Responding to this recommendation, the United Nations General Assembly created the *United Nations Environment Program* (UNEP) to serve as a coordinating body for global environmental protection initiatives.

Despite continual budgetary restrictions, UNEP has made valuable contributions in the form of environmental assessment and management. It pioneered Earthwatch (discussed above), the environmental assessment program envisioned by the Stockholm Conference. Further, UNEP has been prominent in the drafting of environmental regulations at both the international and national level. In support of these functions, it has served as a worldwide disseminator of environmental information.

Intergovernmental Organizations

A wide range of transnational governmental institutions formulate and encourage public and private compliance with global environmental policies. Some deal exclusively with environmental issues while others do so only peripherally. These institutions are by-products of the many global, regional, and bilateral agreements among nations. Because their powers and principles are subject to the consent of sovereign nations, they seldom have strong lawmaking or enforcement powers. Instead, they generally confine themselves to research, information-sharing, and advocacy roles. This section briefly examines a few of the more prominent intergovernmental organizations.

Organization for Economic Cooperation and Development

The *Organization for Economic Cooperation and Development* (OECD) is made up of the countries of Western Europe, Australia, Canada, Japan, New Zealand, and the United States. While the OECD originally was designed to promote economic growth, it later established an environment committee that has been responsible for broad policies of environmental impact assessment. In general, the OECD evaluates and recommends various options its member states may then adopt or reject. This organization has been extremely influential in the development of international environmental regulation. Many of its initiatives have been adopted at the leading environmental conventions.

International Law Commission

Created by the U.N. General Assembly after World War II, the *International Law Commission* (ILC) was charged with developing and codifying international law. In recent years, the ILC has taken a keen interest in international matters and, most recently, has proposed that *willful acts of serious environmental pollution* be regarded as crimes against the peace and security of mankind.

World Health Organization

The *World Health Organization* (WHO) has established regional centers around the globe to assist in eliminating epidemics and illnesses and improving the quality of housing and hospitals. It collects and disseminates health information and works to upgrade worldwide health standards. In 1989, a WHO conference adopted the European Charter on the Environment and Health, which insisted that polluters should be held financially responsible for the restoration of the environment.

World Bank

As the primary funding source for most international economic development, the *International Bank for Reconstruction and Development* (World Bank) could greatly influence environmental decision making. It is the leader of a group of international lending institutions (see Chapter 2). Together with these and several regional development banks, the World Bank adopted the Declaration of Environmental Policies and Procedures Relating to Economic Development, which called for the rejection of financing for environmentally destructive projects. Many environmentalists accuse the World Bank of failing to adhere to these standards when confronted with economically desirable project requests.

Nongovernmental Organizations

Intergovernmental organizations, through the multitude of conventions they sponsor, provide the greatest source of international environmental law. They are assisted in this endeavor by the thousands of nongovernmental organizations that regularly lobby for environmental issues. These private institutions are of three general types: (1) *restricted groups* with scientific or professional interests, (2) *research centers* that serve educational and consultative roles, and (3) *advocacy groups* whose membership is open to the general public. By receiving nonvoting observer and consultation status at many international conferences, these nongovernmental organizations are able to help define the environmental agenda.

The role of nongovernmental institutions is not without its critics. For instance, many underdeveloped nations complain that only the well-financed groups that represent the interests of the developed world have any meaningful influence on the formation of international rules. Because effective participation often depends on a high degree of organization and access to the latest information, these complaints may be valid. Still, nongovernmental organizations have been extremely useful in identifying environmental problems and in encouraging international governmental organizations to act.

International Council of Scientific Unions

Composed of 20 constituent unions, the *International Council of Scientific Unions* (ICSU) is a broad-based federation of scientific organizations. It continually updates the available research on environmental issues by forming interdisciplinary committees charged with examining the latest scientific questions. Its Scientific Committee on Problems of the Environment (SCOPE) has been instructed to educate the public as to its influence on the global environment and to offer scientific advice to governments and intergovernmental organizations with respect to environmental problems.

World Conservation Union

Of all the nongovernmental organizations, the *World Conservation Union* (IUCN), formerly called the International Union for the Conservation of Nature and Natural Resources, has had the greatest overall impact on the global environment. Along with ICSU, the World Conservation Union was a moving force behind the Stockholm Conference and has worked closely with UNEP in implementing that convention's action plan. Representing over 60 nations and hundreds of universities and national nongovernmental organizations, IUCN evaluates the status of renewable natural resources and educates the world about conservation measures. In addition to the Stockholm Conference, the World Conservation Union has mobilized support for numerous international conventions involved with the conservation of natural resources.

Worldwide Fund for Nature

The *Worldwide Fund for Nature* (WWF) is an international nongovernmental organization whose objective is to collect and distribute funds for global conservation activities. It has provided financial support for lawsuits attempting to enjoin environmentally destructive projects. However, WWF is perhaps best known for pioneering the concept of **debt-for-nature swaps**. Typically, these transactions involve the purchase of an underdeveloped nation's commercial bank debts by a private organization or a governmental agency in exchange for the debtor country's agreement to promote conservation efforts.

THE NATURE OF GLOBAL ENVIRONMENTAL REGULATION

For several fundamental reasons, intergovernmental organizations have experienced mixed results in their efforts to enforce global environmental regulations. These problems arise from differences in national priorities, the unwillingness of most countries to waive their sovereign powers, and the enforcement difficulties inherent in a world of sovereign nations. These economic and political realities clearly constrain the form and substance of international environmental regulation.

Differing Agendas
International efforts to preserve the environment have been thwarted, in part, because not all nations share the same commitment to environmental protection. One source of discord stems from the view of many underdeveloped nations that a strictly enforced regime of environmental regulations will retard their economic development. And, even among the developed nations, a deep-rooted suspicion exists that many environmental protection initiatives are disguised barriers to free trade.

Conservation and Economic Development

The disparate economic conditions of the developing and the developed nations have proved to be a serious obstacle to international efforts to formulate comprehensive environmental regulations. At one level, the developing nations view conservation efforts as a severe cost in their development programs that was never borne by the industrialized world during its early stages of economic development. They also claim the right to share in the advanced technology of the industrialized world without financial obligation. However, while the developed nations often admit to their responsibility for the current state of the world environment, they generally have refused to permit access to their environmentally safe technology without compensation. In the absence of technological and financial assistance, the developing nations have rejected many environmental initiatives.

Free Trade and the Environment

Environmental regulations are becoming an increasing source of trade friction as strict national regulations frequently are attacked as barriers to free trade. The leading embodiment of international law protecting free trade in goods is the General Agreement on Tariffs and Trade (GATT). While environmental issues were not a high priority at the time the original GATT agreement was drafted, it permits a nation to enforce nondiscriminatory trade restraints when they are necessary to protect human, animal, or plant life. However, these exceptions have been construed very narrowly. Consider the following two cases that examine the national and international controversy accompanying U.S. legislation designed to protect dolphins from domestic and foreign tuna fleets.

EARTH ISLAND INSTITUTE v. MOSBACHER
929 F.2d 1449 (9th Cir. 1991)

■ **FACTS** For unknown reasons, yellowfin tuna in the eastern tropical Pacific Ocean swim below schools of dolphins. Thus, fishing vessels often set their purse seine nets on dolphins to catch the tuna below. Dolphins are frequently killed or maimed in this process. After the United States restricted this method of harvesting tuna, the number of dolphins killed by the U.S. fleet was reduced. However, dolphin slaughter by foreign nations remained a growing problem. Accordingly, the United States enacted specific standards intended to ensure that foreign tuna fishing fleets would reduce the number of dolphins killed. Specifically, the statute mandates a ban on imports of yellowfin tuna products from a foreign nation until it is certified that the nation's incidental kill rate of dolphins is comparable to that of the United States. Under this statute, the comparability findings would be based on the average rate of incidental killings over a one-year period. Despite this provision, the National Marine Fisheries Service (the agency designated to enforce the statute) decided to refrain from imposing an embargo if an offending nation could demonstrate that it met the allowable kill rate during the first six months following the year in which the allowable limits were exceeded. Based on this interpretation, the United States lifted an embargo against Mexico even though Mexico had exceeded the statutory limits. The Earth Island Institute, a nongovernmental environmental organization, petitioned the court to enjoin the importation of yellowfin tuna from Mexico on the grounds that the government's reconsideration of the embargo violated the federal statute.

■ **ISSUE** Should the court prevent the importation of Mexican tuna?

■ **DECISION**   Yes. The government's primary argument is that the six-month reconsideration provision is within the discretion delegated by Congress to the agency for regulatory implementation of the statute. The difficulty with this position is that agencies do not have discretion to issue regulations that conflict with statutory language and congressional purpose. The language of the statute is clear; it requires an embargo unless the incidental killing rates conform to U.S. standards based on a full year's data. The government's reconsideration provision would seem to be further evidence of the administration's lax enforcement of dolphin protection standards against foreign fleets and, as such, is inconsistent with both the language and the purpose of the statute.

Immediately following the *Earth Island* decision, the United States reinstated its embargo against imports of yellowfin tuna from Mexico. The Mexican government then requested a GATT panel to rule on the legality of the U.S. embargo. (The GATT dispute resolution process is discussed in Chapter 2.)

UNITED STATES—RESTRICTIONS ON IMPORTS OF TUNA
GATT Doc. DS21/R (Sept. 3, 1991)

■ **FACTS**   Mexico argued the U.S. import policy on yellowfin tuna violated GATT by imposing quantitative restrictions or quantitative prohibitions on imports. It claimed the embargo was inconsistent with GATT's objectives of maintaining the free flow of goods. The United States responded that its embargo was excepted from GATT's rule against quantitative prohibitions on imports since it was necessary to protect the life and health of dolphins.

■ **ISSUE**   Is the U.S. embargo on yellowfin tuna from Mexico a violation of GATT?

■ **DECISION**   Yes. The embargo of yellowfin tuna is inconsistent with GATT's rules against prohibitions or restrictions on imports. While GATT does include an exception for measures that are necessary to protect human, animal, or plant life, it is not applicable here for two reasons. First, while GATT permits a nation to establish its own human, animal, or plant life standards within its own territory, that discretion does not extend outside its national jurisdiction. If the United States were permitted to impose its dolphin protection standards on tuna caught outside its territory, the door would be open for any country to unilaterally determine the life or health protection standards for the rest of the world. Second, GATT's exception for trade restrictive health standards applies only when those measures are *necessary*. The United States has not demonstrated that its embargo is necessary to protect dolphins. Specifically, it has not shown that it has exhausted all of its dolphin protection options through measures more consistent with GATT's free trade principles, in particular, through the negotiation of international cooperative arrangements.

■ **ETHICAL IMPLICATIONS**   After the GATT panel's decision, the United States may continue to insist that U.S. fleets comply with the dolphin-safe fishing methods, but it may not force foreign fleets to comply. This is likely to give foreign fleets a competitive advantage over U.S. fleets. Would it be ethical for U.S. fishermen to lobby for a repeal of the dolphin protection measure on this basis? Is it ethical for U.S. tuna processors to favor lower-priced tuna imports over the environmentally safer U.S. catches?

FIGURE 16–1   Developing Global Environmental Standards

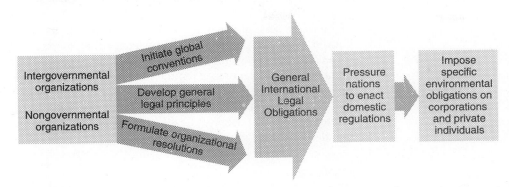

National Sovereignty and International Rules	International regulation often is an unwieldy method of dealing with newly discovered environmental dangers. Customary law and general principles of law develop too slowly to effectively address many health hazards. And international agreements, while easily the greatest source of international rules, seldom impose any precise obligations on national governments. The principle of national sovereignty protects a country from being forced to comply with an international agreement unless it has previously consented to its terms. Historically, few nations have been willing to accept concrete environmental obligations.
Enforcement Difficulties	Enforcing global environmental regulations is extremely difficult for several reasons. First, most international agreements confine themselves to general goals and declarations, rendering them almost impossible to violate. Second, the major polluters in the world are corporations and private individuals; yet the international law regime deals only with the rights and obligations of nations. While national governments may be held accountable for the activities of people and corporations on their territory, the sovereignty principle impedes international enforcement actions. The International Court of Justice is the only judicial forum with the power to conduct international litigation. However, its jurisdiction is voluntary; a nation must consent to the court proceedings.
The Form and Substance of Global Rules	The practical constraints on the creation and enforcement of international agreements define the form and substance of most transnational environmental rules. Rather than establishing precise obligations, most global treaties require adopting countries to cooperate in research, assessment, and monitoring activities. Only on rare occasions, where there has been clear evidence of impending environmental disaster (e.g., the amendments to the Montreal Protocol), have the nations of the world pledged to implement strict regulatory measures. Where environmental treaties have called for nations to impose regulatory requirements, they tend to take one of three broad forms: permits, standards, or lists.

Pollution Permits

Under the concept of **pollution permits,** a nation licenses individuals or corporations to discharge fixed amounts of pollutants over a prescribed period. This technique offers several advantages. First, it allows cleaner plants to sell their permits to heavier polluters. Second, it acknowledges that sometimes it is more cost effective for a company to buy another's license to pollute than to install costly pollution abatement equipment. Licensing regimes may also force nations to more carefully monitor pollution-causing activities and to ensure that potentially dangerous activities are carried out by responsible parties. For example, the *Basel Convention* requires countries to ensure that disposers of hazardous wastes are insured and competent to safely handle hazardous materials.

Standards

Sometimes treaties call on nations to adopt certain environmental **standards**. These may take several forms. For instance, under *emission standards,* the regulation declares the maximum quantity of pollutants that may be discharged, leaving to the polluter the discretion of deciding how to meet that goal. With *product standards,* the agreement defines the composition of certain products. *Process standards* are similar in that they prescribe the precise method by which certain operations can be conducted.

Lists

An extremely common regulatory technique in international environmental law is the use of **lists**. For instance, the Montreal Protocol employs lists of certain chemicals that are unduly hazardous and should be immediately banned or phased out within a prescribed time period. The use of lists has two distinct advantages. First, it avoids the need for too much detail since countries and private parties will know with certainty how materials included on any particular list are to be handled. Second, because of the difficulty in amending any treaty, the adopting parties frequently include any lists of regulated or prohibited activities in an *annex* to the agreement. The treaty then is adopted with the understanding that changes to the annex will not require formally amending the entire treaty. This permits international agreements to quickly adapt to changes in the environment.

DOMESTIC ENVIRONMENTAL REGULATION

The international community recently has exhibited an increasing willingness to tackle environmental issues. However, as we have seen, the international legal system's ability to cope with global problems is severely limited. Thus, the world has witnessed a simultaneous surge in national environmental legislation over the past few years. This section identifies the fundamental design of several of these domestic systems.

Regulation in the United States

The United States has developed an extremely comprehensive scheme of environmental regulations that affect the activities of businesses both within and without the country. This highly developed regulatory system exhibits several fundamental characteristics that greatly affect domestic and multinational businesses.

Multiple Layers of Regulation

Persons doing business in the United States must be prepared for several layers of environmental regulation. Besides a comprehensive set of national laws, most states have developed their own regulatory structures. In many instances, these state laws are even more stringent than their national counterparts. To compound the difficulties for potential polluters, many local governments also have developed environmental standards. To avoid criminal liability and financial disaster, businesses must familiarize themselves with these **multiple layers of regulation**.

Reporting and Recordkeeping Requirements

Most of the regulatory measures enacted within the United States impose onerous **reporting and recordkeeping requirements** on potential polluters. These disclosures must be made to national, state, and local authorities and (with the exception of trade secrets) are made available to the general public. For many commercial projects that require public funding or licensing, the commercial enterprise is required to prepare an **environmental impact assessment** that anticipates possible environmental problems and identifies alternate actions.

Complex Licensing Requirements

Much of the environmental regulation in the United States is characterized by **complex licensing requirements** that must be satisfied before businesses may legally engage in potentially hazardous activities. Before receiving the numerous permits that often are needed for certain ventures (or even to purchase or finance some property), stringent inspection and monitoring requirements may have to be met.

Comprehensive Liability System

Environmental regulation in the United States, perhaps more than in any other country, is characterized by an extremely **comprehensive liability system**. Failure to comply with environmental rules frequently subjects polluters to tremendous civil and criminal penalties. Further, these penalties may be imposed on a wide range of defendants, such as parent corporations, corporate officers and managers, shareholders, and secured creditors. This liability system has encouraged a growing number of foreign plaintiffs to seek redress in the United States for environmental damages that occur in foreign countries.

Regulation in the European Community

Interest in environmental protection has skyrocketed in the European Community during the past 10 years as European leaders have recognized that sustained social and economic growth depends on a principled approach to environmental issues. A comparison of environmental policies in the United States and the European Community demonstrates that, while the two systems have many similarities, they also contain certain important differences.

Underlying Principles

The European Community has established several fundamental policies that guide its environmental protection efforts. Foremost among these principles is the notion that governmental institutions should take **preventive action** to minimize the likelihood of environmental harm. Thus, commercial and industrial activities are carefully monitored and regulated to prevent environmental damage from occurring. Another dominant feature is that environmental policy must be carefully **balanced against economic harmonization** efforts. Finally, a third theme underlying environmental rules in the European Community is that **environmental impact assessments** should be an important component of all governmental policy-making initiatives.

Comparisons with the U.S. System

European environmental regulation is similar to the U.S. approach in that it often occurs at multiple levels. In fact, the member states are permitted to maintain stricter standards than those imposed by the European Community institutions as long as they are not hidden barriers to trade. However, unlike U.S. regulation, the principle of **subsidiarity** prevents Communitywide action unless it can be shown that it would be better able to attain fundamental environmental policies than would national action. The following case examines the conflict that often arises between national environmental legislation and the European Community's goal of removing barriers to trade.

RE DISPOSABLE BEER CANS: COMMISSION v. DENMARK
European Court of Justice, Sept. 20, 1988, [1988] ECR 4607

■ **FACTS** It had long been the practice in Denmark to charge a deposit on the sale of bottles containing beer and soft drinks. The attraction of recovering the deposit was enough to encourage a high percentage of consumers to return the bottles voluntarily, and so the countryside and open spaces were kept free of empty discarded bottles. In the mid-1970s, however, Danish beer manufacturers began to use cans and different shaped bottles. To ensure that the deposit system continued to be effective, legislation was enacted requiring that beer and soft drinks could be marketed only in returnable containers. It

imposed on distributors an obligation to set up and operate a system of deposit and return to encourage the recovery of used containers. Further, all containers had to be approved by the Danish National Environmental Protection Agency. That agency would approve no more than 30 container designs because retailers would not be willing to accept too many types of containers due to increased handling costs. However, to minimize the hardships on foreign producers, the legislation permitted them to market a limited number of drinks in unapproved containers.

■ **ISSUE**   Is this antipollution regulation an unlawful re-striction on the free movement of goods within the European Community?

■ **DECISION**   Yes. Protection of the environment is one of the essential objectives of the European Community, and, as such, it may justify certain restrictions on the free movement of goods. However, measures adopted to safeguard the environment should choose the means that least restrict the free movement of goods. Thus, this regulation violates European Community law if the means employed are disproportionate to its objectives. The obligation to set up a deposit-and-return system is an essential element of a system aiming to secure the reuse of containers. Accordingly, the restrictions it imposes on the free movement of goods should not be considered as disproportionate. However, that is not the case with the approval system. Under the system presently in force, Danish authorities could refuse approval to a foreign producer even if it was prepared to ensure that returned containers would be used again. Because of the limit of 30 approved containers, a foreign producer who wishes to sell in Denmark is compelled to manufacture or use containers of a type already used. The increased cost this might entail may make it very difficult to import products into Denmark. Thus, the approval system is disproportionate to its objectives.

The European Community in 1993 enacted a new Communitywide *packaging waste directive* that will have a costly effect on global businesses. Mirroring a controversial German statute, the law requires all companies to eventually collect and recycle 90 percent of their products' waste packaging. Within 10 years, all packaging that does not comply with the directive's recoverability requirements will be banned.

Communitywide legislation generally is not as comprehensive as national legislation in the United States. Like the international regime examined earlier, European Community environmental laws tend to come in the form of **general directives,** leaving to the member states discretion over how results are to be achieved. (The European Community's regulatory process is described in Chapter 3.) Similarly, neither the European Court of Justice nor the Community institutions have the authority to directly enforce Community legislation against private individuals. Instead, the system is one of **national-level enforcement**.

Eco-labels

As more consumers demanded a cleaner environment, producers responded by using labels that extolled the environmental virtues of their products. Concerned over the possibility that some environmental claims would be false and misleading, most of the world's developed nations introduced formal labeling systems. The European Community, following the lead of several of its member states, developed an **eco-label** in 1992. Under this labeling regulation, producers can apply to have their products declared ecologically safe. If approved by the Community's environmental committee, the eligible producers are then permitted to package their products with the eco-label.

Other Domestic Systems

No single chapter can adequately examine the wide range of national environmental systems that exist in the world today. However, Eastern Europe and Mexico deserve special mention because of their current importance to U.S. international businesses.

Eastern Europe

The countries of Eastern Europe (Poland, Hungary, and the Czech and Slovak Republics) have several things in common. First, their new market orientations have generated a great deal of interest from Western businesses and investors. Second, as a result of their reliance on heavy industry, they form one of the most polluted regions of the world. And third, potential creditors and investors are extremely reluctant to do business there because of uncertainty over who will be held legally accountable for the current ecological condition. The region's past heavy reliance on criminal sanctions to force environmental compliance has led to a general wariness on the part of foreign businesses. Until their regulatory uncertainties are cleared up, many enterprises will delay penetrating this region; however, the growing association between Eastern Europe and the European Community offers a distinct possibility that the two regions soon may follow a similar path in their environmental protection efforts.

Mexico

Environmental regulation in Mexico is in many ways similar to the regulatory structure that exists throughout much of Latin America. Basically, Mexico possesses a comprehensive scheme of environmental laws; however, for economic reasons its enforcement record is suspect. In many instances, poor communications, inadequate training, and manpower shortages prohibit governmental agencies from tracking and punishing illegal behavior. Ratification of the North American Free Trade Agreement is likely to strengthen Mexico's enforcement activities. Environmentalists in the United States lobbied hard for greater cooperation between the United States and Mexico in monitoring and enforcing environmental standards. Further, as U.S. economic interests become more intertwined with the rest of Latin America, a coordinated assault on environmental problems is likely to follow.

Domestic Enforcement Problems and Solutions

Private responsibility for environmental harms varies from nation to nation. Some countries, like Mexico, may have difficulty enforcing their environmental protection laws because they lack the economic means to adequately monitor private behavior. Others lack the motivation, electing instead to encourage economic development despite the resulting ecological harm. Even within the developed world, where environmental commitments are fairly strong, there may be wide differences in how each nation's courts assess private liability. Many legal systems adhere to the more tolerant **negligence** theory, making a corporation or individual liable for environmental injuries only when they are caused by unreasonable conduct. In these countries, a polluter is not legally responsible for unknown harms resulting from conduct that was previously believed to be environmentally safe. A growing number of countries, including the United States, follow the **strict liability** approach, which assesses liability against defendants who exercised some degree of control over the hazard regardless of whether or not they were at fault.

Two problems flow from the wide disparities among domestic regulatory and enforcement activities. First, multinational businesses are likely to move their hazardous

FIGURE 16–2   The Cycle of Poison

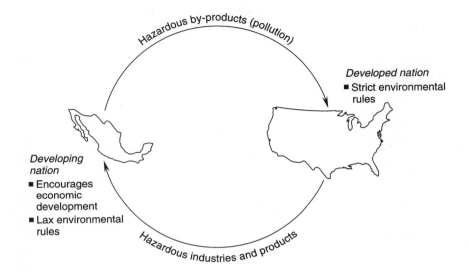

activities from countries with strict regulation to those with lax environmental standards. Second, when one nation bans the use of certain hazardous products (i.e., pesticides) producers may simply export them to countries where they are not banned. In recent years, three devices have been employed to prevent the export of hazardous products and technologies: informed consent, extraterritorial enforcement, and lending restrictions.

Informed Consent

International cooperation, like the Basel Convention (discussed earlier), has made great strides in curbing the export of hazardous wastes from industrialized countries to the Third World. Under this **informed consent** approach, nations have an obligation to inform importing countries of the ecological risks associated with the products or technology they are exporting. The importing nations may then decide if they are willing to expose their people to such risks.

Extraterritorial Enforcement

A fundamental weakness of the informed consent approach is that some underdeveloped countries are willing to become dumping grounds for unsafe products and technologies. Yet the environmental hazards they permit may extend beyond their national borders. To overcome this danger, some nations with strict environmental regulations give their laws **extraterritorial effect**. The United States, perhaps more than any other country, has followed this approach by holding that its laws govern activities conducted in foreign countries. Further, U.S. courts often accept jurisdiction over environmental injury suits brought by foreign plaintiffs who have suffered damages in foreign countries.

DOW CHEMICAL COMPANY v. ALFARO
786 S.W.2d 674 (Sup.Ct. Tex. 1990)

■ **FACTS** Domingo Castro Alfaro, a Costa Rican resident and employee of Standard Fruit Company, and 81 other Costa Rican employees and their spouses brought suit against Dow Chemical Company in a Texas district court. The employees claimed that while working for Standard Fruit on a banana plantation in Costa Rica, they were required to handle DBCP, a pesticide manufactured and supplied to Standard Fruit by Dow Chemical. The employees alleged that this exposure to DBCP caused them physical and mental damages, including irreversible sterility. In response to Dow Chemical's argument that the case should be dismissed because there was little Texas nexus to the injuries (Dow is a Delaware corporation whose principal place of business is in Michigan), the employees cited a state law that they argued gave Texas courts jurisdiction over the dispute. The statute provided: *An action for damages of a citizen of a foreign country may be enforced in the courts of this state, although the wrongful act takes place in a foreign country, if: (1) the law of the foreign country gives a right to maintain an action for damages; (2) the action is begun in this state within the time provided by the laws of this state for beginning the action; and (3) the foreign country of which the plaintiffs are citizens has equal treaty rights with the United States on behalf of its citizens.* [Note: Costa Rica was not a desirable place for the employees to sue because it did not permit attorneys to take cases on a contingency fee basis and capped personal injury recoveries at $1,500.] After the Texas court determined that it had jurisdiction to hear the claim, Dow Chemical requested that the action be dismissed on the basis of forum non

conveniens because the convenience of the parties and the ends of justice would be better served if the dispute was brought in another forum. The employees then claimed the Texas statute prohibited the courts from applying the doctrine of forum non conveniens.

■ **ISSUE** Should the Texas court dismiss the suit against Dow Chemical?

■ **DECISION** No. At issue in this case is whether the statutory language "may be enforced in the courts of this state" permits a court to relinquish jurisdiction under the doctrine of forum non conveniens. Dow Chemical argued that the legislature did not intend to make the statute a guarantee of an absolute right to enforce a suit in Texas. Dow suggested that the language "may be enforced" indicates the legislature's recognition of a court's discretionary power to dismiss. The employees, on the other hand, pointed out that the use of the words "may be enforced" merely made clear that the legislature was not requiring plaintiffs to bring suit in Texas. A review of past cases dealing with this statute supports the employees' position that the legislature has statutorily abolished the doctrine of forum non conveniens in suits brought under this Texas statute. The statute applies in the case since: (1) Costa Rica recognizes the claims these plaintiffs have against Dow; (2) the lawsuit was filed in a timely manner under Texas law; and (3) Costa Rica permits U.S. citizens to bring lawsuits before its courts. Accordingly, the Texas court should not dismiss this claim.

Lending Restrictions

While the extraterritorial approach may be praised for curbing the rise of new "pollution havens," it may be attacked simultaneously as a blatant intrusion into the sovereignty of the importing nations. For this reason, some environmentalists favor a less intrusive approach. They propose that developing nations be persuaded to upgrade their environmental protection standards by attaching such obligations to the credit they receive from international lending institutions. Similar to the debt-for-nature swaps (mentioned previously), these **lending restrictions** would encourage environmentally safe policies through economic incentives.

ETHICAL IMPLICATIONS   While the United States has ruled that DDT is an environmentally dangerous pesticide and banned its use, many countries have not outlawed it. What are the ethical considerations involved in a U.S. company deciding to export the pesticide to one of these countries?

ENVIRONMENTAL BUSINESS MANAGEMENT

Today's global business managers must realize that every aspect of their operations is intertwined with the environment. Pressures from consumers, environmentalists, and legislators have made environmental concerns a strategic part of business decision making. Failure to accept this responsibility may subject business managers to severe legal consequences. This final section briefly examines the legal liability of managers for environmental harm. It then closes by offering several suggestions on how to direct business activities in a responsible manner.

Personal Liability

Criminal Liability

Criminal sanctions for business managers who are responsible for violations of environmental laws are rising. And the increase in extraterritorial application of U.S. law, coupled with greater cooperation between the United States and foreign nations, has helped spread this criminal enforcement to the international arena. Officers, directors, and managers are regularly held liable for corporate crimes under two distinct theories. First, under the **personal participation theory,** anyone who personally participated in the planning or execution of the illegal corporate activity may be held criminally liable. Thus, a manager who knowingly instructs subordinates to illegally dispose of hazardous wastes has committed a crime. Second, directors, officers, and managers also may be subjected to criminal liability under a **derivative responsibility theory.** With this approach, a responsible corporate official may be liable for corporate wrongdoing if he knew or should have known it was occurring, yet failed to act to prevent or correct the situation. This theory places an affirmative duty on managers to monitor what is going on and to make certain their subordinates are complying with the law.

The *Federal Sentencing Guidelines* in effect in the United States have forced judges to treat environmental offenses much more seriously. As a result, the chances are great that corporate officials who are convicted of environmental crimes will actually

FIGURE 16–3 Personal Liability for Corporate Environmental Crimes

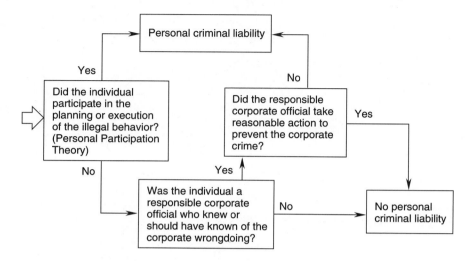

serve time in jail. Such sentences are most likely to be handed out in instances where: (*a*) there was a *knowing violation;* (*b*) the resulting *harm was great;* (*c*) the polluter received a large *economic gain;* and (*d*) there were *repeated violations.*

Civil Liability

Directors, officers, and managers may also be required to pay damages to the victims of environmental harms. Civil liability generally is not imposed under the derivative responsibility theory; instead, it must be shown that the corporate officials personally participated in the conduct that caused the harm. Still, under U.S. environmental protection statutes, private persons have been found strictly liable for the cleanup costs associated with a broad range of environmental harms, including activities that seemed perfectly safe at the time they were performed.

UNITED STATES v. NORTHEASTERN PHARMACEUTICAL
810 F.2d 726 (8th Cir. 1986)

■ **FACTS** Michaels formed Northeastern Pharmaceutical Corporation, was a major shareholder, and was its president. Lee was the company's vice president, the supervisor of its manufacturing plant in Verona, Missouri, and also a shareholder. Michaels and Lee knew that Northeastern's manufacturing process produced various hazardous and toxic by-products. In 1971, one of the shift supervisors at Northeastern's Verona plant arranged to dump numerous 55-gallon drums filled with waste by-products at a nearby farm. Lee approved of this arrangement. Eight years later, the Environmental Protection Agency (EPA) received an anonymous tip that wastes had been illegally dumped and began an investigation. In 1980, the government charged Northeastern, Michaels, and Lee with violating the Resource Conservation and Recovery Act (RCRA), despite the fact that the RCRA was not passed until 1976 (five year after the dumping occurred). Two years later, in 1982, the government amended its complaint against Lee to impose liability for cleanup costs under the Comprehensive Environmental Response, Compensation, and Liability Act (CERCLA), even though that statute was not enacted until 1980. Michaels and Lee argued that they could not be liable under RCRA or CERCLA for damages that arose before those statutes had been enacted.

■ **ISSUE** Can the statutes be applied retroactively to hold Michaels and Lee liable for preenactment cleanup costs?

■ **DECISION** Yes. Cleaning up inactive and abandoned hazardous waste disposal sites is a legitimate legislative purpose, and Congress intended CERCLA to apply retroactively. CERCLA imposes strict liability on any person who arranged for the disposal or transportation for disposal of hazardous substances. As Northeastern's plant supervisor, Lee had actual control over the factory's hazardous substances. The liability imposed on Lee was not derivative but personal. It was not premised solely on his status as a corporate officer or employee. Rather, Lee is individually liable under CERCLA because he personally arranged for the transportation and disposal of hazardous substances and thus actually participated in Northeastern's CERCLA violations. RCRA imposes strict liability on any person who has contributed to the disposal of hazardous substances that may present an imminent and substantial endangerment to health or the environment. Its application here is not retroactive since it imposes liability for present and future conditions resulting from the past acts. Lee is liable as a contributor because he actually participated in the conduct that violated the RCRA; he personally arranged for the transportation and disposal of the hazardous waste. Unlike Lee, Michaels was not personally involved in the actual decision to transport and dispose of the waste. However, as Northeastern's president and as a major shareholder, Michaels was the individual in charge of and directly responsible for all of Northeastern's operations. He had the ultimate authority to control the disposal of Northeastern's hazardous substances and, accordingly, is individually liable.

Responsible Environmental Management	The potential for environmental harm is pervasive at all points in the business management process. New dangers are regularly being discovered in the production, distribution, and consumption of goods. No business—no matter how careful it is—can be certain that today's safe activities will not turn out to be hazardous tomorrow. Still, through responsible environmental management, resources can be managed in a way that reduces the risks of criminal and civil liability and leaves a useful and livable planet for future generations. At least four basic components are essential to such a management scheme: awareness, assessment, compliance, and commitment.

Awareness

As a first step to responsible management, business leaders should acquaint themselves with the multiplicity of standards and procedures imposed by the various legal systems where they conduct operations. However, **regulatory awareness** must extend beyond the existing regulations and anticipate the nature of future legal constraints. This requires an investment in environmental research and an active interest in the lawmaking process.

CONCEPT SUMMARY
Responsible Environmental Management

Awareness	· Become familiar with the regulatory maze · Become actively involved in the lawmaking process · Forecast future environmental regulations
Assessment	· Identify the environmental impact of present and proposed business activities · Identify ways to reduce or avoid unacceptable risks
Compliance	· Perform periodic, objective evaluations of environmental compliance at all levels of the organization · Document the results and report them throughout the organization
Commitment	· Insist on environmental commitment at the highest levels of the organization · Actively communicate the commitment to all levels of the organization · Transform environmental threats into growth opportunities

Assessment

Responsible managers also implement an **environmental assessment program** that forecasts the full effect any activity will have on the environment. This may be performed by inside specialists, outside consultants, or a combination of the two. Through a comprehensive assessment program, businesses may learn how to reduce or avoid unacceptable environmental risks.

Compliance

A successful environmental management program includes a **compliance and reporting component.** This entails periodic *environmental audits* that objectively evaluate environmental compliance at all levels of the organization. To be effective, these evaluations must be carefully documented and honestly reported throughout the organizational hierarchy.

Commitment

Responsible environmental management will not succeed without a sincere **commitment** at all levels of the organization. Starting with the board of directors and the highest corporate officials, a strong message must be broadcast to ensure that environmental considerations are integrated into every phase of business operations. Thoroughly committed businesses are better prepared to take a proactive approach and transform environmental threats into important growth opportunities. For instance, as consumers become more concerned about environmental issues, environmentally compatible products and processes may enjoy a competitive advantage. Similarly, environmentally attuned businesses more readily recognize the growing number of opportunities available in the billion-dollar environmental cleanup industry.

QUESTIONS AND PROBLEM CASES

1. Discuss some of the difficulties that plague international efforts to protect the environment.

2. List the basic sources of international environmental regulation. Which source provides the clearest examples of international law?

3. What is meant by *sustainable development?* What part does it play in the international environmental movement?

4. Environmental law in both the United States and the European Community is characterized by multiple layers of regulation. How does the multilayered system of the United States differ from its European Community counterpart?

5. Because of the many dolphins killed by tuna fishermen using the purse seine method, the United States enacted the Dolphin Protection Consumer Information Act. Specifically, this law make it illegal for any producer, importer, or exporter of tuna products to include on the label of its product the term *Dolphin Safe* if it contains any tuna harvested in the eastern tropical Pacific Ocean by the purse seine method. The Mexican government requested a GATT panel to rule that the labeling law discriminated against Mexico as a country fishing in the eastern tropical Pacific Ocean. Does this labeling law violate GATT?

6. The French government outlawed the growing or importing of produce that was treated with certain pesticides. Mirepoix was charged with violating this statute when it imported into France onions treated with the prohibited pesticide. Mirepoix argued that the French ban constituted an illegal restriction on the free movement of goods within the European Community. The French government argued that the prohibition was permissible since no Community rules existed that regulated the pesticides at issue in this case. Was the French law an unlawful restriction on imports?

7. Park was the chief executive officer of Acme Markets, a retail food chain with approximately 36,000 employees, 874 retail outlets, and 16 warehouses. The Food and Drug Administration (FDA), after a 12-day inspection, notified Park by letter of rodent infestation and unsanitary conditions at Acme's Baltimore warehouse. After receiving the letter, Park conferred with Acme's vice president for legal affairs, who told him the Baltimore division vice president was investigating the situation and would take corrective action. During a follow-up investigation three months later, the FDA found continued rodent infestation despite improved sanitation at the Baltimore warehouse. Park was charged with violating the Federal Food, Drug, and Cosmetic Act. During his trial, the FDA introduced into evidence a letter it had sent one year earlier informing Park of similar problems at Acme's Philadelphia warehouse. Should Park be held criminally liable for the rodent infestation?

8. Baytank Corporation is a bulk liquid chemical transfer and storage facility. Its principal function is to provide interim storage for customers transporting various chemicals. Nordberg was executive vice president of Baytank, and Johnsen was the corporation's safety manager and its operations manager. After the EPA discovered that Baytank was storing hazardous wastes in drums without a permit, it charged the corporation with a knowing violation of the Resource Conservation and Recovery Act. A jury convicted Baytank of the criminal charges. Are Nordberg and Johnsen likely to be found criminally liable also? Explain.

9. Swainsboro Print Works (SPW) borrowed money from Fleet and, in return, gave Fleet a security interest in its textile facility. After SPW filed for bankruptcy, Fleet foreclosed on the facility and contracted with Baldwin to conduct an auction of the building and its equipment. Machinery and equipment were then removed from the site over a six-month period. After inspecting the facility, the EPA discovered 44 truckloads of materials containing asbestos and 700 55-gallon drums containing toxic chemicals. It sued Fleet for over $400,000 in cleanup costs under the Comprehensive Environmental Response Compensation and Liability Act (CERCLA), alleging that Fleet was liable as the owner or operator of the facility at the time the wastes were disposed. Fleet argued that it could not be liable as an owner or operator because of a CERCLA defense for creditors who do not participate in management and hold indicia of ownership primarily to protect their security interest in a facility. Could Fleet be liable under CERCLA despite this defense?

10. The Little Sandy Hunting and Fishing Club held a nondevelopment easement on 3,800 acres of land in east Texas containing high-quality wetlands and wildlife habitat. Concerned that the state of Texas would seize the property under eminent domain and build a reservoir on the site, the club donated the land to U.S. Fish and Wildlife Service to ensure that the wetlands would be preserved in their pristine state. The Texas Water Conservation Authority (TWCA), a nongovernmental organization made up of individuals, firms, corporations, and water districts, wanted the area to be used for the construction of a reservoir. It sued to prevent the transfer, alleging the Fish and Wildlife Service violated federal law by acquiring the property without first preparing an environmental impact statement. TWCA will not have standing to bring its lawsuit unless it will suffer an injury if the transfer is allowed. Does TWCA have standing?

United Nations Convention on Contracts for the International Sale of Goods

The states parties to this Convention:

Bearing in mind the broad objectives in the resolutions adopted by the sixth special session of the General Assembly of the United Nations on the establishment of a New International Economic Order,

Considering that the development of international trade on the basis of equality and mutual benefit is an important element in promoting friendly relations among States,

Being of the Opinion that the adoption of uniform rules which govern contracts for the international sale of goods and take into account the different social, economic and legal systems would contribute to the removal of legal barriers in international trade and promote the development of international trade,

Have agreed as follows:

PART I Sphere of Application and General Provisions

CHAPTER I Sphere of Application

ARTICLE 1

(1) This convention applies to contracts of sale of goods between parties whose places of business are in different States:

(a) When the States are Contracting States; or
(b) When the rules of private international law lead to the application of the law of a Contracting State.

(2) The fact that the parties have their places of business in different States is to be disregarded whenever this fact does not appear either from the contract or from any dealings between, or from information disclosed by, the parties at any time before or at the conclusion of the contract.

(3) Neither the nationality of the parties nor the civil or commercial character of the parties or of the contract is to be taken into consideration in determining the application of this Convention.

ARTICLE 2

This Convention does not apply to sales:

(a) Of goods bought for personal, family or household use, unless the seller, at any time before or at the conclusion of the contract, neither knew nor ought to have known that the goods were bought for any such use;
(b) By auction;
(c) On execution or otherwise by authority of law;
(d) Of stocks, shares, investment securities, negotiable instruments or money;

(e) Of ships, vessels, hovercraft or aircraft;
(f) Of electricity.

ARTICLE 3

(1) Contracts for the supply of goods to be manufactured or produced are to be considered sales unless the party who orders the goods undertakes to supply a substantial part of the materials necessary for such manufacture or production.
(2) This Convention does not apply to contracts in which the preponderant part of the obligations of the party who furnishes the goods consists in the supply of labour or other services.

ARTICLE 4

This Convention governs only the formation of the contract of sale and rights and obligations of the seller and the buyer arising from such a contract. In particular, except as otherwise expressly provided in this Convention, it is not concerned with:

(a) the validity of the contract or of any of its provisions or of any usage;
(b) the effect which the contract may have on the property in the goods sold.

ARTICLE 5

This Convention does not apply to the liability of the seller for death or personal injury caused by the goods to any person.

ARTICLE 6

The parties may exclude the application of this Convention or, subject to article 12, derogate from or vary the effect of any of its provisions.

CHAPTER II   General Provisions

ARTICLE 7

(1) In the interpretation of this Convention, regard is to be had to its international character and to the need to promote uniformity in its application and the observance of good faith in international trade.

(2) Questions concerning matters governed by this Convention which are not expressly settled in it are to be settled in conformity with the general principles on which it is based or, in the absence of such principles, in conformity with the law applicable by virtue of the rules of private international law.

ARTICLE 8

(1) For the purposes of this Convention statements made by and other conduct of a party are to be interpreted according to his intent where the other party knew or could not have been unaware what that intent was.
(2) If the preceding paragraph is not applicable, statements made by and other conduct of a party are to be interpreted according to the understanding that a reasonable person of the same kind as the other party would have had in the same circumstances.
(3) In determining the intent of a party or the understanding a reasonable person would have had, due consideration is to be given to all relevant circumstances of the case including the negotiations, any practices which the parties have established between themselves, usages and any subsequent conduct of the parties.

ARTICLE 9

(1) The parties are bound by any usage to which they have agreed and by any practices which they have established between themselves.
(2) The parties are considered, unless otherwise agreed, to have impliedly made applicable to their contract or its formation a usage of which the parties knew or ought to have known and which in international trade is widely known to, and regularly observed by, parties to contracts of the type involved in the particular trade concerned.

ARTICLE 10

For the purposes of this Convention:

(a) If a party has more than one place of business, the place of business is that which has the closest relationship to the contract and its performance, having regard to the circumstances known to or contemplated by the parties at any time before or at the conclusion of the contract;

(b) If a party does not have a place of business, references are to be made to his habitual residence.

ARTICLE 11

A contract of sale need not be concluded in or evidenced by writing and is not subject to any other requirement as to form. It may be proved by any means, including witnesses.

ARTICLE 12

Any provision of article 11, article 29 or Part II of this Convention that allows a contract of sale or its modification or termination by agreement or any offer, acceptance or other indication of intention to be made in any form other than in writing does not apply where any party has his place of business in a Contracting State which has made a declaration under article 96 of this Convention. The parties may not derogate from or vary the effect of this article.

ARTICLE 13

For the purposes of the Convention "writing" includes telegram and telex.

PART II   Formation of the Contract

ARTICLE 14

(1) A proposal for concluding a contract addressed to one or more specific persons constitutes an offer if it is sufficiently definite and indicates the intention of the offeror to be bound in case of acceptance. A proposal is sufficiently definite if it indicates the goods and expressly or implicitly fixes or makes provision for determining the quantity and the price.

(2) A proposal other than one addressed to one or more specific persons is to be considered merely as an invitation to make offers, unless the contrary is clearly indicated by the person making the proposal.

ARTICLE 15

(1) An offer becomes effective when it reaches the offeree.

(2) An offer, even if it is irrevocable, may be withdrawn if the withdrawal reaches the offeree before or at the same time as the offer.

ARTICLE 16

(1) Until a contract is concluded an offer may be revoked if the revocation reaches the offeree before he has dispatched an acceptance.

(2) However, an offer cannot be revoked:
  (a) If it indicates, whether by stating a fixed time for acceptance or otherwise, that it is irrevocable; or
  (b) If it was reasonable for the offeree to rely on the offer as being irrevocable and the offeree has acted in reliance on the offer.

ARTICLE 17

An offer, even if it is irrevocable, is terminated when a rejection reaches the offeror.

ARTICLE 18

(1) A statement made by or other conduct of the offeree indicating assent to an offer is an acceptance. Silence or inactivity does not in itself amount to acceptance.

(2) An acceptance of an offer becomes effective at the moment the indication of assent reaches the offeror. An acceptance is not effective if the indication of assent does not reach the offeror within the time he has fixed or, if no time is fixed, within a reasonable time, due account being taken of the circumstances of the transaction, including the rapidity of the means of communication employed by the offeror. An oral offer must be accepted immediately unless the circumstances indicate otherwise.

(3) However, if, by virtue of the offer or as a result of practices which the parties have established between themselves or of usage, the offeree may indicate assent by performing an act, such as one relat-

ing to the dispatch of the goods or payment of the price, without notice to the offeror, the acceptance is effective at the moment the act is performed, provided that the act is performed within the period of time laid down in the preceding paragraph.

ARTICLE 19

(1) A reply to an offer which purports to be an acceptance but contains additions, limitations or other modifications is a rejection of the offer and constitutes a counteroffer.

(2) However, a reply to an offer which purports to be an acceptance but contains additional or different terms which do not materially alter the terms of the offer constitutes an acceptance, unless the offeror, without undue delay, objects orally to the discrepancy or dispatches a notice to that effect. If he does not so object, the terms of the contract are the terms of the offer with the modifications contained in the acceptance.

(3) Additional or different terms relating, among other things, to the price, payment, quality and quantity of the goods, place and time of delivery, extent of one party's liability to the other or the settlement of disputes are considered to alter the terms of the offer materially.

ARTICLE 20

(1) A period of time for acceptance fixed by the offeror in a telegram or a letter begins to run from the moment the telegram is handed in for dispatch or from the date shown on the letter or, if no such date is shown, from the date shown on the envelope. A period of time for acceptance fixed by the offeror by telephone, telex or other means of instantaneous communication, begins to run from the moment that the offer reaches the offeree.

(2) Official holidays or non-business days occurring during the period for acceptance are included in calculating the period. However, if a notice of acceptance cannot be delivered at the address of the offeror on the last day of the period because that day falls on an official holiday or a non-business day at the place of business of the offeror, the period is extended until the first business day which follows.

ARTICLE 21

(1) A late acceptance is nevertheless effective as an acceptance if without delay the offeror orally so informs the offeree or dispatches a notice to that effect.

(2) If a letter or other writing containing a late acceptance shows that it has been sent in such circumstances that if its transmission had been normal it would have reached the offeror in due time, the late acceptance is effective as an acceptance unless, without delay, the offeror orally informs the offeree that he considers his offer as having lapsed or dispatches a notice to that effect.

ARTICLE 22

An acceptance may be withdrawn if the withdrawal reaches the offeror before or at the same time as the acceptance would have become effective.

ARTICLE 23

A contract is concluded at the moment when an acceptance of an offer becomes effective in accordance with the provisions of this Convention.

ARTICLE 24

For the purposes of this Part of the Convention, an offer, declaration of acceptance or any other indication of intention "reaches" the addressee when it is made orally to him or delivered by any other means to him personally, to his place of business or mailing address or, if he does not have a place of business or mailing address, to his habitual residence.

PART III   Sale of Goods

CHAPTER I   General Provisions

ARTICLE 25

A breach of contract committed by one of the parties is fundamental if it results in such detriment to the other party as substantially to deprive him of what he is entitled to expect under this contract, unless the party in breach did not foresee and a reasonable person of the same kind in the same circumstances would not have foreseen such a result.

ARTICLE 26

A declaration of avoidance of the contract is effective only if made by notice to the other party.

ARTICLE 27

Unless otherwise expressly provided in this Part of the Convention, if any notice, request or other communication is given or made by a party in accordance with this Part and by means appropriate in the circumstances, a delay or error in the transmission of the communication or its failure to arrive does not deprive that party of the right to rely on the communication.

ARTICLE 28

If, in accordance with the provisions of this Convention, one party is entitled to require performance of any obligation by the other party, a court is not bound to enter a judgment for specific performance unless the court would do so under its own law in respect of similar contracts of sale not governed by this Convention.

ARTICLE 29

(1) A contract may be modified or terminated by the mere agreement of the parties.
(2) A contract in writing which contains a provision requiring any modification or termination by agreement to be in writing may not be otherwise modified or terminated by agreement. However, a party may be precluded by his conduct from asserting such a provision to the extent that the other party has relied on that conduct.

CHAPTER II   Obligations of the Seller

ARTICLE 30

The seller must deliver the goods, hand over any documents relating to them and transfer the property in the goods, as required by the contract and this Convention.

Section I.   Delivery of Goods and Handing Over of Documents

ARTICLE 31

If the seller is not bound to deliver the goods at any other particular place, his obligation to deliver consists:

(a) If the contract of sale involves carriage of the goods—in handing the goods over to the first carrier for transmission to the buyer;
(b) If, in cases not within the preceding subparagraph, the contract relates to specific goods, or unidentified goods to be drawn from a specific stock or to be manufactured or produced, and at the time of the conclusion of the contract the parties knew that the goods were at, or were to be manufactured or produced at, a particular place—in placing the goods at the buyer's disposal at that place;
(c) In other cases—in placing the goods at the buyer's disposal at the place where the seller had his place of business at the time of the conclusion at the contract.

ARTICLE 32

(1) If the seller, in accordance with the contract or his Convention, hands the goods over to a carrier and if the goods are not clearly identified to the contract by markings on the goods, by shipping documents or otherwise, the seller must given the buyer notice of the consignment specifying the goods.
(2) If the seller is bound to arrange for carriage of the goods, he must make such contracts as are necessary for carriage to the place fixed by means of transportation appropriate in the circumstances and according to the usual terms for such transportation.
(3) If the seller is not bound to effect insurance in respect of the carriage of the goods, he must, at the buyer's request, provide him with all available information necessary to enable him to effect such insurance.

ARTICLE 33

The seller must deliver the goods:

(a) If a date is fixed by or determinable from the contract, on that date;

(b) If a period of time is fixed by or determinable from the contract, at any time within that period unless circumstances indicate that the buyer is to choose a date; or

(c) In any other case, within a reasonable time after the conclusion of the contract.

ARTICLE 34

If the seller is bound to hand over documents relating to the goods, he must hand them over at the time and place and in the form required by the contract. If the seller has handed over documents before that time, he may, up to that time, cure any lack of conformity in the documents, if the exercise of this right does not cause the buyer unreasonable inconvenience or unreasonable expense. However, the buyer retains any right to claim damages as provided for in this Convention.

Section II.   Conformity of the Goods and Third Party Claims

ARTICLE 35

(1) The seller must deliver goods which are of the quantity, quality and description required by the contract and which are contained or packaged in the manner required by the contract.

(2) Except where the parties have agreed otherwise, the goods do not conform with the contract unless they:

(a) Are fit for the purposes for which goods of the same description would ordinarily be used;

(b) Are fit for any particular purpose expressly or impliedly made known to the seller at the time of the conclusion of the contract, except where the circumstances show that the buyer did not rely, or that it was unreasonable for him to rely, on the seller's skill and judgment;

(c) Possess the qualities of goods which the seller has held out to the buyer as a sample or model;

(d) Are contained or packaged in the manner usual for such goods or, where there is no such manner, in a manner adequate to preserve and protect the goods.

(3) The seller is not liable under subparagraphs (a) to (d) of the preceding paragraph for any lack of con-

formity of the goods if at the time of the conclusion of the contract the buyer knew or could not have been unaware of such lack of conformity.

ARTICLE 36

(1) The seller is liable in accordance with the contract and this Convention for any lack of conformity which exists at the time when the risk passes to the buyer, even though the lack of conformity becomes apparent only after that time.

(2) The seller is also liable for any lack of conformity which occurs after the time indicated in the preceding paragraph and which is due to a breach of any of his obligations, including a breach of any guarantee that for a period of time the goods will remain fit for their ordinary purpose or for some particular purpose or will retain specified qualities or characteristics.

ARTICLE 37

If the seller has delivered goods before the date for delivery, he may, up to that date, deliver any missing part or make up any deficiency in the quantity of the goods delivered, or deliver goods in replacement of any non-conforming goods delivered or remedy any lack of conformity in the goods delivered, provided that the exercise of this right does not cause the buyer unreasonable inconvenience or unreasonable expense. However, the buyer retains any right to claim damages as provided for in this Convention.

ARTICLE 38

(1) The buyer must examine the goods, or cause them to be examined, within as short a period as is practicable in the circumstances.

(2) If the contract involves carriage of the goods, examination may be deferred until after the goods have arrived at their destination.

(3) If the goods are redirected in transit or redispatched by the buyer without a reasonable opportunity for examination by him and at the time of the conclusion of the contract the seller knew or ought to have known of the possibility of such redirection or redispatch, examination may be

deferred until after the goods have arrived at the new destination.

ARTICLE 39

(1) The buyer loses the right to rely on a lack of conformity of the goods if he does not give notice to the seller specifying the nature of the lack of conformity within a reasonable time after he has discovered it or ought to have discovered it.

(2) In any event, the buyer loses the right to rely on a lack of conformity of the goods if he does not give the seller notice thereof at the latest within a period of two years from the date on which the goods were actually handed over to the buyer, unless this time-limit is inconsistent with a contractual period of guarantee.

ARTICLE 40

The seller is not entitled to rely on the provisions of articles 38 and 39 if the lack of conformity relates to facts of which he knew or could not have been unaware and which he did not disclose to the buyer.

ARTICLE 41

The seller must deliver goods which are free from any right or claim of a third party, unless the buyer agreed to take the goods subject to that right or claim. However, if such right or claim is based on industrial property or other intellectual property, the seller's obligation is governed by article 42.

ARTICLE 42

(1) The seller must deliver goods which are free from any right or claim of a third party based on industrial property or other intellectual property, of which at the time of the conclusion of the contract the seller knew or could not have been unaware, provided that the right or claim is based on industrial property or other intellectual property:

  (a) Under the law of the State where the goods will be resold or otherwise used, if it was contemplated by the parties at the time of the conclu-

sion of the contract that the goods would be resold or otherwise used in that State; or

  (b) In any other case, under the law of the State where the buyer has his place of business.

(2) The obligation of the seller under the preceding paragraph does not extend to cases where:

  (a) At the time of the conclusion of the contract the buyer knew or could not have been unaware of the right or claim; or

  (b) The right or claim results from the seller's compliance with technical drawings, designs, formulae or other such specifications furnished by the buyer.

ARTICLE 43

(1) The buyer loses the right to rely on the provisions of article 41 or article 42 if he does not give notice to the seller specifying the nature of the right or claim of the third party within a reasonable time after he has become aware or ought to have become aware of the right or claim.

(2) The seller is not entitled to rely on the provisions of the preceding paragraph if he knew of the right or claim of the third party and the nature of it.

ARTICLE 44

Notwithstanding the provisions of paragraph (1) of article 39 and paragraph (1) of article 43, the buyer may reduce the price in accordance with article 50 or claim damages, except for loss of profit, if he has a reasonable excuse for his failure to give the required notice.

Section III.   Remedies for Breach of Contract by the Seller

ARTICLE 45

(1) If the seller fails to perform any of his obligations under the contract or this Convention, the buyer may:

  (a) Exercise the rights provided in articles 46 to 52;

  (b) Claim damages as provided in articles 74 to 77.

(2) The buyer is not deprived of any right he may have to claim damages by exercising his right to other remedies.

(3) No period of grace may be granted to the seller by a court or arbitral tribunal when the buyer resorts to a remedy for breach of contract.

ARTICLE 46

(1) The buyer may require performance by the seller of his obligations unless the buyer has resorted to a remedy which is inconsistent with this requirement.
(2) If the goods do not conform with the contract, the buyer may require delivery of substitute goods only if the lack of conformity constitutes a fundamental breach of contract and a request for substitute goods is made either in conjunction with notice given under article 39 or within a reasonable time thereafter.
(3) If the goods do not conform with the contract, the buyer may require the seller to remedy the lack of conformity by repair, unless this is unreasonable having regard to all the circumstances. A request for repair must be made either in conjunction with notice given under article 39 or within a reasonable time thereafter.

ARTICLE 47

(1) The buyer may fix an additional period of time of reasonable length for performance by the seller of his obligations.
(2) Unless the buyer has received notice from the seller that he will not perform within the period so fixed, the buyer may not, during that period, resort to any remedy for breach of contract. However, the buyer is not deprived thereby of any right he may have to claim damages for delay in performance.

ARTICLE 48

(1) Subject to article 49, the seller may, even after the date for delivery, remedy at his own expense any failure to perform his obligations, if he can do so without unreasonable delay and without causing the buyer unreasonable inconvenience or uncertainty of reimbursement by the seller of expenses advanced by the buyer. However, the buyer retains any right to claim damages as provided for in this Convention.
(2) If the seller requests the buyer to make known whether he will accept performance and the buyer does not comply with the request within a reasonable time, the seller may perform within the time indicated in his request. The buyer may not, during that period of time, resort to any remedy which is inconsistent with performance by the seller.
(3) A notice by the seller that he will perform within a specified period of time is assumed to include a request, under the preceding paragraph, that the buyer make known his decision.
(4) A request or notice by the seller under paragraph (2) or (3) of this article is not effective unless received by the buyer.

ARTICLE 49

(1) The buyer may declare the contract avoided:
  (a) If the failure by the seller to perform any of his obligations under the contract or this Convention amounts to a fundamental breach of contract; or
  (b) In case of non-delivery, if the seller does not deliver the goods within the additional period of time fixed by the buyer in accordance with paragraph (1) of article 47 or declares that he will not deliver within the period so fixed.
(2) However, in cases where the seller has delivered the goods, the buyer loses the right to declare the contract avoided unless he does so:
  (a) In respect of late delivery, within a reasonable time after he has become aware that delivery has been made;
  (b) In respect of any breach other than late delivery, within a reasonable time:
    (i) After he knew or ought to have known of the breach;
    (ii) After the expiration of any additional period of time fixed by the buyer in accordance with paragraph (1) of article 47, or after the seller has declared that he will not perform his obligations within such an additional period; or
    (iii) After the expiration of any additional period of time indicated by the seller in accordance with paragraph (2) of article

48, or after the buyer has declared that he will not accept performance.

ARTICLE 50

If the goods do not conform with the contract and whether or not the price has already been paid, the buyer may reduce the price in the same proportion as the value that the goods actually delivered had at the time of the delivery bears to the value that conforming goods would have had at that time. However, if the seller remedies any failure to perform his obligations in accordance with article 37 or article 48 or if the buyer refuses to accept performance by the seller in accordance with those articles, the buyer may not reduce the price.

ARTICLE 51

(1) If the seller delivers only a part of the goods or if only a part of the goods delivered is in conformity with the contract, articles 46 to 50 apply in respect of the part which is missing or which does not conform.
(2) The buyer may declare the contract avoided in its entirety only if the failure to make delivery completely or in conformity with the contract amounts to a fundamental breach of the contract.

ARTICLE 52

(1) If the seller delivers the goods before the date fixed, the buyer may take delivery or refuse to take delivery.
(2) If the seller delivers a quantity of goods greater than that provided for in the contract, the buyer may take delivery or refuse to take delivery of the excess quantity. If the buyer takes delivery of all or part or the excess quantity, he must pay for it at the contract rate.

CHAPTER III   Obligations of the Buyer

ARTICLE 53

The buyer must pay the price for the goods and take delivery of them as required by the contract and this Convention.

Section I.   Payment of the Price

ARTICLE 54

The buyer's obligation to pay the price includes taking such steps and complying with such formalities as may be required under the contract or any laws and regulations to enable payment to be made.

ARTICLE 55

Where a contract has been validly concluded but does not expressly or implicitly fix or make provision for determining the price, the parties are considered, in the absence of any indication to the contrary, to have impliedly made reference to the price generally charged at the time of the conclusion of the contract for such goods sold under comparable circumstances in the trade concerned.

ARTICLE 56

If the price is fixed according to the weight of the goods, in case of doubt it is to be determined by the net weight.

ARTICLE 57

(1) If the buyer is not bound to pay the price at any other particular place, he must pay it to the seller:
    (a) At the seller's place of business; or
    (b) If the payment is to be made against the handing over of the goods or of documents, at the place where the handing over takes place.
(2) The seller must bear any increase in the expenses incidental to payment which is caused by a change in his place of business subsequent to the conclusion of the contract.

ARTICLE 58

(1) If the buyer is not bound to pay the price at any other specific time, he must pay it when the seller places either the goods or documents controlling their disposition at the buyer's disposal in accordance with the contract and this Convention. The

seller may make such payment a condition for handing over the goods or documents.

(2) If the contract involves carriage of the goods, the seller may dispatch the goods on terms whereby the goods, or documents controlling their disposition, will not be handed over to the buyer except against payment of the price.

(3) The buyer is not bound to pay the price until he has had an opportunity to examine the goods, unless the procedures for delivery or payment agreed upon by the parties are inconsistent with his having such an opportunity.

ARTICLE 59

The buyer must pay the price on the date fixed by or determinable from the contract and this Convention without the need for any request or compliance with any formality on the part of the seller.

Section II.   Taking Delivery

ARTICLE 60

The buyer's obligation to take delivery consists:

(a) In doing all the acts which could reasonably be expected of him in order to enable the seller to make delivery; and

(b) In taking over the goods.

Section III.   Remedies for Breach of Contract by the Buyer

ARTICLE 61

(1) If the buyer fails to perform any of his obligations under the contract or this Convention, the seller may:

    (a) Exercise the rights provided in articles 62 to 65;

    (b) Claim damages as provided in articles 74 to 77.

(2) The seller is not deprived of any right he may have to claim damages by exercising his right to other remedies.

(3) No period of grace may be granted to the buyer by a court or arbitral tribunal when the seller resorts to a remedy for breach of contract.

ARTICLE 62

The seller may require the buyer to pay the price, take delivery or perform his other obligations, unless the seller has resorted to a remedy which is inconsistent with this requirement.

ARTICLE 63

(1) The seller may fix an additional period of time of reasonable length for performance by the buyer of his obligations.

(2) Unless the seller has received notice from the buyer that he will not perform within the period so fixed, the seller may not, during that period, resort to any remedy for breach of contract. However, the seller is not deprived thereby of any right he may have to claim damages for delay in performance.

ARTICLE 64

(1) The seller may declare the contract avoided:

    (a) If the failure by the buyer to perform any of his obligations under the contract or this Convention amounts to a fundamental breach of contract; or

    (b) If the buyer does not, within the additional period of time fixed by the seller in accordance with paragraph (1) of article 63, perform his obligation to pay the price or take delivery of the goods, or if he declares that he will not do so within the period so fixed.

(2) However, in cases where the buyer has paid the price, the seller loses the right to declare the contract avoided unless he does so:

    (a) In respect of late performance by the buyer, before the seller has become aware that performance has been rendered; or

    (b) In respect of any breach other than late performance by the buyer, within a reasonable time:

        (i) After the seller knew or ought to have known of the breach; or

        (ii) After the expiration of any additional period of time fixed by the seller in accordance with paragraph (1) of article 63, or after the buyer has declared that he will not perform his obligations within such an additional period.

ARTICLE 65

(1) If under the contract the buyer is to specify the form, measurement or other features of the goods and he fails to make such specification either on the date agreed upon or within a reasonable time after receipt of a request from the seller, the seller may, without prejudice to any other rights he may have, make the specification himself in accordance with the requirements of the buyer that may be known to him.

(2) If the seller makes the specification himself, he must inform the buyer of the details thereof and must fix a reasonable time within which the buyer may make a different specification. If, after receipt of such a communication, the buyer fails to do so within the times so fixed, the specification made by the seller is binding.

CHAPTER IV   Passing of Risk

ARTICLE 66

Loss of or damage to the goods after the risk has passed to the buyer does not discharge him from his obligation to pay the price, unless the loss or damage is due to an act or omission of the seller.

ARTICLE 67

(1) If the contract of sale involves carriage of the goods and the seller is not bound to hand them over at a particular place, the risk passes to the buyer when the goods are handed over to the first carrier for transmission to the buyer in accordance with the contract of sale. If the seller is bound to hand the goods over to a carrier at a particular place, the risk does not pass to the buyer until the goods are handed over to the carrier at that place. The fact that the seller is authorized to retain documents controlling the disposition of the goods does not affect the passage of the risk.

(2) Nevertheless, the risk does not pass to the buyer until the goods are clearly identified to the con-

tract, whether by markings on the goods, by shipping documents, by notice given to the buyer or otherwise.

ARTICLE 68

The risk in respect of goods sold in transit passes to the buyer from the time of the conclusion of the contract. However, if the circumstances so indicate, the risk is assumed by the buyer from the time the goods were handed over to the carrier who issued the documents embodying the contract of carriage. Nevertheless, if at the time of the conclusion of the contract of sale the seller knew or ought to have known that the goods had been lost or damaged and did not disclose this to the buyer, the loss or damage is at the risk of the seller.

ARTICLE 69

(1) In cases not within articles 67 and 68, the risk passes to the buyer when he takes over the goods or, if he does not do so in due time, from the time when the goods are placed at his disposal and he commits a breach of contract by failing to take delivery.

(2) However, if the buyer is bound to take over the goods at a place other than a place of business of the seller, the risk passes when delivery is due and the buyer is aware of the fact that the goods are placed at his disposal at that place.

(3) If the contract relates to goods not then identified, the goods are considered not to be placed at the disposal of the buyer until they are clearly identified to the contract.

ARTICLE 70

If the seller has committed a fundamental breach of contract, articles 67, 68 and 69 do not impair the remedies available to the buyer on account of the breach.

CHAPTER V   Provisions Common to the Obligations of the Seller and of the Buyer

Section I.   Anticipatory Breach and Instalment Contracts

ARTICLE 71

(1) A party may suspend the performance of his obligations if, after the conclusion of the contract, it becomes apparent that the other party will not perform a substantial part of his obligations as a result of:
  (a) A serious deficiency in his ability to perform or in his creditworthiness; or
  (b) His conduct in preparing to perform or in performing the contract.
(2) If the seller has already dispatched the goods before the grounds described in the preceding paragraph become evident, he may prevent the handing over of the goods to the buyer even though the buyer holds a document which entitles him to obtain them. The present paragraph relates only to the rights in the goods as between the buyer and the seller.
(3) A party suspending performance, whether before or after dispatch of the goods, must immediately give notice of the suspension to the other party and must continue with performance if the other party provides adequate assurance of his performance.

ARTICLE 72

(1) If prior to the date for performance of the contract it is clear that one of the parties will commit a fundamental breach of contract, the other party may declare the contract avoided.
(2) If time allows, the party intending to declare the contract avoided must give reasonable notice to the other party in order to permit him to provide adequate assurance of his performance.
(3) The requirements of the preceding paragraph do not apply if the other party has declared that he will not perform his obligations.

ARTICLE 73

(1) In the case of a contract for delivery of goods by instalments, if the failure of one party to perform any of his obligations in respect of any instalment constitutes a fundamental breach of contract with respect to that instalment, the other party may declare the contract avoided with respect to that instalment.
(2) If one party's failure to perform any of his obligations in respect of any instalment gives the other party good grounds to conclude that a fundamental breach of contract will occur with respect to future instalments, he may declare the contract avoided for the future, provided that he does so within a reasonable time.
(3) A buyer who declares the contract avoided in respect of any delivery may, at the same time, declare it avoided in respect of deliveries already made or of future deliveries if, by reason of their interdependence, those deliveries could not be used for the purpose contemplated by the parties at the time of the conclusion of the contract.

Section II.   Damages

ARTICLE 74

Damages for breach of contract by one party consist of a sum equal to the loss, including loss of profit, suffered by the other party as a consequence of the breach. Such damages may not exceed the loss which the party in breach foresaw or ought to have foreseen at the time of the conclusion of the contract, in the light of the facts and matters of which he then knew or ought to have known, as a possible consequence of the breach of contract.

ARTICLE 75

If the contract is avoided and if, in a reasonable manner and within a reasonable time after avoidance, the buyer has bought goods in replacement or the seller has resold the goods, the party claiming damages may recover the difference between the contract price and the price in the substitute transaction as well as any further damages recoverable under article 74.

ARTICLE 76

(1) If the contract is avoided and there is a current price for the goods, the party claiming damages may, if he has not made a purchase or resale under article 75, recover the difference between the price

fixed by the contract and the current price at the time of avoidance as well as any further damages recoverable under article 74. If, however, the party claiming damages has avoided the contract after taking over the goods, the current price at the time of such taking over shall be applied instead of the current price at the time of avoidance.

(2) For the purposes of the preceding paragraph, the current price is the price prevailing at the place where delivery of the goods should have been made or, if there is no current price at that place, the price at such other place as serves as a reasonable substitute, making due allowance for differences in the cost of transporting the goods.

ARTICLE 77

A party who relies on a breach of contract must take such measures as are reasonable in the circumstances to mitigate the loss, including loss of profit, resulting from the breach. If he fails to take such measures, the party in breach may claim a reduction in the damages in the amount by which the loss should have been mitigated.

Section III. Interest

ARTICLE 78

If a party fails to pay the price or any other sum that is in arrears, the other party is entitled to interest on it, without prejudice to any claim for damages recoverable under article 74.

Section IV. Exemptions

ARTICLE 79

(1) A party is not liable for failure to perform any of his obligations if he proves that the failure was due to an impediment beyond his control and that he could not reasonably be expected to have taken the impediment into account at the time of the conclusion of the contract or to have avoided or overcome it, or its consequences.

(2) If the party's failure is due to the failure by a third person whom he has engaged to perform the whole

or a part of the contract, that party is exempt from liability only if:

(a) He is exempt under the preceding paragraph; and

(b) The person whom he has so engaged would be so exempt if the provisions of that paragraph were applied to him.

(3) The exemption provided by this article has effect for the period during which the impediment exists.

(4) The party who fails to perform must give notice to the other party of the impediment and its effect on his ability to perform. If the notice is not received by the other party within a reasonable time after the party who fails to perform knew or ought to have known of the impediment, he is liable for damages resulting from such non-receipt.

(5) Nothing in this article prevents either party from exercising any right other than to claim damages under this Convention.

ARTICLE 80

A party may not rely on a failure of the other party to perform, to the extent that such failure was caused by the first party's act or omission.

Section V. Effects of Avoidance

ARTICLE 81

(1) Avoidance of the contract releases both parties from their obligations under it, subject to any damages which may be due. Avoidance does not affect any provision of the contract for the settlement of disputes or any other provision of the contract governing the rights and obligations of the parties consequent upon the avoidance of the contract.

(2) A party who has performed the contract either wholly or in part may claim restitution from the other party of whatever the first party has supplied or paid under the contract. If both parties are bound to make restitution, they must do so concurrently.

ARTICLE 82

(1) The buyer loses the right to declare the contract avoided or to require the seller to deliver substitute

goods if it is impossible for him to make restitution of the goods substantially in the condition in which he received them.

(2) The preceding paragraph does not apply:

    (a) If the impossibility of making restitution of the goods or of making restitution of the goods substantially in the condition in which the buyer received them is not due to his act or omission;

    (b) If the goods or part of the goods have perished or deteriorated as a result of the examination provided for in article 38; or

    (c) If the goods or part of the goods have been sold in the normal course of business or have been consumed or transformed by the buyer in the course of normal use before he discovered or ought to have discovered the lack of conformity.

ARTICLE 83

A buyer who has lost the right to declare the contract avoided or to require the seller to deliver substitute goods in accordance with article 82 retains all other remedies under the contract and this Convention.

ARTICLE 84

(1) If the seller is bound to refund the price, he must also pay interest on it, from the date on which the price was paid.

(2) The buyer must account to the seller for all benefits which he has derived from the goods or part of them:

    (a) If he must make restitution of the goods or part of them; or

    (b) If it is impossible for him to make restitution of all or part of the goods or to make restitution of all or part of the goods substantially in the condition in which he received them, but he has nevertheless declared the contract avoided or required the seller to deliver substitute goods.

Section VI.   Preservation of the Goods

ARTICLE 85

If the buyer is in delay in taking delivery of the goods or, where payment of the price and delivery of the goods are to be made concurrently, if he fails to pay the price, and the seller is either in possession of the goods or otherwise able to control their disposition, the seller must take such steps as are reasonable in the circumstances to preserve them. He is entitled to retain them until he has been reimbursed his reasonable expenses by the buyer.

ARTICLE 86

(1) If the buyer has received the goods and intends to exercise any right under the contract or this Convention to reject them, he must take such steps to preserve them as are reasonable in the circumstances. He is entitled to retain them until he has been reimbursed his reasonable expenses by the seller.

(2) If goods dispatched to the buyer have been placed at his disposal at their destination and he exercises the right to reject them, he must take possession of them on behalf of the seller, provided that this can be done without payment of the price and without unreasonable inconvenience or unreasonable expense. This provision does not apply if the seller or a person authorized to take charge of the goods on his behalf is present at the destination. If the buyer take possession of the goods under this paragraph, his rights and obligations are governed by the preceding paragraph.

ARTICLE 87

A party who is bound to take steps to preserve the goods may deposit them in a warehouse of a third person at the expense of the other party provided that the expense incurred is not unreasonable.

ARTICLE 88

(1) A party who is bound to preserve the goods in accordance with article 85 or 86 may sell them by any

appropriate means if there has been an unreasonable delay by the other party in taking possession of the goods or in taking them back or in paying the price or the cost of preservation, provided that reasonable notice of the intention to sell has been given to the other party.

(2) If the goods are subject to rapid deterioration or their preservation would involve unreasonable expense, a party who is bound to preserve the goods in accordance with article 85 or 86 must take reasonable measures to sell them. To the extent possible he must give notice to the other party of his intention to sell.

(3) A party selling the goods has the right to retain out of the proceeds of sale an amount equal to the reasonable expenses of preserving the goods and of selling them. He must account to the other party for the balance.

PART IV Final Provisions

ARTICLE 89

The Secretary-General of the United Nations is hereby designated as the depositary for this Convention.

ARTICLE 90

This Convention does not prevail over any international agreement which has already been or may be entered into and which contains provisions concerning the matters governed by this Convention, provided that the parties have their places of business in States parties to such agreement.

ARTICLE 91

(1) This Convention is open for signature at the concluding meeting of the United Nations Conference on Contracts for the International Sale of Goods and will remain open for signature by all States at the Headquarters of the United Nations, New York until 30 September 1981.

(2) This Convention is subject to ratification, acceptance or approval by the signatory States.

(3) This Convention is open for accession by all States which are not signatory States as from the date it is open for signature.

(4) Instruments of ratification, acceptance, approval and accession are to be deposited with the Secretary-General of the United Nations.

ARTICLE 92

(1) A Contracting State may declare at the time of signature, ratification, acceptance, approval or accession that it will not be bound by Part II of this Convention or that it will not be bound by Part III of this Convention.

(2) A Contracting State which makes a declaration in accordance with the preceding paragraph in respect of Part II or Part III of this Convention is not to be considered a Contracting State within paragraph (1) or article 1 of this Convention in respect of matters governed by the Part to which the declaration applies.

ARTICLE 93

(1) If a Contracting State has two or more territorial units in which, according to its constitution, different systems of law are applicable in relation to the matters dealt with in this Convention, it may, at the time of signature, ratification, acceptance, approval or accession, declare that this Convention is to extend to all its territorial units or only to one or more of them, and may amend its declaration by submitting another declaration at any time.

(2) These declarations are to be notified to the depositary and are to state expressly the territorial units to which the Convention extends.

(3) If, by virtue of a declaration under this article, this Convention extends to one or more but not all of the territorial units of a Contracting State, and if the place of business of a party is located in that State, this place of business, for the purposes of this Convention, is considered not to be in a Contracting State, unless it is in a territorial unit to which the Convention extends.

(4) If a Contracting State makes no declaration under paragraph (1) of this article, the Convention is to extend to all territorial units of that State.

ARTICLE 94

(1) Two or more Contracting States which may have the same or closely related legal rules on matters governed by this Convention may at any time declare that the Convention is not to apply to contracts of sale or to their formation where the parties have their places of business in those States. Such declarations may be made jointly or by reciprocal unilateral declarations.

(2) A Contracting State which has the same or closely related legal rules on matters governed by this Convention as one or more non-Contracting States may at any time declare that the Convention is not to apply to contracts of sale or to their formation where the parties have their places of business in those States.

(3) If a State which is the object of a declaration under the preceding paragraph subsequently becomes a Contracting State, the declaration made will, as from the date on which the Convention enters into force in respect of the new Contracting State, have the effect of a declaration made under paragraph (1), provided that the new Contracting State joins in such declaration or makes a reciprocal unilateral declaration.

ARTICLE 95

Any State may declare at the time of the deposit of its instrument of ratification, acceptance, approval or accession that it will not be bound by subparagraph (1)(b) of article 1 of this Convention.

ARTICLE 96

A Contracting State whose legislation requires contracts of sale to be concluded in or evidenced by writing may at any time make a declaration in accordance with article 12 that any provision of article 11, article 29, or Part II of this Convention, that allows a contract of sale or its modification or termination by agreement or any offer, acceptance, or other indication of intention to be made in any form other than in writing, does not apply where any party has his place of business in that State.

ARTICLE 97

(1) Declarations made under this Convention at the time of signature are subject to confirmation upon ratification, acceptance or approval.

(2) Declarations and confirmations of declarations are to be in writing and be formally notified to the depositary.

(3) A declaration takes effect simultaneously with the entry into force of this Convention in respect of the State concerned. However, a declaration of which the depositary receives formal notification after such entry into force takes effect on the first day of the month following the expiration of six months after the date of its receipt by the depositary. Reciprocal unilateral declarations under article 94 take effect on the first day of the month following the expiration of six months after the receipt of the latest declaration by the depositary.

(4) Any State which makes a declaration under this Convention may withdraw it at any time by a formal notification in writing addressed to the depositary. Such withdrawal is to take effect on the first day of the month following the expiration of six months after the date of the receipt of the notification by the depositary.

(2) A withdrawal of a declaration made under article 94 renders inoperative, as from the date on which the withdrawal takes effect, any reciprocal declaration made by another State under that article.

ARTICLE 98

No reservations are permitted except those expressly authorized in this Convention.

ARTICLE 99

(1) This Convention enters into force, subject to the provisions of paragraph (6) of this article, on the first day of the month following the expiration of twelve months after the date of deposit of the tenth instrument of ratification, acceptance, approval or accession, including an instrument which contains a declaration made under article 92.

(2) When a State ratifies, accepts, approves or accedes

to this Convention after the deposit of the tenth instrument of ratification, acceptance, approval or accession, this Convention, with the exception of the Part excluded, enters into force in respect of that State, subject to the provisions of paragraph (6) of this article, on the first day of the month following the expiration of twelve months after the date of the deposit of its instrument of ratification, acceptance, approval or accession.

(3) A State which ratifies, accepts, approves or accedes to this Convention and is a party to either or both the Convention relating to a Uniform Law on the Formation of Contracts for the International Sale of Goods done at The Hague on 1 July 1964 (1964 Hague Formation Convention) and the Convention relating to a Uniform Law on the International Sale of Goods done at The Hague on 1 July 1964 (1964 Hague Sales Convention) shall at the same time denounce, as the case may be, either or both the 1964 Hague Sales Convention and the 1964 Hague Formation Convention by notifying the Government of the Netherlands to that effect.

(4) A State party to the 1964 Hague Sales Convention which ratifies, accepts, approves or accedes to the present Convention and declares or has declared under article 92 that it will not be bound by Part II of this Convention shall at the time of ratification, acceptance, approval or accession denounce the 1964 Hague Sales Convention by notifying the Government of the Netherlands to that effect.

(5) A State party to the 1964 Hague Formation Convention which ratifies, accepts, approves or accedes to the present Convention and declares or has declared under article 92 that it will not be bound by Part III of this Convention shall at the time of ratification, acceptance, approval or accession denounce the 1964 Hague Formation Convention by notifying the Government of the Netherlands to that effect.

(6) For the purpose of this article, ratifications, acceptances, approvals and accessions in respect of this Convention by States parties to the 1964 Hague Formation Convention or to the 1964 Hague Sales Convention shall not be effective until such denunciations as may be required on the part of those States in respect of the latter two Conventions have themselves become effective. The depositary of this Convention shall consult with the Government of the Netherlands, as the depositary of the 1964 Conventions, so as to ensure necessary co-ordination in this respect.

ARTICLE 100

(1) This Convention applies to the formation of a contract only when the proposal for concluding the contract is made on or after the date when the Convention enters into force in respect of the Contracting States referred to in subparagraph (1)(a) or the Contracting States referred to in subparagraph (1)(b) of article 1.

(2) This Convention applies only to contracts concluded on or after the date when the Convention enters into force in respect of the Contracting States referred to in subparagraph (1)(a) or the Contracting State referred to in subparagraph (1)(b) of article 1.

ARTICLE 101

(1) A Contracting State may denounce this Convention, or Part II or Part III of the Convention, by a formal notification in writing addressed to the depositary.

(2) The denunciation takes effect on the first day of the month following the expiration of twelve months after the notification is received by the depositary. Where a longer period for the denunciation to take effect is specified in the notification, the denunciation takes effect upon the expiration of such longer period after the notification is received by the depositary.

Done at Vienna, this eleventh day of April, one thousand nine hundred and eighty, in a single original, of which the Arabic, Chinese, English, French, Russian and Spanish texts are equally authentic.

In witness whereof the undersigned plenipotentiaries, being duly authorized by their respective Governments, have signed this Convention.

B

Article Two of the Uniform Commercial Code (Selected Provisions)

ARTICLE 2   Sales

PART 2 Form, Formation and Readjustment of Contract

§ 2-201.   Formal Requirements; Statute of Frauds

(1) Except as otherwise provided in this section a contract for the sale of goods for the price of $500 or more is not enforceable by way of action or defense unless there is some writing sufficient to indicate that a contract for sale has been made between the parties and signed by the party against whom enforcement is sought or by his authorized agent or broker. A writing is not insufficient because it omits or incorrectly states a term agreed upon but the contract is not enforceable under this paragraph beyond the quantity of goods shown in such writing.

(2) Between merchants if within a reasonable time a writing in confirmation of the contract and sufficient against the sender is received and the party receiving it has reason to know its contents, it satisfies the requirements of subsection (1) against such party unless written notice of objection to its contents is given within 10 days after it is received.

(3) A contract which does not satisfy the requirements of subsection (1) but which is valid in other respects is enforceable

(a) if the goods are to be specially manufactured for the buyer and are not suitable for sale to others in the ordinary course of the seller's business and the seller, before notice of repudiation is received and under circumstances which reasonably indicate that the goods are for the buyer, has made either a substantial beginning of their manufacture or commitments for their procurement; or

(b) if the party against whom enforcement is sought admits in his pleading, testimony or otherwise in court that a contract for sale was made, but the contract is not enforceable under this provision beyond the quantity of goods admitted; or

(c) with respect to goods for which payment has been made and accepted or which have been received and accepted (Section 2-606).

§ 2-202.   Final Written Expression: Parol or Extrinsic Evidence

Terms with respect to which the confirmatory memoranda of the parties agree or which are otherwise set forth in a writing intended by the parties as a final expression of their agreement with respect to such terms as are included therein may not be contradicted by evidence of any prior agreement or of a contemporaneous oral agreement but may be explained or supplemented

(a) by course of dealing or usage of trade (Section 1-205) or by course of performance (Section 2-208); and

(b) by evidence of consistent additional terms unless the court finds the writing to have been intended also as a complete and exclusive statement of the terms of the agreement.

§ 2-203.   Seals Inoperative

The affixing of a seal to a writing evidencing a contract for sale or an offer to buy or sell goods does not constitute the writing a sealed instrument and the law with respect to sealed instruments does not apply to such a contract or offer.

§ 2-204.   Formation in General

(1) A contract for sale of goods may be made in any manner sufficient to show agreement, including conduct by both parties which recognizes the existence of such a contract.

(2) An agreement sufficient to constitute a contract for sale may be found even though the moment of its making is undetermined.

(3) Even though one or more terms are left open a contract for sale does not fail for indefiniteness if the parties have intended to make a contract and there is a reasonably certain basis for giving an appropriate remedy.

§ 2-205.   Firm Offers

An offer by a merchant to buy or sell goods in a signed writing which by its terms gives assurance that it will be held open is not revocable, for lack of consideration, during the time stated or if no time is stated for a reasonable time, but in no event may such period of irrevocability exceed three months; but any such term of assurance on a form supplied by the offeree must be separately signed by the offeror.

§ 2-206.   Offer and Acceptance in Formation of Contract

(1) Unless otherwise unambiguously indicated by the language or circumstances

(a) an offer to make a contract shall be construed as inviting acceptance in any manner and by any medium reasonable in the circumstances;

(b) an order or other offer to buy goods for prompt or current shipment shall be construed as inviting acceptance either by a prompt promise to ship or by the prompt or current shipment of conforming or nonconforming goods, but such a shipment of non-conforming goods does not constitute an acceptance if the seller seasonably notifies the buyer that the shipment is offered only as an accommodation to the buyer.

(2) Where the beginning of a requested performance is a reasonable mode of acceptance an offeror who is not notified of acceptance within a reasonable time may treat the offer as having lapsed before acceptance.

§ 2-207.   Additional Terms in Acceptance or Confirmation

(1) A definite and seasonable expression of acceptance or a written confirmation which is sent within a reasonable time operates as an acceptance even though it states terms additional to or different from those offered or agreed upon, unless acceptance is expressly made conditional on assent to the additional or different terms.

(2) The additional terms are to be construed as proposals for addition to the contract. Between merchants such terms become part of the contract unless:

(a) the offer expressly limits acceptance to the terms of the offer;

(b) they materially alter it; or

(c) notification of objection to them has already been given or is given within a reasonable time after notice of them is received.

(3) Conduct by both parties which recognizes the existence of a contract is sufficient to establish a contract for sale although the writings of the parties do not otherwise establish a contract. In such case the terms of the particular contract consist of those terms on which the writings of the parties agree, together with any supplementary terms incorporated under any other provisions of this Act.

§ 2-208.   Course of Performance or Practical Construction

(1) Where the contract for sale involves repeated occasions for performance by either party with knowledge of the nature of the performance and opportunity for objection to it by the other, any course of

performance accepted or acquiesced in without objection shall be relevant to determine the meaning of the agreement.

(2) The express terms of the agreement and any such course of performance, as well as any course of dealing and usage of trade, shall be construed whenever reasonable as consistent with each other; but when such construction is unreasonable, express terms shall control course of performance and course of performance shall control both course of dealing and usage of trade (Section 1-205).

(3) Subject to the provisions of the next section on modification and waiver, such course of performance shall be relevant to show a waiver or modification of any term inconsistent with such course of performance.

§ 2-209.   Modification, Rescission and Waiver

(1) An agreement modifying a contract within this Article needs no consideration to be binding.

(2) A signed agreement which excludes modification or rescission except by a signed writing cannot be otherwise modified or rescinded, but except as between merchants such a requirement on a form supplied by the merchant must be separately signed by the other party.

(3) The requirements of the statute of frauds section of this Article (Section 2-201) must be satisfied if the contract as modified is within its provisions.

(4) Although an attempt at modification or rescission does not satisfy the requirements of subsection (2) or (3) it can operate as a waiver.

(5) A party who has made a waiver affecting an executory portion of the contract may retract the waiver by reasonable notification received by the other party that strict performance will be required of any term waived, unless the retraction would be unjust in view of a material change of position in reliance on the waiver.

§ 2-210.   Delegation of Performance; Assignment of Rights

(1) A party may perform his duty through a delegate unless otherwise agreed or unless the other party has a substantial interest in having his original promisor perform or control the acts required by the contract. No delegation of performance re-

lieves the party delegating of any duty to perform or any liability for breach.

(2) Unless otherwise agreed all rights of either seller or buyer can be assigned except where the assignment would materially change the duty of the other party, or increase materially the burden or risk imposed on him by his contract, or impair materially his chance of obtaining return performance. A right to damages for breach of the whole contract or a right arising out of the assignor's due performance of his entire obligation can be assigned despite agreement otherwise.

(3) Unless the circumstances indicate the contrary a prohibition of assignment of "the contract" is to be construed as barring only the delegation to the assignee of the assignor's performance.

(4) An assignment of "the contract" or of "all my rights under the contract" or an assignment in similar general terms is an assignment of rights and unless the language or the circumstances (as in an assignment for security) indicate the contrary, it is a delegation of performance of the duties of the assignor and its acceptance by the assignee constitutes a promise by him to perform those duties. This promise is enforceable by either the assignor or the other party to the original contract.

(5) The other party may treat any assignment which delegates performance as creating reasonable grounds for insecurity and may without prejudice to his rights against the assignor demand assurances from the assignee (Section 2-609).

PART 3   General Obligation and Construction of Contract
§ 2-301.   General Obligations of Parties

The obligation of the seller is to transfer and deliver and that of the buyer is to accept and pay in accordance with the contract.

§ 2-302.   Unconscionable Contract or Clause

(1) If the court as a matter of law finds the contract or any clause of the contract to have been unconscionable at the time it was made the court may refuse to enforce the contract, or it may enforce the remainder of the contract without the unconscionable clause, or it may so limit the application of any unconscionable clause as to avoid any unconscionable result.

(2) When it is claimed or appears to the court that the

contract or any clause thereof may be unconscionable the parties shall be afforded a reasonable opportunity to present evidence as to its commercial setting, purpose and effect to aid the court in making the determination.

§ 2-303.   Allocation or Division of Risks

Where this Article allocates a risk or a burden as between the parties "unless otherwise agreed," the agreement may not only shift the allocation but may also divide the risk or burden.

§ 2-304.   Price Payable in Money, Goods, Realty, or Otherwise

(1) The price can be made payable in money or otherwise. If it is payable in whole or in part in goods each party is a seller of the goods which he is to transfer.

(2) Even though all or part of the price is payable in an interest in realty the transfer of the goods and the seller's obligations with reference to them are subject to this Article, but not the transfer of the interest in realty or the transferor's obligations in connection therewith.

§ 2-305.   Open Price Term

(1) The parties if they so intend can conclude a contract for sale even though the price is not settled. In such a case the price is a reasonable price at the time for delivery if
   (a) nothing is said as to price; or
   (b) the price is left to be agreed by the parties and they fail to agree; or
   (c) the price is to be fixed in terms of some agreed market or other standard as set or recorded by a third person or agency and it is not so set or recorded.

(2) A price to be fixed by the seller or by the buyer means a price for him to fix in good faith.

(3) When a price left to be fixed otherwise than by agreement of the parties fails to be fixed through fault of one party the other may at his option treat the contract as cancelled or himself fix a reasonable price.

(4) Where, however, the parties intend not to be bound unless the price be fixed or agreed and it is not fixed or agreed there is no contract. In such a case the buyer must return any goods already received or if unable so to do must pay their reasonable

value at the time of delivery and the seller must return any portion of the price paid on account.

§ 2-306.   Output, Requirements and Exclusive Dealings

(1) A term which measures the quantity by the output of the seller or the requirements of the buyer means such actual output or requirements as may occur in good faith, except that no quantity unreasonably disproportionate to any stated estimate or in the absence of a stated estimate to any normal or otherwise comparable prior output or requirements may be tendered or demanded.

(2) A lawful agreement by either the seller or the buyer for exclusive dealing in the kind of goods concerned imposes unless otherwise agreed an obligation by the seller to use best efforts to supply the goods and by the buyer to use best efforts to promote their sale.

§ 2-307.   Delivery in Single Lot or Several Lots

Unless otherwise agreed all goods called for by a contract for sale must be tendered in a single delivery and payment is due only on such tender but where the circumstances give either party the right to make or demand delivery in lots the price if it can be apportioned may be demanded for each lot.

§ 2-308.   Absence of Specified Place for Delivery

Unless otherwise agreed

(a) the place for delivery of goods is the seller's place of business or if he has none his residence; but

(b) in a contract for sale of identified goods which to the knowledge of the parties at the time of contracting are in some other place, that place is the place for their delivery; and

(c) documents of title may be delivered through customary banking channels.

§ 2-309.   Absence of Specific Time Provisions; Notice of Termination

(1) The time for shipment or delivery or any other action under a contract if not provided in this Article or agreed upon shall be a reasonable time.

(2) Where the contract provides for successive performances but is indefinite in duration it is valid for a reasonable time but unless otherwise agreed may be terminated at any time by either party.

(3) Termination of a contract by one party except on

the happening of an agreed event requires that reasonable notification be received by the other party and an agreement dispensing with notification is invalid if its operation would be unconscionable.

§ 2-310.   Open Time for Payment or Running of Credit: Authority to Ship Under Reservation

Unless otherwise agreed

(a)   payment is due at the time and place at which the buyer is to receive the goods even though the place of shipment is the place of delivery; and

(b)   if the seller is authorized to send the goods he may ship them under reservation, and may tender the documents of title, but the buyer may inspect the goods after their arrival before payment is due unless such inspection is inconsistent with the terms of the contract (Section 2-513); and

(c)   if delivery is authorized and made by way of documents of title otherwise than by subsection (b) then payment is due at the time and place at which the buyer is to receive the documents regardless of where the goods are to be received; and

(d)   where the seller is required or authorized to ship the goods on credit the credit period runs from the time of shipment, but post-dating the invoice or delaying its dispatch will correspondingly delay the starting of the credit period.

§ 2-311.   Options and Cooperation Respecting Performance

(1)   An agreement for sale which is otherwise sufficiently definite (subsection (3) or Section 2-204) to be a contract is not made invalid by the fact that it leaves particulars of performance to be specified by one of the parties. Any such specification must be made in good faith and within limits set by commercial reasonableness.

(2)   Unless otherwise agreed specifications relating to assortment of the goods are at the buyer's option and except as otherwise provided in subsections (1) (c) and (3) of Section 2-319 specifications or arrangements relating to shipment are at the seller's option.

(3)   Where such specification would materially affect the other party's performance but is not seasonably made or where one party's cooperation is necessary to the agreed performance of the other but is not seasonably forthcoming, the other party in addition to all other remedies

(a)   is excused for any resulting delay in his own performance; and

(b)   may also either proceed to perform in any reasonable manner or after the time for a material part of his own performance treat the failure to specify or to cooperate as a breach by failure to deliver or accept the goods.

§ 2-312.   Warranty of Title and Against Infringement; Buyer's Obligation Against Infringement

(1)   Subject to subsection (2) there is in a contract for sale a warranty by the seller that

(a)   the title conveyed shall be good, and its transfer rightful; and

(b)   the goods shall be delivered free from any security interest or other lien or encumbrance of which the buyer at the time of contracting has no knowledge.

(2)   A warranty under subsection (1) will be excluded or modified only by specific language or by circumstances which give the buyer reason to know that the person selling does not claim title in himself or that he is purporting to sell only such right or title as he or a third person may have.

(3)   Unless otherwise agreed a seller who is a merchant regularly dealing in goods of the kind warrants that the goods shall be delivered free of the rightful claim of any third person by way of infringement or the like but a buyer who furnishes specifications to the seller must hold the seller harmless against any such claim which arises out of compliance with the specifications.

§ 2-313.   Express Warranties by Affirmation, Promise, Description, Sample

(1)   Express warranties by the seller are created as follows:

(a)   Any affirmation of fact or promise made by the seller to the buyer which relates to the goods and becomes part of the basis of the bargain creates an express warranty that the goods shall conform to the affirmation or promise.

(b)   Any description of the goods which is made part of the basis of the bargain creates an express warranty that the goods shall conform to the description.

(c)   Any sample or model which is made part of the basis of the bargain creates an express warranty that the whole of the goods shall conform to the sample or model.

(2) It is not necessary to the creation of an express warranty that the seller use formal words such as "warrant" or "guarantee" or that he have a specific intention to make a warranty, but an affirmation merely of the value of the goods or a statement purporting to be merely the seller's opinion or commendation of the goods does not create a warranty.

§ 2-314. Implied Warranty: Merchantability; Usage of Trade

(1) Unless excluded or modified (Section 2-316), a warranty that the goods shall be merchantable is implied in a contract for their sale if the seller is a merchant with respect to goods of that kind. Under this section the serving for value of food or drink to be consumed either on the premises or elsewhere is a sale.

(2) Goods to be merchantable must be at least such as
   (a) pass without objection in the trade under the contract description; and
   (b) in the case of fungible goods, are of fair average quality within the description; and
   (c) are fit for the ordinary purposes for which such goods are used; and
   (d) run, within the variations permitted by the agreement, of even kind, quality and quantity within each unit and among all units involved; and
   (e) are adequately contained, packaged, and labeled as the agreement may require; and
   (f) conform to the promises or affirmations of fact made on the container or label if any.

(3) Unless excluded or modified (Section 2-316) other implied warranties may arise from course of dealing or usage of trade.

§ 2-315. Implied Warranty: Fitness for Particular Purpose

Where the seller at the time of contracting has reason to know any particular purpose for which the goods are required and that the buyer is relying on the seller's skill or judgment to select or furnish suitable goods, there is unless excluded or modified under the next section an implied warranty that the goods shall be fit for such purpose.

§ 2-316. Exclusion or Modification of Warranties

(1) Words or conduct relevant to the creation of an express warranty and words or conduct tending to negate or limit warranty shall be construed wherever reasonable as consistent with each other; but subject to the provisions of this Article on parol or extrinsic evidence (Section 2-202) negation or limitation is inoperative to the extent that such construction is unreasonable.

(2) Subject to subsection (3), to exclude or modify the implied warranty of merchantability or any part of it the language must mention merchantability and in case of a writing must be conspicuous, and to exclude or modify any implied warranty of fitness the exclusion must be by a writing and conspicuous. Language to exclude all implied warranties of fitness is sufficient if it states, for example, that "There are no warranties which extend beyond the description on the face hereof."

(3) Notwithstanding subsection (2)
   (a) unless the circumstances indicate otherwise, all implied warranties are excluded by expressions like "as is," "with all faults" or other language which in common understanding calls the buyer's attention to the exclusion of warranties and makes plain that there is no implied warranty; and
   (b) when the buyer before entering into the contract has examined the goods or the sample or model as fully as he desired or has refused to examine the goods there is no implied warranty with regard to defects which an examination ought in the circumstances to have revealed to him; and
   (c) an implied warranty can also be excluded or modified by course of dealing or course of performance or usage of trade.

(4) Remedies for breach of warranty can be limited in accordance with the provisions of this Article on liquidation or limitation of damages and on contractual modification of remedy (Sections 2-718 and 2-719).

§ 2-319. F.O.B. and F.A.S. Terms

(1) Unless otherwise agreed the term F.O.B. (which means "free on board") at a named place, even though used only in connection with the stated price, is a delivery term under which
   (a) when the term is F.O.B. the place of shipment, the seller must at that place ship the goods in the manner provided in this Article (Section 2-504) and bear the expense and risk of putting them into the possession of the carrier; or
   (b) when the term is F.O.B. the place of destina-

tion, the seller must at his own expense and risk transport the goods to that place and there tender delivery of them in the manner provided in this Article (Section 2-503);

(c) when under either (a) or (b) the term is also F.O.B. vessel, car or other vehicle, the seller must in addition at his own expense and risk load the goods on board. If the term is F.O.B. vessel the buyer must name the vessel and in an appropriate case the seller must comply with the provisions of this Article on the form of bill of lading (Section 2-323).

(2) Unless otherwise agreed the term F.A.S. vessel (which means "free alongside") at a named port, even though used only in connection with the stated price, is a delivery term under which the seller must

(a) at his own expense and risk deliver the goods alongside the vessel in the manner usual in that port or on a dock designated and provided by the buyer; and

(b) obtain and tender a receipt for the goods in exchange for which the carrier is under a duty to issue a bill of lading.

(3) Unless otherwise agreed in any case falling within subsection (1) (a) or (c) or subsection (2) the buyer must seasonably give any needed instructions for making delivery, including when the term is F.A.S. or F.O.B. the loading berth of the vessel and in an appropriate case its name and sailing date. The seller may treat the failure of needed instructions as a failure of cooperation under this Article (Section 2-311). He may also at his option move the goods in any reasonable manner preparatory to delivery or shipment.

(4) Under the term F.O.B. vessel or F.A.S. unless otherwise agreed the buyer must make payment against tender of the required documents and the seller may not tender nor the buyer demand delivery of the goods in substitution for the documents.

§ 2-320.   C.I.F. and C. & F. Terms

(1) The term C.I.F. means that the price includes in a lump sum the cost of the goods and the insurance and freight to the named destination. The term C. & F. or C.F. means that the price so includes cost and freight to the named destination.

(2) Unless otherwise agreed and even though used only in connection with the stated price and desti-

nation, the term C.I.F. destination or its equivalent requires the seller at his own expense and risk to

(a) put the goods into the possession of a carrier at the port for shipment and obtain a negotiable bill or bills of lading covering the entire transportation to the named destination; and

(b) load the goods and obtain a receipt from the carrier (which may be contained in the bill of lading) showing that the freight has been paid or provided for; and

(c) obtain a policy or certificate of insurance, including any war risk insurance, of a kind and on terms then current at the port of shipment in the usual amount, in the currency of the contract, shown to cover the same goods covered by the bill of lading and providing for payment of loss to the order of the buyer or for the account of whom it may concern; but the seller may add to the price the amount of the premium for any such war risk insurance; and

(d) prepare an invoice of the goods and procure any other documents required to effect shipment or to comply with the contract; and

(e) forward and tender with commercial promptness all the documents in due form and with any indorsement necessary to perfect the buyer's rights.

(3) Unless otherwise agreed the term C. & F. or its equivalent has the same effect and imposes upon the seller the same obligations and risks as a C.I.F. term except the obligation as to insurance.

(4) Under the term C.I.F. or C. & F. unless otherwise agreed the buyer must make payment against tender of the required documents and the seller may not tender nor the buyer demand delivery of the goods in substitution for the documents.

§ 2-321.   C.I.F. or C. & F.: "Net Landed Weights"; "Payment on Arrival"; Warranty of Condition on Arrival

Under a contract containing a term C.I.F. or C. & F.

(1) Where the price is based on or is to be adjusted according to "net landed weights," "delivered weights," "out turn" quantity or quality or the like, unless otherwise agreed the seller must reasonably estimate the price. The payment due on tender of the documents called for by the contract is the amount so estimated, but after the final adjustment

of the price a settlement must be made with commercial promptness.

(2) An agreement described in subsection (1) or any warranty of quality or condition of the goods on arrival places upon the seller the risk of ordinary deterioration, shrinkage and the like in transportation but has no effect on the place or time of identification to the contract for sale or delivery or on the passing of the risk of loss.

(3) Unless otherwise agreed where the contract provides for payment on or after arrival of the goods the seller musts before payment allow such preliminary inspection as is feasible; but if the goods are lost delivery of the documents and payment are due when the goods should have arrived.

§ 2-322.   Delivery "Ex-Ship"

(1) Unless otherwise agreed a term for delivery of goods "ex-ship" (which means from the carrying vessel) or in equivalent language is not restricted to a particular ship and requires delivery from a ship which has reached a place at the named port of destination where goods of the kind are usually discharged.

(2) Under such a term unless otherwise agreed
   (a) the seller must discharge all liens arising out of the carriage and furnish the buyer with a direction which puts the carrier under a duty to deliver the goods; and
   (b) the risk of loss does not pass to the buyer until the goods leave the ship's tackle or are otherwise properly unloaded.

§ 2-323.   Form of Bill of Lading Required in Overseas Shipment; "Overseas"

(1) Where the contract contemplates overseas shipment and contains a term C.I.F. or C. & F. or F.O.B. vessel, the seller unless otherwise agreed must obtain a negotiable bill of lading stating that the goods have been loaded on board or, in the case of a term C.I.F. or C. & F., received for shipment.

(2) Where in a case within subsection (1) a bill of lading has been issued in a set of parts, unless otherwise agreed if the documents are not to be sent from abroad the buyer may demand tender of the full set; otherwise only one part of the bill of lading need be tendered. Even if the agreement expressly requires a full set

   (a) due tender of a single part is acceptable within the provisions of this Article on cure of improper delivery (subsection (1) of Section 2-508); and
   (b) even though the full set is demanded, if the documents are sent from abroad the person tendering an incomplete set may nevertheless require payment upon furnishing an indemnity which the buyer in good faith deems adequate.

(3) A shipment by water or by air or a contract contemplating such shipment is "overseas" insofar as by usage of trade or agreement it is subject to the commercial, financing or shipping practices characteristic of international deep water commerce.

§ 2-324.   "No Arrival, No Sale" Term

Under a term "no arrival, no sale" or terms of like meaning, unless otherwise agreed,

(a) the seller must properly ship conforming goods and if they arrive by any means he must tender them on arrival but he assumes no obligation that the goods will arrive unless he has caused the non-arrival; and
(b) where without fault of the seller the goods are in part lost or have so deteriorated as no longer to conform to the contract or arrive after the contract time, the buyer may proceed as if there had been casualty to identified goods (Section 2-613).

§ 2-325.   "Letter of Credit" Term; "Confirmed Credit"

(1) Failure of the buyer seasonably to furnish an agreed letter of credit is a breach of the contract for sale.

(2) The delivery to seller of a proper letter of credit suspends the buyer's obligation to pay. If the letter of credit is dishonored, the seller may on seasonable notification to the buyer require payment directly from him.

(3) Unless otherwise agreed the term "letter of credit" or "banker's credit" in a contract for sale means an irrevocable credit issued by a financing agency of good repute and, where the shipment is overseas, of good international repute. The term "confirmed credit" means that the credit must also carry the direct obligation of such an agency which does business in the seller's financial market.

PART 5   Performance

§ 2-501.   Insurable Interest in Goods; Manner of Identification of Goods

(1) The buyer obtains a special property and an insurable interest in goods by identification of existing goods as goods to which the contract refers even though the goods so identified are nonconforming and he has an option to return or reject them. Such identification can be made at any time and in any manner explicitly agreed to by the parties. In the absence of explicit agreement identification occurs

    (a) when the contract is made if it is for the sale of goods already existing and identified;

    (b) if the contract is for the sale of future goods other than those described in paragraph (c), when goods are shipped, marked or otherwise designated by the seller as goods to which the contract refers;

    (c) when the crops are planted or otherwise become growing crops or the young are conceived if the contract is for the sale of unborn young to be born within twelve months after contracting or for the sale of crops to be harvested within twelve months or the next normal harvest season after contracting whichever is longer.

(2) The seller retains an insurable interest in goods so long as title to or any security interest in the goods remains in him and where the identification is by the seller alone he may until default or insolvency or notification to the buyer that the identification is final substitute other goods for those identified.

(3) Nothing in this section impairs any insurable interest recognized under any other statute or rule of law.

§ 2-503.   Manner of Seller's Tender of Delivery

(1) Tender of delivery requires that the seller put and hold conforming goods at the buyer's disposition and give the buyer any notification reasonably necessary to enable him to take delivery. The manner, time and place for tender are determined by the agreement and this Article, and in particular

    (a) tender must be at a reasonable hour, and if it is of goods they must be kept available for the period reasonably necessary to enable the buyer to take possession; but

    (b) Unless otherwise agreed the buyer must furnish facilities reasonably suited to the receipt of the goods.

(2) Where the case is within the next section respecting shipment tender requires that the seller comply with its provisions.

(3) Where the seller is required to deliver at a particular destination tender requires that he comply with subsection (1) and also in any appropriate case tender documents as described in subsections (4) and (5) of this section.

(4) Where goods are in the possession of a bailee and are to be delivered without being moved

    (a) tender requires that the seller either tender a negotiable document of title covering such goods or procure acknowledgment by the bailee of the buyer's right to possession of the goods; but

    (b) tender to the buyer of a non-negotiable document of title or of a written direction to the bailee to deliver is sufficient tender unless the buyer seasonably objects, and receipt by the bailee of notification of the buyer's rights fixes those rights as against the bailee and all third persons; but risk of loss of the goods and of any failure by the bailee to honor the non-negotiable document of title or to obey the direction remains on the seller until the buyer has had a reasonable time to present the document or direction, and a refusal by the bailee to honor the document or to obey the direction defeats the tender.

(5) Where the contract requires the seller to deliver documents

    (a) he must tender all such documents in correct form, except as provided in this Article with respect to bills of lading in a set (subsection (2) of Section 2-323); and

    (b) tender through customary banking channels is sufficient and dishonor of a draft accompanying the documents constitutes non-acceptance or rejection.

§ 2-504.   Shipment by Seller

Where the seller is required or authorized to send the goods to the buyer and the contract does not require him to deliver them at a particular destination, then unless otherwise agreed he must

(a) put the goods in the possession of such a carrier and make such a contract for their transportation as may be reasonable having regard to the nature of the goods and other circumstances of the case; and

(b) obtain and promptly deliver or tender in due form any document necessary to enable the buyer to obtain possession of the goods or otherwise required by the agreement or by usage of trade; and

(c) promptly notify the buyer of the shipment. Failure to notify the buyer under paragraph (c) or to make a proper contract under paragraph (a) is a ground for rejection only if material delay or loss ensues.

§ 2-505.   Seller's Shipment Under Reservation

(1) Where the seller has identified goods to the contract by or before shipment:

(a) his procurement of a negotiable bill of lading to his own order or otherwise reserves in him a security interest in the goods. His procurement of the bill to the order of a financing agency or of the buyer indicates in addition only the seller's expectation of transferring that interest to the person named.

(b) a non-negotiable bill of lading to himself or his nominee reserves possession of the goods as security but except in a case of conditional delivery (subsection (2) of Section 2-507) a non-negotiable bill of lading naming the buyer as consignee reserves no security interest even though the seller retains possession of the bill of lading.

(2) When shipment by the seller with reservation of a security interest is in violation of the contract for sale it constitutes an improper contract for transportation within the preceding section but impairs neither the rights given to the buyer by shipment and identification of the goods to the contract nor the seller's powers as a holder of a negotiable document.

§ 2-506.   Rights of Financing Agency

(1) A financing agency by paying or purchasing for value a draft which relates to a shipment of goods acquires to the extent of the payment or purchase and in addition to its own rights under the draft and any document of title securing it any rights of the shipper in the goods including the right to stop delivery and the shipper's right to have the draft honored by the buyer.

(2) The right to reimbursement of a financing agency which has in good faith honored or purchased the draft under commitment to or authority from the buyer is not impaired by subsequent discovery of defects with reference to any relevant document which was apparently regular on its face.

§ 2-507.   Effect of Seller's Tender; Delivery on Condition

(1) Tender of delivery is a condition to the buyer's duty to accept the goods and, unless otherwise agreed, to his duty to pay for them. Tender entitles the seller to acceptance of the goods and to payment according to the contract.

(2) Where payment is due and demanded on the delivery to the buyer of goods or documents of title, his right as against the seller to retain or dispose of them is conditional upon his making the payment due.

§ 2-508.   Cure by Seller of Improper Tender or Delivery; Replacement

(1) Where any tender or delivery by the seller is rejected because non-conforming and the time for performance has not yet expired, the seller may seasonably notify the buyer of his intention to cure and may then within the contract time make a conforming delivery.

(2) Where the buyer rejects a non-conforming tender which the seller had reasonable grounds to believe would be acceptable with or without money allowance the seller may if he seasonably notifies the buyer have a further reasonable time to substitute a conforming tender.

§ 2-509.   Risk of Loss in the Absence of Breach

(1) Where the contract requires or authorizes the seller to ship the goods by carrier

(a) if it does not require him to deliver them at a particular destination, the risk of loss passes to the buyer when the goods are duly delivery to the carrier even though the shipment is under reservation (Section 2-505); but

(b) if it does require him to deliver them at a particular destination and the goods are there duly tendered while in the possession of the carrier, the risk of loss passes to the buyer when the goods are there duly so tendered as to enable the buyer to take delivery.

(2) Where the goods are held by a bailee to be deliv-

ered without being moved, the risk of loss passes to the buyer

(a) on his receipt of a negotiable document of title covering the goods; or

(b) on acknowledgment by the bailee of the buyer's right to possession of the goods; or

(c) after his receipt of a non-negotiable document of title or other written direction to deliver, as provided in subsection (4) (b) of Section 2-503.

(3) In any case not within subsection (1) or (2), the risk of loss passes to the buyer on his receipt of the goods if the seller is a merchant; otherwise the risk passes to the buyer on tender of delivery.

(4) The provisions of this section are subject to contrary agreement of the parties and to the provisions of this Article on sale on approval (Section 2-327) and on effect of breach on risk of loss (Section 2-510).

§ 2-510.   Effect of Breach on Risk of Loss

(1) Where a tender or delivery of goods so fails to conform to the contract as to give a right of rejection the risk of their loss remains on the seller until cure or acceptance.

(2) Where the buyer rightfully revokes acceptance he may to the extent of any deficiency in his effective insurance coverage treat the risk of loss as having rested on the seller from the beginning.

(3) Where the buyer as to conforming goods already identified to the contract for sale repudiates or is otherwise in breach before risk of their loss has passed to him, the seller may to the extent of any deficiency in his effective insurance coverage treat the risk of loss as resting on the buyer for a commercially reasonable time.

§ 2-511.   Tender of Payment by Buyer; Payment by Check

(1) Unless otherwise agreed tender of payment is a condition to the seller's duty to tender and complete any delivery.

(2) Tender of payment is sufficient when made by any means or in any manner current in the ordinary course of business unless the seller demands payment in legal tender and gives any extension of time reasonably necessary to procure it.

(3) Subject to the provisions of this Act on the effect of an instrument on an obligation (Section 3-802),

payment by check is conditional and is defeated as between the parties by dishonor of the check on due presentment.

§ 2-512.   Payment by Buyer Before Inspection

(1) Where the contract requires payment before inspection non-conformity of the goods does not excuse the buyer from so making payment unless

(a) the non-conformity appears without inspection, or

(b) despite tender of the required documents the circumstances would justify injunction against honor under the provisions of this Act (Section 5-114).

(2) Payment pursuant to subsection (1) does not constitute an acceptance of goods or impair the buyer's right to inspect or any of his remedies.

§ 2-513.   Buyer's Right to Inspection of Goods

(1) Unless otherwise agreed and subject to subsection (3), where goods are tendered or delivered or identified to the contract for sale, the buyer has a right before payment or acceptance to inspect them at any reasonable place and time and in any reasonable manner. When the seller is required or authorized to send the goods to the buyer, the inspection may be after their arrival.

(2) Expenses of inspection must be borne by the buyer but may be recovered from the seller if the goods do not conform and are rejected.

(3) Unless otherwise agreed and subject to the provisions of this Article on C.I.F. contracts (subsection (3) of Section 2-321), the buyer is not entitled to inspect the goods before payment of the price when the contract provides

(a) for delivery "C.O.D." or on other like terms; or

(b) for payment against documents of title, except where such payment is due only after the goods are to become available for inspection.

(4) A place or method of inspection fixed by the parties is presumed to be exclusive but unless otherwise expressly agreed it does not postpone identification or shift the place for delivery or for passing the risk of loss. If compliance becomes impossible, inspection shall be as provided in this section unless the place or method fixed was clearly intended as an indispensable condition failure of which avoids the contract.

§ 2-514.   When Documents Deliverable on Acceptance; When on Payment

Unless otherwise agreed documents against which a draft is drawn are to be delivered to the drawee on acceptance of the draft if it is payable more than three days after presentment; otherwise, only on payment.

§ 2-515.   Preserving Evidence of Goods in Dispute

In furtherance of the adjustment of any claim or dispute

(a) either party on reasonable notification to the other and for the purpose of ascertaining the facts and preserving evidence has the right to inspect, test and sample the goods including such of them as may be in the possession or control of the other; and

(b) the parties may agree to a third party inspection or survey to determine the conformity or condition of the goods and may agree that the findings shall be binding upon them in any subsequent litigation or adjustment.

PART 6   Breach, Repudiation and Excuse

§ 2-601.   Buyer's Rights on Improper Delivery

Subject to the provisions of this Article on breach in installment contracts (Section 2-612) and unless otherwise agreed under the sections on contractual limitations of remedy (Sections 2-718 and 2-719), if the goods or the tender of delivery fail in any respect to conform to the contract, the buyer may

(a) reject the whole; or
(b) accept the whole; or
(c) accept any commercial unit or units and reject the rest.

§ 2-602.   Manner and Effect of Rightful Rejection

(1) Rejection of goods must be within a reasonable time after their delivery or tender. It is ineffective unless the buyer seasonably notifies the seller.

(2) Subject to the provisions of the two following sections on rejected goods (Sections 2-603 and 2-604),
   (a) after rejection any exercise of ownership by the buyer with respect to any commercial unit is wrongful as against the seller; and
   (b) if the buyer has before rejection taken physical possession of goods in which he does not have a security interest under the provisions of this Article (subsection (3) of Section 2-711), he is under a duty after rejection to hold them with reasonable care at the seller's disposition for a time sufficient to permit the seller to remove them; but
   (c) the buyer has no further obligations with regard to goods rightfully rejected.

(3) The seller's rights with respect to goods wrongfully rejected are governed by the provisions of this Article on seller's remedies in general (Section 2-703).

§ 2-606.   What Constitutes Acceptance of Goods

(1) Acceptance of goods occurs when the buyer
   (a) after a reasonable opportunity to inspect the goods signifies to the seller that the goods are conforming or that he will take or retain them in spite of their non-conformity; or
   (b) fails to make an effective rejection (subsection (1) of Section 2-602), but such acceptance does not occur until the buyer has had a reasonable opportunity to inspect them; or
   (c) does any act inconsistent with the seller's ownership; but if such act is wrongful as against the seller it is an acceptance only if ratified by him.

(2) Acceptance of a part of any commercial unit is acceptance of that entire unit.

§ 2-607.   Effect of Acceptance; Notice of Breach; Burden of Establishing Breach After Acceptance; Notice of Claim or Litigation to Person Answerable Over

(1) The buyer must pay at the contract rate for any goods accepted.

(2) Acceptance of goods by the buyer precludes rejection of the goods accepted and if made with knowledge of a non-conformity cannot be revoked because of it unless the acceptance was on the reasonable assumption that the non-conformity would be seasonably cured but acceptance does not of itself impair any other remedy provided by this Article for non-conformity.

(3) Where a tender has been accepted
   (a) the buyer must within a reasonable time after he discovers or should have discovered any breach notify the seller of breach or be barred from any remedy; and

(b) if the claim is one for infringement or the like (subsection (3) of Section 2-312) and the buyer is sued as a result of such a breach he must so notify the seller within a reasonable time after he receives notice of the litigation or be barred from any remedy over for liability established by the litigation.

(4) The burden is on the buyer to establish any breach with respect to the goods accepted.

(5) Where the buyer is sued for breach of a warranty or other obligation for which his seller is answerable over

(a) he may give his seller written notice of the litigation. If the notice states that the seller may come in and defend and that if the seller does not do so he will be bound in any action against him by his buyer by any determination of fact common to the two litigations, then unless the seller after seasonable receipt of the notice does come in and defend he is so bound.

(b) if the claim is one for infringement or the like (subsection (3) of Section 2-312) the original seller may demand in writing that his buyer turn over to him control of the litigation including settlement or else be barred from any remedy over and if he also agrees to bear all expense and to satisfy any adverse judgment, then unless the buyer after seasonable receipt of the demand does turn over control the buyer is so barred.

(6) The provisions of subsections (3), (4) and (5) apply to any obligation of a buyer to hold the seller harmless against infringement or the like (subsection (3) of Section 2-312).

§ 2-608.   Revocation of Acceptance in Whole or in Part

(1) The buyer may revoke his acceptance of a lot or commercial unit whose non-conformity substantially impairs its value to him if he has accepted it

(a) on the reasonable assumption that its nonconformity would be cured and it has not been seasonably cured; or

(b) without discovery of such non-conformity if his acceptance was reasonably induced either by the difficulty of discovery before acceptance or by the seller's assurances.

(2) Revocation of acceptance must occur within a rea-

sonable time after the buyer discovers or should have discovered the ground for it and before any substantial change in condition of the goods which is not caused by their own defects. It is not effective until the buyer notifies the seller of it.

(3) A buyer who so revokes has the same rights and duties with regard to the goods involved as if he had rejected them.

§ 2-609.   Right to Adequate Assurance of Performance

(1) A contract for sale imposes an obligation on each party that the other's expectation of receiving due performance will not be impaired. When reasonable grounds for insecurity arise with respect to the performance of either party the other may in writing demand adequate assurance of due performance and until he receives such assurance may if commercially reasonable suspend any performance for which he has not already received the agreed return.

(2) Between merchants the reasonableness of grounds for insecurity and the adequacy of any assurance offered shall be determined according to commercial standards.

(3) Acceptance of any improper delivery or payment does not prejudice the aggrieved party's right to demand adequate assurance of future performance.

(4) After receipt of a justified demand failure to provide within a reasonable time not exceeding thirty days such assurance of due performance as is adequate under the circumstances of the particular case is a repudiation of the contract.

§ 2-610.   Anticipatory Repudiation

When either party repudiates the contract with respect to a performance not yet due the loss of which will substantially impair the value of the contract to the other, the aggrieved party may

(a) for a commercially reasonable time await performance by the repudiating party; or

(b) resort to any remedy for breach (Section 2-703 or Section 2-711), even though he has notified the repudiating party that he would await the latter's performance and has urged retraction; and

(c) in either case suspend his own performance or proceed in accordance with the provisions of this Article on the seller's right to identify goods to the contract notwithstanding breach or to salvage unfinished goods (Section 2-704).

§ 2-614. Substituted Performance

(1) Where without fault of either party the agreed berthing, loading, or unloading facilities fail or an agreed type of carrier becomes unavailable or the agreed manner of delivery otherwise becomes commercially impracticable but a commercially reasonable substitute is available, such substitute performance must be tendered and accepted.

(2) If the agreed means or manner of payment fails because of domestic or foreign governmental regulation, the seller may withhold or stop delivery unless the buyer provides a means or manner of payment which is commercially a substantial equivalent. If delivery has already been taken, payment by the means or in the manner provided by the regulation discharges the buyer's obligation unless the regulation is discriminatory, oppressive or predatory.

§ 2-615. Excuse by Failure of Presupposed Conditions

Except so far as a seller may have assumed a greater obligation and subject to the preceding section on substituted performance:

(a) Delay in delivery or non-delivery in whole or in part by a seller who complies with paragraphs (b) and (c) is not a breach of his duty under a contract for sale if performance as agreed has been made impracticable by the occurrence of a contingency the nonoccurrence of which was a basic assumption on which the contract was made or by compliance in good faith with any applicable foreign or domestic governmental regulation or order whether or not it later proves to be invalid.

(b) Where the causes mentioned in paragraph (a) affect only a part of the seller's capacity to perform, he must allocate production and deliveries among his customers but may at his option include regular customers not then under contract as well as his own requirements for further manufacture. He may so allocate in any manner which is fair and reasonable.

(c) The seller must notify the buyer seasonably that there will be delay or non-delivery and, when allocation is required under paragraph (b), of the estimated quota thus made available for the buyer.

§ 2-616. Procedure on Notice Claiming Excuse

(1) Where the buyer receives notification of a material or indefinite delay or an allocation justified under the preceding section he may by written notification to the seller as to any delivery concerned, and where the prospective deficiency substantially impairs the value of the whole contract under the provisions of this Article relating to breach of installment contracts (Section 2-612), then also as to the whole,
   (a) terminate and thereby discharge any unexecuted portion of the contract; or
   (b) modify the contract by agreeing to take his available quota in substitution.

(2) If after receipt of such notification from the seller the buyer fails so to modify the contract within a reasonable time not exceeding thirty days the contract lapses with respect to any deliveries affected.

(3) The provisions of this section may not be negated by agreement except insofar as the seller has assumed a greater obligation under the preceding section.

PART 7   Remedies
§ 2-703. Seller's Remedies in General

Where the buyer wrongfully rejects or revokes acceptance of goods or fails to make a payment due on or before delivery or repudiates with respect to a part or the whole, then with respect to any goods directly affected and, if the breach is of the whole contract (Section 2-612), then also with respect to the whole undelivered balance, the aggrieved seller may

(a) withhold delivery of such goods;
(b) stop delivery by any bailee as hereafter provided (Section 2-705);
(c) proceed under the next section respecting goods still unidentified to the contract;
(d) resell and recover damages as hereafter provided (Section 2-706);
(e) recover damages for non-acceptance (Section 2-708) or in a proper case the price (Section 2-709);
(f) cancel.

§ 2-711. Buyer's Remedies in General; Buyer's Security Interest in Rejected Goods

(1) Where the seller fails to make delivery or repudiates or the buyer rightfully rejects or justifiably revokes

acceptance then with respect to any goods involved, and with respect to the whole if the breach goes to the whole contract (Section 2-612), the buyer may cancel and whether or not he has done so may in addition to recovering so much of the price as has been paid

(a) "cover" and have damages under the next section as to all the goods affected whether or not they have been identified to the contract; or

(b) recover damages for non-delivery as provided in this Article (Section 2-713).

(2) Where the seller fails to deliver or repudiates the buyer may also

(a) if the goods have been identified recover them as provided in this Article (Section 2-502); or

(b) in a proper case obtain specific performance or replevy the goods as provided in this Article (Section 2-716).

(3) On rightful rejection or justifiable revocation of acceptance a buyer has a security interest in goods in his possession or control for any payments made on their price and any expenses reasonably incurred in their inspection, receipt, transportation, care and custody and may hold such goods and resell them in like manner as an aggrieved seller (Section 2-706).

Case Index

Subject Index